D1242332

THE WEHRMACHT'S LAST STAND

THE WEHRMACHT'S
LAST STAND

The German Campaigns
of 1944–1945

Robert M. Citino

UNIVERSITY PRESS OF KANSAS

Published by the University Press of Kansas (Lawrence, Kansas 66045), which was
organized by the Kansas Board of Regents and is operated and funded by Emporia State
University, Fort Hays State University, Kansas State University, Pittsburg State
University, the University of Kansas, and Wichita State University.

Library of Congress Cataloging-in-Publication Data

Names: Citino, Robert Michael, 1958– author.
Title: The Wehrmacht's last stand : the German campaigns of 1944–1945 /
  Robert M. Citino.
Description: Lawrence, Kansas : University Press of Kansas, 2017.
  | Series: Modern war studies | Includes bibliographical references and index.
Identifiers: LCCN 2017026680 | ISBN 9780700624942 (hardback : alkaline paper)
  | ISBN 9780700624959 (ebook)
Subjects: LCSH: Germany—Armed Forces—History—World War, 1939–1945. |
  World War, 1939–1945—Campaigns—Western Front. | World War, 1939–1945—
  Campaigns—Eastern Front. | Germany—History, Military—20th century. |
  BISAC: HISTORY / Military / World War II. | HISTORY / Military/ General. |
  HISTORY / Europe / Germany.
Classification: LCC D757 .C597 2017 | DDC 940.54/21—dc23
LC record available at https://lccn.loc.gov/2017026680.

British Library Cataloguing-in-Publication Data is available.

Printed in the United States of America

10 9 8 7 6 5 4 3 2 1

To Roberta
For Keeping It Real

Contents

Illustrations

Photographs

Acknowledgments

Writing this book found me in a state of professional transition. I composed it in three places: Carlisle, Pennsylvania, where I was fortunate to serve as the Harold K. Johnson Visiting Professor in Military History and Strategy at the US Army War College; Denton, Texas, where I finished up a seven-year stint on the faculty at the University of North Texas; and finally New Orleans, Louisiana, where I am the Samuel Zemurray Stone Senior Historian at one of America's greatest educational institutions, The National World War II Museum.

For that reason alone, the number of people who gave me help and support on this project is a large one. In chronological order, Professors Michael Neiberg and William T. Allison were my mainstays at the War College: erudite, hard-nosed about the finer methodological points of scholarship, and wonderful, caring friends. At UNT, I must mention Harold Tanner, China scholar extraordinaire, confidant in trying times, and dear friend, along with brilliant younger colleagues like Sandra Mendiola Garcia, Jennifer Jensen Wallach, Michael Wise, and Christopher Fuhrmann. Here in New Orleans, the former president and CEO of The National World War II Museum, Dr. Gordon "Nick" Mueller, and his successor, Stephen Watson, have both been more generous to me than words can convey, and I am deeply grateful to them for bringing me to the museum and to this wonderful city.

My work in professional military education has also brought me many worthy colleagues: Colonel Ty Seidule, the head of the History Department at the US Military Academy at West Point, and retired US Army colonels Gian Gentile, currently senior historian at RAND, and Kevin Farrell, the CEO of Battlefield Leadership. All are men of leadership and vision, and I am proud to count them among my friends. Thanks also to General Mark A. Milley, the Chief of Staff of the US Army, for inviting me to address his August 2016 Futures Seminar in Washington, DC. The chief is an avid and omnivorous reader and a sharp thinker, as I discovered during the Q&A!

All through the project, Michael Briggs, formerly the editor-in-chief at the University Press of Kansas, was at my side with advice, encouragement, and the occasional shoulder to cry on. And as the current work comes to fruition, I find myself establishing the same warm relationship with his successor, Joyce Harrison. I know how fortunate I am: I could not have worked with a better press in the course of my career.

I owe a special debt of gratitude to Christian Ankerstjerne, my friend from Denmark, and Seth Paridon of The National World War II Museum, who provided me with expert assistance in assembling the photos for this book. I am fortunate to have so many experts for friends.

Finally, let me turn to the personal side. My wife, Roberta, is a wonderful human being, companion, and adviser. Nothing I do would have meaning if not for her. From Cleveland to New Orleans, with more stops between than I can count, she has been at my side, and once again I know how lucky I am. My daughters—Allison, Laura, and Emily—continue to delight me with their every word and gesture, and the new additions to our family, Laura's husband, Eric, and Emily's husband, Johan, have only made our Christmas reunions richer and more memorable. I cannot thank all of you enough for your love and support, each and every day.

THE WEHRMACHT'S LAST STAND

Introduction

The Weight of History

Ponder for a moment this dramatic scene from the pages of German history. A long, expensive, and bloody war is nearing its end. Enemy armies are driving on Berlin itself, and life and death seem to hang in the balance:

* * *

BERLIN. *"Finally . . . finally!" the leader muttered under his breath. He savored the news that had just arrived in his headquarters. His bitterest and most determined adversary had died after a long and debilitating illness. He knew what that meant: a body blow to the enemy, a wound so grievous that it just might tear apart the coalition he was facing. The news from the fronts had been horrible of late, so bad that he could feel his own fragile health deteriorate with each new dispatch. He couldn't eat or sleep; he trembled. The slightest disruption—a sudden noise, a defeatist comment, a long face among his entourage—worked him into a rage that might come on suddenly but took a lot longer to depart.*

He knew that the men at the front were still holding out, fighting bravely and to the death. But their ranks were full of teenagers and old men and mercenaries, not to mention wounded soldiers who should still be convalescing in hospital. They were certainly not the men of five or six years ago, when he had started this whole adventure. One bloody campaign after another, especially the last two years of ceaseless combat, had worn them down.

His own generals were useless against such odds. Useless! At best they were orthodox and dull, at worst incompetent and—as he now knew—disloyal. They

1

had never believed in him, and that was why defeat was staring them all in the face, why Russian armies were marching on Berlin this very instant. He hated them for their weakness. He hated them all.

If not for him, where would they be? Only his iron will had held them together when nothing else could. He had pulled them through disasters, huge and well-supplied armies coming at them from all directions, a world of enemies howling for their blood—blows that would have broken a lesser will or destroyed a lesser man altogether.

But now it had finally happened. The miracle he had been waiting for. No, "waiting for" didn't go far enough. Somewhere deep in his soul, he'd been expecting it. A last-second reprieve. He had triumphed after all. He savored the sweet taste of vindication, then snorted a single joyless laugh. Such a change of fortune might have caught some men by surprise, but he had too much faith in his own star. Providence had always guided him, and like so many times in the past, fortune had smiled on him at the last possible minute.

He turned back to his maps, noting the twists and turns in the front, his enemies closing in on him, the thin line of defenders in front of Berlin. But it no longer mattered.

He had won after all. Fate had given him a sign.

* * *

The reader will have no difficulty guessing the provenance of this famous mise-en-scène. The date is April 12, 1945, and the "leader," of course, is the Führer, Adolf Hitler.[1] The dictator has just received news of US president Franklin Roosevelt's death, and for a brief moment, the bulletin had galvanized the morose mood in Hitler's headquarters—the Führerbunker deep under Berlin. The man whom the German press spuriously called "Rosenfelt" (a reference to his allegedly Jewish ancestry) had been a determined enemy of Nazis and National Socialism long before the war. Once in the fight, Roosevelt had concentrated the enormous military, financial, and industrial power of his country against the enemy in Europe, even to the extent of placing the struggle against Japan—the real target of the American people's hatred—on the back burner.

And now America's leader was dead. With Hitler's nemesis gone and a virtual unknown about to take office, the Grand Alliance facing Germany might be wavering. The coalition had been an unnatural thing to begin with—an uneasy marriage of capitalists and Bolsheviks. Perhaps now it might collapse altogether. Indeed, Hitler had been selling this notion to his entourage for months, but no one had believed him. Those present in the gloom during the final moments of the Third Reich now had no choice but to believe. One of them wrote: "We felt the wings of the Angel of History rustle through the room."[2]

However, the reader's guess is likely wrong. In the scene's original incarnation, at least, the date was not 1945, but 1762. The beleaguered "leader" was not Hitler, but the *roi-connétable* (soldier-king) of Prussia, Frederick II. The dead adversary was not the president of the United States, but the Tsarina of all the Russians, Elisabeth II.[3]

The king had just suffered through a very bad year, and five years into the Seven Years' War, Prussia seemed lost. Defeated on all fronts, worn down by the superior resources of his enemies, Frederick could see the end approaching and even declared repeatedly that he would not survive defeat—he intended to kill himself. The Tsarina's death and the succession of her Prussophile son Peter III to the Russian throne changed all that. At the last second, a lost war passed into the win column. The Miracle of the House of Brandenburg would enter the history books, and King Frederick II would go down in history as the Great.[4]

This book will look at a similar, apparently lost war: the fight of the German Wehrmacht against the Allies from January 1944 to May 1945. It bases its argument on a relatively simple premise: history matters. It matters to the way people view their own lives and problems. It matters to the things they say and the things they do. Very often—and Germany's situation in the last four years of World War II is a classic example—we do not so much experience things as *re-experience* them. This principle is especially true with regard to one of the most pressing questions of World War II: What kept the German army going in an increasingly hopeless situation? What kept the General Staff planning, the commanders commanding, and the soldiers fighting—even when the situation clearly seemed hopeless?

Over the years, historians have posited various answers. The traditional view places Hitler front and center. A man of magnetism and charisma, Hitler seems the key reason that Germany fought on when most nations would have cracked. The irresistible, steely gaze of his blue eyes was proverbial, especially in the memoir literature of the German military and political elite. Hitler, his generals and ministers claimed, could make them do things they did not really want to do. Albert Speer is the classic example, an educated and apparently smart man who turned to jelly, so he tells us, in the Führer's presence. Hitler appears in Speer's memoirs as Mephistopheles, offering fame and wealth and career if Speer/Faust will only bow down and serve him.[5] Moreover, the generals had taken a personal oath to Hitler, a fact they never failed to mention when defending their loyal service to the Third Reich. They had taken other oaths, however—to the constitution of the Weimar Republic, for example—which they seemed to take rather lightly, as the mood suited them. And what of the generals' responsibility to the men under their command, who died in the tens of thousands in senseless operations up to the very last day of the war? Was that bond not a kind of oath?[6] Finally, to the notion that they were afraid of Hitler (another fact that enters the discussion from time to time): if there is one thing we can say with assurance about German officers, it is that they were absolutely fearless, and they proved it by leading from the front and dying in great numbers—some 220 generals in the course of the war.[7] It is simply difficult to believe that they were afraid of Hitler.

In contrast to this unsatisfying personalist explanation, other scholars point to the role of ideology and to National Socialist indoctrination as the heart of Germany's prolonged resistance.[8] Here we may be on firmer ground. It is now clear that the Wehrmacht professed a strong, even fervent belief in Nazi ideology, racism, and anti-Semitism, and that was as true for the ordinary German soldier (the *Landser*, he was called, the German equivalent of "GI Joe") all the way up to the General Staff. At least on the Eastern Front, the Wehrmacht really did believe that it was fighting a crusade against Jewish Bolshevism and that it was justified in casting off all moral restraint and engaging in mass murder in order to win it. The notion that the army fought a clean fight, while the Waffen-SS (the armed SS) carried out battlefield atrocities and the *SS-Einsatzgruppen* ("SS action teams") shot civilians wholesale, is no longer credible. The German army murdered its way east, then did so again as it fought its way back west. Today, the crimes of the Wehrmacht are among the few settled questions in the historiography of the war.

A third explanation for the army's steadfastness is a simpler argument from history. By the twentieth century, the Germans had evolved a distinct military culture, or "way of war."[9] Starting in the seventeenth century with Frederick William, the "Great Elector" of the Duchy of Brandenburg, Prussian rulers recognized the vulnerabilities of their small, impoverished state. Prussia was the *Macht in der Mitte* ("power in the middle"), surrounded by potential enemies and lacking clearly defined or defensible boundaries.[10] Neither its geography nor its resources would allow it to fight and win a long war of attrition. On the contrary, Prussia had to find a way to fight wars that were "short and lively" (*kurtz und vives*).

For Germany, the solution to the problem lay in a way of war they called *Bewegungskrieg*: "war of movement." It stressed maneuver on the operational level—using large units like divisions, corps, and armies to strike the foe a sharp, annihilating blow within weeks of the opening of the campaign. Using "separated portions of the army" (*getrennter Heeresteile*) that operated independently but united on the day of battle to hit an opponent in the front, flanks, and rear, German commanders like Frederick, Field Marshal Helmuth von Moltke (the Elder), and Field Marshal Erich von Manstein won some of the most dramatic battlefield victories in history.[11] The desired end was a battle of encirclement (*Kesselschlacht*, literally, "cauldron battle"), which aimed not merely to surround enemy forces but to destroy them rapidly through a series of concentric (*konzentrisch*) operations.

The German way of war required brisk maneuver, high levels of aggression, and a flexible system of command that left initiative in the hands of the man in the field as opposed to the headquarters in the rear. German analysts at the time described their command system as the "independence of the lower commander" (*Selbständigkeit der Unterführer*),[12] although the term *Auftragstaktik* (mission tactics) has become more common today among scholars and military professionals.[13] In other words, the higher commander devised a general mission (*Auftrag*), then left the means of achieving it to the officer on the spot. Independence of the lower commander was a useful force multiplier for an army that needed it, allowing the Prussians to decide, react, and move more rapidly than their enemies.

And the Germans had been doing it ever since, developing a sense of superiority over neighboring armies, fighting one aggressive campaign after another, seeking the enemy's flank and rear not in a merely tactical sense but on the operational level—surrounding and destroying entire enemy armies. When German officers thought of "war," they thought of *Bewegungskrieg*. In that sense, the last two years of the war—with the Wehrmacht still on the prowl, still seeking attacks against every target of opportunity, still trying to fight the war of movement—were merely the continuation of a very long, very old story.

But perhaps the officer corps needed to think a bit more deeply about its predicament. Hard-hitting *Bewegungskrieg* worked well often enough for Prussia but was by no means a panacea. The classic illustration of its strengths and weaknesses was the Seven Years' War from 1756 to 1763. In 1757, Frederick the Great assembled a huge force and invaded Bohemia, pounding the Austrian army in front of Prague and driving it back into the city with a series of aggressive attacks. His own losses had been high, however, and when the Austrians sent an army to relieve Prague, Frederick attacked it, too, at Kolin. It may have been his own fault, or the fault of overambitious Prussian subordinate commanders, but Frederick's intended attack on the Austrian right flank degenerated into a frontal assault against a fully alerted adversary who outnumbered him 50,000 to 35,000. Accurate Austrian fire mauled the Prussians, and Frederick and his army had to retreat in disarray.

With the Austrians resurgent, the Russians advancing from the east, and the French moving on him from the west, Frederick was in serious trouble. He retrieved the situation by two of the most decisive victories of the era, crushing the French at Rossbach in November 1757, where another ambitious subordinate, cavalry commander Friedrich Wilhelm von Seydlitz, played the critical role; and at Leuthen, where Frederick's keen penchant for maneuver resulted in the entire Prussian army appearing in dramatic fashion on the perpendicular against a weakly defended Austrian flank. Finally, in August 1758, he warded off the Russian army at Zorndorf, a murderous encounter that saw him march his entire force clear around the Russian flank to attack from the rear.[14]

Frederick had saved himself for the moment, but his foes refused to make peace, and the strategic situation remained dire. Still ringed by powerful enemies, his only hope now was to fight from the central position: holding secondary sectors with smaller forces (commanded ably by his brother, Prince Henry), rushing armies to whichever sector seemed most threatened, bringing the enemy to battle, and giving him a bloody nose. His opponents, especially the Austrians, grew skilled at countering, and on one occasion—at Hochkirch in October 1758—they gave him a "shock and awe" moment he never forgot.[15] But they never lost their wariness of him, and he never stopped attacking, whether the disastrous assault at Kunersdorf in August 1759, the impressive victory at Liegnitz in August 1760, or the attempted flank-march on the enemy's rear at Torgau later that year in November.

We should also note that he failed. By the end of 1761 Frederick was staring disaster in the face. The Austrians had just stormed the Silesian fortress of Schweidnitz. The Russians had overrun East Prussia and had taken the major Pomeranian fortress of Kolberg after a well-conducted siege. Worst of all, the cash that had sustained him thus far in the form of English subsidies was about to vanish with the fall from power of William Pitt the Elder. And then in January 1762, the Tsarina died. Weeks later, Peter III was signing a separate peace with Prussia.

Frederick the Great had survived, but perhaps he should also be known as "Frederick the Lucky."

The Problem: Fighting a Lost War

The Germans never did solve the problem of what to do if *Bewegungs-krieg* failed and quick victory eluded them. Their inability to do so haunted them in World War I, and in the latter years of World War II they found themselves in the same old trap. After a spectacular opening to the war, in which the Wehrmacht smashed every army it met, the conflict settled into a familiar pattern, with Germany fighting a "poor man's war" (*Krieg des armen Mannes*) against the world's most powerful empire, Great Britain; the greatest land power, the Soviet Union; and the world's financial and industrial giant, the United States.[16]

The Wehrmacht first paid the piper in front of Moscow in December 1941, enduring a thrashing at the hands of a Soviet counteroffensive commanded by General G. K. Zhukov that inflicted massive casualties and for a time threatened to destroy German Army Group Center altogether. Things went from bad to worse in 1942 with the catastrophe at Stalingrad and the encirclement and destruction of the German 6th Army, the largest in the German order of battle by far. The hammer fell at Stalingrad virtually the same moment as General Bernard Law Montgomery's signal victory at El Alamein in Egypt, which mauled another Axis field army (Field Marshal Erwin Rommel's *Panzerarmee Afrika*), making November 1942 a dark month indeed for the Wehrmacht.[17]

By 1943, most German officers realized the war was lost. The Western Allies had landed in North Africa at the end of 1942 and—after an initial hiccup for the US Army at Kasserine Pass—the British and American armies cleared the Axis armies out of their Tunisian beachhead. Axis clumsiness in the delicate timing of littoral warfare delayed an evacuation until it was no longer feasible, and the Axis went down in Tunisia in May 1943 with the loss of all hands, a shocking level of sacrifice for a nondecisive sector.[18]

The Allies followed up the win at Tunis by invading Sicily in July, then landed on the Italian mainland in September. The former overran Sicily and forced Mussolini from power; the latter drove Italy out of the Axis, a body blow to the German strategic position.[19] A weak power with little in the way of a military tradition, raw materials, or industrial base, Italy was still Germany's main ally in Europe, and the only one even approaching Great Power status. The Germans reacted to Italy's collapse by initiating Operation Axis, the occupation of Italy, the disarming of the Italian army, and the interning of hundreds of thousands of former soldiers for forced labor in the Reich. Often praised for its speed and decisiveness, Operation Axis was in fact a brutal act of aggression, and its principal result was to force the Germans to deploy an entire field army, and eventually an army group, to defend the Italian peninsula—perhaps the last thing the Wehrmacht needed in 1943.

Events in the east compounded these disasters. The last great German offensive in the Soviet Union, Operation Citadel, took place in July 1943. It was a classic German operation: meticulous preparation, mountains of tanks, a *konzentrisch* maneuver scheme against the city of Kursk. Unfortunately, it was also a complete and utter misfire, hitting a brick wall of deeply echeloned Soviet defenses and lurching to a full stop within days.[20] The Soviets coolly held, then counterpunched hard both in the north against Orel and to the south against Belgorod, inflicting massive casualties—again—and throwing the Germans back into a retreat that did not stop until the Dnepr River. The Soviet pursuit was so close by this point—literally nipping at the heels of the retreating Wehrmacht, with intermingled columns and operational confusion of the most unimaginable variety—that the Germans were unable even to hold the line of the great river. By the end of September, the Soviets were across the Dnepr at numerous places, eventually linking up to form a huge bridgehead on the western bank. In November, Soviet forces fought their way into Kiev, liberating the mother of Russian cities, but an attempt to break out of the Kiev Salient to the west came to grief against a skillfully conducted and very aggressive defensive stand by the German XXXXVIII Panzer Corps under General Hermann Balck. One of the Wehrmacht's most able Panzer commanders, Balck inflicted a heavy blow on the Soviets between Zhitomir and Brussilov, encircling and destroying the Soviet 1st Guards Cavalry Corps and the 5th and 8th Tank Corps. Closing the Zhitomir *Kessel* ended the operational sequence that had begun at Kursk.[21]

While their focus for 1943 was in the south, the Soviets were active elsewhere across the great front as well. Army Group North spent the year handing over divisions, tanks, and equipment to the fierce fight for survival in the south. By July, the army group—two complete field armies, the 18th on the left and 16th on the right—had just forty serviceable tanks, and the number shrank to seven by September. The army group commander, Field Marshal Georg von Küchler, repeatedly tried to draw divisions out of the front line to create a reserve, but the usual result was an order from Hitler or the General Staff removing the division from Küchler's authority altogether. On October 6, the Soviets made them all pay with a brisk assault by 3rd Shock Army toward the key road and rail junction of Nevel. Soviet staff had honed the ability by now to target a German weak spot, and the designated victim this time was the hapless 2nd Lufwaffe Field Division, deployed on the seam between Army Groups North and Center. The 2nd Lufwaffe melted away under a storm of heavy artillery and rocket fire, and soon the Soviets were pouring through Nevel and heading west. They had, for the moment, pried apart 16th Army (on the right of Army Group North) from 3rd Panzer Army (on the left of Army Group Center).

Tough back-and-forth fighting ensued before the Germans closed the gap in November, but the Nevel scrap was one more sign of their plight in the Soviet Union. The Wehrmacht was outnumbered in manpower, but even more so in tanks, artillery, and heavy equipment. And with German rear areas crawling with agents and partisans, the Soviets never had a problem finding weak divisions, operational seams, or incomplete defenses to attack. Moreover, when the Soviets penetrated these vulnerable sectors, the first concern of the German army or group commander was usually to draw in and protect the integrity of his own formation, rather than maintain contact with neighboring formations. His generals bristled when Hitler sent Führer Order No. 10, telling them to "consider it a point of honor" to keep in contact with friendly forces on their flank. The generals viewed Hitler's recommendation as an insult to their professional acumen, but indeed they often seemed to forget this basic operational concept. In private, Hitler was more pointed. Nevel, he spat, was a *Schweinerei*—a "rotten mess."[22]

For the Germans, the same description might apply to all of 1943. True to their form, they had spent much of the year on the attack. The war may have changed, but it was the same old Wehrmacht, still trying to do the same thing it had done in the war's first three years, perhaps the only thing it knew how to do: fight *Bewegungskrieg*. This was an army that stressed fighting power (*Kampfkraft*) over less glamorous aspects of warmaking like administration, logistics, and intelligence. And though the Germans historically produced great philosophers of war like Karl von Clausewitz, Moltke the Elder, or General Hans von Seeckt, they also had an abiding respect for the man of action. General Paul Conrath of the Hermann Göring Parachute Panzer Division, for example, the formation that gave the US Army all it could handle during the invasion of Sicily, once summed up his art of war in fairly nonartistic terms: "You want an immediate, reckless rush [*sofortige Drauflosmarschieren*] at the enemy," he declared—"that's me."[23] Conrath's self-description could stand as the Wehrmacht's motto for 1943. Facing disaster, it remained kinetic, hyperaggressive, and dangerous.

By 1943, rational calculation told the senior officers of the Wehrmacht that the war was lost, and they admitted it often enough in their records and writings, both contemporary records and later memoirs. But tradition, reinforced in a thousand different ways, urged them all to keep the faith and to keep going. And here, yet another old Prussian tradition played a key role in crystallizing their attitudes: the *Totenritt*, or "death ride."

At the battle of Mars-la-Tour in the Franco-Prussian War, Prussian III Corps under General Konstantin von Alvensleben launched a reckless attack against the main body of the French Army of the Rhine under Marshal Achille Bazaine.[24] Alvensleben's men were soon in trouble, facing both greater numbers and superior firepower. Facing disaster, he ordered an immediate charge by the 12th Cavalry Brigade under General Friedrich Wilhelm von Bredow to restore the situation. Even though Bredow had a clear line of sight to the unbroken French gun line in front of him, he obeyed the order, muttering "*koste es, was er wolle*" ("It will cost what it costs," or perhaps more evocatively, "whatever it takes"):

> Having at his right the three squadrons of the 16th Uhlans, under Major von Dollen, men of the *Alte Mark*, and to his left those of the 7th Cuirassiers, under Major von Schmettow, men of Halberstadt, he gallops across the highway up the steep path of glory. The squadrons wheel to the right, advance, and in full gallop they dash at the foe. Now their batteries are reached, and the artillerymen, amazed by this unexpected maneuver, are cut down.[25]

Bredow did indeed silence the French guns and save the III Corps, but then he ran into a second line of infantry and suffered heavy losses to French small-arms fire. By the time the brigade returned to its start line, it had lost over half its strength, perhaps 420 men out of 800.[26]

The French were the first to describe Bredow's attack as a *chevauchade de mort*, but German writers soon took up the phrase—and the *Totenritt* was born.[27] The death ride was an order that a commander obeyed no matter how dim the prospects for success or what it was going to cost him or the men under his command. It existed in a realm beyond rational discourse or sober reflection. It was the culminating point of innumerable old Prussian traditions that emphasized the importance of spirit and will over crass material factors, notions that harkened back to Frederick, Field Marshal Gebhard Leberecht von Blücher, or Prince Frederick Charles, a bold commander in the Franco-Prussian War who once uttered the immortal words, "You aren't beaten until you feel that you are, and I didn't have that feeling."[28]

The Work: Death Ride

This book will analyze German military operations in World War II during the sixteen months from January 1944 (with simultaneous Allied offensives at Anzio and in Ukraine) until May 1945, the collapse of the Wehrmacht in the field and the Soviet storming of Berlin.

We will begin, appropriately enough, in the east, the theater that eventually swallowed the Wehrmacht whole. The year 1944 would begin with massive Soviet attacks breaking across the front. A great January offensive by all four Soviet army groups (also referred to as "fronts") in the south cleared Ukraine, encircling two German corps at Korsun in February 1944, overrunning the large German tank and supply depot at Uman in March, and reconquering Crimea in April. Our focus will be on the greatest *Kesselschlacht* of the Ukrainian campaign: the battle of the Korsun Pocket.

From there we turn westward, to Italy. In any other war in human history, the German defense of the Italian peninsula from 1943 to 1945 would receive epic treatment as one of the largest and most destructive campaigns of all time. In World War II it barely seems to register. A secondary and geographically separated theater; no real strategic target at stake; hostile forces facing off over someone else's homeland: all these factors have conspired to remove the Italian campaign from most accounts of the war. But Italy mattered, not only for the sheer number of casualties (nearly 750,000 including both sides) but also for the pressure it put on a Wehrmacht already bleeding to death and certainly not capable of sustaining such losses. The focus here will be on the Allied landing at Anzio, the ferocious set of German counterattacks that nearly broke the beachhead, and the immense Allied offensive, code-named Diadem, that finally smashed the German position south of Rome. In the end, Italy was one front too many for the Wehrmacht. The German theater commander there, Field Marshal Albert Kesselring, has a reputation today as a defensive genius, and in a purely technical sense he did put up a successful defense against all odds.[29] But it is still fair to ask: Exactly what was Marshal Kesselring defending in Italy?

As bad as the situation was on the Eastern Front, Hitler and the High Command of the Wehrmacht (*Oberkommando der Wehrmacht*, OKW) could not afford to dwell on it. The OKW's gaze soon turned farther westward with the Allies' invasion of France at Normandy on June 6, 1944, which is detailed in Chapter 3. Usually portrayed in terms of its difficulty, complexity, and risk, Operation Overlord seemed very different to the Germans. Trying to defend France with too few men, too few divisions, and meager mechanized reserves, army officers faced the campaign without a great deal of optimism. German propaganda boasted of the Atlantic Wall, a fortified rampart that would repel the Allied landing, but in truth—as our detailed recounting of the first day of the invasion will show—it didn't even come close to blunting the assault.[30]

This catastrophic year for the Wehrmacht was hardly half over, however. Chapter 4 will shift back to the east. The Allied D-Day landing is, for Americans, the best known episode of the entire war, especially now that the "greatest generation" memory industry in the United States has gotten hold of it.[31] What happened in Byelorussia in June 1944 dwarfed Overlord by any reasonable yardstick: the sheer geographical sprawl of the operation, the sizes of the land forces involved, and the level of destruction it wrought on the Germans.[32] During the successful Soviet January offensives in Ukraine and at Leningrad, German Army Group Center had gone mostly untouched. With Soviet progress on both its northern and southern flanks, the army group now lay in a gigantic bulge toward the east, with Soviet forces threatening it from the Baltic region in the north and the Pripet Marshes in the south. The four component armies were not only holding extended fronts; they had surrendered their reserves and virtually all their Panzer divisions to shore up creaking fronts to the north and south. In the iron logic of the Eastern Front, this threadbare sector became the target for the next Soviet offensive—perhaps the most successful campaign by any force in military history. Operation Bagration demolished not merely a German army but an entire army group, "a far greater catastrophe than that of Stalingrad,"[33] and still rewards careful study—if only to ask how an officer corps as skilled as that of the Germans could have fallen prey to such an absolute debacle.

With the Allies ashore successfully in the west and Soviet armies rampaging through Byelorussia, we will pause, remove ourselves from the operational action for a moment, and discuss in some detail the attempt of a relative handful of German officers to assassinate Hitler. The focus of this excursus will be on a few critical questions. Why were so few officers on board with the conspirators? Why did so many of them stay loyal to Hitler? What was the real significance of the "oath" in German military history? Could German officers ever be justified in disobedience?

Chapter 5 will shift back west, where another highly mobile campaign was taking place. The great Allied breakthrough offensive, Operation Cobra, ruptured the weakened German line, and the victors spent August motoring at top speed in open space across France. Hitler's order to launch a great counterattack by his Panzers toward Mortain collapsed almost immediately. As a result, most of the German force in the west, including virtually all of 7th Army and 5th Panzer Army, found itself herded into a small pocket near Falaise. It looked like the campaign in the west was finished. Indeed, with the Wehrmacht broken in both east and west, it seemed that perhaps the war might be over.

But it wasn't over. Chapter 6 will return to the east, where Field Marshal Walter Model was knitting a front back together after the disaster in Byelorussia. No sooner had he done so, however, than the Soviets launched another massive offensive, this one striking Army Group North Ukraine in Galicia. After slashing through the front line and encircling another large German force at Brody, the Soviets wheeled north and stood poised to cross the Vistula River, take Warsaw on the run, and perhaps continue their drive to the east. Model was about to have an even tougher test.

Chapter 7 will open with the broken remnants of the German army in the west scurrying back to the German border. They were panic-stricken and had thrown off all discipline, at least for the moment. The mood in General Dwight D. Eisenhower's Allied headquarters was giddy with optimism about ending the war before Christmas. Not for the first time, however, the Wehrmacht was able to right itself. Under a new commander—Field Marshal Model, no less—the Germans fought a series of tough defensive battles at Arnhem, Aachen, Lorraine, and the Hürtgen Forest and managed to reestablish a defensive position along the fortified Siegfried Line. To many German officers it was like a miracle, and to the Allies an almost inexplicable disappointment. In fact, as we shall see, it was neither.

The pursuit across Western Europe brought Allied armies to the German border, but they were an exhausted lot operating at the end of an increasingly long logistical chain. Prussian-German armies had a long history of counterpunching exhausted enemies, and Hitler chose this moment for the Wehrmacht's last great offensive of the war, the subject of Chapter 8. Operation *Wacht am Rhein* would revisit the site of Hitler's greatest victory, the Ardennes Forest, a relatively quiet sector of the front where Allied divisions were resting, taking in replacements, or getting used to life in the field. With the OKW stripping the rest of the contested fronts to gather the assault divisions, the Germans assembled three armies for the assault. They would smash American defenses in the Ardennes, cross the Meuse River, and seize Antwerp, the main Allied supply port in Europe. The attack eluded US intelligence services, enjoyed complete surprise, tore a great hole in the American line—and fizzled. The Ardennes offensive was a perfect encapsulation of how far the Wehrmacht had fallen, how much the US Army had improved, and how different the war of 1944 was from that of 1940.

Chapter 9 will bring us to the New Year, as the war came to a rapid, bloody climax. We will trace the origins and course of the last great German offensive of the war, the nearly forgotten Operation *Nordwind* ("Northern Wind"), and see what a close call it was. We then move east, as the Soviets launched two simultaneous offensives in January, one that overran East Prussia and a second that lunged out of the Vistula bridgeheads and drove all the way to the Oder River, 300 miles in two weeks. For the first time, the horrors of land warfare came to the German civilian population, as a revenge-minded Red Army wasted no opportunity to visit atrocities upon them: vengeance being offered here as an explanation but certainly not as an excuse. By now, the Soviets had a potent doctrine for offensive warfare known as "deep battle," a carefully choreographed assault involving multiple waves (called "echelons") pounding home the attack along the same relentless axis until achieving a complete breakthrough. But the Germans had by now recovered from the collapse of the previous summer. Fighting on home ground with a greatly shortened front, they contested every yard, quite literally, and the loss of life for everyone involved in these campaigns—Germans, Soviets, civilians—was prodigious.[34] We might say the same for the great Soviet campaign in Southeast Europe, rolling up through Hungary (January 1945) and Austria (March), and, in the case of the Hungarian capital Budapest, conducting a siege of a great city with the entire civilian population trapped inside.[35]

We will write about the final days of the German Wehrmacht in Chapter 10, as Germany's two-front war finally merged into one single, inescapable fate. The last great Soviet thrust from the Oder to Berlin was a classic example of planning, power, and ruthless execution, and it set up the main event: the urban fight for Berlin. Pressing ahead over those final few city blocks generated a bloodbath for all concerned—a fitting ending to this most horrible of wars.

The Wehrmacht fought to the end, as it had always promised it would: *koste es, was er wolle*. At no point in the entire year and a half under discussion did Germany have a hope of winning the war, and the officers of the High Command knew it—the operations chief of the OKW, General Alfred Jodl, for example, or Colonel Adolf Heusinger, Jodl's counterpart in the Operations Section (*Operationsabteilung*) of the General Staff. The army was outnumbered and outgunned on every level, its training standards had collapsed, and it was increasingly reliant upon second- and even third-rate formations like *Volksgrenadier* divisions or *Volkssturm* battalions, not to mention foreign manpower, even to form a cohesive line. Every move it made in the west was under enemy air observation and bombardment, and Allied strategic airpower was bombing its rear areas—cities, factories, railroad marshaling yards—into smithereens. German engineers might design amazing weapons in this phase of the war—the Pzkw. Tiger II heavy tank, the Me-262 jet fighter, the Me-163 rocket aircraft, the V-1 buzz bomb, and the V-2 rocket, for example—but the Reich's industrial plants, relying on millions of slave laborers in underground factories, could never produce them in the numbers required to make a difference on the battlefield, nor could the transportation system ship them to the front, nor was there enough fuel to use them.

Going down in the face of a mechanized juggernaut in east and west, the Wehrmacht had little to offer beyond its traditional human qualities. Key elements of the classic German way of war may well have been dead by 1944. The *Kesselschlacht* was no longer a possibility, and the idea of independent command (*Auftragstaktik*) seemed like a distant memory to officers who were being hauled before "courts of honor" after the attempt to kill Hitler in July 1944.[36] But the Prussian army had a long wartime history of holding on grimly and fighting against the odds, and that tradition was very much alive. *Hartnäckigkeit* (stubbornness), *Beharrlichkeit* (tenacity), *Rücksichtslosigkeit* (ruthlessness), *Kaltblütigkeit* (coldbloodedness), and *Willenskraft* (strength of will): these were the powerful watchwords of 1944–1945.[37]

Historians often accuse Hitler of "unprofessional and defective"[38] decision-making in his insistence on holding every position to the last man and gun, designating every town a fortress (*Festung*), every village a fortified place (*feste Platz*), and "fighting for every meter of earth."[39] Such talk was irrational, yes, but the Führer's pose—standing defiantly against the odds, facing a world of enemies, and shaking his fist at fate—was very much in the tradition of Frederick the Great. The regime had spent a great deal of time and energy posing itself as the rightful successor to Old Prussia, most famously in staging the Day of Potsdam in 1933, and now in its demand to "hold at all cost" (*halten um jeden Preis*). Like Prussian leaders of old, the Third Reich was summoning its officers to do or die, and the call instinctively appealed to many of them, especially those in the field.[40] Indeed, their response might not even have been entirely conscious. And when news of Roosevelt's death hit the bunker in April 1945, it might well have seemed like the second "Miracle of the house of Brandenburg."[41]

Whatever long-term factors from the Prussian past were at work, however, issues of more recent vintage were equally important. One thing that kept German officers fighting was their fear of the Red Army's revenge if it broke into Germany. They knew exactly what they had done to the Soviet Union and had good reason to be worried, and the atrocious behavior of Soviet troops in Germany offers all the justification required for this point. Another factor was the Allied declaration in early 1943 of Germany's unconditional surrender as a principal war aim. By now, the Allies had decided that Hitler had not acted alone in launching the war; the Junkers of the German officer corps had aided and abetted him. And since the war began, Hitler's own atrocious behavior had closed off the possibility of any sort of negotiated peace. Like it or not, Hitler and the generals were all in it together. Indeed, Hitler spent a great deal of money during the war bribing his generals—giving them fat payments and immense landed estates, the infamous "dotations"—in order to keep it that way.[42]

But the most important issue keeping the generals going was the specter of 1918. If there was one searing experience that every man in this officer corps shared, it was the end of World War I, when, they were convinced, the army had stood on the edge of victory until a stab in the back (*Dolchstoss*) by the politicians and by an assortment of antinational traitors on the home front—pacifists and socialists, Spartacists and Jews. The *Dolchstoss* wasn't true, and indeed, it was the German Army High Command itself, under General Erich Ludendorff, who first demanded peace in the fall of 1918.[43] But calling the "stab in the back" false is not the same thing as saying that the German officer corps didn't believe it. Human beings have an infinite capacity for believing falsehoods, fairy tales, and self-justifying rationales for their own failure, and here also the officers of the Wehrmacht were all too human. This time, they swore, they would not weaken or waver: they would fight on till the end, till midnight, "even five past midnight," if that's what it took.[44]

And that's exactly what they did.

1

In the Cauldron: The Battle of the Korsun Pocket

Introduction

It is January 30, 1944—the start of another bad day in the middle of a hard winter. German soldiers stand in a forest clearing, somewhere southeast of the Ukrainian hamlet of Korsun.[1] They have just received news of disaster.

* * *

LOCATION UNDISCLOSED—JANUARY 30, 1944. *The clock says 2:00 P.M. The thermometer? Well, let's just call it cold. A small group of German infantry*—Landser *in the vernacular, "ground pounders"—stand huddled around a map table in a small forest clearing.*

"Damn it," the captain shouts, "we have to get out of here now!"

He slams one meaty fist down on the table, sending the map flying. He is big, raw, and fearless and has a Knight's Cross to prove it, the coveted Ritterkreuz. *His men don't see him as much of a talker, and most of what he does say can't be printed in a family newspaper.*

But now, a tap seems to open and the words pour out of him in a torrent. "We've got to get out of here," he yells again, "while we're still close to friendly lines, and our horses and equipment are in good shape!" He pauses, looks around at the others. "It's life or death." He is shouting now. "We can do it! One battle, one march, and we're out of here!"

The captain is done talking. He has used up his quota of words for the entire month. Silence. No one answers. Somewhere in the distance, a machine gun barks. Theirs? Ours? The men stand there rooted, eyes cast down. He has said everything there is to say. Every single Landser *standing around the table knows exactly what the big man is talking about.*

Two days ago, Russian attacks south of the Dnepr River drove into their deep right flank and linked up with another Russian column coming around their left. They are cut off, trapped, encircled. They all know the word: Kessel, *the German word for "cauldron" or "kettle." They don't need to read a map. They can feel it.*

They are trapped in a filthy, freezing mud hole, and if they don't get out of here soon they are all going to die.

* * *

The German Army and the *Kesselschlacht*

Throughout European military history the battle of encirclement—*Kesselschlacht*—had been a German specialty.[2] Early monarchs like Frederick William (the Great Elector of Brandenburg) or Frederick the Great of Prussia had always maneuvered aggressively to attack the vulnerable flank of adversaries. They had succeeded as often as not, in victories at Warsaw in 1656, Fehrbellin in 1675, Hohenfriedeberg in 1744, and Leuthen in 1757.[3] In the decades following the Napoleonic military revolution, the Chief of the Prussian General Staff, Helmuth von Moltke, went one step farther, planning campaigns involving widely separated armies, often hundreds of miles apart, deploying them on the arc of a great circle, advancing concentrically, and aiming them at a central point. The goal was to find and fix the main body of the enemy army in place with one or two armies, while the remaining one crashed into its flank or rear. While no campaign ever unfolds completely to plan, Moltke had also succeeded—at Königgrätz against the Austrians and at Sedan against the French—in crushing his enemies both times and creating a unified German Reich in the process.[4]

World War I had seen them at it again, attempting a super-*Kessel* of all French forces in the west during the opening days of the conflict. The world knows that operational conception as the Schlieffen Plan, but in fact no hard-and-fast plan existed.[5] Rather, the Germans opened the war conducting business as usual, with separate field armies operating independently and seeking targets of opportunity on which they could close concentrically. They came within an ace of winning that campaign, bludgeoning four of France's five armies and nearly trapping and destroying the French 5th Army at Namur in late August 1914. The German commanders closed the jaws of their pincer just a mite too slowly, however, and the French had managed to slip away. The German misfire at Namur—not the more famous Battle of the Marne—was the decisive event of the failed campaign in the west.

The Germans were able to take some consolation by events on their Eastern Front, however. On virtually the same day they were meeting frustration at Namur, they trapped, encircled, and destroyed a Russian field army at the battle of Tannenberg.[6]

In the opening two years of World War II, the German army fought its aggressive way of war, now made immeasurably more effective by the addition of modern tanks and aircraft, nearly to perfection. The German Panzer formations smashed the first eight enemy armies they met (Polish, Norwegian, Danish, French, Dutch, Belgian, Yugoslav, and Greek), and the world had to introduce a new word, *blitzkrieg* ("lightning war"), to describe what it was seeing. The Wehrmacht mauled a ninth adversary, the British army, which survived only by a hurried evacuation under fire from Dunkirk, the last European port still in its possession in the 1940 campaign. When British forces returned to the continent, landing in the Balkans to help defend Greece, the Germans mauled them again, and once again they survived only to beat a hurried evacuation under fire, this time to the island of Crete. Here they were the victims of a massive German airborne assault, Operation Mercury, and they had to evacuate *again*, this time back to Egypt. The tenth enemy was the Soviet Red Army, which in the first six months of the German invasion of the Soviet Union, Operation Barbarossa, suffered the shocking total of 4 million casualties, 3 million of them taken as prisoners of war in one giant *Kesselschlacht* after the other: Bialystok, Minsk, Smolensk, Kiev, Bryansk, and Vyazma.[7] The Wehrmacht met its eleventh adversary—the US Army—on an obscure rock formation in Tunisia called Kasserine Pass in February 1943, and it, too, was a humbling experience for the victim, with the US II Corps, comprising much of America's fighting strength in the North African theater, handled very roughly.[8]

In all these German victories—still an impressive and improbable achievement these many decades later—the operational package was more or less the same. German mechanized columns—tanks, mechanized infantry, and self-propelled artillery closely supported by Stuka dive-bombers—made breeches in widely separated sectors of the defender's line, drove deep into his rear areas, then wheeled in a pincer maneuver (*Zangenbewegung*), linked up, and encircled him. The point was not merely to surround the foe or starve him into submission. A *Kesselschlacht* was not a siege. Establishing a ring around the hostile force was merely the necessary preparation to attacking him from widely separated compass points, chopping up the encirclement into smaller portions, and finally smashing him. "Concentric (*konzentrisch*) operations," German commanders called this phase of the fight.[9]

If things went well, the *Kesselschlacht* was brutal, quick, and inexpensive, certainly cheaper than pushing the opponent back in a bloody frontal assault, then having to do it again when the defenders reestablished a cohesive line a few miles up the road. Historically, the Germans sniffed at the latter as an "ordinary victory," a slugfest that failed to solve anything.[10] An ordinary triumph was, by definition, the herald of a longer war. Long wars inevitably turn into wars of attrition, however, and a war of attrition was the one thing that Germany, situated in a difficult neighborhood in Central Europe ringed by powerful enemies who could outman and outproduce it, did not believe it could afford. The war of movement ending in a *Kesselschlacht* was not so much a choice, then, as a necessity, a constraint imposed by circumstances of time, space, and resources.

Scholars and military buffs alike may argue about the precise turning point of World War II. In many ways, this is a fool's errand. Such a great global conflagration can hardly have turned on a single, discrete event. The German failure to destroy the British Expeditionary Force at Dunkirk certainly had its long-term implications, but it hardly set the Allies on the road to victory. General G. K. Zhukov's 1941 Moscow counteroffensive gets us closer: it not only ended the German threat to the Soviet capital once and for all, it smashed Army Group Center, inflicting hundreds of thousands of German casualties, and shattered the Wehrmacht's reputation for invincibility—one of its strongest assets in those early war years.[11]

Seen through the long-term lens of German military history, however, only one campaign punches all the buttons: a big defeat, mass casualties, a great hole rent in the German position on the eastern front that the Wehrmacht would never really be able to mend, and a battle that marked a shift in the German war in the Soviet Union from a strategic offensive to a strategic defensive. It was a *Kesselschlacht*, only this time in the wrong direction and with the roles reversed. That battle was at Stalingrad.[12] As Soviet armored spearheads drove in the flanks of the neighboring armies and met up at Kalach-on-the-Don, the German 6th Army still fighting inside Stalingrad found itself in a position that was historically unique for German armies. It was not merely defeated: defeats had happened many times before, at places like Hochkirch, Jena, the Marne, and Amiens. But as the commander of the German 6th Army, General Friedrich Paulus, sat down to write his dispatch that evening, he probably realized how strange his words sounded. His message was as chilling as the winter wind just then beginning to blow across the Volga River. *Armee eingeschlossen*, he began. The 6th Army was surrounded. For the first time in history, a German army sat inside the cauldron.[13] And it died there.

Defeat in the Ukraine: The Soviet Offensives of 1943

The debate over Paulus's decisions within the Stalingrad *Kessel* will never end.[14] He might have attempted a breakout early but didn't. Indeed, lacking much in the way of mechanized transport or even horses, and with hardly any fuel for his Panzers, a breakout would have involved a mass infantry charge across a flat plain against well-supplied Soviet opposition, and it almost certainly would have resulted in a great slaughter. Instead Paulus sat, insisting that he was only following Hitler's orders to defend Stalingrad and fight to the last man. Then again, he might have surrendered in December when his situation had become hopeless as food, water, and medicine were running out inside the cauldron. By January most of his men were so sick that by the time he did give in (in the first days of February 1943), they died in droves in their first weeks in Soviet captivity. But what Paulus did or did not order was almost beside the point. The German High Command tried to supply the pocket from the air, but it was too large and the air assets too meager even to come close. It tried to launch a relief attempt from outside the pocket, Operation Winter Storm, but could barely assemble much more than a single Panzer division for the attempt. With a breakout, and relief from the outside, proving to be a chimera, Paulus had few good options. Sometimes, in particularly painful military situations, there really is nothing to be done.

The defeat and destruction of a German field army in a campaign of maneuver—one capped by a *Kesselschlacht*, no less—was a milestone. Even the apparent recovery in the winter campaign of 1942–1943, culminating in Field Marshal Erich von Manstein's "backhand blow" (*Schlag aus der Nachhand*) against the Soviet armies hurtling toward the Dnepr and the recovery of Kharkov, could do little to hide the fact.[15] As a major offensive force on the Eastern Front the Wehrmacht was done, a fact confirmed by the collapse of Germany's one major offensive that year, Operation Citadel (*Zitadelle*) against the Kursk Salient. Despite its brawny historical reputation "as the greatest tank battle of all time,"[16] Citadel was in fact an utter fiasco for the Wehrmacht.

It turned into an operational misfire that chewed up what was left of Germany's armored reserves that year and gave the Soviets a strategic opening to launch a full-on counteroffensive in the Ukraine—an entire slew of offensives, in fact. Starting in the summer with attacks on the Orel Salient (Operation Kutuzov)[17] and Belgorod (Operation Polkovodets Rumyantsev),[18] Soviet tank armies tore open great chunks of the German line and sent the entire defensive front on the southern wing reeling in reverse.

Even an obstacle like the mighty Dnepr River didn't stop the Soviets. Exhausted German soldiers, who had been withdrawing in the face of superior forces for months as summer turned into fall—and who expected to find succor behind the river—some sort of "eastern wall" (*Ostwall*), concrete bunkers, gun emplacements, a cup of hot coffee, anything at all—were sorely disappointed when they arrived to find . . . nothing. "The disappointment of the troops was gigantic," wrote General Nikolaus von Vormann, commander of the 23rd Panzer Division, "and it was a shocking thing to see."[19] Vormann himself had been part of the harrowing retreat to the Dnepr, and all he wanted as he led his division back across the river through the burning factory districts of Dnepropetrovsk, the last major German formation to cross, was to have "one night's sleep where I didn't have to worry about Russian tanks waking me up."[20]

He was as disheartened as his men by what he found. Hitler and his brain trust back in Berlin had deliberately left the Dnepr unfortified, for fear of weakening the defensive spirit of the army fighting in the east. Hitler didn't want his commanders or men looking over their shoulders, constantly seeking the safety of a fort, blockhouse, or bunker. As the Führer saw it, an army in a fortified line was an army that had ceased to fight, and building a fortified line in the rear was an invitation to retreat "because then my generals only look behind them."[21] It should be added, however, that fortifying a river as long as the Dnepr, an engineering project of major proportions requiring resources and manpower that Germany no longer possessed, was probably impossible anyway.

Consequently, as 1943 was drawing to a close, the Soviets crossed the Dnepr at numerous places, first at Bukrin, south of Kiev, then at Tcherkassy, Kremenchug, and Dnepropetrovsk, eventually linking up to form an immense position on the western bank. They crossed the great river on the fly and often drove on to the west without even bothering to consolidate their bridgehead. As 1943 ended, a massive Soviet force consisting of four well-equipped army groups ("fronts" in Soviet parlance) was in action against the tattered Wehrmacht in Ukraine. On October 20, 1943, the four shed their former geographically descriptive names (the Voronezh, Steppe, Southwest, and South Fronts) for simpler monikers and now became, north to south, the 1st, 2nd, 3rd, and 4th Ukrainian Fronts. In a way, their new anonymity made them all the more terrifying—a sign of the Soviet Union's apparently inexhaustible supply of men and materiel, a tangible representation of the Soviet mass man.

The Wehrmacht tried to hold in front of the lower Dnepr, where the river makes its great turn to the west before flowing into the Black Sea, by establishing a straight north-south "chord position" (*Sehnenstellung*) from Zaporozhye down to Melitopol and thence to the Sea of Azov. But like every one of the German attempts to make a stand in the fall of 1943, this one too was half-hearted and essentially hopeless, involving little more than plunking down 6th Army, only recently reconstituted after the destruction of its ill-fated namesake at Stalingrad, in front of the onrushing Soviets. The 6th Army's commander, General Karl-Adolf Hollidt, was a solid operator, but this defensive operation was doomed from the start. On the situation maps, Hollidt was holding the so-called Wotan Line, but in reality it consisted of little more than a hastily dug antitank ditch and some disconnected trenches for the infantry. The lack of terrain cover—this was the beginning of the bare Nogai Steppe—gave his men the impression of being offered "on a silver platter" to Soviet fire, in the words of the German official history.[22] A well-coordinated offensive by the five armies of Soviet 4th Ukrainian Front, commanded by Marshal F. I. Tolbukhin and spearheaded by over 800 tanks and the entire Soviet 8th Air Army, blew away 6th Army and cleared the great steppe all the way up to Kherson at the mouth of the Dnepr. This rapid westward plunge also saw Soviet forces cover the top of the Perekop Isthmus, thus closing off access to the Crimea and isolating the combined German and Romanian units of Army Group A holding in Crimea. Like so many other German formations that fall, Army Group A was on at least its third life in the Russian campaign, having earlier been extricated from potential tombs in the Caucasus in late 1942 and the Kuban in October 1943. Now, just a few months later, the executioner—in the form of Soviet 51st Army stationed at Perekop—was once again sharpening his ax.

While the entire Dnepr campaign had been a catastrophe of epic proportions for the Wehrmacht, the entire sorry mess might well have been avoided, or at least alleviated, if the orders out of the Führer's headquarters in Rastenburg, East Prussia, hadn't been so dreadfully predictable. By now, the great struggle for command between Hitler and his generals was over, and it had ended in a decisive victory for the former. Having careened into disaster on the eastern front, Hitler was no longer interested in mobile operations (*bewegliche Kampfführung*), or indeed in conducting "so-called operations" at all. Rather, "hold at all costs" had become his order of the day—*Halten um jeden Preis!*— the same command that he was convinced had saved the army during the horrible winter of 1941–1942.[23] The 6th Army might well have fought a more mobile operation in the Nogai Steppe, for example, giving ground, avoiding the initial Soviet blow, then launching some sort of counterattack against the advancing enemy's mechanized columns as they drew down on their stocks of ammunition and fuel. At the very least they might have gotten out of the way of Tolbukhin's great offensive. Instead, they sat and allowed the Soviets to overrun them. Indeed, trying to hold the big bend of the Dnepr at all was senseless: the Germans had nowhere near enough troops, equipment, or supplies.

Once again, the German front in the east was stretched to the breaking point. Soviet forces were ranging far to the west, while sizable German formations were still deployed hundreds of miles forward to the southeast, trying to hold the Dnepr bend. In one controversial case, German units of the 1st Panzer Army were still perched over the Dnepr, holding a shallow and ultimately indefensible bridgehead at Nikopol. Hitler wanted it for its precious manganese ore, although since the region had become a war zone it was highly unlikely that the Germans were going to be extracting or shipping much of the stuff westward.

The front held by Army Group South in Ukraine was nowhere near to being a north-south line, the angle that would have been most economical in terms of the space to be held and the German forces available. Rather, the German line cut obliquely and lazily clear across Ukraine, more or less running on the diagonal. The Wehrmacht was attempting to hold the longest line of all, a kind of hypotenuse, and the rigors of the Pythagorean theorem were beginning to tell.

There were voices in the German command structure, to be sure, who could read a map and who could see the folly. The Chief of the General Staff, General Kurt Zeitzler, served Hitler loyally and was a fervent Nazi, but he was also a competent and energetic staff officer. They called him *Kugelblitz* ("ball of lightning").[24] Since taking over the position in late 1942, he had been urging a general retreat in the Soviet Union to a more defensible position: perhaps a more or less straight south-north line from Nikolaev at the mouth of the Ukrainian Bug

River to Kiev on the Dnepr, thence north to Polotsk on the Dvina, then along the western shores of Lake Peipus (laid out by nature almost precisely north to south), and from there to the narrows of the Narva Isthmus, fronted by the river of the same name. Each of the pegs in Zeitzler's so-called Panther position (*Pantherstellung*) had a river in front of it and thus possessed some value-added terrain benefit. And while linking the pegs wouldn't have been easy, it would have been operationally superior to the current suicidal policy: trying to defend against vastly superior Soviet armored forces on an open plain.[25]

Frontline officers echoed these staff recommendations. Field Marshal Erich von Manstein was commander of Army Group South and had been trying to sort things out in his sector since taking over in the wake of the Stalingrad debacle. The problem remained what it was: German forces were holding exposed positions far to the south and east, on his Army Group's right flank, while the Soviets were smashing into his left flank, which lay far to the west. Again and again, they harried the Germans back and threatened to break through, wheel to the south, and trap all of Army Group South against the shores of the Black Sea or the Carpathian Mountains. Manstein had mastered the problem in the winter of 1943 with a *Rochade*—a "castling maneuver" adopted from chess that brought 4th Panzer Army out of the Donbas (on his right) and shifted it to his left for the successful blow against the Soviets at Kharkov. But he knew now that a greater readjustment was necessary. The Wehrmacht could not continue to hold a tremendous balcony (*Balkon*) jutting to the east with the meager forces available. He had to abandon the Dnepr bend, pull back in the south, and establish a shorter line.

Unfortunately, such plans also meant giving up large amounts of territory all along the line, something that as supreme commander Hitler simply refused to countenance by this point in the war. The strategic equivalent of his tactical orders "to hold at any price," Hitler's stance has been the target of a great deal of hostile commentary, starting in the postwar memoir literature of the German generals and then echoed in the West by literally hundreds of historians. From the purely operational standpoint, a shorter line would free up divisions that Zeitzler and Manstein could feed into the starving German reserve pool and use to plug the holes that were springing up all over the front.

But retreats in both the far southern and far northern reaches of the Russian front not only offended Hitler's meager tactical insight—gleaned from his long-ago experiences on the Western Front in World

War I under far different conditions—they also had real and grave strategic implications. Hitler was not a military genius, as he proved over and over again in this war, but he did know a few things that his generals seemed to ignore. The more ground he gave in the sector of Army Group North, the sooner Finland would treat with the Allies and leave the war. Likewise, the closer the southern front came to the border of Romania, the more likely that Romania would leave the war. Indeed, events would bear him out on these very points in the course of 1944. The complaints from Army Group South commander Manstein that Hitler was allowing politics to trump military necessity, like the rest of Manstein's memoirs (and those of the other generals), seem out of place set against the military tradition of Clausewitz and the notion that war is "merely the continuation of politics by other means."[26] Like all the German field commanders, Manstein wished to fight a war without politics, as that "independent thing" that Clausewitz warned against.[27] He apparently didn't realize (or perhaps didn't care) that a Germany shorn of its Axis allies would have been utterly incapable of continuing the war at all. The Finns, Romanians, and Hungarians were contributing a considerable percentage of the manpower on the Eastern Front, and holding any sort of defensive line without them was impossible.

While its commanders bickered over strategy—something none of them seemed to know much about—the German army fell apart on the Eastern Front. Outgunned, outmanned, and outclassed by a better-equipped adversary, sitting out on a flat, featureless plain without much in the way of defensible terrain or fortifications, the Wehrmacht was reeling backward in confusion and fighting for its life.

From the Dnepr to the Carpathians: The Soviet Winter Offensive

The Soviets' fall offensive in late 1943 never really stopped; rather it blended seamlessly into the winter offensive of 1944—a monstrous series of attacks from the Baltic to the Black Sea. This series of "consecutive operations" represented a milestone in the maturation of Soviet doctrine as it had developed since the 1920s.[28] Each operation alone was a heavy blow that threatened to tear the Germans' defensive front asunder once and for all, but undertaking them simultaneously presented the Germans with problems of resources, men, and energy that Hitler and the High Command never did solve.

The focus of the Soviet attack—its *Schwerpunkt*, the Germans would say—lay in the south. There, the Soviet winter offensive saw all four Ukrainian fronts driving ahead at full throttle, bursting with weapons, confidence, and a sense that the enemy was on the run. All six of the Soviet tank armies—the most powerful formations in the Red Army's order of battle, the ones almost always tasked with spearheading the assault—were present in this sector, another sign that it was the main Soviet effort. The Red Army had a three-to-one numerical superiority throughout the Ukraine, although a combination of skillful deployments and deception operations to confuse German reconnaissance often made it much higher in designated breakthrough sectors. And frankly, to undermanned German infantry formations in the front line, it might as well have been ten-to-one, or even infinity.

Facing four Soviet army groups were four German armies in the Ukraine, and while a Soviet front was smaller than a German army group, it wasn't that much smaller. They were, north to south (and thus left flank to right flank), the 4th Panzer Army, 8th Army, 1st Panzer Army, and 6th Army, and so we can summarize the operational matchups in rough fashion:

> 1st Ukrainian Front v. 4th Panzer Army (General Erhard Raus)
> 2nd Ukrainian Front v. 8th Army (General Otto Wöhler)
> 3rd Ukrainian Front v. 1st Panzer Army (General Hans-Valentin Hube)
> 4th Ukrainian Front v. 6th Army (General Karl-Adolf Hollidt)

All four German armies were, more or less, a mess. The Soviets had beaten them all badly in the fall. All four had taken part in the demoralizing retreat to and over the Dnepr, where they expected to find rest and succor but had found only disappointment. All were understrength, undersupplied, and in a serious state of demotorization, with the number of vehicles in the field far below assigned levels. By the end of the year, Army Group South contained just 328,000 men, plus another 109,000 from the Axis allied forces (Romanian and Hungarian formations), along with foreign volunteers, represented in units like the 5th SS Panzer Division *Wiking*, for example. While Army Group South contained no fewer than fourteen of Germany's precious Panzer divisions, the fourteen together had only 199 tanks between them by the end of the year, or roughly fourteen tanks per division.[29] Its eleven infantry divisions were a shadow of what they were supposed to be, almost all of them whittled down to the fighting strength of a regiment or so.

In absolute terms, this force was nowhere near large enough to man the 900-kilometer meandering line along the Dnepr, especially when the enemy was so much better supplied. Soviet 1st Ukrainian Front alone contained no fewer than 831,000 men, about twice as many as all of Army Group South combined, and total Soviet manpower levels in Ukraine amounted to 2,230,000. The picture wasn't much better in the air, where 2,600 Soviet combat aircraft faced the 625 planes of the understrength 4th Air Fleet, a situation made even worse when we consider that 4th Air Fleet had to do double duty, providing cover not only for Army Group South's overextended line, but also for Army Group A, then trapped far to the south in Crimea.

For all these reasons, the mood in the German ranks was sour. Colonel Oldwig von Natzmer was a divisional staff officer in late 1943, and he didn't like what he was seeing:

A degree of exhaustion has infected all portions of this unit, up to and including the regimental staffs, so badly that we simply cannot overstate it. The result of these unceasing battles is that most of the officers and almost all the non-commissioned officers are falling apart. The men are so apathetic that it is entirely the same to them whether they are shot by their own officers or by the Russians. Whether we can hold our current positions, or any other, is completely unclear. The number of men actually in the trenches is so small that one man deployed in a rifle pit can usually not even see his neighbor.[30]

And this was a description of an elite unit, the *Panzergrenadier* Division *Grossdeutschland*. But how elite could commanders such as Natzmer expect to be when one of his battalions, the composite "1st Grenadier," was holding a sector 2.3 kilometers wide with eight noncommissioned officers and fifty-seven men? As Colonel Natzmer concluded rightly in his clipped Prussian style: "Commentary superfluous."[31]

For all these reasons—the moral and material state of the troops, the absurdly overstretched line, the vast imbalance in numbers—the Soviet winter offensive hit hard. The initial blow came on Christmas Eve 1943 on Army Group South's left, or northern flank, with the forces of Soviet 1st Ukrainian Front under Marshal N. F. Vatutin breaking out of their already massive Kiev bridgehead and smashing into the thin gray line of Raus's 4th Panzer Army. In their respective memoirs, both Manstein and Raus said they saw it coming in advance, with Manstein claiming that he could see "heavy weather" brewing up in the northern sector of his front,[32] and Raus listing all the various measures he had taken to parry the impending Soviet thrust: deploying the newly formed 18th Artillery Division to Zhitomir; pulling General Hermann Balck's XXXXVIII Panzer Corps out of the line and assembling it near Korosten; forming a combat-ready *Kampfgruppe* out of the shattered remnants of 10th Panzergrenadier Division, which was then refitting west of Berdichev; and reinforcing the local reserves along the Kiev-Zhitomir Highway.[33]

On paper, Raus's list is impressive, indeed, but if he and Manstein really did predict the time and place of the blow, it certainly was not evident from the course of the battle. Vatutin had a massive, well-supplied force in hand, with no fewer than seven rifle armies in his first (or breakthrough) echelon, with two tank armies (3rd Guards Tank Army and 1st Tank Army) in his second (or exploitation) wave. With nine armies against one, Vatutin crashed through the thin forward crust of 4th Panzer Army along the Kiev-Zhitomir Highway, broke into the clear by day two, and pried open a massive, 50-kilometer breach in the German lines that Raus had no chance of refilling. The increasing fighting quality of the Red Army was visible on all levels. The concept of deep battle, with assault forces echeloned in depth and fed in along the same axis of attack, now finally proved its worth, with a gifted and experienced officer corps doing the planning and a much-improved logistical network sustaining the intensity. Rather than a simple reliance on mass, for example, Soviet commanders from division on up invariably employed forward detachments as their attack spearheads.[34] Preceding the main body by 20–50 kilometers, they were responsible for maintaining the momentum of the advance, overrunning installations in the German rear, and breaking up counterattacks before they began.

The dilapidated 4th Panzer Army was unable to resist. Within days, Vatutin's spearheads were fanning out in an arc and seeking their deep operational targets, the cities of Korosten, Zhitomir, and Berdichev. By the end of the week of fighting, the Soviets had driven almost 60 miles beyond their start line, 4th Panzer Army was in a free fall, Army Group South had lost contact with Army Group Center, and Soviet forces were ranging in open space along two axes of advance. The first was along the southern edge of the vast Pripet Marshes. Holding the line here—literally responsible for the cohesion of the entire German defensive position in the east and preventing a Soviet drive on Brest Litovsk—was a handful of Hungarian light security battalions deployed along the swamps. The terrain was wretched, and so the Soviet advance, while 100 kilometers wide and representing a threat to 4th Panzer Army's left flank, was therefore relatively tenuous, but the danger of separating the two German army groups from one another was real.

The second axis was more immediately dangerous. Vatutin had already inserted his second echelon, 1st Tank and 3rd Guards Tank Armies, into the fight after the rifle armies had made the breakthrough.[35] They were now careening to the southwest against intermittent German opposition, bashing in 4th Panzer Army's right flank and heading for Vinnitsa, where Manstein had established his headquarters, and Uman, which held the principal tank depot for Army Group South. Armies tend to be prudent in their placement of such facilities, locating them well away from sources of imminent danger, but apparently the Wehrmacht was having trouble keeping up with the pace of deep battle. Manstein now had to shift his headquarters from Vinnitsa to Ternopol, 140 miles to the west, but relocation of the Uman facility was simply impossible on such short notice. Finally, a short hop for the Soviets in this sector would not only separate 4th Panzer Army from its neighbor to the southeast (8th Army under General Wöhler), but would also place the Red Army atop the two principal German railroads supplying both Army Groups South and A: in other words, it would constitute a strategic disaster of the first magnitude.

Manstein had taken a few days to recognize the scale and scope of the Soviet offensive—yet another sign that the attack had surprised him. Now, just a few days into the battle, 4th Panzer Army was threatened with encirclement on its northern and southern flanks. He reacted with his usual operational alacrity, however, and began to draw up his countermoves. Few generals in history had his level of self-confidence, and even in a profession known for big egos, his might have been the biggest of all.[36] What might have looked like a disaster to a lesser mortal, he felt, was in reality merely a problem, one to be fixed by readjusting and shortening the line, freeing up reserves, forming a counterattack force at the decisive point, and then—when the moment had ripened—launching a counterblow against the Soviets when they were beginning to lag in momentum, fuel, and replacements. His plan was a reprise of his signature move in this theater, the same maneuver that had restored the integrity of the front at the end of the 1942–1943 operational sequence and won the smashing victory at Kharkov. It was time, once again, for a *Rochade*.[37]

This time, the chess piece Manstein intended to move was the 1st Panzer Army, under General Hube, one of the most aggressive, gifted, and trusted commanders in the German stable. He had lost an arm fighting on the Aisne in 1914 and was known to his men not by the typical title of the "old man," but more respectfully as *der Mensch*: "the man."[38] Manstein wanted Hube in the thick of the fighting, and he needed 1st Panzer Army to help stave off 4th Panzer Army's collapse. Unfortunately, Hube was still deployed far away to the southeast, holding down the operationally senseless bridgehead over the Dnepr at Nikopol. Manstein planned to order 1st Panzer Army out of the Dnepr bend, rail it rapidly to the northwest, and plug it in to save 4th Panzer Army from catastrophe. Hollidt's 6th Army, back over the big river after its own brush with mortality in the Nogai Steppe in the fall, would take over Hube's sector along with his own, freeing up 1st Panzer Army for the transfer. Manstein was courting risk all over the place. Could the already overburdened rail lines handle the traffic? Would the Soviets detect the shift and launch an offensive at Nikopol to pin Hube in place? Above all, would Hube's army arrive in time to make much of a difference, or would he simply be swept up in a rout that looked all too certain from where Manstein stood on New Year's Day 1944? Risk had historically been part of the German war of movement, however, and at any rate there was nothing to be done about it. Manstein's plan may have been risky, but given Army Group South's dire straits, it may well have been the only hope by this point.

The field marshal had one final decision to make, however. As he and his capable chief of staff, General Theodor Busse, bent over their situation maps that last week of December 1943, 4th Panzer Army was already verging on lost-cause status. The Soviet offensive had torn open two large holes, a 60-mile gap on 4th Panzer's left (northern) wing and a 45-mile breach on its right. Fixing the former problem was important, of course, but it was also a task for higher command echelon, indeed, for the High Command of the Army (OKH) back in Rastenburg—the only authority that could coordinate the various army groups. The High Command had been dealing with the problem of the Pripet Marshes, the "gap in the Wehrmacht" (*Wehrmachtsloch*), as they called it, since 1941. The great swamp had become a nest of partisan activity, but it was unlikely to house large Soviet mechanized formations or be the avenue for a general breakthrough. The latter Soviet breach, however, was dangerously close to a vital German vein: Vinnitsa, Uman, and the rail lines upon which the entire German southern wing relied for supply. To Manstein, therefore, the decision was clear: 1st Panzer Army had to deploy on the right flank of 4th Panzer, slipping into the yawning gap between the 4th Panzer Army and the 8th Army under General Wöhler and plugging the Uman Gap.[39]

The *Rochade* was yet another model piece of German administrative and staff work. Busse drew up the orders on December 29, but nearly a week was required before the new arrangements came into being on January 3, 1944. The complexities involved were enormous. Because of Soviet pressure all along the front, 1st Panzer Army couldn't move west as a whole. Rather it had to leave several of its infantry divisions in place in the Dnepr bend, where they now came under the command of 6th Army. Meanwhile, Hube, his headquarters, and his 17th Panzer Division railed to the northwest and took control of the various units that Manstein had managed to assemble for a counterstroke. These included III Panzer Corps and 6th Panzer Division (transferred to Hube from 8th Army) and 4th Mountain Division and 101st Jäger Division from the XLIV Corps of the 6th Army. By January 4, Busse and company had completed this complicated series of transfers, hand-offs, and redeployments and had managed to place a sizable force in the Uman Gap, led by one of the Wehrmacht's most skilled commanders of mechanized forces. Soviet columns were still motoring south into the gap, unaware of the danger.

Before Manstein could put this operational scheme into play, of course, he had to receive the Führer's permission. As always, that task promised to be harder than it sounded. His first dispatches to Hitler in the opening days of the offensive—replete with demands for more troops, retreats from various sectors, complete freedom of action for his army group, and abandonment of the Dnepr bend and Crimea—had led to some of Hitler's most biting commentary about his generals: how "operating" was merely another word for retreat, a "bunch of hot air" (*geschwollenen Ausdrücke*), an incantatory phrase chanted by his generals when things got tough.[40] Why didn't Manstein just call his intended "counteroperation" by its correct name, asked the Führer: "running away"?[41] Retreat had become a "real mania" with all of them, he complained: "Everybody back!" How easy it was for Manstein to suggest giving up Crimea, for example. "If he were actually responsible for the Crimea, then the decision wouldn't be so easy."[42] Hitler was willing to toss Manstein a gaggle of infantry divisions, two from Army Group A, currently doing nothing in Crimea, and one from Army Group North, as well as a Panzer division from Army Group Center, but he would not approve a general reorientation of the front or any real shortening of the line.

The follow-up to such a long-distance contretemps was, as always, a summons to Rastenburg, with Hitler calling Manstein to a face-to-face meeting. The field marshal flew to East Prussia on January 4 and took part in the Führer's briefing that afternoon. The ensuing meeting was one of the most interesting in German military history, one that not only illustrated all the problems of twentieth-century German warmaking but also, in many ways, hearken back to the past as well. Manstein had flown to Rastenburg intending to put big issues on the table. He had a list that went well beyond the current Soviet offensive (to which, he felt, he had already devised an answer). Items on the checklist included the evacuation of the entire Dnepr bend, a pullback from the troublesome "balcony," and the creation of a shorter and more sensible deployment for Army Group South. Moreover, it was clear to Manstein that there was no long-term hope of holding on to Crimea. The 17th Army (part of the neighboring Army Group A) was the main German formation in the peninsula, and it needed to pull out of its isolation before the Soviets launched an offensive in order to rejoin the main fight on the continent proper, perhaps to be inserted on Manstein's northern flank near Rovno. Finally, Manstein wanted to revisit a topic he had mentioned to Hitler before: the appointment of a supreme commander (*Oberbefehlshaber*) for the entire Eastern Front, a leader who would have complete freedom of action to command as he saw fit. And it should come as no surprise that Manstein knew only one man with enough innate operational genius, ruthlessness, and fire in the belly to do the job: himself.

In *Lost Victories* (*Verlorene Siege*), Manstein describes the January meeting in a manner typical of the postwar German military memoir, with a great deal of emphasis on Hitler's eyes ("the single attractive feature in his otherwise coarse face"),[43] hints of suggestive, hypnotic or even demonic power on the part of the Führer ("like lightning, the idea of an Indian snake-charmer hit me"),[44] the "wordless struggle" of wills that ensued between the two men,[45] as Hitler used his steely gaze to wage a kind of spiritual "guerrilla war" (*kleingekriegt*) against his visitor. Manstein describes his own behavior in heroic terms: speaking boldly, asking for a private meeting without the usual crowd of adjutants, stenographers, official historians, and hangers-on who attended the situation conferences, requesting the right to "speak frankly" ("By all means," Hitler answered tersely),[46] and then telling the Führer that it wasn't only the "superiority of the enemy" that was causing defeat but also "the way that we are being led."[47]

Brave words if true! But, in fact, it is impossible to verify the details in Manstein's account. Only one other man was present, Chief of the General Staff Zeitzler, and he left behind no report. What we can say is that Hitler refused to countenance any retreat, either in the grand style, or even on the tactical level. He also rejected in toto the notion that he was unfit to command and that someone else, even someone as gifted as Manstein, would be able to rescue the Eastern Front and reverse the course of the war. Even Manstein's narrative, moreover, one not at all friendly to Hitler, has the Führer making some telling points. "The field marshals don't even obey me!" he declared. "Do you think they'd obey someone like you, for example, any better?"[48]

Hitler was absolutely right. His field marshals in this war were an obstreperous bunch, and army group particularism was a real problem for the Wehrmacht, most especially in the east. As Hitler pointed out, however, "I can at least fire them if need be, but no one else would have such authority."[49] No one knew the overall situation like Hitler did, once again a fair enough statement, the Führer's strategic and operational blind spots and errors notwithstanding. Manstein claims to have had the last word ("The orders I give *would* be followed!") before Hitler broke off the conversation and left the room.[50]

Let us for the moment assume that the basic contours of the conversation are true, even if Manstein has reshaped, polished, and embellished the details to make himself look more confident and forceful. The January 4 meeting was a watershed in German military history. Both antagonists had defended their corners effectively. Manstein argued for the independence of the military commander in the field, one of the oldest Prussian-German traditions of all and a crucial component of the operationally focused German way of war. It is easy to sympathize with him, the proven professional having to fend off meddling from the amateur—and that, by and large, is how military historians have viewed it. Indeed, it is how they have viewed all of Hitler's interference with his commanders and with operational matters in general: siding with the military men and condemning Hitler.

Against Manstein's traditional point of view, however, it is only fair to point out that Hitler was arguing the more modern case here. The Führer claimed supremacy for the political leadership over the purely military realm, with the civilians in control and with politics (whether domestic politics or foreign affairs) always trumping operations. Civilian supremacy over the armed forces is one of the bedrocks of modernization, and, indeed, it is difficult to say that a state can be truly modern without civilian control over its military establishment. Hitler was an awful man, a mass murderer and a monster, but in refusing to accept Manstein's offer and hand over direction of the war to a uniformed officer, he was acting no differently from any other political leader in this war. World War II in Europe was a civilian-directed war.

By this point, moreover—and ever since the failure to destroy the

Soviet Union in a single campaign in 1941—Germany's problem was not merely military. The Reich needed more sensible political leadership; that is to say, it needed a regime that was more rational, humane, and willing to adjust its ends to the available means. It needed strategy as well a strategist to formulate and execute it. What Germany needed in 1944—what it had needed all along—was not more of Manstein but rather a better Führer: a more reasonable and responsible political leader in the saddle. But the irony, of course, is that a better Hitler probably would never have started this war in the first place.

Rochade 2.0

The session broke up without a meeting of the minds, and yet Hitler did nothing to derail the operational conception Manstein had already worked out. Indeed, Manstein had worked out the plan certain that the pressure of events would force Hitler to accede to it. Moreover, it didn't involve actually surrendering territory: it was simply a matter of switching this army (1st Panzer Army) here and forcing that one (6th Army) to extend its front, even though it was already dangerously overstretched, like all the other German armies in the south. Manstein had tried to use the plan as an opening for his larger conception—"final freedom of maneuver on the Army Group South's right wing in the Dnepr bend and a strengthening of the Army Group's northern wing"—but had failed.[51]

Nevertheless, Field Marshal Manstein had at least laid the groundwork for limited success. Using forces transferred from the other army groups (including two more infantry divisions from the already hard-pressed Army Group North), as well as those mechanized units now assembled under the command of 1st Panzer Army and inserted to the right of 4th Panzer Army, Manstein formed three assault groups against the Soviet armies driving hard toward Uman and Vinnitsa. By mid-January, he had VII Corps to the east of the Soviet spearheads, III Panzer Corps to the south, and XXXXVI Panzer Corps (recently transferred from France) to the west, all under the command of General Hube. Manstein had prepared a traditional German greeting for the Soviets: the *Kesselschlacht*, with concentric (*konzentrisch*) thrusts forcing the enemy to defend in several directions at once, first paralyzing and then destroying him.

The Soviets had no idea that it was even happening. They were in full-on pursuit mode, with three armies abreast (38th, 1st Tank, and

40th) driving hard on their objectives. All three armies had been fighting sustained combat for nearly three weeks, however, their edge was dulled, and stocks of field supplies, ammunition, and perhaps human energy were beginning to run low. All offensives eventually peter out, of course, a point made by Clausewitz when he coined the term "culmination point," that moment when the offensive has achieved all it can and begins, at first imperceptibly, to ebb. But moving beyond the great philosopher, it is clear that ending an offensive had become a systemic problem for the Soviet military. Soviet commanders steeped in the doctrine of deep battle tended to drive on until they imploded from their own overstretch and exhaustion (or until the Germans caught them in a vise). This time, it was a little bit of both.

The German blow hit 40th Army—on the left of the Soviet offensive array, tasked with taking Uman—first, as concentric thrusts from III Panzer Corps and VII Corps on January 15 took it simultaneously in its right and left flanks. The converging German spearheads first linked up, cutting off 40th Army from supply and communications, then turned inward onto their adversary and began the assault proper. German Panzers caught their Soviet counterparts by surprise, often strung out in road column, and the superior training and quicker reaction time of the German tank crews did the rest. The chaos of such a battle was nearly total, with individual tank battles swirling hither and yon in a low-information environment in which telling friend from foe wasn't as easy as it sounded. Moreover, the Soviets still vastly outnumbered the Germans, and even an encircled enemy tank brigade could still be a dangerous enemy if it had a full day's supply of ammunition. One divisional battle diary summed it up perfectly: "In the battle sector of the 17th Panzer Division, it's not exactly clear at the time 'who is kesseling whom.'"[52] Once the Soviet armor was out of the picture, the Panzers could take their time destroying the thin-skinned vehicles of the Soviet supply columns and headquarters formations. In a week it was over, 40th Army was gone, the Germans had closed the eastern half of the Uman Gap, and the city of Uman itself (and the great German tank depot there) was safe for the moment.

The other two Soviet armies (38th and 1st Tank) heading toward Vinnitsa suffered the exact same fate as their confrères in the last week of January, this time caught by converging thrusts of III Panzer Corps and XXXXVI Panzer Corps. The concentric attack began on January 24, with the German spearheads linking up near the village of Oratov four days later and encircling the better part of both Soviet armies. From there it was another three solid days of fighting, at the end of which Hube's Panzers had deleted both 1st Tank and 38th Armies from the Soviet order of battle. The battle in this sector was notable for the German employment of a Heavy Panzer Regiment (*Schweres-Panzer-Regiment*) under the command of Lieutenant Colonel Dr. Franz Bäke. Consisting of forty-six Mark V Panther and twenty-four Mark VI Tiger tanks, *Hummel* and *Wespe* self-propelled artillery, as well as a battalion of Panzergrenadiers, Bäke's regiment became the terror of the battlefield, accounting for no fewer than 268 Soviet tanks with the loss of only four of his own.[53] The Wehrmacht often receives criticism for its tendency to rely upon a smaller number of excellent tanks, as opposed to concentrating on the mass production of lesser vehicles, as the American and Soviet armies did. In this case, however, it would be interesting to sample opinion from those Soviet survivors on the receiving end of Doctor Bäke's fire. The title was deserved, by the way: Bäke had been a dentist in civilian life.

The German revival was neither the first nor the last time that the Wehrmacht had apparently risen from the dead to strike a killing blow. Kerch, Kharkov, and Sevastopol in the spring of 1942, Manstein's counteroffensive toward Kharkov in 1943, and now Uman: this was an army with impressive recuperative powers. Indeed, its elite units—the Panzer divisions and Waffen-SS formations—still held a clear tactical superiority over their adversary (even the Soviet Guards formations). Unit cohesion remained exemplary, even in the face of massive casualties. The realm of military "software" remained a German strength. Soldier education and training, initiative within all ranks, the bond between leaders and led: the Wehrmacht had few peers in the world at the time. And perhaps for the first time in the war with the Soviet Union, German hardware was keeping pace. Tanks like the Panthers and Tigers reigned supreme wherever they appeared across the Eastern Front, and they racked up frightening kill ratios against the Soviet T-34s that still formed a preponderance of Soviet frontline armor.

Unfortunately for the Germans, this tactical and materiel superiority was true only of a small number of elite divisions. The overall picture at the front was one of Soviet strategic dominance. The Red Army had more divisions, more armored divisions, more mechanized infantry, and vastly more artillery than the Wehrmacht. It could hurl into battle wave upon wave of tanks and infantry, guns, and aircraft. The last item bears special mention. Destroyed on the ground in the initial German invasion of 1941, the Red Air Force by 1944 had now established dominance in the air, especially in the designated breakthrough sectors of an offensive.[54] Indeed, this very real Soviet numerical superiority became a kind of excuse for the Germans. One reads it again and again in the memoir literature of the German generals. Note, for example, the number of times that Manstein references the Soviet "hydra" in his recollections.[55] You could kill one head, he notes, but others would immediately rise to the fore. Despite his brilliance, Manstein suggests, he was doomed to be swamped by Soviet numbers.

But tactics (an area of German superiority) and strategy (where the Soviets held the high cards by 1942) were not the only two levels of this war. A crucial middle ground still existed between them: the operational. And in this realm, any analysis must be much more cautious. Operational-level warfare is the ability to plan a campaign: to muster the available formations, concentrate them for different tasks—feint, assault, pursuit, to name just three of many—and then to launch them into a cohesive campaign plan that advances the armed forces toward their strategic goal. An operation is the bridge between tactics (fighting the individual engagement or battle) and strategy (fighting the overall war, including economic planning and resource allocation). This operational level of war had once been one of the Wehrmacht's key strengths, but now the Red Army was dominating in this aspect. Carefully planning the campaign, identifying weak sectors in the German line, then smashing into those soft spots with overwhelming force, with assault formations arrayed into multiple, sequential echelons: this was the Soviet operational art.

But the Germans still had strengths on the operational level as well. The ability to react to the Soviet onslaught, courting weakness at some spots in order to concentrate on crucial ones, a sense of timing: Manstein demonstrated them all in closing the Uman Gap. Certainly the German *Kesselschlacht* was not all it could have been. A lack of infantry in the attacking formations meant that the Germans could forge no true ring around their beaten adversary. Large numbers of Soviet personnel managed to escape the trap, although they did so in a wild, panicked flight that saw them abandoning all their equipment. The final numbers for the second phase of the operation were 8,000 Soviet dead along with 5,500 prisoners; even if we assume that the Soviets suffered similar casualties in the first phase, we are still left with relatively paltry figures by Eastern Front standards. On the materiel side of the ledger, however, Hube's assault destroyed no fewer than 700 Soviet tanks and 680 artillery pieces and antitank guns and mauled fourteen Soviet rifle divisions and five mechanized corps. As an operational achievement, conceived in extremis and designed literally overnight,

Manstein's second *Rochade* was an impressive achievement, stopping the offensive of 1st Ukrainian Front in its tracks.

But was it a victory? Answering such a simple question is surprisingly difficult. Manstein had stopped the seemingly irresistible advance of 1st Ukrainian Front, to be sure, but only at the cost of bleeding neighboring formations. Army Groups North, Center, and A had all contributed divisions to the defense of Army Group South, involuntarily and under protest, and all would pay the price in the coming months. The German official history, written almost seventy years after the battle, offers a sober estimate of the impact of Manstein's last great counterattack. While willing to credit the field marshal with a clear eye, a clever operational conception, and the boldness to "stake everything on a single card," the final verdict is somewhat less than breathless in tone: "Nevertheless, in view of the overall threatening operational situation, it would be inappropriate to speak of a victory. Rather, it was a defensive success, brought about by offensive means (*offensiv herbeigeführten Abwehrerfolg*), which prevented or at least delayed a great catastrophe."[56]

Indeed, as soon became clear, the Wehrmacht had not won anything in front of Uman; rather it had merely weathered what was only the first phase of an operational avalanche: a vast continuing Soviet offensive against Army Group South. Manstein's counterstroke had routed two Soviet armies, a commendable achievement under any circumstances. Unfortunately, the Red Army had seventy-one armies in the field at the time (sixty combined-arms formations, five shock armies, and six tank armies). For Army Group South, the ordeal had only begun.

Encirclement at Korsun

It could have happened almost anywhere on the extended German front west of the Dnepr in the winter of 1944. The tattered German formations west of Tcherkassy just happened to draw the unlucky number.[57]

The Soviet offensive against Army Group South was a comprehensive effort, and while Manstein had successfully warded off the threat to Raus's 4th Panzer Army, the entire Army Group was still in an untenable position. The next army down the line to the south was the 8th, under General Wöhler. Its center lay far to the north of the rest of the Army Group, still sitting along a 40-kilometer stretch of the Dnepr River, while its left (where it linked up with 1st Panzer Army) and its right (where it had only the most tenuous connection to 6th Army) lay far to the south. It was an impossibly severe salient, a bulge so pronounced that any trained staff officer looking at the map would be appalled, as was most of Manstein's staff. There had been the usual imbroglio with Hitler about pulling it back, with Hitler insisting that it hold its position along the river. The Führer had something in mind once the weather turned better—a great offensive, perhaps even a drive to retake Kiev—and thus holding a piece of the river seemed essential. The thoughts were utopian, of course, and they point out how Hitler's hold-at-all-cost orders, far from being a defensive and static strategy, were almost always grounded in an overaggressive, offensive strategic context, as he dreamed of offensives that would never come. Manstein put it best when he wrote that the German front line in this position resembled "a sack," which offered the Soviets a golden opportunity to launch a pincer maneuver and "to tie it off in the south."[58] Wöhler had a reputation for coolness under fire. He was going to need it in the next difficult month.

Indeed, even as battle was raging in the Uman Gap, the Soviets launched a major assault on 8th Army. On January 5, 2nd Ukrainian Front (under Marshal I. S. Konev) attacked the army's deep-right flank, driving on the industrial city of Kirovograd. The plan was to encircle the German defenders, 5th Guards Army passing south of the city, 53rd Army to the north, and 5th Guards Tank Army as the second echelon. The Soviets made rapid progress in both sectors, and no wonder. German defenses were woefully thin: the 10th Panzer Division defending at Snamenka northeast of the city had just 3,700 men to cover 18 kilometers, while 2nd *Fallschirmjäger* Division (in position to the northeast, at Novgorodka) had just 3,200 to defend a 21-kilometer front. The Soviets broke through easily on day one of the offensive, and Kirovograd itself fell on January 8. Nevertheless, the overwhelmed defenders belonging to the German XXXXVII Panzer Corps managed to fight their way out of the intended encirclement and build a new defensive front to the west of the city. Deep snow, the order of the day on this front, on balance probably hampered the Soviet attackers— relying on lightning speed and surprise—just enough to create a window of survival for the Germans, and spirited attacks by the battle-groups of the *Grossdeutschland* Division held open the escape route for XXXXVII Panzer Corps just long enough.[59]

Despite the relatively positive result for the Germans, Kirovograd had been a desperate fight and a near run thing, epitomized by one traumatic moment when Soviet T-34 tanks, with infantry on board and firing wildly in all directions, broke into XXXXVII Panzer Corps headquarters at Mala Vyska. Adjutants, staff officers, and administrative personnel alike had to put down their pens and maps, grab rifles, and fight as infantry squads to clear out the penetration.[60] Moreover, even though the Soviets had failed to encircle a sizable German force in Kirovograd, the bulge formed by 8th Army (and elements of 1st Panzer Army, as well) was now even more pronounced than it had been, with the Soviets ever closer to tying off the "sack" at the base.

And starting on January 24, that was exactly what they did, launching a well-coordinated offensive involving both 1st Ukrainian and 2nd Ukrainian Fronts, with the inestimable Marshal G. K. Zhukov in overall command, responsible for coordinating the operations of the two army groups. As always by this point in the war, the Soviets took few chances. Konev's 2nd Ukrainian Front would hurl massive force against the southeastern corner of the bulge: 5th Guards Tank Army, the 52nd, 53rd, and 4th Guards Army, supported by 5th Air Army, and, de rigueur for Soviet offensives in 1944, a massive artillery barrage. Vatutin's 1st Ukrainian Front would contribute the freshly organized 6th Tank Army, so new that German intelligence had not yet picked up its existence, against the southwestern face of the bulge, with 2nd Air Army and artillery flattening the defenses. The plan was simplicity itself: concentric drives from opposite directions, a linkup of the two forces at some yet to be determined midpoint, the exact location depending on which army made the swifter thrust—and thus the encirclement and destruction of the German formations within the "sack." But along with simplicity and operational elegance went overwhelming force: 336,000 men, 500 tanks, 5,300 guns, and over 1,000 aircraft.[61] (See Map 1.1.)

The operation commenced on January 24 and, once again, broke through everywhere on day one. German intelligence at army and army group levels had seen the offensive coming, but with manpower already stretched to the limit and materiel scarce, the frontline defending formations had, in the words of the German official history, "no way to prevent the Soviet maneuver."[62] Although the situations maps show the 3rd, 11th, and 14th Panzer Divisions in play for the Germans, for example, each of these "divisions" had little more than the strength of a battalion. The Soviets, too, had been bloodied in the fighting of the previous weeks, but they still held a preponderance of strength on both attacking axes. General Nikolaus von Vormann, commanding XXXXVII Panzer Corps, witnessed the assault by 5th Guards Tank Army from the east, and he described what he saw in terms that still vibrate with the shock of being overwhelmed and overrun, as Soviet

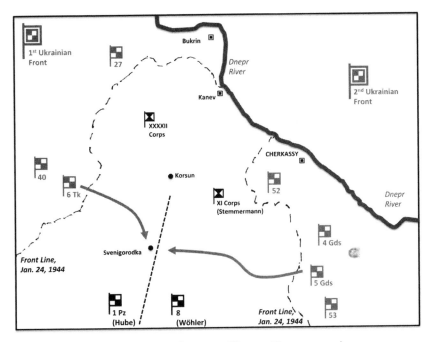

Map 1.1 In the *Kessel*: The Encirclement at Korsun (January 1944)

spearheads made a clean breakthrough of the thin German defenses near Kapitanovka:

> Without any consideration for their own losses—in the truest sense of those words—the Red flood rolled over the tanks and artillery of the 3rd, 11th, and 14th Panzer Divisions around noon, heading west, even as the German tanks fought with all guns blazing. An amazing, dramatic, shocking image! There was really no other way to put it: the dam broke and the great unending flood inundated the plain, as the Panzers, surrounded by a few grenadiers, stood there like rocks in the tide. Our amazement grew in the afternoon hours, as cavalry units in close formation galloped west through our barrage. An improbable spectacle from a long forgotten age![63]

Indeed, Vormann had a front-row seat to a rare occurrence in the European theater in World War II: a cavalry formation operating as part of the modern combined-arms team. In this case, he was watching the headlong westward advance of the V Guards Don Cavalry Corps "Red Banner" (consisting of the 11th, 12th, and 63rd Cavalry Divisions).

Events on the other side of the great bulge were more of the same, as 6th Tank Army made a clean breakthrough at the village of Bojarka and headed east. Nevertheless, by day two of the offensive, both attacking Soviet armies were motoring—if slowly—in the clear and heading toward a linkup. The meeting of the two spearheads came on January 28 near the town of Zvenigorodka, along the little river known as the Gniloj Tikic. The entire, sizable German force to the north was now surrounded, their home for the next few weeks a roughly circular pocket centered on the town of Korsun. The Soviet winter offensive of 1944 had beaten the Germans badly since its opening on the previous Christmas Eve, to be sure, tearing great gaps in the German defenses, inflicting punishing casualties, hurtling forward seemingly at will with an apparently inexhaustible reservoir of men, guns, and tanks. Nevertheless, the Wehrmacht had managed to escape disaster thus far, benefiting from a combination of defensive tenacity, minor Soviet missteps, and the weather. Now the hour had struck. For the forlorn German troops trapped in the Korsun Pocket, the reckoning was at hand.

The Korsun *Kessel*

The forces trapped inside the pocket consisted essentially of two corps, XXXXII to the west, attached to 1st Panzer Army, and XI to the east (8th Army), trapped in a space just 75 kilometers wide, with a circumference of some 250 kilometers. Since the two corps had belonged to different armies, the German High Command decided to form a new, unitary command, combining both corps into a single formation under the XI Corps commander General Wilhelm Stemmermann—and thus dubbed the Stemmermann Group (*Gruppe* Stemmermann). The best estimates place troop levels inside the *Kessel* at 53,000 to 58,000 men, the latter figure if one counts the 5,000 or so Russian "auxiliary volunteers" (*Hilfswilligen*, or "*Hiwis*") as part of the haul. All told, six divisions were present, although none of them were up to full strength, not after the horrendous fighting of the past few weeks. For the record, they were the 57th, 72nd, 88th, 112th, and 389th, along with the 5th SS Panzer Division *Wiking* ("Viking"), a high-morale outfit consisting of non-German Nordic volunteers, along with the Belgian SS Brigade *Wallonie* ("Wallonia"), and an ad hoc formation known as Corps Detachment B (consisting of the consolidated remnants of other, previously destroyed divisions and thus of limited fighting value). All told, the encircled formations had just twenty-six tanks, fourteen self-propelled guns, and some 240 guns, hopelessly inferior to the force surrounding them.[64]

The Soviets completed the encirclement with their armor on January 28, but it took at least three more days for the infantry armies to hustle up to the front and begin to solidify the inner ring around XXXXII and IX Corps. Typically, an encircled force has the best chance to break out in the first week, but the Germans failed to jump. While we can blame Hitler, who in his typically bombastic style now dubbed the Korsun Pocket a "fortress on the Dnepr" (*Festung am Dnepr*) to be held at all costs, another, more elemental factor was at work. On the night of February 1–2, the winter cold suddenly broke and a sustained warm front rolled over the battlefield. Warm weather is normally good news for armies. Here in the Dnepr River basin, however, and in much of the Soviet Union, it spelled trouble: the thaw caused mud, and mud slowed down everyone. Just when the Wehrmacht's formations in the newly formed *Kessel* needed lightning maneuver and deftness for a potential escape, they were sunk in a morass.

Even more serious, German attempts to relieve the pocket from the outside now had to struggle through the dense, sticky mess. On firm ground, German mechanized units always got the better of their Soviet counterparts. Their tanks—especially the Panthers and Tigers—had vastly superior main guns and armor, their crews had better training, and their commanders were more flexible. Mud negated virtually all those advantages, however. The staff of Army Group South had reacted quickly to the formation of the *Kessel*, assembling III Panzer Corps and XXXXVII Panzer Corps for a relief effort within days. The two forces looked impressive on paper, containing no fewer than nine Panzer divisions. But what could either one do when the Panzers had to struggle through one "mud-march" (*Schlamm-Marsch*) after the other, with one battalion making just eight kilometers in twelve hours, or when individual Panther tanks could make only 3–4 kilometers on a full tank of gas, or when tanks sank up to their hulls in the mud during the day, then were entombed as if in concrete when the mud froze during the night? The full panoply of Eastern Front mud stories has survived from the Korsun Pocket: infantry losing boots in the sticky muck and struggling forward barefoot, barely making a kilometer an hour; Panzers dragging one another forward through the mud instead of getting at the enemy; entire days wasted while some tanks schlepped canisters of gasoline forward for the others. The only saving grace was that the mud probably kept Soviet armor from driving on to the west and leaving the Korsun Pocket even more isolated than it already was, and it also hampered any Soviet attempts to drive into the *Kessel* and split it up into smaller, more digestible pieces.[65]

Still, the pocket was only 25 miles from the principal relief column of III Panzer Corps, coming up from the south.[66] It is a testimony to German tank design and troop tenacity that, even with the mud, the first relief attempt on February 4 (Operation Wanda) broke through Soviet defenses almost immediately. But the direction of the attack was northwest, part of an overly complex attempt to encircle the Soviet encirclers, and it eventually broke down in the face of Soviet resistance.

A second relief attempt on February 11 drove more or less directly into the heart of the Kessel, and Soviet attempts to block it led to one of the great tank melees of the war, with the superior German tanks inflicting punishing losses on the Soviets. In the van was the Heavy Tank Regiment of the deadly dentist, Lieutenant Bäke, fighting alongside a battlegroup of 1st Panzer Division, *Kampfgruppe* Frank. Their target was Hill 239.0, the dominant height to the southwest of the *Kessel*. The Soviets recognized its importance as much as the Germans did, and once again a brawl unfolded on February 16, with Panthers and Tigers going up against Soviet T-34s and the new "Josef Stalin" tank. The fight left both sides bruised and bleeding. *Kampfgruppe* Frank lost every single one of its company commanders and platoon leaders, and Bäke's Tigers chewed up every Soviet tank they met. But even Bäke couldn't achieve much on fuel tanks that were sucking air by the end of the day. As in so many times in this war, the German drive petered out tantalizingly close to a crucial objective: the Volga River bank in Stalingrad, Alexandria in North Africa, the key gateway city of Ordzhonikidze in the Caucasus campaign. In this case, Bäke's Tigers were quite literally out of gas. His laconic after-action report was an exemplar of understatement: "Supply was the difficulty. The troops had no rations for days, the tanks lacked fuel and ammunition."[67] They had reached the village of Oktiabr, just a few hundred meters short of Hill 239.0 and about eight kilometers (less than five miles) from their comrades trapped in the Korsun Pocket.

Inside the *Kessel*, the troops had endured something akin to the famous five stages of grief: denial, anger, perhaps some private spiritual bargaining with the Almighty, depression, and, no doubt for some, a final acceptance of their fate. Some got mad at their commanders, some bickered senselessly with their comrades, some withdrew into themselves. The units cohered, however, a trait that would endure until the end of the war, even when defeat was inevitable and the fight had become truly hopeless. They stayed together when communications failed, when Soviet attacks had driven them into a smaller and smaller pocket under nearly constant artillery bombardment, when the Soviet air force raged and thundered overhead and the Luftwaffe disappeared, when the promised air supply of the pocket failed to deliver even half the supplies they required. They stuck together when Soviet aircraft dropped millions of propaganda leaflets into the pocket from the National Committee *Freies Deutschland* and the League of German Officers (*Bund Deutscher Offiziere*) urging them to surrender and promising them humane treatment once they did.[68]

Likewise, their officers resisted personal appeals from their former brother-in-arms, General Walther Seydlitz, a tough character they all respected who was taken prisoner at Stalingrad and had turned against the Hitler regime with a vengeance.[69] They refused to treat with a Soviet envoy who came into the pocket under a white flag of truce and proffered a surrender ultimatum. The German regimental commander whom he met casually offered him a cigarette, no doubt to demonstrate just how comfortable things still were in the pocket. The Soviet commander brought out his own cigarette case and made a counteroffer, likewise refused, making sure the Germans noted the tsar's eagle and the noble seal on the tin. The officers observed all the gentlemanly niceties, shared a bubbly glass of Sekt, and the delegation departed.[70] The Germans never did answer the ultimatum.

Certainly, the cracks were beginning to show. Rumors flew in the ranks. Help was on the way. Their officers were leading them to the slaughterhouse. Hitler would never allow a division of his SS to go into captivity and was sending a relief column immediately. But more numerous than the rumors were the questions. Why haven't we been mentioned in the Wehrmacht dispatch (*Wehrmachtbericht*) lately?[71] Have they written us off? Why haven't they come and gotten us out yet? The knew only the bare outline of the relief attempts already undertaken, that the drive of XXXXVII Panzer Corps had barely gotten untracked, while III Panzer Corps had apparently driven to the very edge of the *Kessel*, but not much more than that. And in their uncertainty, the soldiers grumbled and complained about their plight, as soldiers have done from time immemorial: "We criticized, blamed, and scolded—swearing like troopers," one of the survivors remembered.[72] A near riot broke out when a horde of wounded soldiers overwhelmed a single *Kübelwagen*—the Wehrmacht's equivalent of the jeep—sent to transport the wounded from the fighting front to a primitive receiving station in the center of the pocket. Who could blame them? Even the fighting soldiers in the Korsun Pocket were completely unprotected and sleeping under the stars. The plight was far worse for the unlucky wounded.

And then suddenly came a day that seemed like salvation to all of them. On February 15, General Stemmermann received the miraculous news from Army Group South headquarters: the time had come for the breakout. Manstein had decided, for once, to defy Hitler's orders, not to consult him beforehand, and to order the troops inside the Korsun Pocket to make a break for it on the night of February 16–17. The code word for the breakout, naturally enough, was "Freedom."[73] By now there was no real choice. The pocket was shrinking daily. Soviet attacks along the perimeter had shrunk it to an oblong gash no more than eight kilometers long and five kilometers wide, still containing some 45,000 soldiers and a handful of tanks and guns. Indeed, German troops had evacuated the town of Korsun itself and thus surrendered the only workable airfield they had. With Soviet pressure growing daily and without hope of resupply, the encircled force could not stay where it was. The relief columns had stalled. Salvation lay only in the breakout.

The news spread rapidly and worked like a tonic on the exhausted, filthy, and frozen troops. "Enough of these broken men," one would later write, "enough of this constant talking about death." He knew they would get through—they had to. It was time to "throw your heart over the hurdle," he felt, and ignore all those "crippling premonitions":

> We are breaking out! It will be soldiers who will win the battle, not just uniform-wearers. What do the Russian antitank guns mean to us? What do the enemy reinforcements standing between our relief spearheads and us have to say? The number of tanks and guns behind the enemy infantry will burst like a bubble if we apply the necessary force. Up till now it's been defense, now it's attack, a redeeming, unwinding, concentrated attack of the greatest magnitude, with a force that will be overwhelming in its fighting spirit, aiming at our target: freedom. That is what we think.[74]

The breakout plan was a desperate one, to be sure. General Stemmermann formed his ragged divisions into three assault columns: Corps Detachment B on the right, 72nd Infantry Division in the center, and 5th SS Panzer *Wiking* on the left, with 57th and 88th Divisions making up the rear guard.[75] If all went well, they would follow on to the breakout point once the initial assault had pierced the Soviet defenses. The assault wedges themselves were among the most unusual formations in German military history, each consisting of three echelons. The first was the "bayonet echelon," which would assault the Soviet lines with no preliminary maneuver, no fire preparation, and lowered bayonets. This tactical approach was essentially the mirror image of the one practiced by outclassed Soviet infantry in 1941, who had often done the same thing to break out of German encirclements, linking arms, bellowing "hurra!," and charging for the nearest point in the German line. Hopefully they would make up in surprise and shock what they lacked in weaponry, firepower, and modernity. The second echelon deployed heavy weapons and tanks, at least those that could be muscled out of the mud. The third consisted of the artillery and the impedimenta: supply columns, trucks, and horse-drawn *panje* wagons that littered any modern army's rear area.[76] All these columns and echelons were heading for the same objective: Hill 239.0, the "receiving point" where friendly forces of the III Panzer Corps would take them in. Since speed and surprise were of the essence, the German command made the controversial decision of leaving behind 1,500 of their most severely wounded, along with a few medics and sanitary personnel who vigorously protested their new orders.[77]

Against a powerful and well-supplied Soviet adversary, the Korsun breakout attempt might appear doomed. But as a great philosopher once observed, war is the province of uncertainty in which you can never really be sure of anything; the operation opened with a rousing success. The first echelon charged forward in a headlong rush late in the evening of February 16. The men really did shout "hurra!" as they charged home, brandishing little more than their machine pistols, rifles, and bayonets. They really did catch the Soviets napping—operating in the mud and cold and snow was as taxing on the Soviets as on the Germans. Almost before they knew it, the German first echelon had broken through the Soviet defenses and was heading southwest.

Paradoxically, the very success meant the end of any considerered operational plan for the breakout. No one—certainly not the rank and file—cared any more about the schedule, or the order of approach, or the timetables. The second and third echelons followed in a rush, and then on came the rear guard: a great surging mass of humanity at least 40,000 strong, all crammed into a box a few kilometers square and streaming down the few good roads toward Hill 239.0, their comrades, and freedom. *Gruppe* Stemmermann, an organized military formation just an hour ago, had fallen apart, and in the course of the rush forward Stemmermann's car took a direct hit from a Soviet shell, killing the general instantly. Command and control thus broke down completely at the very moment when it was most required, and only the "elementary flow of the mass" determined the course of the action.[78] The German force inside the Korsun Pocket had exited the realm of war and had crossed back over into the state of nature, where survival is the prime directive and rational thought recedes. And the weather fit the grim situation perfectly, unloading a furious blizzard onto the scene, adding to the meter or so of snow that was already on the ground.

And yet, one thought still guided them all, a compulsion perhaps, an idée fixe: Hill 239.0 meant freedom. It was just a few miles up the road, and the van of the surging German horde was approaching it soon after midnight February 17. Certainly, they were under fire from both flanks, but no one had expected that breaking through such a narrow corridor was going to be easy. Just a few more kilometers, though, and they would be out. They could make out the dim shape of the big height just ahead. Their friends were waiting. A sense of euphoria grew. Codeword "Freedom!"

Then the hillside erupted with a roar: Soviet artillery and machine guns and one tank round after the other, slamming into the defenseless mass of foot soldiers surging forward, a scene of "sheer horror," as the German official history later described it.[79] Standing guard at the very "gate of freedom" was an impenetrable line—a wall, really—of Soviet tanks. Within minutes, the dead covered the ground, thousands more Germans were surging to the front to join them—only to meet death in their turn—and a collective panic ensued. Within minutes, Soviet tanks ratcheted the terror upward by rolling forward to crush everything in their path: *panje* wagons, the dead and wounded lying on the ground, and desperate men trying to run away. Bringing the carnage to a peak was the 5th Cossack Cavalry Corps, charging into the German mass, riding down unfortunate soldiers and hacking away with their sabers. German forces, including heavy tanks, were on the other side of that hill, quite literally. As a crow flies, it couldn't have been more than 500 yards, but on this grisly night they might as well have been on another planet.

Trying to sort out what had happened is not easy. Most of the men in the pocket clearly thought that Hill 239.0 was in German hands. Manstein and his staff at Army Group South believed, when they sent the breakout orders to Stemmermann on February 15, that Bäke's Tigers and Panthers would be able to take the hill the next day. Neither they nor the command staff of III Panzer Corps could have predicted the fuel shortages that cropped up at the worst possible moment, halting the final lunge toward the objective. Likewise, no one, with the possible exception of Clausewitz himself, could have foreseen the unlucky breakdown in radio communications between III Panzer Corps and General Stemmermann that prevented him from learning about Bäke's failure. Even had he known, however, he might have found it impossible to rescind the breakout order that so galvanized his men in the pocket.

Slaughtered in front of Hill 239.0, the human flood turned away. Who can describe the decision-making process? The term "mob psychology" has always been a contradiction, but as if following the explicit order of a phantom commander, much of the breakout mass now swerved south. No doubt the survival instinct was in play—desperate to remove themselves from Soviet fire, and facing the well-defended village of Dzurzhentsy to their north, the Germans really had no choice. Onward they came, once again like a wave, with two streams parting around the village of Pocapincy, then rejoining once past it, heading south, now turning west, toward the village of Lisjanka. They had apparently hit a temporary seam in the Soviet defensive ring—the dark of night had made a confusing situation even more perplexing for all the participants. They had gone around Hill 239.0, circumvented the obstacle, and, once again, freedom beckoned. They all knew that Lisjanka was German-held.

All they needed to do now was cross a river.

The Gniloj Tikic was at high water now, some 2–3 meters deep and 25 meters across. The water was icy, with jagged floes on the surface and a steep, slick western bank. They had gotten there in one piece: elements of all three original breakout columns were present en masse—thousands of men and growing. But as their numbers mounted on the eastern bank of the river, they formed a lucrative target for Soviet artillery, and they could see Soviet tanks beginning to arrive from the north as well. There was no option: thousands of men plunged into the icy waters of the Gniloj Tikic. Many drowned in their panic; many were killed in the water, machine-gunned or blown apart by tank and artillery shells; too many got across to the other side yet failed to gain a purchase on the steep, icy bank and fell back into the water. Hundreds drowned within a few meters of safety. But many, once again an improbable number given all that happened earlier that night, also got across to safety. Even modern weaponry can't kill everyone, and the Germans did have the advantage of mass. The survivors still had to walk the few kilometers to Lisjanka, headquarters of III Panzer Corps, shivering in their wet uniforms, the icy cold, and the snow. It was, in a grim way, a fitting ending to their ordeal.

Analyzing Korsun

Timing is everything, they say. The next day, February 17, III Panzer Corps finally fulfilled its mission and took Hill 239.0, allowing remnants of the breakout force, still milling around or hiding in various states of confusion, to escape to freedom. If the Germans could only have coordinated their two operations, the relief column and the breakout, a bit more effectively—a mere matter of fine-tuning—they might have eluded the disaster. But, in fact, military operations are all about fine-tuning, and it is precisely fine-tuning that separates successful operations from debacles like this one. Perhaps a military force that doesn't have enough fuel and whose radios break down in the Russian winter and whose tanks can't navigate the mud—the three key elements in this brutal timing and communications misfire—has no business at all fighting in the Soviet Union.

The battle of Korsun soon turned into a battle of rival narrative—actually a contest of lies. The Soviets got their lie in first. They claimed to have won a total victory at Korsun—to have shut the *Kessel* so tight that not a single German soldier got out alive. As 2nd Ukrainian Front commander Konev put it:

> We took all the necessary measures so that not a single hitlerite could escape from encirclement. To break through four defensive zones—two on the inner and two on the outer encirclement front—and besides this, to pass the tank-proof areas and antitank artillery in the center of the corridor was impossible. . . . By the morning of February 17 the enemy grouping was finished with. Tens of thousands of German officers and men paid with their lives for the senseless and criminal stubbornness of the nazi Command which rejected our ultimatum for surrender.[80]

But virtually every one of Konev's sentences is false, as were his absurd claims to have killed 130,000 Germans in the battle and destroyed over 600 tanks. If the two standard Wehrmacht infantry corps involved in the fight along the Dnepr actually possessed 130,000 men and 600 tanks in the first place, it is likely that Konev would have been on the defensive and perhaps even running for his life. Indeed, we know now that majority of the men in the pocket—some 36,000 men out of the 58,000 present—were able to flee in that final, mad rush. Along with another 4,000 wounded who were flown out in the course of the fighting, the Wehrmacht managed to extricate nearly 40,000 men.[81]

Some of the German success was simply fortuitous timing. The breakout, for example, had caught the Soviets in the midst of redeploying their troops around the pocket for the final assault. As the weeks dragged by and his armies still had not reduced the encirclement, Stalin had gotten impatient—rarely a happy development within the Soviet high command—and his commanders in the field spent much of the campaign bickering. Konev worked overtime to undercut Zhukov, who was in overall command, while both men spent a great deal of effort maligning Vatutin (1st Ukrainian Front) as a sluggard and blaming him for the allegedly slow pace of the operation. In this Darwinian struggle for survival, Konev came out on top with Stalin precisely by making the kind of absurd promises that he later claimed to have kept: he vowed that he would tie up the Germans so tightly that none could escape, and then he would kill them all. As Konev rearranged his forces for the final drive to split up and crush the pocket, however, the Germans were able to hit numerous seams, gaps, and holes in the defensive rings, with the tragic and bloody exception of the direct route to Hill 239.0. In the end, Korsun was a Soviet victory but a failed encirclement, an "ordinary victory" that fell short of a true battle of annihilation.

But in a deeper sense, Konev was right. Even if Korsun didn't rise to the level of a Stalingrad on the Dnepr, it had been a disaster for the Wehrmacht all the same. The Germans in the pocket had to abandon all their equipment and armor, a loss that the Wehrmacht, already mired in a poor man's war, surely could not afford. The escapees were also so morally and physically wrecked that they were unfit for immediate further duty. It was not simply a matter of plugging them back into the line. As fighting formations, XI and XXXXII Corps had temporarily ceased to exist, creating yet another open wound that would trouble the Wehrmacht for the rest of the winter.

Konev's bloated claims for Korsun were the soul of moderation, however, compared to what the Germans had to say about it. As often with Nazi propaganda, an initial, relatively factual account soon blossomed into something quite different. The first notifications on February 18–19 spoke of "reestablishing communications" to a "strong German battlegroup" that had been "cut off for weeks," an operation that had succeeded despite "numerous enemy counterattacks" and the "most difficult terrain." All that was true enough, but by February 20 the dispatch from the Führer's headquarters in Rastenburg began to lurch into more familiar and bombastic rhetorical terrain: "The absorbtion of the liberated divisions is complete. The formations of the army and Waffen-SS who have been cut off since 28th January, under the leadership of General of Artillery Stemmermann and Lieutenant General Lieb[,] fought a heroic defensive struggle, resisting the onslaught of far superior enemy forces and breaking through the enemy encirclement in a bitter series of battles." Korsun, so the new line read, was "another shining example of heroic endurance, bold offensive spirit, and self-sacrificing comradeship in the history of German soldiering." The ensuing weeks saw a parade of honors for the brave warriors of the Korsun Pocket—including receptions with the Führer, promotions, and medals.

But, in fact, the battle of the Korsun Pocket was a debacle for the Wehrmacht. We should leave the final word to General Vormann, who commanded XXXXVII Corps in its failed relief attempts into the pocket. As always, the closer one stood to the action, the more difficult it was to lie about what had happened. "Nimble propaganda," he would later write, "obscured and twisted the fact that we had lost a great battle and suffered heavy losses."[82]

Conclusion: In the Cauldron

Despite the controversy over numbers, however, Korsun was a fitting curtain-raiser to the war's final phase in the east. Indeed, we may go so far as to label it the *typos*—the typical battle of the era. The opening phase of the Russo-German war—the first six months of Operation Barbarossa in 1941—saw the Wehrmacht in high gear, trapping its Soviet adversary in a series of massive encirclements. But the Wehrmacht's logistics—never a front-burner item in the German way of war—had been grossly insufficient to maintain fighting strength into the winter, and the drive burned out short of its objectives. The next two years handed the German army one punishing defeat after the other: Moscow, Stalingrad, Kursk, and the post-Kursk Soviet offensives. Nevertheless, the Wehrmacht was still able to launch great offensives in that second phase: toward Stalingrad, into the Caucasus, and against Kursk. (See Map 1.2.)

Now those days were gone. In the third phase, all that was left, ap-

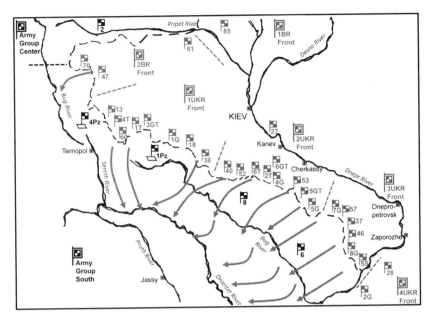

Map 1.2 Slaughter in the Ukraine (March–April 1944)

parently, was the ability to slither out of traps and survive hair-raising brushes with death like the one at Korsun. The entire Eastern Front had become a *Kessel*—a seething cauldron—and many formations of the German army would spend the final two years of the war in a series of desperate attempts to escape from Soviet encirclements.

The 1st Panzer Army under General Hube managed to do just that in March and April. Surrounded near Kamenets-Podolsk by vastly superior forces of 1st and 2nd Ukrainian Fronts, Hube stayed calm, organized his force into two great combined arms columns, and prepared a breakout. Deciding upon the direction was the main problem, and Hube and his superior, Manstein, spent days pondering which way to go. The southern flank of 1st Panzer Army was sitting on the Dniester River to his south, and Hube's first thought was to cross the mighty river and use it for shelter. To the west lay difficult terrain in the form of a series of north-south rivers: the Smotrych, the Zbrucz, and the Seret. This was by far the tougher route, an unappealing slog with stops and starts for each watercourse. In the end, together they made the difficult decision to head west, believing that the unorthodox operational choice would catch the Soviets by surprise. Zhukov, in overall command of Soviet operations in this sector, was indeed expecting

Hube to cross the big river to his south, rushed most of his reserves to the Dniester sector, and never did get his forces positioned correctly.

Starting his breakout on March 24, Hube moved in bounds: punching a hole in the Soviet defenses with his tanks, keeping pursuing Soviet forces at bay with his antitank guns, pulling out the rear guard at the last moment, then heading up to the next river line. Hube's decision to mingle the arms was crucial. An all-mechanized grouping, he knew, would tend to range on ahead and leave the marching infantry isolated in the rear, and that would court disaster. What was necessary here was not a bold rush but a systematic approach, one step—and one river—at a time. In the end, Hube prevailed, and his "wandering pocket" managed to reestablish contact with a mechanized relief column of the II SS Panzer Corps (containing the 9th and 10th SS Panzer Divisions) on April 6.

Manstein's reward for his part in this brilliant operational conception was his dismissal. By now, Hitler had had enough. The never-ending arguments, Manstein's constant demands for more men, more divisions, and more tanks, his cheeky suggestions that Hitler should relinquish command of forces in the east and let Manstein run the war on his own: all these had contributed to turn the relationship between Führer and field marshal toxic. Hitler also took advantage of the moment to remove another thorn in his side, General Ewald von Kleist of Army Group A, who like Manstein had become increasingly critical of the operational scheme in the east. Hube's reward, by contrast, was a summons to Berchtesgaden to receive the Knight's Cross with Oak Leaves, Swords, and Diamonds, then the highest decoration in the German array. He didn't have long to enjoy it, however. His plane crashed soon into the return flight from Germany and Hube was killed.

But even as these dramatic events were playing out to the south, the Soviets had already encircled another sizable German force in the city of Ternopol.[83] With the German position in Ukraine crumbling and no end in sight, Hitler issued Führer Order No. 11 on March 8. His decree allowed for the creation of so-called strongholds (*feste Plätze*) at the front, cities, towns, and villages that were to "allow themselves to be encircled and thereby tie up as much enemy strength as possible."[84] Ternopol, in the 4th Panzer Army sector, was the first of these supposed breakwaters. Attacked on March 9 by forces of 1st Ukrainian Front and declared a stronghold on March 10, the town had no defensive fortifications of any sort or, even, an airfield for ferrying in supplies. It had a sizable garrison—six battalions of infantry, some 4,600 men—but few heavy weapons, artillery, or antitank guns. Basic rations were lacking, and drinking water, especially, was in short supply. The first commandant, General Hans Schrepffer, took one look at his new command, decided the situation was hopeless, and immediately messaged Hitler to that effect. Actually, he first had to requisition a radio, since the new stronghold lacked a workable communications net. His recalcitrance got him fired, unsurprisingly. His replacement, General Heinrich Kittel, arrived in Ternopol and came to the same conclusion as Schrepffer, requesting permission to evacuate Ternopol. Hitler denied the request, and a second series of Soviet attacks surrounded the city on March 23.

There are few times in World War II that the Wehrmacht could be described as operationally inept, but Ternopol was one. The dispatch of a resupply truck convoy under Colonel Werner Friebe, accompanied by a Panzer battalion and two Panzergrenadier battalions, collapsed before it even got started. The trucks and suplies were still 130 kilometers away, back in Lemberg, by the time *Kampfgruppe* Friebe was ready to roll. The tanks set out anyway—not to resupply Ternopol, let alone to evacuate the unlucky German troops still stuck there or to remain there as a reinforcement for the garrison. Instead, the operation devolved into a relief attack: an operation undertaken in the vague hopes of causing the Soviets some undetermined level of damage. Even by those minimal standards, the mission of *Kampfgruppe* Friebe was a misfire, meeting strong resistance, artillery and antitank fire, and heavily mined roads that reduced the foward motion of the Panzers to a crawl. After heavy lossses, including the death of a regimental commander and two battalion commanders, Friebe called the whole thing off. It was just as well that the trucks hadn't shown up, he later remarked bitterly. Soviet fire would have torched every last one of them.

And so the Ternopol tragedy played out. With Soviet artillery emplaced on the high ground around the city and firing over open sights, shells rained down and German losses mounted. By April 1, just over half of the 4,600 defenders had become casualties. The German pocket was shrinking steadily under the pressure of concentric attacks by five Soviet divisions, and General Kittel was dimissed. The third commandant in twelve days, General Egon von Neindorff, made the same request as his two predecessors and received the same response. By now Soviet bombardment was uninterrupted—including mortars, guns of all calibers, and air attacks. The center of Ternopol became an inferno, with some 1,500 German troops compressed into a zone less than 1,000 yards across, every inch of which was being combed by Soviet fire. A final German relief attempt on April 12, once again by

Kampfgruppe Friebe, faltered in the midst of a sudden heavy rainstorm that turned roads to mud. Friebe got within a few kilometers of the city, but no closer, and had to surrender Ternopol's defenders to their fate.

Almost all died: 4,545 out of the original 4,600.[85] As Friebe's Panzers churned slowly forward, they met small groups of shell-shocked, stumbling victims, nearly unrecognizable as German soldiers. Ten men here, another five there, seven more up the road: the fifty-five men lucky enough to have broken out of the inferno.

Ternopol was a tiny battle by Eastern Front standards, and today it is one of the many forgotten battles of World War II. Despite its size, however, the debacle tells us all we need to know about the sorry state of the Wehrmacht by early 1944. Certainly, the Germans could still fight, and they would continue to display their tactical and operational prowess to the bitter end of the war. German Panzer and mechanized formations were still the elite fighting formations on either side in this war. Otherwise, ponder this toxic combination of attributes: a Supreme Commander who was completely out of touch, out of his depth, and increasingly irrational; an impotent General Staff that had sunk to the level of pure administrators rather than advisers; a corps of once-savvy field commanders who shook their heads at the latest ridiculous order out of Rastenburg—but usually did what they were told anyway; and finally, millions of ordinary soldiers who were willing to fight for the cause and die at their posts—and who were about to get that chance. Trapped in a hopeless war, the Wehrmacht was marching to the graveyard.

2

In the Mountains: The Battle for Italy

Introduction

History never lies far beneath the surface of current events. We like to think we are free agents, making our own decisions and determining our own path. In fact, we often march in the footsteps of those who have gone before.

It is early in the fifth year of a great war. Battles are raging in the mountains, the defenders are barely hanging on, and their commanders are conferring.

* * *

LOCATION AND DATE UNDISCLOSED. *The Supreme Commander was always smiling. Was he an optimist? Or was it just a leadership tool, a mask he wore as the occasion demanded to instill confidence in his subordinates? Or perhaps he was actually enjoying this?*[1]

Certainly, the Lagekarte *(situation map) offered little reason to smile. As always by this point in the war, the situation was bad, the prognosis negative. The Allies held all the advantages: men, tanks, endless waves of aircraft, and, as always, a vast superiority in artillery. Their guns never seemed to stop firing, and their ammunition supply was apparently inexhaustible. Armies were not the only players on the Italian front. US industrial production was omnipresent. The Allies may have been driving on Rome, but the sources of their strength were the furnaces, forges, and lathes of far-off places like Cleveland or Pittsburgh.*

The divisional commander never smiled. Prussians rarely did. He was a tough man, and so was his division—the 29th Panzergrenadiers: *armored infantry. Relentless in the attack, steady in the defense. They had gotten it done in Sicily, schooling the American and British armies during a fighting retreat, and they'd been doing it since the Allies landed in Italy. The Grenadiers had been in one tough scrap after the other during the retreat from Salerno: first the slog back to the Volturno River, then the Bernhard Line, and behind that one the Gustav. But the 29th had stood up to every assault, every air raid, every terrifying bombardment.*

Now they were tired, and so was their leader. He could read his men, and right now he didn't like what he was seeing: their stumbling steps, ragged uniforms, dirty beards. They looked more like a criminal gang than modern soldiers.

It was time for General Walter Fries to make his report to the Supreme Commander. He took a long breath.

"The Monte Lungo position is untenable. We have a handful of exhausted companies facing two enemy divisions, both of which are being frequently relieved. The Allied divisions are nearly twice as strong as ours, and their artillery and its fantastically abundant supply of ammunition is in the ratio of ten to one against us."[2]

He was getting if off his chest. Even the hardest have to do that occasionally.

Supreme Commander–Southwest Field Marshal Albert Kesselring shook his head. He'd heard it all before—lack of men, weapons, air cover—but there was nothing he could do about it. Fries was one of the best divisional commanders in the stable, however, and his men needed him at his sharpest. It was time for Kesselring to play his trump, something that he knew would be just the kick in the pants that Fries needed.

"Look," Kesselring said, his smile forced, a bit brittle now. "I know I'm only a Bavarian. You're the Prussian. But I don't recall the Prussians ever asking how strong the enemy is. No: only where he is!"[3]

* * *

Material inferiority? A hopeless mission? Strategic uncertainty? The German campaign in Italy had them all. But the fight in the mountains also had a defending army steeped in a particular tradition, one that emphasized the supremacy of willpower over weapons, of tenacity over technology, and of winning the fight (*Gefecht*) no matter how badly the war might be going.

Why Italy?

Sometimes it is tempting to stand back for a moment, try to gain some distance, and ask: "What were they all doing here?" Why were twenty Wehrmacht divisions in Italy fighting the Allies—the US and British armies, along with contingents from New Zealand, Free France, Poland, and more? Where were the Italians? What was Germany's strategic purpose? What was at stake for them all in the Apennines and the Abruzzi?

The standard answer is: "Not much." As so often in wartime, one thing had seemingly led to another, one decision generating the next in a logical, almost lockstep fashion.[4] The Allies had launched their first great amphibious invasion of the war into French North Africa (Operation Torch) in November 1942. The decision was controversial, especially within the command echelon of the US Army, and President Franklin D. Roosevelt eventually had to force it through against the will of his chief military adviser, General George C. Marshall. The latter wanted a direct blow against the Germans, an amphibious landing in France and a thrust into the Reich. Staff studies—Operation Sledgehammer in 1942, Operation Roundup in 1943—soon showed that Allied troops were nowhere near ready for a cross-Channel landing in 1942, however.[5] They lacked the manpower, the experience of planning such a complicated undertaking, and the specialized equipment a landing would require. The Dieppe landing in August 1942, in which the Germans shot to pieces an attempt by Canadian 2nd Division to seize the fortified port, showed just how difficult such an operation could be.

Nevertheless, the president thought it essential to get US forces into battle against the Axis somewhere in 1942, and North Africa seemed to be the only possible place. Supporting him in his decision was the British prime minister, Winston Churchill, a promoter of a peripheral strategy that would nibble around the edges of Hitler's Europe, rather than attempt to blast directly into it. A landing in North Africa would also place Allied forces in the rear of Field Marshal Erwin Rommel's *Panzerarmee Afrika*, then facing off against British 8th Army at El Alamein in Egypt, and clear North Africa of Axis forces once and for all. With the war more than three years old and counting, Torch was a fairly minimal program for the Allies, an incremental rather than decisive strategic gain. But with the cross-Channel landing postponed indefinitely, it was the only real option.

The Allies landed successfully in Algeria and Morocco, overran the Vichy French defenders, and then smashed Axis forces in Tunisia. But success changed nothing on the strategic level. The Allies were now trapped in a causative loop that forced them to do the same thing again and again. Tunis led to the invasion of Sicily in July 1943 (Operation Husky), and Sicily to the invasion of mainland Italy. What else could the Allies do? Marshall's desired invasion was still in the planning stages and would not be ready for another year. No state fields great armies and deploys massive fleets in wartime so they can sit around and do nothing. The post-fascist Italian government of General Pietro Badoglio was already deep in armistice discussions with the Allies.[6] If the Allies could stage a landing and coordinate it precisely with the moment of Italian surrender, perhaps they could seize the entire long peninsula. Juicy targets beckoned: the airfield complex at Foggia in the south, major cities like Naples, Rome, and Bologna, or even the massive industrial zone of the Po River valley, if they moved quickly enough.

The Allies invaded Italy in September 1943, with British 8th Army landing under General Bernard Law Montgomery in Calabria (Operation Baytown) and the US 5th Army under General Mark W. Clark just south of Salerno (Operation Avalanche). Salerno lay in the southern portion of the peninsula, so Avalanche was a conservative plan, but it offered a good, sandy beach that would allow the Allies to seize the great port of Naples early in the fighting. Aiming anywhere farther north would also have placed the Allied forces outside the range of land-based aircraft deployed in Sicily—a risky move.

Conservative or not, the Allied campaign opened in disastrous fashion, with the Italians bungling their surrender, the Germans occupying the entire country and disarming the 2 million–man Italian army (Operation *Achse* ["Axis"]), and the Panzers nearly crushing the American beachhead south of Salerno.[7] Once the Allies made it ashore, hopes for some kind of grand operational pincer, with Montgomery's army racing up out of Calabria and trapping the Germans against Clark's force, foundered on the rocks of hesitant command decisions, bad roads, and forbidding mountain terrain. Montgomery, never a ball of operational fire, squeezed his army into narrow Calabria, and even small German rear guards were able to delay him. Clark, for his part, was experiencing the growing pains of his first field command, and his handling of the landing and subsequent battle of the beachhead was less than sure.

Clark survived, Montgomery eventually managed to come up into Italy proper, and the Germans had to withdraw their defensive ring around Salerno and pull back to the north. The Allies took their initial strategic objectives, Naples and Foggia, on the same day, October 1. Despite all their advantages in materiel, however, the invaders now found themselves experiencing nothing but frustration in Italy. They bore the burden of attack and soon discovered the joys of campaigning in this mountainous theater.[8] With the weather worsening, the mountains looming overhead, and the Germans everywhere on the high ground looking down on them, the Allies slowed to a crawl and then halted altogether 80 miles south of Rome.

Of course, the Wehrmacht also had a say. At the time of the Allied invasion, the Germans had sixteen divisions in the peninsula, divided into rival commands: Field Marshal Erwin Rommel's Army Group B at Garda in northern Italy and Field Marshal Albert Kesselring's High Command South (*Oberbefehlshaber-Süd*, or *OB-Süd*) farther down the boot, headquartered at Frascati, just south of Rome. To Rommel, defending Italy anywhere south of Rome was foolish. Given the enemy's control of the sea, holding in the south would amount to an invitation for an Allied amphibious landing, or a series of them, to cut off and destroy the defenders. The only thing worth defending in Italy, Rommel felt, was the Po River valley, Italy's population, resource, and industrial heartland. Indeed, some members of his staff felt that the smart thing to do was to construct an impregnable fortified zone in the Alps and let the Allies try their luck at it.

Kesselring argued the opposite. Defending the broad line of the Po Valley, or even the Alps, would require divisions that Germany could no longer raise. He had staff studies in hand that indicated he could hold in the south with a far smaller commitment of forces—just nine divisions in the line and two in reserve. While Kesselring was already well known in the German command for his relentless optimism, he also had operational logic on his side. The easiest place to defend the peninsula was at its "waist" (*Taille*) south of Rome, where Italy was at its narrowest.[9] Moreover, of all Hitler's commanders in late 1943, Kesselring was one of the few who was actually promising to hold his ground, and he must have seemed like a ray of sunshine to an increasingly disillusioned Führer. Here, Hitler realized, was the "stander" (*Steher*) he had been looking for, a determined commander who would follow orders to defend in place rather than constantly begging for permission to retreat. Finally, the shaky Allied performance at Salerno, especially that of the US Army, and the slow pace of the Allied drive north to the Volturno River, sealed the debate within the German High Command. On November 21, Hitler made his decision, sending Rommel and Army Group B to France to organize its defenses against an Allied invasion, naming Kesselring Commander in Chief Southwest (*Oberbefehlshaber Südwest*, or *OB-Südwest*) and giving him command of Army Group C, tasked with defending Italy as far south as possible.[10] With the Wehrmacht outnumbered in men and materiel, increasingly outclassed by Allied motorization and airpower, and bleeding from a thousand cuts on the Eastern Front, the last thing it needed was another major land campaign, but in the unpredictable twists and turns of war, it had one now.[11]

The Wehrmacht Ascendant: On the Gustav Line

The Italian campaign was unique in World War II in that both sides viewed it primarily as an economy-of-force operation, a subsidiary rather than a decisive theater. Both the Germans and the Allies were trying to tie up as many enemy divisions in Italy as possible while using as few of their own, and both of them viewed the fighting in Italy only in terms of its impact on the upcoming campaign in Western Europe. German strategy aimed to prevent the Allied divisions in Italy from taking part in the imminent Allied invasion in the west, and the Allies likewise wanted to prevent the German formations in Italy from reinforcing the invasion sector. And, in fact, both sides believed they were doing just that.

Unfortunately, their quests were mutually exclusive, and it was (and still is) difficult to determine who succeeded and who failed. It takes divisions to tie up divisions, of course, and the result was a rapid and significant buildup of forces on both sides. The Germans, for example, went from fielding a single army in theater in the course of the fighting, the 10th, to a two-army array, adding 14th Army to the order of battle in January 1944. Employing an entire army group in Italy was a significant overcommitment of force for what was essentially a sideshow. Likewise, the Allied landing at Anzio added VI Corps to the forces deployed in Italy, and in the course of the desperate fighting to defend the beachhead, the corps grew to the size of an army. While every division used by either side in Italy was lost for the big show that everyone knew was coming, the Germans had a far greater need for those divisions, especially considering the flotsam and jetsam of "eastern battalions" and "static divisions" they deployed in France to meet Operation Overlord. A one-for-one trade in a war of attrition helps the side with more men, more weapons, and more robust logistics. In that sense, the Italian campaign made more sense for the Allies. But the Allies, too, could have used more divisions for the decisive campaign in France, and even today, the question of "who tied up whom?" can yield varying answers—and will always remain the great strategic conundrum posed by the Italian campaign.

Italy did serve one unequivocal function, however. For an army focused so relentlessly on the conduct of operations in the field, to the near exclusion of other, less kinetic considerations of warmaking like strategy, logistics, or intelligence, Italy was an opportunity to do what Germans did best: fight battles. The strategic situation may have been a mess, but in Italy the Wehrmacht would have an opportunity, once again, to demonstrate its traditional prowess, to highlight the superiority of its *Kampfkraft* (fighting strength), and to humiliate its adversaries in one battle after the other.[12] Here, perhaps, was the last place in the war where German field commanders could win battlefield laurels in the traditional sense.

They were a diverse bunch, these generals: inveterate optimists like Kesselring or hard-charging Panzer commanders like Eberhard von Mackensen,[13] as well as refined intellectuals like Frido von Senger und Etterlin[14] or tough guys like Traugott Herr.[15] What they all shared was a tradition of aggressive battlefield command. Whether on the offensive or the defensive, carrying an assault or fighting a delaying action, they brought maximum aggression to bear. Even in a hopeless cause— perhaps especially in a hopeless cause—tenacity (*Beharrlichkeit*) was the ultimate virtue.[16] Yes, the Allies were beating them back on all fronts, and the same thing would eventually happen in Italy, but the officers of the Wehrmacht were doing the only thing they knew how to do. They were "fighting forward" even as they were "moving back" (*vorwärts kämpfend rückwärts gehen*), conducting a defense, in other words, but a particularly pugnacious one.[17] Their enemies would look on them all with a kind of awe, and the postwar literature in the West would overflow with praise for their performance. In the overall scope of the war, Italy meant little, perhaps, but in the narrow confines of the peninsula, the Wehrmacht won its most important victory of all: the battle to be remembered.[18]

For all the questions we can raise about the wisdom of waging this campaign, the ferocity of the fighting in Italy in 1944–1945 was second to none. The campaign was a classic example of what the Germans call a *Stellungskrieg*, a "war of position." By definition, movement, or at least large-scale maneuver, was absent, fire was dominant, and both sides typically measured their gains in yards rather than miles. Kesselring had his troops dig a series of defensive positions across the peninsula: first along the Volturno River, then the Bernhard Line (the Winter Line to the Allies), and behind it the main position, the Gustav Line. All were more or less the same, a tangle of bunkers, concrete blockhouses, machine-gun nests, and disguised artillery emplacements, with many of the positions blasted out of the sheer rock face of the high Apennines. The mountains themselves formed Italy's rocky spine, spilling out numerous rivers flowing west to the Tyrrhenian Sea or east to the Adriatic. All of the watercourses ran perpendicular to the Allied axis of advance and therefore presented serious military obstacles, especially the four that covered the length of the Gustav Line: from west to east the Garigliano, Gari, Rapido, and Sangro. And finally, anchoring the line and standing directly in the path of the Allied advance, was one of the war's most famous defensive bastions: Monte Cassino. All told, the Gustav Line ran 80 miles from sea to sea as the crow flies, starting at Minturno on the west coast to Ortona on the east, the latter captured by Canadian 1st Infantry Division after a gritty block-by-block fight in December 1943.[19] Eighty miles is not a lot of maneuver room for the attacker, but if the Allies wanted to win this campaign, they had little choice but to bull ahead frontally.[20]

Covering those 80 miles was the German 10th Army under General Heinrich von Vietinghoff-Scheel, an experienced Panzer commander who led a division in the Polish campaign and a Panzer corps in both the Yugoslav campaign and Operation Barbarossa. Vietinghoff had the XIV Panzer Corps (General Senger) west of the Apennines in front of US 5th Army; LXXVI Panzer Corps (General Herr) to the east of the mountains, in front of the British 8th; and an ad hoc formation, *Korpsgruppe* Hauck (a slightly reinforced 305th Division named for the divisional commander, General Friedrich-Wilhelm Hauck), forming a liaison in the high mountains between the two corps. The Wehrmacht was sitting on the defensive and enjoyed every one of the benefits bestowed by what Clausewitz called the "stronger form of warfare." Even in this fifth campaigning season of the war, German divisions still possessed enormous reservoirs of unit cohesion and staying power in battle, even in the face of Allied superiority in materiel and fire. Whether it originated in a solid replacement system that returned wounded men to their original unit (rather than an anonymous replacement pool, as in the US Army), or a familial, father-son relationship between the ordinary grunt (*Landser*) and his officers, or a still-strong, almost messianic faith in Hitler, German unit cohesion was the key to the war lasting as long as it did—and it would be present in spades in Italy.

Indeed, cohesion became all the more crucial as manpower and material resources declined. A tour of 10th Army at the start of 1944 can be revealing. Vietinghoff's two corps were understrength and exhausted, and despite their designation as a Panzer corps, they had precious few tanks between them. The accepted narrative in American and British sources emphasizes Allied difficulties in this campaign, but in every way the Wehrmacht had it worse: fewer supplies, poorer logistics, a longer assignment in the field with no rest or relief. Supply lines, usually consisting of a series of serpentine mountain roads, were under nearly constant Allied air attack, and as a result it took longer to feed German troops, to evacuate their wounded, and to bring up replacements. Hot food was a rarity, and water and medical supplies were nearly always in short supply. In sum, most German formations in Italy were good for little more than positional defense and the occasional tactical counterattack, but they were incapable of taking part in a grand offensive.

Upon taking over XIV Panzer Corps, for example, General Senger visited the command post of his 3rd *Panzergrenadier* Division. The commander, General Fritz-Hubert Gräser, was a flinty old Prussian who had lost a leg in combat during World War I, and yet he still could not resist the lure of visits to the most exposed portions of the front line.[21] But Senger could see troubles in the division. During the retreat from Salerno, the "number of men missing didn't seem to be in harmony with the difficulty of the fighting" and was far in excess of neighboring divisions.[22] The manpower was disparate, with many ethnic Germans (*Volksdeutschen*) from occupied Poland.[23] They were currently serving a military probation in the Wehrmacht, very much second-class soldiers without possibility of promotion. They were also hearing from relatives back in Poland of high-handed treatment by Nazi Party officials. "Special treatment according to 'racial principles' did nothing to raise the morale of the troops," Senger concluded.[24] Even the elements of the division from the Reich proper seemed shaken by the ordeal they had all been through—from Sicily to Salerno and now into the wild Apennines. It had been a time of "many setbacks and uninterrupted retreats," and even a soldier who was a "credulous and loyal follower of Hitler"—and most of them still were—couldn't quite figure out how this parade of failures was supposed to add up to triumph in the end.[25]

The 3rd *Panzergrenadier* had a unique problem set, certainly, but virtually every unit on the front had its own problems. The disaster at Stalingrad still infected the army; no fewer than three of the divisions in Italy had met their demise in the Stalingrad *Kessel* and had been rebuilt, either from cadre and former enlisted personnel who had managed to escape encirclement, or from whole cloth.[26] The 305th Division (*Korpsgruppe* Hauck) was one. It seemed solid enough, and Hauck had taken special care in choosing his regimental and battalion commanders. But like all late-model German infantry divisions, it was weak in antitank assets and mobile reserves and lacked experience in cooperation with the Panzers. Another Stalingrad unit was 44th Division (actually the *Reichsgrenadier-Division Hoch- und Deutschmeister*), under General Friedrich Franek. Recently re-formed, the 44th was inexperienced in combat, inept at combined-arms cooperation, and not at all configured for winter warfare in the mountains. It spent its first months in the line swapping out its horses for mules and desperately trying to keep dry and warm. The 94th Division, on the extreme right of XIV Panzer Corps, was yet another Stalingrad rebuild. Its commander, General Bernhard Steinmetz, was one of the last officers to fly out of the Stalingrad pocket. By all appearances, the 94th was capable, but it had a very difficult dual mission, not only defending its sector of the front but also guarding a long stretch of the seacoast behind it in case of an Allied amphibious landing. In every case, however, these were 1944-model German infantry divisions, consisting of only six battalions (three regiments of two battalions each), compared to the Allied (and former German) standard of nine, and it was the infantry battalions themselves that held the line and that did most of the fighting.

But even the best divisions in the German array, such as the 15th *Panzergrenadier* and 29th *Panzergrenadier*, faced a more fundamental challenge in Italy: "The distinguishing characteristic of the fighting that led to the penetration of the Winter Line and the start of the Cassino battles was that the enemy held the initiative (*das Gesetz des Handelns*). At no location where the enemy launched a serious attack were the German divisions able to maintain their so-called positions. As a result, it was impossible to raise their morale through successes."[27] Indeed, these are problems with every *Stellungskrieg* or, as Senger put it, a linear "frontal defense."[28] As every German commander knew from World War I, one day in the trench or rifle pit comes to seem very much like the next—a monotonous routine that cannot help but erode morale. Danger and death are ever-present, however, and over time the survival instinct can supplant the spirit of aggression and risk-taking. Living day to day in such primitive accommodations, in this case a hole hacked out of the side of a mountain, can turn a soldier's mind more and more to the question of creature comforts. He begins to think, in Senger's words, that "things will be better in the rear," an irreversible crossover point for the cohesion of the defense."[29] These were the very reasons why Prussian and German commanders over the centuries always tried to avoid positional fighting.

A final challenge was the nature of the fighting in Italy: not only a *Stellungskrieg*, but mountain warfare as well. Neither side had much experience, with few actual mountain-trained units appearing in the opposing orders of battle. The Germans were not holding a line so much as a series of semi-isolated strongpoints. Divisions almost never fought as formed units, but instead as individual regiments or battalions. The correct placement of defensive positions took a trained eye and experience, since the geographical crest of a mountain is not necessarily the military crest. A special problem was the tendency, early on, to dig in on the forward slope of the mountain (the *Vorderhang*, in German), an intuitive solution that emphasized holding the high ground and looking directly down into the valley ahead. But the Germans soon learned that deploying on a forward slope was nothing more than an invitation to a plastering by Allied artillery. Hard experience taught commanders that it was usually best to exploit the *Hinterhang*, the reverse slope, with mere observation posts on the forward slope. The point was to let the adversary crest the mountain, then to shoot him up as he descended the other side and was silhouetted sharply against the rocky face.[30] As Marshal Kesselring pointed out, however, there are mountains and there are mountains—tall craggy peaks and lower rounded ones—and what passed for sound tactics in the *Hochgebirge* (the high mountains) was not necessarily the same as in the medium ones, the *Mittelgebirge*. In the end, he concluded, "there is no formula."[31] It came down to feel, in other words, to that same *Fingerspitzengefühl* (the coup d'oeil in French)—the ability to size up terrain at a glance—that was a part of the repertoire of every experienced field commander.[32]

Once the *Landser* had mastered the elements and the mountains, or at least reached an uneasy compromise with them, he had to face the Allies. Analyses of the fighting strength of the US and British armies are legion. Both had their weaknesses: for the British, a tendency toward school solutions, with phase-lines and strict sequencing of operations that were arguably the last thing in the world one needed in mountain warfare; for the US Army, a certain amateurishness, especially among the commanders, and indeed the Americans were still weeding out officers who had risen too high, too fast in the most rapid military expansion of all time. Relations between the two allies could be tense from time to time, with the British accusing the Americans of rushing ahead half-cocked without proper planning, and the Americans accusing the British of having the slows and of pausing every day at teatime. On the personal level, the US 5th Army commander, General Clark, had little use for his superior, General Harold Alexander of 15th Army Group, and for the British in general, and in the course of the fighting he became almost insanely jealous that the British were trying to steal his thunder and get to Rome first (an absurd thought if you study a map of Italy). Clark's counterpart, Montgomery, along with Monty's successor, General Oliver Leese, cordially returned Clark's contempt, and there is little doubt that the ill will filtered down the chain of command into the ranks of the enlisted men.

Their feuds, mutterings, and silly contretemps were meaningless, however, compared to the Allied advantage: absolute materiel and fire superiority over the Germans. The almost limitless industrial potential of the United States was now in play, with tanks, trucks, guns, aircraft, and extremely well-equipped troops flocking to Italy from all points. The British may have been running short of manpower by 1943, and the fighting in Italy saw them relying more and more on Commonwealth and Imperial troops from Canada, New Zealand, South Africa, and India. But fighting alongside the US Army and sharing in American largesse, the British, too, became a kind of firepower colossus, at least in relation to the German troops who opposed them. Add supremacy in the air—both in the tactical realm of ground support and the operational-strategic realm of interdiction and attacks on German supply—and Allied firepower was the German nightmare.[33]

Of course, materiel superiority and even firepower are merely potential advantages. An army has to turn them into something, transforming supplies and ammunition into combat effectiveness. Making that change happen—learning to fight high-intensity, combined-arms warfare—was the real problem for the Allies. Exhibit A was the January 20–22 battle of the Rapido River (which, according to German accounts, actually took place on a small tributary of the Rapido, the Gari).[34] Clark intended to launch yet another attack on the Gustav Line to draw German attention and reserves from the impending Allied landing to the north at Anzio two days later. His plans called for a two-corps assault: British X on the left, crossing the Garigliano River, and US II on the right, crossing the Rapido/Gari chain. The British would hit first with three divisions: 5th Division crossing the Garigliano near its mouth, at Minturno; 56th crossing five miles upriver, at Castelforte; and 46th doing the same at Sant'Ambrogio a few miles farther up. The mission of the British crossings was to force the German defenders—Senger's XIV Panzer Corps—to commit its reserves, thus weakening other sectors of the line.[35]

With British X Corps guarding the left flank, US II Corps would spring into action—carrying out the main assault. Spearheading the assault was US 36th Division, a National Guard unit from Texas under the command of General Fred Walker. The plan was to carry out an assault crossing of the Gari under cover of a massive smoke barrage.

Once the Texans had secured a bridgehead near Sant'Angelo village, engineers would lay down two bridges, allowing 1st Armored Division (General Ernest Harmon) to cross the river and head for Frosinone in the Liri River valley—the relatively open highway to Rome. The shock, Clark hoped, would unhinge the Germans long enough for the Anzio force to land successfully, perhaps even force Kesselring to remove a division or two from the vicinity of Rome to deal with this new threat from the south.

Clark's plan was controversial from the start. The US II Corps commander, General Geoffrey Keyes, was a sound tactician, one of the best in the US Army in the opinion of many of his colleagues. He thought the operational scheme was overly complex and unsafe. Crossing the river would be difficult enough, but even if it succeeded, those who managed to get across would be stuck "in a fishbowl" exposed on all sides to German fire.[36] General Walker of the 36th, likewise, had already had a bellyful of fighting under Italian conditions: the rotten elements, the impossible terrain, the tenacious defenders always perched above and in front of him. He spent the week before the attack scribbling jeremiads in his diary, predicting that the operation would be a disaster, and in the manner of these things, it is highly likely that he communicated his unease to the men underneath him. "I'll swear I do not see how we can possibly succeed in crossing the river near Angelo when that stream is the MLR [main line of resistance] of the main German position," he wrote.[37] But neither he nor Keyes was able to sway Clark, and in the end they gave up trying and followed their orders.

The British attack opened on January 17, a carefully planned set-piece operation that typified the British approach. Making all their preparations under cover of darkness on a moonless night and crossing the Garigliano in silence, 5th Division got over the river before the German defenders could even react. Supporting the direct crossing was a battalion-strength amphibious landing 2,000 yards behind the mouth of the river, using both amphibious trucks (DUKWs) and dedicated landing craft (LCTs). The German 94th Division defending the Garigliano was overstretched, tasked with defending its front and guarding a 30-mile stretch of coastline back to Terracina. Much of the German defensive line in this sector consisted of little more than an outpost line (*Gefechtsvorposten*). While General Steinmetz was organizing the first of many counterattacks to drive back the British or at least contain the bridgehead, a massive artillery barrage heralded the crossing of British 56th Division upriver. Here, too, the 94th's thin gray line had to give way. British X Corps had carved out a bridge-head some two miles deep and 10 miles wide and had placed ten bat-talions across the Garigliano, a potential springboard for exploitation. Only on the right, where the narrow coastal plain transitioned into the mountains, was there trouble, with 46th Division starting late, meeting a swift river current that snapped the ferry cables, and facing strong German resistance. After three thwarted attempts to cross the river near Sant'Ambrogio, the divisional commander, General John Hawkesworth, abandoned the operation.

Despite the 46th's misfire, the German situation was grave enough. If the Allies breached the Garigliano at its mouth, they could unhinge the entire Gustav Line, and the fast road to Rome would lie open to their mechanized forces. Senger contacted Kesselring, bypassing his immediate superior Vietinghoff for greater speed, and demanded rein-forcements for the sector. Kesselring didn't have much to spare—the Wehrmacht rarely did in Italy—but he immediately dispatched the 29th and 90th *Panzergrenadier* Divisions, then resting and rehabilitat-ing near Rome, to the Garigliano front. The two divisions made up virtually the entire reserve of Army Group C.[38] Also headed to the Garigliano was the headquarters of XI *Fallschirmjäger* Corps, under the command of General Alfred Schlemm, to coordinate newly established defenses (and counterattacks) along the front.[39]

If Clark's intent was to tie down German divisions to his front and to get the German command to commit its reserves, then he had suc-ceeded. He also had an opportunity that he could exploit through a flexible alteration of his original operational plans: shifting US forces to the Garigliano front, getting them into the British bridgehead cap-tured by X Corps, and attempting a breakout. But Clark wasn't satis-fied with good fortune. Sadly, he wanted more: an American success, a crossing of the Rapido, and a drive into the Liri River valley. Rather than exploit success, he stuck to his original plan, with the 36th Divi-sion crossing the Rapido and the 1st Armored passing through it into the clear.

As every student of this campaign knows, the crossing of the Rapido on the evening of January 20 was a catastrophe—a legendary failure in the annals of the US Army. The defenders, the 15th *Panzergrenadier* Division under the command of General Eberhard Rodt, were well-blooded veterans of Sicily and Salerno. The unit immediately in the way of the American assault, the 104th *Panzergrenadier* Regiment, sat everywhere on the high ground, and its observers on Monte Cassino could observe every inch of the Gari winding its way beneath them.

They laid out their firing positions cleverly, not in a strictly linear fashion, but in what Senger later called a "zigzag," so that US engineers and troops were already coming under a murderous flanking fire as they slithered down the muddy approaches to the meandering river, with the Wehrmacht's dreaded calling card, the MG-42 machine gun, sawing away and wreaking havoc.[40] The crossing itself, carried out in inflatable rubber boats, was under fire the entire time, and those GIs who did get over the river, slithering up the muddy bank on the far shore, bore out Keyes's "fishbowl" prediction. Senger, for his part, called it a "fire trap" (*Feuerfalle*)—direct German fire of all sorts slashing into the shallow American bridgehead from a 180-degree arc.[41] Within an hour, hundreds of US troops were dead or dying, and the attack had stalled with small bridgeheads on the far side of the Gari.

Attempts to renew the attack the next day were equally futile, as was the idea to insert Harmon's tanks directly into the mix as part of the assault force (a departure from the original phased plan). The Germans added insult to injury by landing a direct artillery hit on Walker's command post on January 22. Already, losses among the two regiments who spearheaded the operation, the 141st on the right and the 143rd on the left, were grievous, somewhere in the range of 2,000 men. A final idea, to get the division's third regiment, the 142nd, into the fight, soon collapsed. The regiment was too far back to get up to the Rapido in a timely fashion, and it was just as well; the 142nd would simply have added to the casualty list.[42]

By the end of the third day, the battle of the Rapido was over. The front line was just about where it had been when the bloodletting commenced, and harsh recriminations within the American camp had already begun. The finger-pointing continued for the rest of the war and would culminate in a postwar congressional hearing into Clark's conduct of the battle. In fact, there was plenty of blame to go around. Clark had drawn up a rigid plan dependent above all else on strict timing, then refused to depart from it even when opportunity knocked. Indeed, rather than question his own plans, Clark blamed the British 46th Division for moving too deliberately and thus unhinging the entire operation. Walker was a walking prophet of doom during the planning process, and it hardly bodes well for the success of any operation when the divisional commander goes around asking witnesses to sign affidavits against his own commanding officer. The corps commander, Keyes, didn't think much of the plan when he first saw it yet did very little to try to change Clark's mind. In the end, however, the failure was systemic. The US Army, for all its surfeit of firepower and modern equipment, had forgotten the fundamentals of preparatory scouting, surprise, and concentration, had blundered into a cul-de-sac of fire, and by the end of the action had paid the price.

The German performance during the Garigliano-Rapido sequence, by contrast, was solid from top to bottom. The British attack at the river's mouth caught local commanders by surprise, but the response from all command echelons was swift. Steinmetz was sending hastily organized *Kampfgruppen* into battle within hours of the British crossing, throwing his two outnumbered grenadier regiments against two complete British divisions; Senger came up to 94th Division's sector the morning of the British assault, and within hours he was on the phone to Kesselring calling for 29th and 90th *Panzergrenadier* Divisions as reinforcements, leapfrogging his own army commander in the process. Vietinghoff later approved Senger's action: time, after all, was of the essence. Kesselring and his planners, including his meticulous chief of staff, General Siegfried Westphal, had to wrestle with Senger's request. Dispatching the two divisions would leave the Rome sector without reserves, potentially disastrous in the case of an Allied landing. As Westphal put it, a "bitter struggle now began over the two divisions":

> It was extremely difficult for the Army Group to find the correct decision. Was the situation . . . in fact so critical as 10th Army viewed it, and had we in consequence to take a risk near Rome? Or should the Army Group hold off in sending help, and allow things on the 10th Army front to take their course? If the breakthrough the 10th Army feared took place, however, we would have sustained damage that we could not put right.[43]

But for all Westphal's agonizing, the "bitter struggle" he describes took less than a day. Indeed, it was the model of dispatch. Senger was still at 94th Division's command post when he phoned Kesselring early on the morning of January 18. Kesselring got the request, phoned Vietinghoff to discuss the situation a little after 9:00 A.M., and made the decision by the afternoon. In the end, Kesselring sent down the 29th and 90th *Panzergrenadier* Divisions. By January 20, 29th *Panzergrenadier* was in battle, launching a counterattack out of Ausonia that not only brought the once-threatening British attack to a standstill but also drove back 56th Division nearly to Castelforte. As always, rapid decision-making and vigorous follow-through were the hallmarks of German command.

As to the German view of the Rapido, so inept had the American attack been that the German commanders involved—Vietinghoff of 10th Army, Senger of XIV Panzer Corps, Rodt of 15th *Panzergrenadier* Division—barely even noticed it. While the assault was taking place, all three believed that the Americans were conducting some kind of reconnaissance in force by a reinforced assault column at company or battalion strength rather than a full-blown assault. Not until late on January 22, when the firing had died down and the Germans could count the American dead, not to mention the 700 US prisoners of war they had captured over the Gari, did they realize the scale of the fight: "Neither the 15th Panzergrenadier Division nor the [XIV Panzer] Corps was fully aware at the time of the extent of the opponent's failure. Only the US Congressional inquiry into the 36th Division's costly attack brought clarity to the situation. The German leadership took very little notice of this attack, since it caused them so little worry."[44] Indeed, repulsing the US attack required "neither local reserves of the 15th Panzergrenadier Division or reserves from other parts of the front."

It's one thing to strive and to lose. Every honorable attempt courts failure. But it is quite another to launch an attack that no one on the other side even notices. Such was the Wehrmacht's tactical ascendancy on the Rapido River.

The War of Movement? Anzio

In the very midst of the Wehrmacht's great defensive triumph on the Rapido, however, the Allies served it a reminder of just who held the strategic initiative in Italy. The Italian campaign had initially been a British idea, and Prime Minister Winston Churchill monitored every step of it like a parent supervising a child. Despite the massive Allied investment of wealth, resources, and industry in Italy, their returns so far had been modest, and getting things moving again was the first Allied operational problem as 1944 dawned. By now, however, the Anglo-American alliance had a great deal of experience at amphibious landings, and it was almost inevitable that they decided to try one here in Italy. (See Map 2.1.)

Operation Shingle was an attempt to outflank the Gustav Line by landing at Anzio in the German rear, a little over 30 miles south of Rome.[45] The intention of the landing was to sever German 10th Army's lines of communication and supply, lever the Wehrmacht out of the Gustav Line, and seize Rome. In a broader sense, Shingle was an Allied

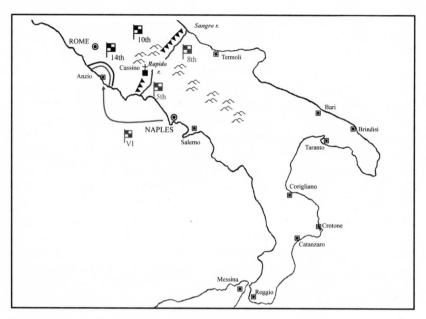

Map 2.1 Failure: The Allied Landing at Anzio (January 1944)

attempt to restore movement to the deadlocked front by exploiting the real Allied advantage in littoral warfare: amphibious mobility.

The operation was ill-fated from the start. By January 1944, men, supplies, and equipment were departing the Mediterranean for the great landing in Normandy, and Italy was becoming the sideshow it was always destined to be. Landing craft, in particular, the sine qua non of Allied amphibious warmaking, were in short supply. The Americans had never been enthusiastic about this campaign in the first place, and now, with American power taking over the Western Allied coalition and with Operation Overlord—the Allied landing in northwest France—imminent, they were being increasingly insistent about limiting further commitments to a secondary theater. Overlord had been General Marshall's solution to defeating Germany almost since the moment that Hitler had declared war on the United States, and he was not about to see it weakened into a half-measure for lack of the necessary equipment.

The fatal decision to land at Anzio has generated controversy ever since it took place. Indeed, from the start, Shingle was at war with itself: an attempt to land a shattering blow that would break the deadlock in Italy, but a limited operation short on resources, troops, and purpose. Rather than a deep strike to achieve strategic surprise and maximum impact, the Allies decided on a relatively shallow envelopment some 60 miles up the Italian boot, making Shingle something between a tactical end run and an independent front. Rather than a full-scale, two-army landing like Operation Husky, Shingle involved only a single corps, the US VI (General John P. Lucas), with British 1st Division (General W. R. C. Penney) landing to the left of Anzio-Nettuno and US 3rd Infantry Division (General Lucian K. Truscott Jr.) to the right. While follow-on forces stood ready (US 1st Armored and 45th Infantry Divisions, along with the usual array of parachute infantry regiments, Rangers, and commandos), the initial burden would fall on the two infantry divisions.

In such a tight situation leadership is critical. Critics then and since have pointed to the US commander tapped to lead Shingle. Lucas worried too much, felt too deeply, and hesitated to act in combat. Consider this assessment, by the greatest American historian of the Italian campaign; Lucas "hardly looked the part of the warrior chieftain":

> He was pudgy and gray, with a brushcut widow's peak, wire-rim spectacles, and a snowy mustache of the sort favored by French general[s] in World War I. He puffed incessantly on a corncob pipe, and carried an iron-tipped cane given him by Omar Bradley. "Fifty-four years old today," Lucas had told his diary on January 14, "and I am afraid I feel ever year of it." One Tommy thought he seemed "ten years older than Father Christmas." Lucas gave an Irish Guardsman the impression of "a pleasant, mild, elderly gentleman being helped out of [a] layer of overcoats."[46]

Even one of his staff officers noted that Lucas "never seemed to want to hurt anybody—at times, almost including the enemy," and Lucas himself once admitted that "I am far too tender-hearted ever to be a success at my chosen profession." Even his nicknames—"Sugar Daddy" and "Foxy Grandpa"—are a far cry from "Stonewall," "Black Jack," or "Stormin' Norman."[47]

The commander with whom Lucas would cross swords was one of the most aggressive in the Wehrmacht, General Eberhard Mackensen. The scion of one of Germany's greatest World War I commanders, Field Marshal August von Mackensen, Eberhard had been born to command, inheriting all of his father's knightly and monarchist traditions, with an admixture of National Socialist ruthlessness that would have been foreign to the elder man. There can be no doubt as to the son's operational talent. The war thus far had seen him serving as chief of staff of the German 14th Army in Poland, chief of staff of the 12th Army in France, and commander of III Army Corps (an element of 1st Panzer Army) in Army Group South during Barbarossa. During the 1942 campaign, III Panzer Corps sealed off an immense Soviet encirclement at Kharkov in May. During the main event of the summer, Operation Blue, Mackensen was at the point of 1st Panzer Army's drive into the Don bend, and then again for the drive into the Caucasus in August. His last offensive saw III Panzer Corps driving on the gateway city of Ordzhonikidze and coming within a single mile of taking it—his war had taken him 1,600 miles away from Berlin at the time, farther that any commander in the army. He was as good a Panzer commander as the Wehrmacht had in 1944, a man tailor-made to torment an amphibious landing and to guard the road to Rome.

Turning Anzio into a personal dual—Lucas versus Mackensen—is unfair, however. Lucas's army commander, Clark, was unsteady, waffling back and forth between optimism and pessimism over the upcoming operation. On the very eve of the landing Clark gave one of the strangest pep talks in military history: "Don't stick your neck out, Johnny," he told Lucas. "I did at Salerno and got into trouble."[48] Lucas saw his missions changing again and again—rarely a good sign of the planning echelon's operational confidence. His orders originally called for him to "advance and secure" the Alban Hills (Colli Laziali in Italian), the crucial high ground to the north of the landing site, and to "be prepared to advance on Rome."[49] But the hills lay 20 miles inland. Securing them while holding the original beachhead was unrealistic for a force of just two divisions. Then, just ten days before the landing, Lucas's orders shrunk. Now he was to "advance on Colli Laziali," with no mention of seizing them, no timetable, and no reference to Rome.[50] "You can forget this goddamned Rome business," Clark told him.[51] Finally, as if to underscore the ill-fated nature of the upcoming operation, a prebattle practice run for 3rd Infantry Division south of the old Salerno beaches on January 19 degenerated into utter chaos: the LSTs hit the wrong beaches, and an entire artillery battalion of 105mm howitzers was lost at sea. Even the divisional commander, General Lucian Truscott, the very model of a can-do US Army officer—and a man who once summed up his leadership philosophy in the pithy phrase "no son of a bitch, no commander"—wondered if Shingle was going to be a suicide mission.[52]

Given all these problems, it is surprising that the Allied landing at Anzio-Nettuno at 2:00 A.M. on January 22 was the smoothest of the entire war. As Naval Task Force 81 approached the coastline—250 ships carrying 40,000 men and 5,200 vehicles—it met with utter silence from the landing beaches. The standard Allied preparatory bombardment—barrages of rocket fire from specially equipped landing craft and over 1,200 aircraft sorties—evinced no reaction at all. The assault forces were expecting all the nightmarish features of a storm landing: minefields, barbed wire, machine-gun fire, long-range artillery. Instead, the landing and the formation of a beachhead "had the character of a peacetime maneuver," as one German analyst put it.[53] German ground fire was practically absent. A pair of coastal defense battalions enjoying some rest from the Gustav Line offered token resistance, and so did a few small antiaircraft units. Allied troops rounded up all of them in the first hour of the landing. By afternoon, Allied engineers had opened the port of Anzio for business, and British and American troops were streaming ashore—36,000 men by the end of the day. The British pushed ahead two miles inland on the left, the Americans three miles on the right. The Alban Hills beckoned to the north, and the road to Rome lay open. Casualties in the course of the day were, for an operation of this size, near zero: 13 killed, 97 wounded, and 44 missing.

Indeed, the landing had taken the Germans completely by surprise. Just days before, Kesselring had sent away the troops entrusted with protecting Rome from an Allied amphibious assault, dispatching 29th and 90th *Panzergrenadier* Divisions to the south to seal off the threatened British breakthrough along the Garigliano River. For the previous three days (January 19–21), the field marshal had placed the forces under his command on emergency alert, but, warned by his staff of unnecessarily tiring the troops, he had called off the alert scheduled for January 22. Kesselring was not alone, however. Admiral Wilhelm Canaris, the chief of German military intelligence (*Abwehr*), had visited Kesselring's headquarters in Frascati a few days earlier and had reported that he didn't see "the slightest sign of an imminent landing in the near future." The level of ship traffic in Naples, Canaris stated, was thoroughly normal. "You can sleep easy tonight," he told the assembled staff.[54]

Now the sector between Anzio and Rome was, for all intents and purposes, undefended. Histories of the campaign are filled with criticism of what the Allies did next. They came ashore, dug in, and sat, and that was as true of US 3rd Division, defending Mussolini Canal on the right flank of the beachhead, as it was of the British 1st, which came ashore and promptly dug in on the left. Lucas himself seemed dazed with relief that it had all gone so smoothly. "I could not believe my eyes," he later wrote, and he made no attempt at the time to kick either one of his divisions into gear.[55] His orders from Clark regarding the Alban Hills were just vague enough to encourage his inaction, a posture to which he was temperamentally inclined, anyway. And so they all stayed put, sitting on a secure beachhead with no Germans in front of them, for three full days (January 22–24). A German judgment that the whole operation was "very strongly focused on security" seems apt.[56]

In the end, however, Shingle failed not because of Lucas but because of the boldness, rapidity, and decisiveness of the German reaction. Over the centuries, Prussian-German commanders had prided themselves on such things: recognizing the inherent uncertainty of war, accepting sudden changes of fortune, crafting improvised solutions on a shoestring and within hours. Indeed, Germany's high-velocity operations always seemed to be careening between disaster and decisive victory: Frederick the Great, in particular, had made a career of it at places like Hohenfriedeberg (1745) and Rossbach (1757). Now Kesselring, a Bavarian, saw his chance to turn catastrophe into triumph and to enter the Pantheon. The Allies wanted to restore the war of movement (*Bewegungskrieg*) through the Anzio landing, but they were fighting the very people who had invented it. For OB-Südwest Kesselring and the staff of Army Group C, it was scrambling time.

And scramble they did. The Allies landed at Anzio-Nettuno at two in the morning. Within the hour, the operations chief for the army group (staff position Ia), Colonel Dietrich Beelitz, had awakened Chief of Staff Westphal with news of the landing. Contingency plans were already on the books in case of "a large-scale landing near Rome," and Westphal now gave the code word: "Richard." By the time Westphal awakened Kesselring and briefed him on developments, at 5:00 A.M., the machinery was humming. Kesselring got things moving locally by ordering Luftwaffe General Maximilian Ritter von Pohl, in command of Rome's antiaircraft defenses, to deploy every 88mm gun he could scrounge to form a screen south of Rome, to protect against a breakout by Allied armor from the bridgehead and a subsequent drive on the capital. Pohl's screen was in place by noon.

Meanwhile, divisions from the four corners of Italy and beyond were already streaming toward the Anzio bridgehead. They came first from 10th Army, currently holding the Gustav Line: 71st Division, which had started the New Year in Istria and was now in the process of deploying on the Cassino front; and the main body of the 3rd *Panzergrenadier* Division, which had only recently been ordered from Rome to the Gustav Line and now reversed course. Elements of both divisions reached the bridgehead by the morning of January 23 (day two of Shingle). Trailing behind were the support units: two field artillery battalions, a heavy artillery battalion, a heavy antitank (*Panzerjäger*) battalion, the reconnaissance battalion of 26th Panzer Division, as well as two battalions of 1st *Fallschirmjäger* Division. They would arrive in the course of the day on January 23. By evening, more formations had come in: a reinforced regiment of the Hermann Göring Panzer Division, another one from 15th *Panzergrenadier* Division, a motorized engineer battalion, and an antiaircraft battalion. Orders had already gone to General Vietinghoff at his 10th Army command post to withdraw 26th Panzer Division from the British 8th Army front and send it to Anzio, and soon after he received the same orders for the headquarters of LXXVI Panzer Corps.[57]

With such disparate forces hustling up to the bridgehead, and with "every meter counting," Kesselring paid special attention to command and control.[58] First, he placed all available forces under the tactical command of General Ernst Schlemmer, a Luftwaffe staff officer in Rome, who hastily improvised a small staff. *Gruppe* Schlemmer was in action within a single day. On January 23, the staff of I *Fallschirmjäger* Corps under General Alfred Schlemm took command of the defenses. Schlemm was in the saddle until January 25, when the staff of 14th Army under General Mackensen arrived from northern Italy to take command, the third German commander at Anzio in three days.

Meanwhile, troops were also coming down to Anzio from northern Italy: 4th *Fallschirmjäger* Brigade, still in the process of being formed, from the Terni-Spoleto sector; 65th Division from Genoa; 362nd Division from Rimini; and two reinforced regiments from 16th SS *Panzergrenadier* Division *Reichsführer-SS*. The High Command of the Armed Forces—the OKW—sent its own units, including 715th Division (Motorized) from southern France, detached from the High Command West (*OB-West*), and 114th *Jäger* Division from the Balkans, taken from High Command Southeast (*OB-Südost*). So did the Replacement Army (*Ersatzheer*) in Germany: Infantry Regiment *Lehr* (a demonstration unit held by Hitler in high tactical repute), two *Panzergrenadier* Regiments, the 1027th and 1028th, and a heavy Panzer battalion equipped with Tiger tanks.

It was an impressive display of both planning and improvisation, and it looked all the better when we consider the fact that the Allies had maintained firm control of the skies over Italy. With road and rail traffic bound to entice Allied fighter-bombers closer to the deck, virtually all movements to the threatened zone took place at night. Strict traffic control and solid organization were of the essence, and so was the use of Italian trucks whenever possible, to put a modicum of doubt into the minds of Allied pilots about whom exactly they were bombing. The result was the placement of a solid defensive line at Anzio far quicker than the Allies thought possible. Rather than the anticipated two weeks for deploying the 65th and 362nd Infantry Divisions, for example, the Germans had them in place on January 26, day five of Operation Shingle: the 65th south of Rome, the 362nd in the coastal sector stretching north from the mouth of the Tiber.

None of these divisions arrived all at once and intact. Virtually every one had something missing—a detached regiment, battalion, or support unit. The 65th Division, for example, was missing its 164th Regiment and was fighting as *Kampfgruppe* Pfeiffer, named for the divisional commander, General Helmuth Pfeiffer. The 3rd *Panzergrenadier* Division, likewise, was missing its 8th Grenadier Regiment and was identified as *Kampfgruppe* Gräser (for General Fritz-Hubert Gräser) on situation maps. The 71st Infantry Division lacked its 211th Grenadier Regiment, the 362nd Infantry Division its 954th Grenadier Regiment. It was all a colossal improvisation, and the result was what 14th Army Chief of Staff General Wolf-Rüdiger Hauser called "a colorful mix" and a "motley crew."[59] This wasn't how you normally played the game: individual battalions of various units flowing in from all directions, this regiment matched up with that one, placed under a commander who might not have been familiar with either one. "In general it is undesirable and disadvantageous to tear apart units," Hauser noted, "since besides many other drawbacks the morale and battle worthiness of the individual components suffers."[60] But there was no avoiding it in these helter-skelter circumstances.

Despite the problems, Mackensen's 14th Army came together as rapidly as any force in history. As he arrived at the front on January 24, the general already had a three-division picket in a crescent around the beachhead: 65th Infantry Division on his right, defending the line of the Moletta River in the west, 3rd Panzergrenadier Division in the center, defending Albano, and the Herman Göring Panzer Division on the left, masking Cisterna, Valmontone, and points east. While none of these divisions were complete, the position was cohesive enough. With reinforcements arriving by the hour, Mackensen soon was in command of a solid, two-corps battle array: I *Fallschirmjäger* on his right along the Moletta, under General Schlemm, containing the 65th and 4th Fallschirmjäger Divisions; and LXXVI Panzer Corps on his left, under General Traugott Herr, a Panzer commander and one of the Wehrmacht's legendary fighting figures. Herr had taken a chunk of shrapnel to the head in front of Nalchik during the Caucasus campaign in November 1942, but it barely seemed to slow him down. He had fought hard at Salerno and during the retreat to the Gustav Line. Now his four divisions (3rd *Panzergrenadier*, 362nd Infantry, 71st Infantry, and Hermann Göring Panzer) held most of the line at Anzio, a position stretching east from the Albano Road, then bending south to the sea behind Mussolini Canal. Behind Mackensen's two corps stood a pair of very fine divisions, the 29th Panzergrenadier and the 26th Panzer. All told, the Anzio line was one of the most solid German defensive positions of the war.

With the Allies established on land and 14th Army up and running, the battle of Anzio proper began. As on the Gustav Line, here, too, the iron grip of *Stellungskrieg* clamped down on all the armies at Anzio. The Wehrmacht divisions on the front line were understrength, thrown together almost randomly, and outclassed in materiel, but they displayed the same cohesion, grit, and battle-worthiness as ever. In addition, the Germans sat everywhere on the high ground around a very shallow Allied beachhead just 7 miles deep and 15 miles wide, could observe every square inch of the Allied array, and were able to bring down a murderous artillery fire by all calibers at any point they chose. Besides the regular field artillery batteries, the Germans had *Werfer* rocket batteries and heavy guns of the 14th Army reserve (the *Heeres-artillerie*), including 210mm mortars, 220mm and 240mm cannons, and even a pair of 280mm Krupp heavy railway guns, firing a 560-pound projectile with a range of 40 miles.[61] Finally, for perhaps the last time in this war, the Wehrmacht could bask in the benefits of air support. Although Allied aircraft held a 10:1 superiority in numbers, the Anzio sector was so small that even the remnants of the Luftwaffe could intervene with effect: smashing ground forces, troop transports and ships at sea, and, most spectacularly, Allied ammunition dumps on land. Air strikes sunk the destroyers HMS *Janus* with the loss of 159 men on January 23, badly damaged the destroyer HMS *Plunkett* (killing 53 sailors) on January 24, and sunk the hospital ship *St. David* that same night, killing 96.[62]

The Allies, by contrast, once again bumped up against the limitations of materiel superiority. Indeed, what use were all those tanks, guns, ammunition, and planes when the men themselves could hardly move by daylight? Allied artillery greatly outnumbered the Germans. In one three-day stretch of battle (February 2–4), the Germans counted a grand total of 135,000 Allied shells hurled against them. Still, seeking out hostile firing positions hidden in the mountains—the Allies task—was very different from pulverizing soft targets out in an open plain. The typical GI or Tommy sitting in the "bitchhead," as he might have called it, had to endure a great deal: the constant feeling of being watched, the seemingly random death dealt out by the German gun, the need to walk in an irregular half-crouch, half-crawl, with the helmet jammed down as low as it could go—the famous "Anzio amble." Operational possibilities ran the gamut from slim to none. The Allies faced a river on the British left, the Moletta, two pieces of high ground in the center, the Alban Hills and the Volscian Mountains, and the malarial Pontine Marshes on the right. Benito Mussolini's regime had drained the marshes in a well-publicized display of fascist vigor, but the Germans had reflooded them on the occasion of Italy's surrender. All of these factors could not help but generate a feeling of helplessness that gnawed at the spirit of the GI and Tommy and tore down individual and unit morale. "Anzio was a fishbowl," an American participant wrote. "We were the fish."[63]

In such a demoralizing situation, the commander is crucial. General Lucas was an uninspiring figure, however, and his choice of command posts mirrored his own falling spirits—from a respectable two-story villa in Nettuno to a former Italian army barracks behind an enormous sandbag wall and finally to a wine cellar in one of the caves that honeycombed subterranean Anzio. Burrowed into his hole, he had little to offer his men, even the often-underestimated fillip of stirring words. Neither did General Clark. He paid a visit to the beachhead on January 29 and was almost killed when his PT boat came under attack by an American minesweeper, USS *Sway*. Those who met him in those days noted a certain jumpiness and a noticeable droop in the left side of his mouth. It was a classic sign of stress—like the facial tic that the German general Friedrich Paulus developed during the ordeal at Stalingrad—and Clark himself noted with some unease that he was losing his hair.

For nearly four months, neither side was able to move the front line significantly one way or the other. That is not to say they didn't try. By the end of the first week, both sides were ready to pull the trigger on offensives: the Allies to break out of their coastal prison, the Germans to drive their adversary into the sea. On January 30, its ninth day at Anzio, VI Corps went over to the offensive, a general advance with the British on the left and the Americans on the right, aiming to seize the Alban Hills and to "prepare to continue the advance on Rome." With the Germans bulking up in the front lines for their own attack, however, the Allies hit tough resistance from the start. Penney's British 1st Division managed to slice open a narrow penetration up the main north-south artery, the Anzio-Albano Road (Via Anziate) toward Campoleone, but promised support on his left from Harmon's US 1st Armored Division never materialized. Aerial reconnaissance had declared the area suitable for tanks, but that's not what Harmon found: "What seemed on the aerial photographs to be a series of dimples or minor indentations turned, when my tankers got there, to be gullies fifty feet deep." With January rains turning the ground into a "gluey mess," 1st Armored was unable to develop any momentum, and the combined attack stuck fast south of Campoleone, with the British crammed into an untenably narrow salient just 1,000 yards wide at its narrowest.[64]

The American attack misfired early. Spearheading the assault toward the key crossroads town of Cisterna were Major William O. Darby's 1st and 3rd Ranger Battalions, the newly trained elite of the US Army. Using irrigation ditches to get forward, they managed to infiltrate the German front line. Unfortunately, due to a series of navigational errors, they popped up in the middle of positions occupied by the Hermann Göring Panzer Division. In the ensuing melee, the Germans destroyed both battalions, with only six of the original 800 men returning.[65] It was perhaps another example of the US Army's tendency to overplan, to find a place in every operation for every possible unit or formation, including Ranger and Airborne regiments, without regard to the suitability of the mission. Despite the opening disaster, Truscott's 3rd Division attacked anyway, slowly grinding the Germans back to the north, trading an advance of three miles on a seven-mile front for 1,000 casualties and falling well short of Cisterna.

The Germans experienced much the same in reverse during their attack on February 4. The plan was classically German in conception: concentric thrusts from all compass points with the Anzio Road as the *Schwerpunkt*. The order of battle reflected the mixed-up nature of the German force, with nary a full division present. Rather, *Kampfgruppe* Pfeiffer (elements of 65th Infantry and 4th Fallschirmjäger Divisions) moving in from the west; *Kampfgruppe* Gräser (portions of 3rd Panzergrenadier and 715th Infantry Divisions) straight down along both sides of the road from the north; and *Kampfgruppe* Conrath (the understrength Hermann Göring *Fallschirmjäger* Panzer Division) from Cisterna in the northeast.[66] Unfortunately, the Allied attack not only disrupted the German timetable; it also took ground that was essential as a staging zone for the German offensive.[67] The first attack by 14th Army, therefore, was a partial blow (*Teilangriff*) rather than a full-blown attempt to drive the Allies into the sea.

The main order of business was the reduction of the so-called Campoleone Salient, which was actually a rail-thin and tactically absurd position—"like a finger pointing to the north," as the Germans described it. The British probably should never have retained it in the first place, since it was impossible to hold in the long term. Once the Germans had Campoleone, they could launch a second-stage attack down to Aprilia at the base of the salient. Here lay a group of stone buildings controlling all the roads in the area, called "the Factory" by the Allies. General Penney had crammed an entire brigade into the tip of the salient, the 3rd Infantry Brigade (1st Division), with another brigade, the 24th Guards, on the salient's left flank and the 2nd Infantry Brigade on the right. The attack should have been one of the Wehrmacht's signal triumphs. An army trained to fight the *Kesselschlacht* could not fail to recognize the opportunity that offered itself. Two converging drives—each less than a mile—would cut off the base of the salient and trap Penney's 1st Division inside, cutting it off from outside supply and rendering it helpless for the kill. The Wehrmacht had done it many times before in similar circumstances, and with elements of three German divisions present—the 65th moving in from the west, 3rd *Panzergrenadier* and 715th from the east, all fighting together as *Kampfgruppe* Gräser—the battle of Campoleone should have been a turkey shoot.

In fact, it was anything but. The 3rd *Panzergrenadier* led things off, hitting the tip of the salient, but the British fought them to a standstill. German attempts later in the day to pinch off the salient at the base succeeded temporarily, with 65th and 715th Divisions linking up and cutting off British 3rd Brigade. But a series of counterattacks, from inside the salient and by 168th Brigade from the outside (part of the newly arrived British 56th Division), reopened the path to 3rd Brigade. The Germans were never able to close it again—and no wonder. All day long, Gräser's assault forces had found themselves under a furious artillery barrage. With the German assault essentially coming down along a single road, Allied artillery and naval guns had a juicy selection of targets. Naval artillery was a particularly galling affair for German ground forces, as it had been in Sicily and Salerno alike. Naval guns firing at tanks and infantry are the very definition of an unfair fight, a demoralizing experience for those targeted even if they survive. The day ended with the British still holding fast, although 3rd Brigade evacuated its exposed position that night and retreated to Aprilia at the base of the salient. The two armies had traded losses, some 1,500 men apiece, on a very small piece of ground. While both sides could mass fires in the defense, they were essentially unable to do so in the attack, since the Allies were invulnerable at sea and the Germans nearly so in the mountains. Like the entire Anzio beachhead, Campoleone was a military version of Hell's Half Acre—a field of slaughter with limited possibilities for the attack.

Gräser's assault was a disappointment on every level. Perhaps it was the irregular command structure and the incomplete nature of the divisions under his command. Perhaps it was the terrain. The ground west of the salient was the same pockmarked field that had frustrated Harmon's American armored division a few days before. Perhaps it was British pluck and determination in the defensive; no army did it better, even when overmatched in numbers and materiel. The plan itself, a direct thrust down the straight road to Anzio, was a problem. Whatever the reasons—and it was likely a combination of all of them—the German attack was a disappointment rather than the quick and bold coup Mackensen envisioned.

In the next days, Mackensen saw the same story repeated all over the field. He launched a second *Teilangriff*, this one by Hermann Göring and 26th Panzer Divisions, out of Cisterna toward Monte Rotto on February 5, and, finally, a third against Buonriposo Ridge, to the left of the Anzio-Albano Road, by a reinforced regiment of 65th Infantry Division on February 7. Both were reruns of the bitter struggle for the Campoleone Salient. The attacks made initial gains, then bogged down into close positional fighting, even hand-to-hand, and then stuck altogether in the face of an Allied artillery blizzard. Again, the casualties were heavy: thousands of men on each side for a mile or so of advance.

By the final stage of the offensive, an attack toward Aprilia, the pattern was familiar. The initial assault managed to push the British back a mile or so. While the Germans managed to take the Factory and hold it against repeated Allied counterattacks, they could go no farther. Once again, Allied firepower was the solution to German aggression. Hauser, the army chief of staff, later argued that while it was important to attack, in order to seize and hold the initiative, these preliminary attacks had been "hard and casualty-laden." He continued: "The battles showed us that we could conduct attacks against the enemy's far superior artillery and his domination of the air—characterized by his heavy employment of bombers and fighter-bombers—only at the expense of heavy casualties."[68] The failure had to have been particularly bitter for Mackensen, a Panzer leader who in late 1942 had jockeyed an armored corps hundreds of miles in two weeks on a headlong dash into the Caucasus, capping off the drive with the conquest of the Soviet oil city of Maikop. Then he had been riding free and clear; now he was scrounging for every inch he could get.

Mackensen's Blow: Operation *Fischfang*

What to do? "The question," Hauser wrote, "was whether German forces, despite the losses they had suffered, could conduct a decisive attack against the beachhead, before the opponent could bring in substantial new reinforcements." Timing was crucial, but "time was undoubtedly working for the enemy." Currently, 14th Army had 125,000 men; Allied VI Corps just 100,000. But Allied reinforcements (US 45th Infantry Division, for example) were pouring into Anzio, and the situation called for haste. But it also required planning: "Any such attack required sufficient forces and such good preparation that it had a realistic prospect of success. Germany's overall situation made it doubtful whether we could assemble sufficient forces for a renewed attack if a first decisive attack failed, as the [14th] army commander had already pointed out." Haste and caution stood in conflict. "Under these mutually contradictory demands," he wrote, "choosing the right moment for the attack was not easy."[69]

Like the Allies, the Germans were suffering their own form of command dissonance. Mackensen was getting more and more dour by the day. An experienced troop commander, he recognized the situation at the front for what it was: a *Stellungskrieg* with fire dominant and the human factor recessive. Kesselring was the optimist, pushing for an early renewal of the offensive—what Hauser described as an "attack-mania" (*Angriffshetze*). Mackensen had forgotten more about land warfare than Kesselring ever knew, however. Both men recognized that fact, and their relations grew increasingly testy. Mackensen chafed under Kesselring's position as a "joint" commander (a mere fiction in Italy). The *Luftwaffe* was hardly present, and the German *Kriegsmarine* was altogether absent. Kesselring was an air force officer commanding troops in an all-army theater—nothing more, nothing less.

The debate ended in the only way possible: with a decision by Hitler and the OKW. The Führer and his operations chief, General Alfred Jodl, felt the time was right for a new blow at Anzio. It was Hitler's latest epiphany. He would shatter the beachhead once and for all, and success would stand as a warning to the Allies about the prospects for their upcoming invasion of Western Europe. Of course, neither he, nor Jodl, nor any other officer from OKW had actually been to the beachhead or inspected the conditions there. Like so many operational orders emanating from the brain trust in Rastenburg, this one bore little relationship to battlefield reality.

The OKW plan handed to the force at Anzio was Operation *Fischfang* ("Fish Haul"). The assault was yet another direct thrust from north to south, along the Anzio-Albano Road, to split the bridgehead and "then tear it apart from the inside."[70] The attack would consist of two "waves" (*Welle*). The first, or breakthrough, echelon consisted of 3rd *Panzergrenadier* Division, the 715th Infantry Division, and the newly arrived 114th *Jäger* Division. The spearhead was another newly arrived unit, the Infantry Regiment *Lehr*, a demonstration and test-bed unit for new equipment and tactics. *Lehr* would attack on a very narrow front, just 3.5 miles wide, as a way to quickly overwhelm the defenders. The second echelon included the 26th Panzer Division under General Smilo von Lüttwitz and the redoubtable 29th *Panzergrenadier* Division under General Fries, along with a battalion each of Mark V Panther and Mark VI Tiger tanks (1st Battalion/4th Panzer Regiment and 508th Heavy Panzer Battalion, respectively). This was the exploitation echelon, its mission to shoot the gap in the Allied defenses pried open by the first. Mackensen was to strip nondecisive sectors of the line of weapons and equipment to outfit the main force for the big battle and to have units on the flanks (4th *Fallschirmjäger* Division and Hermann Göring Panzer Division) carry out local raids as a diversion to fix Allied forces to their front. To mislead the Allies further as to the precise point of the attack, 26th Panzer and 29th *Panzergrenadier* Divisions were to carry out vigorous reconnaissance patrols near Cisterna, with the men fitted out ostentatiously in their black Panzer-force uniforms. Once the fight was under way, the two divisions would shift to their jumping-off positions astride the Anzio Road.

Later, every German officer at Anzio—Kesselring, Westphal, Mackensen, Hauser—would blame it on Hitler.[71] The Führer, they claimed, had dragged them all into it, imposing a flawed operational conception, choosing the wrong unit as the spearhead (*Lehr* was a newly arrived unit with little knowledge of local conditions), and attacking on too narrow a front. While it is always tempting to blame Hitler, we should note that *Fischfang* was exactly the same thing that the generals on both sides at Anzio had been doing: blasting up and down the same Anzio Road. The Germans had no choice. As much as they might have preferred it, they could not attack the flanks of the beachhead. A flanking fight involved deploying near the coastline, thereby ensuring a quick introduction to Allied naval guns. The direct line along the road was not only "the shortest route to the decisive point on the coast,"[72] it was also the best tank country in the beachhead. And so a frontal assault it was, and some sort of frontal assault it would have been no matter who had drawn up the operational plan. And with a solid wall of artillery firing in support of the defenders, somewhere on the order of 25,000 shells a day to just 1,500 for the attacking Germans, *Fischfang* was guaranteed to open to a very noisy reception.

Or perhaps it is better to say that it barely opened at all. A general barrage by virtually every German gun deployed around Anzio kicked off the offensive at 6:30 A.M. on February 16. As always, German assault formations moved forward with will and spirit, especially Infantry Regiment *Lehr*. But Allied firepower soon responded, and the attack down both sides of the road to Anzio met "extraordinarily strong resistance" from the start. German estimates cite a twenty-fold Allied superiority in guns, although it might have seemed like a thousand to one to a *Landser* at the front. German Panzers, moving up with the infantry in combined-arms teams, struggled to get forward. It was cold, but not cold enough to give the ground a good, hard freeze, and so the Panzers were road-bound throughout the day, their attacks channeled (*canalisiert*) into predictable and opposable paths. Even in areas where the ground was solid enough for tank operations, a tangled network of gullies blocked their advance.

With artillery (including naval guns) a key advantage for the Allies and German Panzers stymied by the terrain and ground conditions, the burden of attack fell almost completely on the German infantry—a recipe for a bloody attritional struggle rather than a breakthrough. In the course of the day, attacks by the first wave—3rd *Panzergrenadier* Division and the 715th Division, spearheaded by Infantry *Lehr*—managed to throw back the forward Allied companies of the British 56th and US 45th Infantry Divisions. Losses on both sides were heavy—again reflecting big firepower on a very small front. But the weight of Allied fire eventually began to tell on *Lehr*, not merely in a physical sense but also in a moral one. The fear of battle, an increasing feeling of helplessness, a sense of bewilderment at having been snatched from the homeland and tossed into a "great battle of materiel" on unfamiliar ground: all these worked together to ground *Lehr* down. By day's end, the Germans had ground forward less than a mile south out of Aprilia. The Allied line was everywhere intact, and VI Corps still had not inserted its reserve, the tanks of Harmon's US 1st Armored Division.

Despite a gloomy first day, the Germans, too, held uncommitted reserves: the second echelon—29th *Panzergrenadier* and 26th Panzer Divisions. The German command spent the night of February 16–17 debating how best to employ them: Kesselring was for inserting them into battle the next day, Mackensen and LXXVI Panzer Corps commander Herr wanted to wait and see. The first day told Mackensen that the offensive was going to take longer than he had planned. Perhaps another day of wearing down the Allies would create more favorable conditions for a breakthrough and a bold thrust down to Anzio. In the end they compromised. The first wave would continue attacking during the night, giving the enemy no respite: probing, infiltrating the Allied line where possible, supported by the Panzers. Come daybreak, they would see where they were and make plans for the second wave accordingly.

By dawn day two of Operation *Fischfang*, the compromise looked like a stroke of genius. German night attacks had pried open a gap between the US 179th and 157th Infantry Regiments just before midnight, then exploited the gap with reserve infantry and some sixty tanks. Dawn saw the Germans again on the assault, ripping a 1-mile-deep by 2-mile-wide gash in 45th Division's front, hardly the stuff of legend, but then again, Anzio itself was only eight miles away. Turning an Allied operational problem into a near catastrophe, the 179th attempted to withdraw from the attack in the afternoon, in broad daylight and in direct German line of sight, an inept move that brought down an avalanche of German fire and inflicted heavy casualties. The great crisis of the battle was upon the Allies, and they spent the day doing what they had done when facing a similar disaster and a crumpled beachhead at Salerno—blasting away with all the firepower they could muster: artillery, naval gunfire, repurposed 90mm antiaircraft guns, and tank guns from 1st Armored Division.

Artillery, of course, was business as usual at Anzio. The crisis called for more, and the Allies got it: no fewer than 730 sorties from the XII Tactical Air Command, perhaps the greatest day of ground support in military history up to that point. Capping things off was carpet-bombing: 341 B-24 and B-17 bombers, escorted by 176 P-38s and P-47s, dropping over 1,100 tons of bombs on the tiny field.[73] Despite the sky raining down bombs, Kesselring ironically had to issue a general order to use artillery ammunition as sparingly as possible. Allied bombing of the Alps had put a serious hurt on the Italian rail network, temporarily halting shipments to Anzio. The order can hardly have come as good news to frontline German troops pinned down under Allied fire or hugging the earth for survival. Again, Allied fire had a moral as well as physical impact on the Wehrmacht. German forward momentum first slowed, then stopped, and day two ended with the Germans once again well short of a clean breakthrough.

Now the Germans were facing the crisis. Losses had been staggering. The first-wave divisions—3rd *Panzergrenadier*, 715th, and 65th Divisions—were ghosts. Their infantry battalions, the backbone of a division's fighting strength and usually 700 men strong, had 120–150 apiece. They had not broken the Allied front, and they were not going to. But Mackensen still had two fine, untouched mechanized divisions in his reserve: 29th *Panzergrenadier* and 26th Panzer. Both were at full strength and led by aggressive commanders—Prussians of the old school (Fries for the 29th, Lüttwitz for the 26th). German forces almost never admitted defeat before they had inserted their final reserve; the course of the war thus far had shown it again and again. General Heinz Guderian's 2nd Panzer Army before Tula in December 1941, Field Marshal Erwin Rommel at the three successive battles of Alamein, and General Mackensen—the very man on the spot at Anzio—leading the charge toward Nalchik in the Caucasus campaign in November 1942: while German commanders rarely *defended* to the last man, they almost always *fought forward* to the last man. Hauser summed up the conundrum this way:

> We had to decide on the evening of February 17 whether we should call a general halt to the attack, or whether the insertion of the two second-wave divisions might offer a chance for success. Apart from the fact that our superiors had ordered a continuation, the army also believed that we had to try everything to force the decision in our favor. The enemy too had suffered badly in these days, despite his incredible material superiority. But we could not possibly break off a half-won battle at five minutes to midnight.[74]

"Five minutes to midnight"—*Fünf Minuten vor zwölf*—was a German slogan, a buzzword ever since World War I. They had all convinced themselves that breaking things off prematurely, lack of will, and loss of nerve by a few key individuals had robbed them of the victory they deserved in that earlier war—General Helmuth von Moltke at the Marne, for example. The end of the war in 1918, with its specious notion that the German people—or at least its pacifist, socialist, and Jewish elements—had "stabbed the army in the back" on the verge of victory was like a religious belief to them. This time, they swore, they would fight things out to the inevitably victorious end. The decision to continue the fight at Anzio had little to do with the operational situation—numbers, guns, tanks, terrain. Rather, inserting the second wave was an act of faith, a belief that a strong will could overcome even the most hopeless situation. Kesselring, Mackensen, Herr, and all the rest of them were shaking their fists in defiance: at the Allied armies, at the naval guns, at the heavy bombers. They were shaking their fists at fate.

When the attack came on day three of *Fischfang*, it very nearly crumpled the Allied line. Mackensen had two mechanized divisions abreast—a huge force by Anzio standards—and spent the day riding them hard, probing for weak spots, and shifting his *Schwerpunkt* as he glimpsed opportunities. German artillery played a key role from its hidden positions in the mountain, and for once the Germans had enough tanks at the point of impact. Once again, the Germans tore a gash in the Allied front, overrunning the hard-luck US 179th Infantry Regiment and heading south toward the objective that now seemed within their grasp.

By afternoon they had hustled the defenders back to the "Corps Beachhead Line"—a fortified position anchored on the hill mass just north of Anzio. General Lucas has taken criticism for his lackluster leadership, but the Beachhead Line might just have saved the Allied position at Anzio. All day, February 18, fighting raged along the lateral east-west road (*Strada* 82) on Lucas's final position. The focal points of the slaughter were a crossroads position called the "Flyover" (actually an overpass where *Strada* 82 crossed over the Anzio Road) and a tangled mass of sandstone rock to the right of the Flyover known as "the Caves."[75]

This was literally the last ditch for the Allies—and the last gasp for the German 14th Army. For the Allies, every step backward was another step closer to disaster, and as they stood on that final line on *Strada* 82, there were less than seven miles away from the ocean. But only a single mile behind them lay the command post of the 45th Infantry Division, and if the tanks of 29th *Panzergrenadier* overran it, then the battle was as good as over. For the Germans, every bound forward brought them closer to victory, but it also brought down more accurate Allied fire. Allied guns in the Padiglione Wood just south of *Strada* 82 were well under a mile away, so close that British and American gunners were practically delivering their shells by hand. A Tiger tank was a fearsome thing in 1944 until it took a direct hit from a field artillery piece—then it became just another wreck littering the Anzio Road. And as the day wore on, the Germans were experiencing a familiar problem: penetrations in the center with less progress on the flanks meant they were driving themselves into a cul-de-sac of Allied fire, bad enough under normal conditions and now firing with real desperation. By the German high-water mark later in the afternoon, when a few Panzers actually passed under the Flyover before being drilled by US antitank fire, casualties in the assault divisions—26th Panzer and 29th *Panzergrenadier*—were approaching 40 percent. German 65th Infantry Division, fighting almost nonstop for a month, could now muster a grand total of twenty-six officers and 871 men, and the situation was similar across the board. The forward drive tapered off—then stopped.

Nightfall saw German dreams of victory at Anzio dead. Rather than a dramatic breakthrough, they had tapped "a small wedge" in the Allied line up to *Strada* 82. As Hauser put it:

> The force of the attack (*Angriffswucht*) was broken. The hard strug-gles of the following days would try to consolidate the flanks of the attack wedge, but a resumption of our own great offensive was no longer realistic. The initiative gradually passed to the enemy, the number and strength of his counterattacks increased, the effect of his powerful munitions and air force led not only to casualties, but also to a clear diminishing of our physical and moral strength.[76]

The "great battle of materiel" (*Materialgrossschlacht*), the German at-tempt to crush the Allied beachhead at Anzio, was over. Each side, in a single sanguinary month, had suffered around 20,000 casualties on a battlefield the size of a closet, but no decision was imminent.

The Wehrmacht had failed—but how close it had come! It is com-mon today to see World War II as a done deal, with an outmanned and outproduced Germany fighting a hopeless war from the outset. At least two things about that notion are specious. First, war is an inher-ently unpredictable enterprise, with twists, turns, and surprises by the day; chance and uncertainty abound. We cannot pay lip service to such Clausewitzian concepts and then flip over and declare the outcome of World War II to be inevitable from the outset. Was Hitler's war a gam-ble? Absolutely: a *va banque* wager at exceedingly poor odds; a disaster for the world and for Germany. Was defeat inevitable? Absolutely not.

Second, the thin line that separated victory from defeat in at least a half-dozen major operations in World War II should give anyone pause to think that the end of World War II was foreordained. The line came in various colors and names: a thin khaki reconnaissance screen of Tommies guarding the open desert flank in front of Alex-andria during the Alam Halfa battle in August 1942; brave Ivans in monochrome brown holding a couple hundred yards of riverbank in Stalingrad later that year, while their comrades to the south stopped the Germans in the Caucasus a single mile from the Ossetian Military Road leading into the big oil fields; and now, perhaps most surprising of all, a battered bunch of guys named Joe wearing olive drab, dug in at the Flyover and the Caves. When it counted, guarding their command post and their gun line in the Padiglione Wood, they stood up. With 29th *Panzergrenadier* Division, Tiger tanks, and three hundred years of military tradition bearing down on him, Joe had met the last charge of the Prussians and blunted it. None of it was inevitable—something that you could simply wait for. Someone had to *do* it, and 45th Infantry Division at Anzio was that someone. The margin, however, was far too narrow to speak of "inevitability."

Solving the Problem: Conceiving Operation Diadem

Anzio was a demoralizing situation for everyone on the Allied side, from Churchill on down, and they wound up doing what armies often do in such circumstances: they fired the general. On February 22, the indecisive Lucas was out and the more determined General Truscott was in, but the operational situation was unchanged. For their part, the Germans tried one more blast against the beachhead, this one by the Hermann Göring Panzer Division, coming down from the Cisterna region on February 29. It collapsed immediately in an orgy of Allied artillery fire and achieved nothing beyond killing or wounding another 3,500 German soldiers. Like fighting on the Gustav Line, Anzio was now officially a stalemate.

In a twist of operational irony, the solution to the deadlock was for the Allied armies to break through the Gustav Line and rescue VI Corps at Anzio. It was a complete reversal of the original mission, in which the Anzio landing was meant to unlock the Gustav Line. Western military histories describe a series of three desperate "battles of Cassino": the first, January 24–February 11, featuring a combined attack by US 34th Division and the French Expeditionary Corps; a second, February 15–18, that included the controversial aerial bombardment of the Benedictine monastery atop the mountain and a failed assault by 4th Indian Division (part of the New Zealand Corps); and finally a third, March 15–24, by the entire New Zealand Corps (2nd New Zealand and 4th Indian Divisions). In fact, the Allies were on the attack almost constantly in this period. The "first battle of Cassino" took place on the heels of the US disaster at the Rapido, and when one offensive ends on February 11 and the next begins on February 15, separating them conceptually can be difficult.[77]

However we periodize the fight for Cassino, as one long struggle or several discrete ones, it was a nightmare for both sides. Certainly, it was yet another outright failure for the Allies. There is nothing in battle more dramatic than a great mountain looming overhead, waiting to be conquered, and yet, even after multiple tries, it was still there, looming. Something else was looming as well: Operation Overlord, and it would not do for the Allies to have an open, bleeding wound in existence before the great trial of strength in the west.

The Germans, by contrast, had reason to be pleased. Even when called upon to maintain a two-army array, splitting supplies, reinforcements, and replacements between two fronts, they had held their positions, bottling up the Allies at Anzio and on the Gustav Line. Their one major operational decision—deploying the 1st *Fallschirmjäger* Division under General Richard Heidrich to defend Cassino—proved to be inspired. A meticulously trained, high-morale division, skilled in small unit fighting and completely at home in even the most chaotic tactical situation, the paratroopers were an ideal choice. They dug in deep, first in the town and on the mountain, then in the ruins of the monastery, which Allied bombing turned into a rubble-strewn natural fortress. In this miniature Stalingrad, they turned back all attempts to dislodge them, blocking American, French, British, New Zealander, Gurkha, and Indian troops alike, generating massive frustration (and casualties) in the Allied camp.

But examining Cassino more deeply reveals serious problems for the Wehrmacht. During the months-long sequence, one burned-out set of Allied divisions replaced another, first the 34th Infantry Division and the French, then 4th Indian Division, and finally 2nd New Zealand. All that time, no one was replacing the 1st *Fallschirmjäger* Division, which continued to fight, bleed, and die in the ruins of the town and monastery. Heidrich's battalions dwindled to the size of companies and then platoons, and the division might have collapsed were it not for the divisional clerks and truck drivers who clamored to get into the fight.[78] While Cassino was a heroic epic for both sides, it must not blind us to the truth: the Allies were relentlessly attriting the Germans, and the same thing was true at Anzio. In Italy, both sides were taking losses that only one side could afford. "Affording" military casualties is an ugly concept, especially for the men in the line, and no one likes to talk about it or admit it is happening. Every modern war has fronts in which attrition is the raison d'être, however, and a materiel-intensive *Stellungskrieg* rarely ends well for the side fighting a poor man's war.

Six weeks of relative quiet on the front followed the third abortive attempt to take Cassino in March. Not until May did General Harold Alexander, commanding Allied 15th Army Group, devise a solution to the entire Italian mess. He decided to concentrate both of his armies, Clark's US 5th and British 8th (now under General Oliver Leese) on the western sector opposite Cassino and the Garigliano River line, virtually denuding the Adriatic front in order to launch a massive attack along a narrow, 20-mile front. He also reinforced the Anzio bridgehead, shipping in the US 34th Division in March and the US 36th in May. The bridgehead was now bulging with no fewer than seven Allied divisions: some 150,000 men in all, much closer to a full field army than a corps. Alexander's plan, Operation Diadem, called for twin offensives—one through Cassino and one out of Anzio—to catch the German 10th and 14th Armies between two fires and maul them both.[79] (See Map 2.2.)

Diadem was the signal moment of the Italian campaign. Up to now, the Allies had conducted a broad front advance, divisions abreast, with each one essentially facing off versus a single German division at a time. The advantage of the broad front is that it creates an even, consistent position without weak spots or fissures. With German divisions usually more aggressive and experienced than the Allies, however, the broad-front approach was also likely to be slow, costly, and sometimes even risky for the attackers. Finally, advance on a broad front made it difficult for the Allies to employ their materiel superiority, since Alexander, Clark, and Leese had to parcel out supplies more or less evenly across the front. The broad front made sense for an Allied force obsessed with security, but not one seeking a decisive victory, and the conservative approach had played a key role in the attenuation of the Italian campaign.

Diadem was a reversal of course, with 90 percent of Allied combat strength gathered west of the Apennines. Clark's 5th Army held the left of the Allied battle array, crammed into a zone just 12 miles wide, with US II Corps (General Keyes) on the left and the French Expeditionary Corps (General Alphonse Juin) on the right. Leese's British 8th Army (Leese) deployed to Clark's right, with XIII Corps (General Sidney C. Kirkman) and Polish II Corps (General Władysław Anders) also jammed into a very narrow corridor, and Canadian I Corps (General E. L. M. Burns) in reserve. Those five corps, arranged across a 20-mile front, represented the business end of Diadem. Weary of

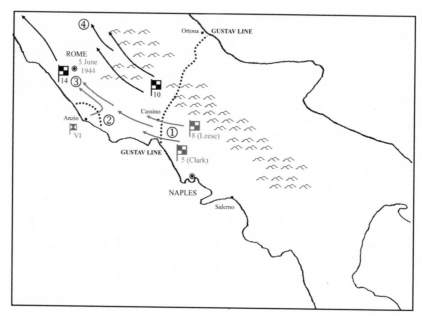

Map 2.2 Diadem: Smashing the Gustav Line (May 1944)

stumbling up the Italian boot a mile at a time, the Allies were going for broke in order to smash the Germans before summer. A wildly unbalanced line; denuding some portions of the theater in favor of a massive concentration of force on narrow, carefully selected decisive points; courting risk in some sectors in order to gain advantage in others: after a long process of trial, error, and heartbreak, the Allies had discovered operational art.

Indeed, Diadem was at least the third time the Allied camp had made this discovery. The Red Army had recognized the importance of all the above factors for years before the war and, by the time of the Stalingrad counteroffensive in 1942, Operation Uranus, was launching its offensives on often shockingly narrow fronts, overwhelming the Wehrmacht in chosen assault sectors, then exploiting the gaps torn in the German line with second- and third-echelon forces. The Western Allies did not have the same prewar doctrinal tradition as the Red Army, but they too had unlocked the secret during the Third Battle of El Alamein, when Montgomery's 8th Army had the unenviable task of chewing through Rommel's defenses in the narrow corridor between the Qattara Depression and the Mediterranean Sea. His solution, Operation Lightfoot, featured a main blow by a phalanx of four assault divisions of XXX Corps attacking on a 6-mile front, supported by infantry tanks and backed by a massive display of air strikes and artillery. Now Alexander was planning something very similar.

Pouring 90 percent of one's fighting strength into a single sector was a risk, doubly dangerous against a fast-reacting force like the Wehrmacht, with Panzer divisions and aggressive commanders ready to pounce on any sign of weakness. Operational art could work against the Germans, provided two preconditions were met. The first was that the Allies had to hold the initiative (*Gesetz des Handelns*), with the Wehrmacht no longer capable of large-scale offensives, and that was true in Italy. The second was the ability to deceive the Wehrmacht through secrecy, deception operations (called *maskirovka* by the Soviets), and careful counterintelligence work. If the Germans were able to detect the unusual levels of massing on a single, 5-mile stretch of front, they would be better able to devise defensive countermeasures. They had failed to do so at Stalingrad, where the Soviets assembled their assault forces in night marches of great distance and employed dummy forces and false radio reports, and they had failed at El Alamein, where a deception operation gave at least some indication that Montgomery's main blow was about to fall in the southern sector of the front.

And they failed again this time. The Allies were planning for another offensive at the Gustav Line—that much was obvious, but little else was. The French Expeditionary Corps, for example, dropped completely off Kesselring's situation maps in the run-up to Diadem. Since it had a reputation as the finest Allied fighting force, especially in mountain fighting, the field marshal needed to know where it was in order to pinpoint the *Schwerpunkt* for the upcoming Allied offensive. More generally, Kesselring completely missed the dramatic redeployment of Allied forces in Italy, a complicated series of redeployments, transfers, and boundary-shifting between formations that brought the entire British 8th Army across the Apennine Mountains from east to west. The Allies indulged in a whole series of deception operations—movements at night, march and noise discipline, dummy landing craft, and a great deal of bogus radio traffic generated by Canadian signalers to make Kesselring think another amphibious landing was in the offing, perhaps a shallow envelopment at Civitavecchia, 40 miles north of Rome, or deeper at Livorno, another 125 miles farther up the boot. The amphibious deception fed Kesselring's own suspicions, making it doubly effective. All told, some 250,000 Allied soldiers were on the march in one direction or another, and the pre-Diadem German intelligence failure was one of the most egregious of the war.

Of course, it wasn't the first or last time that the Wehrmacht was caught napping in this war. Pre-Barbarossa estimates of the size of the Red Army in 1941 were so low they weren't even in the ballpark, and the same thing happened again before Operation Blue, the Stalingrad offensive in 1942. A force as kinetically focused and as operationally obsessed as this one tended to be less interested in the quieter aspects of modern warfare, areas like intelligence-gathering, counterintelligence, and logistics. The Germans certainly had the agencies, organs, and trained personnel to perform these functions—Admiral Canaris of the *Abwehr*, for example, or Reinhard Gehlen of "Foreign Armies East" (*Fremde Heere Ost*), the famous "12th Section" of the German General Staff.[80] They just didn't employ them particularly well, nor did the field commanders or the staff view them as especially critical. The enemy always lay to the front—everyone knew that—and Prussians never asked how many, only where.

Breaking the Wehrmacht: Diadem in Action

The operational plan for Diadem was simplicity itself: parallel drives by both allied armies straight ahead, moving generally northwest, to shatter the Gustav line and head toward Rome and beyond. When the main drive was well under way and time was right, the super-sized VI Corps was to launch its own offensive, breaking out of the bridgehead and linking up with the US 5th and 8th British Armies driving up from the south. Alexander hoped that this "one-two punch"—the first against the Gustav Line, the second out of Anzio—might "destroy the right wing of the German 10th Army and drive the remnants of the 10th and 14th Armies into the area north of Rome."[81] Nearly a half-million Allied troops, not to mention the 4,000 combat aircraft of the Mediterranean Allied Air Forces under US General Ira C. Eaker, were about to try conclusions with the 80,000 men of Vietinghoff's 10th Army, the 70,000 of Mackensen's 14th, and fewer than 500 planes all told.

German dispositions themselves had hardly changed at all since January. On the 10th Army line, Vietinghoff had two corps, Senger's XIV Panzer Corps on his right and LI Mountain Corps under General Valentin Feuerstein on his left, with *Kampfgruppe* Hauck holding a long front along the now quiet Adriatic front. Each had two divisions in the line, for a total of four badly depleted German divisions arrayed abreast—the same four who had been out here a long time by

May. The 1st *Fallschirmjäger* Division was probably the best of the lot, still holding down the fort at Cassino, but it was something of a mess by this point, down to less than 1,000 men in the line and unlikely to receive replacements anytime soon. To the north, 14th Army was no more robust. Mackensen had the same two-corps array he'd had since the landing: I *Fallschirmjäger* on his right, under General Schlemm, and LXXVI Panzer Corps on his left, under General Herr. The same five divisions who had been holding the line since day one—4th *Fallschirmjäger*, 65th, 3rd *Panzergrenadier*, 362nd, and 715th—were still in place, though a great deal more brittle than they had been back in January.

Between these two German armies—the basic components of Kesselring's Army Group C—lay the reserve. It was not much of one, certainly: a mere pair of divisions. They were good units, though, Fries's 29th *Panzergrenadier* and Lüttwitz's 26th Panzer. Both were battle-tested and unlikely to panic even under the hammer blows of a better-supplied enemy, as they'd proven before. Kesselring's principal decision would be when and where to insert them. While he enjoyed what campaign analysts like to call the benefits of the "central position," able to operate on "interior lines" to smash the first enemy force to come within range, then to turn and do the same to the other one, it was highly unlikely he was going to be able to hit anyone very hard with a mere two-division reserve.

Diadem opened on the night of May 11. The four-corps phalanx of the 5th and 8th Armies lurched into action behind a pulverizing artillery barrage—1,060 guns on 8th Army's front and 600 on 5th Army's—accompanied by thousands of aerial sorties. Allied fire blanketed German frontline troops, command posts, and lines of communication alike. The British later claimed to have fired 476,413 shells in the course of the fighting, and to at least one forward German *Landser* it seemed "as if someone had switched on the lights." Diadem had come as a complete surprise, and the German command once again found itself scrambling from the start. Unlike the last time they had all been surprised by an Allied stroke—just a few months earlier at Anzio—this time the scramble failed. In fact, even to speak of the "German command" may be misleading in this unique historical moment. So quiet was the Gustav Line in early May that most of the key men weren't even present. Kesselring's chief of staff, Westphal, was on convalescent leave; German 10th Army commander Vietinghoff was on his way to Germany to receive a decoration personally from the hands of the Führer. The commander of XIV Panzer Corps, General Senger, was nearing the end of a monthlong leave at home, and the figure who would usually take over in the absence of the commander, Colonel Hans-Georg Schmidt von Altenstadt, chief of staff of XIV Panzer Corps, was also likewise on leave. Even if the German command had been present, Allied artillery put both 10th Army and VIX Panzer Corps headquarters out of commission in the opening minutes of the battle.

With the commanders either gone or en route to the front, the first few days of Diadem saw no dramatic German counterstrokes, none of the Wehrmacht's rapid reaction, and few major redeployments. The unlucky four German divisions on the Gustav Line sat and took the blow of the hammer. Each of these understrength units faced an entire, heavily reinforced Allied corps, and, lacking central direction, they had little choice but to fend for themselves. On the coast, 94th Division held the Garigliano Line versus US II Corps; to the left, 71st Division held the Monte Majo massif, facing the French Expeditionary Corps; the next division in the line, 44th Division, held the line of the Rapido, the same bloody river that the Americans had tried to force back in January, against British XIII Corps; and finally, on the extreme German left of the Diadem sector, Heidrich's 1st *Fallschirmjäger* Division held the ruins of Cassino against Polish II Corps.

While the opening days of Diadem featured hard fighting here and there, on the operational level, at least, the allies made a complete and total breakthrough within days. The French got through first, driving toward Monte Majo, with British XIII Corps crossing the Rapido to its right and US II Corps the Garigliano to its left.[82] When frontline divisions radioed Kesselring to request reinforcements, fire support—anything, really—Kesselring told them to fend for themselves and to create their own reinforcements by thinning out less threatened portions of the line—a "true counsel of despair." Only in the north, the extreme right of the Allied battle array, was there a holdup. Here a game Polish II Corps—eager not only for combat but also for revenge on the Germans—suffered a bloody repulse at the hands of the paratroopers holding Cassino. By now, the paras of 1st *Fallschirmjäger* must have felt like they had a lease on the place—and they didn't seem eager to move out. With the rest of the Gustav Line giving way, however, the Cassino position no longer fulfilled any real operational purpose, and therefore Kesselring ordered what was left of 1st *Fallschirmjäger* Division to evacuate Cassino on the night of May 17.[83]

Through it all, we cannot say that Kesselring had been particularly active in arranging countermeasures. His initial reaction to Diadem was disbelief. His own prognostications had been so off, and he had solid mechanized divisions—the Hermann Göring Panzer Division and the 90th *Panzergrenadier*—dispersed all over Italy, guarding beaches against amphibious landings that never came. But with the Allies in full fury all across his front, the Gustav Line cracking into pieces, and many of his key subordinate commanders still hurrying to get back to their posts, Kesselring could do little beyond the obvious: summoning 29th *Panzergrenadier* and 26th Panzer Divisions, and his Army Group C reserve, from their perch at the Anzio bridgehead in order to bolster the line in the south. They began arriving in driblets almost immediately but could do little to salvage the situation.

And now the climax of the campaign had arrived: the breakout from Anzio. The small cockpit now bulged with Allied forces—seven and a half reinforced divisions' worth—while German defensive strength was pretty much what it had been in January. Material inferiority and the constant strain of trying to do more with less was generating real friction within the German command. Mackensen's no-nonsense realism had never harmonized with Kesselring's increasingly manic optimism, and now a fundamental operational difference had arisen between the two. Kesselring believed that an Allied breakout would aim toward the town of Valmontone, in order to cut off Highway 6 and thus sever German 10th Army's line of retreat as it straggled up from the south. Mackensen thought otherwise. Once the Allies had broken out, they would head toward the Alban Hills, wheel left, and get on Highway 7, the most direct route to Rome. Both were reasonable propositions, but operational disputes were now bleeding over into the realm of personal animosity. Hitler's meddling didn't help—suggesting that Mackensen's army create a false front, pulling back from the front line just before the main bombardment, then counterattacking Allied assault formations as they came up, a relic of World War I–style linear thinking that had little place on a modern, mechanized battlefield.

In fact, nothing would have helped. It had taken a while, but the Allies were finally firing on all cylinders—tactical, operational, and strategic: an army-sized VI Corps under a highly competent commander, Truscott; massive fire support from artillery, air, and naval assets; a solid deception operation code-named "Hippo" that succeeded in deceiving the Germans into thinking that the main attack was coming in the British sector on the left of the beachhead; and even purpose-built new equipment like the "Snake," a long tube filled with explosives to detonate German minefields. Against this show of strength, guile, and invention, the Germans could offer what they always did: the fighting strength (*Kampfkraft*) of five weakened divisions. While Mackensen had heavily fortified his defensive position and echeloned it in some depth (1–2 kilometers), he had no reserves (which Kesselring had already dispatched to the south), and without reserves to counterattack Allied penetrations and plug holes, 14th Army was fighting without a backstop and, frankly, without hope.

The breakout began on May 22. Of several alternative possibilities, Truscott (and Clark, his army commander) had chosen Operation Buffalo, an initial thrust northeastward toward Cisterna, followed by a drive on Valmontone to cut off 10th Army's retreat, and Alexander had approved it. Clark also had Truscott draw up alternate plans, however, since he did not believe that a single Allied corps, even a big one, had much chance to trap an entire German army ("the Boche is too smart," he confided to his diary). The others were Operation Grasshopper (a drive almost due east to link up with 5th Army as it came up along the coast); Turtle (another attack up the Anzio Road to the Alban Hills); and Crawdad (a drive left, or southwest, of the Alban Hills, the shortest route as the crow flies to Rome).

What happened next has become part of the US Army's mythology of World War II. After three days of bitter fighting, US 3rd Division splintered the German 362nd Division defending Cisterna and took the town, at a cost of 3,000 US casualties. With no German reserves available, the loss of Cisterna meant the loss of the beachhead, and the Germans began to pull back. US forces coming down from Anzio linked up with those of II Corps near the bombed-out village of Borgo Grappa on May 25.[84] US 5th Army now formed a united front against the Germans. The path to Valmontone and Highway 6 seemed to be open. Already, armored patrols of the US 1st Armored Division were probing far into the German rear, heading toward Giulianello. The destruction of 10th Army seemed imminent. At this point, General Clark intervened, with fateful consequences.

The legend goes something like this: lusting for the personal glory of seizing Rome and possessed of a suspicious Anglophobia, Clark now went renegade. On May 26, he ordered Truscott to institute alternate plan Turtle and to wheel VI Corps almost 90 degrees to the left from northeast to northwest. Rather than continuing his drive toward Valmontone, cutting off Highway 6 and blocking the retreat of the German 10th Army, Truscott was to drive on Rome as rapidly as possible. The decision has generated a great deal of criticism, like so much in the Italian campaign, with Clark accused not only of disobeying a direct order from his commander, Alexander, but also sabotaging the operational plan and saving German 10th Army from certain destruction.[85] One analyst has labeled Clark "neurotic," another called him "troubled to the point of paranoia," and a third condemned Clark's wheel as "one of the most misguided blunders made by any Allied commander" in the war.[86]

Such judgments remain typical in the literature. The only problem with them is that they ignore the Wehrmacht, arguing that if the Allies had but taken Valmontone they would have destroyed 10th Army. But all sorts of operational questions arise: Would the Germans really have allowed that to happen? Would they not have reacted in some way to an Allied thrust on Valmontone? Would they not have attempted a breakout? Or sought an alternate route north? Could a forward US Army patrol, even an entire infantry battalion, hold Valmontone in a maneuver battle against what were sure to be desperate German attacks to retake it and reopen Highway 6?

In fact, encircling 10th Army was never a high probability. Vietinghoff already had the force in full retreat, and there are many roads north beside Highway 6.[87] The operational situation was confusing, even chaotic, and the Anglo-American armies had already proven that they operated best in a controlled, set-piece environment, with clear sector lines and phased advances. In the end, Diadem had to be satisfied with mauling the Germans rather than destroying them outright. Perhaps the best proof of the nonevent of "Clark's blunder" is that the Germans do not seem to have noticed it at all. Certainly they could see the importance of the various roads and of Valmontone. But in none of the relevant documents or memoirs—Kesselring's, for example, or those of his chief of staff, Westphal—do we read a word of the "miracle of Valmontone" or the incredible Allied operational blunder that had led to it, and these are memoirs that dissect every last Allied command mistake in full living color. Kesselring, in particular, spends much of his memoir criticizing operational decisions on both sides (except his own, which he deems to be invariably correct). Mackensen never wrote a memoir for this period, but the Allied turn to Rome seemed perfectly normal to him: he had predicted they would do it all along. Or take Senger: if any German commander on the line should have understood the significance of the sudden Allied wheel away from Valmontone, he was the one. His XIV Panzer Corps would have been the first to be rounded up if the Allies cut off 10th Army's line of retreat. But once again, "Clark's blunder" doesn't fit into his analysis:

The attempt to exploit out of the Anzio beachhead and cut off the path of retreat of the XIV Panzer Corps had misfired. Nevertheless, we cannot conclude that Field Marshal Alexander's suggestion to attack with strong forces out of the beachhead toward Valmontone would have been more correct. Such an action would only have destroyed XIV Panzer Corps if it had been able to pin the corps in the vicinity of Frosinone or drive through Valmontone [another 14 miles] to Subiaco, which would have met serious terrain difficulties.[88]

Not one of them—solid operators all—discusses the focus on Rome as a blunder. Italy's greatest city and communications hub, Rome was a legitimate target, even a strategic target. They all seem unaware—and, indeed, who can blame them? Slithering out of a trap by the skin of their teeth was just another day at the office for German commanders by 1944. In Italy, facing two Allied armies coming on from opposite directions, the Wehrmacht did it again, surviving yet another near-death experience and living to fight another day.

The Italian Campaign and the German Way of War

Rome fell to the US 5th Army on June 4, but the fighting in Italy went on. The hammer blows of Diadem had taken their toll, and neither the 14th nor the 10th Army could make a stand against the pursuing Allies. Kesselring dismissed Mackensen as commander of 14th Army—even though the latter's pessimistic assessment of the operational situation had been correct—and replaced him with General Joachim Lemelsen, but it barely mattered. The port of Civitavecchia fell on June 7, the Viterbo airfield complex on June 9, and by June 20 the Germans were back on a hastily dug line centered on Lake Trasimeno, some 90 miles north of Rome. By early August the Allied pursuit had driven them back to the line of the Arno River, anchored on the cities of Pisa and Florence, and by the end of the month the Wehrmacht was sitting on the forbidding "Green Line" (or Gothic Line) from Massa on the western coast of Italy to Pesaro on the eastern. Here was a secure position they would hold against all Allied attacks until 1945—a restoration of *Stellungskrieg*.[89]

Despite the disappointing ending, it was one of the great pursuits in military history. By August, the Allies stood 300 miles north of where they had been in May. Unfortunately, Allied strategy had now reduced

Italy to a theater of the second rank, and two entire corps (the US VI and the French Expeditionary) had shipped out to take part in Operation Anvil, the invasion of southern France. As 1944 drew to a close, the Allied commanders in Italy had to shelve their grandiose plans for a drive farther north, to Bologna, the Po River valley, or perhaps even into Austria. As always in Italy, reality had a way of setting in.

Evaluating the Wehrmacht's performance in the Anzio–Cassino–Diadem operational sequence is a complex undertaking. German forces had faced off against dual threats for nearly four months, defending themselves successfully on the Gustav Line and the Anzio beachhead, and even while facing a hopeless strategic situation they had made the Allied armies pay dearly for every step forward. The 1st *Fallschirmjäger* Division had distinguished itself, defending Cassino bravely against all comers, but so too had the garden-variety infantry formations, the 44th and 71st and 94th Divisions on the Gustav Line and the 65th and 362nd Divisions at Anzio. The mechanized units, General Fries's 29th *Panzergrenadier* Division, in particular, were as fine as any unit on either side in the entire war: flexible, aggressive in the attack, and steadfast on defense. Even as their fronts collapsed under the weight of Diadem, with their headquarters crushed under Allied bombs and their paths of retreat nearly severed, all these formations had endured. They were particularly skilled at forming improvised battlegroups (*Kampfgruppen*) and rear guards that managed to hold up the pursuing enemy just long enough for the main body to continue the retreat to the north until it could reform along the Gothic Line. For all these reasons, military historians have lavished praised on the Wehrmacht's defensive stand in Italy and on Field Marshal Kesselring, in particular, routinely describing him as a defensive genius.

If we look at the Italian campaign as a whole, however, another startling fact comes to mind: the Wehrmacht had no choice but to defend, since it had clearly lost its ability to attack. From the moment the Allies invaded Italy, the Wehrmacht had met the Allies' every move forward with an immediate and vigorous counterattack. During the invasion of Sicily in July 1943, the US Army wound up with a Panzer division in its face within hours of the landing. In September 1943, the landing force at Salerno faced *six of them* within a few days and came very close to being driven back into the sea. The same thing happened at Anzio: a powerful attack on the beachhead featuring mechanized forces and Panzers that once again came within a hair of success. From Frederick the Great, with his preference for "short and lively wars" and his insistence that "the Prussian Army always attacks," down to

General Paul Conrath of the Hermann Göring Panzer Division, who once summed up his art of war as "an immediate, reckless rush at the enemy," Prussian-German armies lived by the offensive, launching aggressive attacks along concentric lines.

But those keeping score will note that none of them had worked. The Allies survived German mechanized attacks at Sicily, Salerno, and Anzio. Allied numbers, fire superiority, battlefield skill, and experience: all conspired to rob the once irresistible German mechanized attack of its force. *Kampfkraft*—the concept of "battle strength" that was the essence of the Wehrmacht at war—wasn't what it used to be. Kesselring's chief of staff, Colonel Westphal, put it best. "The blanket," he said, "had become too thin," using an old peasant expression for hard, lean times.[90] In fact, "after almost five years of war, the troops were no longer capable of prosecuting a successful attack. Grass grew on the graves of the majority of commanders we had trained during peacetime. Their successors could not consistently coordinate the fire of the various weapons, or achieve the maximum concentration in combat."[91] His phrase—"no longer capable of prosecuting a successful attack"—no longer *angriffsfähig*: ominous words indeed for the German way of war.

For Westphal, the second, abortive attack at Anzio—smothered in a blizzard of Allied fire almost before it got started—was the key moment of the war, a turning point "similar to August 8, 1918."[92] Indeed, he traveled to Berchtesgaden at the time to deliver the news to Hitler in person. After giving Westphal a rap on the knuckles ("So this is the general who's been running down my troops!"), Hitler was concerned enough to summon twenty-two more officers from Italy ("from company chief to divisional commander") to hear their accounts of what had happened at Anzio. General Fries of the 29th *Panzergrenadier* Division was part of the assemblage.[93] Even after they gave him the same gloomy accounts—no air support, inferiority in artillery—Hitler remained dubious: "We can't draw conclusions from the course of the fighting up to now," the Führer concluded. "It would be like declaring bankruptcy."

Italy was the theater where the Wehrmacht finally went bankrupt, and the long process of liquidation began.

3

On the Beach: Normandy and Beyond

Introduction

The great British prime minister of the Victorian era, Benjamin Disraeli, once allegedly spoke of "lies, damn lies, and statistics"—arguing that people can use numbers to back up almost any case they like. We live in a world of statistics, a barrage of figures, percentages, and numbers, and most of us learn to be pretty cynical about them.

But sometimes numbers don't lie. It is early 1944, and a member of the Wehrmacht's brain trust is wrestling with the figures.

* * *

LOCATION AND DATE UNDISCLOSED. *The Planner liked his facts and figures, his tables and numbers, his charts and graphs.[1] This was what war was all about, he felt: not thundering along in a Panzer or Stuka or leading an infantry Zug into battle, but cold, careful planning. Planning based on the numbers.*

Maybe that was why he felt so distracted lately. He looked at the number at the bottom of the sheet of paper.

"280."

An impressive total: the number of divisions he currently had in the field. A massive force, surely enough to handle any crisis or to defeat any enemy. He felt a momentary thrill contemplating the power of the number.

But the thrill soon faded, leaving the Planner with a vaguely unsettled feeling. He'd been playing with the figures all night, and it wasn't getting any better. The numbers didn't lie, nor did they fool him. He began to jot down more figures, his pen moving decisively on the paper like a knife whittling away at a good piece of wood.

"The Balkans: 25 divisions."

Again, that unsettled feeling.

"Norway: 12 divisions."
He swallowed hard.
"Italy: 27 divisions."
General Alfred Jodl, the operations chief for the High Command of the Wehrmacht, had long ago memorized all the numbers. It wasn't like they changed every day. He was frowning. He knew what came next. He ran his hand through his thinning hair, felt his shiny, balding head. He suddenly felt small, powerless. He continued to scribble:
"Ostfront: 156 divisions."
He stared at the number, marveling at it.
His task that evening was to draw up preliminary plans for the defense of France in the event of an Allied invasion. "In the event?" There was no question of it! They were coming. The Führer knew it, Keitel, Rundstedt—they all did.
General Jodl looked one last time at the totals, then did some simple math. Take 280, subtract the others. He had sixty divisions left—ten Panzer divisions, and a few solid infantry divisions. But a large number—at least twenty-five—were second- or third-rate units without any organic transport. Old men. Convalescents. Frostbitten victims from the last Russian winter. The army had more than enough of those, he thought bitterly. Foreigners enrolled in the Wehrmacht who were fighting for dubious motives. He estimated thirty good divisions, give or take.
He exhaled slowly. He wasn't sure exactly how many divisions the Western Allies would be bringing to France, but he knew one thing: when the Big Invasion came, the number would probably be higher than thirty.

Turf Wars: The German Command in France

It's tempting to ask: How did the Germans foul this one up so badly?

After almost four full years of planning, the German defensive campaign in France was a fiasco. The Wehrmacht opened badly and then careened into complete disaster within weeks. The quality of the effort was consistent from top to bottom: a hopelessly muddled command structure, a force that would charitably be described as second-rate, and a botched operation from the initial deployment to the final rout. From strategy down to tactics and at all stops in between, France was the theater where the Wehrmacht's "genius for war"[2] vanished, where "Hitler's legions"[3] fell apart, and where "the devil's virtuosos"[4] played like amateurs. On the French coast, the military tradition that had given the world Frederick the Great, Carl von Clausewitz, and Helmuth von Moltke suffered one of the most humiliating defeats in its long history.

Let us begin at the top. Fighting a global, multifront war wasn't easy on the best of days, but the Germans hadn't made it any easier on themselves by developing a bizarre and convoluted system for running theirs. Each of the three services had its own high command: the *Oberkommando des Heeres* (OKH) for the army, the *Oberkommando der Marine* (OKM) for the navy, and the *Oberkommando der Luftwaffe* (OKL) for the air force. A joint staff stood watch over all three, the High Command of the Armed Forces (*Oberkommando der Wehrmacht*), with Hitler himself acting as the Supreme Commander of the Armed Forces (*Oberbefehlshaber der Wehrmacht*), theoretically the source of all authority, decision-making, and strategic planning.[5]

So far, so good—except for one structural problem: the army was vastly larger than the other two services; in fact, it was larger than both of them put together. The Third Reich was a land power as the first two had been, as Germany was always destined to be, and victory or defeat in this war was always very much in the hands of the land force. In fact, Hitler had created the OKW back in 1938 not as a way to rationalize military planning or to make sure that the armed forces were strong across all three domains of land, sea, and air. Rather, he intended the formation of the OKW as a means to limit the influence and authority of the army, whose officer corps he viewed as a decadent remnant of the old Junker aristocracy—a conservative force that would never be comfortable with his radical designs. The navy and the air force understood their role in the new command drama, and Admiral Erich Raeder, his successor, Karl Dönitz, and Field Marshal Hermann Göring—high commanders of the Kriegsmarine and the Luftwaffe—could almost always be relied upon to form a united front against the army in discussions on resource allocation, manpower, even operational planning.[6]

Since the OKW wasn't designed to run the war efficiently, it didn't. Some German operations were truly joint, like the complex triphibious invasion of Denmark and Norway in April 1940.[7] Most were not. The fighting in the Soviet Union, in particular, was essentially an all-army show. The Luftwaffe's contribution was a supporting one, and as its losses grew, its influence on the fighting diminished until it was practically invisible.[8] The navy could provide very little assistance to a continental struggle waged in the very heart of the Eurasian landmass and therefore limited its contributions to defense of the Baltic and Black Sea ports, to running supplies to the German and Romanian forces occupying Crimea, and later to various evacuation operations.

By 1942, a de facto division of responsibilities had evolved. The army, through the OKH and the Chief of the General Staff (first General Franz Halder, then General Kurt Zeitzler), was responsible only for operations in the east.[9] The other fronts became "OKW theaters"— areas in which the army was expected to fight, but over which it had no real jurisdiction. They included Norway, occupied France, Finland, the Balkans, Crete, North Africa, and Italy. Splitting the war into two parts had enormous implications, none of them good. A single German division, for example, might be fighting in Russia (under OKH authority), then receive transfer orders to France (from the OKW), and then be ordered back to Russia again (OKH). The result was a nightmare of competing jurisdictions and bureaucracies, which only a direct appeal to Hitler could solve.[10]

Adding another level onto this already complex system was the creation in early 1942 of yet another high command, this one for Western Europe, France, and the Low Countries. With US entry into the war in late 1941 and increasingly strident Soviet demands for the opening of a second front, it seemed clear that Western Europe was going to be the target of an Allied amphibious invasion at some point in the not too distant future. In March 1942, Hitler issued Directive (*Weisung*) No. 40, declaring that "the European coasts face the strong danger of enemy landings in the near future." Amphibious warfare—either offensive or defensive—required close cooperation between all three services. "Coastal defense is a task for all the armed forces, and requires close, seamless cooperation between the various services," he declared.[11] A joint command was necessary. Hitler now appointed Field Marshal Gerd von Rundstedt to be Supreme Commander West (*Oberbefehlshaber-West*, or OB-West) and simultaneously gave him command of Army Group D, embracing all German ground forces in the west: 15th Army on the Channel coast, 7th Army in Normandy and Brittany, and 1st Army along the Atlantic coast and the Bay of Biscay.[12] In August 1943, with Italy wavering and the Italian forces occupying southern France no longer reliable, the Germans stood up a new army, the 19th, to guard the Mediterranean coast, and it too came under the command of Army Group D.

Since then, the forces under the command of OB-West had waxed and waned in size, but mainly the latter. Battles of unimaginable scope were raging in the Soviet Union, while a sizable occupation force, some twenty-five divisions by summer 1942 and growing by the month, languished on soft duty in France. Like all occupation forces, the Germans in France settled in, got comfortable, and grew sloppy—a dream assignment for any soldier lucky enough to pull it. Meanwhile, hard-pressed German army commanders in the Soviet Union desperately needed reinforcements and knew where they could get them: from the inactive "army in being" in France, an immense force currently doing nothing.[13] Ever since 1942, "the hard-pressed and always under-manned Eastern Front looked with envy at the army in the west, which seemed to be sleeping (*schlafende*). As each crisis arose, commanders in the east demanded the surrender of this pointless reservoir of forces in the west. In the need of the moment, these demands were usually granted."[14] Divisions came and went, fresh ones leaving for the east, burned-out ones coming back, and the constant to-ing and fro-ing made any kind of operational planning to defeat an Allied invasion impossible. From January to October 1943, for example, no fewer than thirty-eight divisions left France for the Eastern Front, and no one could predict when it would end.

While OB-West was doing little but serving as a manpower reservoir for the Eastern Front, the British were turning up the operational heat in the theater. British commandoes, heeding Winston Churchill's directive to "set Europe aflame," launched a series of flashy commando raids: Vaasgo (Vågsøy) Island in Norway in December 1941 (Operation Archery); the German radar station at Bruneval in February 1942 (Operation Biting); St. Nazaire in March 1942 (Operation Chariot); and the fortified port of Dieppe in August 1942 (Operation Jubilee).[15] Each raid, successful or not, heightened anxieties within the German command that the big one was imminent: a general Allied landing on the coast. The spectacular Allied attack on the dry dock at St. Nazaire, for example, which culminated in the detonation of the explosive-laden destroyer HMS *Campbeltown* in the mouth of the channel, seemed so threatening that Hitler and the OKW decided that something had to be done.[16] They would construct a great system of coastal fortifications in the west: no fewer than 15,000 concrete bunkers, 600,000 conscripted French laborers, large-scale flooding of coastal territories, and a completion date of May 1943. It was the birth of the Atlantic Wall.

Even as the Atlantic Wall grew in size and scope, however, German defenses in the west continued to languish. In the summer of 1943, a dismayed Rundstedt decided to undertake a comprehensive inspection of his command, looking at issues of manpower, coastal fortifications, deployment, supply, communications, and preparation against airborne landings. The results, laid out in a detailed report to Hitler in October 1943, were discouraging, to say the least.[17] Rundstedt laid out the possibilities for an allied attack: a main attack on the Channel coast, perhaps in connection with secondary attacks against Normandy and Brittany, a landing on the Mediterranean coast, or a combined attack from the Mediterranean and Atlantic coasts. With so few reconnaissance assets in hand, any landing would almost certainly be a surprise and most likely get ashore in several places.[18] The defensive posture could not be static, therefore, but rather aggressive. Sufficient reserves had to be present to launch an immediate counterblow (*Gegenstoss*).[19] "If the enemy has time to establish himself, throwing him out again is usually difficult."[20]

Unfortunately, adequate and concentrated (*schwerpunktmässig*) defenses existed only in the sector of the 15th Army, charged with defending the Channel coast and the Pas de Calais. The rest of Rundstedt's vast, 2,000-mile front was "weakly occupied and hopelessly incomplete in terms of construction"; in fact was barely more than a "picket" (*Sicherung*) and in some cases only a "watch" (*Beobachtung*).[21] Divisional frontages were so large that they bordered on the absurd—over 80 miles for the 18th Luftwaffe Field Division in the 15th Army Sector, for example, or 60 miles for the 266th Infantry Division in the 7th Army—creating a thin crust of defenders without any tactical or operational depth. Moreover, the troops were second-rate, either too young or too old or too sickly, and were "not suited to conduct a war of movement (*Bewegungskrieg*) against such a well equipped enemy," especially if he attacked with strong forces on what Rundstedt called "an American scale."[22] Artillery was a motley collection of captured weapons: French, Danish, Belgian, Polish, Dutch, Soviet, Yugoslavian, and especially Italian. Across the board, the west was a secondary front. Lack of fuel, lack of airpower, lack of a fully mobile operational reserve: the news was bad everywhere. Rundstedt closed with a quiet but unmistakable warning. On average, his units in the west were only conditionally ready for combat, but "if the day of the great attack comes," Rundstedt promised to do all that was possible "with the available means." It was a hardly a ringing affirmation.[23]

Historians accuse Hitler of never listening to his officers in the field, but this time he did, or at least he seemed to. Just a week after reading Rundstedt's report, on November 3, 1943, he issued Führer Directive No. 51:

The hard and expensive battle against Bolshevism over the past two and half years has required the mass of our military strength and effort. Such was the scale of the danger and the overall situation. Now the situation has changed. The danger in the east remains, but a greater one has arisen in the West: the Anglo-Saxon landing! In the east, the size of the theater allows even an extreme loss of territory without landing a deadly blow on one of Germany's vital nerves.

Not so in the west!

"Not so in the west!"—*Anders der Westen!*[24] If the enemy cracked through German defenses here, the results would be incalculable. By spring of 1944, or perhaps even earlier, the Allies were going to launch an attack on Western Europe, Hitler warned, and the time had come to stop weakening the west in favor of the other theaters and to make sure that it was prepared for the decisive struggle: "All units and formations in the west and in Denmark, as well as all the newly raised Panzer, assault guns, and antitank formations in the west, may not be released for duty on other fronts without my express approval."[25] If the enemy did force a landing on the western coast, then it would be necessary "to launch an even more forceful counterattack," and that required a "high-quality, fully mobile force that was capable of launching a successful attack."[26]

There was that phrase again: "capable of conducting an attack" (*angriffsfähig*). It was the same descriptor that had governed German operational planning at Sicily, Salerno, and Anzio. For the Wehrmacht, defense was always a temporary condition, and victory was always the result of a bold, aggressive, and *angriffsfähig* force. Once the coastal formations had absorbed the initial blow of the landing and brought the Allies to a halt, the mobile and armored reserves would go into action, smashing into the still unsteady beachhead from multiple and concentric directions and crumpling it. Without such a capability, the campaign in France was hopeless. Indeed, any campaign was hopeless.

Along with its general strategic guidelines, Directive No. 51 addressed key issues on the operational level. Where would the Allied landing take place? Where should forces lie in wait to launch the aggressive counterattack that would drive the interlopers into the sea? A series of supplementary instructions followed. Führer Directive No. 51a, issued by Field Marshal Wilhelm Keitel, the chief of staff of the OKW, stated that the Allied buildup in southern Britain was complete and foresaw a landing either on the Channel coast or Normandy

at any time after mid-February. All available reserves were to reinforce the threatened sectors, including the Hermann Göring Panzer
and the 90th *Panzergrenadier* Divisions. Later Führer Directives (No.
51b and No. 51c) reinforced the ban on any divisional transfers out of
OB-West and handed Rundstedt supreme authority for all tactical matters within a so-called battle-zone (*Kampfzone*) along the French and
Belgian coasts.[27]

While Directive No. 51 and its codicils seemed to be a sensible response to the problem of defending the west, the overall strategic situation robbed them of any real impact. First, the Red Army celebrated
the New Year of 1944 in its typical fashion by launching a series of
massive offensives in Ukraine, involving all four of their heavily armored fronts (army groups) in the sector. Successive hammer blows
culminated in the final loss of the Dnepr Line, the encirclement of
most of the German 8th Army in the Korsun Pocket, and the near destruction of Field Marshal Erich von Manstein's Army Group South.
The ban on transferring any units out of the west, as sensible as that
might have seemed in isolation, soon had to give way to the military
reality of a multifront war. Beset by superior enemies east, west, and
south, there was little that the High Command could do except plug
the most dangerous hole at the moment, and that meant taking divisions from quiet France, or divisions that had been previously ear-
marked for duty there, and shipping them to the hot spot of the week.
By the end of January 1944, the Allies landed at Anzio, Hitler issued
Directive No. 52 calling for a "tough and merciless struggle" against
the enemy in Italy, and the two divisions mentioned by name in Directive No. 51a (90th *Panzergrenadier* and Hermann Göring) were soon on
their way to Italy.[28] The crisis in the east also continued unabated, and
Hitler's new operational scheme—the creation of "strongholds" (*feste
Plätze*), that individual divisions were to defend to the last man—was
hugely expensive in terms of manpower and would continue to suck
units out of *OB-West* for the foreseeable future.[29]

Rather than send even more troops, Hitler decided to stand up yet
another military command in France, perhaps the last thing the theater needed at the moment. In December 1943, Field Marshal Erwin
Rommel and Army Group B arrived on the scene. Having lost the
power struggle with Field Marshal Albert Kesselring for the command
in Italy in November, Rommel and his staff had been sitting idle. Now
Hitler sent them to the west to inspect the coastal fortifications in
Denmark, Flanders, the Channel coast, Normandy, and Brittany and
to evaluate their readiness to oppose an Allied invasion. Rommel is

a much-beloved character in the English-speaking world today, but his presence in France was redundant and anomalous. The Germans already had an army group in France (Army Group D), along with a commander (Rundstedt). Now the OKW had inserted Rommel into the mix, giving him command over the two German armies in the northern sector (the 7th and the 15th), thereby depriving Rundstedt of his two largest formations. Rommel was soon demanding full military authority in the entire theater, and it seemed clear to Rundstedt and his staff that Hitler had brought the younger Rommel to the theater to create a rivalry, a situation that was guaranteed to generate disagreement and even personal animosity between the two field marshals. Rommel didn't even report to Rundstedt but rather to Hitler directly, and, according to the orders from the OKW, had complete "freedom of action within his Army Group sector."[30] One of Rundstedt's staff officers called it a "rubber order" (*Gummibefehl*), an elastic proviso that the ambitious Rommel could twist and turn to his own advantage.[31] Rundstedt still had command authority over the two armies in the south (the 1st and 19th), but both were small and weak, and at any rate the Allied blow was unlikely to fall in either of their sectors.

By the spring of 1944, a full-fledged turf war was under way.[32] With Rommel clearly making a play for command over all land forces in France, Rundstedt was on the verge of becoming supreme commander in name only and of slipping into redundancy in his own theater.[33] "As Commander in Chief West, my one authority was to change the guard in front of my gate," he told one of his interrogators after the war.[34] He saw little use for a joint command with no actual control over the troops, and in fact he considered resigning if the command muddle continued. As a stratagem for self-preservation, but also to create a more sensible chain of command, Rundstedt in late March requested the creation of another army group in France alongside Rommel's Army Group B, consisting of the two German armies deployed in the south (now designated *Armeegruppe* G). The new command structure would limit Rommel's own ambitions to the command of his own army group, give him operational command of the armies in northern France, but also confirm Rundstedt's own status as OB-West, a central command overseeing two army groups. Hitler agreed, and indeed the logic was inescapable. The new command structure was at least a "partial victory" (*Teilsieg*) for Rundstedt and his staff.[35] Unfortunately for the Germans, this regularized and more balanced command structure came into effect only on May 10, 1944—less than a month before the Allied invasion. The Germans had been snoozing in France for nearly four years. Now, with the Allies on the verge of boarding their ships, the Wehrmacht was once again doing a last-second scramble.

Forlorn Hope? Defending France

On the surface, the Germans seemed to be holding some high defensive cards as they prepared to repel the Allied invasion of Western Europe in 1944. (See Map 3.1.) These included a Supreme Command with two army groups under it: Army Group B in northern France under Rommel, and Army Group G in the south under General Johannes Blaskowitz, (who last commanded an army in Poland in 1939 and had been placed on ice since then in a variety of administrative posts and occupation duties).[36] Each army group contained two armies, a balanced array of four armies in all: 7th and 15th in the north, 1st and 19th in the south. The total number of men standing guard in the western theater varies by the source, but it was large: 865,000 for the army; 326,000 for the Luftwaffe; 102,000 for the navy; and another 100,000 in the Waffen-SS and police—well over a million men in all. With support troops thrown into the balance, the total was larger still—more than 1.5 million.

But appearances can be deceiving, and behind the facade of German readiness lay a whole host of problems. Let us begin with quantity. Those 1 million men formed sixty divisions, again a sizable sum, but their task was to cover no fewer than 2,000 miles of coastline: from Holland into the English Channel, then down the French coast and the Bay of Biscay, and finally into the Mediterranean and northern shore of the inland sea all the way to the Italian border. The Wehrmacht also had to defend Denmark, as unlikely a site as it seemed for an Allied landing, and, in fact, Rommel performed a thorough inspection of Danish invasion zones in December 1943. It had to defend the Hook of Holland and the Channel coast and the mouth of the Loire, even the French Riviera. Since a typical World War II division might, at best, defend 10–15 miles of front, the size of the German force was manifestly inadequate, as it would have been even if France were only half its actual size. As a German staff officer put it, "nowhere were the coverages narrow enough or deeply echeloned for defense in a major battle."[37] Even in the (relatively) well-off 15th Army, for example, divisions were holding 20-mile frontages; in more weakly defended sectors like Brittany, the frontages were over 100 miles per division. The average frontage in France—all fronts, all divisions—came to about 60 miles

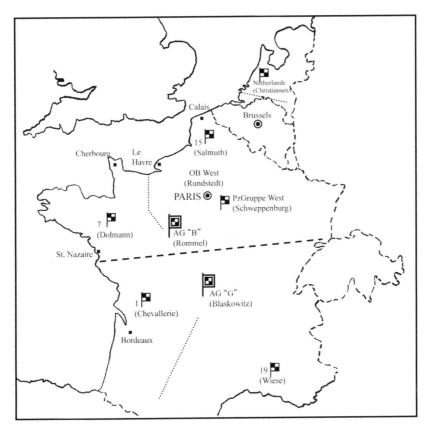

Map 3.1 Hopeless Task: Defending France (June 1944)

of beach per division, or about five times the recommended breadth. Fuel was in such short supply, moreover, that regimental commanders could make only one inspection visit per month to their far-flung component battalions, and some of them even rode horses—hardly a favorable omen for the great mechanized campaign that was to come.

Superior quality of the troops can often offset lack of numbers, and quality had been a traditional Prussian-German strength, but not this time. These were German divisions of the 1944 type, with only six maneuver battalions each, rather than the more robust nine-battalion divisions that the Wehrmacht had used to conquer Europe in the early war years. Many units were sent to France to recuperate from the ordeal of the Eastern Front, and while they were counted on *OB-West*'s roster sheets, their combat strength for the moment was near zero. In fact, France became a grab bag of diverse manpower. All the problems Rundstedt identified back in October 1943 were still present, perhaps even worse: overage conscripts; third-degree frostbite cases convalescing in the west; ethnic Germans from the occupied territories (*Volksdeutsche*); and even men suffering from various stomach ailments. In the midst of the campaign, OKW would form an entire division from this last category, the 70th, known to wags as the "Stomach Division" (*Magen-Division*), or sometimes the "White Bread Division." It was not uncommon to see officers wearing various prostheses.[38]

Perhaps most striking was the noticeable presence in France of "eastern battalions" (*Ost-Bataillonen*), consisting of volunteers, conscripts, and former prisoners of war from the Soviet Union who had signed up for a hitch in the Wehrmacht rather than languish in a POW camp. In the autumn of 1943, some forty-five battalions from the East—Cossack, Georgian, Caucasian, Turkmen, Volga Tatars, Azeris, and more—flooded into *OB-West*, and they would make up a considerable portion of the Wehrmacht's infantry fighting strength in the Normandy campaign (eight out of the forty-two infantry battalions in LXXXIV Corps, to give one example). From the start, however, the High Command debated their worth, never fully trusted them, and made sure that they always fought under strict German control, usually with a German battalion deployed on either side of them.

Finally, about half the formations in France were so-called static divisions (*Bodenständig*), quite literally "rooted to the ground" on which they stood.[39] Composed of manpower from the categories listed above and provided with very limited means of transport, usually a few horse-drawn wagons, they had a dual mission: to resist the initial Allied landing as long as possible, and then to die in place. They had less artillery, fewer heavy weapons like machine guns and mortars, and no reconnaissance battalion, since their mission did not call for them to move. We may regard the 709th Division as typical. The men in this division had an average age of thirty-six, two of its battalions hailed from Soviet Georgia, and its area of operations was the northern and eastern shore of the Cotentin Peninsula, some 150 miles long.[40] In the end, the 709th (like most of the other German infantry divisions in France) were good for nothing more than positional defense. And while they would perform that limited role admirably, most were absolutely incapable of attacking—no more *angriffsfähig* than their far-better armed compatriots had been in the meat grinder at Anzio.

If the ground force was tattered, the others branches of Rundstedt's joint command were even worse. The Kriegsmarine had begun the war hopelessly outnumbered, and by now it had not a single heavy unit (a battleship or cruiser) to oppose the Western Allies. The competent authority for the invasion theater, *Marine-Gruppen-Kommando West* (Navy Group West) under Admiral Theodor Krancke, was little more than a paper command containing a few dozen swiftboats (*Schnelle-Booten*, or S-Boats), light torpedo craft opposing the greatest armada in history.[41] The Supreme Commander of the Navy (*Oberbefehlshaber der Kriegsmarine*), Admiral Karl Dönitz, tried to fill in the gap between the navy's mission and its actual capabilities with increasingly fanatical rhetoric. "Attack them! At them! Sink them!" he commanded. "A U-Boat that causes losses to the enemy during the landing has accomplished its highest mission and justified its existence, even if it dies in the attempt." It was language that the German official history admits "was a bit reminiscent of the deployment of Japanese kamikaze flyers."[42] And that is the truth: on the morning of D-Day, the Allied fleet contained 6,939 vessels from eight different navies, including a total of 1,213 warships. Facing the onslaught were precisely 31 German S-Boats, carrying a total of 124 torpedoes between them. They were unable to exert any impact at all on the landing—nor should anyone have expected them to.

The situation in the air may well have been worse. Once again, there was the fiction of a Luftwaffe command in the theater, a 3rd Air Force (*Luftflotte* 3) under the command of Field Marshal Hugo Sperrle. While Sperrle was by all accounts an active and energetic officer, he had little to contribute to the defense. In fact, he was unable even to provide OB-West with basic information on aircraft numbers or potential reinforcements; that was closely held information guarded jealously by the Supreme Commander of the Luftwaffe (*Oberbefehlshaber der Luftwaffe*), Field Marshal Hermann Göring, isolated from the front at his Karinhall estate northeast of Berlin. But even without precise numbers, Rundstedt knew that the situation was bad. German air formations had taken a mauling in air battles above the Reich during the spring of 1944, and aircraft, well-trained crews, and especially fuel were all in tight supply. No German flight was capable of penetrating Allied airspace over the British Isles, and, consequently, OB-West was as blind as Field Marshal Kesselring had been in Italy before the Anzio landing. During the D-Day landing, *Luftflotte* 3 had just 319 operational aircraft to its name and managed to put only 90 bombers and 70 fighters into the air, a tiny figure compared to the more than 3,000 aircraft (2,434 fighters and fighter-bombers and 700 light and medium bombers) that the Allies sent over the Channel that morning.[43]

Rundstedt's joint command had a final problem, however, and again it lay in the area of command relationships. Put simply, the field marshal had no authority over the naval or air assets in his theater. Only Krancke could order ships to sea and direct a convoy, and he took his orders only from Dönitz. As OB-West, Rundstedt had authority only in matters that had to do with the coastal defenses on land. Rundstedt could request Krancke's cooperation (*Zusammenarbeit*) and hope that the Kriegsmarine would comply, but he had no power to issue orders. The same was true for air force planning. Like Krancke, Field Marshal Sperrle was not Rundstedt's subordinate but instead reported back to Göring. Again, in matters of personnel, tactics, and operations, Rundstedt could make known his requirements and request for cooperation, but *Luftflotte* 3 was compelled only to "weigh" these considerations, not to obey. Only in issues related to coastal defense—tactical air support, antiaircraft (German: *Flak*) ground units, or radar installations—did OB-West have any control over the air assets within his theater.

Anyone with a passing familiarity with bureaucratic institutions and their jealousies will recognize the pitfalls immediately. Jointness was a myth within the Wehrmacht. With the army dominant over everything else, the sister services naturally guarded their prerogatives fiercely. Absurdities could result. German coastal artillery batteries, for example, were naval assets as long as they were firing out to sea. Once the enemy had made landfall, those same guns came under the command of the army, although no one on the German side seems to have given a great deal of thought to the complex procedures involved in such a transition. Simple issues of battery construction could take up precious man- and planning-hours. The navy wanted pure coastal artillery, concentrating on targets at sea, with the appropriate range-finders and optical equipment. The army, backed by Hitler, wanted multipurpose coastal guns that could fire not only on targets at sea but also swivel around to engage Allied paratroopers or ground forces that had broken through the first line of German defenses and were heading inland. Hitler and the army won the debate, of course, forcing the navy to design batteries whose functions it did not fully understand. Given their numerical and material weakness, German air and naval assets were destined to be bit players in the drama to come, and the tortured nature of the German command structure made the situation much worse than it had to be. Able to recommend but not to compel, Supreme Commander Rundstedt "was unable to create a firm, unified command in the west."[44]

An outnumbered force, low-quality troops, a chain of command so awful it could only have been created on purpose: the Wehrmacht in France was in deep trouble. But perhaps the Atlantic Wall would save the day? Since being put in charge of the coastal defenses in late 1943, Rommel had done his usual energetic job, sowing millions of mines, constructing bunkers for the static divisions, and planting tens of thousands of sharpened poles ("Rommel's asparagus") in fields to block airborne and glider landings. Perhaps his signature device was the "Czech hedgehog"—three steel rails bolted together in the form of a tripod—which Rommel used as antiboat obstacles and submerged at all the likely landing sites. A primitive antitank device that the state of the art had long since made obsolete, the hedgehog had the advantage of being cheap. The Germans had mountains of them sitting around. A classic poor man's weapon, the submerged hedgehog was enough of a threat to force the Allies to change their landing scheme from high tide to low tide, a more complex and time-consuming process.[45]

At some points, the defenses could be imposing, the monstrous "offensive battery group" at Cap Gris Nez in the Pas de Calais, for example: the Lindemann Battery (three 406mm guns), the Great Elector Battery (four 280mm guns), the Todt Battery (four 380mm guns), and the Friedrich August Battery (three 303mm guns).[46] And overall, the numbers were impressive enough: 12,247 fortifications of various sorts constructed on the Atlantic and another 943 in the Mediterranean; 500,000 beach obstacles of various sorts, over 6.5 million mines, heavily fortified *Festungen* ("fortresses," in key ports like Cherbourg, Brest, and Antwerp), smaller *Stützpunkte* ("strongpoints"), and individual *Widerstandsnesten* ("resistance nests") as far as the eye could see. They were all the work of hundreds of thousands of forced laborers conscripted from the civilian population. "It's high time that we put the thousands of do-nothings in Denmark, Holland, France, and Belgium to work on building the fortifications and that we do it with ruthless energy and hardness," Jodl had snarled in late 1943—and he had gone on to do just that.[47]

Rommel's fixes and improvements were almost all tactical ones, however, and he could not overcome the inevitable inconsistencies in constructing a fortified position of this magnitude. While the number of fortifications may have been impressive, the size, equipment, and armament of each one was a crapshoot, depending on which materials and guns happened to be available locally. Captured weapons were everywhere, and even today a battlefield tour of Normandy shows visitors numerous examples of French artillery batteries in German service. Moreover, the tactical utility of many of the positions was questionable, since the outfit responsible for designing and building them, the Organization Todt (OT), was not particularly well versed in the military's requirements in terms of fields of fire or line of sight. As always, manpower continued to be a problem—in fact, *the* problem. Some of the most imposing bunkers on the landing beaches (at Omaha, for example) were sitting empty on the day of the Allied invasion—always a deflating experience for tour groups. Given the fact that the allies had their choice of landing sites, the Germans would have had to fortify every stretch of beach in France to be truly secure, and they never came close. Nor was it even possible to do so, no matter who was in charge of the Atlantic Wall.

Finally, every German planner knew that any wall was only as robust as the force defending it, and it is possible to detect a certain skepticism even among the true believers in the army. Rundstedt must have heard enough muttered comparisons between the Atlantic Wall and the failed Maginot Line that he decided to remind his armies in the field that the contexts of 1940 and 1944 situations were very different, that German soldiers would never waver in their duty as the French had, and that anyone who *did* waver was going to be in big, big trouble. He didn't want to hear excuses for failure or complaints about lack of ammunition and supplies. Anyone shirking his duty or failing to hold out to the last would be in for "rough handling," up to and including the death penalty.[48] But even as he was threatening to put his own men to death, perhaps Rundstedt, too, was wavering: he ordered the construction of a secondary defensive position well inland, running along the Somme and Marne Rivers to the Saône Canal and thence to the Swiss border.

The basic German strategy for defending France against an amphibious invasion was virtually the same as it had been in Italy. The defenders needed to administer a thrashing to the invaders early on—that is, as they approached the coast and as soon as they landed. Rundstedt's missive to his subordinate commanders in February 1944 stressed that "our advanced position is the sea, the best tank trap of all."[49] Forward defense required strong forces on the coast, deeply echeloned and hunkered down in well-fortified installations. They needed to be able to fight the invaders on their own at least temporarily with local reserves, holding up Allied progress long enough for mechanized forces to assemble and throw the invaders back into the sea. Every coastal unit had to be ready to defend the position to the last man, Rundstedt declared: "We don't give way in the western sector."[50] Allied superiority at sea and in the air were facts, but tough fortifications and the inherent battleworthiness (*Kampfwert*) of the German soldier would have to suffice.

No assessment of the Atlantic Wall can be complete, however, without a mention of its most ridiculous component, the place where sober operational planning blended into the theater of the absurd: the small Channel Islands of Guernsey, Jersey, and Alderney. Seized after the 1940 campaign and the only English-speaking territory actually conquered by the Wehrmacht in World War II, they had become a Hitler obsession by 1944. Having taken the islands, he felt it absolutely essential to defend them, and the thought that Churchill might launch a commando raid to win them back became a nightmare. While holding the islands brought Germany no material advantage, their loss would have been a propaganda boon to the Allies. Consequently, fortifications sprang up all over the islands, at the main cities like St. Peter Port on Guernsey and St. Helier on Jersey, along with numerous locations along the coast. Even today, visitors to the islands are stunned by the sheer volume of bunkers, batteries, and strongpoints: 613,000 cubic meters of concrete, guns of all calibers, Skoda antitank positions, gigantic searchlight emplacements, foreboding watchtowers that look like something out of a medieval fantasy novel. These charming little islands might well have been the most heavily fortified spot on the planet by 1944.[51] But more important, they are how the entire world might look if the Third Reich had won the war—and, we should add, a completely worthless outlay of manpower, material, and effort.

Given the overall weakness of the German position—the infantry divisions no longer capable of attack, the Kriegsmarine and Luftwaffe impotent, the incomplete nature of the fortifications—the defense of France essentially came down to a handful of Panzer divisions, just ten in all. Their placement was absolutely critical to the success of the defense, and, indeed, the issue led to a major row within the High Command. Rommel knew how difficult it was to operate under Allied air attack. He had seen it in the desert, and on one frightening occasion a British bombing raid had caught him in the flat plain south of Alam Halfa. He survived but never forgot the trauma. Attacks by the RAF, he wrote, "literally nailed my army to the ground, making impossible any smooth deployment or timely thrust." Fighting an enemy with control of the air, to Rommel, was akin to "a force of natives from the bush fighting modern European troops, under the same conditions and with the same chances of success."[52] Nonstop enemy bombing forced all movement to take place at night. As a result, he wanted the Panzers to be close to the water's edge at the moment of the landing. Such a course would be the only chance of smashing the landing, he felt, by hitting the Allies in their most vulnerable moment: as they waded and staggered ashore. If the Panzer divisions were held too far inland, they might not get into the fight at all.

His superior, Rundstedt, was a more conservative figure and more given to the orthodox solution. He planned to group the Panzer divisions into a strong, centrally located reserve, ready to smash the Allies as they advanced inland. Rundstedt identified the weakness of Rommel's approach: if the Wehrmacht guessed wrong about the location of the Allied landing site, the Panzer divisions—the most valuable units in the German order of battle—would begin the battle hopelessly out of position. Once again, the danger existed that they might never reach the battlefield at all. Moreover, Panzer formations deployed along the coast would have been highly vulnerable to naval artillery, something Rommel had not yet experienced. Assembling them into any sort of operational *Schwerpunkt* for a later battle would have been very difficult. As in all such thorny operational debates, there was no ideal solution. Once again, it was the price that Germany had to pay for trying to fight a global war with inferior resources: almost all of the problems eventually became insoluble.

In the end, there was a compromise, and like all compromises it was the only sensible solution and it satisfied no one. Each army group got three Panzer divisions to deploy as it wished, while the other four went into a newly established central reserve, Panzer Group West (*Panzergruppe West*), under the command of General Leo Geyr von Schweppenburg. Authority to commit the divisions of the Panzer Group to action, however, lay with the High Command of the armed forces, the OKW alone, that is to say, with Hitler himself. And even this oft-maligned proviso made a certain kind of sense: let the High Command see which way the battle was developing before agreeing to commit the reserves.

The Germans therefore headed toward D-Day facing a world of problems. To be sure, there might be wildcards in the deck. To give just one instance: all through 1944 the bedrock German assumption had been that the Allies would land on the coast of the Pas de Calais, the shortest hop across the Channel and the most direct route into Germany. Consequently, the 15th Army defending this sector was the strongest in the German battle array. In April, however, Hitler suddenly seemed to have an epiphany, perhaps "an example of that famous intuition of his," as his deputy chief of operations, General Walter Warlimont, put it, or perhaps he had confidential sources of intelligence that he did not share even with his staff. He suddenly decided that Normandy was on the list of "probable landing targets" and ordered its immediate reinforcement and the strengthening of beach defenses.[53] A few units arrived, with the 6th *Fallschirmjäger* Regiment deploying in the Cotentin along with the 91st Air-Landing Infantry Division (*Luftlande Infanterie-Division*), both intended primarily to combat enemy airborne landings. But even Hitler could not build fortifications overnight, redirect artillery batteries, or produce Panzer divisions that did not exist. While every military operation is a gamble—and an amphibious invasion on this super-sized scale especially so—the Wehrmacht was in a bad way as it faced the great test of arms in June 1944.

Perhaps the situation was hopeless, but one couldn't tell from the words or actions of the German officer corps in 1944. While they later filled memoirs with a sober accounting of how hopeless the situation had been—analysis that is objectively true, given the lopsided balance of forces—they were singing a very different refrain at the time. Firm faith in the cause, unshakable belief in the ultimate victory if only they hung tough, protestations of loyalty to their supreme commander, threats against anyone too lukewarm in their devotion: this was the mood of the day, a foul and defiant temperament. Few reasonable people today consider Rundstedt to have been a loyal Nazi. Rather, he has a historical reputation as a traditionalist—"the last knight" or sometimes even "the last Prussian"—whose aristocratic hauteur could barely stomach Hitler and the uncouth party ruffians and fanatics (*Bonzentum*) grouped around the Führer.[54] But Rundstedt himself was spouting rhetoric in the run-up to the Allied invasion that often rivaled Hitler's in its intensity and hatred. They all were. However the officer corps may have chosen later to remember it or to write it up in memoirs—how they knew that the war was lost and how they chafed under Hitler's inane orders—commanders like Rundstedt were actually abetting it. From Jodl hissing dark threats against malingerers in the occupied territories, to Rundstedt demanding that the coastal formations hold each position to the last man, to Dönitz calling upon his sailors to kill themselves for the Reich, to the constant threats emanating from every level of the command structure to shoot their own men if they shirked their duty, the eve of the great invasion was the time for bluster, tough talk, and fanaticism.

Invasion Planning

It was an article of faith within the German officer corps that Allied commanders tended to make war with the concept of security uppermost in their mind, rather than boldness, aggression, and daring. A preference for caution was the greatest Allied weakness, German commanders believed, since it often prevented them from exploiting their vast material superiority in manpower and weapons. "Give me that force," many German officers would comment in the course of the war, "and I'll end the war in three weeks." But perhaps it is more accurate to say that the Allies tended to wage their war prudently—a sensible posture for the side with more resources and manpower—and that Allied planners generally weighed risk and opportunity in a rational, rather than reckless, fashion.

While we know the actual course of the Allied landing, consider the possibilities. A force truly obsessed with its own security might have chosen to land on a weakly defended portion of the French coast (in the Bay of Biscay, for example). The sector of German 1st Army, under the command of General Kurt von der Chevallerie, was responsible for the entire coastline from the mouth of the Loire to the Spanish border, a stretch of over 250 miles, and he possessed exactly four divisions—the 158th, 708th, 159th, and 276th. But a landing at Bayonne or Bordeaux, no matter how safe, was also a doorway to nowhere, requiring a long trek across southern France to arrive at anything approaching a strategic target. Landing in 1st Army's sector, in other words, would have been a low-risk, low-reward venture for the Allies, and both the Allied command and the OKW treated it as such.

By contrast, a landing along the Channel coast at the "Calais step" (the Pas de Calais) would have been an explosive undertaking from the start. Here was the most direct route across the Channel and the most direct route into Germany, and the Germans consequently had the largest and most powerful of their four armies in France, the 15th, under General Hans von Salmuth, an army commander with experience on the Eastern Front. Salmuth had five corps in the line: LXXXIX, LXXXII, LXXXXI, LXVII, and LXXXI, moving right to left along the Pas de Calais. The five of them together contained eleven divisions directly in the line, plus another seven in the army's reserve to launch immediate counterattacks or to serve as a backstop in case of a setback. Landing against the 15th would have been a high-risk, high-reward operation. The Allies did everything they could to encourage the Germans to think that the main landing would come here, launch-

ing Operation Fortitude South—a fictional First US Army Group under the command of General George S. Patton Jr.—including dummy
deployments and falsified radio traffic.[55] It is unclear to this day how
much impact any of it had, but it barely matters. It is more accurate to
say that the Germans remained wedded to a belief that the Allies would
land in the Pas de Calais because that was what they would have done.
It was the bold choice, in other words, and German commanders had
historically never believed that timid decisions were a suitable path to
victory.

Somewhere in the middle of the high-risk/low-risk spectrum lay
the Normandy sector. For the Allies, Normandy was near enough to
Germany to be attractive, but not so close as to be the most heavily
defended. It was within the range of Allied airpower and also possessed
a suitable major port in Cherbourg. From the German perspective,
even a successful Allied landing in Normandy was remote enough that
it did not require defenses of the first rank. Normandy (along with the
eastern shore of the Cotentin Peninsula) was the medium-risk, me-
dium-reward choice, in other words. In fact, the Germans might have
had more to do with the eventual Allied choice of Normandy than the
Allies themselves. As the various planning iterations had taken place
on both sides, German defenses in the Pas de Calais had grown so thick
and so rapidly that a landing on the Channel coast seemed less and less
likely to succeed.

Normandy was part of the sprawling operational sector of the German 7th Army, under General Friedrich Dollmann. The 7th had to
guard not only Normandy from the mouth of the Seine westward but
also the entire Cotentin Peninsula (both sides of it), and then all of
Brittany down to the mouth of the Loire River. Dollmann had four
corps, including eleven divisions and a mobile brigade, a theoretically
formidable force. But two of his corps, the XXV and the LXXIV, were
in Brittany, and one, II *Fallschirmjäger* Corps, was in the reserve. That
left a single corps along the coast that the Allies actually intended to assault: the LXXXIV under General Erich Marcks, holding the beaches
stretching from the mouth of the Vire River in the west to the Orne
in the east.[56] The Allies would hit a corps, therefore, and not even a
very powerful one. Marcks had four divisions under his command, but
one of them, the 319th Infantry, was guarding the Channel Islands of
Guernsey and Jersey against an Allied assault that never came, and two
others, the 709th and 716th, were static divisions with all the attendant
problems in mobility, firepower, and cohesion. When we boil it down,
LXXXIV Corps had precisely one serviceable, all-purpose division in

its order of battle, the 352nd Infantry Division, which Marcks plunked down in the center of his battle array along the Calvados coast in front of Coleville-sur-Mer. Whether it would be enough to stop the Allies should they attempt to land in Normandy was the big question.

The Invasion

The D-Day landings on June 6, 1944 (code-named Operation Neptune, part of the broader campaign plan known as Operation Overlord) have become a venerated part of Anglo-American military lore, and for understandable reasons.[57] The sheer size and scope of the operation, the drama of liberating a continent from Nazi terror, the heroism of the assault troops on that fateful day: D-Day was indeed an epic, and perhaps it requires a poet, a modern-day Homer rather than a mere historian, to sing its glory adequately.

From the perspective of the German army, however, there was no romance whatsoever, just the uninspiring spectacle of a once-proud military establishment that was now grossly inferior to the power of the enemies it faced and no longer up to the challenges it had set for itself. The Allies landed at five invasion beaches along a 50-mile stretch of the Normandy coast. Four of the beaches lay between the Vire and the Orne Rivers on the Calvados coast (code-named, west to east, Omaha, Gold, Juno, and Sword), while the fifth one loomed far to the west on the Cotentin Peninsula (Utah). The operation was a model of coalition warfare. Two of the beaches (Utah and Omaha) were American, two (Sword and Gold) were British, and one (Juno) was Canadian. They were the spearheads of two separate armies—US 1st Army to the west and British 2nd Army to the east—and the initial landings would see them facing a single, understrength German corps, Marcks's LXXXIV, consisting of one standard infantry division and two static formations. The United Nations had finally arrived to put Europe right, and the Wehrmacht was now facing down the "power of two global empires," as a contemporary German article put it.[58]

On the extreme right of the Allied landing, the US 4th Infantry Division, the spearhead of VII Corps, landed at Utah against minimal opposition. While the landing craft drifted well south of the planned zone, the foul-up barely mattered. A flooded zone behind the beaches, crossed only by narrow causeways, had been troubling to Allied planners, and so the Utah landing included drops by two complete airborne divisions in the interior of the Cotentin (the 82nd landing east of Pont

l'Abbé and the 101st north of Carentan) to block German reinforcements from coming up and sealing off the causeways. The paratroopers,
too, drifted all over the place, fought a number of famous and spirited
company-sized engagements against startled German troops, suffered
very heavy losses, and, once again, barely mattered to the overall operational picture. Defenders of the airborne arm have actually resorted
to arguing that the extreme scatter of the drops had a kind of mesmer-
izing effect on German responders, since they were unable to make out
any kind of discernible *Schwerpunkt* for the Allied landing, but such an
argument was, and is, ridiculous. The real problem for the Germans at
Utah was the tiny force they had deployed to guard against an Allied
landing this far west, little more than pickets from the understrength
709th Static Division under the command of General Karl Wilhelm
von Schlieben. By day's end, US forces had landed 21,000 men at a cost
of only 197 casualties and penetrated inland almost five miles.

The Allies' landing was equally successful on the extreme left flank.
At Sword, British 3rd Division came ashore between Lion-sur-Mer
and Ouistreham against patchy resistance from yet another substan-
dard static division, the 716th, under the command of General Wilhelm Richter.[59] British technology played a role here, with twenty-five
duplex-drive (DD) amphibious tanks launched along with the assault
infantry. Twenty-one of them made it ashore, and so the British were
able to fight a combined-arms battle from the start. Accompanying the
3rd Division into battle were a host number of attached units, the 27th
Independent Armoured Brigade, the 1st Special Service Brigade, Free
French commandos, the No. 41 (Royal Marine Commando), and elements of the famous 79th Armoured Division with its specially modified tanks, or "funnies": the Sherman Crab equipped with a mine flail,
the AVRE, firing a 40-pound explosive charge known as the Flying
Dustbin, and the Crocodile, a Churchill tank with a flamethrower in
place of the standard turret gun. And here too there was airborne support, with the British 6th Airborne Division dropping east of the Orne
River to protect the beachhead's eastern flank from German counterattack. A small glider force also seized intact both the Bénouville
Bridge over the Caen Canal and the Ranville Bridge over the Orne
River, a little operation that was nevertheless a marvel of operational
daring, precision flying, and a spot-on landing.[60]

DDs and funnies notwithstanding, the crucial factor on Sword was,
once again, the lack of German infantry. Richter's division was only
some 8,000 strong, or just about half strength, in other words, lacking
heavy weapons, and covering an 8-mile stretch of coastline with exactly

four weak infantry companies, some of them consisting of *Osttruppen*, low-quality troops from the east. The German units facing the British at Sword were a handful of companies from the 736th Regiment, dispersed in strongpoints and incapable of battlefield maneuver. They fought in their initial positions and died there, but they couldn't have retreated even if they wanted to. Even as a delaying force, the impact of Richter's division was minimal. Anglo-American historians often criticize the Sword landing for its failure to penetrate farther inland and capture Caen, Normandy's principal city, but no major amphibious landing in history has ever stormed a great city on day one—the troops are exhausted, their units intermingled, and confusion reigns—and this one was no exception. At Sword Beach, the Allies had to be satisfied with getting a massive force ashore—over 28,000 men—with minimal casualties.

At Gold Beach, the center of the five landing sites, British 50th (Northumbrian) Division landed against the same sporadic resistance faced at Utah and Sword. Once again, the landing hit elements of Richter's unlucky 716th Static Division, although a battalion of its neighbor to the west, 352nd Infantry Division, also took part in the fighting. The Atlantic Wall here might have been formidable, with two large batteries emplaced at Mont Fleury (four 122mm guns) and Longues-sur-Mer (four 150mm guns), but neither of the positions was complete by D-Day and British naval gunfire soon smashed them both. The landing went smoothly, with most of the damage done by precisely two German guns, an 88mm at La Rivière and a 75mm at Le Hamel, and once again Britain's DD tanks and other funnies gave a good accounting of themselves. While the 50th Division also failed to reach its D-Day objective, the town of Bayeux, it did secure the key coastal town of Arromanches, a much more important target in the long run. Arromanches was the intended site of a massive artificial harbor, or Mulberry, a floating hunk of concrete that would come over from Britain in the next few days. The Mulberry was an ingenious solution to the monstrous logistical problem of sustaining a great mechanized force in Normandy. By the end of June 6, the British had landed nearly 25,000 men at Gold and were advancing inland with relatively light casualties, just 700 for the entire day's fighting.

At two beaches the Allies met significant initial opposition. At Juno, sandwiched between Gold to the west and Sword to the east, Canadian 3rd Division landed between the towns of Courseulles-sur-Mer and St. Aubin. Juno was a star-crossed landing in many ways: the weather was rough, with high surf breaking up the formation of the landing craft; the landings were up to a half hour late, enough time to alert the defenders fully; and the seas proved too rough to launch the DD tanks. The late start made the landing more of a high-tide affair: the now-submerged beach obstacles took their toll of landing craft, and as the tide rose, the beach shrank, causing dangerous levels of crowding as follow-on waves of men and equipment joined the original assault force. Once ashore, the Canadians had to fight their way up to and over a seawall just to the left of Courseulles under murderous German fire. Once again, as at Gold and Sword, the enemy was a handful of companies from the 716th Static Division. While they managed to inflict heavy losses on the initial assault wave, the belated arrival of Canadian tanks, dispatched directly from their landing craft onto the beach instead of swimming ashore as designed, provided the equalizer, as did two regiments of the Royal Canadian Artillery. Once the Canadians launched a determined push into Courseulles itself and began clearing the town house by house, the initial spirited German opposition melted away. Despite the rough start, the Canadians managed to get 21,000 men ashore that first day. Casualties had been heavy among the assault waves, but overall losses were in rough harmony with those at Gold and Sword, some 1,000 men. And while Canadian 3rd Division did not reach its objective of Carpiquet airfield to the west of Caen, the Canadians did make contact with British troops from Gold Beach on their right, the first two landing sites to link up and form the seed of a unified Allied beachhead in Europe.

The landing at Omaha Beach nearly ended in disaster for the US 1st and 29th Divisions—and for Operation Neptune more generally. Here the Allies hit not static troops but regular infantry, Colonel Ernst Goth's 916th Grenadier Regiment, part of the 352nd Infantry Division under General Dietrich Kraiss.[61] The German defenders sat in a naturally strong position, a kind of semicurved amphitheater with steep bluffs looming over the beach, and fortifications like the concrete hulk known as *Widerstandsnest* 62 (WN 62) were less than 100 meters from the water. The overcast weather reduced the accuracy of the bombardment, the choppy sea sank twenty-seven of the thirty-two DD tanks almost immediately after they were launched, and for all intents and purposes the first assault wave hit a fully alerted defense that was almost completely untouched by preparatory fire. American intelligence had only recently discovered the presence of the 352nd Division in Normandy, but the information had not yet filtered down to the tactical level. From the moment the Americans hit the beach, at 6:30 A.M., machine-gun fire erupted from the resistance nests, mowing down the first wave, slamming again and again into milling masses of US infantry desperately trying to find cover behind the tiny rocky ledge at the waterline known as the "shingle." Within ten minutes, the beach was littered with the dead and the dying.[62]

Like all amphibious landings, unfortunately, Omaha had all the operational subtlety of an assembly line. The first wave met disaster, but there was literally no way to impart that information to the next waves already at sea in their landing craft. The engineers weren't far behind the infantry, and command elements began to show up soon after. The arrival of heavy weapons units (artillery, antiaircraft, and antitank) only added to the congestion. Their weapons were useless for the time being, and the personnel had to fight as infantry. The density of the American landing—with men, tanks, guns, and equipment of all sorts herded together onto an absurdly small stretch of beach—turned every German mortar shell into a weapon of mass destruction. Still, the Americans kept coming, compounding casualties and threatening to sink the operation altogether. The US beachmaster had to close the beach two hours into the landing, a sign that things had gone badly wrong. General Omar Bradley, the US 1st Army commander, floating offshore on the cruiser USS *Augusta*, thought so, too, and actually considered ordering an evacuation, a dicey move under fire that would certainly have ended in a bloody catastrophe.

At the very moment that Bradley was mulling his options, however, the situation was looking up. The original plan, to crush the Germans with preparatory bombardment, then waltz off the beach into the French interior through the gaps in the bluff, the so-called draws, had failed utterly. Recognizing that unhappy fact, commanders and men alike had to devise a backup plan, and to do so under fire, in shock, wet and exhausted. They did have enough of their wits about them to recognize one thing: if they stayed on the beach they were dead, and if they didn't know it, they had commanders willing to tell them, men like General Norman Cota, the assistant commander of 29th Infantry division, or Colonel George A. Taylor of 16th Infantry Regiment. Gradually a few intrepid men began to creep forward. The draws were too heavily defended, and so they channeled their attack toward the bluffs looming overhead, and indeed, the best recent research on Omaha characterizes this "battle of the bluffs" as the decisive moment of the landing. With the support of US naval gunfire—always the infantry's best friend in such circumstances—they managed to infiltrate past the concrete strongpoints, attack them from the rear, and scale their way up the heights, some 600 or so men by noon. At the very moment that Bradley was thinking of calling it off, US forces had already penetrated German defenses in numerous places and neutralized a number of the most troublesome coastal strongpoints. Once up the bluffs, they could call fire down into the draws, kill or drive off the German defenders there, and restore Omaha Beach to something resembling the original plan. With combat engineers clearing gaps in the German minefields and beach obstacles, by the end of the day US troops were passing through the draws into the villages of Colleville and Vierville and trudging into the interior of Normandy. Behind them lay the bodies of over 2,000 dead—the bloodiest beach by a considerable margin.

An American epic? Certainly. From the German perspective, however, the view is less dramatic. Holed up in its bunkers, the Wehrmacht's contribution to the battle at Omaha Beach was essentially to sit in place and shoot, and it did so quite well. The 916th Grenadier Regiment (and the neighboring formation on its right, the 726th Grenadier Regiment) laid down an impenetrable wall of fire early on, although the intensity slackened in the course of the day as ammunition ran low and Allied naval gunfire pounded away. Tourists to the site today marvel over the apparent power of the German forts—WN 62 and the others—and they are sights to behold as living remnants of the famed Atlantic Wall. But like the wall as a whole, WN 62 was less than it seemed. The bunker did hold an assortment of mortars, antitank, and antiaircraft guns, many of them foreign weapons of French or Polish origin, but the small garrison's most important task was to direct fire from batteries situated well inland, not to oppose the landing itself. One of its two casemates was completely empty, since the Germans never had enough artillery pieces to go around. The main contribution of WN 62 to the defense was a mere handful of men manning machine guns. One of them, Corporal Heinrich Severloh, later claimed to have fired no fewer than 12,000 rounds from his MG42 that day and to have been personally responsible for the deaths of 2,000 Americans.[63] He was either misremembering or exaggerating these numbers, of course, since they are obviously absurd. But even his fantastic claims help to illustrate an important point. The real German need in that summer of 1944 was not more concrete or bunkers or watchtowers. The Germans needed more soldiers, more men willing to wield weapons, more divisions willing to die to hold a piece of ground. They needed more Severlohs. A mighty construction effort had built a wall that the Germans could never hold given the manpower constraints of a multi-front war.

Even epics deserve the truth. Had there been a single German maneuver element present near the beach, or even a handful of tanks as at Salerno, the battle for Omaha would almost certainly have ended in disaster for the Americans. Since neither of the two German regiments present on Omaha could maneuver, they had very little chance of driving even a badly mauled landing force into the sea in those first terrible hours. The Germans trusted in their Atlantic Wall, but walls rarely work in war, and certainly not under modern conditions. Walls try to defend everything, but in the immortal words of Frederick the Great, "He who defends everything defends nothing at all."[64] In one day of combat, the Allies had negated two years of German construction and had put over 150,000 men ashore. Within three weeks, the number would top 800,000. Allied casualties on that first day, which might well have been awful, were in fact reasonable, perhaps 10,000 in all. The eternal lesson of Omaha Beach? If you want to defend a piece of ground, build an army.

The German Reaction to the Landing

For years, the Germans had been formulating plans for how to react to an Allied landing in the west, and two basic operational schemes vied for supremacy. Some wanted to follow Rommel's lead and fight a desperate, even frantic defense with predeployed Panzer divisions at the water's edge; others echoed Rundstedt's call for a coordinated counterattack by a powerful central reserve of Panzer and mechanized formations. When the time came to go into action, however, the Germans didn't follow either scheme. Rather, their main-force units spent the first few days of the campaign racing back and forth across Normandy, attempting to put out whichever fire seemed most threatening at the time and to form a cohesive defensive front—all characteristic behaviors for a materially inferior force fighting an adversary who holds the initiative. At no time were they able to launch a coordinated counterattack, and nowhere did they threaten the integrity of the Allied beachheads. Call the German reaction to the D-Day invasion the "Great Fizzle." In the end, Allied armies had faced far worse threats to their survival at Salerno and Anzio.

It is true that the Allied landing in Normandy surprised the Germans. With the Luftwaffe no longer capable of providing a detailed operational picture through reconnaissance flights, and Germany's surface navy all but driven from the Atlantic Ocean and the English

Channel, solid information had been hard to come by during the weeks before the invasion. The weather that first week of June had been miserable—cold, blustery, and raining—and without reliable weather information from the Atlantic the Germans could not know a crucial fact that Eisenhower and his staff did: forecasts called for more moderate weather on June 5–6. Even armed with the "most important weather forecast in history," however, Eisenhower had a hard time pulling the trigger. He knew that he might actually be staking the existence of his armies—indeed, of the entire free world—on a weather report of all things. In the end, thankfully, the forecasters were right. When asked in later years about the reasons for Allied success in Normandy, Eisenhower would provide the ritual answer ("We had better meteorologists than the Germans"), and he wasn't simply being glib.[65]

But surprise doesn't provide a complete answer. Salerno had surprised the Wehrmacht, and an iron ring of Panzer divisions had almost smashed the beachhead in the following days, at the same time as the Germans were having to multitask by occupying Italy and disarming a 2 million–man Italian army. Anzio, too, had completely surprised the Germans, forcing their commanders in Italy to gather men and formations from across Germany and occupied Europe and to assemble the 14th Army almost from scratch. Once again, German mechanized formations were soon in action, striking the beachhead aggressively and coming far too close to crumpling it for Allied comfort. From the old Prussian days—the Great Elector and his Brandenburg army double-timing across Europe from west to east to confront the Swedes at Fehrbellin, for example, or Frederick the Great doing the same in the opposite direction in 1757 to fight the Franco-Imperial army at Rossbach, to give just two examples—reacting against surprise and overcoming it through an ever-more rapid and decisive response had been a German military tradition for centuries.

So something else must have been at work here. Perhaps it was a case of bad luck? Certainly, war is always a gamble, and "no other human activity is so continuously or universally bound up with chance."[66] The Germans might have used the few days' grace they felt they had in that first week of June in any number of ways: a last-second shoring up of weak sectors in the defense, fine-tuning deployments along the beaches and readying forces for potential counterattacks, even giving a last-second pep talk to the troops. Instead, the crucial evening of June 5–6 became a travel day for far too many commanders. After all the furious activity and preparations, and the wrangle over the command structure and the Panzer divisions, D-Day actually caught many of the concerned commanders away from their posts, engaged in other pursuits that, for the moment, seemed more important.

General Dollmann, commander of 7th Army, for example, had called a meeting of his division commanders for June 6 in Rennes, where they were to take part in a planning wargame (*Planspiel*) designed to test various operational responses to an Allied airborne landing in Normandy. Most of Dollmann's officers were en route to Rennes when the reports of Allied airborne landings in Normandy came in, a bit after midnight: Kraiss of the 352nd Infantry Division; Richter of the 716th Static Division; General Heinz Hellmich of the 243rd Coastal Division; even General Rudolf Graf von Schmettow, commander of the 319th Infantry Division on the Channel Islands.[67] Each of them got their recall messages and headed back immediately to their command posts.

Only one of the scheduled participants, General Schlieben of the 709th Static Division, did not get the recall while on the road. He was already in Rennes, having driven the more than 100 miles from his headquarters near Valognes in the north-central Cotentin the night before. As he came down to begin the game, around 6:30 A.M., Dollmann's orderly gave him the formal announcement: "The wargame had been canceled. All commanders must return to their units immediately."[68] It was the first that Schlieben had heard that the continent was under attack—more than five hours after the first paratroop landings. He now scurried back to his division, already facing the Allied landing at Utah Beach to its front and two divisions' worth of scattered American paratroopers deep in its rear.

Nothing illustrates the swirling chaos of that early morning better than the demise of General Wilhelm Falley of the 91st Air-Landing Infantry Division. Driving to Rennes in the dark early morning hours in his Mercedes staff car, along with his aide Major Joachim Bartuzat, the general sensed that something was wrong. Air attacks were far heavier than they had been recently, and he could clearly hear the shocking roar of thousands of engines in the night sky. He ordered the car turned around and raced back to his command post at the Château Haut near Bernaville, a few miles west of Sainte-Mère-Église. As his car pulled onto the grounds, he ran into a blaze of gunfire from US paratroopers of the 508th Parachute Infantry Regiment (part of the 82nd Airborne Division). At this point the sources diverge. Either Falley was killed by gunfire, or a point-blank bazooka round tore off the back of his head, or his car swerved and hit a wall, killing him instantly.[69] The sources agree that Bartuzat was somehow injured and thrown from the car and that a paratrooper shot the major dead as he reached for his Luger pistol (and was perhaps begging for mercy at the same time). The airborne force was an improvised band, fittingly enough, made up of paratroopers from the 82nd who had drifted badly during their drop and were now lost in the timeless countryside of the Cotentin Peninsula. This brief encounter was an almost Clausewitzian ideal of the fog and friction of war: the surprised fighting the confused.

The most famous German commander of the war was likewise missing in action at the moment of the landing. After all the work and energy he had put into the defenses in the west, not to mention his ambitions for supreme command in the theater, Field Marshal Rommel was away. He had left his headquarters at La Roche Guyon on the right bank of the Seine the day before to take personal leave in Germany and, to celebrate his wife's birthday, give her a present: a pair of shoes he had purchased for her in Paris.[70] He also hoped for yet another meeting with Hitler on the Obersalzberg, the Bavarian mountainside retreat, both to persuade the Führer to grant him more authority over the Panzer divisions, the latest round in this apparently never-ending dispute, and to complain about the persistent shortages of men and materiel on the Atlantic Wall. An early morning phone call from his chief of staff, General Hans Speidel, put the field marshal in the picture, and Rommel was soon motoring to the west at top speed in his Horch staff car. He did not arrive back at La Roche Guyon until early evening on June 6, however, by which point this historic day of destiny had all but wrapped up. He might have taken an aircraft and gotten back earlier, but flying had long ago become too dangerous for German commanders anywhere within range of the Allied air forces, and in fact regulations now strictly forbade it.

Such scenes have become part of the mythos of the D-Day landings. Rommel heads home to Herrlingen for a birthday party in the family circle and misses the invasion. The 7th Army's divisional commanders assemble to play a wargame, then must rush back to their headquarters to play out a much more deadly version. Falley and Bartuzat are killed in the opening minutes of the campaign, by an unknown enemy, before the general had given a single command or order. Sometimes it seems like the Wehrmacht's ready rating on June 6 was hovering near zero. What can we say when we read that commander of the 21st Panzer Division, General Edgar Feuchtinger, supposedly received the sobering news of the invasion in the midst of a romantic tryst in Paris and that he rushed back to the front with his paramour still in tow to send his division into battle?[71] Or that Adolf Hitler, the Führer himself, couldn't be bothered to get up early in the morning, even when he was supposed to be running a global war? Or that his aides and staff officers in the OKW, his operations chief General Alfred Jodl foremost among them, refused to wake Hitler to get permission to insert the reserve Panzer divisions into battle at a time when they might have made a difference?

But let us ask the key question: Would they have made a difference? The momentary absence or presence of a commander from his headquarters matters little in the modern era. Radio and telephone communications suffice to keep him in the picture, and, indeed, every single commander mentioned above, except Hitler, apparently heard about the invasion in something approaching real time. Moreover, no army in the world had historically invested as much authority in its staff officers as this one did, in particular the chief of staff and the operations officer (the staff "Ia," in German parlance). The chief of Army Group B, Colonel Speidel, was not only a trusted friend and confidant to his commander, Rommel; he was a skilled operator and a workhorse in his own right. We might say the same for General Max-Josef Pemsel, chief of 7th Army, or even Colonel Fritz Ziegelmann, Ia of the 352nd Infantry Division facing the Americans at Omaha whose account of the fighting is still the primary source from the German side. A large number of German unit commanders may have been absent at the start of the D-Day fighting, but that hardly implied any sort of operational paralysis.

The problems were not simply surprise or bad luck. Systemic factors ran far deeper. The German force was too frayed, the command system too convoluted for rapid response. No matter who was present or absent, no matter who was sleeping or awake, the Wehrmacht was heading into the big operation virtually blind—that is to say, practically stripped of airpower—and therefore without even the most fundamental aerial reconnaissance. As a result, getting a fix on exactly what was happening at the front was far more difficult that it should have been. The German operational reaction to the landing might not have been much more rapid even if Hitler had been wide awake or Rommel present in person.

Stymied: The Demise of *Kampfgruppe* Meyer

Nothing illustrates the German operational problem on June 6 better than the saga of the 352nd Infantry Division. Its three regiments were drawn up in a sensible defensive posture, with two up, along the waterline, and one behind, in reserve. The 914th Grenadier Regiment under Lieutenant Colonel Ernst Heyna held the divisional left along the mouths of the Douve and Vire Rivers; the 916th Grenadier Regiment (Colonel Ernst Goth) to its right defended what was about to become Omaha Beach, stretching roughly from Maisy and Grandcamp in the west to Coleville-sur-Mer in the east; the 915th Grenadier Regiment—identified on German situation maps as *Kampfgruppe* Meyer (for the regimental commander, Lieutenant Colonel Ernst Meyer), stood back in reserve. For operational purposes, the regiment immediately to the right, the 726th Grenadier Regiment under Colonel Walter Korfes (part of the 716th Static Division), was also subordinate to the 352nd Division. Deployed immediately to the east of Coleville-sur-Mer (and thus sharing in the defense of Omaha Beach), the 726th would also have to bear the brunt of the British and Canadian landings. Taken together, then, the Wehrmacht defended what it called "Coastal Defense Sector Bayeux" with four Grenadier regiments: the 914th on the left, the 916th in the center, and the 726th on the right, with the 915th (*Kampfgruppe* Meyer) in reserve—and that is how the Wehrmacht, unaware of which Allied invasion beach was which until well after the war, wrote up its D-Day accounts.[72]

So strapped for troops and divisions were the Germans on D-Day, however, that *Kampfgruppe* Meyer was actually serving as the reserve for LXXXIV Corps, rather than playing a more typical role as a backstop for its own division. General Marcks didn't have any divisions to spare, a more typical corps-level reserve. *Kampfgruppe* Meyer's employment in the course of June 6 was therefore crucial to the shape of the fighting. Allied paratroopers began dropping in Normandy and the Cotentin after midnight, and the 914th Grenadier Regiment on the German left was soon engaged in tough and confused fighting with elements of the 101st Airborne north of the key crossroads town of Carentan. A little over an hour later, around 2:00 A.M., a new report came into LXXXIV Corps headquarters from the 914th Grenadier Regiment of "strong airborne landings in the Vire River basin south of Carentan," a far deeper penetration than the original drop and a real threat to separate the 352nd Division from its neighbor to the left, the 709th.[73] Indeed, a drop south of Carentan would have put US airborne forces about halfway to one of the key crossroads towns in lower Normandy, one that would play a key role in the fighting later on: Saint-Lô.

The report was disturbing enough that General Marcks ordered *Kampfgruppe* Meyer to ride west to the assistance of 914th Grenadier Regiment in clearing out this threat from the Americans. By 3:00 A.M.,

Meyer and his men were on the road, his regimental infantry loaded onto French trucks and accompanied by the division's bicycle-mounted Fusilier Battalion. The Germans later complained that the French drivers were clearly unenthusiastic about motoring into battle in the middle of the night and that many of them slowed things down by claiming engine trouble, but this may well be more special pleading of the sort that filled the postwar German reports. The real problem for all concerned may simply have been trying to navigate Normandy's narrow country roads in the middle of the night, the same problem that the Americans were having in the wee hours of the morning and the same problem that bedevils travelers to the battle sites even today. At any rate, Meyer's force crept, rather than drove, to the west. His battlegroup was still on the road at 5:00 A.M., at which point the 914th Regiment was reporting "very hard" (*sehr hart*) fighting with American airborne forces for the Orne bridges west of the Brévands sector, and still on the road at 6:00 A.M., when the sun came up and the vast Allied invasion fleet came into view. It was clearly a "systematic landing by powerful forces," as Ziegelmann described it. "The 'invasion' had begun for real."[74]

By this time, the threatening situation south of Carentan, the original reason for *Kampfgruppe* Meyer's journey to the west, was now receding in importance on the list of General Marcks's problems. The divisions of his LXXXIV Corps were under attack everywhere: 709th Static Division in the Cotentin, 352nd Division between Vierville and Coleville-sur-Mer, and 716th Static Division at a whole host of places stretching from Arromanches in the west to Le Hamel, Courseulles-sur-Mer, Lion-sur-Mer, and Ouistreham to the east. Allied naval fire was ranging deep into his rear positions—penetrating as far south as the Isigny-Bayeux Road well inland. And just as Marcks was trying to process this awful list of threats, a new report came into his Corps headquarters just after 7:00 A.M.: there had been no airborne drops south of Carentan, after all. It had been a mistake of some sort—a rumor, a jumpy patrol, a typo on the report, "südlich" (south) when it meant "nordlich" (north): it could have been anything. A reconnaissance flight could have clarified the ground situation for the Germans in ten minutes, of course, but recon flights were impossible under the present state of Allied supremacy in the air. Indeed, the Luftwaffe hardly played any role at all on June 6.

What to do now? The US landing at Omaha had been smashed—that much was clear to the Germans—and the 352nd Division was more than holding its own. A report into corps headquarters from the commander of *Widerstandsnest* 76, located at Pointe et Raz de la Percée, west of Omaha Beach, was emphatic:

It's low tide on the beach before the bluffs at St. Laurent and Vierville, and the enemy is pinned down and seeking cover in front of the defenses in the coastal zone. A large number of vehicles, including ten tanks, stand burning on the beach. The troops who are supposed to clear the beach obstacles have ceased their activity. The offloading of the landing craft has stopped and the vessels themselves are holding their positions further out to sea. Fire from our defensive works and artillery has been effective and has inflicted heavy losses on the enemy. Very many dead and wounded lie on the beach.[75]

The commander of the 916th Regiment, Colonel Goth, confirmed the report. He had prevented a landing on a broad front, and the defenses had held firm. His losses had been heavy, however, especially to Allied naval gunfire, and he also seemed to be under some sort of commando attack at Pointe du Hoc, where commandoes had scaled the steep rock face using rope ladders. He was sending out an assault force of forty men to clear up the situation at Pointe du Hoc, but he was going to need reinforcements to hold his main position.

While the defenses were holding at Omaha, however, the Allies were very much on the march to the German right. The British had landed on a broad front, penetrating the beach defenses of the 726th Regiment and shattering the 441st Ost-Battalion, a unit that was shaky enough to begin with and now had to bear the brunt of some of the heaviest fighting on D-Day. Allied tanks had already gotten ashore and were heading inland toward Meuvaines and Crépon. An armored breakthrough threatened. Once in the clear, an armored force could wheel to the west, seize Bayeux, and roll up the entire unprotected eastern flank of the 352nd Division. If German reinforcements didn't arrive soon to attack the British at Meuvaines and throw the invaders back into the sea, LXXXIV Corps's entire position was in danger. Indeed, preinvasion German exercises had often practiced this very counterstroke. The only force currently available to carry out such a counterattack was *Kampfgruppe* Meyer, however, but it was currently heading west—that is to say, away from the threatened zone, with orders to fight an enemy south of Carentan who was not in fact there.

Once apprised of the gravity of the situation, General Marcks made the necessary adjustments and ordered Meyer's force to double back.

The *Kampfgruppe* was now to head east at speed to a deployment area at Esquay, east of Bayeux, and from there attack north toward Meuvaines and Crépon. Success would drive the British back or destroy them and secure the endangered right flank of the 352nd Division. Meyer got the order at 9:00 A.M.: "Counterattack by reinforced grenadier Regiment 915—direction Crépon."[76] Once again, he had 352nd Fusilier Battalion in tow, plus the 1352nd Assault Gun (*Sturmgeschütz*, StuG) Battalion, containing ten 75mm self-propelled guns, and an antitank battalion of twelve guns.

Carrying out this simple order proved to be anything but. The Allies had been ashore for over two hours, and the British already had a secure foothold at Gold Beach. The counterattack sector was under Allied naval gunfire, and Meyer's force had to take a circuitous route south of Bayeux rather than move directly up the main road. Before it launched its attack, it had to subordinate the units already there—remnants of the 441st Ost-Battalion and the 1st Battalion, 916th Grenadier Regiment. All these things took time. At 11:00 A.M., moreover, nature intervened. The weather suddenly changed. The clouds lifted, the skies cleared, and the sun appeared. All these usually welcome omens of battle had just the opposite reading for the Germans. As Ziegelmann saw it,

> After a short time, the first fighter-bombers [the dreaded "*Jabos*," short for *Jagdbombern*] made their appearance and began to beat down the far-flung march columns of the 915th Grenadier Regiment. Movement stopped, since more and more fighters appeared. The attempt to oppose these fighters by 1st Flak-Regiment south of Grandcamp had only meager success, since numerous squadrons of bombers were covering the operational sector, and some of the guns had been buried alive. . . . Continuous attacks by the *Jabos* had also made practically any movement along the coast impossible. The telephone lines from the division to the regiments had been working up till now, but enemy air activity was leading to extensive interference, so that we now had to employ radio troops (with delays for encoding!).[77]

Meyer's moment had come and gone. The clock slipped closer to noon, and once again he had to report that, due to ongoing Allied air attacks, he had to postpone his decisive counterattack until 2:00 P.M.

That deadline came and went as well, since elements of Meyer's

Kampfgruppe—one whole battalion, in fact—had still not reached the deployment area for the counterattack at Villiers-le-Sec. In fact, much of Meyer's unit was stretched out along the roads behind him, either pinned to the ground or taking cover under a rain of Allied bombs and strafing. Meyer himself had just reached Bazenville to the west of Villiers-le-Sec at 3:00 P.M., when elements of the British 50th Division went over to the attack, Sherman tanks in the lead, fighter-bombers thundering overhead. They easily overran the German spearhead and assembly area, killing Colonel Meyer in the melee. Both the commander of the 532nd Fusilier Battalion and the 1352nd *StuG* Battalion also went missing in action, and soon the bulk of the regiment was in a hurried retreat to the west. To declare the counterattack of *Kampfgruppe* Meyer a failure is inaccurate. Indeed, it had never even started.

To the Shore: The Ride of the 21st Panzer Division

Although the Germans failed to defend their beaches that morning, they did manage to launch one counterattack. One of the Panzer divisions fought its way to the front, launched an attack, and drove all the way to the sea.

The backbone of German defensive strategy in France, and indeed the Wehrmacht's only hope for a successful campaign, was the Panzer division. To be precise, nine Panzer divisions and one *Panzergrenadier* division stood ready in the western theater, containing no fewer than 1,400 tanks and self-propelled guns in all. The just-concluded May compromise adjudicated by Hitler had split this armored force into three discrete clusters. Beginning in the north, Rommel's Army Group B had three divisions, formed into the XXXXVII Panzer Corps (General Hans Freiherr von Funck):

21st Panzer Division—St.-Pierre-sur-Dives
2nd Panzer Division—Amiens
116th Panzer Division—Pontoise

Rommel had deployed one of the divisions, the 21st Panzer, in the 7th Army sector in Normandy, while 2nd and 116th Panzer supported the sector of the 15th Army.

In southern France, Blaskowitz's Army Group G also included three Panzer divisions, formed into the LVIII Panzer Corps under General Walter Krüger:

2nd SS Panzer Division *Das Reich*—Montauban
9th Panzer Division—Nimes
11th Panzer Division—Bordeaux

All three of the divisions in Krüger's corps were veterans of the murderous fighting on the Eastern Front, however, and were currently in southern France not so much to defend the sector in case of Allied invasion as to rest, rebuild, and incorporate replacements, new tanks, and equipment. They were not prepared for hard fighting at the moment, and, indeed, that's precisely why they were deployed in this quiet region of France.

Finally, there were the four divisions of *Panzergruppe* West, under the *command* of General Leo Freiherr Geyr von Schweppenburg for purposes of training and administration, but under the direct operational *control* of the OKW for purposes of insertion into combat. Even moving them required Hitler's express permission:

1st SS Panzer Division *Leibstandarte Adolf Hitler*—Turnhout
12th SS Panzer Division *Hitlerjugend*—south of Caen
17th SS *Panzergrenadier* Division *Götz von Berlichingen* (Thouars)
Panzer *Lehr* Division—Nogent le Rotrou

To add to the complexity of the command arrangements, the four divisions also constituted the I SS Panzer Corps, under *SS-Oberstgruppenführer* (equivalent to the army rank of "General") Josef "Sepp" Dietrich. Functioning as a Führer reserve, I SS Panzer Corps was scattered across France, without a recognizable geographical center of gravity, or *Schwerpunkt*. The 1st SS Panzer Division was at Turnhout in eastern Belgium, for example, while 17th SS *Panzergrenadier* stood at Thouars, near the city of Tours in central France, and Panzer *Lehr* began the campaign in Nogent le Rotrou, just northeast of Le Mans.

Lack of a *Schwerpunkt* might not have been crucial, however, since the corps was never intended to function as a unitary whole or fight under a single command. In fact, the organization of the Panzers was an almost perfect example of what political analysts have called the "polycratic" nature of the Nazi state, with competing offices and layers of authority, and with quarrels over competency the norm, quarrels that could be adjudicated only by Hitler himself.[78] Polycracy had long been the norm in the civilian affairs of the Third Reich but, by 1944, had become business as usual within the military as well, with standard divisional and corps organizations topped by a command structure that can only be described as baroque. The armored reserve in France contained two separate and independent ground armies, the regular army (the *Heer* portion of the Wehrmacht) fighting alongside the Waffen-SS, with neither force subordinate to the other; a Panzer corps commander, Dietrich, possessing four divisions over which he had no real control; and a *Panzergruppe* commander (Geyr) theoretically commanding the same divisions as I SS Panzer Corps, but likewise with no actual authority over them.[79] Condemning the system as inefficient is an understatement. Rather, it was illogical and defective. Once again, however, we need to bear in mind that neither efficiency nor logic was the purpose of creating these multiple and squabbling command echelons. Rather, their purpose was to strengthen the authority of the Supreme Commander of the Wehrmacht, Hitler himself.

Ten Panzer divisions sounds like a large number, and indeed it had the potential to be a mighty force in aggregate. Even single Panzer divisions were capable of prodigious feats of arms on the Eastern Front, especially when counterattacking Soviet forces that were advancing rapidly and outstripping their logistical network, and there was no telling what ten might achieve. A careful look at the map of Western Europe in conjunction with these divisional deployments, however, soon cuts the number down to size. Subtract the three divisions undergoing replenishment in the south of France under Army Group G, then the three in *Panzergruppe* West located in Belgium and central France, and, finally, the two that Rommel had deployed behind 15th Army. None of these eight were close enough to the invasion beaches to make a difference on D-Day.

That left precisely two mechanized divisions to respond to the massive Allied landings. The 21st Panzer Division under General Feuchtinger, a component formation of Army Group B, deployed at St.-Pierre-sur-Dives, about 20 miles southeast of Caen; 12th SS Panzer Division *Hitlerjugend* (under the command of General Fritz Witt and forming part of the OKW Reserve), lay farther south and east of Normandy, in the triangle between Louviers, Dreux, and Vimoutiers. Given the geography of the campaign, both were potential threats to the British and Canadian landings only; the Germans had no Panzer division close enough to the beaches in western Normandy to make a difference against the Americans.

Again, it might seem simple to group these two divisions together and make a run at the invasion beaches. In war, however, even the simplest thing can be difficult.[80] Not only did the two divisions belong to separate commands, requiring separate permissions for insertion into battle; their deployment sectors were also far too widely separated for effective cooperation. No matter who was giving permission, the 12th SS Panzer Division was still more than a day's march from Caen on June 6. Indeed, the early-morning hours found the division ordered toward Lisieux, a full 30 miles away. It would finish the day falling in on the German defensive line to the west of Caen. Ironically, Witt's division was originally stationed in Lisieux back in April, but concern that the town lay too close to the beaches and would thus be exposed to the full fury of Allied preparatory bombardment in the event of an invasion had resulted in a decision to pull the unit back into the French interior. And indeed, lest we shake our heads at yet another incomprehensible German mistake, Allied bombing on the night of June 5–6 actually did destroy Lisieux. Had the Hitler Youth Division remained, it might well have shared the town's fate.[81] As always in this campaign, enemy airpower was a problem to which the Wehrmacht had no real solution.

And then there was one: one Panzer division deployed close enough to counterattack the Allied beachhead on D-Day. Like so many of the other German divisions in France, the 21st Panzer was a troubled unit in 1944. The commander, General Feuchtinger, owed his status to his loyalty to the regime and his ability to curry favor with the Führer's minions. One of his regimental commanders, Major Hans von Luck, described him as having "no combat experience, and none at all of Panzer units."[82] His pull in Berlin did allow him to procure high-quality officers for his division like Luck, often yanking them out of other assignments they truly desired. He was also able to get the division topped off with manpower before D-Day, some 16,200 men. But Panzer divisions do not produce strength by their manpower, and all the pull in the world can't forge more steel or produce more tanks. The 21st rode into battle, therefore, with a motley pile of equipment: tanks of foreign manufacture, mainly Czech pieces, *Beutewaffen* captured from former enemies, and Panzer Mark IVs, a tank that had been state of the art in 1941–1942 but was now showing its age.

The division reacted to D-Day briskly enough. British paratroopers and glider-borne troops of the 6th Airborne Division were dropping all around it, and 21st Panzer went into action against them on the right bank of the Orne in the early morning hours. Both sides found themselves in a tough fight, particularly around the town of Ranville, and the early morning darkness and the swirling confusion of the operational situation only added to the mix. With the break of dawn came the Anglo-Canadian amphibious landings at Gold, Juno, and Sword Beaches, however, and now the thing to do was to disengage the division from its fight with the airborne and get to the beaches. That was certainly the opinion of General Erich Marcks, commander of LXXXIV Corps. His entire defensive sector was melting away under the Allied onslaught, and only an armored counterattack could put things right. The 21st Division was under Army Group B, however, and Rommel's permission was necessary to get it into the fight. But Rommel was still on his way back to the front, and Speidel, Rommel's chief, wasn't the sort to yield to the first loud voice demanding reinforcements. Even if he had yielded, it would have been no small matter to disengage the 21st from its cramped, close-quarters fight with the British paratroopers on the right bank of the Orne, regroup the Panzers, and shift them to the left bank for a concentrated counterattack. Such operational gymnastics take time, and they become even slower and more hair-raising when performed under enemy air attack.

As a result, 21st Panzer Division's day was a series of delays. The division came under the command of LXXXIV Corps a little after noon. Marcks now ordered Feuchtinger to leave his 125th *Panzergrenadier* Regiment (*Kampfgruppe* Luck) east of the Orne to continue the antiairborne clearing mission and to shift his 22nd Panzer Regiment (Colonel Hermann Oppeln-Bronikowski) and his 192nd *Panzergrenadier* Regiment (Colonel Joseph Rauch) to the other side of the river, head toward Caen, and drive north against the Allied landings. But it took two and a half hours to move the 10-mile stretch from the Ranville sector through Caen to the front. Every man and vehicle had to squeeze through the eye of the needle in Caen over the few remaining undestroyed bridges, the sky was crawling with Allied *Jabos*, and losses in both machines and men were heavy. Colonel Oppeln would later claim to have lost no fewer than fifty tanks in the course of that short drive, and while his estimate almost certainly errs on the high side— like all German claims of materiel losses in Normandy—the approach march was hellish enough. Allied airpower was a nightmare, but almost as damaging to the speed of the German approach was the demand that 21st Panzer Division maintain radio silence during the march—a security measure that seems sensible enough but a real brake on progress now that every minute mattered.

While Oppeln was still struggling to bring his regiment on line, the enemy was also on the move. Elements of the Canadian 9th Brigade (Canadian 3rd Division) and British 185th Brigade (British 3rd Division) had orders to head south toward their D-Day objective: the city of Caen. The zone of operations was the open plain between Caen and the sea, a battlespace in which even slight undulations or rises in the ground could take on massive tactical significance. On Périers Ridge and at the village of Biéville-Beuville, the British attack came to a halt against remnants of the 716th Static Division, backed by a handful of 88mm antitank guns—the nemesis of British armor in the desert and still a fearsome enemy in Normandy. British forces showed improvements, as well, with tanks and artillery working together in effective combination, and they managed to take both the ridge and the village. The British had burned themselves out getting there, however, and their drive petered out just three miles north of Caen.

It was 4:00 P.M. when it finally happened: the main event—the culmination of all those hours of planning, controversy, and angst within the German command. Around 4:20 P.M. on D-Day, the Germans finally launched a Panzer attack on the Allied beachhead. Oppeln's 22nd Panzer Regiment was on the right, elements of Rauch's 192nd *Panzergrenadier* on the left. Morale in both regiments was high, and so was confidence. Oppeln himself was a skilled Panzer commander with a reputation for hard drink and for dodging the Grim Reaper.[83] On no fewer than three occasions in the course of this war, he had survived direct hits on his tank and managed to walk away without a scratch. His men no doubt thought that their colonel lived under a lucky star. Perhaps he would pull them all through. After all those months of waiting, the enemy had arrived, apparently serving himself up on a platter with the sea at his back. Oppeln knew what was at stake—or at least he should have after General Marcks surprised him at the regimental command post and ordered him into battle immediately.[84]

The assault began in earnest at 4:20 P.M., with Oppeln's Panzers rolling north toward Périers Ridge. The tanks were mainly Panzer Mark IVs, older models now upgraded with a high-velocity 75mm gun, although in most of the other relevant metrics—speed, armor, optics—the state of the art had long passed them by. Trundling along behind the Mark IVs came the infantry on halftracks, along with self-propelled guns of various calibers mounted on the reliable French Lorraine 37L tracked chassis. The regiment moved out with verve, and it was as always an impressive sight: the army that had invented mechanized, combined-arms warfare once again on the prowl, apparently irresistible in the advance. While many of the men in the 21st Panzer Division may have lacked experience, their officers and commanders had all been here before, many times, and we can properly describe them as fearless.

The British defenders they faced were not the same as they had met in Africa, however. The units were blooded, the commanders more seasoned, and the support weapons far more effectively coordinated. Holding Périers Ridge in force was a complete battalion, the Shropshire Light Infantry. It had dug itself in deeply, its positions were well hidden, and a full complement of heavy weapons was ready to fire in support: 6-pounder antitank guns, Firefly tanks, a Sherman variant with a powerful, high-velocity 3-inch (17-pounder) gun, and self-propelled artillery. The Shropshires held their fire until the Germans came to the foot of the ridge, then opened up with a full spectrum of weapons. One Mark IV after another went up in flames, with six destroyed in the opening minutes of the engagement on the German right, then nine more on the left near Mathieu. Within ten minutes, the surviving German tanks were scrambling toward whichever gully, copse, or farmhouse they could find, desperately seeking cover. Both sides would trade fire and losses over the course of the next hour, but British fire had broken the momentum of the Panzer attack, and the beachhead was safe. Oppeln's luck had run out.

Although the 22nd Panzer Regiment had run into a buzz saw, things went much more favorably on the left of the German attack. Here the 1st Battalion of Rauch's 192nd Regiment managed to strike the seam between the British and Canadian forces, slashing into the operational gap between Juno and Sword Beaches and driving ahead. Forward they rode against little enemy opposition or fire, their path ahead eased by the attention being drawn by Oppeln's abortive Panzer attack taking place to their right. Within the hour they reached the sea at Lion-sur-Mer and Luc-sur-Mer, splitting the Allied beachhead, separating Juno Beach from Sword, and linking up with joyful elements of the 716th Static Division who were still hanging tough in their bunkers along the coast and who probably thought that they were goners. In so doing, Rauch had grabbed a laurel wreath denied to all the other German division commanders fighting against Allied amphibious landings. General Paul Conrath of the Hermann Göring Division on Sicily; General Rudolf Sieckenius of the 16th Panzer Division at Salerno; General Walter Fries of the 29th *Panzergrenadier* at Anzio: all of these capable and aggressive commanders had launched furious attacks against recently landed Allied forces with the intention of driving them back into the sea—and all of them had fallen short of their objective. If we could gather them in a room, they would no doubt commiserate with each other about their shared experience: the ceaseless blizzard of Allied fire, enemy air forces filling the sky, unchallenged by the Luftwaffe, the anger of their men at the "unfair fight" versus naval gunfire. But now, for the first time, the gods of war were apparently smiling on the Wehrmacht, as the rush of events apparently caught the Allies napping.

Rauch had reached the sea, traditionally a marker of victory. But, we might ask, to what end? Here the Germans came face-to-face with the real problem of littoral warfare, that is, fighting on or near the coast. The German operational schema on World War II was typically a breakthrough on a narrow front, through which friendly mechanized forces passed on into the enemy's rear, prior to surrounding him in a battle of encirclement, or *Kesselschlacht*. But a breakthrough to the coast was a breakthrough to nowhere. Friendly forces that hit the water's edge simply reached a *Nullpunkt*—point zero, the end of the line. Panzer formations could not exploit through such a gap, not unless they had found a way to swim out to sea, and all that was left was a drive to the west or east in order to crumple the bridgehead from one of its flanks. Unfortunately, such a maneuver had to take place along a coastal bluff or beach, quite possibly the last terrain in the world in which one would choose to employ mechanized forces. In Rauch's case, a follow-up drive into the right or left flank of Juno or Sword would have meant a flank march along the seashore, with any German assault column amounting to little more than a perfectly silhouetted parade of targets that would have had Allied naval commanders licking their chops and adding up their kills. Even if German tanks had broken through at Périers and Biéville and had been available to reinforce Rauch, Allied naval gunfire would probably have resulted in the complete destruction of both German regiments.

At any rate, anything that Rauch *might* have done soon became a moot point. With the 22nd Panzer Regiment halted in the face of British fire, with no other mechanized forces available, and with fire pouring into the German position from both sides, Rauch was in an untenable position. The coup de grâce, fittingly, hit the Germans from the air. Around 9:00 P.M., with Rauch still holding his position at the water's edge and divisional commander Feuchtinger trying to decide what to do next, a gigantic force of aircraft passed overhead. The British were reinforcing their airborne bridgehead east of the Orne River with the largest glider force of all time—250 craft, their towplanes, and dozens more fighters flying escort. They passed directly over Luc-sur-Mer en route to their destination, and, inevitably, some of them landed in the rear of the German position. Fearing an Allied encirclement, Feuchtinger now ordered Rauch's 192nd Regiment to retreat from its forward position and to rejoin the main body of 21st Panzer

Division along Périers Ridge. His snap judgment was controversial among his colleagues, with one of Rundstedt's staff officers later stating that "it is open to question whether the decision was correct."[85] Even if Feuchtinger had decided to hang tough that evening, however, Rauch's oceanside battlegroup consisted of little more than a single battalion, and it was going to be facing massive opposition once the sun came up the next morning. Reinforced Allied divisions with strong armored support stood on either side of the narrow penetration, and the massive naval armada in front was once again ready to function as a heavyweight grand battery. Rauch was riding high when he reached the sea on the afternoon of June 6, but the 192nd Regiment ended the day by slinking back down to the south, leaving the remnants of the 716th Static Division to their unhappy fate.

Conclusion: The Longest Day

D-Day ended in total defeat for the Germans. The Allies crossed the water with impunity, came ashore smoothly at four of their five beaches, and even at the fifth (Omaha) they had already pressed inland by evening. Allied losses had been manageable, German casualties heavy. The fighting had demolished General Marcks's LXXXIV Corps, the formation defending the landing sector in the Cotentin and Calvados sectors. The frontline divisions, the 709th and 716th Static and the 352nd Infantry, had suffered grievously. The twin rocks upon which the OKW had constructed its defensive strategy in the west—the Atlantic Wall and the Panzer divisions—had both failed. The Allies pierced the defensive wall within minutes, and only a single Panzer Division managed to get to the beach and actually launch an attack on June 6 itself. While the attackers had not reached their planned objectives for the day, such a failure was a matter for an internal Allied conversation. It does not constitute any sort of validation for German arms. D-Day was a disaster for the Wehrmacht.

Finding a list of reasons for the German failure is a straightforward process. Commanders at all levels made errors. The absence of German leaders from their headquarters is a favorite trope of the literature, and many students of the campaign really do seem to believe the "Hitler slept in" thesis, that is to say, that a great battle was lost because the Supreme Commander was in bed and his subordinates were afraid to wake him. But other problems arose in the course of the day. From Rundstedt on down, German commanders had difficulty deciding whether the invasion was the real thing or a diversion, then they had equally serious problems identifying the Allied *Schwerpunkt*. As a result, they responded to all sorts of false alarms about allied airborne drops, and they dispatched the only real corps reserve, the 915th Grenadier Regiment (*Kampfgruppe* Meyer), on a back-and-forth trudge across the Norman countryside, sending it first west toward Carentan to deal with a phantom threat, then back to the east through Bayeux to attack the flank of the British landing at Gold Beach. Likewise, the day ended with General Feuchtinger making a false read on the British glider drop east of the Orne, believing that he was facing encirclement and thus deciding to pull back the 192nd Regiment from the position it had won on the coast. Hitler sleeping in; local commanders having to beg for multiple command echelons and competing jurisdictions for the tanks; Panzers setting out on the road to attack, then being called back because someone had failed to give permission to insert them: all these things really did happen.

But did they lead to the Germans' loss on D-Day? Let us recall that the Allies, too, made their share of blunders. Allied intelligence services famously failed to identify the presence of the 352nd Infantry Division on Omaha Beach, to give one example, and the landing there had been a near fiasco. The US 82nd and 101st Airborne Divisions experienced operational problems in the past—the drop onto Piano Lupo in Sicily, for example, or at Avellino in the Salerno campaign. The drop into the Cotentin was the worst of all, generating maximum scatter, maximum confusion, and very heavy friendly casualties. Indeed, every big military engagement in history is filled with misreads, misperceptions, and outright blunders of all sorts. Well-trained, well-equipped, and flexible military establishments usually manage to compensate for them. And as for those ten German mechanized divisions in France? It is simply untrue to say—as legions of historians have since 1944—that Hitler's obstinacy prevented them from getting to the beaches on D-Day. Nine of them were too far away to arrive on day one. Only one division (the 21st Panzer) was close enough, and it duly attacked the Allied beachhead. Yes, if the Germans had managed to line up all ten mechanized divisions on the Calvados coast on June 6, they might have handled the invasion more roughly than they did. But such a one-sided deployment was possible only in a fantasy world.

The mirror image of the "bungling Germans" thesis has been an explicitly heroic Allied narrative. Tied to the rise of "greatest generation" rhetoric, heroic analysis emphasizes the invaders' martial brilliance. The young men who stormed Omaha or Courseulles or scaled the sheer face of Pointe du Hoc take center stage, and museums, politicians, and reenactors sing their praises. Certainly, Allied soldiers, sailors, and airmen yielded to no one in valor on D-Day (or any other day). But what of the Germans? Manning a bunker at water's edge, under a rain of enemy naval gunfire and air raids, knowing that no help was on the way, and fighting a battle without hope: all these things took a certain amount of bravery, too. Even those whom the German accounts spend the most effort maligning—French truck drivers or the soldiers of the Ost-Battalions, for example—went well above and beyond their military duty that day. And take the 352nd Infantry Division, the supposedly "full-strength" or "nine-battalion" or "veteran" division on Omaha Beach. All these designators appear in the literature on the battle, yet none of them are true. The 352nd was a 1944 infantry division, built on the remnant of a division destroyed on the Eastern Front. It was short on everything: veteran officers, ammunition, fuel. The replacements in the ranks were 19–20-year-olds, the class of 1925/26, who often arrived at the front in a state of malnourishment or ill health and who couldn't make a field march longer than 10 miles. The hardiness of outdoors life and a healthy diet of milk from the Norman countryside raised physical standards, but the men of the 352nd were inexperienced until their baptism of fire on June 6.

Alongside notions of Allied valor comes praise for Allied military genius and expertise in planning. Historians assert that the Germans fell prey to all sorts of brilliant enemy diversionary stratagems and deceptions. Operation Titanic, for example, dropped 500 dummy parachutists into Normandy and often gets credit for luring *Kampfgruppe* Meyer to Carentan. On the strategic level, Operations Fortitude North and Fortitude South (part of the overall deception plan, Operation Bodyguard) aimed to confuse the Germans about the actual site of the landing. Fortitude North created a fictional British 4th Army preparing to invade Norway, while Fortitude South did the same for a landing on the Channel coast. It is unclear even today what impact they had. After all, the Germans needed no special urging to think that the Channel coast was the likeliest site for an Allied landing.

In the end, neither individual German mistakes nor Allied superiority in smarts or bravery won D-Day. The victory went to sheer, raw power. The Allies had finally learned to transform their wealth and industrial superiority into combat power at the front. Beginning on D-Day, Allied firepower—far more lavish and concentrated than even the Soviet version—turned Normandy into a burning cauldron. Thousands of ships, ten of thousand of sorties, and the elements of nine divisions were in play on the Allied side that morning, and millions of men waited in the wings as follow-on forces. To resist this onslaught, the Germans could present only three divisions: two static units useful for fortress duty only, utterly unsuited for high-intensity fighting, and a single infantry division.

Despite the modern tendency in the United States and Great Britain to romanticize D-Day, the Allies on June 6 wielded a sledgehammer and swatted a fly: exactly what you should do, if you can.

4

In the Middle: The Smashing of the Central Front

Introduction

History repeats itself, Karl Marx once noted, before adding an important addendum: "the first time as tragedy, the second time as farce."[1]

* * *

FRANCE—AUGUST 1870. *The scene is the battlefield of Mars-la-Tour, a moment immortalized in a thousand retellings and, no doubt, embellishments.[2] A foolhardy attack on the French army west of Metz by the Prussian III Corps under General Konstantin von Alvensleben had misfired badly. Alvensleben believed he had only a French rear guard in his sights, but in fact his corps had taken on most of France's Army of the Rhine. One thing the French could do in this war was to dish out the fire, courtesy of their high-powered Chassepot rifles and even the occasional Mitrailleuse volley gun. Alvensleben's assault troops, first the 5th Division under General Ferdinand von Stülpnagel and then the 6th Division under Baron von Buddenbrock coming up on the left, were soon reeling back in confusion, leaving thousands of their dead and wounded on the field.*

The III Corps was in extremis, outnumbered many times over and with the only potential reinforcements—the Prussian X Corps—still nearly a day's march away. Alvensleben's own artillery was starting to come up from the route of march, but wheeling the batteries into position would take hours, and at any time even the simplest French counterattack threatened to destroy his corps. With disaster staring him in the face and his corps on the ropes, Alvensleben made his decision. He summoned General Friedrich Wilhelm von Bredow, commander of 12th Cavalry Brigade, and ordered him to lead an immediate cavalry charge against the French gun line.

Bredow knew what the order meant. Horses against fire could generate only one outcome: a Totenritt—*a death ride. He had his orders, however, and at the very least the sacrifice of his brigade—two fine regiments, the 16th Uhlans and the 7th Cuirassiers—might take some of the pressure off the hard-pressed III Corps. But the death ride wasn't really about sober calculation. As Bredow saddled up and rode off into the lore of the Prussian army, there were those who heard him mutter a simple phrase, half-resignation, half-defiance. "Koste es, was er wolle," he said: "Whatever it costs," or better, "Whatever it takes."*[3]

* * *

JULY 1944. *The staff meeting had already careened into absurdity in the first hour.*[4] *They always seemed to, nowadays. Every front had collapsed or was about to. A two-front war? Hardly! More like an all-front war* (Allfronten-krieg).[5] *The Allied beachhead in the west now encompassed a sizable portion of northwestern France, and a breakout was imminent. Kesselring's beaten forces in Italy were still retreating northward at top speed, and who knew where that would end? And as for the east . . . there were no words.*

Heusinger didn't know what to say. He was chief of the Operations Department (and at least temporarily chief of the great General Staff, filling in for the exhausted General Kurt Zeitzler), but Hitler no longer wanted to "operate," as he had said on at least two dozen occasions in the past few months.[6] *Hitler wanted commanders and men who would stand fast. Stay put. Hang tough. Heusinger could tick off the phrases in his head. Hitler didn't care if his officers were competent or not. He wanted them to be hard. Tenacious. Ruthless. Yes, especially that last one. "Ruthless"* (rücksichtslos) *had always been one of the Führer's favorite words.*[7]

But somehow, Heusinger didn't think that being ruthless or fanatical was going to get it done this time. Army Group Center, about one-third of the total front in the east, had collapsed under a gigantic Soviet offensive. Everyone in the German High Command had known that an offensive was coming, but the details—when, how, exactly where: those were the problem. They had all guessed wrong on the location of the first Soviet attack, and that meant that everything that followed—reaction, employment of reserves, the dispatch of reinforcements—had all been a colossal foulup, a complete and utter mess, a Durcheinander. *And now the front had cracked wide open.*[8] *Two complete armies—9th and 4th—practically wiped off the map, a third one shattered; one supposed "fortress" after the other falling to the enemy; a single Panzer division sent to retrieve the situation practically vanishing in the tumult. Even now, Soviet tank armies were ranging far to the west, encircling some German formations, but simply flattening others. Minsk was in Soviet hands again—not two weeks ago it had been the headquarters of Army Group Center! And there were no signs of slowing the avalanche. Vilnius, the Baltic states, the port of Libau: Soviet possibilities seemed endless.*

So that was why they were all here—the Führer and his staff. How to close this gigantic gap, this Loch *between Bobruisk and Vitebsk, where Army Group Center used to be?*[9] *The new commander on the spot, General Model, wanted to shift divisions from the southern portion of the front to the center. Heusinger knew that was a bad idea—it was clear that the Soviets were about to launch yet another attack in the south as well. He also knew where there were fresh divisions to be had, however: in the sector of Army Group North, currently holding a vast and overextended front on both sides of Lake Peipus. The staff up there had been requesting permission for months to pull back to the line of the Dvina River: a shorter line, easier to hold, requiring half the manpower and freeing up 4–5 divisions for action elsewhere.*[10]

All sound arguments, but Heusinger barely got any of it out before Hitler intervened. The Führer was back to his favorite topics. Treason. Betrayal. The "mysterious" nature of the collapse in the east. Ordering immediate investigations of every single commander involved. No one was going to pull back anywhere! "The generals will do their duty or I'll force them to!"[11] *Göring nodding his head in agreement, as well as Dönitz, Keitel, Jodl—all the rest of them.* "Zu befehl, mein Führer!"[12] *Staff meetings were always a competition between sober planning and bloodlust against perceived enemies of the regime, especially the generals.*

Suddenly, Hitler's gaze fixed on the map. He pointed. There. Vilnius. We'll hold them there. Heusinger slumped a bit, involuntarily. He knew what was coming next. Hitler was about to create another "fortress," a stronghold, a fester Platz. "We'll need a really hard man here," *the Führer bawled.*[13] *A proven commander. His voice rose.* "Get me General Stahel. We must hold Vilnius!"

Heusinger could almost predict the next phrase.

"Koste es, was er wolle!"[14]

* * *

There it was again: "whatever it costs." The phrase runs like a golden thread through the history of the Prussian-German army, from the Great Elector of the seventeenth century to the great collapse in 1945. Prussia rarely fought from a position of material strength, and neither did its successor, Germany. Hohenfriedeberg and Rossbach and Leuthen, Königgrätz, and Tannenberg: the greatest wins in German military history had all been victories against the odds. A willingness to do "whatever it took" could act as an equalizer against a force of greater size but lesser will, and indeed the Prussian army had built its military reputation on just such calculations.

But sometimes, as in Bredow's death ride or Stahel's doomed attempt to hold Vilnius, or even the entire failed German war in the Soviet Union, an overreliance on will and determination could also be a ticket to oblivion, an ethereal and subjective substitute for a firmer objective reality. It could become a kind of *Täuschungsmanöver*—a vast "deception operation," but this time you wound up fooling only yourself.[15] Numbers, resources, allies: all the quantifiables needed to make sound strategic judgment simply faded away into the ether. Numbers didn't matter, nor did reality. All you needed was a strong will, a firm jaw, and a grim determination to see the thing through. You needed to do or die.

By 1944, the Wehrmacht could have used a smaller pool of determination and willpower—it had more of than enough of those—and a much larger number of fresh divisions.

Operation Bagration: Planning and Misperception

The great catastrophe of 1944 began, as did so many others in the Wehrmacht's war in the Soviet Union, with a German intelligence failure. The Soviet winter offensive of 1943–1944 had badly mauled Army Group South and at times threatened to shatter it altogether. The Soviets had concentrated their drive against the left, or northern, wing of Army Group South, attempting to separate it from its neighbor to the north, Army Group Center. And indeed, the Red Army had come within a hair of a decisive victory in this operational sequence, driving far to the west and lapping around the city of Kovel, the hinge between the two army groups. A breakthrough here would have put Soviet tanks on the road to Warsaw, and few German formations would have been there to oppose them. Hitler had declared Kovel to be a *fester Platz*, however, and the Germans managed to hold, just barely. Kovel was one of the few times that a German stronghold functioned as intended—both as a breakwater on Soviet momentum and a means of tying up Soviet formations that might otherwise be joining in the offensive. The subsequent relief of the city in April 1944 by German forces marked the end of the crisis, as the rains came and movement across the front halted. The Wehrmacht had once again weathered a storm.

By now, any relief for the Germans could only be temporary. Along with their offensive in the south, the Soviets opened the 1943–1944 winter campaign launching strong attacks against Army Group North, the Novgorod-Luga Operation. Army Group North was an operational shell by this time, not a functioning, vigorous field force. The crisis in the south had forced it to hand over one division after the other to Army Group South, and it no longer had a single tank in its order of battle. Attacks by two Soviet army groups (the Leningrad and Volkhov Fronts) shattered it, combining brute force—always the Red Army's calling card—with a certain amount of finesse. Indeed, the offensive began with an entire army, the 2nd Shock, transported by sea into the zone of the Oranienbaum bridgehead, a narrow sliver of coastline that the Germans had never been able to overrun.[16] The Soviet attack hit hard initially, cleaving a great gash between the German 18th Army on the left and the 16th Army on the right and threatening to separate Army Group North from Army Group Center altogether. Within the first week, both German armies were running for their lives. The 18th Army, in particular, fought in desperation mode, with Soviet forces coming at it from its front (east), its left flank (north), and even from its left rear (the 2nd Shock coming down from Oranienbaum). While the Soviet offensive pushed both armies back to the "Panther position" stretching from the Narva bottleneck on the Gulf of Finland to Lake Peipus and points south, the effort stopped just short of destroying Army Group North. One authoritative source describes the Soviet pursuit as "slow and fumbling" and "poorly coordinated," although a combination of densely forested terrain and the brutal cold of the northern winter no doubt played a role.[17] At any rate, after a near-death experience, the Germans were able to restore the cohesion of their front. New German leadership also contributed to the defensive success, as Field Marshal Walter Model arrived to replace the Army Group commander, General Georg Küchler. Model already had a reputation as the "Führer's fireman"—a skilled defensive commander able to master any crisis and restore even the most hopeless cause. His work done here, Model now headed south to take over Army Group South, then passing through its own trial by fire, from Field Marshal Erich von Manstein. Despite the less than stirring ending for the Soviets, the Novgorod-Luga Operation did succeed in finally breaking the German ring around the encircled and starving city of Leningrad.

While they hammered away in both north and south, however, they also launched a series of frontal attacks against Army Group Center. Although involving significant Soviet forces, the operations were uncoordinated, shifting from one *Schwerpunkt* to the next, and sloppily executed. The commander of the army group, Field Marshal Ernst Busch, skillfully parried them by transferring divisions from nonthreatened sectors and hurling them against the Soviet penetrations. Like everyone in the German command, however, he too was concerned about the Soviet drive against the northern wing of Army Group South. Yawning gaps between army groups were more than a tactical or operational problem. They could have real strategic implications. Facing the possible separation of his army group from its neighbor to the south, he worked on forming a powerful reserve, the LVI Panzer Corps under General Friedrich Hossbach, by stripping mechanized divisions from parts of Army Group Center that seemed relatively quiet. It was a classic example of accepting risk in nondecisive sectors in order to concentrate strength at the *Schwerpunkt*. Busch now dispatched LVI Panzer Corps to the far southwestern corner of his area of operations, and Hossbach's divisions played the key role in the relief of Kovel in April.[18]

With impressive Soviet progress on the northern and southern flanks, but much less in the center, the front had now taken on the curious shape of a question mark. Army Group Center formed the hook, a vast semicircular bulge centered on Minsk and looping lazily out to the east. The "Byelorussian balcony," the Germans called it. Army Group South, now split in half into Army Group North Ukraine under Field Marshal Walter Model and Army Group South Ukraine under General Ferdinand Schörner, lay far to the west and served as the stem. Here, the Soviets were holding a vast forward position of their own, a "Ukrainian balcony" that was an ideal springboard for a renewed attack.[19] This sector still held the majority of Soviet armored strength on the Eastern Front, concentrated against Model's Army Group North Ukraine. Particularly crucial to German intelligence estimates was the confirmed presence of Soviet tank armies and perhaps even the formation of a new front headquarters, always the most reliable indicators of Soviet offensive intentions.

Indeed, the shape of the front was an entirely appropriate symbol of German uncertainty. The Wehrmacht's planners at every level—army, army group, OKH, the Foreign Armies East intelligence office (*Abteilung Fremde Heere Ost*) under Colonel Reinhard Gehlen—were all certain that the summer would bring a renewed Soviet offensive on a grand scale. But just where would the blow land? Out of the myriad possibilities on this vast front, two potential scenarios soon crystallized: a Balkan solution (*Balkan-Lösung*) and a Baltic solution (*Ostsee-Lösung*). Both shared the same logical starting point: a Soviet offensive against Model's Army Group North Ukraine. As envisioned, the Soviets would launch a great armored thrust through the Galician gap between the Pripet Marshes and the Carpathian Mountains and, once through the bottleneck, would carry out a gigantic wheel, either to the left (the south) into the Balkan Peninsula or to the right (north) toward the Baltic Sea.[20] In either direction, a Soviet breakthrough offered the enticing possibility of encircling multiple German army groups. The Balkan solution could spell doom for Army Groups North Ukraine and South Ukraine, and perhaps even Army Groups E and F, then occupying Greece and Yugoslavia, respectively. The Baltic option, by contrast, threatened to encircle Army Groups Center and North, trapping and destroying them against the shores of the Baltic Sea in a vast encirclement. A drive to the coast in this sector would also leave massive Soviet forces well placed to carry out a follow-on drive toward Berlin. Either way, the Germans told themselves, the Soviet summer offensive of 1944 would be more than a mere "operation." It would aim at strategic effects, perhaps even an early end to the war.[21]

Divining Soviet intentions with any precision was no easy matter, however. Not only did German intelligence have to tease out the secrets of one of the world's most secretive regimes; the almost complete disappearance of the Luftwaffe and the lack of German aerial reconnaissance turned the entire process into a kind of black-box mystery. Essentially the Germans wound up relying on deduction, educated guesswork, and a kind of strategic empathy: trying to place themselves in the shoes of Stalin and his planners. From these perspectives, the Balkan solution seemed logical enough. After all, why would the Soviets have launched all these attacks on the southern front for nearly a year—ever since the German failure at Kursk, really—if they didn't intend to go south eventually? A breakthrough near the city of Lvov (German Lemberg) and a drive over the San River would put Soviet armored formations across the Carpathian Mountains and give them access to the fertile Hungarian Plain, the gateway to Central Europe. Moreover, Kremlin watchers in the German command could point to traditional Soviet, and even Tsarist Russian, strategic aims in the Balkans, including control of the strait, access to the Mediterranean Sea and to warm water ports, and the seizure of the Ploesti oil fields. The last objective was crucial: the Reich couldn't carry on the war for very long without Romanian oil.

But the Baltic solution held its own attractions. Here, the danger was a Soviet armored breakthrough at Kovel, the "hinge" (*Scharnier*) between Army Groups North Ukraine and Center. A renewal of the Soviet attack as soon as the ground dried out seemed like a logical way for the Soviets to reinforce success. Once through at Kovel, a quick Soviet wheel to the right between Warsaw and Brest could have Soviet tanks reaching the Baltic coast on the Danzig-Königsberg line in no time. Moreover, during this second-stage drive to the north, the vulnerable western flank of the Soviet maneuver would have the Vistula River serving as a protective barrier. The final result would see Army Groups North and Center cut off from communications and supply and thus ripe for destruction—a super-Stalingrad, the greatest *Kesselschlacht* in history. As one analyst noted, this northern option exerted a kind of fascination on German planners that went well beyond a purely objective analysis into the realm of the psychological. To all of them from Hitler on down, a Baltic solution seemed to resemble nothing so much as a monstrous reverse image of their own great victory over the Western powers in 1940, the *Sichelschnitt* maneuver, the "cut of the scythe" through the Ardennes Forest and the drive to the English Channel, replete with a super-sized Dunkirk on the Baltic at the end.[22] In other words, the Baltic solution was what they, themselves—the German command—would have done if they were sitting in the Kremlin, and for that reason it became the official expectation within the Wehrmacht's planning cells. They well knew how badly weakened the fighting of the previous year had left them. If they had an adversary on the ropes, they would go for broke. One grand blow and a potentially decisive result, even an end to the war: How could Stalin resist the temptation?

And so the Germans denuded the rest of the Eastern Front of its Panzers in order to strengthen the sector of Army Group North Ukraine. Eventually all but one of Army Group Center's Panzer divisions was transferred to Field Marshal Model's front. Some of it was personal. Model stood high in Hitler's favor.[23] He was no operator but a "stander," a commander who would hold a piece of ground no matter the cost, and he usually got what he asked for, even if neighboring army groups starved. But as always, personality was only a piece of the problem—a small one. In a sense there was no choice. With the Wehrmacht now wedded to a "stand fast" and "hold at any price" mentality, German planners had to guess right about Soviet intentions.[24] They had to face strength with strength. They had to match the Soviet offensive concentration with a defensive concentration of their own (*Schwerpunkt gegen Schwerpunkt*).[25] The post-Kursk Wehrmacht no longer held the initiative to launch a great offensive of its own. Equally, it no longer had the mobile forces to wait for the opening Soviet moves and then react, in the style of Field Marshal Erich von Manstein's "backhand blow" (*Schlag aus der Nachhand*).[26] The German official history of World War II describes Manstein as "operating after the fact" (*operieren a posteriori*). By the summer of 1944, however, strong German defensive forces had to be in place from the start. They had to operate a priori, in other words, bulk themselves up on the very spot the Soviets had chosen for their offensive, and then stop the Red Army in its tracks from the outset.[27] The Wehrmacht had to pick its spot, and it chose Army Group North Ukraine as the most likely sector for a renewed Soviet offensive and thus the spot where the defenses had to be strongest.

As it turned out, the German brain trust guessed wrong. The Soviets had no intention of launching either a Balkan or a Baltic campaign, no desire to risk the war on a one-shot, all-or-nothing drive for glory. Instead, the Soviet High Command (Stavka) decided upon a carefully sequenced series of operations.[28] In chronological order, they included offensive blows against the Finnish army in Karelia, a second against Army Group Center in Byelorussia (designated Operation Bagration), along with subsidiary operations against Army Group North; a third against Army Group North Ukraine in front of Lvov; and finally, a fourth against Army Group South Ukraine in Romania. By the end of the sequence, Soviet offensives would engulf all four German army groups in the Soviet Union. The Red Army had grown so powerful that it finally could achieve its doctrinal ideal—first formulated in the 1920s—of "consecutive operations." Modern armies were too large and too resilient to be dispatched with a single blow, no matter how powerfully it landed. In the Soviet vision, one offensive after the other would stretch German resources to the limit, force the Wehrmacht to shuttle its meager reserves across the map, and keep the Wehrmacht right where the Soviets wanted it: in a tentative and reactive mode. And, in fact, as the preparations for these multiple offensives went forward in spring 1944, high confusion reigned in German intelligence circles. Try as they might, they could not discern a single, lone *Schwerpunkt* as they had expected. Rather they saw at least a half-dozen potential ones, and virtually every German army in the Soviet Union could report strong enemy activity across its front.[29] German intelligence was, as one source puts it, "like a bloodhound on the hunt whose instincts are blocked because he sees three equally distant hares."[30] And so, again and again, a confused German planning process that was unable to achieve objective certainty returned to its original intuitive conception. The impending Soviet offensive would target Army Group North Ukraine.

One last piece of the puzzle was necessary to make German confusion complete and the coming disaster inevitable. For the first time since 1941, another development was competing with the Eastern

Front for priority in men, weapons, and attention. In late 1943, Hitler's Führer Directive No. 51 had granted operational priority to the new Western Front that he expected the Allies to open in 1944. For the time being, the sprawling Eastern Front became a kind of subsidiary theater—as fantastic a notion as that seems to us. On the eve of the invasion, a kind of "auto-suggestive euphoria" had taken hold in the Führer's camp, to use Albert Speer's memorable phrase.[31] If the Wehrmacht could destroy the Allied landing, Germany would win the war. The landing itself saw the euphoria peak. Hitler was in an apparently ecstatic mood, according to the OKW's deputy chief of the operations staff, Colonel Walter Warlimont: "With an utterly carefree smile, and with the bearing of a man who has finally gotten the opportunity to settle up with his opponent, he approached the map and, in unusually broad Austrian dialect, uttered the simple phrase, 'So . . . it's on.'"[32] The decision would come not in the east, therefore, but in the much smaller western theater, where it was still possible to prosecute "a short but mighty campaign" (*einen kurzen aber wuchtigen Waffengang*) and win a rapid victory, perhaps a subconscious reference to Frederick the Great's preference for the "short and lively" (*kurtz und vives*) war.[33] They apparently all believed it—Keitel, Jodl, Göring, Dönitz—or at least they professed to and acted as if they did. Propaganda Minister Josef Goebbels boasted openly of a "new Dunkirk" to drive the Allies from the continent, and domestic opinion as sampled by the Sicherheitsdienst (SS security service) reflected the same optimism. The Allied invasion had ended "a period of unbearable tension and oppressive uncertainty."[34]

Moreover, for the first time in a while, Hitler's conception was not without a certain operational and historical logic. Germany had always faced the nightmare of fighting on two fronts, and the logical thing had always been to exploit the advantages of the central position and to operate on interior lines, sitting patiently in the middle, then smashing the first enemy army to come within reach. Frederick the Great had made a career out of it, and Alfred Graf von Schlieffen, still the exemplar of the brilliant planner to this generation of German officers, had argued the identical point on numerous occasions. Indeed, the preference for seeking out the nearest enemy and smiting him had been at the root of German strategy in World War I. The problem in the east was long-term, not susceptible to the quick solution, while the Wehrmacht could, conceivably, win the campaign in the west in a single day. And once it had done that, who could tell what might happen? Hitler's plan was to "strike in the West while holding in the

East" (*Im Westen schlagen, im Osten halten*), smash the Allied landing, then turn east with thirty to thirty-five divisions and reconquer the Wehrmacht's big loss in 1943–1944: Ukraine.[35] Indeed, this plan was the entire reason that he had decided to change the name of the German formations fighting on the southern wing to Army Group North Ukraine and Army Group South Ukraine. The names represented his pledge and plans for 1944–1945.

Two notions, therefore, dominated German thinking as the summer approached. First, the main Soviet offensive would strike south of the Pripet Marshes and target the operational sector of Army Group North Ukraine. Second, Germany could still win the war through a successful campaign in the west. These two ideas dictated the operational situation on the Eastern Front. It meant that the entire German operational reserve on the Eastern Front—no fewer than eighteen Panzer and *Panzergrenadier* divisions—was deployed to the south of the Pripet, to backstop the Germans defenders facing the expected Soviet offensive.[36] These divisions were not the product of new levies in men or a sudden rise in productive capacity. Rather, they came from Army Groups North and Center. The latter, especially, sent one division after the other to the south, contributions that included the entire LVI Panzer Corps. It departed Army Group Center just weeks before the start of the Soviet offensive.

Even more serious than the lack of an *operational* reserve was the fact that the Wehrmacht no longer had a *strategic* reserve in the east. There was no pool of fresh divisions on which the Germans could draw as the situation demanded. The army's strategic reserve was 1,400 miles away, fighting in France. Here were the ten mechanized divisions whose precise placement had generated so much controversy within the High Command, including the oversized and heavily reinforced divisions of the Waffen-SS. The west also soaked up some two dozen more solid infantry and *Fallschirmjäger* divisions. Even if the western army managed to win a rapid victory over the Anglo-Allied forces, however, the Reich still faced a "window of vulnerability" in the east.[37] Loading those divisions and shipping them clear across the European continent promised to be a chore for the already overloaded German rail net. Indeed, it was possible that the Soviets might win a signal victory long before help arrived.

The standard narrative of the Red Army's 1944 summer offensive stresses the success of Soviet deception (*maskirovka*) efforts.[38] Soviet skill at such battlefield-shaping activities has become proverbial within the historical literature. But hiding something as large as this grand offensive wasn't possible, now matter how careful or devious they were, or how many dummy tanks and trains they erected to fool enemy reconnaissance.[39] The Germans could clearly see men and materiel flowing away from Army Group North Ukraine's front toward Army Group Center. Indeed, intelligence reports from the latter's armies were filled with detailed information on the Soviet buildup. The four component formations of Army Group Center (3rd Panzer Army, 4th Army, 9th Army, and 2nd Army, moving north to south inside the Byelorussian balcony) all saw the same thing. In 2nd Army's sector, on the right of the bulge, the Soviets were clearly redeploying away from the army's right wing (where it joined Army Group North Ukraine) and toward the left (where it linked with 9th Army holding the front of the bulge). On the other side of the army group, the 3rd Panzer Army sector, reconnaissance could detect a massive Soviet buildup opposite the city of Vitebsk. The site of heavy fighting deep into the spring of 1944, Vitebsk was already encircled on three sides with a very narrow supply lifeline to the rest of Army Group Center. An orthodox solution would have been to abandon the city or to retreat at the first sign of Soviet attack; Hitler's was to declare it a *fester Platz*, to garrison it with no fewer than three German divisions, and to demand that they hold the place to the death. The same situation obtained along the front of the 9th Army, where two Soviet thrusts toward Bobruisk were brewing, and the 4th, still holding a wide, shallow bridgehead over the Dnepr anchored on Orsha and Mogilev. Here lay the main artery in this part of the Soviet Union, the Minsk-Smolensk Rollbahn, and 4th Army command became ever more convinced that the Soviets would use it as the main axis of their imminent offensive. As with Vitebsk, all three threatened cities—Bobruisk, Orsha, and Mogilev—became *feste Plätze*, each with a one-division garrison. By June, the so-called fortresses had tied up a total of six German divisions, a considerable number. Army Group Center contained only thirty-eight divisions in all. Hardest hit by these mandatory deployments was the 3rd Panzer Army, which lost three of its eleven divisions to the *fester Platz* at Vitebsk.[40] (See Map 4.1.)

Soviet *maskirovka*, therefore, had not necessarily masked the buildup for Operation Bagration. Plenty of observers noted it officially and unofficially. Unfortunately, the higher one moved up the chain of the German command, the more tenuous became the grasp on the realities of the front. Frontline divisions and corps reported what they saw, all dutifully recorded in the war diaries of the four German armies deployed in Byelorussia and then passed up to Field Marshal Busch, the

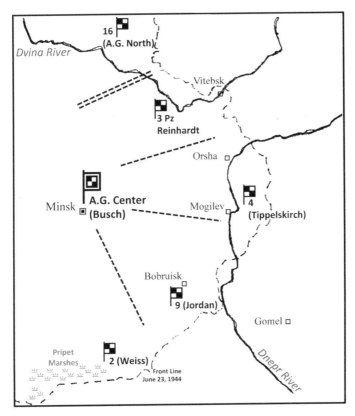

Map 4.1 Threadbare: German Defenses on the Central Front (June 1944)

army group commander. And here they stayed. Busch tried to fight the good fight at first. During a briefing at the Führer Headquarters at Rastenburg on May 20, he passed along the reports of Soviet activity to his front and requested permission to begin construction of fortified positions in the army group's rear. Perhaps Army Group Center might even carry out a planned withdrawal from its most exposed positions over the Dnepr (the sector of 4th Army) to disrupt the timetable of Soviet offensive plans. At the very least, a withdrawal to prepared positions back over the Dnepr would remove German frontline divisions from the killing zone of the Soviet artillery barrage. All of these prudent suggestions earned the field marshal a tirade from the Supreme Commander, however, with Hitler sneering that Busch must be "another one of those generals who always seemed to be looking over his shoulder."[41]

Busch was, if anything, a true believer in the Führer and the "historic mission" of National Socialism, and these mocking words must have cut him to the quick.[42] Four days after Hitler chewed him out, Busch issued orders to the four armies under his control "expressing the unmistakable will of the Führer that the Army Group maintain and hold its current positions on the eastern front under all circumstances."[43] The thing to do now, Busch declared to them, was to fortify the present positions, create a firm defensive *Schwerpunkt*, and fight it out on the front line, no matter what the Soviets threw at them. He even went so far as to discourage any more "defeatist"—that is to say, accurate—intelligence reports from observers at the front.[44] A certain resignation seemed to have set in, with Busch once expounding to Colonel Peter von der Groeben, his operations chief (Ia), on the difficulty of objecting to Hitler's orders. "Groeben, I am a soldier," Busch remarked. "I have learnt to obey."[45] Perhaps he was obeying against his better judgment—that certainly seems to be the case—but he obeyed.

Operation Bagration was about to begin. The Soviets had assembled their greatest concentration of offensive power yet. The force included four separate fronts (army groups), no fewer than 15 field armies (14 infantry armies and 1 tank army), 118 rifle divisions, and 43 tank divisions. Over 6,000 tanks, nearly 7,000 combat aircraft (5,683 aircraft from five air armies, along with 1,000 bombers from eight air corps of the Long Range Bomber Force), 24,000 guns and mortars lined up hub to hub, and 2,300 Katyusha multiple rocket-launchers stood ready to smash the threadbare German defenders in the Byelorussian balcony. All told, the Red Army had concentrated 1,254,000 men for the operation. Supplying this monstrous force was a fleet of no fewer than 70,000 trucks, many of them 2.5-ton Studebakers from the United States, part of the Lend-Lease Program.[46] In its way, Bagration rivaled the original German invasion of the Soviet Union, Operation Barbarossa. While fewer men were involved, the Soviets had managed to assemble more than twice as many tanks in Byelorussia as the Germans had possessed along the entire front in 1941. Since those dark days, the Red Army and Red Air Force had become a "militarized juggernaut."[47]

Meanwhile, on the German side of the line, things were falling apart. "The entire front was overtaxed; the reserves sat in a false position, and the army group was forbidden from carrying out any sort of mobile defense," wrote Dr. Hermann Gackenholz, the editor of Army Group Center's war diary.[48] Most divisions were at a fraction of their assigned strength, and the infantry in the front line was fighting from sketchy field fortifications, slit trenches, and a handful of bunkers. Behind the lines, Hitler's orders and Busch's obedience had halted the construction of any sort of fortified lines—the Bear Line along the Dnepr, or an intended line along the Berezina River farther to the rear.[49] There were supposedly 849,000 men in the army group, but that was total strength (*Iststärke*). The number included all sorts of personnel who did not fight: 103,000 Soviet "auxiliary volunteers" (*Hilfswillige*), for example, the 309th Field Training Division, the legion of bureaucrats and administrators of the new German empire in the east, the thousands of wounded in the hospitals, and more. Compared to this fictive strength, the *Tagestärke*—the number of men ready to fight on a given day—was a great deal lower, a mere 486,000 fighters, to be precise, or about 40 percent the size of the Soviet adversary they faced.[50] If we subtract the German 2nd Army—which was not a target of the initial Soviet assault, the number shrinks further, to 336,000 men, about a quarter the size of the Soviet force. One analysis of General Hans Jordan's 9th Army on the eve of the battle computes a density of just 143 German soldiers per kilometer of front or, put another way, "approximately 350 men in the way of each Soviet division" of 6,000 men.[51]

The manpower situation was horrible, but the equipment deficit was even worse. Even today, the numbers can be difficult to accept. Facing those 6,000 or so Soviet tanks were precisely 118 German Panzers, 56 of them belonging to the 20th Panzer Division, the lone Panzer division in Army Group Center, and the remaining 62 with the 4th Army. Assault guns (the *Sturmgeschütz*, or StuG) were present in slightly higher numbers—377 in all.[52] The turretless design and fixed main gun of the StuG rendered it unsuitable for any sort of mobile tank battle, however, and the fact that the Wehrmacht was pressing it into service as a surrogate tank was yet another sign of distress. Indeed, the designation "Panzer" had ceased to have much meaning by now. The XXXXI Panzer Corps (part of 9th Army) contained three straight-leg infantry divisions, and the 3rd Panzer Army had not a single tank to its name, just 76 StuGs. Things were no better in the air, where *Luftflotte* 6, the Luftwaffe formation assigned to Army Group Center, could field only a fraction of the strength of the Soviet air force, 61 fighter planes to 2,318, to give one example. But even if tanks and aircraft had been present in greater numbers, neither the army nor the Luftwaffe had enough fuel to keep them going. On the ground as well as in the air, demotorization (*Entmotorisierung*) was the order of the day, a sad state of affairs for the force that had pioneered mechanized combined-arms operations.[53]

Peering back in time, it is almost possible to drum up sympathy for those four German armies, outnumbered, demotorized, and forsaken by their high command. Sitting there in that lazy, vulnerable bulge east of Minsk, they were practically offering themselves up to destruction. One modern authority has declared Army Group Center in 1944 as "no longer capable of conducting operations," and it is difficult to argue with that judgment.[54] The greatest hammer in military history was about to come down, and the Wehrmacht seemed oblivious. Perhaps it was no longer completely cognizant of its surroundings, no longer fully compos mentis. Hitler was hapless as a supreme commander, but his planners and aides in the Supreme Headquarters in Rastenburg, as well as a sizable contingent of the field commanders, share the blame for this one. They had left the realm of reality and were now trapped in a fantasy world of their own preconceived notions. And, as always when military leadership goes astray, their men would pay the price.

Full-Spectrum Dominance

An operation the size of Bagration does not simply begin with a starter's gun, and, indeed, the precise date that the Soviet offensive opened can vary by the source. (See Map 4.2.) Most German sources identify June 22, 1944, and link the date explicitly to the third anniversary of Operation Barbarossa.[55] The leading western authority on the Red Army disagrees, however, in favor of a series of staggered dates.[56] First came a wave of partisan attacks in the German rear, beginning on the night of June 19–20. From a nuisance in the eastern campaign's opening phase, the *partisansky* had grown into a serious threat by now, with the Germans estimating the number of irregulars operating in the rear areas of Army Group Center at 143,000 men, encompassing 150 brigades and forty-nine independent battalions. These irregulars attacked all the usual targets: railroad junctions, bridges, repair sheds, map depots, communications facilities, and more. They carried out no fewer than 9,600 attacks with improvised explosive devices in that first night, cutting entire stretches of the rail line from the front to Minsk and points west and shutting down more than a thousand transportation nodes. They reinforced their success the next night with another 2,500 reported explosions. Most did fairly limited damage, and German repair crews soon arrived on the scene. But the engineers could not be everywhere at once, and supply traffic for Army Group Center shut down for more than 24 hours, a real operational achievement in the oft-debated history of partisan attacks.

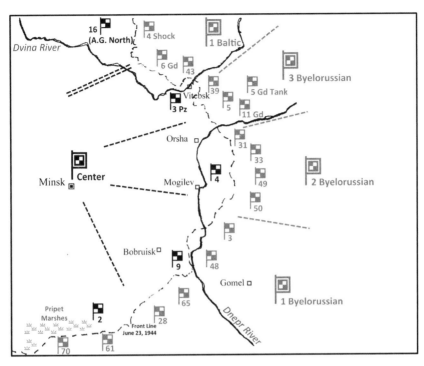

Map 4.2 The Avalanche: Operation Bagration (June 1944)

The second stage opened on the night of June 21–22, a skillfully synchronized combination of heavy bombing attacks against targets in the German rear, once again concentrating on vulnerable points in the communications and supply network, with attacks by Soviet reconnaissance battalions. Soviet commanders feared the very possibility that Busch had suggested to Hitler—a German pullback just before the start of the Soviet offensive—and feared that an artillery bombardment of the front line might land on empty trenches and represent a horrendous waste of ammunition. Aggressive probing attacks in battalion strength seemed to be an ideal solution. If the Germans had abandoned their positions, then that was all to the good and the main operation could commence. If reconnaissance discovered that the Germans were still in place, then Soviet artillery could open up and pulverize them. As it turned out, the initially tentative probes represented one of the most successful reconnaissance operations in history. Moving forward after the briefest of opening barrages—just sixteen minutes in the 1st Baltic Front sector, for example—they penetrated almost everywhere, fighting forward three miles deep into the German defensive zone. Fighting went on through the day, as bypassed German regiments in the front line realized what was taking place and attempted to restore communications to their flank or rear, or as local German reserves launched hasty counterattacks. As night fell, Soviet commanders inserted specially trained night-fighting squads to keep the pressure on and to "hold the Germans by the throat."[57] The Soviet insertion of these elite units, along with the severity of the fighting, seemed to German defenders to mark the start of a general offensive. Thus German sources, along with virtually all of the English-language histories constructed upon the German narrative, have traditionally identified June 22 as the start of Operation Bagration.

In fact, it was not until the early morning of June 23 that the offensive proper began, as the Soviets launched their main-force units into action. Even these many years later, summarizing an undertaking of such vast geographical size and scope challenges the limits of human understanding. On the surface, the operational matchups appeared to be fairly symmetrical. A simple listing of the formations involved yields the following:

Soviet		*German*
1st Baltic Front	v.	3rd Panzer Army
(General I. Kh. Bagramyan)		(General Georg-Hans Reinhardt)
3rd Byelorussian Front	v.	4th Army
(General I. D. Cherniakhovsky)		(General Kurt von Tippelskirch)
2nd Byelorussian Front	v.	9th Army
(General G. F. Zakharov)		(General Hans Jordan)
1st Byelorussian Front	v.	2nd Army
(General K. K. Rokossovsky)		(General Walter Weiss)

The reality was a great deal more complex, however. Reducing Bagration to a series of one-on-one encounters oversimplifies the situation and fails to do justice to the complexity of the Soviet plan. So vast was the operational conception that Stalin and the Stavka decided to employ two "coordinators," Marshals G. K. Zhukov and A. M. Vasilevsky, with the former responsible for the 1st and 2nd Byelorussian Fronts in the south, and the latter for the 3rd Byelorussian and 1st Baltic in the north.[58] The presence of coordinators bestowed a degree of fine-tuning on Soviet planning that had been absent in previous operations. Rather than a series of individual frontal blasts, Bagration was able to mass multiple fronts against specific key objectives. In the north, Bagramyan (1st Baltic Front) and Cherniakhovsky (3rd Byelorussian Front) would cooperate in a concentric attack upon German 3rd Panzer Army, for example, while Cherniakhovsky and Zakharov (2nd Byelorussian Front) did the same to German 4th Army. In the far south, meanwhile, perhaps the most gifted operator in the Soviet officer corps, General Rokossovsky, would have multiple missions.[59] First, he was to hold the German 2nd Army at bay with a pair of corps, then mass the right wing of his 1st Byelorussian Front for a blow against the German 9th Army, and finally prepare his left wing for a second-stage assault into eastern Galicia against Army Group North Ukraine (the Lvov-Sandomierz Operation, in Soviet records). It's not easy to be in multiple places at once, but Rokossovsky was going to try. Thus, a more accurate operational précis for Bagration looks closer to the following:

Soviet		*German*
1st Baltic Front		
and	v.	3rd Panzer Army
3rd Byelorussian Front (right wing)		
3rd Byelorussian Front (left wing)		
and	v.	4th Army
2nd Byelorussian Front		
1st Byelorussian Front (right wing)	v.	9th Army
1st Byelorussian Front (center)	v.	2nd Army
1st Byelorussian Front (left wing)	v.	Army Group North Ukraine (follow-on operation)

While the Red Army was doing it best to match individual commanders and formations with appropriate objectives, the Wehrmacht was moving in the opposite direction, becoming more and more faceless. All of the German armies in Army Group Center had become interchangeable by June 1944, filled with vastly overstretched infantry divisions, second-rate Luftwaffe field divisions, light security formations, and mediocre leadership. Along the combined front of 3rd Panzer Army, 4th Army, and 9th Army, the sectors targeted by the Soviet offensive, thirty-eight divisions of the Wehrmacht were spread out along 660 miles of front, averaging more than 17 miles apiece. Those extended frontages were bad enough, but making matters worse was an operational reserve that hovered around zero. Jordan's 9th Army, for example, had a single division (the 707th Security Division) in its reserve. The 3rd Panzer Army, likewise, could call upon a single division (the 95th Infantry). Tippelskirch's 4th Army had nothing at all, and Weiss's 2nd Army (guarding the southern face of the Pripet Marshes) possessed only the 4th Cavalry Brigade and the Hungarian 1st Cavalry Division. The reserve of Army Group Center, responsible for covering this entire vast area, consisted of the solitary 20th Panzer Division, still refitting after heavy losses in the previous spring; yet another lone infantry division, the 14th; and the 60th *Panzergrenadier* Division *Feldherrnhalle*, still in the process of being formed when the Soviets launched their offensive.[60] Busch parceled out these units as reasonably as he could: deploying the 20th Panzer Division behind Bobruisk in the 9th Army sector and assigning the 14th Infantry Division and the unready 60th *Panzergrenadier* to the 4th Army in its exposed position across the Dnepr, but his reserve component was so small that it barely mattered.

As the four attacking fronts launched the assault, individual Soviet commanders had to make a decision: to employ the immense artillery bombardment they had planned and risk slowing the progress already being made, or to dispense with the bombardment and thereby risk running into untouched German defenses. The decision varied by sector. General Bagramyan, for example, split the difference by bombarding only where the reconnaissance probes had encountered resistance and canceling it elsewhere—a touch of finesse for a military establishment we still tend to caricature as relying on brute force alone. Whether the commanders employed their artillery or not, Soviet ground-attack aircraft flew in support in unprecedented numbers. Hundreds of Shturmovik ground-assault aircraft, heavily armored machines that could sustain shocking amounts of damage and still stay in the air, flew thousands of sorties in those opening days.[61] So difficult was the Shturmovik to bring down that helpless German infantry sitting under the rain of bombs cursed it as the "cement bomber" (*Zementbomber*) or the "flying tank" (*fliegender Panzer*). The ungainly craft smashed German frontline positions, bunkers, and strongpoints and also ranged far into the rear against headquarters, communications, and supply installations. Their attacks were practically unopposed. German *Flak* was meager and German aircraft altogether absent from the sky over most of the front.

The Death of the 3rd Panzer Army

The result was a breakthrough of epic proportions, virtually everywhere, as the frontline German defenses collapsed on the first day and Army Group Center tumbled down like a house of cards. (See Map 4.3.) Moving around the bulge from the north, the narrative for each of the three German armies was nearly identical. In the sector of 3rd Panzer Army, initial Soviet attacks concentrated on the small but sharp German salient around the city of Vitebsk, a *fester Platz* held by the four divisions of the LIII Corps under General Friedrich Gollwitzer.[62] Already on June 22, aggressive Soviet reconnaissance detachments penetrated German defenses northwest and southeast of Vitebsk. The next day, June 23, saw Soviet artillery and aircraft mercilessly pound the city, as well as those sectors of the German front that were still intact. The artillery bombardment was the greatest of the Russo-German war: over two hours of steady drumfire by thousands of guns of all calibers, with 200 gun tubes and rocket launchers deployed per kilometer. The big guns roared with complete impunity, absent any fear of German counterbattery fire or air attack, a trauma that simply broke German resistance and morale. Once the bombardment lifted, the Red Army went over to the attack. Wisely avoiding a frontal attack on Vitebsk, the assault formations of the 6th Guards and 43rd Armies (from 1st Baltic Front) and 39th and 5th Armies (from 3rd Byelorussian) smashed in the flanks on either side of the city. The initial blows fell on German IX Corps on the left and VI Corps on the right, inflicting massive casualties. On some portions of the front, the Germans attempted a hasty retreat, but in others the weight and skill of the Soviet attack simply crushed them. By June 24, the front had collapsed and the Soviets had encircled Vitebsk, trapping LIII Corps and a major portion of 3rd Panzer Army's fighting strength—the 246th Infantry, 4th Luftwaffe, 6th Luftwaffe, and 206th Infantry Divisions. With LIII Corps cut off and erased from the order of battle, a yawning gap existed in the very center of 3rd Panzer Amy's line—nearly 25 miles wide and getting wider by the hour—between IX Corps in the northwest and VI Corps in the southeast. Soviet Mobile Groups and Cavalry Mechanized Groups were now motoring in the clear inside the gap, driving at speed to the south and southwest toward Minsk. German hopes of closing the gap were nil, since there was no reserve. By day two of Operation Bagration, the Soviet offensive had destroyed 3rd Panzer Army, crumpling it like a paper bag, an unprecedented event on the Eastern Front.

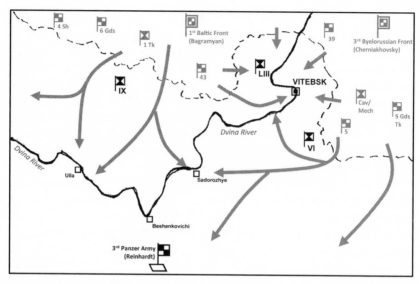

Map 4.3 The Vitebsk Stronghold (June 1944)

While the Soviets were hard at work closing the ring around Vitebsk, the German command was talking itself to death. With Soviet armor lapping around both his flanks, the commandant of *fester Platz* Vitebsk, General Gollwitzer, phoned his 3rd Panzer Army commander, General Reinhardt, for permission to pull back and at least attempt to escape destruction. Just a few months previously, Reinhardt had successfully defended the city from Soviet attack in the spring, and the German press had fêted him as the "Victor of Vitebsk."[63] Now, just two days into the Soviet offensive, he could see that situation was already hopeless. He agreed to Gollwitzer's request and soon was on the phone with Field Marshal Busch, pleading for approval to retreat from Vitebsk. The army chief of staff, General Kurt Zeitzler, had just arrived to confer with Busch, having flown to Minsk in the early morning. Busch told him the startling news that the Soviet attack had shattered 3rd Panzer Army and that LIII Corps wanted permission to retreat from Vitebsk. Zeitzler flew back to the Obersalzberg—a very busy day!—to plead the case with Hitler directly.

Of course, Hitler refused. Vitebsk was a *fester Platz*, and that was that. As they argued, the Soviet spearheads on both sides of Vitebsk were drawing closer and closer to cutting the last remaining road out of the city. Zeitzler telephoned General Reinhardt in Hitler's presence, and the general confirmed that it was only a matter of minutes until the Soviets shut the door and condemned the four divisions of LIII Corps to a grisly end. The arguments droned on, with both sides reciting lines that must have seemed very familiar to them by now—until another message came in from Reinhardt. The Soviets had encircled Vitebsk. Only now, far too late in the day, did Hitler agree to a withdrawal from Vitebsk. Even now, however, he held firm to his original conception, approving only a partial retreat. One division, the 206th Infantry under General Alfons Hitter, was to hold the city while the mass of LIII Corps broke out to the west.[64]

Hitler's belated order of June 24—with some divisions retreating while the 206th Division carried out a complicated relief in place along the rest of the encircled front—would have been difficult enough during a peacetime exercise. Under the bombs and the shells and the confusion, however, the directive simply generated chaos. The absurdity of the situation peaked with Hitler phoning Reinhardt and ordering him in all seriousness to parachute a staff officer of 3rd Panzer Army into Vitebsk solely for the purpose of handing the fortress commandant, General Gollwitzer, written orders to hold the *fester Platz*. Reinhardt refused outright to force "a general staff officer or any other soldier of the 3rd Panzer Army" to jump into Vitebsk.[65] Only one man was suitable for the mission—Reinhardt himself—and he was ready to go if the Führer required it. The army commander's readiness to kill himself apparently satisfied the Führer and he rescinded his order, but only after keeping Reinhardt waiting on the phone for what must have been ten very long minutes.

Perhaps Hitler was right to suspect that the army wasn't carrying out his orders, however. General Gollwitzer, the corps commander in Vitebsk, had never trusted the *fester Platz* concept in the first place. He was the latest in a line of veteran, hard-headed German field commanders to scoff at the notion. Hitler's order reached him on June 25: "The 206th Division will hold Vitebsk until relieved."[66] But Gollwitzer wasn't buying any of it: the ability of 206th Division to hold the town alone, the ability of the rest of the Corps to break out without the combat power of the 206th, and especially the promise of any impending relief. He had inquired into this very subject back in April, when Busch appointed him commandant of Vitebsk, and Busch had made it quite clear to him back then that no reserves would be at hand. Already Gollwitzer could see the signs of panic inside Vitebsk. The commander of the 6th Luftwaffe Division, for example, General Walter Peschl, was slumped in his command post—Gollwitzer thought it might be the first stage of a nervous collapse—and there was no telling what might happen if the mood started to filter down to the ranks.[67]

Gollwitzer decided to disobey the order: all four divisions would break out. He no doubt knew that the situation was hopeless, and, indeed, the possibility of a successful breakout was receding by the hour. Soviet forces were fighting their way into Vitebsk amid bitter street fighting, and the ceaseless bombardment was taking its toll. Moreover, heavy Soviet mechanized forces had already driven 50 miles beyond Vitebsk, and a foot-mobile formation like LIII Corps was going to have a hard time outracing Soviet tanks. At any rate, on June 26 at 5:00 A.M., LIII Corps launched a breakout attempt in the general direction of Ostrovno, some 35 miles southwest of Vitebsk. Abandoning virtually all their equipment, the remnants of four heavily blooded divisions began to filter out of the burning city. The initial thrust seemed to surprise the Soviets, who had not yet drawn the ring tight on this side of Vitebsk. The region immediately southwest of the city was wooded and offered a modicum of cover. But once the sun came up, the escapees had to break cover—and the slaughter began. Packets of desperate German soldiers raced across fields and hills, recoiled from Soviet opposition, then doubled back to try again by a different route. Tiny but desperate battles raged for possession of crossroads and lake defiles, copses, and tiny villages.

German command and control broke down within minutes of departing Vitebsk. Gollwitzer had no contact with his subordinate divisions, and they, in turn, had lost their regiments and battalions. Soviet airpower ruled the skies, transforming road movement into a nightmare for the Germans, and Soviet ground formations were able to block the most obvious cross-country routes and river crossings. "Like hares before the hunt we raced across the open field, bullets chirping around us," one *Landser* reported.[68] By the end of June 26, some German soldiers were 10 miles southwest of Vitebsk, but they were going no farther, and Ostrovno and safety were nothing but distant mirages. Soviet attacks had pinned most of the escaping Germans into a tiny perimeter, German ammunition was running low, and Soviet artillery and tank fire were raking every square inch of the position. At 3:45 A.M. on June 27, LIII Corps radioed in that "breakthrough by night under personal leadership of the commanding general has started favorably." This was the last message from LIII Corps.[69] Some 10,000 men went into Soviet captivity, all that was left of the corps's original 28,000. The prisoners included Gollwitzer, picked up at the head of a small group of a few hundred men. Like so many of his officer confrères, he would remain a Soviet prisoner until 1955. The fighting in Vitebsk itself ended on June 29, with the Soviets reporting 5,000 German corpses in the city.

The 3rd Panzer Army had fallen apart. Of its three original corps, VI Corps on the right had been pushed so far to the south under relentless Soviet pressure that it had come under the command of the neighboring 4th Army, and LIII Corps in the center had vanished. General Reinhardt now commanded just a single component formation, the IX Corps. Containing two divisions at the start of the Soviet offensive, the 252nd and a division-sized conglomerate (designated Corps Group D), the corps was now swollen with the flotsam and jetsam of the army's rear area—security formations, railroad personnel, students from the Artillery Weapons School, as well as remnants of units already shattered by the fighting. Indeed, it was as much a refugee camp as a field army. The corps commander, General Rolf Wuthmann, had requested permission to retreat behind the Ulla River early on in the fighting. Busch at first denied the request, then hemmed and hawed, then gave his approval. By now, the Soviets were breathing down IX Corps's neck, and the result was not so much a retreat as a "wild flight" back to the Ulla.[70] By the time 252nd Division got to the river, Soviet air attacks had destroyed all the bridges, and not for the first or last time in this war German troops had to strip down and swim across a river under enemy fire, fighting neither for glory nor for strategic position but simply for survival. Large numbers drowned, and many of the division's survivors were now barefoot. It had come to this.

Kesselschlacht: Destruction of 4th Army

The 4th Army (under General Kurt von Tippelskirch) began Operation Bagration in an impossible tactical position.[71] It formed the tip of the Byelorussian Salient, bulging out to the east. With much of the army packed into a vulnerable bridgehead over the Dnepr River, even a local retreat had the potential to degenerate into a panicked rush for a small number of bridges. The 4th Army's initial strength wasn't much higher than its ill-fated neighbor to the north, the 3rd Panzer Army. Three corps stood on the line (XXVII, XXXIX Panzer, and XII, moving north to south), containing nine divisions of varying quality, almost all infantry. Reserves were minimal, consisting of little more than the 14th Infantry Division and the not-yet-ready 60th *Pan-*

zergrenadier Division *Feldherrnhalle.* Like the rest of Army Group Center, 4th Army had no Panzer component. The divisions were holding impossibly overstretched sectors, and once again the High Command had decided to bestow on certain cities the designation of *fester Platz*—in this case Orsha on the army's left wing and Mogilev in the center. Each city received a garrison of one division—78th Assault Division for Orsha and elements of the 31st Infantry Division for Mogilev—as well as the familiar orders to hold out to the last man and to die in the ruins of the city if need be.

Unfortunately, this utterly threadbare army happened to be sitting on some valuable real estate. First, it was defending along the most important road in the Soviet Union: the Moscow–Smolensk–Minsk Highway. Control of this main artery (the *Rollbahn,* the Germans called it) was crucial to supplying military operations in either direction. Much of the fighting during the first six months of Operation Barbarossa had taken place along this single artery, in fact. Where once the Wehrmacht had seen the Rollbahn as the path to Moscow, however, the Red Army now viewed it as crucial to an eventual drive on Minsk. Second, 4th Army sat astride an important land bridge, the 50-mile gap between the Dvina and Dnepr Rivers. Orsha on the Dnepr was particularly important in this context as the key to securing the land bridge. Control of the land bridge would let the Soviets feed men, equipment, and supplies forward for follow-on offensives without having to rely upon bridge traffic over the two major rivers. For both of these reasons, 4th Army was a principal target of Operation Bagration.

The Soviet assault opened on June 23, with elements of the 3rd Byelorussian and 2nd Byelorussian Fronts attacking simultaneously. The artillery kicked things off with a monstrous two-hour avalanche of fire that vaporized the frontline trenches and the men inside them, flattened bunkers, and detonated ammunition dumps. Even veterans of the Eastern Front would later say that they had never seen anything like it in terms of intensity or accuracy. The fire lifted and the rifle divisions attacked—elements of the 3rd Byelorussian Front on the right and the 2nd Byelorussian Front on the left. The former, under General Cherniakhovsky, was landing the main blow, hurling three complete armies (the 5th, 11th Guards, and 31st)—twenty-five rifle divisions and eleven tank brigades in all—against the XXVII Corps sector just north of Orsha, sitting on the left wing of 4th Army. The assault penetrated the first line of the corps defenses almost immediately, and that evening the Germans had to bring 14th Division up from the reserve into the line. The Soviets responded the next day by inserting their tank brigades en masse, and within hours the tactical penetration had widened into an operational breakthrough. By June 25, Soviet tanks had broken into open space and were pouring west. The 4th Army had lost contact with 3rd Panzer Army to the left, the gap widening from 25 to 50 miles by the second day, and Soviet armor now had a clear shot into 4th Army's rear.

To the south, 2nd Byelorussian Front, under the rookie commander Zakharov, was the weakest of the four Soviet fronts. Zakharov's task was a secondary one: to attack the Dnepr River bridgehead frontally and to pin 4th Army in place near Mogilev. Success would prevent 4th Army from redeploying or responding quickly enough to the massive breakthrough on its left. But even in this sector, defended by German XXXIX Panzer Corps (four weak infantry divisions and yet another so-called Panzer formation without tanks), the combination of a formidable opening bombardment and a robust assault by two armies, the 49th and 50th (sixteen rifle divisions and two tank brigades), was more than the German defenses could handle. By noon, the initial assault had smashed through two defensive positions of the German 337th Division. With the line in danger of cracking open altogether, corps command inserted the only reserve it had, the 60th *Panzergrenadier* Division *Feldherrnhalle*. With the division still in the process of being equipped and much of the manpower consisting of untrained replacements, it fought about as well as one could expect—that is to say, not well. Indeed, it broke in the course of a single day's fighting on June 24 and embarked on a panicked flight to the rear, toward Minsk.[72]

With 4th Army's left wing broken at Orsha, its center collapsing at Mogilev, and contact lost with the neighboring 9th Army to the south, army commander Tippelskirch requested permission on June 25 to withdraw back across the Dnepr. Whether he could save 4th Army was open to question, but a retreat would at least break contact temporarily and ease the worst of the murderous Soviet pressure to his front. He certainly had to do something, however. The Soviets had broken through north of Mogilev and enemy tanks were pouring toward the Dnepr. When permission was not forthcoming, Tippelskirch decided on his own accord to order a general retreat not to the Dnepr but to the Dnepr Barrier (*Dnepr-Schutzstellung*), a fortified line in front of the river. Impossible to hold as a permanent position, it would at least give the frontline troops a short breather. But even this partial solution drew the wrath of his army group commander: "You are violating Hitler's orders," Busch hissed.[73] He ordered Tippelskirch to return the troops to the original front line and ended by saying: "Report back when you're finished."[74]

The only trouble was that Busch's order was impossible. The front line as originally constituted hardly existed. That was precisely why Tippelskirch had ordered the retreat in the first place. The German official history excoriates Busch for his "losing touch with reality" here, no doubt out of his fondness for Hitler, and the claim seems fair:

> The only possible result of an order of this kind, in view of the chaotic situation and the collapsing front, would have been an indescribable mess. The German divisions had just begun a retreat, pursued by an onrushing enemy, who at many places had already overtaken them. And now they were supposed to stop their movement in the dead of night, turn around, and launch an attack in the opposite direction! The old positions had already fallen into Soviet hands.[75]

Stymied when he acted openly, Tippelskirch turned to subterfuge. He drew up new operational orders halting the retreat while specifying that "the troops are to stand fast on all sectors of the front that have not been attacked, until they are attacked by superior enemy forces and forced back."[76] As formulated, the working order gave his corps commanders a back door to continue their retreat to and over the Dnepr.[77] All of them were under attack by "superior enemy forces." Issuing orders had become a kind of a nod-and-wink game: enough "stand fast" rhetoric to satisfy the High Command, with enough flexibility to continue to operate at the front. Clear language, a firm purpose, saying what you mean, and meaning what you say: these are the requisites of military command—but none still had a place in the Wehrmacht.

Tippelskirch's small victory here could do little to stanch the bleeding. What began as a retreat soon turned into an ordeal. As his army pulled slowly back toward the river, the sandy trails and tracks that passed for roads in this part of Byelorussia were soon choked with men, equipment, and horses. Progress was excruciatingly slow, not least because the Germans were not alone in the rush to the Dnepr. Soviet formations were also on the march—often on the same roads—and the fighting was bitter and incessant. Soviet tanks and infantry repeatedly sliced up German march columns or overran rear guards; the Germans had to deploy from road column into fighting formation over and over again. Units became intermingled on the march, and there was not a single German division left fighting as an intact unit. Communications from army to corps and corps to divisions broke down early. Worst of all, as the weary columns stumbled toward the Dnepr, they learned to their dismay that Soviet spearheads had reached the river the same time, were already crossing, and were heading west in a hurry. There would be no respite, no halt at the Dnepr—the fondest hope of every soldier who has ever crossed a river during a hard retreat. If they were going to survive, they had to keep going, over the Dnepr and beyond.

On June 26, with 3rd Panzer Army shattered and 4th Army barely breathing, Field Marshal Busch flew to Berchtesgaden to report to Hitler. If any field commander in the Wehrmacht had struck a bargain with the Führer, it was Busch. He was not an incompetent commander, but he had given orders that he knew were objectively incorrect and that withheld permissions for courses of action he knew were right. He had done what Hitler told him to do, no matter how inane. He had tied up division after division in the defense of fantasy fortresses. He had ordered half-strength infantry divisions to ward off massed tank attacks. He had listened to dying men begging for permission to retreat and told them to stay where they were and die. He had run Army Group Center straight into the ground, and he had done so in Hitler's name. Perhaps he believed that obedience absolved him of another responsibility: the lives of the men under his charge.

Now it was time to survey the wreckage and figure out what to do next. Busch doesn't appear to have sugarcoated or deceived Hitler as to the depth of the disaster; indeed, the collapse was so catastrophic that he had no option but to own it. The conference was a typical one by this point in the war. The participants wasted far too much time discussing Hitler's obsession, which was the only operational detail he seemed to care about: the strongholds of Orsha and Mogilev. Hitler still wanted them held—a fantastic notion by now—with German troops retreating to the Dnepr and with the Soviets already across the river. In fact, both were about to fall to the Soviets, Orsha on June 26 and Mogilev (with 31st Division) the next day. But Busch did get the main point across. Both of 4th Army's flanks had been caved in, Soviet armored spearheads had passed far to the west, deep into the army's rear, and the danger of encirclement was real. Hitler burned divisions like matchsticks—losing them never phased him in the slightest—but the encirclement of an entire army reeked too much of the debacle at Stalingrad. He now gave Busch permission to pull 4th Army back behind the Berezina River, provided that the retreat took place "in stages."[78] The town of Berezino, site of the principal bridge over the river, lay 110 miles to the southwest of Orsha and 60 miles to the west of Mogilev. Minsk lay another 60 miles beyond. Whether the battered remnants of 4th Army would make it that far was an open question.

And so 4th Army began its last and most disastrous anabasis: the long march to the Berezina River and thence to Minsk. No one will ever write its epic, nor should they. Indeed, it was a tawdry spectacle of human suffering, an army far away from home falling apart. As the *Landers* trudged along on foot through the dark forests and poorly mapped bogs of Byelorussia, Soviet tank columns motored all around them, sometimes slashing directly through the march columns, swooping in and out at will, shooting up German transport and picking off stragglers. Road movement along the Berezino-Minsk Road was nearly impossible by day, due to the omnipresent Soviet Air Force, and it was even more dangerous at night. The partisans were everywhere: bands of men and women who traveled light, who knew every inch of the landscape—the shortcuts, ambushes, and cul-de-sacs—and who had sworn death to the invader—although they often seemed to enjoy a bit of grisly sport with their German captives before dispatching them. One day on this death march was much like the next: blasting through Soviet roadblocks, leaving a rear guard, and moving forward a short bound, then having to stop to do the same thing over and over again, losing kinetic energy and men the whole way. One source describes the march to Berezino as "no longer a retirement, not an orderly withdrawal, rather a mass of men hysterically fighting their way back through an extended area of forests and swamps, crisscrossed by many rivers and streams whose crossings had already been destroyed, over mostly poor roads, in tremendous heat, without adequate provisions, and threatened from all sides."[79] That just about covers it.

The main body of 4th Army began arriving at the town of Berezino on June 30. Here they finally got one piece of good news: German troops—a shaky amalgam of shattered units and rear area personnel—were holding a small bridgehead over the river. The town stands a little more than 30 miles downstream of Borisov, the site of Napoléon's crossing point in November 1812, the battle in which Marshal Ney handled the rear guard of the Grande Armée so effectively that the emperor dubbed him "the bravest of the brave."[80] Indeed, not all that much had changed between 1812 and 1944. Armies still invaded Russia at their peril, getting out of the country was more dangerous than getting in, and a great army trying to cross a river over a single bridge is an automatic recipe for congestion and chaos. The ragged columns converged on the spot from three general directions—XXVII Corps from Orsha in the northeast, XXXIX Panzer Corps from Mogilev in the east, and XII Corps from Rogachev in the southeast. As the vehicles, horses, and tens of thousands of men from thirteen intermingled divisions jostled toward the bridge, the situation threatened to descend into utter chaos. The crossing point was under constant fire from Soviet artillery, and the sudden appearance overhead of Soviet aircraft, bombing and strafing with impunity, led to outbreaks of panic within the crowd milling below that were not easy to quell. As one survivor remembered it:

> No one was safe from the Russian aircraft. We were moving toward the Berezina bridge on the Rollbahn. Every now and then the planes appeared over the Rollbahn and worked over the thickly packed columns.
>
> We moved about three kilometers farther until we were just short of the Berezina Bridge at Berezino. Here the whole thing stopped. A mass of vehicles of all sorts, horse-drawn and motorized, cannons, howitzers, supply trucks, assault guns, Panzers, light and heavy flak, stretching our as far as the eye could see, column upon column on the Rollbahn before the bridge—behind one another, beside one another, left and right of the Rollbahn up to 100 meters out. Everyone was trying to get to the crossing. If only we could get to the other side of the river! We just had to get out of this dangerous spot. The later it got, the more dangerous it became. Get across! Safe and Sound! . . . And now our unfriendly comrades are back in the air—about twenty of them! Shooting up vehicle after vehicle! . . . We couldn't understand how we escaped without being hit. Every minute seemed like an eternity. The Red Air Force just kept unloading.[81]

Indeed, it wasn't long before a direct hit from a Soviet bomber destroyed the bridge. Pioneers worked feverishly under fire to repair it and also built a pair of inadequate temporary bridges, while the 110th Division had constructed its own bridge eight miles to the north near the village of Zhukovets. Yet, even a dozen bridges probably wouldn't have sufficed to untangle the traffic jam here and get things moving with more dispatch.

The 4th Army got across the river by July 2 after three days of hell—only to find itself once more at a decision point. The river offered no cover: no positions, no bunkers, not even a trench system. The exhausted men couldn't stay there, and it was time to restart their long march, this time toward Minsk. Soviet mechanized and tank forces had already crossed the river to the north and south of Berezino, however. Their eyes were on a bigger prize: not a single field army, but all of

Army Group Center. The Soviets, too, were heading ultimately toward Minsk, and at a much faster pace. Thus, as 4th Army shook itself back out into some sort of rough march order and began the weary slog to Minsk, they had Soviet forces everywhere: in front of them, blocking the roads; behind them, nipping at their heels and overrunning the rear guards; on both vulnerable flanks, requiring the detachment of men to march security duties; and finally and most decisively, in the air. In operational terms, the Germans had the 3rd Byelorussian Front to their north (31st Army) and 2nd Byelorussian Front to their south (33rd, 49th, and 50th Armies). German 4th Army was already encircled—a "wandering *Kessel*," to be sure, still on the move generally westward—but a *Kessel* all the same. They even had Soviets *among* them. According to numerous reports from within the ranks, spies dressed in the uniforms of captured German officers were providing false directions and bogus information to the marching columns.[82] By July 4, Soviet attacks had split the wandering *Kessel* into three parts: a westerly one at Gatovo, with elements of the 110th Division; a second at Dubniki, with the remnants of three divisions, less that 10 miles east of Minsk; and a third, larger one near Pekalin, about 15 miles farther out, that held at least six divisions.[83] That day, dire news began to filter into the pocket that the ostensible destination of 4th Army (Minsk) had fallen to the Soviets. The 4th Army's chances of reaching Minsk had never been high, but now the retreat had lost whatever purpose it once had.

Once again, 4th Army stood at a decision point. On July 5, one of the most depressing war councils in the long history of the German army took place inside the Pekalin Pocket. The corps commanders of 4th Army—General Paul Völckers for XXVII Corps, General Vincenz Müller for the XII—summoned all the surviving generals to a conference in order to review their shrinking options.[84] The commander of 4th Army's remaining corps (XXXIX Panzer), General Robert Martinek, was already dead, killed near Mogilev along with his successor, General Otto Schünemann, and the corps chief of staff.[85] Everyone present agreed that organized resistance had become impossible. The men were exhausted, supplies were running low, and the trucks and tanks were so short of fuel that many commanders had already issued orders to destroy them. Soviet formations were ranging far to the west of Minsk, toward Molodeczno northwest of the city and even southwest toward Baranovichi, more than 100 miles from where they were standing. At first, they decided to form the mass of men in this tiny pocket, just seven miles long by three miles wide, into two rough and

ready "corps," one under Völckers and one under Müller, still bearing the designations XXVII and XII Corps, respectively. Völckers
would lead XXVII Corps to the west, bypassing Minsk to the south,
while Müller and XII Corps would pass to the north of the great city.
Reorganizing the chaotic horde of men milling around would require
time, however, and Soviet fire was raking every inch of the pocket. The
council eventually settled on a backup plan: allow individual divisions
to break out on their own and hope for the best. The decision wasn't
so much a plan as a nonplan—but there was really nothing to be done
at this point.

The breakout began at 10:30 P.M. on July 5 and met with initial
success.[86] They always did, since maintaining a 360-degree watch was
nearly impossible for formations holding an encirclement. Hope soared
for a few hours, then collapsed the next morning. Soviet tanks seemed
to be everywhere, partisans sniped from every suitable position, and
German columns became disoriented on the swampy, forested, and
largely roadless terrain. Over the next three days, the Soviets relentlessly flushed out and rounded up their quarry, capturing both Völckers and Müller along with some 50,000 men—all that was left of 4th
Army. Regular Red Army formations had problems of their own operating in this vast wilderness, however, and the confusion on both sides
was boundless. Fighting would continue for a week to liquidate German survivors in the Byelorussian swamps, and the partisans played an
increasingly larger operational role befitting their knowledge of local
conditions.

Overall, just enough friction crept into the Soviet pursuit to allow
small groups of German soldiers to find cover here and there during
the day, to march at night, and to repeat the process over the next days
and weeks. Miraculously, some managed to evade their pursuers and
made it back to the safety of German lines. These were the legendary
Rückkämpfer, the men who "fought their way back."[87] Some eventually
traveled 250 miles on foot and managed to get back to German territory in East Prussia, and they were still checking in months later—
more than 800 officers and men between August and October, for
example. Soviet peasants often took pity on these ragged scarecrows,
feeding, clothing, and nursing them back to health. Each *Rückkämpfer*
had an epic tale to tell, and their legend played an important role in
sustaining troops of the Wehrmacht facing similar dire straits in the
future. But these rare triumphs of endurance can do nothing to obscure the horrible truth: in a bit over two weeks of fighting, 4th Army
had been reduced from over 100,000 men on June 23 to destruction on

July 8. Historians use the term "battle of annihilation" so often that it has lost whatever meaning or utility it might once have had, and in fact they often use the phrase to mean any impressive or decisive victory.[88] What happened to the German 4th Army in the midst of that steaming, swampy triangle between Orsha, Rogachev, and Minsk was the real thing, however: from being to nothingness.

Blasted: Destruction of 9th Army at Bobruisk

The Soviet offensive against the German 9th Army, defending the southern curve of the Byelorussian Salient, did not open until June 24, a day later than the action to the north.[89] Here all the usual German deficiencies—insufficient manpower, understrength and overstretched divisions, inadequate reserves—were present in spades. The distinguishing characteristic of this sector of Operation Bagration was the commander of the 1st Byelorussian Front tasked with the assault: General Rokossovsky. Only recently is this officer gaining the recognition he deserves as one of Stalin's most gifted and energetic commanders—brilliant in his operational conceptions and ruthlessly determined in executing them.[90] He was also one of those paradoxical figures whom the regime tormented and who wound up serving it faithfully. Originally a cavalry officer, he became one of the military progressives during the interwar era supporting mechanization of the Red Army. Like so many Soviet military reformers in the 1930s, he fell afoul of Stalin. Arrested during Stalin's purges on specious charges of sabotage and treason, Rokossovsky spent two and a half years in prison near Leningrad from August 1937 to March 1940. His interrogators beat him (knocking out nine of his teeth), tortured him (ripping off his fingernails, smashing his toes with hammers), and, on two occasions, stood him up before mock firing squads. For the rest of life, he kept a pistol handy. They wouldn't take him alive a second time (a promise he once swore to his daughter). But perhaps the paradox was more apparent than real. The only realistic alternative to serving Stalin was submitting to Hitler, and given Nazi racial policies—as well as the horrible depredations the Wehrmacht visited upon the Soviet Union—such a course was unthinkable.

Rokossovsky was released from Stalin's hell suddenly and without explanation or apology in March 1940. With the rapidly expanding Red Army in desperate need of experienced officers, he rose rapidly from one command to the next, and he saw action on numerous fronts.

He led V Cavalry Corps during the occupation of Bessarabia, began the war with Germany as commander of IX Mechanized Corps on the southern sector of the front, and commanded an ad hoc mechanized formation (Group Yartsevo) that successfully blunted the German drive east of Smolensk. Stalin gave him command of 16th Army during the decisive fighting in front of Moscow in late 1941, then the Bryansk Front in the summer of 1942. In November, he commanded Don Front—the northern wing of the epic pincer at Stalingrad during the Soviet counteroffensive. He then commanded Central Front at Kursk in 1943, facing down the Germans' own pincer coming down from the north (consisting of General Walter Model's 9th Army) and stopping it dead in its tracks. Even in the early years of the war, at a time that the world seemed in awe of the German blitzkrieg, he seemed relatively unimpressed, reminding his staff that "the German army is a machine, and a machine can be broken."

But now, in 1944, Rokossovsky's 1st Byelorussian Front had become one of the key players in Operation Bagration. His mission was to smash German 9th Army in front of him, then lunge as rapidly as possible for Minsk. During the planning process, Rokossovsky separated himself from his peers by being one of the few senior officers who dared to challenge Stalin. The original Stavka directives had 1st Byelorussian Front carrying out a single great thrust toward Bobruisk from the east. The terrain in the area was a morass of bogs, swamps, and lakes—with the Drut River running directly across Rokossovsky's line of advance—and the movement of mechanized formations and tanks would be difficult at best. For these very reasons, operational simplicity seemed to be the key to success: a single thrust and a frontal assault with massive force. Rokossovsky rejected the original plan, arguing that the Germans would be expecting it. He countered with a plan of his own: a double envelopment, coming up on Bobruisk not only from the east but also from the south.

A scene of high drama followed—one with ominous undertones of personal danger for Rokossovsky. Stalin had grown increasingly suspicious of complicated operational plans during the course of the war, and he told Rokossovsky to reconsider, sending him into the next room to "think it over." Rokossovsky did so, yet he came back and presented the same plan for dual thrusts. Stalin sent him away a second time—this time with two members of the State Defense Committee, G. M. Malenkov and V. I. Molotov. They must have thought Rokossovsky had taken leave of his senses. "Do you know who you are arguing with?" they asked him. Rokossovsky stuck to his guns for a third time, and now even Stalin seemed impressed: "The front commander's insistence proves that the offensive has been fully thought out," he declared, pronouncing Rokossovsky's assurances "a reliable guarantee of success."[91] All Rokossovsky had to do now was succeed, and he knew the price of failure better than anyone in the room.

Rokossovsky's planning for the attack on Bobruisk was meticulous in the all the usual areas—fire, movement, supply—but creative in many more. If Soviet military operations still had one persistent problem in 1944, it was a refusal to consider the importance of terrain obstructions. Perhaps it was a cultural problem. In the Stalinist Soviet system, shock work overcame bottlenecks and blockages, and military commanders were expected to follow suit. The result had been bloody defeats and towering friendly casualties, even in the midst of operations that ended in victory. The terrain south of Bobruisk, in particular, could well have been a death trap for any attacking force unfortunate enough to get stuck in it. Rokossovsky (working with Marshal Zhukov, the designated coordinator for Operation Bagration's southern sector) had to find a way for tanks and men to cross the marshes, bogs, and swamps. For weeks before the offensive, Soviet engineers and thousands of infantry built causeways out of logs for the tanks, often just below the Drut River waterline. The tanks themselves would roll into battle laden with brush and logs to fill in any gaps and to bolster weak areas. The infantry, too, carried mats made of brush, rolling them out as they went, which enabled them to negotiate the soft ground.[92] Often labeled a surprise to the Germans and another triumph of Soviet *maskirovka*, it was hardly that. The German 9th Army's reconnaissance repeatedly noted Soviet preparations, engineering, and building activities taking place to the south of Bobruisk. Such intelligence hardly mattered, however: German aircraft or long-range artillery—assets that would normally impede enemy engineering activities like bridge- or causeway-building—were nowhere to be found in 9th Army; indeed, they were hardly present at all in Army Group Center.

Likewise, while the schema for Rokossovsky's great assault was similar to that of his brethren to the north, just enough differences crept in to place his personal stamp on the operation. The attacks by reinforced reconnaissance forces, leading off on June 23, were the same as elsewhere, and though they didn't penetrate the German line to any extent, they did draw in 9th Army's local and tactical reserves to the front. Such presence in a forward position made them easier meat for the great Soviet bombardment that Rokossovsky laid on, starting at 2:30 A.M. on June 24 and concentrated initially against 9th Army's left wing north of Rogachev (XXXV Corps under command of General Friedrich Wiese). The barrage was even shorter than up north, just forty-five minutes, yet dwarfed the other fronts in its intensity:

> For three-quarters of an hour shells of every caliber hailed and hammered down, howling and hissing on trenches, strongpoints, resistance nests, battery positions, and command posts. Scarcely a square meter of ground was left unchurned. The grenadiers in their devastated positions dared not raise their heads and the gunners couldn't get to their guns. Field telephone lines were shot up and shredded and most of the radio equipment was knocked out—no more communications.[93]

Suddenly, the fire lifted on the front and shifted to targets in the rear, while hundreds of Shturmovik ground-attack planes appeared overhead to keep battering the German front. Then two heavily reinforced and tightly packed Soviet armies (the 3rd and the 48th) launched Rokossovsky's planned assault.

German soldiers on XXXV Corps's front line looked on, astonished, as Soviet tanks and infantry drove toward them along avenues of approach thought to be impassable. The Soviet *Schwerpunkt* was suitably massive. Rokossovsky had massed twenty-seven infantry battalions, reinforced by fifteen pioneer companies on a very narrow, 3-mile front while targeting just three German battalions. The Soviets broke into the German position, and the close-quarters fighting was desperate from the start. Recognizing the seriousness of the situation on his left flank, German 9th Army's commander, General Jordan, took a dramatic step: he ordered 20th Panzer Division into combat east of Bobruisk to shore up the wavering XXXV Corps.

The 20th Panzer was part of Army Group Center's reserve, the only Panzer division in all of Byelorussia. A veteran division containing seventy-one Mark IV Panzer tanks, upgraded to the 75mm high-velocity long gun, the 20th had enough shock potential and firepower to do a great deal of damage. Moving into battle late in the afternoon of June 24 under the command of General Mortimer von Kessel, the Panzers immediately began to deal out punishment to the huge mass of Soviet T-34 tanks north of Rogachev. German tanks might have been grossly outnumbered, but they still held a qualitative edge in training, target acquisition, and rate of fire. The situation was looking favorable when General Kessel received a radio message from army group headquarters: Field Marshal Busch ordered him to halt his attack immediately, turn 20th Panzer Division around almost a full 180 degrees, and head at top speed to the region south of Bobruisk. Trouble, it seemed, was brewing on German 9th Army's right flank.[94]

And trouble there was. A few hours after the big Soviet attack at Rogachev, Rokossovsky launched his second thrust toward Paritchi, almost due south of Bobruisk. Once again, the combination of reconnaissance attacks, thousands of massed guns firing a brief but terrible 40-minute barrage, and the arrival of hundreds of Shturmoviks overhead obliterated much of the front, with follow-on attacks by massed infantry armies (the 65th and 28th) smashing into what was left of the German defenses. Holding the line here was XXXXI Panzer Corps under General Edmund Hoffmeister—yet another misnamed and Panzer-less German formation. Within hours, Soviet assault troops had torn open a great gash in XXXI Panzer Corps, 18 miles wide and 6 miles deep. Rokossovsky could smell blood now and immediately inserted his second echelon, the 1st Guards Tank Corps. By evening, Soviet tank attacks had widened the gap to 30 miles. Rokossovsky had already decided to insert the third echelon, the Cavalry-Mechanized Group, the next morning.

To the German command, the plight of XXXV Corps at Rogachev now receded in importance compared to the breakthrough at Paritchi. That realization was the factor that led Field Marshal Busch on the afternoon of June 24 to call the commander of 20th Panzer Division and order him to turn around. General Kessel was to launch a counterattack southward from Bobruisk to restore the catastrophic situation on the front of XXXI Panzer Corps. He obeyed the order immediately, got the division back into column, turned it around 180 degrees, and headed toward the south. The distance from the Rogachev front, on the extreme north wing of 9th Army down to Paritchi, was almost 100 kilometers, with roads clogged by administrative personnel, staff cars, and civilians desperate to avoid the fighting. Kessel was swimming against the tide the whole time. Attempts to go off-road landed the tanks in trackless swampland and came to nothing. The ride lasted all through the night of June 24–25. The 20th Panzer Division reported for duty to the commander of XXXXI Panzer Corps, General Hoffmeister, at 6:00 A.M., although the exertions of the march had whittled seventy-one tanks down to just forty. Hoffmeister ordered the division into combat, and the Panzers immediately entered the fray against Soviet tank spearheads just west of the village of Slobodka. The German Panzers once again confirmed their reputation for lethality, destroying no fewer than sixty Soviet tanks in the course of the day's fighting, while suffering negligible losses of their own. But even sixty destroyed tanks amounted to nothing more than *ein Tropfen auf den heissen Stein*, as the Germans say—a "drop in the bucket." A Panzer division was a precious resource to the Wehrmacht in 1944, and having one run around for the better part of 48 hours was an egregious command error. It spent too little time in either the northern or southern sectors to achieve much on either one. General Jordan may well have overreacted to the original Soviet attack on XXXV Corps, inserting his reserve without waiting for the operational situation to ripen and reveal itself. And then Busch might have overreacted in turn by canceling 20th Panzer Division's original mission near Rogachev and sending it to the south. The odds of 20th Panzer Division defeating or even delaying 1st Byelorussian Front for long were nil, however. Perhaps we lay those odds at 71-to-900—the approximate number of tanks in the division compared to those operating under Rokossovsky. Numbers can lie, they say, but not numbers like these.

By June 27, massive Soviet forces were driving ahead in the clear and lapping around both sides of Bobruisk; encirclement seemed imminent. The city had become a magnet for German forces in the area and was soon packed with some 70,000–80,000 men: remnants of shattered divisions, administrative personnel, supply troops, headquarters for formations whose manpower had vanished in the maelstrom. The Soviet air force was in the air all day, bombing and strafing, and Soviet artillery and rocket launchers worked around the clock, smashing Bobruisk building by building and eventually brick by brick. Like Vitebsk, Orsha, and Mogilev, Bobruisk was on the books as a *fester Platz*, and it possessed the exact same qualities as the other ones, that is to say, none at all: no fortifications to speak of, no stockpiles of supplies or ammunition, no heavy artillery, no dedicated garrison troops. The reaction of the German High Command to the catastrophic situation that it had created was all too typical. At 9:00 A.M., with the Soviet pincers just about to close, 9th Army received permission to launch a breakout from Bobruisk. No sooner had the word gone out to the men in the ranks than a second message came in at 9:15 A.M.: breakout canceled. The level of disorder momentarily went off the charts—new arrivals were still streaming into Bobruisk, others were in the first stages of organizing a breakout, while still others were attempting to obey orders and go into an all-around defense. Sullen depression and wild panic in equal measure now gripped the German force. The commander of the 134th Division, General Ernst Philipp, shot himself, and undoubtedly so did some of the anonymous *Landsers* trapped in the city, not to mention Soviet Hiwis, the auxiliary civilian volunteers working for the Germans.[95] At 4:00 P.M. came a third order reverting back to the original 9:00 A.M. directive: breakout permitted. "We've gone completely haywire!" commented Jordan ruefully. "What a madhouse!" his chief of staff muttered.[96] Even now, Hitler insisted that one division remain behind to hold Bobruisk for a few more days, with the 383rd Division getting the happy news. None of this talkfest really mattered, however. While the commanders chattered, Soviet tanks corps had linked up and closed the ring around Bobruisk. The 9th Army, according to the entry in the war diary for June 28, "has ceased to exist as a fighting unit."[97]

Now began the death throes. A mass breakout was a fantasy. The Bobruisk pocket held 80,000 unsupplied men, among them 5,000 wounded; a handful of tanks from the 20th Panzer Division; and thousands of noncombatants. They were under constant fire from heavy weapons and air attack; communications within the army had broken down, and most of the men were fighting without any higher direction or command. The plan was for the breakout to start at 11:00 P.M. and take place along the western side of the Berezina River, moving generally to the north. But with much of the city in flames, finding a suitable jumping-off point proved impossible. There are accounts—too many simply to dismiss—that as they huddled together and waited for H-hour to strike, German soldiers sang the old nineteenth-century patriotic hymn *O Deutschland hoch in Ehren*—"Oh Germany High in Honor."[98] They joined the rolls of past Prussian-German soldiers who felt themselves moved to song on the battlefield. Both Frederick the Great's victorious army at Leuthen in 1757 and Moltke's host on the stricken field at Königgrätz in 1866 had sung the Lutheran hymn *Nun danket alle Gott*—"Now Thank We All Our God"—two of the most dramatic scenes in the long history of German arms. German soldiers had no reason to be thankful in the ruins of Bobruisk, however, and their gesture was no paean to victory. Indeed, they were singing a threnody.

The first wave ventured out at 11:30 P.M. As always, there was the sweet initial taste of freedom. They were no longer helpless but moving purposefully, breathing fresh air, with no enemy in sight. About four kilometers up from the city they met their first enemy roadblock. They fired wildly, charged forward, and overran it. Again and again, the mad rush forward brushed aside minor Soviet opposition, pickets, and roadblocks, still hugging the Berezina. Hopes were rising, undoubtedly—but unfortunately so was the sun. Dawn brought wave after wave of Soviet ground attack aircraft, with over 500 planes appearing in a single hour. They screamed in for low-altitude attacks, since the Germans on the ground had no antiaircraft guns, and they handed out a merciless pummeling to the defenseless marchers below. As the main column lost cohesion and scattered into smaller groups, Soviet tanks arrived on the scene, dispatched the remaining German Panzers and assault guns, and began to turn the riverbank into a blood-soaked killing ground. Some of the German force—a surprising number, in fact—managed to take advantage of the swirling chaos of the moment to slip away to the northwest, eventually reaching Svisloc, some 60 miles northwest of Bobruisk. Here they met friendly forces and escaped the Soviet trap. A handful of others, a few hundred perhaps, joined the ranks of the legendary *Rückkämpfer*, finding their way to safety in the most improbable ways—living off of green berries, rotten potatoes, and gleanings from the wheat fields and slaking their thirst by licking the dew from the grass in the morning. Soviet forces slaughtered the rest of the Bobruisk *Kessel:* the nearly 5,000 wounded still lying in the city, as well as stragglers who failed to leave until it was too late, the remainder in the dark forests and endless bogs along the Berezina. The Soviets later claimed to have counted 73,000 German dead, wounded, and prisoners in and around Bobruisk, and that horrible number seems just about right.

The destruction of the three German armies more or less still in their frontline positions was just the first stage of Operation Bagration. With a 250-mile gap yawning where Army Group Center used to be, the Red Army could now do what its doctrine had long prescribed: it could go deep, as far and as fast as it logistics would permit. With Rokossovsky's 1st Byelorussian Front coming up from the south, Cherniakhovsky's 3rd Byelorussian Front coming down from the north, and Zakharov's 2nd Byelorussian moving in directly from the east, the Soviets succeeded in sealing off a monstrous über-*Kessel* at Minsk on July 3. The great city held the headquarters of Army Group Center, and thousands of noncombatant German personnel were still pulling out as the Soviets were pulling in, with all the typical attendant scenes of road congestion, confusion, and panic. The Germans were headed for Lida, some 100 miles west of Minsk, where they established their new army group headquarters. Minsk itself lay in ruins, its factories demolished, its water and electrical systems wrecked. The fall of Minsk was the death knell for all German forces still alive in the big Byelorussian bulge. Individual formations might well break through a picket of Soviet divisions immediately to their front, but not from an iron ring of Soviet fronts lying 100 miles behind them. Indeed, no sooner had the Soviets taken Minsk than they dispatched their tank armies and corps far beyond the city, driving them hard to the west. The remains of the German 3rd Panzer, 4th, and 9th Armies had become an operational afterthought.

As three German armies died and Army Group Center dissolved, Hitler and his staff were essentially paralyzed, although it is difficult to imagine a successful counter to the Soviet offensive. Massed reinforcements—the only possible salvation for the Wehrmacht in Byelorussia—were simply not available. The mechanized divisions that might have formed the operational reserve were sitting hundreds of miles away to the south of the Pripet Marshes, assigned either to Army Group North Ukraine (General Model) or Army Group South Ukraine (General Ferdinand Schörner). Divisions this far away would require rail transport, a slow process even if enough rolling stock and rail capacity could be found to handle them. The strategic reserve was over 1,300 miles to the west, facing the Western Allies in Normandy. The sum total of reinforcements the Germans were able to scrounge thus consisted of precisely two Panzer divisions trying to beat back fifteen Soviet armies. Neither was able to achieve much significant on the operational level.

The first division to arrive was 12th Panzer Division. At the start of Bagration, the division was part of Army Group North. As always by this point, the Wehrmacht was robbing Peter, since the 12th Panzer was the last remaining Panzer division in Army Group North. The unit stood at something less than half strength, with a single battalion of tanks, just forty-four in all, and these were Panzer IIIs and IVs, not the more modern Mark V Panthers or Mark VI Tigers. Detraining at Marina Gorka on June 28–29, the division gamely launched a drive to the southeast the next day. The mission was the relief of the 9th Army penned up in Bobruisk, and while the Panzers never came close to the city, they did get about halfway there, opening up a narrow corridor toward the town of Svisloch, sitting on the river of the same name. The small armored thrust got just far enough to meet the tip of the corridor carved out by elements of XXXXI Panzer Corps that had broken out of Bobruisk. The 12th Panzer managed to hold the door open just long enough for some 10,000 ragged *Landsers* to get out. They were a pathetic sight, these sole survivors of the 9th Army—unshaven, hungry, and thirsty. They were alive, however, the one bright spot in the utter debacle of Bobruisk.

The second division to arrive on the scene was 5th Panzer. Detached from Army Group North Ukraine and ordered to Byelorussia, the 5th entrained at Chelm on June 25. The trip was well over 300 miles, and the trains were under attack by Soviet fighter-bombers and partisans the entire way. The division's original mission was to close the 100-mile gap between 3rd Panzer Army and 4th Army, a notion so unrealistic that it bordered on fantasy. It detrained on June 27 at Borisov on the Berezina, where the Germans still held a bridgehead on the far bank. The division was as well equipped as any Panzer division on the Eastern Front: fifty-five Panzer IVs and seventy of the feared Panzer V Panthers. Within its narrow sector, it stopped the Soviet drive cold. In the first six days of fighting, 5th Panzer Division destroyed nearly 300 Soviet tanks, mainly from the 5th Guards Tank Army under General Pavel Rotmistrov—the same unit that had fought at Prokhorovka during the climax of the Battle of Kursk. Indeed, a few days into the fighting, the Germans intercepted a Soviet radio message that advised: "If you make contact with the 5th Panzer Division, withdraw immediately!"[99] But counting tank kills is essentially a tactical concept, and the odds of 5th Panzer having any real operational impact—unhinging the Soviet pincers on Minsk, for example—stood somewhere around zero or, perhaps more accurately, 125 to 1,810: the number of tanks in the 3rd Byelorussian Front at the start of Bagration. Stymied at Borisov, the Soviets simply passed columns north and south of the German bridgehead, threatened 5th Panzer with encirclement, and forced its retirement to the region west of Minsk.

Summing Up

From the start of the Soviet offensive to the fall of Minsk and Vilnius, precisely twelve days had passed. In roughly two weeks of fighting, powerful Soviet blows had demolished an entire army group, smashed three German armies containing twenty-eight divisions, and inflicted nearly 300,000 casualties. The front was now 200 miles to the west of where it had been at the start, although in many places the Wehrmacht could still not speak of a "front"—the defenses had not yet cohered. Operation Bagration was more than a victory. It was *the* victory, perhaps the greatest single win in all of military history, and certainly a more painful defeat for the Wehrmacht than Stalingrad. Soviet military power and expert planning, combined with German ineptitude on all levels save the tactical, had brought them all to this pass.

The German errors are easy enough to point out. Hitler's insistence on a fixed defense (*starre Verteidigung*) and his mania for creating *feste Plätze*—bogus fortress cities that deliberately allowed themselves be encircled—was senseless. The Soviets simply bypassed them with their tank spearheads, cutting off tens of thousands of German infantry while staying focused on operational targets in the depth of the German position. The wrong German guess about the *Schwerpunkt* was another crucial misstep. The High Command deployed virtually the entire mechanized reserve against an expected Soviet offensive into Galicia against Army Group North Ukraine. While the Soviets did launch such an attack (the Lvov-Sandomierz Operation), they did not do so until July 13, by which time Army Group Center had already ceased to exist. Finally, the notion of treating the sprawling Eastern Front as a secondary theater for the time being was simply bizarre. Hitler and Jodl wanted the Wehrmacht to "strike in the west and hold in the east," but in the end the Germans lacked the forces to do either one successfully.

Likewise, operational schemes came and went. Hitler and the OKW wanted an attack south out of Latvia to restore contact between Army Groups North and Center. In the current configuration of the front, however, with Army Group North holding an extended front from Narva through Lake Peipus on down to the middle Dvina, it could spare only one or two divisions for the attack. The army command was certain that such a small concentration was bound to fail. A grander operational scheme from the Chief of the General Staff, General Kurt Zeitzler, also came to naught. The Zeitzler plan called for evacuating Estonia and most of Latvia and retreating behind the lower Dvina River. Such a move would not only protect Army Group North from getting trapped in Estonia; it would also halve the length of the army group's front. Zeitzler could then use the freed-up forces, five or six divisions, to launch a truly crushing blow against the flank of the Soviet drive on Minsk.

The plan foundered on two rocks. The first, of course, was Hitler's refusal to countenance a major withdrawal of any sort. He had Admiral Dönitz backing him this time, since a retreat from the Estonian littoral would allow the Soviet Baltic Sea fleet to break out of the Gulf of Finland and operate once again against German shipping. Likewise, Germany would lose its shale oil as well as the testing ground for new experimental U-boats on which so many of Hitler's hopes rested. The second rock that sunk the Zeitzler plan, however, was time. Zeitzler didn't formally present the plan to Hitler until June 30, by which date it was probably already too late. The withdrawals, regroupings, and attack preparation would have taken another three to four days even for an army renowned for the brisk pace of its staff work, by which time Minsk had already fallen to the Soviets.

Reducing the collapse of Army Group Center to this or that operational decision or magic moment isn't enough, however. The Wehrmacht's problems ran far deeper and were thus far more intractable. In his classic study *Problems of the Kesselschlacht* (*Probleme der Kesselschlacht*), General Edgar Röhricht identified the real difficulty of defending against Operation Bagration:

> A defender made up of foot-mobile divisions alone stood now on the broadest possible front, in a strictly linear defense, without depth and without reserves, and this in the fifth year of a war whose operations were more and more dependent on the employment of a constantly increasing number of armored and motorized forces. This anachronism gave a distinctive character to the events that followed.[100]

From 1939 to 1941, the Wehrmacht had redefined modern military operations—incorporating mechanized forces and aircraft en masse to achieve shockingly rapid and decisive victories. Other armies worldwide had soon followed suit, or tried to. By June 1944, however, this same Wehrmacht had devolved into a flabby mass of infantry formations of indifferent quality. As Röhricht saw it, an army that had once epitomized modernity had somehow become an "anachronism," no longer fully of its time, no longer representing the cutting edge or the state of the military art.

By mid-July, the Eastern Front was "bleeding from a thousand wounds," in the words of the historian of the German General Staff, Walter Görlitz. "No one could tell what tomorrow might bring," he added, although it was almost certain to be bad.[101] As the remnants of the Wehrmacht reeled back to the west and the few desperate *Rückkampfer* ate wild berries and licked the morning dew off of leaves to stay alive, the Soviets staged a grand celebration. In one of the war's more bizarre set-pieces, Stalin paraded 57,000 ragged German prisoners of war through the streets of Moscow on July 17, as if in a Roman triumph of old.

Precisely three days after that, Adolf Hitler presided over a staff briefing at his Führer headquarters in the Wolf's Lair in Rastenburg, East Prussia.

Excursus: The Plot

"Friction," Clausewitz wrote, is "the concept that differentiates actual war from war on paper," the unruly aspect of war that "makes the apparently easy thing difficult."[102]

* * *

RASTENBURG, EAST PRUSSIA—JULY 20, 1944. *The noon staff meeting* (Mittagslage) *is taking place in the Wolf's Lair. They are all gathered here, like always: Hitler, Jodl, Keitel, Heusinger, Luftwaffe Chief of Staff Korten, aides and adjutants and advisers, even a pair of civilian stenographers.*[103] *The last have become fixtures at these sessions ever since things began to go wrong on the Eastern Front, and Hitler grows increasingly paranoid that his underlings are twisting his words. Twenty-four men in all, gathered into a single 40-foot by 18-foot room, most of them clumped around the giant oaken map table in the center. Maps and charts are spread everywhere; also planning documents and briefing notes—the organized chaos of a German staff meeting circa 1944.*

General Heusinger briefs the situation on the Eastern Front. Bad news everywhere. Amy Group North Ukraine is in free fall against a monstrous Soviet attack toward Lemberg (Lvov). Soviet spearheads are lapping around both flanks of XIII Corps and threatening to encircle it near Brody. Army Group Center is still falling back out of Byelorussia and into Poland, but at least it finally appears to be coalescing again after the catastrophic defeats of the past month. Then again, who can say? The Soviet tank armies—always the best indicator of the Red Army's offensive intentions—are off the situation map for the time being. Luftwaffe reconnaissance has been worthless—indeed, so has the entire Luftwaffe of late.

Another officer enters the room. A twenty-fifth man. It is not an unusual event. Officers come and go all the time during these interminable meetings. Some of the participants notice this one, though. Colonel Claus Schenk Graf von Stauffenberg is a war hero, with the wounds to match. One of the participants at the briefing, General Walter Warlimont, later remembers him as "the very incarnation of a warrior, frightening and imposing at the same time."[104] *You can tick off the dues he's paid just by looking at him: left eye, right hand, two fingers on the left hand. Like so many officers of the Wehrmacht in this war, Stauffenberg has fallen prey to Allied airpower, caught in a strafing run by a squadron of Australian P-40 Kittyhawk fighters near Mezzouna during the Tunisian campaign.*

Stauffenberg has reason to be there. The Führer wants a report on the activities of the Replacement Army (Ersatzheer), the military office charged with scraping together new divisions to replace those chewed up in the fighting at the front. At the moment, however, Hitler is more interested in the Eastern Front briefing and declares that he will hear the report from the Replacement Army later. Stauffenberg stays for a moment and then excuses himself. He has to make an urgent phone call. He leaves his briefcase under the map table and exits. Another officer, Colonel Heinz Brandt, steps up to take his place. Brandt is Heusinger's aide, producing the pertinent maps and documents when called upon.

Heusinger is still speaking—a half-hour, forty minutes. The Soviets may be heading for East Prussia. He and Hitler bicker about whether the exposed eastern province is in danger. Field Marshal Model and Gauleiter *Erich Koch have sworn that not a single Russian will step foot inside the province, Hitler declares. Heusinger isn't so sure. At any rate, what if the Soviets decide to target Army Group North? The two begin to bicker again, this time about the correct operational posture in the Baltic States—to defend them in their entirety or to pull back to a shorter position along the Dvina River. It is 12:42 P.M. "If the army group doesn't pull back from Lake Peipus," Heusinger is intoning, "catastrophe may well be . . ."*[105]

And then it happens. A blinding explosion. Smoke and flame everywhere. The oak table blown sky-high. Blood, gore, body parts. Panic. Screaming.

Keitel's voice rising above the din: WHERE IS THE FÜHRER?[106]

Stauffenberg had placed an explosive device, a one-kilo block of plastic explosive, in his briefcase. A bomb of that size going off in an enclosed room will do a great deal of damage, and this one certainly has.

Stauffenberg is certain that Hitler is dead. He and his aide, Lieutenant Werner von Haeften, drive off, bluff their way past a couple of checkpoints on the way to the airfield, and are in the air on board a Heinkel He-111 aircraft by 1:00 P.M. They are flying to Berlin to take part in the military coup in the capital, an uprising that will overthrow the Nazi regime, bring an end to the lost war, and perhaps save Germany. Other plotters within the officer corps are already in the process of seizing power in Paris.

Stauffenberg and Haeften do not know it, but in true Clausewitzian style, just enough little things have gone wrong to unhinge the plan for Operation Valkyrie (Unternehmen Walküre)*. The sweltering noontime heat of a July day brought a change in venue. Rather than holding the staff discussion in the closed concrete bunker—the usual choice—the briefing was moved to the main hall of the Wolfsschanze, a much larger room with doors, windows, and thinner walls. Stauffenberg's blast has blown out the walls, expending much of its kinetic energy more or less harmlessly outward. If the bomb had gone off in the closed confines of the concrete bunker, the force would have vaporized everyone inside. Likewise, after Stauffenberg leaves his briefcase and departs, Colonel*

Brandt apparently nudges it behind one of the table legs, further muffling the explosion and reducing its impact. Finally, the plan had originally called for two bombs. Setting the complicated chemical fuses is tricky business for a man with one hand, however, and Stauffenberg runs out of time before the staff meeting. He has just finished prepping bomb number one in the restroom when one of Keitel's aides, Sergeant Werner Vogel, raps on the door to remind him that the meeting was about to start. As a result, bomb number two misses its rendezvous with destiny. Once again, had it been ready to go, everyone in the room would almost certainly have died instantly.

For all these reasons, only four of the twenty-four men in the room are killed, and none of them are named Adolf Hitler. General Günther Korten, the Luftwaffe chief, is dead. So too is the man who nudged the briefcase under the table, Colonel Brandt. So is one of the civilian stenographers, Heinrich Berger. Hitler has burst eardrums—like virtually everyone in the room—and other superficial wounds, but he is alive.

Within twelve hours, Stauffenberg and Haeften themselves will be dead, executed a bit after midnight by an improvised firing squad in the courtyard of the Replacement Army headquarters in Berlin, the Bendlerblock, the shootings illuminated by the headlights of a truck. Many others who are involved in the plot and know that they are about to be found out commit suicide. All over Germany, the regime begins rounding up officers and civilian officials implicated in the attempted coup and summarily shooting them. The ripples from Rastenburg will include drumhead courts-martial by an Honor Court of the Army (Ehrenhof des Heeres), *show trials in front of a newly established People's Court* (Volksgerichthof), *and executions that will continue up to the very end of the war.*[107]

* * *

In a world of exploding bombs and shells—tens of millions of them on land, sea, and in the air—setting one off in Hitler's headquarters might seem like the simplest thing. But as Clausewitz noted, sagely, in war "even the simplest thing is difficult."

Fahneneid: The Oath, Disobedience, and the German Military Tradition

Perhaps the most shocking aspect of the attempt on Hitler's life was the negligible impact it had on the rest of the fighting. Despite the instability in the rear, the army at the front stayed steady. The commanders continued to command, the staffs continued to plan and administer, and the soldiers soldiered on. In the days following July 20, certainly, a mood of uncertainty had gripped many field officers. The attempted murder of the Supreme Commander was bound to shake the faith of even the most loyal and dutiful soldier. "Would the front still hold? Would the soldiers fight as they had before?" wondered General Bodo Zimmermann, the Ia on the staff of OB-West. Within a week, however, he had the answers to those questions and more. "The front fought on," he noted with relief, "as if nothing had happened."[108]

But something had indeed happened. The vast majority of the Wehrmacht—the officers and men in all three services—responded to the bomb plot with incredulity and even anger. Most of them saw Stauffenberg and the other conspirators, heroes to right-thinking people today, as traitors who deserved every horrible punishment they received. The condemnation is easy enough to explain in the case of the enlisted ranks. The *Landsers* were fighting and dying in droves all over the map, often under the most horrific battlefield conditions. Now they found that some of the high-ranking officers tasked with planning and supplying their operations, men living comfortably and safely in the rear, were more interested in trying to kill Hitler than they were in discharging their professional military duties. Personal survival, not German national redemption at some point in the future, was the obsession of the frontline fighter. Indeed, few of them felt the need for redemption. The vast majority of soldiers still believed in their Führer and his historical mission. "Thank God it wasn't a *Landser*," General Hermann Teske's driver told him, and there is little doubt that he was speaking for the mass of enlisted men.[109]

The attitude of the officer corps was more complex and requires deeper exploration. Many of them had viewed Hitler as a vulgar upstart from the beginning of his political career, mocking his lower-middle-class background, his years as a homeless street person in Vienna, his gauche manners. General Rudolf Christoph Freiherr von Gersdorff, a cavalry officer from an old Silesian aristocratic family who at one point tried to kill Hitler via a suicide bomb, remembered meeting the Führer for the first time at a reception at the Reich Chancellery in March 1939 and noticing how common he was, how ill at ease he seemed ("he sat there tugging on his fingers in visible embarrassment and seemed incapable of starting a conversation"), and how noisily he slurped his vegetable soup.[110] The officers shared many of Hitler's goals, however—defiance of the Treaty of Versailles, rearmament, restoration of Germany's Great Power status—and they had supported him as long as his success lasted. Some of them fell away as the war approached.

"The fool actually wants to start a war," commented Stauffenberg in 1939.[111] But it was only a few. They had been muttering privately for over a year about Hitler and his amateurish military decisions ever since Stalingrad, often doing so in the most explicit terms. They criticized what looked like operational and strategic drift in the war effort. A few were appalled at the deliberate and systematic mass murder of the Jews.

General Warlimont admits in his memoirs that, when he thought of the "fountain of misfortune" that Hitler's leadership had brought forth, he often thought of killing the Führer himself, although he quickly adds that such fantasies never went beyond the "pale cast of thought" (quoting the German translation of Shakespeare's *Hamlet*).[112] In private conversations, at least, many of them admitted that the war was lost and accused Hitler of leading Germany to ruin. A small number of them had actually said as much to the Führer's face. General Siegfried Westphal had reported in person after the abortive German counterattacks at Anzio, for example, declaring that "the blanket had become too thin and too short" and that the German army was no longer "capable of prosecuting a successful attack."[113] Rommel had done so in writing, just before falling victim to an Allied air attack on July 17 ("The unequal struggle is drawing to a close").[114] And so had General Wolfram von Richtofen, the commander of *Luftflotte* 2 in the Mediterranean theater and a hard-core true believer. Contrary to our modern fantasies about what disagreeing with Hitler must have entailed, he could often appear quite reasonable in face-to-face exchanges. In smaller groups, at least, he could be "open and relaxed," and after hearing Richtofen out, for example, he posed a simple, but daunting counter-question: What prospect did Richtofen see of obtaining an acceptable peace for Germany?[115]

Despite all their qualms about Hitler's leadership, however, only a few members of the officer corps saw fit to move into the ranks of the active resistance. The total amounted to 185 officers in all, and just thirty-nine generals out of the Wehrmacht's thousands. "Since the generals haven't gotten anything done up to now," Stauffenberg told his uncle and confidant, Nikolaus Graf von Üxküll-Gyllenband, in 1943, "it's time for the colonels to step in."[116] The nonactors would later put forth various explanations in their postwar testimony and memoirs. They abhorred the notion of breaking their oath to Hitler, they claimed. They considered conspiracy in wartime to be an act of treason. They could not simply abandon their duty in the face of the approaching Soviet army. They believed that the German people and their own soldiers would reject any plot against the Führer. They were merely soldiers. They were only following orders.

Whichever specific rationalization they chose, however, their judgment on July 20 was nearly unanimous. The attempt to kill Hitler had been a crime. Field Marshal Model, for example, called the plot "the greatest possible disgrace for the Prussian-German General Staff."[117] He also remarked to Teske, his chief of transport in Army Group Center, that it had been "more badly prepared than the Kapp Putsch," the 1920 military uprising against the Weimar Republic that was still the gold standard for slipshod, banana republic–style military intervention in civilian politics.[118] General Lothar Rendulic, commander of the 20th Mountain Army in Finland, remembered that "the first reaction was the sharpest possible rejection of such a deed at the very moment that the military situation was passing through such a dangerous crisis." The troops, he said, now realized that "certain circles were trying to stab them in the back," fell words indeed for a historically minded German officer.[119] General Friedrich Wilhelm von Mellenthin, chief of staff of XXXXVIII Panzer Corps, was "dumbfounded that a German officer could make this attempt, particularly at a time when the men of the Eastern Front were waging a life and death struggle to stem the advance of the Russian hordes." He and his fellow officers "were disgusted to hear of this attempt on Hitler's life and indignantly refused to approve of it."[120] Teske himself joined in the condemnation ("As a general staff office at the time I was outraged over the attempted assassination"), but he also offered another, quite standard explanation of why he had not enlisted in the ranks of the resistance. He had simply been too busy: "I could not understand my old friends Stauffenberg and Mertz. While my doubts about the Supreme Commander were increasing, I had neither the time nor the power to think these through to the end. The professional demands of those days were so great that they absorbed the necessary engagement with the larger military predicament or the more general role of the German people and their role within Western Civilization." In the end, Teske said, he "knew little of the homeland."[121] Like most staff officers in the field, he had only been there three weeks in the past eighteen months.

Finally, there were some who rejected not only the substance but also the manner of the attempted killing. "Neither the officers nor the mass of the soldiers could accept the way it happened," argued General Bodo Zimmermann, who was the Ia of *OB-West* in July 1944: "Broad circles at the time did not understand how officers, of all people, could attempt such a treacherous murder and why the chief plotters then tried to flee to safety. It is only possible to understand this point of view by considering the historical and traditional development of the German army officer corps. Nothing like this had ever happened in its history. Chivalry (*Ritterlichkeit*) instinctively rejected the chosen method." It would have been far easier to understand, Zimmermann concluded, "if the plotters had advanced to the deed with an open visor and with pistol in hand."[122] He later gave a vivid description of the views within the officer corps of the July 20 plot and where the weight of opinion fell:

> Those with insight, who had followed developments since the start of the war with real concern and who now saw fate approaching, as well as those who simply wanted the war to end: these groups breathed anew and summoned up new hope. Opposing them, however, was a great mass of those who thought differently, be it from inner conviction or from prudence, perhaps even from personal economic reasons. . . .
>
> The broad-minded thought: this is the beginning of the end, a frightening beacon (*Fanal*)! The stalwarts said: it is good that the criminal reactionaries have unmasked themselves and that we can make a clean sweep of them. We can only win the war if we remove all saboteurs.[123]

In the end, it almost always came down to the violation of the oath. On the surface, such an argument seams reasonable enough. The vow, the solemn oath, the word of the gentleman: these are the very bedrock of civilization, and not just Western or German civilization. Where would we be without them? Those who read the memoirs of the German generals often find the argument convincing. Any honorable man would struggle when faced with such a choice. An officer could do the right thing by his conscience, or he could remain true to the vow he had sworn to the Führer. He certainly could not do both.

But using the oath as an excuse becomes problematic when we remember just who it is we are discussing. These were German officers, men raised and trained in the Prussian tradition. They were officers taught to assess a situation (*Lage*), understand the mission (*Auftrag*), and then find their own path forward with a bold decision (*Entschluss*). Modern analysts credit them with the birth of "mission command" (*Auftragstaktik*), that is, acting independently within the context of a commander's mission to devise the best and most efficient way to succeed.[124] In fact, we might take this point even farther. The Prussian tradition emphasized the "independence of the lower commander" (*Selbständigkeit der Unterführer*).[125] The Prussian-German tradition, often caricatured as "the obedience of a corpse" (*Kadavergehorsam*), actually carved out a great deal of room for free-thinking initiative on the part of field commanders, and indeed the greatest victories in its history were almost always bound up with that freedom. A list of German officers who had disobeyed explicit orders from their superiors—up to and including their sovereign king or emperor—would fill a book.[126] The foundational battle of the Prussian army—the triumph over the Swedes at Fehrbellin—began with the Prince of Hesse-Homburg launching an outnumbered attack on the Swedish positions against explicit orders from the Great Elector. Frederick the Great had a stable filled with obstreperous officers who saw no problem in unhinging the king's operational plans, most notably General Christoph Hermann von Manstein at Kolin. The pageant of Prussian military history presents with a veritable hall of fame: Friedrich Karl, the Red Prince, at Königgrätz; General Hermann von François at Stallupönen; General Heinz Guderian on the drive across northern France. The ethos of this officer corps was to do what was necessary and then report it later up the chain of command, when it was too late to countermand the order.

Disobeying an operational order and breaking an oath are two different things, of course, but the Prussian-German officer had also broken plenty of solemn oaths over the years. The officer caste had famously taken an oath to Kaiser Wilhelm II, for example, but they broke it in 1918. With revolution sweeping across the country and Wilhelm anxious to know if the army would fight to defend his throne, German frontline commanders actually held an "Army parliament" (*Armeeparlament*) to decide his fate.[127] Consisting of regimental, brigade, and division commanders from each of the ten German field armies closest to Imperial Headquarters at Spa, it met on November 9, 1918. The chief of the operations section of the General Staff, Colonel Wilhelm Heye, summarized the findings to the emperor: "The troops are still true to Your Majesty, but they are tired and indifferent. They want only rest and peace. They will not march against the homeland; also not with Your Majesty at their head. They also will not march against Bolshevism. Above all they want an end to hostilities; therefore every hour is important." Wilhelm was unimpressed. Could the army even undertake an orderly march home without him? Heye again: "The army will march home alone under its generals. In this respect, it is still solidly in the control of its leaders. And if Your Majesty marches with them, it will seem proper and pleasing to them. The army only wants no more fighting either inside [Germany] or outside."[128] Pressing the point one more time, Wilhelm finally asked the larger question. He was the Supreme War Lord, and hadn't the army "sworn an oath of loyalty (*Fahneneid*)" to him?

At this point, the first quartermaster general, Wilhelm Groener, weighed in with a splash of cold water. His exact wording has remained controversial. "In this situation such an oath is only a fiction," he supposedly declared (*Der Fahneneid ist jetzt nur eine Idee*). Other accounts have him being even more pointed: "Oath to the colors? War Lord? These are only words, an idea." Whichever version is correct, his sense was clear. The cohesion of the army and the survival of the Reich (in that order) were more important than the officer corps's sworn fealty to the emperor.[129]

After the revolution of 1918, these same oath-breaking officers took a new oath, this one to the Weimar Constitution. They broke that one, too, early, often, and almost nonstop for the fifteen years of the interwar period. They took part in secret rearmament projects that not only violated the Versailles pact but also the constitution. They formed *Grenzschutz* units—border guards that allowed the interwar German military, the Reichswehr, to evade the disarmament clauses of the treaty. They conspired to organize a so-called Black Reichswehr that appeared nowhere on either of the army rolls or the Weimar budget, and then approved the murder of those accused of leaking information on the conspiracy to the government.[130] They built training facilities for forbidden weapons in the Soviet Union—a flying school at Lipetsk and a Panzer school at Kazan. Men of old aristocratic families with titles to match, they had no particular affection for democracy. They despised it, in fact. At best they were "rational republicans" (*Vernunftrepublikaner*), supporting the Weimar state until the time was right for a monarchical restoration or a military dictatorship.[131]

The army subverted the Republic in numerous other ways, sometimes quite blatantly. It refused government orders to suppress the Kapp Putsch, for example, a military coup in March 1920 that attempted to overthrow the infant Republic. When called upon to act, the chief of the army command, General Hans von Seeckt, actually snubbed his civilian superior, War Minister Gustav Noske, telling him: "Troops do not fire on troops. Do you perhaps intend, Herr Minister, that a battle be fought before the Brandenburger Tor between troops who have fought side by side against the common enemy? . . . When Reichswehr fires on Reichswehr, then all comradeship within the Officer corps has vanished."[132] The solidarity of the army, in other words, took precedence over the defense of constitutional government in Germany.

Finally, in 1932–1933, a clique of army officers—Generals Kurt von Schleicher and Kurt Freiherr von Hammerstein-Equord and Colonel Oskar von Hindenburg (son of the former field marshal and current president of the Republic, Paul von Hindenburg)—played key roles as power brokers in bringing Hitler to power. Senior army officers yearned for a restoration of order and discipline in German life, and they were especially concerned about the threat from the left. They saw Hitler as a fellow nationalist, a bit crude, but one who could win the masses to the nationalist and conservative cause. His opposition to Marxism, his plans for German rearmament, his anti-Semitism: all these things harmonized well with the essentially premodern worldview of the officer corps. Indeed, the support of aristocratic army officers was crucial in allowing Nazi propaganda to declare that the new Hitler regime was carrying out both a "legal revolution" and a "conservative revolution" in accordance with constitutional norms. One of the new regime's first actions was the famous Day of Potsdam, when it melded the traditional, Old World symbology of Prussia to the order of the swastika, a reassuring sign to millions of ordinary, patriotic Germans. How radical could Hitler really be, many asked, if he had managed to get the Junkers on board? All of these political activities, too, were violations of the oath the officers had taken to the Weimar Constitution.

For the classical oath-breaking moment in Prussian-German military history, however, we need to go back to December 1812. Napoléon's Grand Armée was stumbling out of Russia after having been largely destroyed in the retreat from Moscow. Prussia was a French ally at the time and had contributed a corps to the Russian campaign: 20,000 men under the command of General Hans David von Yorck. The Prussians hadn't seen much hard fighting in Russia, campaigning in the Baltic region as part of Marshal Etienne MacDonald's army group and reaching Riga in October. Henceforth, Yorck remained relatively inactive save for the occasional skirmish with the Russians, and, indeed, some sort of tacit agreement may have existed, requiring the Prussians "to do only what honor demanded."[133] The entire time, the Russian command was peppering Yorck's headquarters with calls to defect. With the collapse of Napoléon's campaign in December, Yorck began a withdrawal back to Prussia, but he was under constant pressure from the Russians, who threatened to get around his southern flank and cut off his line of retreat.

The years since the catastrophe at Jena had been an era of Prussian reform, but the new currents in state, society, and culture had barely touched Yorck, the scion of an old Pomeranian family with links to the most reactionary elements in the Prussian state. Obedience stood high on his list of virtues, but so too did Prussian patriotism and a hatred for the French occupier. As the Russian army approached East Prussia, its commander, Johann von Diebitsch, continued to urge Yorck to abandon the French alliance and perhaps even to switch sides. Diebitsch was a Prussian who had entered Russian service in 1801, and serving as his adjutant was another Prussian officer by the name of Carl von Clausewitz. Yorck dutifully reported these contacts to the king of Prussia via messenger, but before he heard back the Russians cut off his rear guard and requested a meeting. Late on Christmas Day, Yorck, Diebitsch, and Clausewitz met in person. Yorck hesitated even now to take the fateful step; Diebitsch and Clausewitz hinted that, short of defecting, Yorck might simply remain neutral and step aside, allowing the Russian army to continue its advance. The meeting was testy, and the mood was not lightened by the obvious antipathy between the Prussian reformer Clausewitz and the more traditionalist Yorck.

On December 29, Yorck received his answer from the king, but it was disappointingly vague: "non-specific instructions and no response to the Russian overtures."[134] On his own initiative now, he decided to leave the French alliance and to adopt a posture of neutrality. On December 30, 1812, he and Clausewitz hammered out the terms of an agreement at Yorck's headquarters at Tauroggen (today Tauragė in Lithuania), about 40 kilometers northeast of Tilsit. The Convention of Tauroggen began the chain of events by which Prussia and Russia signed a military alliance, the Treaty of Kalisch, in February 1813, and Prussia joined the Sixth Coalition against the French emperor. Friedrich Wilhelm III was furious when he heard the news, issuing orders for Yorck's dismissal. With the French in occupation of Berlin and the kingdom virtually defenseless, the king's anger is understandable. Presented with a fait accompli and with his own subjects spoiling for a war of liberation against the French, however, Friedrich Wilhelm had no choice but to accede to Yorck's bold stroke and to rescind the dismissal orders.

Tauroggen became one of the legendary moments in the history of Prussian arms. Every senior officer of the Wehrmacht knew the details of the story by heart. Their military education from the cadet schools on up had pounded Yorck's heroism into their heads. In certain situations, there can be a higher good than following orders, even when those orders were issued by the supreme leader. Yorck knew the risk he was taking, and it is worth highlighting:

> Gentlemen, I do not know what I shall say to the king about my action. Perhaps he will call it treason. Then I shall bear the consequences. I will put my grey head willingly at the feet of His Majesty, and gladly die knowing that I have not failed as a faithful subject and a true Prussian.[135]

And yet he had acted anyway. Prussian discipline can generate even "direct rebellion" given the right circumstances. And this heroic moment in Prussian military history was the work of three traitors, three oath-breakers. Yorck had no constitutional authority to reorient Prussian foreign policy. Diebitsch was a turncoat leading Russian armies in an invasion of Prussia, and his adjutant Clausewitz, too, was a traitor. So, too, were the thousands of Prussian officers and men who joined the "Russian-German Legion" to fight against Napoléon.

Conclusion: A Yorck for 1944?

This Prussian tradition of disobedience in the interests of serving a higher cause had one final flowering on July 20, 1944. Indeed, some of the oldest and most famous family names in Prussian-German history studded the ranks of the conspiracy: Helmuth James Graf von Moltke, Hermann Henning von Tresckow, and even Peter Graf Yorck von Wartenburg, a direct lineal descendant of the man of Tauroggen. Hitler saw the bomb plot as an attempt by "the Reaction," a very old-school conspiracy of Junkers, officers, and especially the General Staff, to bring an end to the National Socialist revolution once and for all and to replace it with a more conservative regime, perhaps some form of military dictatorship.[136] The leader of the German Labor Front, Dr. Robert Ley, sounded the note clearly in a radio speech broadcast on July 22, blaming the "blue-blooded swine" (*blaublütige Schweinehunde*) for the dastardly deed and promising to settle accounts with them once and for all.[137]

But the bomb plot was only a temporary and partial recrudescence, not a true revival of independent thought and action. In the course of Prussian-German military history, apparently, there were oaths and then there were oaths. Some of them were malleable and some were rigid. Some one could break and others one could not. Loyalty to one's oath depended on the situation, and if anyone should have been aware of that fact, it was the senior officer corps of the Wehrmacht. When we consider the very small number of officers who took part in the plot to overthrow the Nazi regime, it becomes clear that many officers used their oath as a device, a means of rationalizing their inaction. By now they had identified with the regime and with their Führer. They commanded wartime armies of unimaginable size, and Hitler was paying them well to do so, including large payments under the table ("dotations," they were called, hearkening back to the gifts of cash and land that the old Prussian monarchs granted to those who had performed loyal service, but now perverted into something indistinguishable from a bribe).[138] But even if Hitler hadn't been showering them with money, the generals might well have fought on anyway. Unlike 1918, they were determined to fight this war out to the end: *koste es was er wolle.*

Emulating Yorck would not have been easy in 1944. The Red Army was not coming as a liberating force, but as an avenger. Army officers knew well the kinds of policies they had been carrying out in the Soviet Union. They knew that a reckoning was at hand. The reaper was coming, and the harvest would probably include their own careers, fortunes, and even lives. On the other side of the two-front war, the conspirators who tried to kill Hitler had won little sympathy in the Western Allies' camp. Indeed, for US and British policy makers, from Roosevelt and Churchill on down, the notion of an uprising by militarists and monocled Junkers held sway. The *New York Times* described the conspirators as a sinister gang "whose only hope is for a quick peace that will leave them with the nucleus to begin building for the next world conflict."[139] John Wheeler-Bennett, the noted British historian who had cultivated contacts in Germany on behalf of the government, noted that "the killing of Germans by Germans will save us from future embarrassments of many kinds."[140] And, of course, the Allies had declared at the Casablanca Conference in 1943 that they were pursuing nothing less than the "unconditional surrender" of the Axis powers. And so the generals stayed loyal, remained in the field, and oversaw a final year of doomed and disastrous military operations that inflicted untold suffering on the soldiers under their command, on Germany, and on Europe.

Even so, there is such a thing as a moral imperative. As Yorck had stated at the time, you may look like a traitor, but you "bear the consequences," and you die knowing that you did what you could. Let us leave the final word on the subject to one of the most respected officers in the Wehrmacht, Field Marshal Gunther von Kluge, Rundstedt's successor as OB-West. In July 1944, General Gersdorff tried to convince Kluge to enter into independent negotiations with the Allies, urging him to establish radio contact with US General Omar Bradley, commander of the US 12th Army Group. In other words, he wanted Kluge to seize the day, march in the footsteps of old Yorck, and try something quite similar to what the latter had done at Tauroggen.

Kluge was having none of it. "Gersdorff," he said, "if this goes sideways, then Field Marshal von Kluge will be the biggest idiot in world history."

"*Herr* Field Marshal," responded Gersdorff, "like all great men of world history, you're standing before a choice: either to be condemned by history or to enter into history as a savior in a moment of dire need."

Kluge put a hand on his underling's shoulder. "Gersdorff," he said, "Field Marshal von Kluge is not a great man."[141]

In the end, far too few of them were.

Despite its reputation for bristling with Panther and Tiger tanks, the 1944–1945 Wehrmacht employed a motley assortment of equipment. This Marder II light self-propelled antitank gun (here fighting in Hungary) was one of a vast family of vehicles based on the prewar Czech Pz Kpfw 38(t) chassis. Courtesy of the Christian Ankerstjerne Collection.

Captured "German" equipment in Normandy, actually a French Hotchkiss H35, two Renault UE tractors, and a Marder. Courtesy of the Christian Ankerstjerne Collection.

Captured *Jagdpanzer* 38 Hetzer light tank destroyer, another Pz Kpfw 38(t) offshoot. Courtesy of the Christian Ankerstjerne Collection.

Captured Grille 150mm self-propelled artillery, one more use of the versatile Pz Kpfw 38(t) chassis. Courtesy of the Christian Ankerstjerne Collection.

Two Marder 38Ts of 17th *Panzergrenadier* Division next to the church of Roncey in Normandy, where the division's rear guard came under attack by Allied fighter-bombers. Courtesy of the Christian Ankerstjerne Collection.

A young paratrooper of the 3rd *Fallschirmjäger* Division stares in disbelief after his capture by American infantry near the Ardennes Forest in early 1945. Courtesy of The National World War II Museum.

A King Tiger of the 501st SS Heavy Tank Battalion clatters down a road near Kaiserbaracke. While attempting to cross a bridge at Stavelot, days later, King Tiger 222 was knocked out by a US M-10 tank destroyer. Courtesy of The National World War II Museum.

Men of the 17th SS *Panzergrenadier* Division *Götz von Berlichingen* head into battle near Carentan on June 13, 1944. Courtesy of The National World War II Museum.

Young, confident mortarmen of the 17th SS *Panzergrenadier* Division *Götz von Berlichingen* advance through the hedgerows near Saint-Lô and Carentan on June 13, 1944. The men carry the tube and base plate for the 81mm mortar. Courtesy of The National World War II Museum.

Two views of Rommel. An unusually contemplative Field Marshal Erwin Rommel gazes out of a window in his home near Herrlingen, Germany, in 1944. Courtesy of The National World War II Museum.

The man of action roaring off to the scene of the action in his staff car. Courtesy of The National World War II Museum.

Besichtigungsreise am Atlantikwall

Generalfeldmarschall von Rundstedt bei einer Lagebesprechung anhand einer großen Karte

, .-Aufn. Valtingojer   61828   Presse-Hoffmann

Field Marshal Gerd von Rundstedt takes a tour of the Atlantic Wall with members of his staff prior to the Allied invasion of France. Courtesy of The National World War II Museum.

Two paratroopers of *Fallschirmjäger* Regiment 6 keep watch near St. Come du Mont, June 8, 1944. Courtesy of The National World War II Museum.

American soldiers inspecting the hull of the unfinished E-100 super-heavy tank prototype, a 140-ton monster with 200mm of frontal armor. Courtesy of the Christian Ankerstjerne Collection.

A Tiger II heavy tank of *Schwere SS-Panzer-Abteilung* 101. Its crew abandoned it in Jemappes, Belgium, in 1944 after running out of fuel. US engineers removed the gun after GIs captured it. Courtesy of the Christian Ankerstjerne Collection.

Abandoned Tiger I of *Schwere SS-Panzer-Abteilung* 101 in Marle, France, being inspected by US forces. French resistance fighters stand to the right. Courtesy of the Christian Ankerstjerne Collection.

Tiger on the prowl. Propaganda photo of a Tiger II, intended to demon-strate the rugged cross-country ability of the tank—the very thing it lacked. Courtesy of the Christian Ankerstjerne Collection.

SS-Brigadeführer Fritz Witt salutes officers of his 12th SS Panzer Division *Hitlerjugend*, June 1944. Witt took command of the new division in July 1943. He was killed by a barrage of British naval gunfire at his command post near Venoix, France, on June 14, 1944. Courtesy of The National World War II Museum.

German prisoner with bruised and bloodied face. Anzio, Italy, January 1944. Courtesy of The National World War II Museum.

5

In the West: The Campaign in France

Introduction: A Case of Auto-Suggestive Euphoria

In book 1, chapter 3 of his classic work *On War*, Clausewitz attempts to define the elusive concept of "military genius."[1] Rather than relying upon a common understanding of genius as native intelligence or preternatural brilliance, Clausewitz locates genius within "strength of mind or character": the ability to size up a situation rationally and come to a rapid and firm decision.[2] Indeed, he warns against the man of excessive passion, "whose feelings ignite as rapidly and violently as gunpowder, but do not last."[3] Mercurial emotions "are useful neither for practical life nor for war," warns the Prussian sage.[4]

* * *

BERCHTESGADEN—1944. *They'd all heard it before. The Leader was on a roll.*[5]

"We're bleeding the Russians white! The retreats of the last month have given us an immeasurable advantage, since we no longer have to defend such a gigantic area. And we know from our own experience how exhausted the Russians must be after their hurried advance. Think of what happened to us in the Caucasus! Just like the Russians back then, a turning point is still possible for us today. It's even likely. Think about it! They've lost 15 million men according to our figures. It's monstrous. They can't survive the next blow. They won't survive."[6]

The all stared at him. Silent. Dumb. They knew that he wasn't finished.

"Jet fighters! Masses of them. V-weapons!" V for Vergeltung, *they knew: "vengeance." He would soon unleash them against England. "Then you'll see how 'peaceloving' the British become," he exulted. Just yesterday morning, Admiral Dönitz had promised him the imminent arrival of new advanced U-boats, the Type XXI. They could stay submerged for days and fire eighteen torpedoes in twenty minutes. "Miracle weapons," he called them all collectively.*

226

"We can't compare our situation today to 1918. It's not the same." He paused for effect. *"Even if the enemy thinks it is."[7]*

They knew that one was coming. Always the same comparison. No more catastrophes like 1918. No stab in the back this time. No quitting "at five minutes to midnight."

His eyes were shining . . . as if he were starting to believe his own words. Did he, really? Or was it a form of self-hypnosis? The generals on the staff couldn't tell—not even Jodl and Keitel, the men who were at his side constantly, the ones who knew him best. Not even an educated civilian like Speer. If anyone could have analyzed things objectively, it was Speer.

The Leader's voice was rising now. It was time for the peroration.

"What lies at the bottom now can rise to the top tomorrow! Whatever happens, we'll fight on! It's amazing how much fanaticism even our youngest soldiers carry with them into battle. They know that there are only two possibilities: we either solve this problem, or we will all be destroyed. Providence will never abandon a people who fight so bravely! Frederick the Great also fought through hopeless situations with indomitable energy. They didn't call him 'great' because he won through in the end, but because he stayed brave in misfortune. And the future won't understand me through my triumphs of the early war years, but through the fortitude I showed during the setbacks of the last few months."[8]

The stirring ending: *"Will always triumphs!"[9]*

Even though they'd heard it all before, his words still held a certain power, at least inside this tight inner circle. You could find yourself swept up from time to time, no matter how sober (sachlich) or objective (nüchtern) you tried to be. It certainly beat looking at the hopeless situation maps or statistical tables on manpower, or steel, or aircraft production. They would deny it later, under Allied interrogation: virtually all of them. But at the time, they felt renewed. It was a momentary euphoria, certainly, but refreshing nonetheless.

He came back down to earth. He looked around the room—eyes harder now. A meanness there. Apparently, the pep talk was over.

"But if we lose this war, gentlemen, you'd all do well to get yourself a rope."[10]

* * *

Adolf Hitler's generals often complained that he didn't seem capable of facing the truth. He fled into fantasy worlds, they testified, and he spun yarns about potential victory long after Germany's defeat was certain. Perhaps they weren't listening carefully enough, however. Occasionally, just occasionally, their Führer spoke the absolute truth.

Stymied in Normandy: Panzer *Lehr* Takes a Ride

The campaign in Normandy from D-Day on June 6, 1944, through the eventual Allied breakout in the last week of July is one of the best-known operational sequences in history, especially within the English-speaking world. After the landing—a success purchased with a fraction of the expected friendly casualties—a kind of euphoria suffused the Allied camp. The next six weeks, unfortunately, were the morning after. As at Anzio, the Wehrmacht performed its patented "scramble": whipping divisions together from all over France and shipping them to the danger zone. They managed to form a cohesive defensive line within days, denied the Allies their initial objectives, pinned them up in the relatively narrow confines of Normandy, and fought viciously for every step of ground. To the Allies, the fight for Normandy was a bitter disappointment after the high hopes generated by the successful landing.

Those weeks of fighting were equally as troubling to the Germans, however. The attempt to rush divisions to the front took place in such an attenuated fashion that we might liken it more to a low-speed chase than a rush. While the 21st Panzer Division was already present in Normandy and fought the landing on the first day, other reserve divisions arrived in dribs and drabs over the next week. The pace was much slower than the buildups at Salerno or Anzio, and at no moment were the Allies in danger of facing any sort of operational overmatch. The principal reason for the desultory buildup in Normandy was the firm belief shared throughout the German chain of command—Hitler, Rundstedt, and Rommel alike—that the Normandy landing was a mere "diversionary operation" designed to smooth the way for the real operation: a landing north at the mouth of the Seine River in the Pas de Calais.[11] Despite the mountain of postwar literature blaming the misread on Hitler, or crediting the Allied deception plan known as Operation Fortitude, the Germans held 15th Army in the Pas de Calais for weeks because that is where they would have attacked had they been planning an invasion of Europe from England. Calais was the option with the highest risk and highest benefits—precisely the way the Germans liked to plan operations.

But whether the German High Command released 15th Army or not, getting the divisions to Normandy was going to be difficult. Allied air supremacy made it nearly impossible for German formations to move by day, either by rail or in road column. Take the experience of *Kampfgruppe* Heintz, a regiment-plus of the 275th Infantry Division with artillery, engineers, and *Flak* units attached. Stationed at Redon in southern Brittany, the *Kampfgruppe* received orders on the morning of June 6 to move to Normandy.[12] The distance was 120 miles and should have taken a day or two at most by rail. But Allied air attacks delayed the loading until the early morning hours of June 7. The lead train chugged north and made it safely through the Avranches bottleneck, but it came under Allied air attack at Foligny and was completely destroyed. The second train didn't get even that far. Air attacks destroyed the rail line near Pontorson in northern Brittany, and all personnel had to unload and slog north on foot. Most of the trains en route on June 7 didn't make it past Rennes in central Brittany. Heavy air attacks continued on June 8, blocking various portions of the rail line. German transportation officers tried desperately to reroute the trains to the east through Fougères, but air attacks smashed that line as well. On June 9 the entire *Kampfgruppe* received orders to detrain and head north by truck or foot. In two days and three nights, the formation managed less than 30 miles by rail. Not until the evening of June 11 did *Kampfgruppe* Heintz actually reach Normandy in strength, entering the line near Carentan. A one-day deployment, in other words, had taken five.

Or take, as another example, the two nearest German mechanized divisions. The 12th SS Panzer Division *Hitlerjugend* under General Fritz Witt began the invasion deployed south and east of Normandy between Louviers, Dreux, and Vimoutiers. With a nominal strength of over 20,000 men, *Hitlerjugend* was one of the largest and most powerful divisions on the German order of battle, and it had the equipment to match—no fewer than 91 Panzer Mark IVs and 66 Mark V Panthers, a high number indeed for a German Panzer division by 1944. Panzer *Lehr* Division (General Fritz Bayerlein) was at Nogent le Rotrou near Le Mans. It, too, was a powerful unit: a full manpower complement of 14,699 men, along with 99 Panzer Mark IVs, 89 Mark V Panthers, and even 8 Mark VI Tigers.[13] The two divisions received orders to proceed to Normandy at 4:00 P.M. on June 6, along with the staff of I SS Panzer Corps (General Sepp Dietrich), but both had a long way to go to reach the front that day. *Lehr*, for example, lay some 90 miles south of Caen, while *Hitlerjugend* was a good 50 miles away.

Bayerlein was a thoroughly experienced commander who had served as Erwin Rommel's chief of staff in Africa. No one knew better than he did the importance of haste at a crucial moment. As *Lehr* was preparing to march by 5:00 P.M., Bayerlein knew something else, however. If his division departed for the north just now, while it was still light, Allied airpower would slaughter it. The *Jagdbombern*—fighter-bombers, or *Jabos*—would be on them all in an instant. He wanted to wait, at least until twilight, but the 7th Army commander, General Friedrich Dollmann, insisted on the original march order. The division had to be on the Caen front by the next morning, Dollmann ordered. Bayerlein argued the impossibility of the order. The French Resistance was also active along the march route, blowing up railroad tracks and bridges, supply dumps, and telephone lines. The frequent stops, restarts, and detours the division would have to make would result in a march rate of 5 miles per hour tops, and thus *Lehr* wouldn't arrive until June 8, anyway. At least let it arrive in one piece, Bayerlein argued.

The back-and-forth between the commanders ended in victory for the superior officer (Dollmann), and Panzer *Lehr* set out that evening to ride to the assistance of 21st Panzer Division and throw the Allies into the sea. As Bayerlein predicted, however, the drive north was a nightmare. "I drove with two tanks and two radio vehicles at the head of the central column on the Alençon-Argentan-Falaise road," but within the first hour, as the command staff reached Beaumont-sur-Sarthe, the first *Jabo* attacks forced them to seek cover:

> The columns became more and more disrupted. Since the Army had ordered us to keep radio silence, runners were the only liaison between the columns. As if radio silence could prevent *Jabos* and reconnaissance aircraft aloft from recognizing us. Unfortunately, radio silence did prevent the divisional leadership from forming a true picture of the state of the advance, whether we were moving forward, whether there were bottlenecks or losses, where the spearheads were. I had constantly to detach officers and also drive to the various units myself.[14]

This first air raid put twenty men out of action, as well as twenty to thirty vehicles.

Nevertheless, the division continued to roll north on five roads. All five columns were under Allied air observation the whole way, even after nightfall. By 11:00 P.M., Bayerlein reached the village of Sées, already "lit up like a Christmas tree" by Allied bombing. Three hours later, he and the staff reached Argentan and found more of the same:

> It was as light as day—from fires and explosions. The little town trembled under a rolling attack of bombs. We got through the southern approaches, but then it became impossible to continue.

The street behind us was also blocked. We were trapped in a burning city. Dust and smoke blinded us. We found ourselves in a witch's cauldron. Sparks sprayed over the vehicles. Smoldering beams and collapsed houses blocked our way. And still above us in the sky hovered the aircraft.[15]

Bayerlein had to bring up the pioneers to repair a heavily damaged bridge over the Orne River, a process that took a full hour, and even then it was impossible to get the vehicles forward on the bombed-out and blocked roads. He and his staff dismounted and reconnoitered their way forward on foot. Eventually they decided to abandon the direct march north and head due west, toward the village of Flers, almost 30 miles away. The new route was the long way around to Caen, but they all breathed a sigh of relief as the road was passable and the bombing seemed to be slackening. They reached Flers by 4:00 A.M., headed north, and were in Condé-sur-Noireau, 30 miles south of Caen, an hour later. Here they waited for the rest of the divisional march columns (*Marschkollonen*) to catch up.

And they waited.

Bayerlein looked "far and wide," but "he didn't see a thing"—not a platoon of infantry or a company of tanks. The divisional liaison officer, Captain Alexander Hartdegen, was standing with Bayerlein and the general's driver, Sergeant Kartheus, waiting for the advance guard of the 901st *Panzergrenadier* Regiment. Nothing. "I drove back onto the road," Hartdegen remembered. "The village of Condé was a smoldering pile of ruins. Bombing had destroyed the road bridge and since 5:00 A.M. the *Jabos* were once again tracing their path through the bright blue morning sky."[16]

Bayerlein had a division out there somewhere, in other words, but he had momentarily lost it. And just as communications downward to his division had vanished, so had his upward link to his corps. "*Panzer Lehr* was part of the I SS Panzer Corps," Hartdegen wrote. "All night we had been looking for the command post of Sepp Dietrich, the corps commander, in order to discern his intentions and to receive orders. But we hadn't been able to find the corps command post. It wasn't until late on the afternoon of June 7 that we discovered it in a little wood north of Thury-Harcourt."[17] Dietrich finally gave *Lehr* its orders. Bayerlein was to form a pair of divisional battlegroups (*Kampfgruppen*) and dispatch them to Norrey and Brouay, sitting on the railroad between Bayeux and Caen, by 8:00 A.M. on June 8th. Here they would form up on the left wing of 12th SS Panzer Division and launch an attack on a broad front against the British and Canadians to the north. But yet another *Jabo* attack intervened just as the staff departed for their new command post, killing the driver (Kartheus) and wounding Bayerlein. Not until June 8 did *Lehr* reach the appointed line. Another day passed before enough of its combat elements had arrived to launch an attack, however, by which time a concentrated attack to catch the Allies in a vulnerable moment and drive them into the sea was a mere fantasy.

Even worse, the ride from Nogent to the north on June 6–7 had cost Panzer *Lehr* dearly, especially in terms of equipment. According to Bayerlein's own account, his division lost 85 armored vehicles (halftracks, prime movers, self-propelled guns) out of some 700, and 123 trucks out of 1,000.[18] His heavily armored tanks had come through better. Only five were destroyed (out of the division's complement of nearly 200). Nevertheless, the ride north had been an ordeal rather than a simple movement, and adding to the sting was a small but annoying friendly-fire attack from his own Luftwaffe, the only German aircraft Bayerlein had seen in the course of two days. In all, Panzer *Lehr*'s casualties were commensurate with those of a good-sized battle, his division was already hard-hit, and he had yet to fire a shot.

So Close, So Far: *Hitlerjugend* and the Battle of Carpiquet

General Witt's 12th SS Panzer Division *Hitlerjugend* experienced another form of frustration. The division was a great deal closer to the action on June 6, so close that divisional elements, at least, might have taken part in the fighting on D-Day itself. A confused series of march orders prevented that possibility. The division had originally deployed in Belgium in early 1944, then shifted to the French town of Lisieux, less than 20 miles from the coast, in April. In the course of the dispute over the placement of the Panzer divisions, *Hitlerjugend* moved again, this time some 30 miles farther inland, almost due west of Paris. With the first news trickling in of Allied airborne landings east of the Orne River at 3:00 A.M., Witt alerted the division. Within an hour, it was ready to march. Instead of heading toward the action, however, it now sat for three full hours, awaiting orders, as the High Command sorted out just how it wished to respond.[19] Not until 7:00 A.M. did Witt receive orders to assemble the division at Lisieux, precisely where it had been located back in April, to support the operations of LXXXI Corps. In the course of the march, the orders changed once again, this time to assemble west of Caen in support of LXXXIV Corps. And so the powerful *Hitlerjugend* division spent the first day of the Allied invasion marching fruitlessly to and fro. Night had fallen by the time the division closed up on the left of 21st Panzer Division, with orders to take part in a coordinated, three-division counterattack on the Allied beachhead the next day.

The new plan didn't work out, either. A morning attack by the three Panzer divisions was a fantasy. The 21st Panzer Division on the right was a wreck after its baptism of fire on D-Day and could contribute little to the day's events. *Panzer Lehr* spent June 7 straggling up on the left under attack by Allied fighter-bombers, and not even a solid commander like Bayerlein was quite sure where to find it. *Hitlerjugend* had to go it alone. Nevertheless, the division managed to land the first heavy blow for either side in the campaign for France. The target was the Canadian 3rd Infantry Division. Hustling down from Juno Beach, the 3rd was pressing inland with orders to skirt Caen to the west. The divisional objective for June 7 was the airfield at Carpiquet, just southwest of Caen. Along the way, the Canadians had to pass through a series of obscure Norman towns, blips on the map like Buron, Authie, and Franqueville. The unit in the divisional van was the 9th Canadian Infantry Brigade, and the unit spearheading the 9th Brigade was the North Nova Scotia Highlanders—the "North Novas," in Canadian parlance.[20]

What followed has become one of the best-known episodes of the Normandy campaign. As the North Novas drove south out of Villons, heading southwest on the road to Carpiquet, they were unaware that they were heading directly toward Witt's *Hitlerjugend* division. SS Divisions were in many ways no different from their Wehrmacht counterparts, but they tended to be oversized, topped off with men and materiel in a manner that was quite unusual for the Germans by this point of the war. *Hitlerjugend* was no exception. With a nominal strength of over 20,000 men, it was a division and a half by German standards in 1944, although it mustered fewer men than that in Normandy. Actually, it mustered boys. As the name indicated, *Hitlerjugend* consisted of very young volunteer recruits—16–18 years of age. While they had the enthusiasm of youth, one could hardly call them hardened soldiers, still less an "elite" formation. The commanders and officers were veterans, however, and so too were the noncommissioned officers, and their job was to provide the steady hand. The specific divisional element unit standing in the path of the North Novas, for example, was the 25th *Panzergrenadier* Regiment. Its commander was *Standartenführer* (Colonel) Kurt Meyer, a man with a long and successful combat record in the 1st SS Panzer Division *Leibstandarte Adolf Hit-*

ler who had fought in every major campaign of the war. His nickname was, of all things, "Panzer," although it seems to have come not from a bold armored exploit but from an incident in his youth. Attempting to play a prank on a friend, Meyer fell off the roof of a two-story building and broke just about every bone in his body, but he managed to survive, and his classmates deemed him as indestructible as a tank.

Perhaps he was indestructible—he was certainly confident to the point of arrogance. Examining a map of the Allied landings at midnight on June 6, he scoffed: "Little fish! We'll throw them back into the sea in the morning," which deserves a special entry in any compilation of greatest last words in military history.[21] When the sun came up on June 7, it appeared that Meyer might just get his chance. As he later related the tale, he was at his regimental command post up in the tower of Ardenne Abbey (*Abbaye d'Ardenne*), peering through his field glasses, when he could see opportunity knocking. It was a Canadian infantry battalion heading southwest toward Carpiquet, with tanks in support (fifty Shermans from the Sherbrooke Fusiliers). Meyer had drawn up his own grenadiers in a defensive position in front of the Abbey, facing roughly northwest. The Canadians were, in other words, passing almost directly across his front. Standing high up in his bell tower, Meyer later claimed that it all came to him in a flash: the long, vulnerable road column; the inexperienced unit advancing below as if on parade ground; the vulnerable flank virtually inviting an attack. He could scarcely believe his eyes. "But what is this?" Meyer later wrote. "Am I seeing things?"[22] He was still licking his chops years later when he wrote the account:

> An enemy tank is pushing its way through the orchards of Contest! Now he stops. The commander opens the hatch and scans the terrain. Is the guy blind?
>
> Hasn't he noticed that he's only 200 meters from the Grenadiers of the II Battalion and that the antitank guns are pointed at him? Apparently not. He calmly lights a cigarette and squints through the smoke. Not a shot rings out. The battalion keeps excellent fire discipline.
>
> Aha! Now it's all clear. The tank has thrust forward as a flank guard. Enemy tanks are rolling out of Buron toward Authie. My God! What an opportunity! The tanks are driving clear across II Battalion's front! The unit is offering us its unprotected flank. I give orders to all battalions, to the artillery and to the tanks that are standing by. "Do not shoot! Open fire on my order only!"[23]

It was a spellbinding spectacle, Meyer later remembered. The two armies a few hundred years apart, the voice of tank regiment, *Oberstürmbannführer* Max Wünsche, quietly transmitting his orders, every man in the command post speaking in a whisper. Above all, the long tension and the sudden crash of action:

> An unbearable pressure weighs on us. It has to happen soon. The enemy spearhead pushes past Franqueville, intending to cross the road. I give the attack signal to Wünsche, and can just hear his order, "*Achtung! Panzer marsch!*" Now the tension disappears. Explosions and flashes near Franqueville. The lead enemy tank is smoking and I watch the crew bailing out. More tanks are torn apart with loud explosions.[24]

Meyer's attack had hit the North Novas hard. They experienced the kind of momentary disorientation typical of a force caught by surprise in the flank, taking casualties in the opening minutes and retreating whence they had come, from Franqueville to Authie and then back to Buron. The strike by Meyer's young Panzergrenadiers had saved Carpiquet airfield, at least for the moment. The youngsters whooped and hollered with jubilation back at the command post. They also celebrated their successful battlefield debut in a shameful way, but one entirely typical for Waffen-SS troops of any age or nationality: murdering their Canadian prisoners of war in cold blood on the sacred grounds of the old Abbey.[25]

Meyer's exciting narrative of the attack on Authie-Buron is a classic example of the postwar writings of the German officer corps. The man of action, the instant application of the coup d'oeil that takes in the entirety of the battlefield with a single glance of the eye, the quick decision without waiting for higher authority: Meyer's memoir is a virtual source text for aficionados of independent command. Here is *Auftragstaktik* in all its glory, the rapid process of decision-making and command that made the Wehrmacht (and perhaps even more the Waffen-SS) so feared. Buron-Authie was a tactical situation that seemed purpose-built for a commander like Meyer, one schooled in the Prussian-German tradition of aggressive attack. Meyer was confident that he could would drive forward, scatter the advancing North Novas, then break into the depth of the Canadian position. "Objective," he thought, "the coast."[26]

But, in fact, this practically perfect Prussian moment petered out in the end. There is no doubt that Meyer had struck a blow, but at no time on June 7 had his 25th *Panzergrenadier* threatened to achieve any sort of breakthrough. Indeed, it is questionable if the attack had much of an operational impact at all. The North Novas were not conducting an assault. They were functioning as the advanced guard of the 9th Brigade (and the Canadian 3rd Division). The battalion was probing south on June 7, and its mission was to take Carpiquet airfield if it had a clear shot at it. If the Novas met "heavy resistance" at Carpiquet, however, they were supposed to hunker down on a contour of high ground between Buron and Authie, consolidate, and let the rest of the brigade come up for a more deliberate attack.[27] They met opposition all right—and plenty of it. Their Sherman tanks were no match for German antitank fire, especially of the 88mm variety, and that was a lesson that a lot of Allied tank crews were going to learn in the ensuing weeks. But throughout the day, the Canadians gave as good as they got. Meyer's regiment, too, suffered heavy losses, largely by virtue of superior Canadian artillery, which came into play in strength after some early fumbling. As his own account relates, Meyer's regiment lay under heavy and unnervingly accurate Canadian gunfire for much the day. At one point, as Meyer was speeding along on the motorcycle he was using as an improvised command vehicle, a massive detonation blew him into a bomb crater, and he claims to have lain there next to an equally nonplussed Canadian soldier for some time. Eventually, the Panzergrenadiers took Buron, but here the North Novas stopped them cold. In the course of a tough day, a few minor villages had changed hands. Both sides were exhausted, and it is safe to say that no one was unhappy to see nightfall.

The next two days, June 8–9, featured more fierce fighting with much the same result. The Canadian 9th Brigade, as well as its neighbor to the west, the 7th, was under almost constant attack by elements of three German Panzer divisions (12th SS, 21st, and Panzer *Lehr*). The Germans could not coordinate their attacks, however, and it is no wonder. Canadian firepower, self-propelled artillery, and well-aimed main gunfire from their Firefly tanks dominated the battlefield, and the Germans never did develop any real operational momentum. Enemy fire superiority slowed down everything the Wehrmacht tried to do, and of course it inflicted casualties. But its most grievous effect was on the German ability to synchronize the fire and movement of multiple divisions. The fights at Putot and Bretteville on June 8–9, as well as the battle of Norrey (June 9–10) were slaughter battles, in fact, in which the youthful grenadiers of the 12th SS came up in waves and the steady and well-equipped Canadians mowed them down in the same fashion. Throughout all these battles, the *Hitlerjugend* Division, in particular, attacked recklessly and paid the price. The division used the same tactical approach that had worked so often in the Soviet Union, but it had failed spectacularly here. Colonel Hubert Meyer, the division's Ia, later wrote: "The tactic of surprise, using mobile, fast infantry and Panzers even in small, numerically inferior *Kampfgruppen*, had often been practiced and proven in Russia. This tactic, however, had not resulted in the expected success here against a courageous and determined enemy who was ready for defense and well equipped."[28] Indeed, the Canadians shot them to pieces. "The Germans thought we were fucking Russians!" one of the men in the Regina Rifles later commented. "They did stupid things and we killed those bastards in large numbers."[29]

As a result, a counterattack that might have posed a serious threat to the newly arrived Allies came to a disappointing end. From this point on, German operational orders rarely invoked the traditional formula of "throwing the enemy into the sea." The Allies were here to stay, and the Germans would have to transition from the attack to the defense. From Meyer's perch high up in the Ardenne Abbey tower, he could look north and just barely catch a glimpse of the sea shimmering in the distance. "Panzer" was just 12 miles away from the English Channel, but given the balance of forces, and the Wehrmacht's inability to sustain a successful attack against the Allies, it might as well have been a thousand.

The US Army in Motion: Cherbourg

The first stage of the fighting in Normandy came to a distinct and dramatic end on Saturday, June 10. That was the day that an RAF raid targeted the headquarters of *Panzergruppe West* at the château of La Caine, badly wounding the German commander of the *Panzergruppe*, General Leo Geyr von Schweppenburg. Some say that Schweppenburg, a neophyte at operating under enemy air superiority, had neglected to camouflage his headquarters well enough and that the plethora of radio trucks and staff cars parked outside the château gave away his position. More likely, the raid was a triumph for Allied signals intelligence and for ULTRA. Whatever its origins, the results were deadly. The bombing incapacitated Geyr and killed his chief of staff, General Sigismund Ritter und Edler von Dawans, as well as twelve other staff officers. While Geyr survived his injuries, his headquarters was hors de combat for a full two weeks.[30] The Germans would have had trouble busting the Allied bridgehead even if they could coordinate an attack by every last Panzer division in France. With command and control momentarily dislocated, planning any sort of bold Panzer stroke was impossible.

The decapitation of *Panzergruppe West* was not a one-off, either. Consider this list of German generals fighting in Normandy: General Wilhelm Falley of the 91st Air-Landing Infantry Division; General Erich Marcks, commander of the LXXXIV Corps; General Fritz Witt of the 12th SS Panzer Division *Hitlerjugend*; General Heinz Hellmich of the 243rd Static Division; General Rudolf Stegmann of the 77th Infantry Division. They have much in common. All were competent, hard-driving unit commanders, well schooled in the operational art, trusted by their subordinate officers and men. They were also all killed in the first two weeks of the Normandy fighting: Falley on June 6, Marcks on June 12, Witt on June 14, Hellmich on June 17, and Stegmann on June 18. Marcks, Hellmich, and Stegmann all died in Allied air attacks, the latter two stitched by 20mm shells. Death at the hands of Allied fighter-bombers became so common that German soldiers coined a new term: *Jabo-Tod*, they called it. It wasn't a small-caliber round, and the results usually weren't pretty. Witt's fate was even grislier: obliterated by 15-inch gunfire courtesy of the Royal Navy during a bombardment on his divisional command post at Venoix.[31] All of them joined the ranks of the dozens of German generals and field commanders killed in action in this war. And the number of dead generals could easily have been higher. On July 17, two Canadian Spitfire fighters from 412 Squadron caught Field Marshal Rommel's open Horch staff car tearing along the narrow country road between Vimoutiers and Livarot, killing the driver and wounding Rommel so grievously that the first responders to the wreck thought he was dead. Although Allied histories remember the period as one of hedgerow-slogging, frustration, and high losses, in fact the better-supplied Allies were blooding the Wehrmacht prodigiously from top to bottom. Such was the Wehrmacht's cost of command, the price of waging war against an enemy vastly superior in resources and firepower.[32] "A poor people," Rommel commented to his staff just a few weeks before his brush with death, "shouldn't fight a war at all."[33] German manpower was irreplaceable, of course, but so too were veteran commanders. In killing off the Wehrmacht's officers, the Allies were gouging away at a key German center of gravity.

Indeed, the overall impression of Allied operations once ashore was their methodical nature, their inexorability. For the Americans, house-keeping duties took up the first week or so on shore, with the US Army driving on Carentan in order to unify its two widely separated beachheads, Utah and Omaha. Carentan fell to the US 101st Airborne Division on June 12, and so the Americans could move down to the next objective on their checklist: a drive across the base of the Cotentin Peninsula. The purpose was to isolate the great port of Cherbourg and to cut off German forces to the north. With the Douve River serving as protection to the south, mechanized spearheads of the US VII Corps (General Joseph Collins) broke out of the Utah beachhead on June 14, heading west and reaching St. Sauveur-le-Vicomte on June 16. The next day, US 9th Infantry Division reached the sea. German opposition was minimal, and a brief examination of the battle array shows why. Elements of three German divisions were fighting in the Cotentin. Both the 91st Air-Landing Infantry Division (*Luftlande Infanterie-Division*) and the 709th Static Division were remnants of divisions smashed on D-Day. The third, the 243rd Infantry Division, had originally been a static division but had now acquired limited mobility, and like many of the divisions in the west it was equipped with captured Russian artillery.

One other division was present. Elements of the vastly under-strength 77th Infantry Division were also filtering up into the Cotentin from the division's original location at Saint-Malo. Only three battalions had arrived by the time Collins shut the door behind them, however. The headquarters of LXXXIV Corps now ordered the division back out of the Cotentin, so it could take part in the broader battle then developing in Normandy. The divisional commander, General Stegmann, was relieved. He had seen the outdated fortifications at Cherbourg and saw no hope for a long-term defense of the port. No sooner had he handed off the new orders to his staff, however, than he became the latest victim of *Jabo-Tod*. The commander of the 1049th Infantry Regiment, and the senior regimental commander in the division, Colonel Rudolf Bacherer, now took over the 77th and led the divisional elements on a mini-breakout to the south. They overran surprised US defenders of the 47th Infantry Regiment (9th Division), took 250 US prisoners, and some 1,500 men managed to regain German lines on June 20.

While no one should downplay the toughness of the fighting in the Cotentin, the difficulties occurred only in the tactical realm. Lifting up our gaze to the operational level—the movement of divisions and corps—the Americans moved forward steadily and the Germans did the same in reverse. The same description is apt for the subsequent battle of Cherbourg.[34] The Germans managed to form a thin defensive line across the Cotentin from Barneville in the west through Montebourg in the center to Quinéville in the east, a line that corresponded roughly to intermingled divisional elements of the 243rd, 77th, 91st, and 709th Divisions. In terms of their actual fighting strength, however, they didn't add up to much more than a division and a half. Their orders from the high command were to fight it out for every meter of ground and only to retreat when enemy pressure had become unbearable.[35] Such a posture of delaying resistance (*hinhaltender Widerstand*) is a delicate balancing act, however, requiring experienced troops and a degree of mobility that at least matches the adversary, and German divisions had neither of these prerequisites in Normandy. Indeed, the fully mechanized units of the US Army simply overran the Germans south of Cherbourg, and the defenders neither delayed their adversary nor had enough time to fully prepare the defenses of the port. Declared a "fortress" by Hitler and the High Command, Cherbourg was nothing of the sort. Like virtually all naval fortresses, its strongest ramparts faced the sea, and the landward side had neither the engineering works nor the suitable terrain to support resistance against a better-armed and -supplied adversary.

For all these reasons, the so-called siege of Cherbourg moved in fast motion throughout. US forces began to arrive in strength before the town on June 20, with Collins's three divisions abreast, from west to east the 9th, 79th, and 4th. A multilingual propaganda broadcast on June 21 (in German, Russian, Polish, and French, reflecting the polyglot nature of the Wehrmacht's forces in Normandy) demanded the surrender of the Cherbourg garrison by the next morning.[36] When the newly appointed commandant of Fortress Cherbourg, General Schlieben of the 709th Division, failed to respond, US bombers arrived in strength on the morning of June 22. Collins requested a massive air assault—"air pulverization," he called it—by all eleven groups of the IX Bomber Command.[37] For over an hour, some 375 aircraft flattened the defenses in front of Cherbourg, completely unopposed by German aircraft. The main attack followed immediately afterward. The defenders put up game resistance here and there, but units like the 84th Fortress Battalion or the 549th *Ost*-Battalion had no business in this fight. They were old, half-trained, and already suffering from what Schlieben called "bunker fever."[38] They were in a hopeless situation and they knew it. "Reinforcement is absolutely necessary," Schlieben reported to Rommel, but he knew as well as anyone that none was forthcoming.[39] In fact, preliminary plans to ship 15th *Fallschirmjäger* Regiment from Brittany to Cherbourg by sea had already collapsed when the extent of American bombing damage to the port became clear.

The actual ground fighting started slowly on June 22, with 9th Division driving on Octeville, approaching Cherbourg from the left, while 79th Division headed straight for Fort du Roule and the high ground overlooking the city from the south. On the right, 4th Division was to head for Tourlaville and seal off the Cherbourg sector from the east. Given the sorry state of the port's physical defenses as well as the manpower defending it, there was little danger of the plan going wrong—and it didn't. The 7th Corps made small gains on June 22, penetrated the outer ring of Fortress Cherbourg on June 23, and crumpled the defenses altogether on June 24–25. The occasional last stand, like the one put up by the defenders of the village of La Glacerie two miles southeast of Cherbourg, only brought into sharper relief the lack of resistance elsewhere. Anytime the Americans met resistance, a combination of P-47 Thunderbolt attacks and that old US Army standby—the field artillery—crushed it, at Tourlaville on June 24, Octeville and Fort du Roule the next day. With all three US divisions pushing into the city proper, the end was near. As Schlieben reported on June 24: "Concentrated enemy fire and bombing attacks have split the front. Numerous batteries have been put out of action or have worn out. Combat efficiency has fallen off considerably. The troops squeezed into a small area will hardly be able to withstand an attack on the 25th."[40] And he was right. On June 25, US troops took his command post, an underground bunker at St. Saveur, under direct fire, and so too did Allied naval gunfire. "Loss of town unavoidable in nearest future as enemy has penetrated outskirts," Schlieben radioed to Rommel. "Request urgent instructions." Rommel's response: "In accordance with the Führer's orders, you are to continue fighting to the last round."[41] Schlieben surrendered the next day, June 26, along with the Naval Commandant Normandy (*Seekommandant Normandie*), Admiral Walter Hennecke, and 800 men. Another 400 men in the city itself gave themselves up independently, and forcing the surrender of the garrisons of various fortified works took several more days. Finally, US troops gathered several thousand prisoners outside the city, who had withdrawn to a lonely refuge on Cap de la Hague in the very northeastern tip of the Cotentin. Cherbourg had fallen, and the Allies had their port.

The aftermath of the city's capture is well known. The Germans had achieved one thing while they held Cherbourg. They demolished the place. Hitler had ordered Schlieben to "defend the last bunker and leave to the enemy not a harbor but a field of ruins."[42] He meant resistance to the last ditch, and Schlieben had certainly not done that. But in a broader sense, Cherbourg had become a "field of ruins." US Colonel Alvin G. Viney, the engineer in charge of the port rehabilitation plan, described the demolition as "masterful, beyond a doubt the most complete, intensive, and best-planned demolition in history."[43] Mines, sunken ships, demolitions, systematic destruction of the Gare Maritime, which controlled both electricity and heat for the port, 20,000 cubic yards of masonry dumped into the harbor, destruction of the breakwaters: it was a particularly thorough job. Not until August would Cherbourg be fully open for business.

The very thoroughness of the demolition raises an interesting issue, however. The Wehrmacht could have simply demolished the port in the opening week of the fighting and been done with it. As it was, the High Command sacrificed four full divisions in a hopeless campaign that barely slowed down the American attack, a particularly senseless equation for the Wehrmacht by this point in the war.

Stellungskrieg in Normandy

The operational situation was far different in front of the British and Canadians. Deployed on the open, rolling plain of the Calvados, with the largest city in Normandy, Caen, in their sights, the Anglo-Canadians had the best possibility for a large-scale armored assault to break through the German lines. At the same time, they attracted the strongest part of the German defensive line. Eventually, the Germans deployed seven Panzer divisions, along with four heavy tank battalions equipped with the new Mark VI Tiger tank, to guard the Caen sector, while only two Panzer divisions faced the Americans farther west. As one source describes it,

> The countryside in the British and Canadian sectors—a relatively open, flat, dry expanse stretching from Caen to Paris—was more favorable for offensive warfare. Paradoxically, those conditions made fighting there perhaps more difficult than in the American sector. The nature of the ground and the strategic importance of the area compelled the Germans to mass the bulk of their Panzer units and their best troops in the path of Montgomery's forces.[44]

Montgomery had promised to take Caen on the first day and might well have been able to do so. The typical cautiousness of a just-disembarked force in a major amphibious invasion took hold, however, and British forces hesitated in their drive to the south. The delay on day one was only hours in length, but it was just long enough to permit an improvised attack by the spearhead of the 21st German Panzer division that brought the British to a halt.

The terrain on the US front in the Cotentin Peninsula and western Calvados, by contrast, was an ancient array of small farms, separated one from the other by hedgerows (*bocage*), great earthen embankments topped by thick, twisted hedges 10–12 feet high. They formed an ideal protection for the defenders, and US troops soon learned that charging a hedgerow without a careful prior reconnaissance could be suicide. Moreover, the compartmentalized battlespace meant that the Allies, and especially the Americans, were unable to unfold their full cornucopia of firepower. Every encounter boiled down to a small-unit infantry clash, with machine guns and mortars in support, precisely the spot where the Wehrmacht might still claim a degree of supremacy, or at least a greater degree of experience.

Without giving it a second thought, in other words, the Allies had got it all wrong. The most casualty-averse Allied force was the British, and for good reason. They were fighting with a shrinking replacement pool, especially in terms of infantry. Veteran units like the 7th Armoured or 51st Highland Divisions were tired and apathetic, a problem for the entire British army by now.[45] Some of these men had been fighting for five years by 1944. And these were the very units now facing a solid wall of Panzer divisions, many of them formations of the Waffen-SS. Without any romanticizing of the situation, we might say that the German divisions here were the finest mechanized units in the world. Achieving a breakthrough here was simply impossible without suffering extremely high casualties. No one had planned this. Assigning the beaches in Normandy was a simple function of the preinvasion deployments in Britain. British divisions deployed in eastern Britain, in Kent, and on the southeastern shore of the island, where they had been since the summer of 1940 to defend against a potential German invasion. The Americans deployed where they could find space upon arriving, to the west. And that is how the two forces landed in Europe: the Americans to the west and the British to the east. The richer and more robust partner was stuck in mind-boggling terrain in a relatively secondary portion of the front, while the poorer and more exhausted force faced a solid wall of Panzer divisions in open country.

Even as the Americans were driving on Cherbourg, the main front had already assumed a stable form. A line formed on both sides, with the Allies on the attack more or less constantly and the Germans locked into a pattern of rigid defense (*starre Verteidigung*) on the orders of the High Command. As in Italy, the overall operational form settled into the *Stellungskrieg*, a positional fight, and a materiel- and manpower-intensive slugfest that offered few chances for maneuver or decisive victory. The Americans tried to grind their way through the bocage toward Saint-Lô, and though they made steady progress, it was slow and expensive. Casualties were extremely heavy, 40,000 men in return for a 20-mile advance. Even today, the statistics are striking. During its first six weeks on the continent, for example, US 90th Division took nearly 90 percent casualties in its rifle platoons, "the men who do the scouting, the patrolling, the flank protection, the front-line work," as one US officer put it, and the casualty rate for company-grade officers in the division was even worse—nearly 150 percent over that same period.[46] The 90th was a green unit, but even the more experienced divisions were paying the price for fighting among the hedgerows. The 1st, 4th, 9th, and 25th Infantry Divisions, for example, had casualty rates of 60 percent of enlisted men and some 70 percent of their officers among the riflemen. General Eisenhower was at his plainspoken best in explaining the three factors that were making this all so difficult. "First, as always," Ike wrote, "the fighting quality of the German soldier; second, the nature of the country; third the weather."[47] Indeed, weather seemed to be conspiring against the Allies, too. At no time in the twentieth century had a Normandy summer been this cloudy, rainy, and windy as the summer of 1944.

The British and Canadians to the east, meanwhile, took a run at Caen. Then they did it a second time, and over and over again with increasingly futile results. Montgomery's attempt to send 7th Armoured Division on a "right hook" to outflank Caen's defenses to the west on June 13 led to disaster. Near the quaint little town of Villers-Bocage, the division's 22nd Armoured Brigade fell into a skillfully laid ambush by Waffen-SS Lieutenant (*Obersturmführer*) Michael Wittmann and a company of Tiger tanks, part of the 501st SS Heavy Tank Battalion. Alert to the British advance, Wittmann took his Tiger into a small patch of woods south of the road out of town and waited.[48] He let the head of the British column get within 80 yards, then took out the lead tank with a single shot from his 88mm main gun. Trapped on the narrow road by the flaming wreck, much of the brigade (with fifty-eight Cromwells, equipped with a mediocre 75mm gun) was helpless. Realizing he had little to fear, Wittmann drove parallel to the road, shooting as he went. "For Christ's sake, get a move on!" screamed one British noncom into the radio. "There's a Tiger running alongside us 50 yards away!"[49] At one point, Wittmann actually climbed onto the road, destroying the tanks in front of him, forcing lighter vehicles into the ditch, and even running some of them over. In five minutes, he and his company destroyed twenty-four tanks, nine halftracks, and a mass of towed guns and armored cars. In the end, Wittmann's decision to get on the road and drive into the town was his undoing. His Tiger was disabled by a British 6-pounder antitank shell at point-blank range, and he and his crew had to escape on foot. Nevertheless, Villers-Bocage was yet more proof—if any were still needed—of the tactical supremacy of German mechanized units in 1944, both Wehrmacht and Waffen-SS.

Attack followed attack, but the Germans managed to parry each one. Montgomery's third attempt was Operation Epsom on June 25. Epsom was a much more concentrated thrust by much of British 2nd Army (General Miles Dempsey) carrying out a shorter right hook to the west of the city. The goal was to cross the Odon River and encircle the city from the southwest. It also came to grief, this time at Hill 112, a rise just over the Odon. Not until Operation Charnwood on July 8 did Montgomery succeed in taking the northern half of Caen. The unique feature of this operation was the introduction of Allied carpet-bombing, the use of heavy strategic bombers in the tactical role, to help pave the way for the advance. But even here, enough German forces survived the maelstrom of bombing to limit the British advance to the half of Caen on the northern bank of the Orne River.

The low point of this record of futility was, without a doubt, the disastrous breakout attempt on July 18, Operation Goodwood. A classic set-piece battle gone wrong, Goodwood was a huge operation, carried out by Montgomery's entire 21st Army Group (the 2nd British Army under Dempsey and the 1st Canadian Army under General H. D. G. Crerar). Despite heavy bombing that once again smashed the German front, killing thousands and driving equal numbers deaf and mad, Montgomery's attack got stuck in front of the German positions on a slight rise known as Bourguébus Ridge. Despite everything—the air support, the vast forces at his command, and the constant claims that a breakthrough was just around the corner—Montgomery had failed again. Goodwood, Eisenhower raged, had cost 7,000 tons of bombs in order to gain a total of seven miles and once again had failed to break through.

But what of the Germans? The focus on Allied problems in Normandy is an Anglo-American construct. It fails to take into account the plight of the German forces, the Wehrmacht and Waffen-SS alike. Outnumbered in manpower, vastly inferior in materiel, fighting without air cover, and trapped in a brutal *Stellungskrieg* whose only end could be their destruction, the German forces in Normandy were trapped in the first of many purgatories that would characterize the final ten months of the war. Morale stayed high among the men, and of course the officers stayed loyal, but neither of these factors could alter the facts: Normandy was destined to be a graveyard. Within a week of the successful Allied landing, both Rundstedt, the OB-West, and Rommel, commanding Army Group B, had begun to insist that an officer of the High Command visit the front to witness the hopeless conditions in person.

Nonevent: The Margival Conference

Both men were surprised to receive a communication on June 16 responding to their demand. A representative from the High Command would be arriving tomorrow: Hitler himself. On June 17 the Führer, Jodl, and a small entourage of staff officers flew from Germany to France to meet with the two field marshals who had so disappointed him thus far. The pair had failed to mesh from the start. They never overcame their mutual distrust. They had failed in signal fashion to achieve the operational objective that had been their obsession for nearly a year: driving the Allied invasion back into the sea. Now, near Margival north of Soissons, the Führer had come to call his commanders to account.[50] Neither officer could do much by way of preparation for the meeting. Rommel, for example, had just spent a twenty-one-hour day inspecting troop dispositions in the Cotentin Peninsula and now had to drive 120 miles to Margival.

The meeting took place in a great bunker complex, Command Center W-II. Built by Organization Todt in 1942, W-II was part of that futile mountain of concrete that the Germans had poured into France, a poor man's replacement for sufficient divisions, tanks, and supplies to defend the place. Hitler opened the discussion "in a raised and bitter voice."[51] He expressed his displeasure at the successful invasion, accused the local commanders of mistakes and failures, and demanded that Fortress Cherbourg be held at all costs. But the presentation misfired. Hitler looked "pale and bleary-eyed."[52] He sat, hunched on a stool. He fiddled with his glasses and toyed with a bundle of pencils. His legendary "powers of suggestion" seemed momentarily to have vanished.[53]

Here, for once, was an opening for the generals, and the exchange of views, for once, was frank. Rundstedt spoke briefly, then turned the meeting over to the ground commander, Rommel. The "struggle was hopeless," Rommel said, and "the enemy's superiority on land, on the sea, and in the air" irresistible. He condemned a recent OKW report—apparently taking an Allied communiqué at face value, that the Allied invasion had surprised the coastal divisions "in their sleep" on June 6. In fact, Rommel reported, they had fought "to the last breath in their weakly built fortifications."[54] Like his comrades fighting in the east, he objected to Hitler's senseless declaration of individual ports as fortresses. The number of such places, already a problem in the Soviet Union, had assumed grotesque proportions in the west. Ijmuiden, Walcheren Island, Dunkirk, Calais, Cap Gris Nez, Boulogne, Dieppe, Le Havre, Cherbourg, Saint-Malo, Brest, Lorient, St. Nazaire, La Pallice, Royan, and the Gironde River mouth: sixteen in all, the fortresses tied up no fewer than 200,000 men and irreplaceable stocks of ammunition and materiel. The Allies didn't storm them and often didn't even watch them all that closely, and certainly the fortresses failed to tie up an equal number of Allied troops. Many of them surrendered in May 1945, their garrisons marching into captivity after virtually sitting out the last year of the war. The Wehrmacht could not afford such a "senseless sacrifice of men and materiel," not with the Allies already having twenty-five "highly mobile" divisions ashore and introducing two to three new ones per week. A successful defense in Normandy just wasn't in the cards, and the result for the entire Western Front was incalculable, "especially since neither the Seine River line nor any other rear positions had been built."

"Even if the enemy's conduct of battle seems slow and ponderous," Rommel concluded, "the persistence of his methods and their superiority in all areas is a guarantee of success." A breakout from the beachhead was likely any time now, and the time had come to give the commanders in the west "total operational freedom."[55] Unrealistic decisions formulated "around the green table"—that is to say, by Hitler and his staff sitting around the conference table in Berchtesgaden or Rastenburg—had to end. Commanders at the front deserved the traditional prerogative of independent authority. "You demand our trust," Rommel complained, "but you don't trust us at all."[56]

Not to worry, Hitler promised. Everything was about to change. He had just unleashed the V-weapons on England the previous day, June 16. So terrible would be their impact that they would bring the British people to their knees, making them much more inclined toward peace (*friedenswillig*) than they were at the moment. The V-1 would be the decisive weapon in the struggle. Masses of jet fighters, likewise, were about to come online, which would soon break the enemy's air superiority over both the front and the German homeland. He even broke off his monologue long enough to dictate a press release on the miracle weapons to one of his aides. The situation on the Eastern Front and in the Balkans was stable for the moment. Things had never looked more favorable.

Just at this moment—in an almost exquisite turn of irony—the air-raid siren in the bunker began to shriek. Hitler and company had to rush to the air-raid shelter. It was close quarters for the moment: Hitler, the two field marshals, their chiefs of staff, and Hitler's adjutant, General Rudolf Schmundt. Rommel's *Chef*, General Hans Speidel, claimed that Rommel took the opportunity to discuss the political situation as well as the military one. The field marshal recited the litany of troubles: the wavering German front in Normandy, the threat to Germany once the Allies had broken through, the complete collapse then taking place in Italy, the impossibility of holding the Eastern Front. Germany was isolated, and whatever the propaganda claims, the international situation was dire. It was time to end the war, Rommel insisted. After repeated attempts to change the subject, Hitler brusquely cut off the conversation. "Don't bother yourself about the future course of the war," he hissed, "just your own invasion front."[57]

And then, after a promise to visit Rommel's Army Group B headquarters in the next day or two, he was gone. Rundstedt's chief of staff, General Günther Blumentritt, was up early the next morning, already busying himself with the arrangements for Hitler's trip to the front, when he received the news that the Führer had departed for Berchtesgaden the night before. Apparently, a V-1 had wobbled in flight and went badly off course, heading east instead of west and crashing not too far from the Margival meeting site. While the bomb did little damage and no one was hurt, Hitler used the accident as the reason for his hasty departure. It is equally likely that he intended only a one-day stay all along. Given the utterly fruitless nature of the conversation, a second day would have been a waste of time anyway.

The Margival leadership conference (*Führerbesprechung*) was over. Assessing its meaning isn't easy. Hitler had spouted nonsense for the entire seven-hour meeting (9:00 A.M. to 4:00 P.M.). His talk of miracle weapons, of jet fighters, and of bringing the British to their knees was nonsense by this point in the war—and so was his admonition to Rommel to keep his nose out of politics and stick to the operational side. Hitler hadn't practiced politics in this war since the start of the Russian campaign: no diplomacy, no communications with the opponent, no real peace-feelers. But Rundstedt and Rommel didn't look much better. Their insistence that there could be some operational solution to the problem of their front, as much as military historians would like to believe it, has to be judged against the facts. The two field marshals were battling against a more mobile and better-supplied opponent, whose absolute control of the air rendered even that most basic of military activities—movement—nearly impossible, but this problem didn't even come up in the discussion. Rommel did recommend bringing the war to an end, but he didn't push the point. Margival saw all the participants posturing and saying nothing, a nonevent for a war that had lost all strategic purpose.

Collapse of the Defense: Cobra

The month of July saw the Normandy front in deadlock. On the surface, the operational situation seemed balanced enough. Two German armies stood facing two Allied armies. For the Wehrmacht, the 7th Army deployed on the left (in the west), more or less facing off against the Americans in the bocage. To the east lay *Panzergruppe West* (soon to be renamed 5th Panzer Army), holding the German right wing and barring the British from reaching the open country around Caen and beyond. Deployed against them were two Allied armies. US 1st Army stood on the right, facing the German 7th. British 2nd Army deployed on the Allied left, facing *Panzergruppe West*. The front extended from Portbail on the western coast of the Cotentin Peninsula to just beyond Ouistreham on the Channel coast in the east: a distance of 65 miles as the crow flies, but much more than that, well over 100 miles, given the twists, turns, and bulges of the front.

As always in war, the surface view can be deceiving, and a great deal was actually happening in Normandy. The fighting had been more or less continuous, halted from time to time by the weather more than anything else. A great storm had blown in during June 19–23, for example, which not only hindered operations on the ground but also destroyed the Mulberry artificial harbor in the US sector. The disaster stranded some 800 Allied ships packed with supplies and equipment. Otherwise, the Allies woke up every day and renewed their push toward their objectives: Saint-Lô for the Americans, Caen for the British; the casualties on both sides were high. The pressure that Allied materiel could bring to bear was enormous, and even in a sector where analysts usually criticize Allied operations (i.e., Montgomery's thrashing about near Caen), the Allies forced the Germans to keep their mechanized divisions in the line rather than swap them out for infantry divisions and place them into a reserve. Sepp Dietrich's I SS Panzer Corps was already in France at the time of the invasion. Joining it in the line was II SS Panzer Corps under *SS-Obergruppenführer* Wilhelm Bittrich, detached from Army Group North Ukraine on June 12 and shipped to the Western Front. A journey that should have taken days took instead two full weeks due to the devastated state of the railroads in France, and II SS Panzer Corps did not begin to enter the line until June 29.[58] And indeed, these elite, oversize divisions defended their positions superbly, arriving just in time to blunt Montgomery's latest offensive toward Caen, Operation Epsom. Taking four of the strongest and most mobile divisions in the German order of battle and tying them down to static positional fighting was a not winning hand in the long run, however, and no one on the German side thought it was. Befitting a close *Stellungskrieg* of this sort, the two sides in Normandy were trading losses: 65,000 German to 61,000 Allied by July 1. The latter number broke down to 35,300 American, 22,700 British, and 3,000 Canadian.[59] The former number—the German total—didn't break down at all, of course, and therein lay the problem. The coalition could distribute losses and share the pain, while the Wehrmacht could do neither.

Likewise, beneath the surface appearance of a cohesive front, the Germans spent the first part of July in turmoil. A comprehensive command shuffle was in train, one that would eventually affect the entire army in the west. The 7th Army under General Friedrich Dollmann had borne the brunt of the fighting thus far. His failure in the hopeless defense of Cherbourg had aroused Hitler's ire, and the OKW chief Wilhelm Keitel immediately instituted court-martial proceedings against Dollmann. On June 28, Dollmann, Rommel, and Rundstedt had to report to Hitler in person at Berchtesgaden. Although the field marshals were able to defend Dollmann's conduct and protect him from the noose, they could not save his job. The Führer dismissed him late on June 28, and Dollmann died the next day, either of a heart attack or suicide by poison, we will never know. His successor was *SS-Obergruppenführer* (Lieutenant General) Paul Hausser, one of the

founding fathers of the Waffen-SS before the war and now a grizzled, one-eyed combat veteran of numerous campaigns and much hard
fighting. Hausser had led the II SS Panzer Corps during the battle of
Prokhorovka, the climax of the battle of Kursk and one of the greatest armored clashes of all time. A loyal National Socialist by convic-
tion, his appointment seemed to herald a more energetic and aggressive
prosecution of the campaign.[60]

The other German army in Normandy, likewise, came under new
command. General Leo Geyr von Schweppenburg was still recovering
from the wounds he had suffered in the RAF air raid on his headquarters at La Caine on June 10. Since then, the Panzer divisions had
been languishing, adopting a defensive posture against the British on
the Caen front. Here, too, Hitler and his advisers saw the need for
a more vital and energetic commander. Their choice seemed to be a
good one. General Heinrich Eberbach had commanded 4th Panzer
Division in 1941 and took over the XXXXVIII Panzer briefly after the
Soviet offensive at Stalingrad. Since then, severe wounds had forced
him to alternate between frontline command and less dangerous duties
on the home front: inspector of the Panzer troops for the Replacement
Army from February to October 1943; commander in quick succession of XXXXVII, XXXXVIII, and XXXXX Panzer Corps. Another
serious wound at the end of 1943 brought him home again, this time
as inspector of Panzer troops for the Home Army. Rommel brought
him onto the staff of Army Group B in June. Like Hausser, Eberbach
was a highly experienced veteran with a fearless disposition, a fighting
general. He, too, seemed an ideal choice for the hard days ahead in
Normandy.

The great purge reached even higher, however, to the very top of
the military hierarchy in the west. The Margival conference had convinced Hitler that Rundstedt and Rommel were tired and demoralized,
which was absolutely true. The repeat performance on June 29–30,
with Rundstedt and Rommel traveling to Berchtesgaden in connection with *le cas* Dollmann, had done nothing to change the Führer's
mind. Rundstedt had never been a paragon of enthusiasm. "As long as
the field marshal is grumbling, everything must be in order," Hitler
had once remarked.[61] Rundstedt's dourness and aristocratic hauteur
were on the increase lately, however. Rommel, for his part, had been
a broken man ever since Africa. At Margival, he had committed the
cardinal sins of meddling in politics and recommending peace and had
lost whatever special favor he once enjoyed with the Führer.

Rundstedt went first. On July 2, he received news of his dismissal
as OB-West. His replacement was Field Marshal Günther Kluge.[62]

"Clever Hans," as he was known (a German play on words, since *klug* means "clever"), had seen it all. One of the brightest young officers in the interwar Reichswehr, he commanded the 4th Army in the Polish campaign, then again in the French campaign of 1940, and one final time in Operation Barbarossa. During the crisis in front of Moscow in December 1941, he rose to the command of Army Group Center. At this point, opinions on his reputation diverge. He mastered a very difficult situation and stabilized the line, managing to get Hitler to agree to the necessary withdrawals, but he also proved skilled in casting others in the role of scapegoat. He dismissed his subordinates in droves: General Adolf Strauss of 9th Army, General Erich Höppner of 4th Panzer Army, and even his successor as commander of 4th Army, General Ludwig Kübler. Most damning of all to his historical reputation, he fired General Heinz Guderian as commander of the 2nd Panzer Army, an influential writer in the postwar period who savaged Kluge in his memoirs.

Kluge proved just as "clever" in 1943. This statement is true, however, only if we use the term to imply a certain devious quality. High command in the Wehrmacht during World War II required principles that were elastic and could change from moment to moment. Those present in the planning sessions for Kursk remember Kluge in various ways. Some portrayed him as a commander in wholehearted support of the German offensive (Operation Citadel), mainly because the plan allotted a leading role to his command, Army Group Center. Others show him firmly in support of the offensive *as scheduled*, or firmly in support of the offensive against the breakthrough zones *as originally envisioned*. All three of these planning scenarios were very different things, and agreeing to all three was a real trick. As always, Kluge was able to look good in the eyes of the Führer without earning the contempt of colleagues in the officer corps. In that sense alone, Kluge may well have been the quintessential Nazi officer, despite his often-expressed disrespect and even contempt for Hitler, and despite the number of times he had stated to his colleagues that only the removal of Hitler could save Germany from destruction.

New leadership meant old problems. No commander, no matter how skilled, could buttress the creaking front in the west by now. The month of July saw German casualties double, to a total of 117,000 since June 6. While the Allies could replace their losses, only 10,000 or so German replacements made it to the front in that same period. The constant strain of operating under the shadow of the *Jabo* weighed on everyone. The remains of *Luftflotte* 3 in the west could generate

300–350 sorties per day, while the Allied air forces could perform more than 4,000, and the balance of airpower was only going to get worse, since the Allies had already built no fewer than twelve airbases within their continental beachhead. Eberbach was a tough character, but he was appalled at what he saw, noting how "the substance of our divisions is being eaten away." Kluge seemed to have no illusions either. "We'll hold, and if we don't receive any help to better the situation, we'll die a decent death," he wrote to Hitler on July 21, as the Führer was convalescing from the previous day's bomb attack.[63]

While the Allies were attriting the Wehrmacht nicely, they were becoming increasingly impatient with the static front in Normandy. The beachhead was no longer large enough to hold all the units that Eisenhower had envisioned pouring into Europe. Indeed, the backlog of men, tanks, and equipment still in Britain was huge, some 250,000 men and 58,000 vehicles.[64] Moreover, the V-weapons campaign on which Hitler had placed so many hopes had begun, and the British public was deeply shaken. The death toll in London during the course of July was over 4,200, along with 30,000 wounded and tens of thousands of destroyed buildings. Perhaps even worse than the numbers was the almost complete helplessness of the island under attack. There simply was no counter. The only solution was to overrun their bases and launchpads on the Channel coast. To do that, however, they first had to break out of Normandy.

The plan the Allies eventually devised, Operation Cobra, was at least the fourth iteration of the Allied solution to fighting the Wehrmacht. Attacking the Germans unit versus unit was almost always a failure. Whatever the disparity in numbers or materiel, German divisions usually managed to hold their positions or to withdraw in good order. A broad-front advance, with divisions and corps spread evenly across the attack sector, might drive the Germans back, but such an approach would rarely rupture the German front decisively enough to achieve a breakthrough. The Allies had immense materiel superiority, but turning it into battlefield advantage was no easy task. At El Alamein, Stalingrad, and Cassino, a local battlefield commander managed to figure it out for himself. The honor role thus far included Montgomery (Alamein), Vatutin (Stalingrad), and Alexander (Cassino). Now, a fourth name was about to join the hall of fame: General Omar N. Bradley, commander of US 1st Army.

By mid-July, Bradley and his staff had drawn up a plan that was a conceptual departure for the US Army.[65] Rather than a lockstep, broad-front advance, Cobra was a breakthrough on a very narrow front between Saint-Lô and Périers. Bradley concentrated enough force against this tiny spot to crush it: the entire US VII Corps under General Joseph Collins. The front line consisted of three infantry divisions, the 9th (General Manton S. Eddy), 4th (General Raymond O. Barton), and 30th (General Leland S. Hobbs), although the term "infantry" in the 1944 American context signified a fully mechanized, mobile division, with a level of heavy weapons and artillery support that was unique for the era. Soviet planners would have labeled the assault force the "first echelon," although the US Army didn't use the term. Deployed behind the assault echelon was another powerful three-division array, consisting of 1st Infantry Division (General Clarence Huebner), the 2nd Armored Division (General Edward Brooks), and the 3rd Armored Division (General Leroy Watson). These divisions constituted the exploitation force, a "second echelon," preventing the Germans from sealing off the rupture in their lines made by the initial assault. In terms of personnel, firepower, and logistical support, VII Corps was the equivalent of a Soviet army. Perhaps without being consciously aware of it, Bradley had invented a US version of deep battle.

Bradley managed to go Soviet planners one better, however. With the vast resources of the world's most productive economy at his disposal, he could lay on the materiel support in a way that few other armies could. Leading off Cobra would be a vast carpet-bombing strike, employing an expensive strategic asset (heavy, four-engine bombers) in the tactical role. The number of aircraft involved was staggering: 1,500 heavy bombers and 396 medium bombers of the Eighth Air Force, as well as 350 fighter-bombers of the IX Tactical Air Command. A grand total of 2,246 aircraft were going to be in the air simultaneously over a very small piece of real estate in close proximity to friendly troops on the ground.[66] Both coordination of the flight paths and split-second timing were necessary, and US Army Air Forces planners had to spend thousands of man-hours huddled over their slide rules to get it right.

The target of this vast aerial armada was "five square miles of Normandy hedgerow."[67] Bradley marked off a small rectangle on his planning maps, 6,000 yards long by 2,200 deep, centered on a short stretch of the main road west out of Saint-Lô. The rectangle was the kill zone, but the road was the crucial marker. US bombers would plaster German troops deployed to the south, transforming their defensive front into a killing field. At the same time, the road would serve as a caution marker, preventing fratricide against American troops deployed to the north. Bradley felt that the road would be easily identifiable from the sky, and indeed he wanted the bombers to fly parallel to it for insurance.[68] Once the bombers had plastered the German defenders, US forces would go over to the attack, the first echelon breaking through and heading southwest toward Coutances, the second echelon exploiting through the hole. As planning proceeded, Bradley became more and more confident in its potential. He expanded the offensive to include VIII Corps (General Troy Middleton). Lying to the immediate right of VII Corps, Middleton's force would join the offensive on the second or third day. Driving due south, VIII Corps would encircle whichever German forces happened to lie between it and VII Corps.

Facing this huge and lavishly equipped force was Hausser's 7th Army. By now, it included just two understrength corps. The LXXXIV Corps (General Dietrich von Choltitz) lay in the path of Bradley's intended offensive. The II *Fallschirmjäger* Corps (General Eugen Meindl) lay to the east, toward Caumont. Both formations had been in the line almost continuously since June 6. They were understrength, undersupplied, and increasingly demoralized. The entire 7th Army possessed perhaps seventy-five tanks, most of them belonging to Panzer *Lehr*, yet another Panzer division trapped in a static defensive posture, a mission for which it was neither trained nor configured, without the possibility of relief, refitting, or rest. It had only recently entered the line on July 11, launching an immediate counterattack toward Le Desert in order to slow down the Allied drive on Saint-Lô. Hard fighting had ground it down, especially in tanks. Now it sat between Saint-Lô and Périers, unaware of the avalanche of fire about rain down upon it. In sum, Hausser was hardly commanding a robust defensive position, one with depth and sufficient reserves but little more than a picket line or *Sicherungslinie*, a thin crust of forward positions with nothing behind it but open space. By late July, Hausser could compose a litany of woes:

> Almost all our divisions have been in battle since the beginning of the invasion. The massive superiority of the enemy has badly weakened our own fighting strength (*Kampfkraft*) in both men and materiel (weapons and radio equipment). Our strength no longer suffices to hinder an enemy break-in and to free up sufficient reserves. Support by our own artillery is sufficient as long as we can guarantee the ammunition supply, but that's no longer the case.[69]

The lack of an air force, he knew, was the real problem, weighing down the frontline troops emotionally (*seelisch*), especially as they saw their commanders killed. The increasing youth of the men under his command was a problem. They were inexperienced, he knew, and simply not up to the rigors of a "war of materiel."[70]

Cobra began on a note of Clausewitzian stuttering. The aircraft took off for their targets on July 23, ran into bad weather, and had to be recalled. One group of heavy bombers failed to get the recall notice, however. They flew on to their targets alone, then compounded the error by bombing US troops of the 30th Infantry Division rather than the Germans. The problem was larger than poor technique. Air planners rejected Bradley's plan for a parallel approach along the road—and for good reasons. Flying over an enemy line for any length of time was guaranteed to draw a great deal of fire. Funneling all those aircraft into a tight parallel pattern along the road also proved to be more than even a slide rule could handle. It would have taken the bombers at least two and half hours, and the plan only allotted one. The planners decided instead to come on the perpendicular, reducing their time over German lines but most definitely increasing the chances of fratricide. Unfortunately they either failed to tell Bradley of their decision or Bradley failed to hear what they were saying.

Another day of bad weather intervened, and so Cobra proper did not begin until July 25. The bombers took off again, approached the target box on the perpendicular—and once again bombed US troops. This time the victim was the 9th Infantry Division, along with the 30th Infantry Division, which had the misfortune to be bombed twice by its own air force. General Eddy, 9th Division commander, had to pull out one of the battalions that he intended to use for the assault and hurriedly substituted a replacement. The bombing also killed General Lesley J. McNair, by now commander of the US Army ground forces. He had gone forward to see his troops in action and became the highest-ranking Allied officer killed in Western Europe.

These friendly-fire incidents aside, the bombers also hit their target box—over and over again. First came the 350 fighter-bombers, bombing and strafing the tiny road for 20 minutes. Then the main event: 1,500 heavy bombers—B-17 Flying Fortresses and B-24 Liberators—blocking out the sky, roaring in at 8,000 feet and "drenching the carpet" for a solid hour.[71] Each of the 1,500 bombers dropped forty 100-pound bombs, for a total of 60,000 detonations in 60 minutes—1,000 per minute. Stage three was the advance by Collins's three assault divisions in the forward echelon, backed by the concentrated fire of over 1,000 guns. Then came the fighter-bombers again, flying close-support of the ground troops and raking the "carpet's leading edge." Finally, once VII Corps was under way, the medium bombers came up to hit the "back edge of the carpet" for another 45 minutes. Overly complex plans have a way of imploding, and this one certainly had its share of problems early. Nevertheless, Bradley's Cobra plan married complexity to one of the greatest displays of brute force in military history. Call it "Bradley's constant": 60,000 explosions per hour have a way of solving most operational problems.

Indeed, that carpet-bombing may well have been the longest hour of the war for the Wehrmacht. The bombs were not particularly heavy, mainly 100-pound fragmentation bombs, since Bradley did not want the ground cratered so badly that his troops could not advance over it. They made up for their relative lightness with sheer quantity, however. The rain of bombs—some 4,000 tons in all—pulverized the German front line, inflicting casualties, to be sure, but just as importantly stunning the survivors so that they were momentarily, for minutes or hours, incapable of offering cohesive resistance. Panzer *Lehr* Division bore the brunt. Just before 9:00 A.M., General Bayerlein looked up and could scarcely believe what he was seeing. "Every living person immediately went for whatever cover he could find, and stayed there. The waves of planes kept coming, like a conveyor belt, seemingly without end." The bombs rained down "now before him, now on the right, now on the left, rolling forward relentlessly."

> From 0930 on, he was completely out of communication with all levels, even by radio. About 1000 or 1030 he mounted the pillion of a motorcycle and set out for Les Mesnil Amey by inconspicuous paths he had previously learned. The CP itself was not damaged, but the fields all about were burning and smoldering. Here in an observation post in a heavy stone tower 2 meters thick he watched the next wave of attack. He could see Amigny, on the US side of the lines, and could watch the bomb carpets unrolling in great rectangles. By 1200, nothing could be seen at all, in any direction, so thick were the smoke, dust, and murk.[72]

His front lines looked "like a landscape on the surface of the moon (*Mondlandschaft*), all craters and death," he later remembered. "At least seventy percent of the personnel were out of action, either dead, wounded, crazed, or dazed."[73] The bombing had destroyed many tanks and trapped others in deep craters. Most shocking of all, the force of the bombing had simply tossed some of the Panzers in the air and turned them over on their backs.

Perhaps Bayerlein himself had become momentarily unhinged. The next day, an emissary from the staff of Field Marshal Kluge arrived at Panzer *Lehr* headquarters. The field marshal, the staff officer instructed Bayerlein, insisted that *Lehr* hold its position on the Saint-

Lô–Périers Road. "Hold the line with what?" asked Bayerlein. "This is an order I am bringing you, General," the officer answered. "You must hold: no man may leave the position." So there was to be no retreat, no shortening of the line: resistance to the last man and bullet, as always. Such phrases were by now a very old and very tired song to all German frontline commanders. Timing is everything, they say, and this was probably not the best time to be transmitting such ridiculous orders. Bayerlein was not having it. The most oft-quoted source has the general exploding: "Everything's holding up front. My grenadiers and the pioneers—the antitank men—they're holding. Not a single man leaves his post. Not one! They're lying in their foxholes, still and silent, for they are dead! Dead, do you understand me? You may report to the Field Marshal that Panzer Lehr Division is annihilated." "Only the dead are still holding the line," he concluded bitterly, "and I stay here as ordered."[74]

The first day found the infantry divisions of Collins's VII Corps probing into the cratered rubble against sporadic German resistance. Most US accounts stress the difficulty of the fighting, the resilience of the defense, and the disillusionment of American infantry coming under fire from German artillery untouched by the great bombing. In fact, the defenders were nothing more than the scattered remnants of Panzer *Lehr*—uncoordinated *Kampfgruppen* improvised around a machine-gun or mortar team and a handful of infantry or administrative personnel. By contrast, Collins's corps alone had more men than all of the German divisions facing the American front. Nevertheless, the defenders gave ground slowly, and in fact they had no choice, since they lacked all form of motor transport. There was no high gear for a ruined division like *Lehr*. The second day saw VIII Corps joining the attack, but progress was still slow. On the third day, an increasingly impatient Collins inserted 2nd Armored Division on his left flank, the act that blew the front wide open. German resistance, so tenacious up until that point, was crumbling. American tanks actually crashed into Bayerlein's forward command post at Cerisy, while the general and his staff were hard at work trying desperately to reform their shattered line. The headquarters was a total loss, including radio equipment, maps, orders, and documents of all sorts.[75] The next day came the turn of Panzer *Lehr*'s repair shop, with the US tanks rolling in just as suddenly and the Germans barely managing to destroy the facility, along with the twenty newly repaired Panzers inside.[76]

By the third day, both VII and VIII Corps were driving forward at speed. No army in the world could move as rapidly as a US force that had just cracked open a seam in an enemy defensive position. The Americans had proven it in Tunisia on a small scale, when the 1st Armored Battalion of Lieutenant Colonel John Waters crested a low ridge outside of Djedeida in December 1942 and overran a German airfield packed wingtip to wingtip with Stukas; or on Sicily, when General George S. Patton Jr. took his 7th Army on a top-speed drive clear around the coast of the island, all the way out to Palermo and then all the way back to Messina. Most recently, the Americans had proven their penchant for speed during the breakout from the Anzio bridgehead: heading southeast for the linkup with the Cassino force and northwest toward Rome at the same time. Now, US tanks were tearing through the remnants of the German front line, heading toward the key crossroads town of Coutances. They took Coutances on July 28. Four armored divisions were now in the van: 1st and 2nd from VII Corps and 4th and 6th from the VIII, all hustling down south, with VIII Corps moving along the coast and VII matching it mile for mile to the east, with both corps operating under an irresistible umbrella of close-support aircraft provided by the IX Tactical Air Command. No army stood in their path, but rather the remnants of divisions that had been thoroughly attrited in the line and were no longer capable of fighting *Bewegungskrieg* against a first-class enemy. For the record, from the German left (west) to right (east), they included the 243rd Infantry Division, the 91st Division, the 2nd SS Panzer Division *Das Reich*, 17th SS *Panzergrenadier* Division *Götz von Berlichingen*, and what had been, just a few days ago, the Panzer *Lehr* Division. None of them were fighting by now. While elements of each of these divisions managed, from time to time, to get in the way of the American advance, they rarely held their ground for more than a few hours at a time. The scene was one of unimaginable operational chaos, with columns of both sides intermingled, often on the same road, both heading south. The spearhead of VIII Corps, Combat Command B of the 4th Armored Division, took Avranches, the coastal bottleneck, on August 1, having made the 30-mile lunge down from Coutances in a little over a day. The tanks of VII Corps took the town of Mortain, 20 miles to the east, two days later. Broad vistas now beckoned to the Americans. Having turned the corner at Avranches, they could head west and south into Brittany, or east into France proper. Finally, after fifty-five days of travail and bloodshed, the Allies had broken out of Normandy.

While the US Army has been rightly proud of Operation Cobra over the ensuing decades, an objective analysis requires recognition of the British and Canadian roles. Montgomery's seemingly endless series of offensives toward Caen had twisted German defenses into an unbalanced, even distorted shape. Even in failure, Montgomery kept the vast majority of the German Panzers away from the Americans. Indeed, the Anglo-Canadians kept attacking, up to and during the start of Cobra. The Imperials launched another set of attacks toward Caen on July 18 (Operation Goodwood for the British, Operation Atlantic for the Canadians). Both of these operations failed to break through, but given the immense German armored force in front of them, the failure is not surprising. All these operations made another positive impact, however. They convinced the Wehrmacht command that the Allied *Schwerpunkt* still lay in the eastern sector of the beachhead and that the breakout, when it came, would probably be coordinated with a second amphibious landing in the Pas de Calais. Indeed, so consistent was the pressure put on by the Imperials that it is unclear if the German command realized that events like Charnwood, Goodwood, or Atlantic were separate and discrete offensives. They seemed rather to be part of a nonstop fight, further indication that this was the Allies' main effort, and Wehrmacht commanders felt that only their Panzer divisions were up to the fight. The Germans had believed this from the beginning of the campaign, and Anglo-Canadian attacks kept them believing it right up until the end. And finally, once Cobra began, the British again came into play with Operation Bluecoat, an assault by VIII and XXX Corps (British 2nd Army) coming down south of Caumont and protecting the eastern flank of the Cobra advance. German armor heading west to plug the American breakthrough had to turn and face this new threat. Without all of these Imperial operations, an American breakout on the breadth and scale of Operation Cobra is impossible to imagine. Normandy wasn't some sort of inter-Allied competition, with points carefully tallied and deducted for each of the Allies. It was a military campaign, and analysts must evaluate it holistically, with a cold eye unclouded by bias or special pleading.

Mortain

By the first week of August, Cobra was rolling out at top speed. (See Map 5.1.) The Americans had shredded the defenses of the German 7th Army beyond hope of recovery. Now their highly mobile formations were heading in two directions at once: driving into Brittany and simultaneously passing around the southern flank of the German forces still facing Montgomery (*Panzergruppe West*, now renamed 5th Panzer

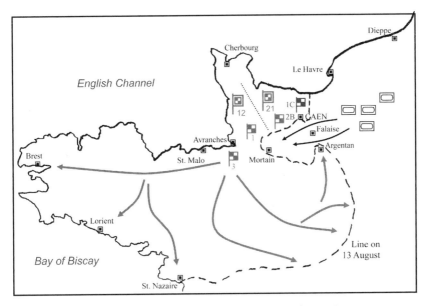

English Channel

Bay of Biscay

Map 5.1 Mortain Counteroffensive: Operation *Lüttich* (July 1944)

Army). German resistance against the Americans was sporadic at best. Cobra had blown a hole in the German line, and there was, for the foreseeable future, nothing left to plug it. A sensible reaction might have been a phased but rapid retreat to form some sort of defensible position, perhaps the line of the Seine River. But there was no Seine Line at the moment, no real defensive construction or fortified bridgeheads. Indeed, even reaching the Seine Line was probably impossible, given the degraded state of German mobility and communications. The Allies were able to move 24 hours per day, but the Germans only at night—and the results of a full-scale race to the Seine would have been predictable.

With the operational situation in tatters, the German High Command decided on a massive counterattack by all available armored reserves. The Panzers would head toward Mortain and, from there, to Avranches and the coast. Operation *Lüttich* ("Liège") was the brainchild of the OKW, a plan drawn up in all its particulars on a map table hundreds of miles behind the lines and then hand-carried to Field Marshal Kluge in the field by General Walter Warlimont of the OKW Operations Section. Its intent was to cut off all of those American divisions already operating in Brittany and south of Avranches, the forces recently grouped into US 3rd Army under General Patton. "All available Panzer units," Hitler ordered, "regardless of their present commitment, are to be taken from other parts of the Normandy front, joined together under one specially qualified Panzer operations staff, and sent into a concentrated attack as soon as possible."[77] The plan created a new command, *Panzergruppe* Eberbach, named for the former commander of 5th Panzer Army, and placed every single Panzer division in Normandy under his control. The thrust toward Mortain would smash the crucial hinge of the Allied maneuver, where all three Allied drives originated: the thrust south out of Normandy, another one west into Brittany, and a third east toward LeMans. Once through, the plan aimed high: "After a successful breakthrough of the enemy, the assault forces will wheel to the north and launch a blow into the deep flank and rear of the enemy forces facing the 7th Army, in order to collapse the enemy's entire Normandy front." As always, Hitler knew how to invoke the nonmaterial factors that were so appealing to his officer corps: "Greatest daring, determination, imagination must give wings to all echelons of command. Each and every man must believe in victory. Cleaning up in rear areas and in Brittany can wait until later."[78] At the very least, Hitler and the OKW believed, Lüttich should smash the US 3rd Army, re-form the line, and bottle up the Allies back in Normandy.

Historians ever since have had a field day criticizing the decision to launch Lüttich, and at times they have even mocked it. The German army once again seemed to be defying reason. If the previous week of combat had proven anything, it was that the Wehrmacht could no long go steel on steel against the Allies. Nevertheless, anyone with knowledge of the long-term patterns of German military history could well have predicted it. The Allied breakout from Normandy had been a devastating defeat, to be sure. But to German staff officers and commanders, Cobra meant something else. The breakout marked the transition from *Stellungskrieg*, the attritional and bloody "war of position," to *Bewegungskrieg*, the swirling "war of movement," laden with opportunity for those commanders bold enough to take advantage. The entire history of the German army had preferenced the latter over the former, for a very simple reason. From the commanders on down to the noncommissioned officers and the ordinary *Landser*, they all believed they were better at it than the Allies—in fact better than anyone in the world. Returning to *Bewegungskrieg*, they recognized, gave free reign to the spirit, allowing human qualities of creativity, invention, and intuition to come to the fore. Material factors receded. Numbers meant little. Genius and willpower could once again dominate. "The break-through was a fact!" wrote one German intelligence officer. "The war of movement had begun." As strange as it may seem, the Wehrmacht had the Allies just where it wanted them. After the war, not a single German officer claimed to have been a supporter of Operation *Lüttich*. Their behavior at the time proved otherwise. Indeed, from Kluge on down, whether harboring doubts or not, they all got on board. Just two weeks after the attempt on Hitler's life, *Lüttich* was a declaration of loyalty to the Führer—and one of the last great acts of will of the Prussian-German officer corps.

There are limits to what willpower can do, however, and *Lüttich* was a dismal affair from its start to its rapid close. Prepping it was a night-mare that involved passing nine Panzer divisions laterally behind the German front. The road network couldn't handle the tank traffic, the Luftwaffe failed to cover, and the units rarely arrived where and when they were supposed to. The Luftwaffe once again failed utterly in pro-viding aerial protection to the ground forces, and the entire prepara-tion took place under Allied air observation and attack. Between the need to jump off the road at the first sight of the *Jabos* and the lack of fuel for the tanks, the divisions hurrying up became snarled in unsolv-able traffic jams on the way to the concentration zone. Some of the intended assault units had to fight their way through an American cor-don even to get to their assembly points. By the time the process was finished, only four Panzer divisions, not one of which was anywhere near full strength, were ready to take part in the offensive. What might have been a good local counterstroke if carried out rapidly had wasted a week in preparation and lost any operational meaning it might have had. Indeed, it barely made sense by the time it was launched. With Patton's 3rd Army already driving rapidly to the east, *Lüttich* was a case of the Wehrmacht putting its head into an Allied noose.

The operational précis was simple enough. *Lüttich* involved elements of four divisions arrayed abreast from north to south: the 116th Panzer (the "Greyhound" or *Windhund* Division), 2nd Panzer Division, 1st SS Panzer Division *Leibstandarte Adolf Hitler*, and 2nd SS Panzer Division *Das Reich*. The plan envisioned a first, or breakthrough, echelon con-sisting of three divisions: 116th Panzer on the right flank, north of the Sée River valley, attacking toward Chérencé; 2nd Panzer Division in the center, breaking through north of Mortain; and *Das Reich* on the left, attacking directly into Mortain itself. Once they had broken the American line, 1st SS Panzer Division would exploit rapidly through the gap to Avranches. But yet another wobble intervened early, when the commander of 116th Panzer, General Gerhard Graf von Schwerin, refused to pass on the attack orders from his corps commander, General Hans von Funck of the XLVII Panzer Corps. As a result, the *Windhund* Division was out of the action at Mortain for most of August 7.[79]

Despite the problems, Kluge duly launched *Lüttich* shortly after midnight on August 7. The attack achieved initial surprise and made moderate progress. The US defense was in the hands of the 30th Infantry Division (General Leland Hobbs), which had recently seen hard fighting at Tessy-sur-Vire. The 30th had only just arrived at Mortain and was still in the process of preparing its defenses, performing basic reconnaissance, and settling into its shallow foxholes. With an early-morning fog grounding Allied aircraft, SS troopers of *Das Reich* broke into Mortain, isolating a US infantry battalion, the 2nd of the 120th Infantry Regiment, and capturing the battalion commander, Lieutenant Colonel Eads G. Hardaway, along with his staff.[80] Much of the battalion still held the high ground outside the city, however, and from Hill 314 they had an unobstructed view down onto the roads below. From here, the men of the "Lost Battalion of Mortain" were able to call down accurate American artillery fire on the advancing Germans. When the fog burned off by noon, the Allied air forces soon got aloft, and ten squadrons of RAF Typhoons had a very lucrative target laid out for them, indeed: wall-to-wall German vehicles on a very narrow front. Today, the claims of Allied airmen to have destroyed 200 German tanks in that one day are no longer sustainable. Indeed, the Germans didn't even have 200 tanks present at Mortain. But airpower did drive the Panzers from the road, forced them to throw on camouflage netting to escape detection, and was thus instrumental in blunting the force of the German attack. On the ground, individual roadblocks of the 30th Division held fast and fought the German advance to a standstill. By the late afternoon of August 7, the German command— Funck, Eberbach, and Kluge—realized that the attack was stuck. Their spearheads had advanced less than five miles in some sectors, just one-quarter of the way to Mortain. It was clear that they were going no farther after making a local dent, some five miles to the north and south of Mortain, but still a full 15 miles from Avranches. Operation *Lüttich*, the final hope for rescuing the Wehrmacht from failure in Normandy, had failed.

In the long annals of German military history, few offensives had misfired as badly as this one had. A planned all-out offensive by nine Panzer divisions had shrunk to a local strike by four. Four became three when the 116th Panzer Division refused to join in. The number of tanks present in the remaining three barely amounted to single full-strength Panzer division under regular conditions. In the face of American artillery and air superiority, German armor could barely move—the traditional strength of German military forces in the field—and in most places small American combined-arms teams managed to stop them cold. Even when the Panzers managed to penetrate American ground defenses, Allied airpower was there to harry them. German infantry fought with its usual élan and drive, infiltrating US defenses at will in numerous spots. The Wehrmacht had nowhere near the necessary amount of trained infantry to make much of a difference in the operational situation, however. An operation intended to strike a decisive blow collapsed within 24 hours.

Lüttich should have been a professional embarrassment to everyone involved in its planning and execution. But, in fact, one reputation came out of the mess unscathed. Count Schwerin of the 116th Panzer Division thought the plan was suicidal from the start. His own division sat on the northern flank of the assault, and with superior American forces bearing down on him from that direction, a drive to the west, against Mortain, seemed senseless. Schwerin was from the old East Prussian aristocracy, the *Junkertum*. His family had been around for a long while, serving the Prussian and German armies for over two centuries. One distant ancestor, Kurt Christof Graf von Schwerin, had been Frederick the Great's most brilliant field marshal. At Frederick's first major battle, Mollwitz in 1744, Kurt Christoph had the temerity to order his monarch to leave the field when he thought that the young man was putting himself in too much danger. In 1944, when corps commander Funck accused the current scion of the family, Gerhard Graf, of having "cold feet," Schwerin became livid: "I will not stand for any insults to myself or to my division," he swore.[81] He then left his command post without reporting his whereabouts, a traditional gesture of contempt from a bygone era, but one that had become quite unusual in the context of twentieth-century warfare. Schwerin had complained before about ridiculous orders, and he would do so again. Unlike many of his colleagues, he never wrote his memoirs and is all but forgotten today. In the annals of the Wehrmacht, he was one of the few officers who could claim to have fought the madness, however, and to have maintained some sense of the old Prussian honor.

The Hell of Falaise

Although forward motion had stopped at Mortain, the High Command ordered the Panzers to keep hammering away on the same spot in subsequent days. (See Map 5.2.) Tenacity (*Hartnäckigkeit*) and persistence (*Beharrlichkeit*) were traditional Prussian virtues, too, but here the result was not only increased German losses in tanks and equipment but also a drastic worsening of the overall operational situation. August 8 was perhaps the crucial day in the campaign. First, having mastered the initial German attack at Mortain, General Courtney Hodges's US 1st Army began to go over to the counterattack. Second, the spearhead of Patton's 3rd US Army, the XV Corps of General Wade Haislip, took Le Mans. The city was the headquarters of German 7th Army, and while *Obergruppenführer* Hausser and his staff managed to escape, they had to abandon the mountain of supplies of all sorts, including irreplaceable stocks of fuel and ammunition. From Le Mans, Patton's army had a clear shot into the rear of the German armies still defending to the north against the British and Canadians. Elements of Patton's army now made a quick wheel to the north, driving toward Alençon, and from there to Argentan. And finally, August 8 was the day that the newly formed Canadian 1st Army (General H. D. G. Crerar) launched Operation Totalize, a drive straight down the Caen-Falaise Road to the south, furnished with all the latest accoutrements of Allied power: two tank divisions drawn up abreast in a massive steel phalanx, with over 600 tanks and 720 gun tubes in a battlespace just 2,000 yards wide.

The Wehrmacht stood on the brink of the precipice. Both German armies from the Normandy campaign, 7th Army and 5th Panzer Army, along with the newly created *Panzergruppe Eberbach*, were facing converging thrusts from four Allied armies. From left to right, pressure from the 1st Canadian, 2nd British, 1st US, and 3rd US Armies was bending the German front back into a very tight jackknife, with the Allied armies in the center (2nd British and 1st US) applying frontal pressure, and 1st Canadian and 3rd US Armies driving in the German flanks. With Patton coming up from Argentan and Crerar coming down to Falaise, only 15 miles would separate the two spearheads. The Allies were on the verge of trapping the entire German force in a fantastic *Kessel*, an encirclement the size of an army group, a remarkable one-shot destruction of the entire German force in Normandy. From there, who knew? Smooth sailing on to Germany. The collapse of the Wehrmacht and perhaps the Hitler regime. An end to the war within weeks. The change of battlefield fortunes in the two weeks since the

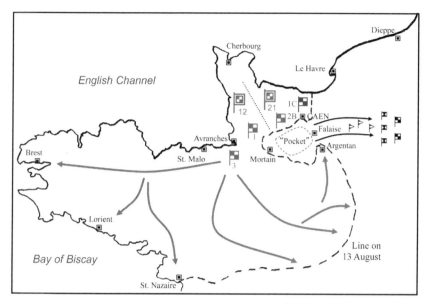

Map 5.2 Death in the West: The Falaise Pocket

start of Operation Cobra was breathtaking, and perhaps some Allied officers were getting a bit giddy.

So began the operational sequence that has gone down into the history books as the battle of the Falaise Pocket. While the Allies enjoyed numerous advantages—operational position, tanks, and absolute dominance in the air—none of their commanders had ever before planned and carried out a land operation so large, so complex, and with so many moving parts. And so it was that things went wrong. The Canadians got halfway to Falaise before Totalize bogged down against the same Panzer divisions that had been blocking the way since June 6. Bradley ordered Haislip's XV Corps to halt at Argentan, then sent much of Patton's army off to the east, racing for the Seine. His reasons later became controversial, and indeed Bradley would provide various explanations for his decision. Whatever his reasoning, the 25-mile-wide Argentan-Falaise Gap stayed open for a solid week. And finally, the Germans were still in the field and still fighting hard for every inch of ground. Perhaps do-or-die battles for survival and existential crises were the only thing that still motivated the Wehrmacht by this point in the war. For all these reasons, the Allies didn't finally seal off the encirclement until August 19, and a large number of Germans, perhaps half the 100,000 men originally trapped, managed to slither out from the Allied jaws.

And so Falaise was not a perfect battle. Nevertheless, discussing Falaise in terms of its failure to encircle the Germans fully—to emphasize what did *not* happen—obscures the enormity of what *did* happen. The Wehrmacht in the west suffered one of the most complete and destructive defeats in military history. As the Allies tightened their grip on the perimeter and slowly closed the gap in the east, they herded the Germans into a smaller and smaller pocket. By August 18, all that was left was a rough rectangle six miles deep and seven miles wide, containing a dense concentration of German troops. The US official history lays it out in detail:

> Inside were the headquarters of the Seventh Army, Panzer Group Eberbach, and the LXXIV and LXXXIV Corps, the II Parachute and XLVII Panzer Corps; the remnants of six infantry division still operating as entities: the 84th, 276th, 277th, 326th, 353rd, and 363rd; one parachute division, the 3rd; three Panzer divisions, the 12th SS, 2nd, and 116th; perhaps two more Panzer divisions, the 1st SS and 10th SS; a number of splinter groups of divisions that had ceased to exist as tactical units and that had been absorbed by other divisions or amalgamated into *Kampfgruppen;* and a mass of stragglers, service elements, and trains.

Moreover, all these units, subunits, and divisional remnants—this horde—lay crammed into the tiniest of cockpits "entirely under the watchful eye and effective fire of Allied artillery and air."[82] The Argentan-Falaise Gap was an escape route for some German units, in other words, but a gauntlet of fire and death for many more. For the Germans, fighting at Falaise meant sitting under a 24-hour rain of steel and high explosives, on a rolling landscape without much in the way of cover. With Allied fire raking every inch of the *Kessel* for a solid week, the level of physical destruction was probably unprecedented in this war. The German forces in Normandy collapsed into a heap of twisted wreckage: artillery, heavy weapons, abandoned or destroyed tanks, all forms of equipment, the detritus of defeat.

Perhaps the real surprise of this hellish ordeal was that the German units inside the pocket kept their cohesion. Some analysts point to the importance of having all the commanders and staff, up to and including *SS-Obergruppenführer* Hausser of the 7th Army, penned up inside the pocket with their men, courting the same amount of risk and enduring the same suffering. In dire circumstances, leaders have to lead. Hausser himself was seriously wounded in the fighting, shot through the jaw. Even the final closure of the pocket by Canadian II Corps on August 19 didn't end the struggle. Bittrich's II SS Panzer Corps launched an immediate relief from Vimoutiers in the east. Working in coordination with a last, desperate breakout from inside, it actually worked to reopen communications with the outside world for another day, allowing another few thousand men to get through. General Eugen Meindl, commander of the II *Fallschirmjäger* Corps, was on point here, actually leading small parties of men in the escape near Coudehard, experiencing all the hair-raising moments one might expect. Perhaps the plight reawakened tactical skills learned decades ago and presumably lost: an eye for ground, personal leadership, the thrill of the hunt (or being hunted). The last few hundred meters were always the worst, especially trying to get across the Dives River barring the escape route to the east. Crossing the Dives was a kind of final purgatory, a picturesque sylvan stream now made gruesome with the dead bodies of men and horses.

Conclusion: Suicide

Field Marshal Kluge was perhaps the most interesting commander in the entire Wehrmacht. He was willing to take bribes from Hitler—huge sums of money that bound him inextricably to the regime—and yet he also tolerated officers on the staff of Army Group Center who openly discussed killing the Führer. Once he knew that the July 20 plot failed, he had the plotters in Paris arrested but admitted he would have supported the coup "if only the swine had died." He was clearly not a Manichaean man, one who lives in a moral world of clear-cut choices, black and white, good and evil. Hitler brought Kluge on board as OB-West in July because the Führer wanted a commander who would carry out orders without the constant static provided by Field Marshals Rundstedt and Rommel. Kluge had done just that, following directives from the High Command that made little sense at the time and that haven't gotten any better with the passing of the decades. Hitler trusted him enough to make him simultaneous commander of Army Group B after Rommel's injury. He obeyed Hitler's refusal to withdraw on any sector of the Normandy line, he ordered no retreats even during Cobra, and then he planned and led the abortive, even ridiculous, Operation *Lüttich*, the counterattack at Mortain. Even when the operation failed to make any headway on day one, Kluge ordered it to continue the next day. He did the same the day after that and more, for a solid week, launching a drive on Avranches that had no chance at all of getting there. Even as US armored divisions were looping around the open southern flank of German 7th Army toward Le Mans, then wheeling north toward Alençon and Argentan, Kluge continued to do the Führer's bidding faithfully at Mortain, a course of action that led directly to the catastrophe at Falaise.

Kluge had committed his share of mistakes, even crimes. On August 15, for once, he doesn't appear to have done anything wrong. He summoned his ground commanders—Hausser, Eberbach, Dietrich, and Funck—to a senior general's conference at the headquarters of 5th Panzer Army, Nécy, which lay eight miles southeast of Falaise. It was time to talk, certainly. All the German field commanders could see a simple defeat rapidly transforming into a catastrophe. Kluge's subordinates dutifully reported, but the field marshal was nowhere to be seen. After three hours of waiting, the meeting broke up and the generals returned to their commands. En route to Nécy in his staff car, Kluge had come under *Jabo* attack and narrowly escaped death. By the time he arrived late that evening, there was no one to be found. The attack had smashed his mobile signal unit, and for a time the German Supreme Commander in the west was out of communications, not only with his own headquarters but also with the higher command echelons. Jodl repeatedly called Army Group B headquarters and asked Kluge's chief of staff, General Hans Speidel, if something had gone wrong, if perhaps Kluge "had gone over to the enemy" (*zum Feind gefahren*).[83]

That same day, Hitler dismissed Kluge from his post, in favor of the great repairman, the one commander who seemed able to master these hopeless causes and reform a front: Field Marshal Walter Model. Kluge first heard the news when Model arrived at Army Group B headquarters at La Roche Guyon. Model handed him a personal letter from Hitler explaining the reasons for the switch: Kluge seemed tired, Hitler noted, worn down by the strain of command, no longer up to the task. The letter ended with a terse directive: Kluge was to report "where he intended to be in Germany."[84] The field marshal interpreted the note, correctly, to mean that he was under suspicion. As he pulled away on August 19 from La Roche Guyon, the command post from which he had led his armies to their doom, artillery from the US 1st Army was already beginning to shell the place. "I won't survive this," he muttered, "being taken away from my troops and leaving them to their fate." The future opened to him with awful certainty. He was going to be the scapegoat for the loss of the west. During a rest stop somewhere between Metz and Verdun, the field marshal swallowed a cyanide capsule and killed himself.

In the years after 1945, historians often discussed the "tragedy" (*Tragik*) of the German officers corps. Torn between their oath to the Führer, their responsibility to the soldiers under their command, and their love of the Fatherland, German officers bravely soldiered on, fighting a good fight, and even winning the admiration of their enemies. Today, a mountain of historical evidence has shredded this image beyond repair. Responsibility to their soldiers? The acquiescence of the officer corps in senseless operational orders sent millions of soldiers to their death in a war long since lost. Love for the Fatherland? Germany would emerge from the war shattered, occupied, and dismembered, with the horrors of the Shoah having besmirched its reputation as a civilized country, perhaps for all time.

Consider Kluge: before his suicide, the disgraced field marshal sent Hitler a letter. The sections of it most often quoted were those that called on the Führer to make peace. The "struggle had become hopeless," Kluge declared. "If your new weapons don't succeed, especially in the air, you must end the war." He invoked the "unspeakable suffering" of the German people and urged Hitler "to make an end to this horror." Less well known is the closing paragraph, Kluge's last words, in a sense: "I take leave of you, my Führer—inwardly closer to you, perhaps, than you have ever suspected—in the knowledge that I have done my duty to the utmost. *Heil, mein Führer!*"[85]

In the end, of their three competing allegiances—Führer, soldier, country—virtually all of the officer corps made the same choice: loyalty to Hitler.[86] And that was a tragedy.

6

On the Run: The East

Introduction: A Lucid Moment

The irrationality of Hitler's war has become proverbial. Obsessive hatreds, unlimited aims, a world of enemies: a recipe for disaster. Yet, on occasion, even Hitler could have a lucid moment.

* * *

WOLFSSCHANZE—JULY 31, 1944. NEAR MIDNIGHT. *The Leader was in a thoughtful mood . . . meditative, almost. A great many things had happened to him lately, all of them bad. The Allied landing in Normandy. The collapse of Army Group Center in the east. The Allied breakout at Avranches.*

And the bomb. Maybe it took a bomb to get the Leader's full attention, to lift him out of his fantasies and put him back in the moment.

Hitler opened the meeting with his customary monologue, surveying the strategic and operational situation on all fronts.[1]

"Jodl, when I think about our great cares today, the first is the stabilization of the Eastern Front. We really can't do much more than that right now. And I ask myself, viewing the overall situation, is it really such a bad thing that we are being pressed together so tightly? There aren't only disadvantages, but advantages."[2]

Jodl hadn't heard this line of reasoning before. The tone was quiet, even moderate, the substance sensible. Talk about contraction, about retreat or surrender of territory, was quite rare in the Wolfsschanze.

"If we can hold on to the area the we currently occupy, it is an area that can sustain us, and we will no longer have these gigantic rear areas. Of course, we must be able to supply the combat groups"—he stumbled for a moment—"the combat troops with the same amount we spent in the rear areas. Then we'll really have a force."[3]

Jodl nodded. It seemed reasonable enough. A smaller front, fewer troops on occupation duties, fewer partisans. Wasting fewer resources on occupation meant more for fighting.

"The narrowing of space isn't always a disadvantage as such, but can be a benefit. But only under one condition: that we really put what we have developed or consumed in this huge area into the fight."⁴

On to the situation in France. More sensible talk: reasonable and clear.

"We have to admit it, and keep it in mind at all times: under the current conditions, it's just not possible to conduct an operation in France, a so-called open-field battle. We cannot do that. We are only able to move some of our formations, and even those only in a limited way. The others can't move at all, and not only because we lack air superiority, but because the formations as such cannot move. They aren't suited to the conduct of mobile operations, either in their armaments or equipment. They can't do it, they don't know how."⁵

And that, too, was true enough. They all knew it—their static divisions in France had no business fighting an enemy as well-equipped as the Western Allies. He went on.

"We can't count our total strength in France solely on the number of divisions that we theoretically have there, but only based on the limited number of formations that are actually able to maneuver, and that's only a very small portion. If the territory wasn't so important, we'd have to evacuate the coast, draw the mobile formations into a defensive position, and defend it stubbornly. But one thing is sure: I only have a certain amount of forces, and they scarcely suffice to defend even this tiny front."⁶

Jodl had just seen the situation map out of France, the Allied breakthrough in Normandy. He nodded in agreement before Hitler went on.

"We have to realize that a turning point can come in France only if we succeed, even for a short time, in reestablishing our superiority in the air. . . . If we could immediately pump in 800 fighters, to give us a total of 2,000, we'd overcome this entire crisis."

There certainly were moments of the old Führer during this meeting. Anger against his generals and the "blood poisoning" infecting the war effort. The plot to kill him had laid bare the entire situation. "How does the enemy learn what we are thinking?" the Führer asked. "How does he counter so many of our moves? Why does he always react so quickly?" Now they knew. This "damned little clique," he called them, "wreckers and traitors." They were all in a stand-or-fall fight to the death—a Hunnenkampf—and the generals, "these lowest creatures in history to wear the soldier's uniform," had been more interested in treason than winning the war.

But the rant soon died down and, at any rate, was probably excusable given what he had just been through. His thoughts turned to foreign policy—the Finns, Turkey, Romania, the Balkans. The attitude of Bulgaria. Operations in Italy. The advisability of holding the Apennine position as opposed to falling back to the Po River.

And then back to the army. He needed younger, more energetic officers. How tired he was of hearing "Mein Führer, we can't do that" from his senior commanders. Good officers were out there, proving themselves in the field every day. "By God we'll go out there and promote them! I'll do it in a second—it's all the same to me. If Napoléon could become First Consul at 27, I see no reason a 30-year old can't become a general or lieutenant general—it's ridiculous! We're conducting a revolutionary war!"[7]

The conversation drifted to his health—not good of late, and the attempted assassination had only made it worse. "I can stand up and speak for a certain length of time, but then I suddenly have to sit down again. I couldn't trust myself to speak to 10,000 people today . . . I might suddenly get dizzy and collapse." He did note, however, that the tremors in his left leg, so severe that they kept him awake at night, had vanished. Apparently the shock of the explosion had done him some good. "Still, I'm not sure," he concluded wryly, "that I would say it's the best remedy."[8]

* * *

After the war, the military and political elite of the Third Reich wrote memoirs that labeled Hitler "insane." In point of fact, rational discussion of wartime strategy took place in the Führer Headquarters all through the war. The strategy was faulty, certainly, and Hitler's epiphanies in July 1944 were showing up awfully late in the game. Labeling him "insane" does an injustice to the war, however, belittling the threat that his movement posed to the world and diminishing the difficulty of the hard struggle to destroy him. The Führer was many things—a criminal, a hater, a murderer—but he certainly wasn't insane. He also wasn't alone in running the war. Every step of the way, he had trained professional officers at his side: weighing options, making plans, aiding and abetting—officers who listened raptly to his every word during wartime and who, immediately afterward, tarred him a "madman."

Model's War: To the Vilnius Pocket

In that July 31 *Lagebesprechung*, Hitler had expressed his hopes that occupying a smaller area of Europe might actually work to the good of the German war effort. He was about to get a chance to test that hypothesis. The war was in the endgame. In 1939–1941 the Wehrmacht was on the march. In 1942–1943 it was on the edge. Now, in 1944, it was on the run.

Hitler and the High Command responded to the collapse of Army Group Center, a disaster almost entirely of their own making, by firing the generals. With the onset of catastrophe in Byelorussia, Hitler dismissed Field Marshal Ernst Busch, perhaps the most loyal field commander he had. Busch had carried out absurd commands that he knew were wrong and refused to do things that he knew were right, anything to curry Hitler's favor, but it hadn't saved his job. Also out was General Hans Jordan, commander of the 9th Army. Jordan's offense was his uncertain handling of the 20th Panzer Division in response to the initial Soviet attack, although he was no clumsier in command than any other officer in Byelorussia that summer. General Nikolaus von Vormann, a Panzer division commander during the great retreat to the Dnepr River in 1943 and commander of XXXXVII Panzer Corps during the relief attempt into the Korsun Pocket, took over 9th Army, more a ragged band at this point than a robust field army. The new commander of Army Group Center was Field Marshal Walter Model.

Model was a dislikable character with a foul temper and an acerbic tongue, but he was also possessed of genuine operational skill. Born in 1894 to a nonmilitary, middle-class family, he fought as a lieutenant in World War I, took a bullet to the shoulder, and won the Iron Cross First Class. Model held a variety of staff and field assignments in the interwar era and commanded 3rd Panzer Division in the 1940 campaign in France. He won his reputation on the Eastern Front, however, taking command of the 9th Army in the midst of the furious Soviet winter counteroffensive of 1941–1942. He managed to hold his ground in the absurdly narrow Rzhev Salient while all around him other German armies were reeling back or dissolving. He defeated all Soviet attempts to overrun the salient in 1942, and then in early 1943 he withdrew 9th Army from the pocket in careful stages. This so-called Buffalo maneuver was a model operation of its type, shortening the front by over 200 miles and freeing up over twenty divisions for use elsewhere on the front.[9] After the failure of the German offensive at Kursk in July 1943, he had to do much the same sort of thing again, this time extricating 9th Army from the Orel Salient in August 1943 in the face of the great Soviet counteroffensive known as Operation Kutuzov.[10]

In personal terms, he was ruthless: to his own officers and men, to the enemy, and to Soviet civilians unfortunate enough to be caught in his zone of operations. During 9th Army's retreat in the summer of 1943, he infamously evacuated the entire civilian population of the Orel district, hundreds of thousands of men, women, and children, with horrendous loss of life. Even Hitler never seemed entirely comfortable around Model. "I trust that man to make it happen," Hitler once declared, "but I wouldn't want to serve under him."[11] Model could, within bounds, disagree sharply with Hitler, talk back rudely, even hang up the phone on occasion. "Who commands the 9th Army, *mein Führer*, you or I?" he had once asked at a time when Hitler was offering a few too many operational suggestions.[12]

Model's most important attribute had little to do with any sort of particular military genius or strength of will, however. Rather, the main factor that propelled him into command was that he was loyal to the core and that Hitler trusted him. The Führer even agreed to let Model keep command of Army Group North Ukraine while taking on Army Group Center, exercising command of the former through his deputy, General Josef Harpe. The decision invested the field marshal with an authority enjoyed by no other German officer on any front in this war. Model had succeeded where luminaries such as Guderian, Rommel, and Manstein had failed, becoming the new warlord from the Dniester to the Dvina.[13] As such, he could shuttle the Panzer and mechanized divisions around and within his immense area of responsibility without wounding the prerogatives of neighboring army group commanders, and usually without any resistance from Hitler. These were the same divisions that he had claimed for himself in the run-up to Bagration, when he was as certain as the High Command that the attack would come against Army Group North Ukraine. Indeed, his constant demand for more divisions back in the spring—demands to which Hitler invariably acquiesced—had been one of the key factors that transformed Army Group Center from a fighting force into an empty shell before the Soviet offensive—and thus one of the reasons for the disaster.[14]

As an operator, Model wasn't much for intricate maneuver and had no record at all of offensive success. Perhaps the timing of his ascent to army and army group command was simply wrong. It is hard to imagine anyone—including Alexander the Great or Napoléon—leading the Wehrmacht to victory on the Eastern Front in 1944–1945. But perhaps it was also his temperament for order and discipline. His preference was always to hold a cohesive front line, no matter how weak it might be in spots, to fortify it strongly with multiple fallback positions, and to form a reserve by ruthlessly combing out rear-area manpower. Once a Soviet attack had revealed its intentions, Model plugged the holes with an immediate counterattack, no matter how small, against the flanks of the penetration. These were rapid attacks, more like raids: get in, do the job, then break contact. They had an impact, however. The

5th Panzer Division, for example, managed to destroy 486 Soviet tanks in just about a month of fighting. Since his art of war lacked a true offensive component, it could not be a recipe for victory, but it could at least ward off catastrophe. Above all, Model was able to avoid any new encirclements for the rest of the summer, and that was no small operational feat. Whether it ranks "among the greatest performances by German commanders during World War II," as one respected analyst called it, is open to question.[15] The Soviets helped by withdrawing their armor from the front and carrying out a broad-front advance with their infantry formations in the van, and even Model had taken note of a certain operational pause in the enemy's approach.[16]

Indeed, Model's appointment changed little in the short term. Massive Soviet forces were on the move in full stride. The German operational reserve that might have stopped them was still south of the Pripet Marshes and was coming up slowly, one division at a time. The strategic reserve was in France, slowly dissolving in the course of an attritional *Stellungskrieg*. Moreover, stage three of the Bagration operational sequence was about to begin. The Soviets had new operational targets in their sights: the city of Molodeczno (50 miles northwest of Minsk) and Baranovichi (90 miles southwest).[17] Both were critical transportation nodes on the rail lines to Minsk, and their possession was absolutely necessary if the Soviets intended to supply heavy forces beyond them to the west. Moreover, each of the cities dominated critical terrain gaps, the relatively open ground passing north and south of the nearly impassable *Naliboki Puschka*, the primeval "wild forest" of northwestern Byelorussia. In operational terms, Molodeczno opened the way to Vilnius, Kaunas, and the Baltic states, Baranovichi to Bialystok, Brest, and Warsaw. For the Germans, the two locales were the final bottleneck, one last chance to slow down the Red Army before it broke into the North German Plain.

And once again, the chances of holding either Molodeczno or Baranovichi were near zero. The Wehrmacht was still fighting "a war of regiments and battalions against armies," as the General Staff described it at the time.[18] The defenders of Molodeczno were a motley collection: remnants of the hard-hit 5th Panzer Division and 2,000 stragglers stumbling in from the Minsk encirclement and placed under the command of VI Corps headquarters. Reinforcements in the form of 7th Panzer Division and 170th Infantry Division were on the way, but not there yet. Molodeczno fell to the 5th Guards Tank Army on July 5. Soviet forces barely paused before pressing on, crossing the Lithuanian border and encircling a German force in Vilnius on July 8, the latest town to be named a *fester Platz*. Model did manage to form a more robust defensive concentration in front of Baranovichi, including the newly formed 4th Panzer and 28th *Jäger* Divisions, along with remnants of 12th Panzer Division. The Soviets countered in force with three armies from 1st Byelorussian Front, the 28th, 48th, and 65th, along with I Mechanized Corps and General I. A. Pliev's cavalry mechanized group. Baranovichi fell on July 8. The Red Army was through the Byelorussian bottlenecks, and grand vistas beckoned: the Baltic states to the north, Poland to the southwest, and between them the German province of East Prussia.

The case of Vilnius is illustrative of the fault-lines between the professional operators on the General Staff and Hitler's more rigid conception.[19] Hitler declared it a stronghold with absolutely no advance preparation. While his staff was recommending abandonment of the city, Hitler was still ordering troops and commanders into it.[20] Indeed, at the very moment that the Soviets were closing the ring, the 2nd Battalion of the 16th *Fallschirmjäger* Regiment was landing at the Vilnius airport. A mobile *Kampfgruppe* sent toward the city under Lieutenant Colonel Theodor Tolsdorff—a legendary fighter who would survive no fewer than fourteen wounds in the course of the war—ran into heavy opposition and went into a *Kessel* of its own near Lentvaris, six miles west of the city. The commandant of the "fortress," Luftwaffe General Rainer Stahel, was the last to arrive, flown in only after the completion of the encirclement. His 4,000-man force had few heavy weapons or artillery and no air cover at all, and no sooner had he arrived than he requested permission to lead a breakout from the Vilnius trap. Hitler at first refused outright: "The nerve of him, to send me a radio message like this! I didn't send General Stahel to Vilnius so he could make a request to break out. He is supposed to hold the city or perish with it: the same thing we demand from any ship's captain. This is cowardice! It's ridiculous! The gentleman has his duty to do. Radio him that!"[21] Perhaps it was the depth of the disaster taking place all around them, or a renewed determination on the part of Hitler's professional advisers to push their ideas, or simply one of the Führer's passing moods, but Vilnius turned out differently from the disasters of Vitebsk and Bobruisk. General Heusinger posed the question to him not as one of victory or defeat, or of holding versus retreating. The men would almost certainly die, he told Hitler, no matter what the Führer decided: "But at least give these men a chance. It's easier to die if you hold your own fate in your hand. It's easier to die in an attack than in a hopeless defense. Give these men hope, and if it can't be avoided, at least make their deaths easier." Still irritated, Hitler grumbled ("Do what you want. You won't save a single life") but gave in and agreed to the breakout attempt.[22] General Reinhardt, commander of 3rd Panzer Army, swiftly assembled a relief column from the 6th Panzer Division and a battalion of Mark V Panther tanks. The Vilnius garrison began the breakout the night of July 12–13, heading west; the relief column left Kaunas the next morning, driving east; and the two linked up near Lentvaris, where the Tolsdorff *Kampfgruppe* was still holding its all-around laager. The breakout saved 3,000 men from the original Vilnius garrison, a demonstration of what might have taken place in the other encircled towns and one of the few definite successes of the entire sorry sequence of Bagration.

The Smashing of Army Group North Ukraine

TO THE BRODY POCKET

As always, however, a local success by the Wehrmacht usually meant a big hole somewhere else in the front.[23] The next sector of the German front to feel the Soviet lash belonged to Army Group North Ukraine, currently defending in eastern Galicia. The German High Command had been expecting an offensive in the sector of Army Group North Ukraine for months. Indeed, they had placed most of the available mechanized forces in the sector to meet such an offensive, one of the factors that had so fatally weakened Army Group Center. Now, with German attention riveted to the disaster unfolding in front of Minsk, the Red Army uncorked yet another of the grand operational blows that characterized the final year of the war. Involving two Soviet fronts, with heavy support from artillery, armor, and air, the Lvov-Sandomierz Operation was, in scale, practically equal to Operation Bagration, and the results were nearly as predictable. The Red Army's prewar doctrine of consecutive operations—irresistible hammer blows, one after the other, directed against carefully selected portions of the enemy's defenses—had now come to full fruition.

As always, the Soviet force was massive. Marshal I. S. Konev's 1st Ukrainian Front stood in the south opposite Lvov with no fewer than ten armies: seven infantry armies and three tank armies, along with a pair of cavalry mechanized groups. To Konev's north stood the left wing of Marshal Rokossovsky's 1st Byelorussian Front opposite Chelm and Lublin. Rokossovsky had five Soviet armies, including four infantry armies and a tank army, along with the small, four-division 1st Polish

Army. Rokossovsky's right wing had played the key role in dismantling German 9th Army at Bobruisk in Operation Bagration, and even now it was supervising an advance far to the west, harrying German 2nd Army in front of it. Conducting a second simultaneous offensive was no easy matter, especially considering that Rokossovsky had half of his front to the north of the Pripet Marshes and half to the south. Indeed, Rokossovky may have been one of the few commanders in the war on either side who could have handled this operational assignment.

The targets of this immense concentration of force were two main component armies of Army Group North Ukraine, 4th Panzer Army in the north under General Walther Nehring, and 1st Panzer Army to the south under General Erhard Raus, facing more or less due east, with the allied 1st Hungarian Army guarding the southern flank. Two German Panzer armies might conjure up a powerful force indeed, but they were nowhere near the strength they had been just a month ago. The army group had already surrendered six Panzer divisions and three infantry divisions to stanch the bleeding in Byelorussia and in Normandy. Replacements hadn't kept pace, with the OKH ordering three untested infantry divisions to the sector: 88th Infantry Division, 28th *Jäger* Division, and 14th SS-Volunteer Division *Galizien* (Galicia), but they were still being acclimatized to the front in early July.[24] As a result, Army Group North Ukraine was a standard model for the 1944 Wehrmacht: a linear formation of weakened infantry divisions, arrayed abreast across far too broad a front, and backstopped by an inadequate mechanized reserve. A force of thirty-four divisions (eight of them Hungarian) on a 450-kilometer front; five weakened Panzer divisions (one of them Hungarian) in reserve; a faux fortified line (*Prinz–Eugen Stellung*) with neither the equipment nor the men to defend it; probably 450 serviceable tanks facing Konev's 2,200 and Rokossovsky's 1,700: business as usual on the Eastern Front.[25]

The weakened state of Army Group North Ukraine, in fact, had already led Model to request a pair of limited tactical withdrawals by 4th Panzer Army. The first was a pullback from the Kovel Bulge, the scene of so much hard fighting back in the spring. The adjustment created a new, shorter line 15 miles west of the city and thus freed up a division or two for the upcoming fight. Tactical retreats were usually nonstarters for Hitler, but he trusted Model implicitly and approved the field marshal's request. More important, giving up Kovel meant abandoning Hitler's original plan to declare the town a *fester Platz*, another accommodation on the Führer's part. Model was obsessed with avoiding the sort of "pre-programmed encirclements" that had eviscerated the

Wehrmacht at Vitebsk and Bobruisk in June.[26] Model's second request was for a minor withdrawal to flatten out a small bulge in 4th Panzer Army's line on its right near Torchin, and Hitler acceded to that one, too.[27]

Not that any of it helped. The offensive to dismantle Army Group North Ukraine took place in successive stages, much like the successful sequencing of Operation Bagration. Konev's turn came first. The marshal envisioned an offensive thrust by his 1st Ukrainian Front, moving forward simultaneously on two axes: one in the north toward Rava Russkaya, and one in the south toward Lvov. Stalin was congenitally suspicious of any overly complex or precious operational scheme, and he had raised objections to Konev's plan during the planning phase. One big thrust would be better, he insisted, and he agreed to Konev's plan: "You are a very stubborn fellow. Very well, go ahead with your plan and put it into operation on your own responsibility."[28] The scene was an almost note-by-note replay of the argument Stalin had with Rokossovsky over the Bagration plan back in May 1944, and Stalin had given in on that one, too. Operational success had bred a more confident Soviet officer corps. The marshals were more and more willing to take on the boss, and Stalin tended to defer to them—the exact opposite of the relational arc between Hitler and his generals.

The thrust in the north came first, aiming to break through the right wing of the German 4th Panzer Army and head for Rava Russkaya.[29] Originally intending to attack on July 14, Konev moved the schedule up a day when his reconnaissance picked up on 4th Panzer Army's limited withdrawals. The combination of a Soviet force still hustling up to the front and a German force in the midst of a withdrawal raised the chaos level a notch for both sides. Konev had always been a bit of a bludgeoner, and perhaps being in command of so much combat power sharpened the tendency. The initial attacks by 3rd Guards and 13th Army went in hastily without artillery preparation and found German frontline positions unmanned. Konev, fearing that the Germans were in the midst of withdrawing into the *Prinz–Eugen Stellung*, now decided to rush the position. Even before achieving a clean breakthrough, he inserted a second echelon, consisting of several infantry corps, into the fight. The result was unimaginable congestion and heavy casualties, and a grinding advance of 12 miles in three days, as the Soviets chewed through the German defenses. The commander of 4th Panzer Army, General Nehring, fought to restore the situation by inserting the reserve 16th and 17th Panzer Divisions into the fray on July 14.[30] They fought with their usual verve, but they were little more than armored battlegroups by now, and at any rate, hasty attacks-from-the-march by individual Panzer divisions no longer sufficed to stop offensive thrusts by multiple Soviet armies. Soviet forces continued their inexorable assault, the Panzers suffered heavy losses and had to yield, and by the end of day three Konev's assault forces had broken through near Gorochow. He now inserted his third (exploitation) echelon, the 1st Tank Army under General M. E. Katukov, directing it first due west toward Rava Russkaya, then wheeling it south to come down on Lvov from the north and northwest.

Konev met equally hard-fought success with a second thrust on July 15, this one by his Lvov grouping in the south, coming up against the left wing of 1st Panzer Army.[31] The attack here met a fully deployed German resistance, and the fighting was even harder and bloodier than it had been to the north. Once again, Soviet assault forces made initial inroads, the Germans struck back with their understrength Panzer divisions (the 1st and the 8th), and the Soviets warded them off only after intense fighting on the morning of July 16. The Red Air Force made itself felt on this sector of the front, with attacks by fighter-bombers slowing down the German counterattacks enough so that the Soviet artillery could zero in. Konev could see German resistance weakening and now made the key decision to insert his 3rd Guards Tank Army (General P. S. Rybalko) into the very narrow penetration he had made in the German lines near the village of Koltuv. By evening, Rybalko's tankers were fighting their way through the absurdly narrow Koltuv corridor in what, at times, amounted to single-file order. This was no way to achieve a decisive breakthrough, and Konev decided to insert a second tank army, General D. D. Lelyushenko's 4th Tank Army, into the defile. In heavy fighting on July 17, this monstrous array of tank forces—led by two of the fiercest armored commanders in the Soviet army—squashed the German defenders in the corridor, broke free, and then lunged far to the west, lapping around the city of Lvov from the south.

Two widely separated Soviet pincers turning inward almost always meant one thing: a German force being trapped between them. The unlucky number this time belonged to the German XIII Corps of General Arthur Hauffe.[32] With 1st Tank Army coming down from Gorochow and 3rd Guards and 4th Tank Armies coming up from the Koltuv corridor, it was clear that XIII Corps was in danger of being encircled. But a sense of urgency seemed lacking in the corps command staff. Hauffe received no orders to withdraw and took no initiative on his own to prevent disaster. He had spent much of the war in administrative posts, most notably as chief of the German military mission to Romania from 1941 to 1943, and perhaps he was simply out of his depth in an operational assignment on this scale. Not until July 18 did orders arrive for XIII Corps to withdraw behind the relative safety of the Bug River—and by then it was too late. The Soviet pincers had already linked up at the village of Busk, encircling Hauffe's entire command near Zloczow, southwest of Brody. Yet another German corps was in the *Kessel*: 454th Security Division, 361st Infantry Division, Provisional Corps C (a division-sized formation containing the remnants of three fought-out divisions, each of roughly regimental strength), 349th Infantry Division, and 14th SS-Volunteer Division *Galizien*.[33] Withdrawal was now out of the question; it was time to break out.

By now, this was a story that ran according to a very familiar script. The Soviets were coming down hard from the north and east, and a morass of swampy bottomland lay to the west. Hauffe had just one direction available, therefore: due south. Here lay XXXXVIII Panzer Corps under General Hermann Balck, one of the most redoubtable commanders in the German army. While the counterattacks by German 1st and 8th Panzer Divisions in the opening days of the Soviet offensive had been stillborn, if any opening existed at all to launch a relief attack, Balck was the man to find it. Hauffe duly arrayed his forces for the drive south. Provisional Corps C was in the spearhead, reinforced by the 249th Assault Gun Brigade. The 349th Infantry Division deployed to its left, ordered to seize the high ground of Hill 334 and protect Provisional Corps C's flank. The remaining three divisions formed a semicircle protecting the northern face of the *Kessel* and waited for their summons to join the rush to freedom. In between them were all the typical impedimenta: supply wagons, trains, artillery, and, of course, the most tragic figures of all: the thousands of wounded who were almost certainly doomed to die one way or the other.

Nothing went smoothly for XIII Corps, neither in the planning nor in the execution of the breakout. On the morning of July 19, the corps chief of staff, Lieutenant Colonel Kurt von Hammerstein, gathered the regimental commanders and issued march orders. While speed was of the essence, once again we see no particular sense of urgency: H-hour wouldn't be until 3:30 A.M. the next morning. Forming up the assault columns took longer than expected. Every movement took place under Soviet artillery and rocket fire, not to mention near-constant attack from low-flying Soviet Mosquito bombers, and the corps took steady losses all day while being herded into a smaller and smaller perimeter.

With five major formations and 65,000 men occupying a rough square five miles on a side, traffic jams and sheer confusion were present in abundance, and the indescribable state of the muddy roads only made it worse. Finally, intelligence was not so much insufficient as it was completely wrong. Colonel Hammerstein had checked off three boxes in his command briefing: there were no formed Soviet units to the south, just light security forces; XXXXVIII Corps was holding a solid front to the south and waiting to open its lines to receive XIII Corps; and 1st and 8th Panzer Divisions had already begun another relief drive toward the pocket and were making good progress. Not one of these statements was true, however, and to this day it is impossible to say what he was thinking or what his commander, General Hauffe, had told him. Hauffe was in constant touch by telephone with 1st Panzer Army headquarters, and he certainly knew the truth of XIII Corps's predicament, but once again, he doesn't seem to have shared it with anyone.

For all these reasons, the breakout didn't begin until well after 5:00 A.M., just before dawn. Although the breakout surprised the Soviets initially (a constant feature of the *Kesselschlacht*, since no force can efficiently patrol the circumference of a circle from the outside), they recovered by early afternoon. German supply troops had not waited for the breakout to begin the dash to freedom, as the plan had specified, but had set out immediately after Provisional Corps C, when it was already broad daylight. The dense truck and wagon columns broadcast the direction of the German breakout, and the Soviets' response was swift: blocking forces in front; constant harassment of the southbound columns from both flanks; and unceasing air and artillery bombardment of the breakout site and the mass of men still milling around inside the pocket waiting to depart. A running back-and-forth battle developed for Hill 334, which changed hands several times. The initial thrust made perhaps five miles before getting stuck, but it was another six miles to safety—and that was six miles too far under the conditions. The Panzer divisions had launched another relief attack, as advertised, but they simply vanished in a sea of Soviet tanks prowling south of the pocket. Indeed, one German battalion (2nd Battalion, 2nd *Panzergrenadier* Regiment, 8th Panzer Division) wound up encircled by Soviet tanks. The battalion fought to its death over the next five days in its own miniature *Kessel*.

A breakout from an encirclement begins as a military operation, but it soon transforms into sheer human drama. As always, command

and control became the first victim. The corps radio net broke down, and so did the bonds of discipline. Each soldier began to make his own decisions about life or death, obedience or disobedience, and all the while the surge of humanity streamed south. The Catholic chaplain of the 454th Division, a Father Bader, later remembered encountering General Hauffe and finding him a broken reed. "Their superiority is too great," Hauffe moaned. "It's not worth it. We can't have the men slaughtered needlessly. Perhaps we'll wait till night. The situation is hopeless."[34] Bader still shuddered years later, after returning from Soviet captivity:

> There was no more command authority in the pocket. The Stalin organs [Katyusha rockets] hammered the tightly packed troops without pause. Low-flying Russian aircraft bombarded the jammed vehicles ceaselessly. Russian guns and mortars surrounded the Kessel and blazed away with all tubes at a fullness of targets. The enemy stormed one German battery after the other, finished off one company after the other. Burning vehicles were everywhere, exploding fuel tanks, wounded and dying men moaning.[35]

In that final spasm of death and destruction, the *Kessel*, Bader wrote, "was as terrifying as the end of the world."[36]

By July 22, it was all over. The German divisions in the pocket and in the breakout attempt to the south had disintegrated, and the surrenders began. The XIII Corps was an infantry formation, heavy on manpower and extremely light on weapons, equipment, and armored vehicles. Those facts account for the speed with which the Soviets were able to chop up the *Kessel* and for the extremely heavy toll in lives. Of the 65,000 men packed into the Brody Pocket, 20,000 were killed or wounded, and at least 40,000 went into Soviet captivity. The Soviets spoke of 30,000 killed and 17,000 captured. Miraculously, some 5,000 German soldiers managed to break out of the ring, filtering through Soviet lines to the south and rejoining the lines of XXXXVIII Panzer Corps. The casualties and prisoners included virtually the entire command staff: the corps chief of staff, Colonel Hammerstein (killed while leading a battalion in a last, desperate assault); the commander of the 361st Division (wounded, then captured); and the commanders of the 183rd and 217th Divisions (missing). General Hauffe suffered a curious fate. The Soviets took him prisoner, but as his guards were frog-marching him off into captivity, he stepped on a mine and was blown apart.

To Warsaw: Rokossovsky's Attack

The catastrophe at Brody opened the door to Galicia to Konev's 1st Ukrainian Front.[37] With the main road (the Rollbahn, the Germans called it) now open to the west, the Soviets took Lvov on July 23 and lunged another 60 miles to Przemysl the next day, effectively overrunning eastern Galicia in a single day. Under immense Soviet pressure, German 1st Panzer Army had to break contact all along the line and execute a hurried withdrawal to escape destruction. The army commander, General Raus, envisioned a "swing-back" maneuver (*Zurückschwenkung*): holding firm on his relatively untouched southern, or right, flank and drawing back his left and center—where the Soviets had done most of their damage. The maneuver was easier said than done, however. For the Germans, one river crossing followed the other—from the Strypa, across the Zlota Lipa, then the Gnila Lipa, and finally the Dniester—with the Soviets nipping at their heels the whole time. For the bruised northern wing, Raus's plan meant disengaging from contact, forming rear guards, and moving at speed through a deeply rural, forested region with an underdeveloped road and communications net. The final lunge to the south saw XXXXVIII Panzer Corps carry out a 27-mile forced march to catch up to the rest of the army and not be caught in isolation. Nevertheless, under Raus's able leadership and that of his corps commanders, all five corps of 1st Panzer Army wheeled back to the left and eventually re-formed a cohesive, 100-mile line behind the Dniester. The new position ran northwest to southeast, from Sambor on the left to Stanislaw (modern Ivano-Frankivsk) on the right, facing a parallel Soviet line from Sandomierz in the northwest to Halicz in the southeast (hence the Soviet designation for Konev's great offensive, the Lvov-Sandomierz Operation).

In extricating itself, however, 1st Panzer Army had opened up a vast gulf with its neighbor to the north, 4th Panzer Army. Under the grip of the iron logic that ruled behavior on the Eastern Front, no one was going to be closing that gap anytime soon. On July 18, five days into Konev's offensive, the Soviets launched yet another offensive, this time by the left wing of Rokossovsky's 1st Byelorussian Front. The target was the other German formation of Army Group North Ukraine, General Nehring's 4th Panzer Army. Rokossovsky was the greatest of all the Soviet operational commanders, a near-perfect balance of brute force and finesse. His offensive out of the Kovel region had plenty of the former, to an almost unimaginable degree. Rokossovsky had five regular armies in his first echelon and the 2nd Tank Army in his second. His divisions attacked on frontages of less than a kilometer, surely some kind of record.[38] He had enough heavy weapons support to devote no fewer than 356 artillery pieces and eighty-three tanks to every single one of those kilometers, while some 1,500 Soviet aircraft swirled overhead. All told, the mass represented a greater concentration of force than anything the Soviets had laid on during Operation Bagration.

The results were predictable: a clean and nearly immediate breakthrough. The defenders "were simply overrun," in the words of the German official history.[39] The thrust aimed at the seam of the two left-wing corps of 4th Panzer Army (VIII Corps and LVI Panzer Corps), driving the former into a northward retreat toward Brest Litovsk and the latter southwest toward the Vistula River. By day two the attackers were in the clear, reaching the Bug River and crossing it on the fly, and by July 22 Rokossovsky had inserted his second echelon, 2nd Tank Army.[40] The VIII Corps, separated from the rest of 4th Panzer Army, now became the right flank of Army Group Center, while LVI Panzer Corps reeled back. The result of these divergent (*exzentrisch*) retreats by the two major formations opened up a 60-mile gap in the German defensive position, through which Rokossovsky was now pouring the armored might of 2nd Tank Army. Soviet tank spearheads took Lublin on July 24 and reached the Vistula the next day. By July 29, 69th Army had crossed over the mighty river and formed a bridgehead on the far bank near the town of Pulawy.

It is no exaggeration to say that the German *Ostheer*—the Wehrmacht's vast Army of the East—now faced its single most dangerous moment of the entire war. Rokossovsky's 1st Byelorussian Front stood on the brink of total victory. He had smashed through Army Group North Ukraine—theoretically the best-defended portion of the German Eastern Front—as if it were not even there. In so doing, he had reunited his front as a cohesive whole for the first time in over a month. The primeval swamp of the Pripet Marshes had separated the two wings of his front, and he had performed the unenviable task of commanding troops and planning operations on both sides of that gigantic morass. He had overcome that obstacle, however, and now he had his choice of targets that were not merely operational. He could, for example, pursue the big solution, that is, a hard wheel to the right west of Brest Litovsk, heading toward the Baltic shore. Such a maneuver would place him far into the rear of both Army Group North and Army Group Center, surrounding well over half the German troops still fighting in the Soviet Union in a kind of *Überkessel*. (Such a maneuver had been the nightmare of the German High Command since

April, when the deployments and planning for summer 1944 had first begun.) Or he could concentrate on a smaller but still significant target: the German 2nd Army. With his right wing attacking 2nd Army frontally and driving it to the west in some disorder, his left could now come up on its rear and bag the entire force—a triumph on the scale of Stalingrad. The 2nd Army had opened Operation Bagration in a relatively quiet and nonstrategic sector, guarding the southern face of the Pripet Marshes. It had thus managed to avoid being swept up in the initial Soviet offensive and the great debacle that had befallen its partner formations in Army Group Center (the 3rd Panzer and 4th and 9th Armies). Now it seemed that its time had come. A pure infantry formation commanded by an officer of no particular distinction (General Walter Weiss), 2nd Army could match its Soviet adversary in neither combat power nor mobility. It was in a kind of operational free fall. It's northern anchor, Bialystok, had already fallen to the Soviets, and while the army's southern anchor, Brest Litovsk, still lay in German hands, Rokossovsky's tanks had already driven far to the west and south of the fortress.

The Red Army was now coming at Weiss's hapless army in four great thrusts. Soviet 70th Army was coming up on Brest Litovsk from the south, soon joined by two other armies (61st Army striking the city from the east and 28th from the north). Swinging far to the south and west, independent Soviet armored formations—XI Tank Corps and II Guards Cavalry Corps, along with support from 47th Army— were heading toward Siedlce, their mission to strike into the rear of 2nd Army and cut off its retreat.[41] The massed power of the 2nd Tank Army had thrust all the way to the Vistula at Pulawy and then turned due north toward Warsaw. And finally, forces of Rokossovsky's right wing were applying direct pressure on 2nd Army, with elements of 65th Army hitting it frontally in a thrust through Kleszczele, just about at the army's midsection between Brest Litovsk and Bialystok. A glance at the situation map would have convinced even the most optimistic staff officer that 2nd Army was doomed. Certainly, Rokossovsky, Stalin, and the Stavka must have thought so. They were already thinking of more distant targets: Warsaw, the bridges over the Narev River at Zegrze and Serock, and trapping the entire northern wing of the German *Ostheer* (Army Groups Center and North).

MODEL'S MOMENT: THE WARSAW COUNTERATTACK

They had failed to reckon with Field Marshal Model, however. At his best when the odds were worst, Model was able to overcome even the hopeless materiel situation, at least temporarily, often with little more than with sheer ruthlessness and determination. He rarely cajoled or inspired; he yelled and bullied. It is unlikely that any commander in the Wehrmacht threatened his subordinates with courts-martial more often than he did—and he had fierce competition on that score. In operational terms, he tossed together whatever manpower he could find, whether they belonged to the same regiment or not, and whether they were trained as infantry or not, and rigged together a cohesive defensive line in any way that he could—anything to slow down Soviet momentum. Then came the counterattack with any Panzer formation he could find, under his direct command and without any form of corps organization. Untangling his battlegroups afterward was often nearly impossible, and a stratagem that deliberately destroyed the orderly chain of command certainly couldn't be a recipe for long-term success. Then again, Model wasn't thinking in the long term. Dealing with the emergency du jour was his specialty. Few did it better, and perhaps no one ever did it better than he did in August 1944.

Model knew that the reeling 2nd Army couldn't save itself and thus required emergency assistance from the outside. A quick glance at the map had already shown him the danger points, and he planned two attacks to relieve them. Hustling the newly arrived 5th SS Panzer Division *Wiking* up to the line, he launched it into an immediate counterattack from the march in cooperation with 4th Panzer Division toward Kleszczele. Catching the onrushing spearheads of the Soviet 65th Army in a set of pincers from north and south, the attack destroyed a great deal of Soviet equipment and armor and stopped 65th Army dead in its tracks for a crucial few days. With the frontal pressure on the army now relieved, 2nd Army had just enough of a respite to continue its retreat to the west more or less unmolested.

The threat to the army's rear was even more serious, but once again Model was up to the challenge. Detaching 3rd SS Panzer Division *Totenkopf* from the north, where it was locked in desperate fighting to rescue what was left of German 4th Army, Model brought it down south. The decision left 4th Army to its fate for the time being, but once again Model was juggling emergencies. *Totenkopf* rushed down to Siedlce, launched an attack with almost no preparation, and savaged the tanks of the Soviet II Guards Cavalry Corps and XI Tank Corps. Soviet equipment losses were once again prodigious—hardly a blip to the Red Army in the long term, perhaps, but the difference between life or death for German 2nd Army at the moment.

In both battles—Kleszczele and Siedlce—Model benefited from

his nearly limitless command authority. Alone among all the German commanders on the Eastern Front from 1941 to 1944, he commanded multiple army groups. He could, therefore, shift the precious Panzer divisions hither and yon as he wished, without reference to higher authority and without having to beg the Führer for permission. Indeed, one last element of this operational sequence showed just how independent the field marshal could be. The High Command's immediate response to Rokossovsky's breakthrough was typical, declaring Brest Litovsk a *fester Platz*. Hitler's language was even more fanatic than usual this time. Brest Litovsk was to be held "until the annihilation (*Vernichtung*) of the garrison," he declared.[42] The German official history notes the date—July 24—and admits that the attempt on Hitler's life just four days before may have had something to do with his increased obstinacy.[43] But the Führer had help this time: the newly appointed Chief of the General Staff, General Heinz Guderian. He had finally arrived at the pinnacle of power that he felt had been rightly his all along, and he wasn't about to engage in an operational dispute with his leader and patron in his first few days on the job. At any rate, it was Model who talked sense into Hitler about Brest Litovsk. Indeed, he was already pulling back both army groups under his command—North Ukraine and Center—as rapidly as they could march without Hitler's permission, and he wasn't going to lose another two divisions senselessly, he declared. Hitler finally agreed, and the divisions nearly trapped in Brest Litovsk managed to break out during July 27–29, not without considerable losses, but nonetheless intact.

Model's performance so far had been sure-footed and decisive as he patched together a front that had appeared hopelessly shredded. Big threats still loomed all over the map, however. The Eastern Front was closer to collapse than it had ever been. Germany had only four German army groups in the Soviet Union, moving from the Baltic to the Danube: Army Groups North, Center, North Ukraine, and South Ukraine. Each one had been smashed, or was about to be. In the north, a Soviet offensive by 1st Baltic Front had caught the seam between Army Group North and Army Group Center and reached the Baltic coast at Tukums in Latvia, about 40 miles west of Riga. The successful Soviet thrust meant that Army Group North, the most threadbare of all four groups, was encircled. The disaster that had befallen Army Group Center requires no further elucidation. Suffice it to say that while it was not at the moment encircled, it had no contact with either army group on its flanks, Army Group North on its left and Army Group North Ukraine on its right. The latter was in the process of being chopped up by Rokossovsky's 1st Byelorussian Front. Currently, Soviet 2nd Tank Army was driving hard to the north along the right bank of the Vistula. Its power was enormous and its vistas limitless. In the first week of August, not a single formed unit of the Wehrmacht stood between 2nd Tank Army and Warsaw, or indeed between the army and the Baltic coast. The destruction of the entire German northern wing seemed imminent. And Warsaw was only the most obvious threat. And finally, in the south, Army Group South Ukraine was seeing disturbing signs in the first week of August of a massive Soviet buildup on its front, directly north of the Romanian city of Jassy. Clearly a major offensive was brewing, a blow that the army group had very little chance of withstanding on its own.

The threat to Warsaw was the most serious by far. A town on the direct road and rail line to Berlin, packed with rear-area installations of all sorts—supply depots, gigantic military hospitals, arms factories: its loss would be a disaster to the Wehrmacht and lead to a full-on logistical collapse. Once again, Model had to perform a kind of triage among his army groups and their constituent armies: who was lightly wounded and worth saving, who had to be written off altogether. With Soviet 2nd Tank Army moving north into a vacuum, backed up by 8th Guards Army and 1st Polish Army, Rokossovsky aimed first to take Warsaw's suburb of Praga on the right bank of the Vistula "off the march," then launch an assault into the Polish capital.[44] The 2nd Tank Army formed a powerful array with three corps abreast: XVI Tank Corps on the left, with its left sleeve on the Vistula itself, VIII Guards Tank Corps in the center, and III Tank Corps on the right. By August 1, the last of the three was already ranging far to the north and east of Warsaw, taking Radzymin and heading for the bridges over the Narew just a few miles away. That same day, 8th Guards Army under General V. I. Chuikov, the hero of Stalingrad (the army had been 62nd Army back then before being honored with Guards status), crossed the Vistula at Magnuszew, establishing yet another bridgehead over the river and threatening Warsaw from the south. Model was doing what he did best, yanking warm bodies out of rear billets and administrative posts and sending them to the front, forming a notional 9th Army in Warsaw, but its fighting strength barely sufficed for a passive defense. Alongside a single German division (73rd Infantry), elements of the 818th Azerbaijani Battalion or the 791st Turkish Battalion were on the line, with diverse training, weaponry, and fighting strength. The 9th Army was already bottling up the Soviets in the Pulawy bridgehead; now it had to do the same at Magnuszew. And finally, to add the final touch that would make the crisis complete, August 1 was the day that the Polish Home Army (*Armia Krajowa*) rose up in revolt in Warsaw to drive out their hated Nazi occupiers and liberate the city before the arrival of the Soviets. The Warsaw Uprising would become one of the most celebrated and controversial episodes of the war.[45]

Indeed, the events inside Warsaw have overshadowed what happened outside the city. With multiple Soviet tank columns hurtling forward and clearly intending some sort of major blow against Warsaw, Model launched one of the great counterattacks of the war. Ruthlessly stripping the front of armor, he was able to concentrate no fewer than four Panzer divisions for the fight. The four seemed to appear "out of nothing," in the words of the German official history, and in fact that was probably how it looked to the Soviets, advancing with a great deal of confidence but without much in the way of reconnaissance or flank protection. Model hadn't spent a lot of time wrangling with Hitler over operational freedom. Instead, the field marshal "simply took it."[46] Model called 19th Panzer Division down from Bialystok, plus the 5th SS Panzer Division and 4th Panzer Division from the previous week's hard fighting at Kleszczele. Finally, he rushed the Hermann Göring Panzer Division, fresh from Italy, almost directly off its trains into battle.

While none of the four divisions was at full strength—in total they amounted to 233 tanks and fifty-four assault guns facing over 800 Soviet tanks of 2nd Tank Army—they made up for it with a perfectly sequenced set of concentric attacks, the standard currency of Prussian-German operational methods for a long, long time. Model dealt with the most serious threat first: the Soviet III Tank Corps, far ahead of its neighboring corps and heading toward the Narew. On August 1, elements of the 19th Panzer Division and 5th SS Panzer Division *Wiking* launched a pincers attack on Okuniew, the former from the west and the latter from the east. They met up within hours and severed III Tank Corps's line of communication. The next day, 4th Panzer Division joined in from the north and the day after that the Hermann Göring Panzer Division from the south. The symmetry, even perfection, of the maneuver deserves mention. The German official history, hardly given to breathlessness or hyperbole, describes a kind of perfection: "four Panzer Divisions attacking concentrically from four directions," and for once the description seems apt.[47] Soviet III Panzer Corps was pressed into a smaller and smaller space and finally torn apart. On August 4, Model loosed a general offensive by all four divisions against Soviet 2nd Tank Army. Catching the Soviets unaware, the Panzers wreaked havoc on their adversary, destroying 550 of the 800 Soviet tanks in the three tank corps that had been attacking Warsaw, and 2nd Tank Army soon had to withdraw from the front for refit and replacements.

Model's counterattack in front of Warsaw has barely entered the historic consciousness, and even the most diehard World War II aficionado might be hard-pressed to identify it. Nevertheless, the victory was crucial on many levels. Model had saved the integrity of the German line of communications, averting what looked like an inevitable logistical catastrophe. He had saved Army Group North Ukraine from almost certain destruction, and that, too, seemed impossible just a few weeks ago. He had brought Army Group Center back to life, which must have seemed like a miracle inside Führer Headquarters, and not only to Hitler. It is no exaggeration to say that he saved the Eastern Front.

Finally, as Soviet pressure in front of Warsaw abated, Model could turn to smashing the Warsaw Uprising inside the city. He declared at the time that his preference was for a "ruthless burning" of the city, "1,000 meters east and west of the main road," since "otherwise, we won't be able get through."[48] In fact, the destruction the Wehrmacht wrought upon Warsaw in the two months it took to put down the Warsaw Uprising was even worse, encompassing some 85 percent of the city's buildings. The Old City of Warsaw that tourists visits today is a re-creation from the communist era, a simulacrum of what once was. The German victory at Warsaw also suggests an answer to the great unanswerable question of the uprising: Did the Soviets deliberately sit across the Vistula and allow the Germans to smash the uprising, crushing Poland's bourgeois elites and enabling an easier communization of the country in 1945? We will probably never have a firm answer to that question. Certainly the German destruction of the main Soviet force at the very gates of the city—an awful reprise of General Josef Pilsudski's "miracle on the Vistula" in 1920—meant that whatever the Soviets may have wanted to do they had little choice but to adopt a passive posture for the time being. The Red Army had just lunged all the way from Orsha to Warsaw—450 miles in just six weeks—and had dealt out a fantastic level of punishment to its German enemy, one of the signal operational achievements of the war. Even the commander admitted toward the end of the campaign, however, that he "was running out of breath."[49] It was time for the Soviets to consolidate their positions along the Vistula, firm up their bridgeheads, and rebuild their strength for their next great lunge to the west—the one that would bring them into Germany.

Model's successes even emboldened the High Command, especially the new Chief of the General Staff, Guderian, to launch Army Group Center into a counterattack.[50] The aim was to restore communications to Army Group North, currently isolated north of Riga. The plan was big, employing two Panzer corps (XXXIX in the north and XXXX in the south), containing no fewer than six Panzer divisions, plus another ad hoc Panzer formation designated *Gruppe* Strachwitz, two brigades under the command of General Hyazinth Graf von Strachwitz, the famous "Armored Count."[51] Operation *Doppelkopf* ("Two Head") was to slice through Soviet defensive positions on and south of the Gulf of Riga and restore a line of supply and communications to Army Group North. The main blow on August 16 by the two Panzer corps misfired, foundering on lack of surprise, Soviet numbers, and the significant antitank defenses that the Red Army had already rushed into the gap between the two German army groups. But a thrust by Strachwitz along the coast toward Tukums on August 20 (with just sixty tanks in all) apparently took the Soviets in this sector completely by surprise.

The Armored Count was a supremely confident commander whom Guderian once labeled "the last cavalryman in the world," a man of "completely unorthodox tactics, always with new ideas, each crazier than the last."[52] Strachwitz had once told a subordinate, "If I say that an antitank ditch doesn't exist for me, then it doesn't for you either," and indeed that phrase has defined him in history.[53] His family was old, well-connected Silesian nobility, and fourteen of his distant forebears had died fighting the Mongols at the decisive battle of Liegnitz in April 1241. But Strachwitz's attack at Tukums wasn't simply a case of a mad aristocrat riding to the hounds. He made sure to contact the German naval command before the attack, and the Kriegsmarine offered the cruiser *Prinz Eugen* and two destroyers (Z-25 and Z-28) for close support. For once, it was the Allies sitting helplessly under a rain of naval gunfire, the bane of the Wehrmacht in the west. *Prinz Eugen* fired off no fewer than 284 rounds from its 8-inch guns in the course of the day, and the destroyers chipped in with hundreds of 5-inch rounds. German records indicate forty-eight Soviet tanks killed in Tukums alone—nearly a complete tank brigade.[54] Strachwitz himself was in the lead Tiger tank, driving his two brigades (Panzer Brigade 101 and SS Panzer Brigade *Gross*) forward in what the official history calls a "wild attack."[55] They fought their way into Tukums and then headed east toward the linkup with Army Group North. On August 21, Strachwitz's Panzers made contact with SS Division *Nordland*, part of German 16th Army. Pressing on, the Armored Count and his little division entered Riga a few days later, where some of the local garrison wondered at the identity of the "lieutenant" with the dirty face, muddy overalls, and unkempt hair. "You're talking to a general in the flesh," he told them.[56]

Model was not in charge of *Doppelkopf*. Hitler had already tabbed him to rescue another bleeding front. This one lay in the west, where the Anglo–American–Canadian force was currently running rampant. The new commander of Army Group Center was General Georg-Hans Reinhardt, moving up from the command of 3rd Panzer Army. The field marshal was leaving behind the familiar haunts of Rzhev, Orel, and Kovel and heading for new ones: Avranches, Mortain, and Falaise. Time would tell if he could work his magic there. Nevertheless, Model could look back on the last month with some pride. Three of Germany's four army groups in the east had been at death's door, and he had rescued each one in the most dramatic fashion. Call it "Model's moment": an operational trifecta.

Army Group South Ukraine: The Second Death of 6th Army

Some numbers are simply unlucky. Certain combinations of the dice—snake eyes or boxcars—are almost never good news to the gambler when they appear, and they always seem to appear at the worst possible moment. Thirteen has traditionally been the unlucky number par excellence, so much so that we still construct buildings without thirteenth floors. The elevator proceeds from Floor 12 to 14, or to "12a" or to "M," the thirteenth letter of the alphabet. Friday the 13th is legendary. So many people stay home from work or otherwise alter their routine (canceling flights, for example) that the US economy loses hundreds of millions of dollars in business on that day alone.

Within the German order of battle in World War II, however, one number seems to be the unluckiest of all: the number 6.

Every student of the war knows the sad fate of German 6th Army. Consider the following narrative description:

* * *

The 6th Army was in deep trouble. Months of constant, grinding combat had sapped it of men and materiel, robbing it of its fighting edge and bringing its frontline soldiers to the brink of exhaustion. The Red Army had just launched a massive counteroffensive, pinning 6th Army in front and working around its left and right flanks. Here stood elements of the 3rd and 4th Romanian Armies, brave soldiers, to be sure, but with nowhere near the equipment, supply, or training of the Wehrmacht. By day's end, Soviet forward detachments—mixed groups of fast-moving tanks, infantry, and motorized artillery—had torn open great gashes in the defensive sectors of both Romanian armies. As always, the Red Army had a "second echelon" ready to exploit the breakthrough, and by day two, the Soviets were already driving forward at speed, lapping around both of 6th Army's flanks and heading for a linkup far in the German rear. On the third day of the offensive, it happened: the Soviets encircled German 6th Army, trapping it within a vast Kessel. *Cut off from home, from retreat, and from supplies, the fighting strength of 6th Army began to plummet—and so did morale.*

Already, members of 6th Army's brain trust—the army commander and his staff officers, along with the corps commanders and theirs—were evaluating the probabilities. How many days? How many men? How much supply and fuel? The math was terrible, and so was the list of operational possibilities. They could stay where they were and hope for a relief offensive by another German army from outside the pocket. Unfortunately, there wasn't one nearby, or even in the same time zone. The Soviet offensive had shattered the Romanians, so no help was going to be forthcoming from that quarter, either. Vague promises of supply by air were already filtering out of Führer Headquarters, but supplying an army this large—hundreds of thousands of men—was a pipe dream. They had one final option, of course. They could all strap on their helmets, form up, and try to fight their way out of the pocket. It wouldn't be easy, fighting through to the west while holding off Soviet attacks from the other compass points, but at least 6th Army would be doing something, and keeping up morale in such an awful situation was critical.

* * *

The gleam of recognition is immediate in any student of the war: General Friedrich Paulus, Operation Uranus, Kalach-on-the-Don— together they form one of the best-known operational sequences in the entire war, the Stalingrad campaign.

But the scene described above was *not* a description of Operation Uranus, the great Soviet counteroffensive at Stalingrad in November 1942. Rather, the date was August 1944, and the Red Army had just launched the Jassy-Kishinev Operation, hardly a household word in the West today. German 6th Army was standing not on the Volga River, as in 1942, but between the Dniester and Pruth. It was fighting not in the Soviet Union, but in the Romanian province of Bessarabia. The army commander was not the ill-fated General Paulus, but a relative unknown to modern memory, the equally ill-fated General Maximilian Fretter-Pico. German 6th Army, encircled and destroyed at Stalingrad in the winter of 1942–1943, reincarnated for the difficult defensive struggle on the southern sector of the front in 1943, and now encircled again, was dying for the second time in eighteen months.

The death of the 6th Army in the distant marches of Bessarabia and Moldavia was not a purely operational matter, but rather it was the latest milestone in the continued dissolution of the Axis. Fascist Italy had departed in September 1943, the first of Germany's allies to drop out and defect. The Germans responded with fury, displaying a level of emotional commitment that they had never shown during the years of their alliance with Mussolini. German forces occupied the entire country, attacked, killed, and imprisoned their erstwhile allies, and executed anyone they found troublesome. The Wehrmacht killed somewhere between 7,000 and 12,000 Italian officers and men in the course of Operation Axis, many of them shot in captivity. Moreover, that operation resulted in over 600,000 "military internees" (*Militärinternierte*), who spent the rest of the war as slaves in the Reich's armament factories.[57] After the killing and enslaving came the pillaging. The loot taken during Operation Axis was prodigious. While the Italian fleet managed to escape, the Germans captured the totality of the equipment of the Italian army and air force: thousands of tanks, guns, mortars, and antitank guns. These "booty weapons" (*Beutewaffen*) would equip Germany's second-line formations for the rest of the war. Taken on its own terms, as a raid for plunder, Operation Axis was a roaring success.

We should keep in mind that looting someone else's arsenal is a far cry from having him fight and die alongside you as an ally, however. The Germans might have avoided the need for Operation Axis altogether by devising strategies to keep the Italians in the war, or at least to keep them in the war longer. But the cultivation, care, and feeding of alliance partners was not a high priority for the Germans, not in this world war, nor the previous one. Indeed, lack of faith in military alliances was one of the long-term patterns of German warmaking, and the roots of this disdain lay deep in the past. As far back as there was a Germany, and before that a Prussia or even a Brandenburg, the armies of the Hohenzollern state had preferred to campaign as lone wolves, making war on their own, viewing alliances not as value-added accretions of strength but rather as limitations on their operational freedom.

Every officer of the German Wehrmacht, for example, knew the historical details of the Fehrbellin campaign of 1674–1675, the birth of the modern Prussian state and army. Frederick William, the Elector of Brandenburg, was campaigning in Alsace in 1674 as a cog in one of the serial coalitions formed to oppose Louis XIV of France. With troops of the Holy Roman Empire, Brunswick, Electoral Saxony, and the Electoral Palatinate all in the field simultaneously, the campaign had proven to be a slow-motion disaster, a parade of endless war-council talkfests, interallied negotiations over the most excruciating details, and missed opportunities to land a blow on their French adversary. The French forces in Alsace, by contrast, were under the strong hand of a single, very capable commander, Henri de la Tour d'Auvergne, Vicomte de Turenne. Throughout the fighting, Turenne acted more decisively, marched more rapidly, and outmaneuvered the allies at every turn. The allies' retreat back over the Rhine in late 1674 marked the final surrender of Alsace to the French.

But the problems of coalition warfare in 1674 ran deeper than operational sluggishness. While Frederick William was marching and countermarching across Alsace, Swedish forces invaded Brandenburg itself in December 1674. The Elector had a small home guard in place under Johann Georg, the Prince of Anhalt, but the force was too small to offer much resistance, and soon the Swedes had occupied the entire country. Facing an existential crisis now, a do-or-die moment, the Elector first canvassed his allies for support (unsuccessfully, of course), then struck camp in Schweinfurt and started back across Germany to liberate Brandenburg. Liberated from encumbering alliances and restraining coalitions, he was a free man: "As he recognized that he would now establish his immediate future by his own good sword, there was no more hesitating. His actions were as bold and rapid as lightning. He could now bring his own energy to bear, free from diplomatic considerations."[58] Frederick William and his fiery commander, Field Marshal Georg von Derfflinger, had to move an army clear across Germany as quickly as possible. With the army traveling light, broken up into smaller columns, and purchasing its supplies along the way (a rarity in those days of squeezing supplies out of the local population), the Brandenburgers covered the route from Schweinfurt to Magdeburg, nearly 200 miles, in just over two weeks—one of the era's great marches. So rapidly had they moved that they caught the Swedes still in winter quarters, dispersed all over the duchy, and completely unready for major operations. The resulting campaign, which brought the rattled Swedes to battle and destroyed them at Fehrbellin, made

Frederick William's reputation and transformed him into the "Great Elector."

Ever since Fehrbellin, Prussian-German armies had distrusted coalition warfare. Indeed, their own preference for high-tempo operations, for bold maneuvers, and for *kurtz und vives* wars that hit hard and wrapped things up quickly were the very antithesis of coalition warfare. Allies, by definition, tend to slow things down, as strategies, orders of battle, and operational approaches are negotiated rather than decreed. A coalition war is almost certain to be a long one, and a long war was something that Brandenburg could not afford. Frederick the Great, for example, signed the Convention of Westminster with Great Britain, but while he was happy to take British subsidies, he rarely listened to operational advice from London. In fact, the British had been dead set against Frederick's preemptive strike against Saxony and Austria that opened the war in 1756. They had signed on with Frederick as a means to avoid war, not to fight one. The Seven Years' War was a global conflict, with all sorts of maritime and imperial ramifications for Britain and France, but Frederick ran the conflict in central Europe very much as a close-hold operation.

Likewise, although Prussia fought as part of a coalition in the latter Napoleonic Wars, we often forget the decision that got it into the those wars in the first place: its hesitance to join the Third Coalition (1804–1807) against Napoléon. During the 1805 campaign, as the Grande Armée crossed the Rhine, took the Austrian entrenched camp at Ulm, and drove deep into central Europe, Prussia sat aloof, confident in the glory and excellence of its army. King Frederick William III stuck to that posture even as Napoléon smashed the Austrian and Russian armies at Austerlitz in December 1805. Prussia now faced Napoléon alone. A series of French provocations—in Napoléon's own inimitable style—followed, as did a Prussian declaration of war on Napoléon (as did Jena, Auerstädt, and the destruction of both the Prussian army and state in October 1806).

Even the debacle of the Jena campaign can obscure the aggressive deployment with which the Prussian army began it. The Prussians under the Duke of Brunswick were sitting at Erfurt, far to the southwest of Berlin, waiting to intercept and destroy any direct move by the Grande Armée into Prussia. Of course, Napoléon moved faster than the Prussians did, positioned himself south of the Thuringian Wood, and drove toward Berlin from an entirely unexpected direction. The Austerlitz-Jena sequence should remind us that a "way of war" is not a strategy, nor a doctrine, nor a replacement for either one. It is instead an ingrained and traditional military culture, imposing repetitive patterns of thought and behavior on the principals involved. A "way of war," in fact, is just as likely to lead to negative strategies and generate seemingly disastrous or even senseless outcomes as it is to bring victory.

But a way of war can also work. Prussia unified Germany in 1864–1871 by fighting a series of wars, creating a new state on the basis of its own military power. Certainly Bismarck was a master diplomat—isolating potential enemies and wisely choosing the time to strike. But unification came not from political maneuvering or coalition-building, but rather from the railroads and rifles of the Prussian state. The war with Austria found the newly formed state of Italy at Prussia's side, but the two fought entirely separate wars on either side of the Alps with no operational cooperation or joint planning. Indeed, the lack of encumbering alliances gave Bismarck and the Chief of the Great Prussian General Staff, Helmuth von Moltke the Elder, a great deal of freedom of movement (politically) and maneuver (militarily). The new state was a giant, to be sure, but the real power center in the heart of Europe—the real element that destabilized Europe for the next forty years and the most important factor in generating another world war—was the Imperial German army. It was an apparently irresistible machine that had found some magical formula to the problem of modern military operations by vast mass armies, able to mobilize more rapidly, strike more forcefully, and beat its enemies decisively within weeks.

Consider the experience of World War I. In the run-up to the conflict, Germany managed to alienate virtually all of its neighbors, until it was left with only one real ally, perhaps the weakest state in Europe: Austria-Hungary. Often blamed on Wilhelm II's boasting and bungling, Germany's world policy (*Weltpolitik*) of building an overseas empire in Africa, Asia, and the Pacific, or brash German behavior in the nearly endless series of diplomatic crises before 1914, the real reason for going into World War I with a lone, lame ally was that the other Great Powers lived in fear of the German army. Certainly German naval-building strength was a factor in driving Britain into the enemy camp, but so too was Britain's fear that Germany was well on the path to armed continental domination.

And so Germany entered the war fighting alongside Austria-Hungary, an unenviable proposition at best.[59] In the course of the war, the Germans tended to ignore their ally, refused to share information about either their deployment schemes or operational intentions (a crucial problem in the opening campaign of 1914), and then had no choice but to ride to Austria's rescue when disaster struck—disasters borne partly out of Germany's own neglect of coalition warfare.[60] Finally, after the near collapse of the Habsburg army in the face of the Brusilov Offensive in 1916, Austria-Hungary became little more than a German client and more of a drain on the Reich's limited resources than a strategic benefit.[61]

The World War I Allies, meanwhile, followed an entirely different character arc. They began the war with deployment plans already in place, the French and Russians to put so many men into the field at appointed times, the British Expeditionary Force to arrive in France within weeks of the outbreak of the fighting. The Allies consulted with one another during the war, with the Chantilly Conference of December 1915 being the best example, about how they intended to proceed. They even agreed during the crisis of spring 1918 to appoint a Supreme Allied Commander over all their armies in the field, the well-regarded Marshal Ferdinand Foch. Despite inevitable hiccups along the way, the Allies began the war with a solid base of cooperation and learned to conduct coalition warfare during the course of the conflict.

In 1939, it happened again. Germany entered World War II with the weakest ally in the field: Italy. Once again, faulty German diplomacy, aggressive behavior, and Hitler's apparently insatiable demands all played a role. But as important as Hitler was to the shape of the political prewar constellation, something more fundamental was at work here. The revival of the German army—still dedicated to high-tempo military operations in pursuit of decisive victory—was the real specter haunting Europe. After the public announcement of German rearmament in 1935, Europe returned to the same dynamic that had generated war in 1914. The key to European affairs was not merely how to integrate the German Reich into a peaceful and stable concert of Europe, but how to integrate the German *army*—with its Prussian roots and its preference for the bold strike—into a peaceful and stable international regime. The quest proved impossible.

As in World War I, so in World War II. Germany spent the early years of the conflict ignoring Italy, had no choice but to ride to its rescue in North Africa and Greece, and fought alongside Italian armies in North Africa and on the Eastern Front. The latter was high-intensity fighting for which the Italians were neither well configured nor trained. Then, when Italy had had enough, overthrew Mussolini, and decided to leave the war, the Germans turned on their ally with great savagery, occupying the country and subjecting the population to brutal reprisals for Italy's "treachery." But the German cry of "*Ver-*

rat!" ("Betrayal!"), uttered by every echelon of the Wehrmacht from the ordinary soldier to the Führer, was utterly false. Indeed, from drawing up plans for a violent coup against the new Italian government that was still part of the Axis with Germany (Operations *Schwarz* and *Student*), to ordering a mission to rescue Mussolini (which would culminate eventually in the raid on the Gran Sasso in September, Operation *Eiche*), Hitler had actually betrayed *his* ally.

Once again, the contrast with the opposing side is striking. The Western Allies fought the war with such a close degree of cooperation that they might as well have been one country. Like any good marriage, they argued from time to time over fundamental strategies, especially over the relative importance of the Mediterranean theater, and sometimes they simply bickered over nothing, but in the end they planned together, fought together, and never did lose a campaign. The Soviet Union remained aloof from the West, gladly accepting Lend-Lease weapons, vehicles, and aircraft but planning and executing operations entirely on its own. On the level of strategy, however, the Soviets did take part in the long string of Allied diplomatic conferences that punctuated the war, with Joseph Stalin attending the gatherings at Tehran, Yalta, and Potsdam. For all the problems the three powers had in working out reasonable strategic and operational compromises, the Grand Alliance was the closest wartime alliance in history.

In short, the German way of war proved absolutely inept in navigating the tricky waters of coalition warfare. And to make matters worse, former members of the German officer corps spent decades after the war blaming the Allies for the defeat. The memoir literature—from Field Marshals Erich von Manstein[62] and Albert Kesselring,[63] Generals Hans Friessner,[64] Maximilian Fretter-Pico,[65] and Lothar Rendulic,[66] and many others—all share an emphasis on the ways the Wehrmacht was let down or betrayed by its allies, especially the Romanians, the Italians, and the Hungarians. Western historians relying upon the memoir literature have followed suit, and today the notion that the Italians were responsible for the loss of North Africa and that the Romanians were culpable for the catastrophe at Stalingrad—both absurd points on their face—continue to dominate the historical narrative of Germany's war. Certainly the minor Axis allies were not up to German standards of equipment, training, and leadership, but their manpower was every bit as good, and all of Germany's allied armies fought very well under extremely trying circumstances.

Making war without allies, planning operations without the interference of coalition politics, relying only your own "good sword":

these were the Prussian-German army's watchwords. In both world wars, the Germans might have paid more attention to their allies, nurturing them, arming them, and "building partner capacity" (in the current parlance of the US Army). They might have worked to keep the Italians or the Romanians in the war longer, for example, and fought side by side in a spirit of loyalty and partnership. None of these things would have been easy to achieve. The Axis allies needed supply and materiel, above all, and the Germans were barely able to supply their own army in a comprehensive way. Still, nurturing the Axis coalition was worth a try. A Nazi foreign policy run by Adolf Hitler and his Nazi minions, a diplomacy characterized by dominance, power, and plunder, was an unusual matrix in which to nurture comradely and trusting relationships among peers, however. Instead, and as always, the Germans actually preferred to go it alone, a foolish preference indeed in modern warfare, and their allies stuck with them only as long as German power impressed and frightened them. These facts help to explain how the Third Reich lost every one of its allies by the end of the war—and how the Axis wound up as a willing coalition of precisely one.

Since joining the war in 1941, Romania had certainly contributed more than its fair share to the German campaign in the Soviet Union.[67] The Romanian army saw hard fighting in 1941, particularly in the two-month campaign to reduce the Soviet port city of Odessa (August–October 1941), during which it suffered nearly 100,000 casualties, as well as in the fighting for Crimea in 1941–1942. In the opening campaigns, the Romanians not only reconquered Bessarabia (the province between the Pruth and Dniester Rivers, lost to the Soviet Union as a result of the Nazi-Soviet Spheres Agreement of 1939) but also acquired broad Soviet territories beyond the Dniester and extending eastward all the way up to the lower Bug River, the district known as Transnistria. By 1942, Romania was bearing an immense share of the Wehrmacht's burden, contributing two of the nine Axis field armies on the southern wing (alongside five German armies and one each from Italy and Hungary). Putting Romania in the "minor ally" box really isn't correct. As one leading authority put it, "Romania is more aptly bracketed in the Axis line-up with Italy than with the minor satellites."[68]

All that began to change in late 1942. Stalingrad was a disaster for the Germans, yes, but also a catastrophe for the Romanians, one from which they never recovered. The Soviets smashed both of Romania's field armies—the 3rd and 4th—in the opening moments of Operation Uranus in November 1942. The two had been holding flank positions on either side of Stalingrad, and their destruction opened a path for Soviet pincers to encircle the German 6th Army inside the city. In the last two months of 1942 alone, Romanian losses topped 100,000 men. The post-Stalingrad fighting saw the Romanians in a harried retreat along with their German and Italian allies, and the first signs that their dictator, Marshal Ion Antonescu, might be rethinking his options and considering breaking with the Axis. In a January 1943 meeting with Hitler, he suggested a compromise peace with the Western Allies in order to concentrate Axis forces in the east. On his return from the meeting, he muttered to an aide, "Germany has lost the wider war. We must make every effort to ensure that we don't lose our own war."[69]

But, in fact—as Antonescu no doubt suspected—that train had already left the station. Disaster upon disaster followed: the loss of Transnistria and the evacuation of as much of the Romanian civilian population as possible; the great retreat back to the Romanian border in the face of the Soviet winter offensive of 1943–1944, covering nearly 250 miles from the lower Dnepr River to the Dniester; and the resulting isolation of Crimea. Army Group A and its component 17th Army were the German formations defending Crimea, but those designations disguise the immense military investment that the Romanians had there as well: two infantry divisions (10th and 19th), two cavalry divisions (6th and 9th), three mountain divisions (1st, 2nd, and 3rd), not to mention the headquarters of 1st Mountain Corps and the Cavalry Corps. The Germans had 165,000 men in Crimea, but the Romanians added the not inconsiderable total of 65,000 more. The Wehrmacht might have cut its losses and fetched 17th Army out of Crimea in good time with minimal losses, but of all the things the Germans did ineptly in this war, amphibious and littoral warfare were perhaps the worst. The fine touch and sensitive timing required for initiating an evacuation, for example, or the detailed planning required for smooth army-navy cooperation: these things simply seemed beyond the High Command of the Wehrmacht. From Hitler and Jodl on down, the OKW tended to prefer land warfare in all its planning, even though it was supposed to be a joint planning group. The collapse of the Tunisian bridgehead in May 1943 was a good example of this conceptual disconnect.

The evacuation of Crimea, almost exactly one year later, was another one.[70] Hitler and his OKW hemmed and hawed, contemplating a withdrawal, then decided to send reinforcements to the peninsula. The Führer was concerned about the international situation, especially the impact that evacuating Crimea would have on the attitude of neutral

Turkey, as well as friendly Romania and Bulgaria. He seemed adamant, and on this occasion no one in the inner circle was able to make the case strongly enough to change his mind. Jodl, Keitel, Zeitzler: all of them were on shaky ground when talk turned to politics. Their focus was relentlessly operational. As a result, precious military resources of 17th Army languished in a kind of operational prison in Crimea while successive Soviet drives on the mainland harried Army Group A (renamed Army Group South Ukraine in April 1944) back to the very border of old Romania. The retreat finally ended on a line running from Târgu-Neamţ in the Carpathians due east to Jassy and Kishinev, then bending to the southeast and running along the Dniester River to the Black Sea.

Moreover, when the Soviets finally decided to clear Crimea, launching a major offensive by 4th Ukrainian Front (General F. I. Tolbukhin) on April 8, 1944, the Axis position collapsed in a week. The Soviets broke through the Perekop Isthmus into Crimea proper, raced down to Sevastopol, and invested the great fortress city—a reverse mirror image of the German conquest of Crimea in 1941–1942 under Field Marshal Erich von Manstein. Tolbukhin's plan also displayed a certain operational acumen along with its brute force: his assault forces crossed the salt marshes of the Syvash, the "Putrid Sea," onto the northeastern shore of Crimea and were able achieve surprise against the Romanian defenders there, while a third army, the Independent Coastal Army, drove out of its bridgehead in the Kerch Peninsula, the easternmost point of Crimea. In the middle of these three powerful armies stood three threadbare corps: the German XXXXIX Mountain Corps defending the Perekop Isthmus, the Romanian Cavalry Corps guarding the narrow crossing of the Sivash, and the German V Corps in Kerch. Just a day before the Soviet assault, the new commander of Army Group A, General Ferdinand Schörner, reported to the OKH that "he guaranteed the long-term defense of the Crimea."[71] That evaluation lay in sharp contrast to the assessment of the man who was actually in Crimea, the 17th Army commander, General Erwin Jaenecke. He declared the situation hopeless and was already demanding permission to evacuate Crimea altogether. (See Map 6.1.)

A few days of fighting proved Jaenecke right. The Axis defenses lay in ruins. All three Axis corps were beating a hurried retreat to Sevastopol. The XXXXIX Mountain Corps had to cross nearly 100 miles of featureless steppe under heavy Soviet air attacks. The V Corps and Romanian Cavalry Corps had it nearly as bad. The former, in particular, had to march practically single file along the very narrow road on

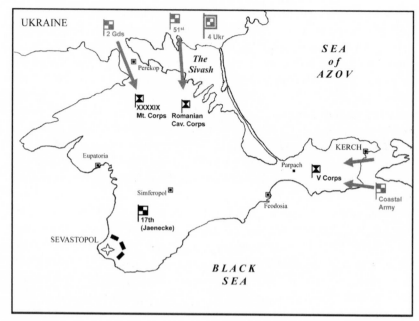

Map 6.1 Death in the Crimea: The Destruction of 17th Army (April–May 1944)

the south coast of Crimea. By April 14, all three had arrived in Sevastopol, bruised and bleeding, and losses had already run into the tens of thousands. Hitler blamed the debacle on Jaenecke, accused the general of having "lost his nerve," and sacked him on May 1 in favor of the V Corps commander, General Karl Allmendinger.[72] The latter took over a sinking ship, however.[73] Three ragged corps without a single tank were hardly going to be able to stand up to a concentric assault by three well-supplied Soviet armies, no matter how determined the defending commander.

Inevitably, what might have been an uncontested strategic redeployment out of Crimea turned into a hasty evacuation under fire—a far more dangerous and expensive thing. When the time came, German 17th Army had no choice but to fight off massive Soviet forces from one direction while waiting for the boats to arrive from the other.[74] The final Soviet assault on Sevastopol commenced on May 5, and four more days of bloody fighting took place before Hitler finally approved of an evacuation on May 9. The German Kriegsmarine and the Romanian navy both fought with their usual efficiency, running one convoy after another to the beaches. The Soviet Black Sea Fleet was as operationally sluggish as ever, so no surface threat materialized, but Soviet airpower and artillery contested the evacuation every step of the way, and Axis losses were high. The Kriegsmarine, up to now the can-do force within the German military establishment, displaying an often senseless level of optimism, soon realized that it was a matter of "saving what we can save."[75] Within days, Soviet bombardment from the land and air had become impenetrable, and on May 10 disaster struck when two German steamers, the *Totila* and *Teja*, carrying nearly 8,000 men between them, fell victim to Soviet air strikes—the former to bombers, the latter to torpedo aircraft. Both ships sank with the loss of all hands.[76] By now, command and control ashore had collapsed, as the shattered remnant of three Axis corps huddled on the beach behind the last ditch at Cape Chersonese—a dense mass of men standing under a murderous artillery crossfire from the Sapun Heights east of Sevastopol, as well as from Severnaya Bay to the north. By the time the navy called off the effort on May 12, it had managed to rescue 30,000 men, about half the force present for the final defense of Sevastopol, a commendable total given the stormy weather and unimaginable confusion on the beaches. The effort had failed more than 12,000 men, however, abandoning them to their uncertain fate in Soviet captivity. More than 10,000 men had died in the course of the evacuation, either in the *Totila* and *Teja* disasters or the dozens of smaller ships lost at sea. The army and navy spent the rest of the war and the ensuing postwar decades pointing fingers at each other, but the evacuation was only the ghastly end to a campaign that had already failed in every possible way. Some 60,000 German and Romanian troops died in the course of that single terrible month of fighting in Crimea, with another 20,000 German troops listed as missing—a sickening casualty total for what one German authority describes, correctly, as a "completely senseless fight."[77] In a rare role reversal, the Red Army suffered far fewer casualties, less than one-third those of the Axis. (See Map 6.2.)

By summer 1944, Antonescu's catastrophic war had come home to Romania. Civilian and military officials alike, along with representatives of the various political parties, were actively seeking a way out of the conflict, abandoning the Axis alliance and even switching sides to the Allies. By July, they had put out peace-feelers to the Soviets. The conspiracy centered around an unlikely character, twenty-two-year-old King Michael—an inexperienced young man whom Antonescu treated with barely disguised contempt. Their opportunity would come in August 1944, when the Soviets launched their last great offensive of the summer. The Stavka had already dealt out punishing blows

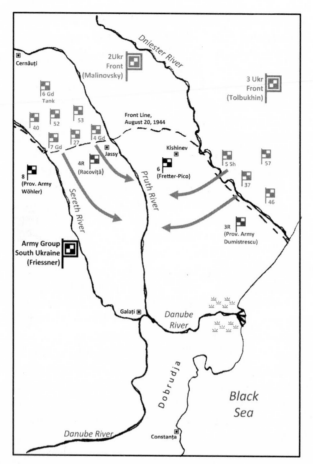

Map 6.2 Sixth Army's Second Death: The Conquest of Romania (August 1944)

to the three other German army groups in the east, and now, almost inevitably, came the turn of Army Group South Ukraine. The Soviets massed two fronts for the Jassy-Kishinev Operation: 2nd Ukrainian under General R. J. Malinovsky on the right, and 3rd Ukrainian Front under General Tolbukhin (transferred from 4th Ukrainian Front after the victory in Crimea) on the left. Together they amounted to just under 1 million men, with 1,400 tanks and assault guns, 16,000 guns, and over 1,800 aircraft in support. Malinovsky would attack southeast toward the Romanian city of Jassy, while Tolbukhin would drive west from his bridgeheads over the Dniester River. Their drives would work concentrically, link up somewhere on the Pruth River, and trap and destroy all enemy forces in a *Kessel*. The plan was simplicity itself, but the vast power the Soviets concentrated gave the Jassy-Kishinev Operation the same grim aura of inevitability as Operation Bagration two months ago or Rokossovsky's attack out of Kovel in July.

The intended victim, Army Group South Ukraine, consisted of four armies, impressive enough on paper.[78] Theoretically, two German and two Romanian armies (the German 6th and 8th and the Romanian 3rd and 4th) stood shoulder to shoulder in defense of the Romanian homeland. In reality, the Romanians were fought out: materially and morally exhausted, fed up with German arrogance, and no longer willing to die in Hitler's war. The German armies were almost purely infantry. During the long summer of 1944, Army Group South Ukraine had lost its Panzer divisions to the maelstrom in Byelorussia. In the three weeks after the opening of Operation Bagration, five Panzer divisions, an infantry division, two assault-gun brigades, and the headquarters of XXXX Panzer Corps all departed Romania for points north. The fighting power remaining to the four armies, therefore, was probably equivalent to only two at full strength, and that was how the Germans constructed their order of battle. Two provisional armies (*Armeegruppen*) were in the field: one pairing German 8th Army (General Otto Wöhler) with the Romanian 4th Army (General Ioan Mihail Racoviţă) and designated *Armeegruppe* Wöhler; the other pairing German 6th Army (General Maximilian Fretter-Pico) with Romanian 3rd Army (General Petre Dumitrescu) and designated *Armeegruppe* Dumitrescu. Boiled down to their essence, therefore, the operational matchups consisted of the following:

Jassy Front		*Dniester Front*
Soviets	2nd Ukrainian Front	3rd Ukrainian Front
	vs.	vs.
German	*Armeegruppe* Wöhler	*Armeegruppe* Dumitrescu

It was an obscure command structure, to be sure, with a potential for disputes and friction of all sorts. Both Hitler and Antonescu agreed to it, however—two congenitally suspicious men, each seeking to ensure that the other would not betray his alliance. Intermingling the troops, often deploying German and Romanian divisions side by side in the front line, seemed the best guarantee against leaving anyone in the lurch.

Indeed, mutual trust was fraying. The two men had an unusually frank exchange of views during a meeting at Führer Headquarters in

Rastenburg on August 5, the last time they would ever see one another.[79] Romania's cities and oil fields were under increasingly heavy air attack, Antonescu complained, and with military transport prioritized, road and rail transport for civilian goods had come to a complete standstill. Antiaircraft resources were scarce, and the number of fighter aircraft opposing the raids, thirty to forty at most, was wholly inadequate. In their last meeting, the Romanian *Conducator* noted, Hitler had promised to hold Crimea, to stabilize the Eastern Front, and even to launch an offensive to reconquer Ukraine. None of these things had happened. Hitler responded by declaring that he would never betray an ally, but he also wanted a clear answer. Was Romania "ready to fight the struggle to the end?" If not, Germany would have to "draw the necessary consequences."[80] For his part, he was ready to "defend each square kilometer of conquered territory fanatically," but he had to be sure of Romanian loyalty.

Antonescu had a great deal more military experience than Hitler, however, and he wasn't buying Hitler's promise of fanatical defense. He had "no doubt," he said "that good intentions always lay behind the Führer's promise to hold the current front line in Moldavia and Bessarabia. As a military man with the corresponding experience, I have to add, however, that we are not the only ones who decide what happens. All of this also depends on the possibilities, and especially on the will of the enemy." As to Romania's loyalty, "Antonescu answered that he had already made it plain he had no doubt whatever in the Führer's intentions. Furthermore, there was no ally as loyal to Germany as Romania. Romania would stay at Germany's side, and would be the last country to abandon the Reich, because it knew that Germany's end meant the end of Romania, as well."[81] The testy meeting droned on for hours, with the two men actually bickering about the rates Romania was paying for German aid and whose cities had been more completely destroyed by Allied bombing. When it was over, Antonescu excused himself from the evening meal. He'd had enough, apparently—and so had Romania.

Looking back at the Romanian campaign of August 1944 is like listening to a recording played back at excessive speed: familiar enough in its essentials, but whizzing by with a giddy energy. The Soviet offensive opened on August 20, launching two concentric drives. Malinovsky's 2nd Ukrainian Front attacked from the northwest, between Târgu Frumos and Jassy. Tolbukhin's 3rd Ukrainian Front attacked from the east, out of the Dniester River bridgeheads the Soviets had previously carved out at Tiraspol. Both 2nd and 3rd Ukrainian Fronts achieved massive and complete breakthroughs within days. Their mutual drives isolated German 6th Army southwest of Kishinev by the third day of the offensive, August 22. The 6th Army tried to extricate itself and beat a retreat back to the Pruth River, but the force was already doomed: a horde of nearly immobile infantry with horse-drawn transport being ridden down by powerful Soviet mechanized columns. The whole thing took barely more than a week. For the second time in this war, the Soviets had destroyed the German 6th Army.

The coup of August 23 in Bucharest, with King Michael having Antonescu arrested, then summoning the dictator's minions one by one to the palace for consultations and arresting them as well, put the final touch on the Wehrmacht's catastrophe. German attempts to put down the coup and keep Romania loyal misfired badly. King Michael first urged his troops not to fire on the Germans, but a Stuka raid on the royal palace soon changed his mind.[82] On August 25, Romania declared war on Germany. The Romanian army duly obeyed its oath to the king and switched sides, fighting alongside the Soviets to clear the Germans out of Romania. Bucharest fell to the new allies on August 23, followed by Ploesti on August 30, and the Germans were gone by the first week of September. The Germans often accused their allies of operational ineptitude and sometimes even cowardice, but the Romanians certainly seemed energized enough in this brief liberation campaign. Perhaps it was all a matter of having the right motivation.

The Germans used the coup as their great excuse for failure, with the Romanian "betrayal" (*Verrat*) featuring prominently in the German literature. The hapless commander of Army Group South Ukraine, General Friessner, titled his memoirs *Battles Betrayed* (*Verratene Schlachten*). But signs of betrayal are hard to come by, and no evidence exists that the Romanians shirked their duty or agreed in advance to stand aside while the Soviets chewed up the Wehrmacht. Rather, the only strategy by which Army Group South Ukraine might have defended itself—shuttling the Panzer divisions as fire brigades to seal off Soviet penetrations of the front line—was no longer operative, since there were hardly any Panzer divisions left in Romania when the Soviets attacked. Whether brought on by Romanian betrayal or German military incompetence, however, the Wehrmacht's losses in this brief campaign had been catastrophic: over 200,000 men, including thousands of German officials, both civilian and military, the administrators of the alliance. And even today, no one knows the fate of the

80,000 Germans who went "missing" in Romania; indeed, so rapid and bewildering was the collapse that these phantom soldiers might as well have vanished into thin air.

Where did Germany lose World War II? With all due respect to the other fronts in Europe, North Africa, and the Mediterranean, there was one front that was merciless in exposing German weakness, one front that allowed the enemy to unfold his total strength and to pose operational problems that the Wehrmacht was helpless to solve. Only one front offered wide-open spaces, an endless plain where the Wehrmacht could never field enough divisions, and where breakthroughs inevitably achieved encirclements of massive German forces. The German way of war had evolved within fairly narrow geographical confines; indeed, all the greatest victories in Prussian and German history had occurred between the Meuse and the Vistula. Fehrbellin, Leuthen, Königgrätz: all had a fairly narrow radius. Leuthen was 65 miles from Berlin, Königgrätz less than 200. Reaching out to the *latifundia* ("broad fields" in Latin) of southeastern Europe and Ukraine, however, to the endless steppes between the Dniester and Volga Rivers played into the hands of an enemy with superior resources. Deploy a Prussian army within its traditional inner zone, and its aggression, operational acumen, and tradition of independent command might very well win out. Plunk it down on the vast southern marches of an overextended Nazi empire, however, or ask it to wage war a thousand miles from home along the Donets or the Bug or the Dniester, and things changed. For the Wehrmacht, the broad fields of the east were the killing floor.

7

On the Run: The West

Recitation

What kept them going? What were they telling themselves? What were they saying to one another? At the end of the day, we can always justify ourselves. We rarely admit mistakes and, even more rarely, our guilt. And we can always come up with reasons to keep doing what we're doing, no matter how ill-advised our actions may seem.

* * *

AT COMMAND POST SOMEWHERE ON THE WESTERN FRONT—JANUARY 1945.[1] *They were a mixed bunch, these three. The oldest was a veteran divisional commander, another led one of the new* Volksgrenadier *(VG) Divisions, a second-rate unit filled with men combed out of the rear areas, or the supply troops, or even, in the case of the lightly wounded, out of a hospital bed. Finally, there was a colonel, a staff officer—or at least he had been until a few days ago, when he received the notice transferring him to the front. He was still trying to acclimate himself. The war seemed orderly enough on maps and charts, but out here, "order" was the last word you'd think to apply.*

The veteran commander had seen enough. "I can't keep trying to show confidence and faith to my troops," he complained. "My people have known me for years, and I've never lied to them." But he was lying now, and he could feel their eyes following him. "I don't want to lose the trust of my men," he said.[2]

The VG commander wasn't having it. "The worse the situation is, the tougher we have to be in struggling through it," he declared.[3]

"How much longer are we going to continue this 'tooth and nail' stuff?" asked the older man. "We're already pressed back to the homeland as it is."

*"That's the wrong question," answered the VG man. "We have no other possibility than to fight on. Let the other side break their teeth on our resistance. We have to hold out, whatever it takes (*koste es, was es wolle*)."[4]*

There it was again—that old Prussian formula. People were saying it a lot lately.

The colonel had been silent up to now. "That's Hitler's view."

"Of course it is," snorted the older man. "The Führer can end the war only if he and his regime step down. The last Kaiser drew the right conclusions. Hitler never will."

"Then we have no choice . . . you said it yourself," said the VG man. "Any talk about ending the war is crazy. We can't call it quits now, we mustn't. We soldiers least of all."

The colonel chipped in. He didn't feel at home yet, not with the frontline fighters. "One other thing to think about. Next summer we'll see more V-weapons, new U-boats, our jet fighters, and new types of Flak. *The optimists think they'll be a last-hour turning point in the war. They say we can't lose our nerve at five minutes to twelve* (fünf Minuten vor zwölf). *"[5]*

Another Prussian formula—handed down from long ago and given new life in 1918.

"I know how difficult it is," answered the older man, suddenly feeling weary. "Whatever! As an old soldier, I know you don't just throw in the towel, but I can't figure it out.[6] I only hope that the higher-ups come up with a decision that's best for the people."

The Volksgrenadier *general jumped back in. "The future of our people stands and falls with the Führer. If fate is against us, then maybe we're done for. At least we've fought to the last . . . ! My men will do their duty, without question, and they won't trouble themselves by thinking too much."[7]*

He was just getting started. He'd gotten his division late in the war, he was still full of fight, and he wasn't about to tolerate negativity or defeatist talk. "If we lose this war, then it's the fault of each man who didn't dedicate himself heart and soul and who didn't believe in the Führer. They stabbed him—and those fighting at the front—in the back."[8]

* * *

Sometimes it seems like they were actors reading lines, reciting formulas that had been written for them by their forebears. Keeping up the fight "whatever it takes" (*koste es, was er wolle*), the demand to "hold out at any cost," the admonition not to quit "five minutes before midnight," even Hitler's serial evocations of Frederick the Great: this was the German army's discourse in the war's latter days. And now, the "stab in the back" was experiencing a revival. Old Prussian traditions were rubbing shoulders uneasily with the darker paranoid fantasies that emerged after 1918. The "stab in the back legend" (*Dolchstoss-legende*) had been one of the things that doomed the Weimar Republic from its infancy. The notion that the army hadn't lost the war in a fair force-on-force contest in 1918, but had been the victim of a foul betrayal by the home front, had become part of the *mentalité* of the officer caste, and all of them shared it to some degree. The threat of being seen as a traitor to the cause—a party to betrayal—was enough to silence many German officers, keep them loyal during one crushing defeat after another, and call them to the colors in the few violent months they had left.

Our *Volksgrenadier* officer was typical, perhaps. Beset by a world of enemies, leading a second-rate division in a lost cause: rational thought should have told him to lay down his arms. Obsessed with memories of 1918, however, he had decided to go down with fists flying, and the ensuing mountain of casualties—most of them German, of course—seemed to bother him not at all.

The Loss of France: Dragoon

Even as the Allies were running riot after Avranches and smashing Army Group B in northern France, they had enough spare men, weapons, and resources to launch another vast amphibious operation in the south.[9] (See Map 7.1.) The original conception for Operation Anvil was a landing on the French Mediterranean coast, scheduled to take place simultaneously with Overlord and thus catch the German defenders of France in a gigantic strategic pincer. Lack of sufficient troops, landing craft, and naval and air support eventually forced the postponement of Anvil, however, leading to a great deal of inter-Allied wrangling between the Americans and the British over the timing, resources, and exact location of the operation. Indeed, the British didn't want to do Anvil at all. Churchill preferred to devote the resources to Italy, with an eye to bringing that attenuated and frustrating campaign—one in which he had invested enormous time, energy, and political capital—to a close. The last thing the Americans wanted was more fighting in Italy, however, and they suspected Churchill of ulterior motives—using the Italian campaign as a springboard for further diversions into the Balkans, primarily. American counsels prevailed, however, yet another sign of the subordinate role that British interests were playing by this phase of the war.

Under a new code-name, Operation Dragoon, the landings took place on August 15. Targeting the French Riviera coastline between Cap Nègre in the west and Fréjus in the east, the Allies put ashore the three divisions of the US VI Corps under the command of General Lucian K. Truscott Jr. on day one.[10] The next day saw three more

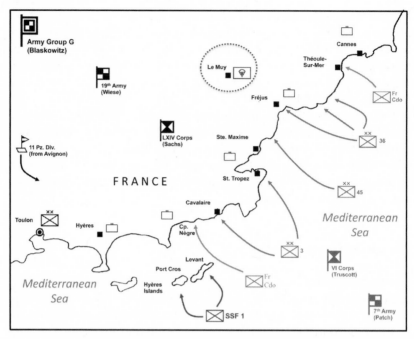

Map 7.1 Anvil-Dragoon: Allied Landing on the Riviera (August 1944)

divisions, the French II Corps (General Edgard de Larminat), come ashore to the left of VI Corps. German resistance was so light as to be nonexistent, and Allied troops, having learned the dangers of delay in previous amphibious landings, were already pushing inland with gusto. By August 18, US tanks had rolled up to Riez, more than 50 miles from the beaches. French forces, driving west with impressive speed, took both the major ports, Toulon and Marseille, within two brisk weeks of fighting, an impressive achievement, indeed. Marseille was nearly 75 miles away from the original beachhead. The participation of French forces was useful politically, demonstrating that the Allied host had come not to conquer France but to liberate it; it also served to galvanize the French resistance, officially known as the French Forces of the Interior (FFI). It had grown increasingly active in the months since Overlord, and the *maquis* (literally, "bush-fighters") ruled the rough terrain of the *Massif Central*. By the opening of Dragoon, in fact, the *maquis* had already surrounded several German garrisons in the interior. Eventually, Dragoon put two complete Allied armies ashore: French Army B (later renamed French 1st Army), under General Jean de Lattre de Tassigny on the left, and US 7th, under General Alexander

Patch on the right, with the two armies eventually coming together into 6th Army Group under General Jacob L. Devers. By any measure, Dragoon was one of the most successful operations of the war: landing an entire army group ashore without tapping the already overburdened Normandy lodgment area, sustaining minimal friendly casualties, and opening the vast port of Marseille to Allied shipping.

Of course, the Wehrmacht had something to do with that. The German defenses in southern France had never been particularly formidable. Army Group G (General Johannes Blaskowitz) had originally consisted of two armies, 1st Army on the Biscay coast and 19th Army defending the Mediterranean. Neither force had been very robust to begin with, and both had individual divisions holding defensive sectors of impossible breadth. Since then, the situation had gotten only worse. The Normandy invasion forced the High Command to fetch fresh divisions from Army Group G, along with tank, assault-gun, artillery, and antiaircraft assets, and transfer them to the north. Most serious was the loss of two of the Army Group's three mobile divisions—9th Panzer Division and 2nd SS Panzer Division *Das Reich*. The ride of the latter to the northern theater became infamous due to the horrific atrocity it wreaked upon the town of Oradour-sur-Glane, blamed for the kidnapping of an SS-man and for harboring the *maquis*. Divisional personnel shot all the men of the village, locked up the women and children in a church, and set fire to it, killing 642 people.[11] This sort of thing may have been business as usual on the Eastern Front, but like the massacre at the Ardenne Abbey in Normandy, Oradour serves as a historical reminder that the brutal ethos of the SS knew no geographical boundary.

By August, most of 1st Army had also departed the south, heading north to become part of the desperate struggle to restore Army Group B's defensive line after Operation Cobra. That left only the 19th Army deployed along the Mediterranean. While on paper it commanded an impressive force of three corps (IV Luftwaffe Field Corps, LXXXV Corps, and LXII Reserve Corps), it was a shadow of what it had been back in June.[12] Then it had contained sixteen divisions, now just seven.[13] The struggle up north had gobbled up its formations and replaced them with diverse troops of dubious fighting value, *Ost*-Battalions and *Hiwi*-Troops and the remnants of divisions chewed up in the Normandy fighting and sent south to rest and refit. The 716th Division, for example, a static formation mauled during the Anglo-Canadian landings, now stood at Perpignan near the Spanish border, on 19th Army's extreme right. The division probably wielded the actual fighting strength of a single US battalion. Its own commander doubted whether the division was strong enough to withstand even a weak attack, and the 19th Army chief of staff rated it "still not ready for action" at the time of the Allied landing.[14]

The same might be said for the rest of 19th Army. Some of the numbers remain astonishing today. The IV Luftwaffe Field Corps on the army's right wing possessed precisely 71 artillery pieces when the Allies landed. The LXII Reserve Corps on the opposite flank had just 28.[15] The single Panzer division available for all of southern France probably had some 100 tanks in all, and it began the campaign deployed on both sides of the Rhône River. The deployment was unfortunate, given the fact that preparatory Allied bombing had destroyed the bridges over the river. As always, German Panzer divisions in France had a strategic mobility rating near zero. Once in battle they always gave a fine account of themselves. Getting them into battle in a timely fashion with Allied aircraft prowling overhead, however, was a problem the Germans never solved.

Despite its manifest weaknesses, 19th Army command was talking tough. "The main line of defense (*Hauptkampflinie*) is and will remain the beach," General Friedrich Wiese told his men, before adding the usual proviso about defending the position "to the last man and the last bullet."[16] In private, he didn't believe that holding out was possible, and neither did his army group commander, General Blaskowitz. Neither commander communicated their doubts to the men under their command, however. To be blunt, the command was exhorting the men to lay down their lives while at the same time realizing that the order was senseless. They kept their men busy fortifying positions as best they could, erecting beach obstacles, and preparing demolitions. There is a certain pathos here: an underarmed force relying on horses and bicycles for its mobility about to try conclusions with a fully mechanized host enjoying complete control of the air. Pathos dissipates, however, when we call to mind the other activities that were keeping the Wehrmacht busy on the verge of Operation Dragoon: hunting down and killing the *maquis*. For the Wehrmacht, the partisan hunt had always been synonymous with atrocity and civilian massacre, and southern France was no different. We should not call them "excesses," since they actually emerged from policy and doctrine.

The great Allied landing on August 15 struck this indifferent German force and soon scattered it. US and British paratroopers led things off, jumping south of Draguignan near Le Muy and dropping almost on top of the headquarters of LXII Reserve Corps.[17] Within hours, they had surrounded the entire corps staff and cut it off from contact with the fighting elements on the beaches. In that sense, the opening minute of Dragoon was the decisive point in the fighting. Allied bombing also severed communications between Army Group G and 19th Army. The 11th Panzer Division took a solid week to assemble itself on the eastern bank of the Rhône and was a nonfactor in the landing phase. Meanwhile, Wiese was broadcasting more senseless orders to his men, ordering an immediate counterattack "to throw the enemy into the sea."[18] The German official history argues that he issued the order for his own "security and justification," that is, so he could later claim to have followed the Führer's orders to the letter, which explains but does not excuse.[19] The situation careened from threatening to disastrous in two days, and on the evening of August 17 the OKW ordered a general retreat of Army Group G to the north, including both 19th Army and the LXIV Corps still arrayed along the Atlantic coast to the west (the remnant of the 1st Army, now departed for the north). The order set nearly a quarter of a million men on the road, 138,000 from 19th Army and 87,000 from LXIV Corps.[20] Left behind were the 13,000-man garrison of Marseille, another 18,000 at Toulon, and another 27,000 miscellaneous personnel, as well as the garrisons of the Gironde fortresses on the Atlantic and the defensive perimeter of La Rochelle.[21] The LXIV Corps had its own problems. Years of occupation duty had rendered it unfit for fighting, or even for marching. Two thousand customs officials swelled its ranks, as did 3,000 railway workers, and even 2,000 female auxiliaries. Ugly outbreaks of panic were common, as were disputes over who got to leave first, who had precedence on the roads, and who got to ride in the scarce number of vehicles as opposed to marching on foot. Discipline crumbled early. The garrison commander of Limoges, General Walter Gleininger, tried to surrender to FFI forces surrounding the town, but his troops broke out against his will, and he shot himself rather than face a court-martial.[22] The LXIV corps commander, General Karl Sachs, was the man in charge of shaking out this motley crew and getting it on the road, and he described the entire experience as a "really shattering image."[23]

Army Group G began its retreat north in two columns: IV Luftwaffe Field Corps (189th Reserve and 716th Infantry Divisions) shuffling up the western bank of the Rhône and LXXXV Corps (198th and 338th Infantry Divisions) coming up on the right. Packed in their midst was a huge array of men whose fighting value in ground combat was nil—navy, Luftwaffe, and administrative personnel numbering in the tens of thousands, and even the fighting forces had to drop all unnecessary equipment and baggage and most of their heavy weapons. Their objective was the region north of Dijon. Here, the columns were to link up with Army Group B, the formation fighting to the north, thus restoring a cohesive defensive line in France from the English Channel to the Swiss border. The retreat was an epic of sorts but, like so many late-war events, has dropped from our consciousness today. That is unfortunate. Dijon lies a full 300 miles north of Marseille, so the distances were vast. The Allies were fully motorized, the Wehrmacht barely so. The Allies had lavish material and logistical support, the Germans 100 tanks and few guns. The Allies were flushed with victory, the Germans a ragged, jittery bunch. The Wehrmacht had once come to France in one of the greatest mechanized operations of all time, but the retreat to Dijon was a slow procession of long, foot-mobile road columns, a kind of double-file march with high vulnerability on both flanks—all the ingredients for catastrophe.

And, indeed, catastrophe seemed to be in the offing. The Allied had great success early in the campaign, overtaking and overrunning German infantry at Aix, Arles, and Avignon and taking 24,000 prisoners. Now they, too, were moving north in two parallel columns, one directly up the Rhône Valley, a second to the east in the general direction of Grenoble. The drive up the Rhône by US 3rd Infantry Division was essentially the "frontal" pursuit of the Germans, pushing them up the main road to the north. A fairly standard retreat/rear guard/pursuit sequence, it was unlikely to result in a decisive outcome one way or the other, since the Allies were merely forcing back their adversary. For that reason, the VI Corps commander, General Truscott, decided to assemble a rapid armored exploitation force, a brigade-sized unit under his assistant corps commander, General Frederic B. Butler.[24] Supported by US 36th Division, Task Force Butler's orders were to ride like the wind out of the bridgehead to the north, then wheel sharply to the west, reach the Rhône Valley, and cut off the German retreat near the town of Montélimar.

Truscott's plan unfolded smoothly and methodically. As the German trudged to the north in the river valley, and the mountains on either side grew steeper (the Provence Alps transitioning into the more forbidding Dauphiné Range), the US 36th Division and Task Force Butler headed to the north out of Le Muy. Butler's tanks made 45 miles on August 18 and nearly the same on August 19 and 20. The ride was classic US military improvisation, a scratch formation using Michelin maps and a Piper Cub plane aloft as guides. Butler *was* riding like the wind, overrunning 1,000 German infantry at Digne-les-Bains, taking the town of Sisteron without a fight, and bluffing his way into the German radio base in the village of Gap by threatening to have the village leveled by imaginary B-17 bombers.[25]

German resistance was everywhere weak, and no wonder. The 148th Infantry Division should have been guarding this sector, but the German High Command had just transferred it to Army Group Italy and ordered it back to the Alpine passes to prevent any Allied drive into northern Italy. On August 21, Truscott ordered Task Force Butler to lunge for Montélimar on the Rhône. Even Butler might have swallowed hard at the order. Montélimar was still 60 miles away. Nevertheless, threading their way through mountain passes, the vanguard of Butler's little band reached the high ground north of Montélimar late that afternoon—a handful of armored cars and Stuart light tanks, followed by an artillery battery. It was one of the war's wildest rides—some 200 miles in just four days. Truscott was pleased: "Georgie P. is not the only one who can cover ground," he chuckled.[26]

Now the US guns unlimbered and began to rain shells down onto Highway 7, the main artery up the eastern bank of the Rhône, unleashing panic within the German columns jamming the road. Sitting wagon to wagon and bumper to bumper, 19th Army was a dense and helpless target, impossible to miss. Within minutes, US artillery fire turned fifty German vehicles into burning wrecks. Fire, in turn, bred panic. Trucks swerved off the roadway, collided, and toppled over. The Wehrmacht enjoyed a high degree of unit cohesion, yes, but this situation was already out of control. Truscott had sprung his trap: Butler coming down from the top, and US 3rd Division pushing up Highway 7 from the bottom. All that remained was to close the jaws of the pincer and yet another German army would be marching off into captivity. Full of confidence, Butler wired Truscott that he was ready to launch a full-strength attack to finish the job the next day.

Sitting on the plain below, 19th Army went into an immobile laager, perhaps the worst of all possible responses to the incipient encirclement. No one ordered it to do so, and it is accurate to say that no one was in command. With radio communications severed, neither Army Group G commander Blaskowitz nor 19th Army commander Wiese were quite certain of their dispositions or those of the Allies. Looking back, Blaskowitz still sounded bewildered by his time on the Rhône. "The immobility of the troops, the absence of any suitable air or land reconnaissance, the failure of our communications net, and the increasing roping off of our freedom of movement by the French resistance" made it impossible to operate. "We had to do everything blind, as if in the pre-technical era," he wrote, "against an opponent with the most modern weapons, systems of command, and means of transport."[27]

Blaskowitz and his command would almost certainly have met their doom in the Montélimar Gorge, were it not for a single German unit. The 11th Panzer Division under the command of General Wend von Wietersheim was the single mechanized division in Army Group G, but timing is everything, and the 11th had gotten to the right place at the right time.[28] That it was there at all was controversial. Discussion had taken place in the highest echelons of Army Group G about having the division make a run for it, escape to the north, and abandon the infantry formations to their fate. Wietersheim had argued against it, and his opinion eventually prevailed. But no one could blame him for wishing to go it alone. The operational situation faced him with a brutal portfolio of missions. He functioned simultaneously as a rear guard to the south, holding off the attacks of the US 3rd Infantry Division; a delaying force to the US 36th Infantry Division coming in from the east; and a hammer to pound Task Force Butler trying to seal off the pocket to the north. In what was by now standard German practice, Wietersheim broke his division down into battalion-size *Kampfgruppen* of all arms. Delaying in the south and east, and making good use of his five 88mm antitank batteries, he managed to hold the Americans at bay. At the same time, he launched a series of counterattacks to the north. Task Force Butler never amounted to more than a light mechanized screen rather than a fighting formation, and Wietersheim handled it roughly, inflicting punishing losses and pushing it back and away from the high ground north and northeast of Montélimar. In the process, 11th Panzer Division opened just enough of a path to get the demoralized main body of 19th Army on the road and back on the move. Despite losses of two-thirds of his Panzers, Wietersheim had prevailed.[29]

Several other factors besides Wietersheim's heroics were also crucial to the successful German escape. Throughout the fight at Montélimar, the Allies were unable to apply any significant pressure on the German march from the western bank of the Rhône. Here, the attackers were not regular Allied troops but the *maquis*. Adept at little war—ambush and raid—they could apply pressure to the Germans but not engage in a standup firefight with Wehrmacht regular infantry. The terrain on that western bank of the river was the rough Cévennes District, the southeastern extremity of the Massif Central, and small parties of German infantry were able to keep the FFI at a distance from the road. The result was a one-sided battle at Montélimar, with the pressure coming mainly from the Americans to the east, but with no real threat from the west. Second, the great lunge into the interior from the Dragoon beaches was already resulting in supply and fuel difficulties—the bête noir of all Allied operations in Western Europe. By the time they even reached Montélimar, US and French troops had already advanced 200 miles in two weeks. Marseille had just fallen, and the great port was big enough to solve the supply difficulties all by itself, but it was not yet on line.

Finally, Truscott's plan might have briefed well and looked good on the map, but neither 3rd Division coming up from the south nor 36th Division from the east showed a great deal of drive in this campaign. The commander of the 36th, General John E. Dahlquist, never really had his division in hand, and it spent the week of fighting scattered all over the place in a vast triangle between Montélimar, Grenoble, and Saint Tropez. Dahlquist wound up on the wrong end of several of Truscott's legendary tongue-lashings, and on one occasion Truscott visited the divisional command post to relieve him, only to be talked out of it. Analysts then and now have scapegoated Dahlquist for the failure to trap the Germans, and even he admitted "I fumbled it badly."[30] US military historians love their villains and heroes and usually place Truscott in the latter camp. But the plan concocted by the VI Corps commander raised its own set of questions. The key element that Truscott devoted to closing the gate, Task Force Butler, was nothing more than a brigade-minus consisting of lightly armored vehicles. Cross-country speed was impressive, as long as it wasn't fighting anything, but once in combat it posed no real problem to the concentrated strength (and the Panther tanks) of Wietersheim's 11th Panzer Division. One recent judgment on the campaign seems apposite: "Task Force Butler had been too weak, the 36th Division too slow, the 3rd Division too cautious."[31]

The post-Montélimar phase of the campaign was something of an anticlimax. The 19th Army continued to stagger north in the first week of September, against US pressure that slackened but never really ceased. The columns passed through Lyon on August 29, Besançon on September 3, and made contact with Army Group B near the French fortress city of Belfort on September 5. The 19th now held the extreme southern point of the main defensive line in France, what Hitler had dubbed the "German position in the west" (*deutsche Weststellung*).[32] The Allies followed into Dijon a few days later and contacted Patton's US

3rd Army north of the city.[33] The linkup of the Overlord and Dragoon forces marked a strategic milestone for the Allies, a return to unity of effort and concentration of force. A massive Allied force—perhaps the most powerful in military history—now stretched from the English Channel to the Swiss border. While Dragoon had failed to trap 19th Army, it had mauled it, and that was just as good. Of the 210,000 Germans who tried to evacuate southern France, 80,000 had been lost in a month, the vast majority of them listed as "missing in action" on German rolls—large-scale surrenders, in other words. The entire campaign, including the pounding that the Allies meted out to the German LXII Reserve Corps in the opening days of the landings and the losses suffered by LXIV Corps in its ragged trek from southwestern France, generated 140,000 German casualties in all.

The number is a monstrous one under any circumstances. It seems even worse, however, when we remember that the Wehrmacht field commanders knew that the battle in the south was hopeless from the outset. The German command in southern France, Blaskowitz and Wiese, along with their respective chiefs of staff—smart, competent officers like General Heinz von Gyldenfeldt for Army Group G and General Walter Botsch for 19th Army—spent the entire Dragoon campaign lying to their men: calling on them publicly to hold the beaches and throw the invaders back into the sea, while privately shaking their heads at the absurdity of it all. Even now, safely back in the main line, they kept lying. The first orders handed down to Army Group G in the new position in front of Belfort spoke of "turning every village in Alsace and Lorraine into a fortress" and fighting the invaders with "fanaticism."[34] The only possible outcome of such orders was another 100,000 German casualties and the eventual abandonment of the position—and both would come to pass in due time. In that sense, the southern France campaign changed nothing. With the Wehrmacht trapped in a tangled web of its own lies, tomorrow promised to be a great deal like yesterday.

The Revival: Model's War

One way to determine the relative urgency of a sector or front in the late war period is to identify the commander. Where did the Führer plant his "standers" (*Stehern*), those fighters whom he trusted to hold out at any price? Their task was always the same: defend their position to the "last man" or the "last bullet," as the new late-1944 formulation had it, "to annihilation" (*Vernichtung*).[35] Field Marshal Ferdinand Schörner was a good example. The commander of XXXX Mountain Corps in the Arctic, he had proven his mettle against superior forces and hideous conditions. "*Arktis ist nicht!*" he told his men when they began to complain about the cold and the desolation—"The Arctic does not exist!"[36] Shifted all the way down south to Army Group A when things looked bleakest and the Soviets were about to bludgeon their way into Crimea, he managed to extricate what German forces he could from the beleaguered peninsula. He moved back up to Army Group North in July 1944 to ward off yet another existential threat in the Baltic region. Finally, with Army Group North shut up in the Courland Pocket, Hitler sent him to command Army Group Center until the end of the war, where he exhorted the *Landser* into battle until the very end.

General Lothar Rendulic fit the same bill. This former Austrian officer commanded a corps in the bitter defense of the Orel Salient in 1943, slaughtered the Partisans in Yugoslavia as 2nd Panzer Army commander in 1943–1944, then shifted to 20th Mountain Army in the high north, where he ravaged the already poor province of Lapland during the long retreat from Finland back into northern Norway.[37] Hitler knew he could count on Rendulic. During the last four months of war in 1945, the Führer shuttled him from post to post: Army Group Courland, then Army Group North, then back to Army Group Courland, and finally to Army Group South (renamed Army Group *Ostmark* just before the end of the war). In diehards like Schörner and Rendulic, Hitler finally had the loyal cadre that he felt had been missing earlier in the conflict.

The greatest of them all, however, was Field Marshal Walter Model. When one of the Wehrmacht's armies or army groups had collapsed, or the defenses in a given sector had exploded into smithereens, when Soviet tank armies or Anglo-American armored divisions were rampaging in the German rear and carrying all before them, Model was in his element. He was the Führer's real fireman. By any reasonable standard, German 9th Army should have fallen victim to massive Soviet attacks in the narrow Rzhev Salient. Model not only held the position, he then managed to extricate the army from the trap in the famous "buffalo maneuver" (*Büffel-Bewegung*). From there, he had moved from one astonishing performance to another. He defended the Orel Salient after the breakdown at Kursk, then propped up Army Group South after Field Marshal Erich von Manstein's dismissal. His greatest achievement was taking over Army Group Center after the catastrophe at

Minsk (while continuing to lead Army Group North Ukraine through its own trial of fire), patching together a line by ruthlessly yanking administrative personnel out of the rear echelons and ordering them to the front, jealously hoarding reserves no matter how much his army and corps commanders screamed for them, then finally launching a perfectly timed counterattack in front of Warsaw in August 1944.

Where other commanders had to lie to their men (and perhaps even to themselves) about the operational situation just to get through another day, Model didn't. He didn't lie because he didn't have to. He was a true believer: in Hitler, in the war, in the evils of Bolshevism, and in the eventual victory to come—but only if everyone had the same amount of determination as he did. In late July 1944, he issued an order of the day to Army Group Center that even today breathes the fires of fanaticism. With Soviet armies standing on the East Prussian border, Model declared to his men that there was "no going back now":

> Tank panic, constant withdrawals without a fight, and the like are signs of weak spirit and cowardice, which can have no place in the heart of a German man. Each of us must remember our old superiority as eastern fighters! For three long years we eastern fighters have beaten the Soviets or stood up to them unshakably, in order to keep Bolshevism away from Germany.
> Cowardice has no place in our ranks!
> There must be no doubt: he who wavers has forfeited his life!
> We are fighting for our homeland, for our women and children![38]

"No soldier in the world may be better than we, the soldiers of our Führer, Adolf Hitler!" he declared, and there can be little doubt that he considered himself the best of all.

Based on his reputation as the defensive specialist par excellence, his new appointment in mid-August reveals a great deal about how Hitler and the High Command viewed the situation at the front. The Western Allies had broken through at Saint-Lô and then Avranches, foiled the German counteroffensive at Mortain, then mauled two main German armies, most of the Wehrmacht in the West, at Falaise. A gigantic Allied mechanized force was rolling across northern France, heading for the Seine River bridges and Paris. And from there, who knew how far they might get? Hardly a single German formation stood between Paris and the German border. Replacements were meager, reinforcements nonexistent. The OB-West in France, Günther von Kluge, had already slipped into a downward personal spiral, on the verge of suicide. The situation was hopeless.

In other words, it was Model time. The field marshal opened his tenure as Army Group B commander with a typical blur of activity. A stream of telegrams issued forth from his headquarters at La Roche Guyon, both to those above him and to subordinates. From the former he demanded reinforcements, and lots of them: 270 more tanks and assault guns immediately, twenty-five replacement battalions to fill the ranks, 9,000 tons of fresh supply, six new Panzer brigades. "The force is burned out," he warned General Jodl, "and without filling these minimal demands, no one should expect it to achieve much of anything in combat."[39] Above all, the "enemy's absolute supremacy in the air" had to be overcome—and soon. Model recognized the limits of the possible in all of this, of course, but he had also learned in his previous commands that making maximal demands on the OKW almost always paid off. Model could leverage Hitler's support in a way that no other field commander could, and he knew that OKW would make sure to feed Army Group B even if other forces had to go hungry. Certainly, a certain cynicism about the overall impact on the war effort was present in Model's calculations. Allocating resources among the army groups was Hitler's business, however, and Model would probably have argued that it was a free competition. If he proved better at the game than his colleagues, well, that was their fault. While Model was pestering the OKW, moreover, he was also firming up his authority over the armies under his command, demanding dedication to the cause, ordering them to take matters "more firmly in hand," and warning them that he "condemned any neglect in the sharpest possible terms." For those in the know, such language carried with it an undeniable threat. As always, Model's command style conjured up the image of the court-martial.

But having an in with the boss and threatening subordinates could only do so much. Model's original concept for Army Group B—and Hitler's original order to him upon handing him his new command—was to organize a defense along the Seine. Such an idea soon proved impossible, however. Model had three armies on line, more or less—with an emphasis on the "less." The remnants of 7th Army held a 50-mile stretch of front due south of Honfleur at the mouth of the Seine to L'Aigle. General Heinrich Eberbach was the commander after *SS-Obergruppenführer* Paul Hausser's serious injury in the Falaise Pocket. The 5th Panzer Army (*SS-Oberst-Gruppenführer* Sepp Dietrich) then bent sharply eastward, holding the line from L'Aigle to the western outskirts of Paris and facing almost due south. Finally, 1st Army (General Kurt von der Chevallerie) had recently arrived from the coast of the Bay of Biscay and now held the sector from Paris to the upper Seine in the southwest. To the rear lay the once-powerful 15th Army (General Hans von Salmuth), still tucked into the Pas de Calais. It once possessed four robust corps and sixteen divisions, back in the day when the Germans felt that the Pas de Calais would be the main site of the Allied landing. Now it had only six divisions, having surrendered a good dozen of its units to the fighting in Normandy and receiving a couple of replacements in return. All of Model's formations were "armies" in name only, badly bruised, lacking in manpower and equipment, and, outside of a few SS units, sagging in morale. The Canadian 1st and British 2nd Armies were pressing Model frontally, and US 3rd Army under General Patton was wheeling sharply to the left (i.e., to the north). By August 22, Patton had slashed through the line on the map where 5th Panzer Army was supposed to be and had gotten divisions over the Seine at Melun (downstream from Paris) and Mantes-Gassicourt (upstream). By August 25, Patton also had elements of 4th Armored Division far to the southeast along the Seine at Troyes. And finally, with the end of the battle of the Falaise Pocket, US 1st Army (General Courtney Hodges) had hurried up to the front, tucking itself between the Canadian 1st Army and Patton's 3rd US and heading toward Paris. The German commandant, General Dietrich von Choltitz, had orders from Hitler to defend the city to the last and turn it into a field of ruins (*Trümmerfeld*) if need be, along with "the demolition of residential housing, public execution of resistance ringleaders, the evacuation of area involved in the fighting."[40] Instead, he chose to negotiate and surrender the city to elements of the French 2nd Armored Division of General Philippe Leclerc de Hauteclocque on August 24. The next day, the main body of the French 2nd Armored arrived, as well as the US 4th Armored Division.

Choltitz will always remain an enigma.[41] Often portrayed in a heroic light for saving Paris, he was anything but that. On August 29, just four days after being captured, he admitted to a fellow captive, General Wilhelm Ritter von Thoma, that he had carried out Hitler's order to liquidate the Jews in Crimea "down to the very last detail."[42] He had apparently come to see the lunacy of continued resistance, however. He did good work in Paris, ignoring an immoral order and rescuing Parisians from a great deal of pain and suffering. Destroying Paris was never an option, not with the relatively small number of troops under his command—fewer than 20,000 men for a sprawling urban area. Choltitz certainly could have made the city suffer, however: starting fires, destroying water and electrical systems, and demolishing bridges over the Seine, destroying Notre Dame. Once can easily draw up a list of a hundred officers of the Wehrmacht who would have tried.

Facing overwhelming strength on the ground and harried every waking hour by Allied airpower, Model gave ground where he had to and put up rear guards wherever he could. His most pressing task was to get his most battered army—the 7th—back across the Seine in one piece, with 5th Panzer Army taking over its front and covering the retreat. He would then wait and see what the Allies were up to before deciding upon his next move. Perhaps the time might be right for a counterattack. The Allies had been on the move for a solid month of high-intensity combat and top-speed maneuver and would have to shift into a lower gear at some point. By now, Model could already detect a bit of an Allied slowdown. Patton's swing to the north, carried out with all his customary brio, had actually crossed the march route of the 2nd British Army as it was driving toward the Seine at Louviers. Disassembling the resultant traffic jam took a full two days, during which forward movement came to a halt. Field Marshal Bernard Law Montgomery was the 21st Army Group commander overseeing the Anglo-Canadian advance, and he was, in the words of one German analyst, "apparently more concerned with neatly maintaining his lines of advance than he was with the advance of the Americans, which might have had a destructive impact on the German retreat." Monty simply wasn't "flexible enough for this form of *Bewegungskrieg*."[43] But two armies crossing each other's route of march requires bungling at various levels, all the way up to the army group commanders (not only Montgomery but also General Omar N. Bradley of the all-American 12th Army Group, Patton's superior) and possibly even the Supreme Allied Commander, General Eisenhower. Maintaining the sector boundaries and the phase lines was almost always an Allied priority, not just Montgomery's.

Despite that bit of friction in the Allied advance, the retreat across the Seine was yet another gut-check moment for the Wehrmacht, one more do-or-die drama carried out under heavy pressure on the ground and overwhelming pressure from the air. Like everything the Germans tried to do in 1944, it was easier said than done. In many ways, the operational problem resembled southern France. Most Germans were trudging on foot, their morale shot for the moment, and were short of everything. The Allied enemy was motorized, confident, and flush with supplies of all sorts. Moreover, Allied bombing had destroyed virtually every bridge over the Seine prior to the invasion, so the operation was not simply a river-crossing. Rather, the Wehrmacht had to rely on a system of ferries, a well-organized one to be sure but no replacement for a few solid bridges. With Allied planes aloft constantly, the Germans had to make all their transfers at night, huddling under cover during the day. The last week of August thus saw the once proud German host of 7th Army slinking back across the Seine, one vessel, rowboat, or amphibious Volkswagen at a time.[44]

Against all odds, 7th Army made it back over the river. Lack of inter-Allied cooperation played a role in the success. So did a handful of tough defensive stands in front of the Allied bridgeheads over the Seine by *SS-Oberst-Gruppenführer* Sepp Dietrich's 5th Panzer Army, along with *Kampfgruppen* made up of elements from the 49th Infantry and the 18th Luftwaffe Field Divisions. The 49th held the front at the Vernon bridgehead, with 18th Luftwaffe at Mantes-Gassicourt, both enjoying the support of a handful of Mark VI Tiger tanks. They managed to contain the Americans long enough to stave off disaster for the 7th Army and even to reduce them slightly in size. A planned attack against the right flank of US 3rd Army—seemingly unprotected once Patton wheeled north—proved abortive, however. OKW wasn't happy, Model reprimanded Dietrich for a seeming lack of drive, and Dietrich spat back that he wasn't "some little schoolboy you could pull up by his ears."[45] Model finally closed the circle of discontent by reminding Hitler that toughly worded orders alone wouldn't get things done, since the Panzer divisions under his command were nothing but "torsos"—cadavers, in other words.[46] And indeed, the 1st SS, 12th SS, and 2nd Panzer Divisions between them could call upon a grand total of ten tanks in the last week of August.

Model's success in extricating the remnant of 7th Army could not mask a bigger problem. He was managing to knit Army Group B back together, with 5th Panzer Army on his right, 1st Army on his left, and 7th Army recuperating to the rear. Nevertheless, he could do nothing about the yawning gap on this left flank—that is, to the left of 1st Army. The army group's flank was dangling in the air, without terrain protection or a neighboring formation to protect it. Army Group G was at that very moment fighting for its life at Montélimar in the Rhône Valley, and the odds of survival were still quite long. No sooner had Model met the emergency on his right flank, therefore, than he shifted practically every Panzer division he could find to the left—or at least the remnants of his Panzer divisions—to oppose Patton's 3rd Army, which was still motoring in open space, driving ahead rather than fighting. Model also wheeled back 1st Army until it was deployed west to east and facing almost due south. At the very least he was able to lengthen his flank, increase the distance Patton would have to go to outflank him, and perhaps buy some more time. If Patton turned southeast toward Dijon, 19th Army was doomed, and without the 19th Army, holding the German border was going to be impossible in any case. Having an enemy army in the seam between the two German army groups in France was courting disaster. Model knew it, but there was really nothing to be done.

Otherwise, he knew that it was time to retreat. He might hold the Seine, but he knew that he had to evacuate all his troops from the position west of the river—the "bridgehead" in the parlance of Führer headquarters—at once.[47] His intentions contradicted Hitler's, but Model began the preparations anyway. He didn't go begging the staff in Rastenburg for permission but simply reported his actions to them afterward. What meager reserves he could scrounge up would deploy between the Seine and the Somme Rivers. He hoped to restore some order to the ranks, slow down the onrushing Allies, reinsert 7th Army into the line when it was ready, and then wait for replacements and reinforcements from the homeland. The OKW had promised them for weeks now, but they were maddeningly slow in arriving. All in all, it was a sound plan of action, and considering the situation he had faced two weeks ago upon taking over Army Group G, Model seemed to be working yet another defensive miracle as the Wehrmacht's horrible August mercifully came to an end.

Not yet, however. Even while Model was ferrying elements of 5th Panzer Army back over the Rhine, the Allies launched a general offensive by all four of their armies.[48] US 1st and 3rd Armies led things off on August 26, crashing through the shaky left wing of German 1st Army south of Paris, concentrating between Melun and Troyes. Nine well-supplied American divisions (the entire VII, XX, and XII Corps, left to right) were on the business end, facing little more than an "extended German outpost line" made up of elements of 48th Infantry Division and the 17th SS *Panzergrenadier* Division *Götz von Berlichingen*.[49] The 48th fell apart immediately at Melun, the 17th SS the next day at Troyes, and the Americans were through the line. A moment of high drama ensued. Where would they go? A wheel to the southeast toward Dijon might shatter Germany's strategic position in the west with a single blow, and so it was no doubt with some relief that Model saw the Allies turn northeast.

Still, the Allies had the pedal to the floor. They now had a phalanx of four armies abreast, and all of them were driving forward with energy:

1st Canadian and 2nd British on the left (21st Army Group), US 1st and 3rd on the right (12th Army Group). The power of the Allied drive was overwhelming. While all of Model's armies reeled back in some confusion, 5th Panzer Army, holding the line from the coast to the outskirts of Paris, was the formation in the direct line of fire. Towns, cities, and bridges fell in a rush. The 1st Canadian Army (General H. D. G. Crerar) took Dieppe on September 1—a fitting thing, given the tragedy of the Canadian raid on the port in August 1942—and reached the mouth of the Somme River at Abbeville on September 3. The Canadian thrust had isolated every one of the smaller Channel ports: Boulogne-sur-Mer, Calais, Dunkirk. British 2nd Army (General Miles Dempsey), advancing on the Canadian right, took what was virtually a World War I memory tour: Amiens, Arras, Lille, crossing the border into Belgium at Tournai on September 3 and reaching Brussels that same night.[50] Still pushing northeast, Dempsey's XXX Corps took the megaport of Antwerp. Working in close cooperation with units of the Belgian resistance, British 11th Armoured Division broke into the city so suddenly that the German defenders had no time for demolitions.[51] The harbor installations on the northern bank of the Scheldt River thus fell into Allied hands undamaged, even though the crucial Albert Canal bridges on the northern edge of the city remained in German hands.

Adding to the value of this movement, the British advance to the Scheldt had cut off the German 15th Army (now under the command of General Gustav Adolf von Zangen), which still lay to the south of the river on the Breskens Peninsula, while the Allies were already north of it.[52]

For US 1st Army, the travelogue included Château-Thierry, St. Quentin, and Cambrai. Hodges crossed into Belgium and was approaching Mons on September 2.[53] Command and control had clearly broken down in the German 5th Panzer Army, and the allies had captured the army commander, General Heinrich Eberbach, on August 31. With an immobile German mass in front of him, General Hodges sprung his trap: XIX Corps continued to head northeast while VII Corps wheeled suddenly to the north. The spearheads of the two corps linked up on September 2, trapping elements of six German divisions in and around Mons and taking 24,000 prisoners. While the haul in POWs was meager—a sign of how worn-down German divisions were by this point in the fighting—Hodges's Mons Pocket deserves respect as the only encirclement the Allies managed to pull off during the entire campaign in France.[54] And finally, the forward drive of 3rd

Army allowed General Patton to revisit the towns and battlefields of his youth in a rush: Reims, the Argonne Forest, Châlons-sur-Marne, St. Mihiel, Verdun. By September 3, he was over the Meuse between Verdun and Commercy. It had been a heady experience for the great cavalryman: a high-speed joyride across the French countryside in which "a jeepload of soldiers who had missed a turn in the road might capture a village"[55] and American GIs raced one another to the next French village to get "first shot at the cheers, the cognac, and the kisses."[56]

The Allied achievement since leaving the Seine on August 26 was one of the greatest operational victories of all time. They had landed a great blow and smashed a German field army, always an event worthy of recognition. They had launched a great pursuit that saw British 2nd Army, for example, advance no fewer than 225 miles and still have the reserves of energy at the end to slash its way into Antwerp before the Germans could destroy the port. Hodges had come nearly as far, and he had capped his operational sequence with an impressive little *Kesselschlacht*. And from where Patton sat over the Meuse, he was just about 50 miles from the Mosel, Metz, and the prewar German border.

He was also out of gas. So were they all.[57] The incipient logistical crisis that had been dogging the Allies since they landed in Europe had now become real. The US Army had conquered Cherbourg early, but the Germans had demolished it and only now was it beginning to function, and the entire Allied war effort in Europe still relied on the lone Mulberry artificial port still in service. The Allied breakout had been an operational triumph but a logistical disaster, sending Allied armies farther and farther away from their bases and thus lengthening their supply lines by the day. Rail transport, by far the most efficient system for bulk haulage, was not a possibility, not after the pasting the American air forces had delivered to the French rail system. The Allies resorted to a system of truck convoys, like the famous Red Ball Express, or even aerial supply, but trucks could never replace a functioning railroad net, and air supply was, and always would be, an emergency improvisation, not a reliable logistical pipeline. By late August 1944, more than 160 Allied ships were waiting offshore to be unloaded.[58] Since then, the Allies had added two more burdens: the capture of Paris, a city of 4 million people whom the Allies had to feed, clothe, and shelter; and a shockingly rapid, weeklong bound deep into the European interior. The former placed immense demands on the Allied supply services—at least 2,400 tons per day in emergency supplies alone.[59] The latter had extended the length of Allied supply lines well beyond the reasonable. From where General Patton stood at the moment, at Verdun, he was about 300 miles from the Normandy beaches where Allied stevedores were off-loading his supplies.

Possession of Antwerp, with its capacity of 40,000 tons of cargo per day, would have solved Allied supply problems all by itself, but the encircled German 15th Army sat on the Breskens Peninsula on the southern shore of the Scheldt Estuary, blocking off Allied access to the inland port. Like all Allied commanders, Montgomery's eyes had been on the main prize: trying to maintain momentum toward the Rhine and Germany proper. The painstaking littoral complexities of reducing an individual port had been far from his mind. While it's fair to say he had taken his eye off the ball on this occasion, any other commander in the Allied camp would probably have done the same. But the Allies had definitely missed a chance here, and Antwerp remained closed for the next two months. The 15th Army managed to extricate itself from encirclement, with the Kriegsmarine rushing every small vessel it could find—minesweepers, small steamers, trawlers—to the narrow inlets, bays, and ship channels of the estuary and evacuating the troops stuck south of the Scheldt. Allied pressure was minimal. The 1st Canadian Army directly opposite Breskens was strewn up and down the coast, reducing the minor Channel ports of Boulogne, Calais, and Dunkirk; antiaircraft batteries on Walcheren Island kept the Allied air forces at bay (although the Germans did have to evacuate most of their troops by night), and the Allied navies apparently did not wish to risk operations in the narrow waters of the estuary. During September 4–7, the German navy's 1st Coastal Division managed to evacuate 25,000 men, 550 vehicles, and 44 guns, most of them making the short, 3-mile hop from Breskens to Vlissingen (Flushing) on the southern shore of Walcheren Island.[60] The total for the entire evacuation (September 4–24) amounted to nearly 120,000 men, 7,000 vehicles, and 700 guns, in exchange for minimal German naval losses (18 small ships, including 6 fishing vessels).[61] The evacuation of the 15th Army was nothing less than a German Dunkirk, taking place a short hop up the coast from the British near disaster in 1940. Even though the army had gone, however, the Germans still held the Breskens bridgehead (64th Infantry Division), Walcheren Island (70th Infantry Division), and the South Beveland Peninsula, a former island linked to the mainland only by a railroad causeway (245th Infantry Division). In other words, the Germans still had an iron grip on the shipping lanes into and out of Antwerp. Walcheren Island would continue to hinder Allied supply and operations well into November.

Exerting control during that action-filled week was not easy, but

Model did his best. Ordering a tough stand by a hastily deployed *Kampf-gruppe* in a key crossroads village, deploying divisional remnants to man a roadblock and cost the Allies a day or two, launching a pinprick counterthrust by four or five Panzers: this was Model's way of war in September 1944. More important than any of those tactical moves, however, was simply keeping his army group together and in the field. From his new headquarters at Arenberg, just across the Rhine from Koblenz, Model was monitoring a collapse. The retreat out of France had turned into a rout, with an air that recalled the great Prussian collapse of 1806. Thousands of stragglers, men separated from their units, rear-echelon and administrative troops overseeing the occupation who had suddenly become superfluous, truck columns carrying both supplies and plunder: all were racing east amid scenes of confusion and panic, without clear orders and with little purpose beyond getting home. Supplies and equipment were disappearing at a record pace: 1,500 cubic meters of fuel and ninety-one tractors in the 1st Army sector, for example, along with untold oceans of French brandy—indeed there was an aura of drunken menace in these wild columns. The war diary of the LXXXIX Corps described the situation in the corps sector succinctly as "unworthy and disgraceful for the German army."[62]

Model moved on two tracks to stop the dissolution. First, he took the extraordinary step of issuing a proclamation "To the Soldiers of the Western Army!" and placing it along major retreat routes and even distributing it to his troops via airdropped leaflets.[63] He urged the men not to lose faith:

> We have lost a battle, but I say to you, we are still going to win this war! I cannot say more at the moment, although I know that troops have many burning questions they'd like to ask. Despite everything that has happened, let no one disturb or take away your strongest, most confident belief in Germany's future.[64]
>
> . . .
>
> You must be conscious of the seriousness of these hours and days. This moment will separate the men from the wimps.[65]

Appealing to their "soldierly honor," he urged stragglers to return to the colors and to report to the nearest command post, or simply to join back up with the nearest fighting unit they could find. They shouldn't wait to be told what to do, standing around "with your hands in your pockets," but decide on their own "what is the best and most correct in this situation" and do it.[66] It was up to each individual, each man "whose heart was in the right place: a calm word, a sensible idea, practical advice in the right moment will give to countless others the necessary support, assurance, self-reliance, self-confidence, and correct bearing."[67]

> The enemy has lost battles for four years. For the first time he has won a battle against us. He has not won it because he is smarter, braver, and better. He's not a magician. He can't be everywhere. If we add together all the tanks that the panic-mongers claim to see, then the enemy would have 100,000 tanks. In reality they are often only small spearheads. Defensive barriers of various sorts can increasingly hold them up. The rumors usually hurt us more than these armored spearheads.[68]

"Keep in mind," he concluded, "that in this moment everything depends on winning the time the Führer needs to bring new troops and new weapons into action. They will come! Soldiers, we must give the Führer the time!"[69]

The voice of a fanatic? Perhaps—or perhaps a reflection of his own increasingly heavy drinking.[70] But it seemed to have its effect. Wartime stragglers and the routed almost always seek order, direction, and purpose. Bewildered by defeat and perhaps somewhat ashamed of their flight, they are often waiting for a reason to return to the ranks. Wehrmacht units in France were no exception, often more bewildered than beaten. Gradually the rout began to subside. Meanwhile, for those who remained unmoved by Model's stirring words, he provided the usual horde of disciplinary personnel: Wehrmacht Patrol Service (*Streifendienst*), field gendarmes, and specially assigned staff officers whose task was to halt the flight, whip stragglers back into fighting shape, and punish deserters.

Model could see other signs of order. For the past three weeks, he had been dual-hatted as the *Oberbefehlshaber-West* and commander of Army Group B. Running the joint force and being responsible for ground operations were probably beyond the abilities of any one man. Model much preferred to be a ground force commander only, and the arrival of Army Group G after its anabasis from the south necessitated a change at any rate. On September 5, the OKW separated the two commands and appointed a new OB-West (or rather the old one): Field Marshal Gerd von Rundstedt, called out of retirement for one last encore. Rundstedt had never displayed any particularly operational brilliance, and he didn't now. He trusted his gifted and energetic chief of staff, General Siegfried Westphal, however, and the new OB-West freed up Model to concentrate on Army Group B's land fight.[71]

Model also knew, for the first time with certainty, that reinforcements were on the way. Two veteran divisions—the 3rd and 15th *Panzergrenadier*—were moving up from Italy, a theater where the Wehrmacht was still wasting a great many solid units. Moreover, Hitler had ordered the organization of twenty-five new *Volksgrenadier* Divisions, and four of them would arrive in the west in mid-September.[72] The *Volksgrenadier* were units after Model's own heart: six-battalion divisions consisting of the remnants of units burned up in Russia, administrative personnel combed out of rear areas, and even the lightly wounded, all organized around a battle-hardened veteran cadre. Equipped with few of Germany's increasingly scarce heavy weapons, they possessed a relatively large number of submachine guns and automatic weapons. They also had a liberal supply of the cheap but effective antitank weapon known as the *Panzerfaust*. The *Faust* was a single-shot weapon, handheld and requiring little training to use beyond an infantryman's steady nerve. By design, then, close-in defense was the forté of the *Volksgrenadier*. What was once an emergency improvisation on Model's part had now become German army policy. They were an unpredictable bunch, these *Volksgrenadiers*, not surprising given the diverse origins of their manpower and the haste with which they had arisen. Many divisions would give a good accounting of themselves in positional defense, but rarely would they be able to prosecute a successful attack. Moreover, their very existence was an affront to the notion of careful, long-term planning. The wounded should be resting and gathering their strength, not fighting, and no modern army can long exist without a secondary army of administrators, logisticians, and clerks.

Model even had a new army in his array, the 1st *Fallschirmjäger* Army under the command of the veteran paratroop leader, General Kurt Student. Formed officially on September 2, it deployed along the Albert Canal, the crucial water barrier linking the Scheldt and Meuse Rivers. The stretch between Antwerp and Maastricht was just one of many yawning gaps in the Western Front, but it sat along one of the shortest routes into Germany. Student only had a pair of weak divisions at the beginning (the 85th, a casualty of the fighting to reopen the Falaise Pocket, and the 719th, one of the static divisions guarding the Dutch coast), along with a handful of antitank units.[73] The 176th Division was scheduled to arrive shortly, but it was a so-called sick division (*Krankendivision*) made up of recent convalescents, men with severe allergies, or other various handicaps. Finally, Student was able to get his hands on 10,000 superfluous Luftwaffe personnel, as well as six *Fallschirmjäger* regiments in various stages of training. Three of the latter he grouped into a very loose division, the *Fallschirmjäger-Division Erdmann*, named for its commander, General Wolfgang Erdmann, but later redesignated 7th *Fallschirmjäger* Division, the fourth division in his improvised battle array. Twenty more *Flak* batteries would arrive from Germany within the week to form the backbone of his defensive strength. The guns had been part of the antiaircraft defenses protecting German cities against Allied bombers, but the emergency in the west had to take precedence. Likewise, an airborne headquarters and staff like Student's was a strategic asset, inserted for highly specialized missions and then withdrawn for the next use. Inserting it into a defensive position and forcing it to comport itself as line infantry was another tradeoff: trading long-term planning in exchange for momentary security. If the gap over the Albert Canal wasn't closed, however, there wasn't going to be any need for long-term planning. The Allies were going to be in the Ruhr, Germany's industrial heartland.

Despite the continuing problems, no less an authority than General Omar N. Bradley noted a revival of German fighting power. "Montgomery winced as we did over the sudden reappearance of German opposition on his front," he wrote. Bradley credited the sudden recovery to a single man whom he described simply as "a Prussian"—Field Marshal Walter Model. In "one of the enemy's more resourceful displays of generalship, Model stemmed the rout of the Wehrmacht," Bradley wrote. "He quieted the panic and reorganized the demoralized German forces into effective battle groups. From Antwerp to Épinal, 260 miles south, Model had miraculously grafted a new backbone on the German Army."[74]

That he had. Nevertheless, the revival came at a price. Burning out strategic assets, hounding the wounded from their hospital beds, stripping cities of antiaircraft defenses: all of these stratagems were strategic dead ends. Under nearly unbearable pressure on all fronts, the Wehrmacht was beginning to eat itself.

The Stand

The Allies made one last attempt to maintain their forward momentum—an offensive by Montgomery's 21st Army Group featuring the greatest airborne drop of all time. Montgomery drew up Operation

Market Garden in early September, and Eisenhower signed off on it on September 10.[75] The plan intended to leverage the advanced state of the Wehrmacht's disintegration by landing no fewer than three airborne divisions deep in the rear of the German defenses in the Netherlands. The paratroopers would move first, seizing the bridges over the numerous Dutch rivers and canals (Operation Market), acting as a carpet over which British XXX Corps (Guards Armored, 43rd Wessex, and 50th Northumbrian Divisions) could roll smoothly forward to the north (Operation Garden). The objective was the great bridge over the Lower Rhine (*Nederrijn*) River at Arnhem, 50 miles distant. They were to reach the Rhine by the third day and link up with the paratroopers there. From here, the British would wheel to the east toward the Ijssel River, cross it, and head toward Germany. With the Rhine crossed, no major terrain obstruction would block Montgomery's access into the North German Plain. If all went well, XXX Corps (and the entire British 2nd Army) would have a clean shot into the German interior and an open path from the north into the Ruhr.

Arnhem has generated its own industry of books and analyses, most dwelling on the problems of the plan itself. Montgomery was aiming to do too much, analysts have argued. He had three airborne divisions plus a brigade (US 82nd and 101st Airborne and British 1st Airborne) heading toward five bridges: one bridge each over the Wilhelmina Canal near Son and the Zuid Willemswart Canal near Veghel, a bridge over the Meuse (*Maas*) River at Grave and one over the Waal River at Nijmegen, and finally the grand prize, the Rhine bridge at Arnhem. The Allies had to secure all five, quickly and before the Germans could detonate them, or the operation would fail. Three out of five, four out of five: not good enough. Since sufficient transport aircraft did not exist to carry the entire force at once, it would drop in waves: the men on day one and most of the heavier equipment and artillery over the next three days. This meant a requirement for clear weather for all four days, a very tenuous thing in the early Dutch autumn.

Those were Market problems. Garden had its own set. The land drive by British armor had to proceed over a single road, the elevated highway from the Neerpelt bridgehead over the Meuse-Scheldt Canal in the south through Eindhoven, Grave, Nijmegen, and finally Arnhem. Off road to either side was trouble: marshes and bogs and woodlands utterly unsuited for mechanized operations. The Guards Armored Division spearheading the drive would by definition create a long, thin penetration with vulnerable flanks on either side, even if it succeeded in making a clean breakthrough. Multiple objectives, high complexity, risk all over the board, weather requirements, a single road: it all added up to failure, many argue. Montgomery was wrong to plan it, they say, and Eisenhower was wrong to approve it. Both men were seduced by the vision of wrapping up the war before Christmas, and Market Garden seemed to offer the only possibility. But World War II in Europe, we now know, was never likely to have a happy or clean ending.

In emphasizing Allied decisions and Allied planning, however, we miss the real reason Market Garden failed. "The enemy gets a vote" is one of the enduring clichés of military analysis, but it endures because it is true: the Germans made it fail. The Wehrmacht was in the process of recovering its equilibrium, their intelligence services had detected Allied activity in the Eindhoven region, and the troops were on a heightened state of alert for Allied airdrops. Indeed, an entire Panzer corps was resting and refitting in the Arnhem region, the II SS Panzer (9th SS Panzer Division *Hohenstaufen* and 10th SS Panzer Division *Frundsberg*), commanded by *SS-Obergruppenführer* Wilhelm Bittrich. Often depicted as a "surprise" to the British, the German presence was apparently known to Montgomery, but the Germans were in such sorry shape after their "mauling in Normandy," he later wrote, that he hadn't worried too greatly about them.[76] And once again, as always in this period of the war, Model's role was conspicuous. Indeed, Market Garden virtually landed on top of him.

The British drop zone on the Rhine lay to the west of Arnhem, at Oosterbeek, where Model and his staff were meeting in the Park Hotel. When the first planes flew overhead, no one was unduly disturbed. Allied bombers were part of the everyday scene in Europe. Then the bombs began to fall, blowing out the windows and sending the entire command staff of Army Group B sprawling to the floor. The bombs continued to fall, and as they ran out of the collapsing building the sky was black with Allied aircraft. Model's operations chief, Colonel Hans von Tempelhof, received a call informing him of the size and scope of the Allied airborne drops. He passed the information on to Model. "Clear out!" Model shouted. "Rendezvous at Terborg!"[77] Just that quickly, the staff was in action, reassembling within the hour at the small village about 25 miles east of Arnhem. Within the next hour, Model was personally directing German countermeasures, barking orders into the phone—he had no other tone in dealing with his subordinates—ordering the troops in place to launch immediate counterattacks and also summoning reinforcements up to the front.

Market Garden had begun well, but the operation was already

doomed. The Allies launched it on September 17 in broad daylight, a benefit of having complete air superiority over the battlespace, and virtually all of the units were dropped on time and on target. Allied airborne casualties had been extremely light: 2–3 percent, whereas 25–30 percent was the reasonable preoperation estimate. The 101st Airborne Division dropped just north Eindhoven, seizing the first two bridges and opening the gate for XXX Corps, which began its drive north just 45 minutes after the drop and contacted the 101st late on the first day. Elsewhere the situation was dicier. The 82nd Airborne Division secured the Maas River bridge at Grave, but not the Waal bridge at Nijmegen, and was already coming under attack near the latter by the 10th SS Panzer Division *Frundsberg*. The British 1st Airborne Division landed some six miles to the west of Arnhem, near Oosterbeek, in order to avoid the heavy *Flak* emplacements in Arnhem itself. This was the landing that had disturbed Model's meeting. From here, the division's orders were to advance to the east, secure the railway bridge over the Rhine at Oosterbeek, then the floating ship bridge (the "pontoon bridge" in most accounts) two miles to the east, and then on to the main objective, the road bridge in Arnhem itself. But the British came under fire almost as soon as they landed, courtesy of the 16th SS *Panzergrenadier* Training and Replacement Battalion under *SS-Obersturmbannführer* Sepp Krafft. Within 90 minutes of the landing, *Kampfgruppe* Krafft, only 435 men in all and many of them only half trained, had a solid blocking position set up between Oosterbeek and Arnhem. Soon joining them were "alarm companies" of the 9th SS Panzer Division *Hohenstaufen* under the leadership of Lieutenant Colonel Ludwig Spindler, commander of the 9th SS Artillery Regiment. *SS-Hauptsturmführer* Klaus von Allwörden's 9th SS Pioneer Battalion was also rushing to the scene. Within hours of the British landing, these three hastily formed *Kampfgruppen* (Krafft, Spindler, and Allwörden) managed to stop the British drive on Arnhem.[78] The manpower was, to put it politely, diverse: troops of the Replacement Army, superfluous naval personnel, Luftwaffe ground crews.[79] Military historians and buffs alike marvel at the improvisatory genius of the Wehrmacht in World War II, and often their enthusiasm seems overblown. In fact, they usually rely for evidence on the memoirs of the German commanders themselves. Arnhem was the real thing, however: a handful of men, a pair of machine guns, a few mortars and vehicles, and voilà—the Germans had stamped a *Kampfgruppe* out of the clay.

The British did manage to push their way though Oosterbeek toward the rail bridge, but no sooner had they gotten a platoon onto the bridge than the Germans successfully detonated and destroyed it. Only small elements of the division—a few hundred men of the 2nd Airborne Reconnaissance Battalion under Lieutenant Colonel John Frost—were able to reach the northern end of the road bridge in Arnhem by the evening of the first day. After attempts to cross the bridge withered in the face of heavy German machine-gun fire from the southern end, Frost set up a small perimeter on his side of the river. His troops silenced the guards in the bridge towers and also shot up four trucks loaded with German infantry that tried to cross the bridge from the southern end. By the evening of the first day, each of the opponents held one end of the bridge—a frustrating situation for both. But overall, the Germans held the upper hand, having split 1st Airborne into two pockets: a larger one at Oosterbeek containing the divisional main body and a smaller one at the northern end of the Arnhem traffic bridge, containing the reconnaissance battalion. Hemmed into a pair of isolated perimeters on the northern bank of the Rhine, 1st Airborne dug in and waited for relief.

Relief was nowhere in sight, however. Everywhere the Allies were meeting stiff opposition. Operation Garden, in particular, was having difficulty getting untracked, and by the second day of the operation XXX Corps was locked in a desperate struggle against concentric German attacks from both sides of the narrow corridor along the Eindhoven-Arnhem Road, a stretch that came to be dubbed "Hell's Highway." The 59th Infantry Division led the German charge from the west. The 59th was one of those units of 15th Army recently evacuated from the trap on the Scheldt. From the east, the newly formed 107th Panzer Brigade arrived from the east—one of a slew of the small but powerful new Panzer formations being raised in the Reich. The 107th consisted of three companies of Panther tanks, an antitank (*Panzerjäger*) company, and a Panzergrenadier battalion. Coordinating operations against the eastern side of the corridor was the headquarters of LXXXVI Army Corps, still another survivor of the Scheldt. Indeed, the troops of the so-called German Dunkirk were present here in strength, with parts or all of five divisions taking place in the defeat of Market Garden.

While the battle raged for the highway, British 1st Airborne was surrounded outside of Arnhem and dying one squad at a time. Incessant German attacks, spearheaded by the tanks of the 9th SS Panzer Division, inexorably drove in the divisional perimeter. By the morning of September 21, the Germans had overrun the British forces at the northern end of the bridge after three days of resistance. Eighty-one paratroopers had died in the fighting—all the rest were wounded or taken prisoner. That same day—already too late—reinforcements arrived south of the Rhine in the form of the Polish 1st Independent Parachute Brigade under Brigadier Stanislaw Sosabowski. The Poles dropped into a bloodbath. German fighters and *Flak* shot down five fully loaded C-47s, and bad weather turned back forty-one more. The Poles dropped near the ferry site at Heveadorp on the southern bank, only to find that the Germans had already sunk it. The fully alerted defenders soon hemmed the Poles into a narrow enclave on the southern bank of the Rhine—yet another *Kessel*. Radio communication between Sosabowski and divisional headquarters (just a mile away) failed early. The Poles were doomed: in fact, *everyone* was doomed if Operation Garden didn't get to Arnhem soon.

Unfortunately, Garden was having all kinds of problems and finally petered out altogether short of its objective. At several points in the fighting, the Germans actually cut XXX Corps's supply lines back to Neerpelt. The British were able to reopen the path, but these efforts took valuable time. As always, Allied firepower helped XXX Corps grind forward, and the British did manage in the course of a week of difficult fighting to reach the first four crossings. The Oosterbeek *Kessel* continued to hold out valiantly but hopelessly. What had started as a 3,500-man fighting force was now down to less than 2,000, and 1,400 wounded men lay inside the pocket with medical supplies dwindling. The senior British medical officer, Colonel Graeme Warrack, even negotiated a truce with the Germans to evacuate the most heavily wounded.[80] By September 25, the Germans had heavy armor in play (Tiger II tanks), and the end was near. The British even managed to get to the southern bank of the Rhine, and while they could not cross the mighty river without a bridge or ferry, they did manage to deliver a handful of assault boats. The remnants inside the Oosterbeek *Kessel* attempted to retreat back to the southern bank of the river, but too few men could. German fire destroyed what was left of the division, and Market Garden was over.

The attempt to jump the Rhine had failed. The sense of euphoria in the Allied camp—palpable just two weeks before—dissipated almost as rapidly as it had arrived. The bubble had burst, and it was now clear that final victory over Germany was going to have to wait until 1945. But why had Market Garden failed? Certainly the plan was risky, overly complex, and more suitable for a map exercise than an actual field battle against a live opponent. The commander of the British 1st Airborne Division, General Brian Urquhart, was correct when he wrote that "too much reliance was placed on armour and on the main axis."[81] All sorts of things had gone wrong, moreover: the fair weather turned, radios failed, and a full copy of the British operational order fell into German hands. American writers with a special dislike of Montgomery have, over the decades, indulged in a certain schadenfreude over his failure. Finally, the insufferable one had been laid low, caught in a trap of his own making.

But remember the old saw: the enemy gets a vote. Market Garden opened just two weeks after one of the most ignominious defeats in German military history. Even a week before the Allied drop at Arnhem, German columns were scurrying out of France without order or discipline. The men were no longer listening to their officers and seemed only to want an end to the war and a chance to return home. They looked more like fugitives than a modern army, a coarse *Soldateska*: unshaven, unkempt, and inebriated on looted cognac. Not in its worst moments in World War I—not even at the very end—had a German field army ever approached the devolved state of the 1944 model in the west.

But what a difference two weeks can make! In that brief span, the Wehrmacht had righted itself, restored its discipline, and regained its sense of purpose. Now it had won a clear and indisputable defensive victory over the Western Allies—the very thing the Führer had been calling for (and predicting) since the landings back in June. The Germans re-formed their lines, foiled a well-supplied Allied stratagem, and mauled an Allied airborne division, killing 1,500 and taking another 6,500 prisoners (out of a 12,000-man unit). Total Allied casualties numbered over 16,000, German less than half that (somewhere around 6,500). As these relatively small casualty figures indicate, Arnhem was a pocket battle within the grand scheme of World War II. Its implications and impact, however, were massive. The Wehrmacht had served notice that it was still game, still in the field, and still a force to be reckoned with. It wasn't the return of Rundstedt, or the fanaticism of Model, or even the fear of draconian punishments that had done it, as much as each of these played a role. Rather, the victory over Market Garden was proof that enough German soldiers—company grades, noncommissioned officers, and enlisted men alike—still found the Hitler regime worth fighting for. No matter how distasteful that judgment appears in retrospect, no one can discuss the historical problem of the Wehrmacht honestly without recognizing that fact.

Perhaps it was all a matter of timing. When Montgomery was planning Market Garden in early September, the Wehrmacht had apparently fallen apart, and all sorts of risks seemed reasonable enough. When he attempted to execute it a short time later, that favorable moment had vanished. Toward the end of the previous global war, on August 22, 1918, Field Marshal Sir Douglas Haig surveyed the dissolving German forces to his front and noted that "risks which a month ago would have been criminal to incur ought now to be incurred as a duty."[82] Perhaps Montgomery—a student of history—was thinking of these very words as he contemplated his options in early September. If so, he had gotten things exactly backward, and Montgomery was neither the first nor the last commander to fall victim to Clio's caprice. Market Garden made perfect operational sense on September 10 but none at all on September 17.

The Last *Stellungskrieg*

The stand at Arnhem solidified the Western Front for three full months. From September to December 1944, the German army fought its last great *Stellungskrieg*. (See Map 7.2.)

In mid-September, when the great Allied forward rush finally abated, the German front in the west resembled a great number 7. Starting on the English Channel, it ran west to east along the Scheldt (with the Germans still blocking access to Antwerp from their perch on Walcheren Island) to just below Arnhem on the Rhine and thence to Aachen. It then bended sharply down, turning almost 90 degrees to the south, running through Aachen, to the Hürtgen and Ardennes Forests, and holding a position in front of the Moselle Gate (*Moselpforte*) and the city of Trier, where the Moselle River valley runs sharply to the northeast toward the Rhine and the city of Koblenz—an ideal pathway into the Reich. From here, the Moselle fronted the line through Thionville, Metz, and Nancy, one of the few sectors where terrain actually anchored the German line. Moving south, 19th Army held a line in front of the Belfort Gap (the Burgundian Gate—*Burgundische Pforte*, to the Germans), the valley that separates the Jura Mountains to the south from the Vosges Mountains to the north, and, once again, offered a relatively unobstructed route into Germany. Overall, the line was about 600 miles long, and finding sufficient strength to man it in force was still a problem. OB-West reported on October 15 that the forty-one infantry and ten mechanized divisions manning the front line corresponded to the actual strength of twenty-seven infantry and just six and a half Panzer divisions. Weak or not, the Germans had re-

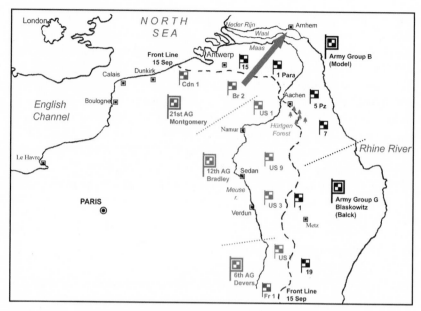

Map 7.2 Coming to a Halt in the West (September 1944)

established a cohesive front line, and with maneuver having eased for the moment (and rarely possible due to fuel constraints), the Allies had little choice but to attack it frontally.

In the center of the front, the Wehrmacht now made its stand on the defensive position protecting the Reich's western border of 1937, the Siegfried Line (colloquially, the West Wall). While theoretically good news for the German soldier, the Siegfried Line was not complete in any real sense, and, indeed, the very notion of an impenetrable line or wall was an illusion within the context of mechanized combined-arms warfare. The Germans had given proof in their conquest of France in 1940 that even the most sophisticated defensive position (the Maginot Line in that case) was only as effective as the army manning it. While the line may have been proof against the weaponry of 1938–1939, when the Germans had built it, the ordnance in 1944–1945—heavier bombs, higher-velocity tank guns—was able to make short work of most of the concrete emplacements. Indeed, the army had already stripped the West Wall of much of its weaponry and equipment before 1944 to feed the insatiable demands of construction on the Atlantic Wall. The High Command had begun a vast program of construction back in August to strengthen the line and had conscripted a people's levy (*Volksaufgebot*) of 160,000 civilians to do the job: boys from the Hitler Youth (*Hitlerju-gend*), young women from the League of German Girls (*Bund deutscher Mädel*), workingmen from the Reich Labor Service (*Reichsarbeitsdienst*), and the Organization Todt. Overseeing the project were the Gauleit-ers of the various districts. As the war came home, Nazi Party officials jumped at the opportunity to take more of a hand in running it. The trouble was that they were not under the supervision of the army. No one could hold a Gauleiter to standards or to order him to cooperate with his neighbors, and chances were that he knew little of the tech-nical intricacies of fortification construction such as terrain, lines of sight, or overlapping fields of fire. The resulting Siegfried Line had thousands of bunkers, but they were strewn about haphazardly, and the line as repaired tended to lack cohesion and systematic design. With its concrete pillboxes and imposing bunkers, barbed wire and "dragon's teeth" tank traps, the Siegfried Line was at least a psychological but-tress to the Wehrmacht, to be sure, and that was particularly impor-tant to the new *Volksgrenadier* divisions and young soldiers coming up to defend it. Years of propaganda about the West Wall had invested it with a kind of "mystical significance" and a "belief in its impregnabil-ity." Less impressed were the troops retreating *to* the line after their ordeal in France. They expected "a firm position they could defend and troops already present" to take them in. What they got was quite a bit less: "No wire obstacles, no mines, no weapons in the bunkers, even worse, some sections completely run-down and neglected, the commu-nications net dismantled, technical facilities missing or unusable, no security garrison, no trained technical personnel or fortress troops." The overall impression, wrote a German staff officer, was "dreary" (*trostlos*), and it's safe to say that not a single German officer in the west felt that the army could hold the position—not with the forces at their disposal.[83]

What followed was a very tough fall for all concerned. The Allied force in Europe had now grown to seven armies—a massive and mag-nificently equipped force. Montgomery's 21st Army Group (or better described, perhaps, as the Northern Group of Armies), had the same two armies, 1st Canadian (Crerar) and 2nd British (Dempsey), facing roughly north toward the Netherlands. Bradley's 12th Army Group (Central Group of Armies) now had three armies abreast, the newly formed 9th (General William H. Simpson), the 1st (Hodges), and the 3rd (Patton). Finally, the newly formed 6th Army Group (Southern Group of Armies) under General Devers contained the US 7th Army (General Alexander Patch) and French 1st Army (de Lattre). The ensuing decades have not reduced the aura of power that emanated from this great host, overflowing with manpower, materiel, and technology alike. That sense of potency was particularly true of the US Army. The Americans had come a long way from Tunisia, when they could field but a lone corps. Now they had four armies in the field of the Allies' total of seven (plus a fifth, the French 1st Army, which was a US creation down to the uniforms and tanks). They were paying for the war, and increasingly they were dictating its strategy.

Eisenhower had the whole array battering forward in his patented broad-front advance. Strip away the details for a moment and the strategic goals become clear. Montgomery was heading north toward a crossing of the Lower Rhine. Bradley was heading east toward Germany, the general direction being Frankfurt am Main. Devers was covering Bradley's flank. Since the Allied drive lacked a point of main effort—the *Schwerpunkt* to the Germans—it is not surprising that the advance turned into an ordeal. The fighting tended to be a slow, firepower-intensive grind that slaughtered the Germans while also generating heavy Allied casualties. While the Allies could afford their losses and the Wehrmacht could not, no one in the Allied command was particularly happy about it. Just like the Germans, the Allies, too, began combing out rear areas for warm bodies to keep infantry companies up to their allotted strength. Things got tense—and not for the first time—between Montgomery and Eisenhower, with the former demanding the appointment of separate commanders for the sectors north and south of the Ardennes. Eisenhower rejected Monty's implication that the campaign up until now had been some sort of failure, pointing to the rapid liberation of France and the swift march to the German border. In the end, Montgomery had to accept that a lack of fuel—a problem due not least to his failure to open Antwerp—had forced the Allies to conduct limited operations across the board, even as Eisenhower and his Supreme Headquarters Allied Expeditionary Forces (SHAEF) were planning a decisive offensive in 1945.

Nevertheless, the Allied armies never really stopped moving forward. Montgomery and his Anglo-Canadian forces had their hands full throughout autumn clearing out the Scheldt Estuary. They managed to overrun the South Beveland Peninsula in late October and to assault Walcheren Island itself in the first week of November. By now, Walcheren was a mess. Allied heavy bombers had destroyed the dikes on the island weeks before, and much of the landscape was submerged when the Germans finally surrendered it to the British on November 8. Three more weeks passed while the Royal Navy swept mines laid in the Channel, and it was not until November 28 that the first Allied convoy put in at Antwerp. Crerar's Canadians also managed to finish off the German garrisons in the smaller Channel ports of Le Havre (September 12), Boulogne (September 22), and Calais (October 1), although Dunkirk would hold out until the end of the war.[84]

Hodges's 1st Army, meanwhile, made two tries at Aachen, a first (unsuccessful) one in September and a second (much more powerful) one in October. The city fell only after hard, block-by-block fighting, featuring heavy casualties on both sides. Among the worst casualties: the city itself, most of which was completely destroyed by US bombing and artillery fire.[85] Hodges subsequently launched a series of bloody attacks into the Hürtgen Forest (*Hürtgenwald*) just south of Aachen, 50 square miles of dense fir and pine stands, winding trails, and, of course, tenacious Germans defending. Eschewing even a hint of maneuver (difficult in any case given the terrain), 1st Army assaulted the forest frontally in late September and kept attacking it. Forward progress was glacial and casualties high, and the chief impact of the fighting was to grind up a series of American infantry divisions—the 9th, 28th, 4th, and 8th—a potentially serious problem for a US Army that had decided to fight the entire war with the relatively small number of ninety divisions.[86]

To Hodges's south, Patton was having a very tough fight in Lorraine, a campaign of bad roads, rotten weather, and above all fierce German resistance in front of the fortress of Metz. Patton was utterly out of his element in this grinding campaign. A commander built for the high-speed chase, Patton was at his worst here: in a bit of a funk, rarely communicating with subordinates, and hardly intervening at all in day-to-day events. Opening his attack on September 27, Patton was not able to take Metz until November 22, but the last of the outlying forts did not surrender until December 13.[87] The 3rd Army took almost three full months to move forward 46 miles into Lorraine. To Patton's right (south), the neighboring 6th Army Group had better luck, with General Devers prosecuting a vigorous and well-planned campaign in Alsace, first driving Army Group G (now commanded by General Hermann Balck) to the Vosges Mountains in October and then back to the Upper Rhine in November. The Free French 1st Armored and 9th Colonial Divisions liberated Mulhouse (Mühlhausen) just north of the Swiss border on November 22, while General LeClerc's Free French 2nd Armored Division liberated Strasbourg the next day, pushing up to the Rhine crossing at Kehl. Between those two advanced positions, Balck continued to hold a sizable salient west of the Rhine around Colmar—the Colmar Pocket to the Allies. Of all the Allied armies, those of Devers's army group were the only ones on the German Rhine in strength in December 1944. He wanted to cross the river and break into the Reich, and there are some analysts who believe that Eisenhower should have given him the go-ahead.[88] But a breakthrough on the extreme right (southern) wing of the Allied battle array made little sense in the context of overall Allied strategy, and Devers had no choice but to cool his heels.

To the Final Briefing

At this point in the narrative, the astute reader will note the relative absence of details regarding the Wehrmacht—and for good reason. In a *Stellungskrieg* of this sort, the more powerful side is able to seize and hold the initiative. The fight may have been a difficult one, but the Allies were holding all the high cards. They were on the offensive almost constantly and everywhere. Their attacks aimed at fairly limited objectives rather than a decisive breakthrough. Any meaningful breakthrough would have to wait until the Allied command sorted out its supply problems. And Eisenhower and his staff were in the process of doing just that. The great port of Marseille was already up and working, as was Antwerp a bit later. The current frustrating stage of the fighting—the "Hürtgen phase," we might call it—was only a temporary annoyance. The last great offensive, and victory over Germany, was certain to come in 1945.

For the Germans, however, the shift to *Stellungskrieg* in late 1944 was no small matter. If the Wehrmacht could not find a way to break the chains of positional warfare, then the Allies would grind it into powder. German activity during the last three months of 1944 was reduced almost completely to defending tenaciously, launching the occasional local counterpunch, then retreating under unbearable pressure with heavy losses—far heavier than the Allies were suffering in the attack. Clausewitz famously described the defense as the stronger form of warfare, and in some ideal sense it is. The truth of that statement in practice, however, is entirely situational. Chronically understrength units, second-rate manpower, thinly stretched divisions with very meager reserves, and an enemy in control of the air: it was no wonder that all of the arrows on the situation maps were pointing backward into Germany. The Wehrmacht had slowed the Allies down, but it never stopped them altogether. Nor could it.

The German army was still hanging together after its momentary collapse in September, but occasionally cracks became visible. The commander of 116th Panzer Division, General Schwerin, tried to surrender the city of Aachen to the Americans without orders or permission from above. He was a brave and sensible man, and he didn't want to see Aachen destroyed for no reason. He actually left a letter at the local post office "to the American commander" that asked him to spare the townspeople unnecessary suffering (and got in a bit of trouble when the Americans didn't press the attack and the SS discovered the letter). Schwerin had done it before—refusing the senseless attack orders back in Mortain—and has been called "one of the few German generals with any guts."[89] General Balck, Army Group G commander, found one of his artillerymen so drunk on duty that he had the man summarily executed (and went to prison for it after the war).[90] Balck also noted an officer squirreling away fuel to enrich himself on the black market (but the perpetrator was a general, so he didn't get punished like the poor gunner).[91] Still, such events were fairly rare. Despite the defeats, discipline was holding.

But there was a more profound problem here. If we can boil down the German way of war to a single term or concept, it is *mobility*. The art and science of *Bewegungskrieg*—the war of movement—had been the basis of Prussian and German military campaigns for centuries. Prussian-German armies maneuvered. That was the chief ingredient in their success, one of the main factors that had transformed Prussia from an imperial sandbox into one of the Great Powers. The books were filled with legendary feats: The Great Elector leading an army by sleigh across the frozen waters of the Curonian Lagoon (*Kurisches Haff*) into the deep flank and rear of the Swedes in the winter campaign of 1678–1679; Frederick the Great marching his army clear around the Austrians' southern flank at Leuthen in 1757—his movements cleverly hidden by a line of forests and hills—and suddenly emerging to strike a mortal blow from a completely unexpected direction; Moltke the Elder coolly enduring a rough morning at Königgrätz even as the Austrians—whose rifled artillery on the Chlum Heights were tearing apart one of his armies—didn't suspect that he had a second force on the way, about to lay them low with a flank attack. Such were the great exploits depicted in Prussian military history.

Since German unification in 1871, the German army had written its own entries into the book: Tannenberg and Łódź in 1914, Poland in 1939, France in 1940, the Balkans and Crete in 1941. The Prussians had not chosen this way of war in any conscious way. Rather, this particular way of war had chosen them. An army that could maneuver rapidly—highly mobile under the command of aggressive officers acting on their own initiative—could win big battles early, and winning big battles early was one way that a relatively small and poor state could actually win wars. One way? No: the only way! Certainly, Prussia couldn't afford to fight long wars like France, Russia, or Austria could, but it could fight wars that were *kurtz und vives*, in Frederick the Great's memorable phrase: short and lively.

What *couldn't* Prussia do? Fight and win a *Stellungskrieg*. The opponents were larger, sprawling states with reserves of wealth and manpower that Prussia couldn't touch. For a Prussian commander or his later German descendant, fighting a *Stellungskrieg* meant losing slowly. They would fight such a war only when they had to and go back on the offensive as soon as possible. They had to break through the enemy's defenses, not merely for the sake of doing so but as a means to reestablish the open-field campaign, where their traditions, superior training, and flexible system of command could once again come to the fore. Every campaign in Prusso-German history taught them the same lesson: *Stellungskrieg* was an aberration, a degenerate form of war. *Bewegungskrieg* was normative, healthy, and the only means to ultimate victory. This belief was as true in 1944 as it was in 1757 or 1866, and it is almost impossible to conceive of World War II ending without one last, great German offensive—one final draw of the card.

And so it was that Adolf Hitler summoned his generals to the Eyrie (*Adlerhorst*), his bunker complex near Bad Nauheim, deep in the Taunus Mountains in central Germany. Great plans were afoot, fell deeds were imminent, and massive German armies were already on the march to their assault positions. The final briefing was at hand.

An MG-42 gunner of *Fallschirmjäger* Regiment 6 advances near St. Come du Mont on June 8, 1944. Units of FJR-6 attacked elements of the US 506th Parachute Infantry Regiment over a period of two days, inflicting heavy casualties. Courtesy of The National World War II Museum.

A young soldier of the 91st *Luftland* Division, his helmet covered with a piece of US parachute camouflage, stares toward enemy lines in the heavy fighting around Utah Beach. Courtesy of The National World War II Museum.

The strain of constant combat evident in his face, a hardened veteran of *Fallschirmjäger* Regiment 6 takes cover alongside a comrade during the heavy fighting near the town of Carentan in June 1944. Courtesy of The National World War II Museum.

Panther of the Panzer *Lehr* Division, knocked out near Le Désert, Normandy, on July 11, 1944. Courtesy of the Christian Ankerstjerne Collection.

Knocked-out Panther of the Panzer *Lehr* Division in Normandy being inspected by US forces. Courtesy of the Christian Ankerstjerne Collection.

US soldiers, accompanied by a Light M5 Tank, pass a knocked-out Panther in Normandy. Courtesy of the Christian Ankerstjerne Collection.

Well-drilled Waffen-SS grenadiers take cover in a ditch alongside a road to avoid incoming fire early in the fighting for Normandy. Courtesy of The National World War II Museum.

A Panzergrenadier of *Kampfgruppe* Hansen moves down a drainage ditch past burning vehicles of the US 14th Cavalry Regiment near the Poteau road junction during the Battle of the Bulge. Courtesy of The National World War II Museum.

A *Sturmgeschutz* IV of the 17th SS *Panzergrenadier* Division *Götz von Berlichingen* moves behind advancing Panzergrenadiers near the town of Saint-Lô in Normandy shortly after the Allied invasion. Courtesy of The National World War II Museum.

Dug-in Nashorn tank destroyer. Courtesy of the Christian Ankerstjerne Collection.

Very young paratroopers of the 3rd *Fallschirmjäger* Division move along the road to Carentan to engage US forces. The division took massive casualties in the withdrawal from the Falaise Pocket in August 1944. Courtesy of The National World War II Museum.

Captured Sd Kfz 251 armored personnel carrier, modified by US forces to mount a Calliope 4.5mm rocket launcher. Courtesy of the Christian Ankerstjerne Collection.

Destroyed Wirbelwind self-propelled quad 20mm antiaircraft gun. Courtesy of the Christian Ankerstjerne Collection.

Pz Kpfw IIIs and Pz Kpfw IVs from 233rd Reserve Panzer Division in Viborg, Denmark. The group includes an early-war, short-barreled Pz Kpfw IV, which were still in use with secondary units. Courtesy of the Christian Ankerstjerne Collection.

Soldiers riding a *Sturmgeschütz* III assault gun at a mountain pass. Courtesy of the Christian Ankerstjerne Collection.

German infantry armed, respectively, with a *Panzerschreck* (*left*) and a *Panzerfaust* on the Western Front. Courtesy of the Christian Ankerstjerne Collection.

Sturmgeschütz III assault gun and Sd Kfz 252 ammunition carrier. Courtesy of the Christian Ankerstjerne Collection.

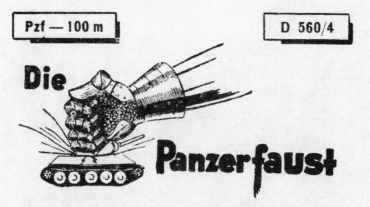

Pzf — 100 m   **D 560/4**

Die Panzerfaust

Die Panzerfaust ist D e i n e Pak! Du kannst mit ihr jeden Panzer bis auf Höchstentfernungen von 150 m abschießen. Je näher Du ihn aber herankommen läßt, um so sicherer erledigst Du ihn. Lies Dir dies Merkblatt richtig durch, dann kann Dir, wenn es darauf ankommt, nichts passieren.

Wie sieht die Panzerfaust - 100 m aus?

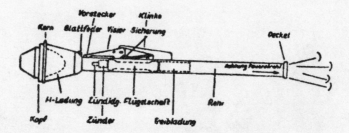

Der Kopf enthält eine H-Ladung, die jeden zur Zeit bekannten Feindpanzer durchschlägt, auch an der dicksten

Panzerfaust manual. Even as the Wehrmacht demotorized, it continued to produce innovative and deadly weapons. Courtesy of The National World War II Museum.

German prisoners of war are marched through the destroyed streets of Aachen following the city's capture by the US 1st Army in late October 1944. Women and civilians make up part of the column. Courtesy of The National World War II Museum.

A very young member of the Waffen-SS following his capture by Americans in the Ardennes. By the end of 1944, most of the crack SS Panzer divisions were filled with young, inexperienced recruits who nevertheless fought with tenacity and fanaticism. Courtesy of The National World War II Museum.

Sixteen-year-old Hitler Youths taken prisoner during 2nd Armored Division's drive through Lichtenburg. The lad at right still wears a swastika. Courtesy of The National World War II Museum.

8

The Last Battle

The Eyrie

On the eve of the battle of Leuthen in 1757, Frederick the Great summoned his officers to a meeting in the tiny Silesian village of Parchwitz. There he addressed them, steeling them for the ordeal to come.[1] Snow was falling that December morning, and the king looked anything but regal. He was weak, stooped with fatigue, and his uniform was ragged and unkempt. He usually preferred the civilized niceties of the French tongue, but he spoke in plain German this time.

The time had come, he told them. Outnumbered two to one, he had decided to attack the Austrian army in front of him. "We must beat the enemy, or be buried in front his batteries."[2] He reminded them of their heritage, recalled the honorable service they had provided his dynasty in the past, invoked the great family names of Prussian military history.[3] In the most telling moment of the Parchwitz address, he even gave them permission to leave if they didn't think they were up for the struggle. "You can go home, and I won't reproach you," he said quietly.[4] A dead silence enveloped the room. He had deliberately offended them, impugned their honor. The very idea of stepping out was repugnant to all of them. One of those present, Major Konstantin von Billerbeck, called out, "Yes, if you're a scoundrel—now's the time!"[5] Billerbeck, an officer of the Prince Henry Regiment, carried weight with his comrades. He had once fended off an attack by 4,000 Croat irregulars on a key Prussian supply column with just 200 musketeers. And now, his bold cry silenced the room.

"Hah! I knew it," the king smiled broadly. "I knew that none of you would desert me."[6] He didn't smile very often—the common touch wasn't one of his strengths. But he sensed victory in the room. He had gathered them to himself, formed them into his personal bodyguard, willing to do or die. It was a brilliant piece of political theater.

He took his leave. "Now good luck, gentlemen: tomorrow we either beat the enemy, or we will never see each other again."[7]

Almost two hundred years later, in 1944, the commanders of the Wehrmacht gathered at the Eyrie on a dark December day. They had obeyed the summons to hear their Führer speak. These men were the spiritual heirs of Leuthen. No, more than that! Some of them were the *actual* heirs—direct lineal descendants of the men who had fought under Frederick. Ever since the Seven Years' War, Prussian noble families had developed a habit of rating their precedence and prestige on a macabre scale: counting how many of their ancestors had died serving under Frederick in that bloody and protracted conflict. They could recognize the gravitas of the moment. As in 1757, a great coalition was bearing down on the Fatherland with superior forces, a long war seemed as good as lost, and their leader was summoning them all to a last grand attack, a last attempt to prove their "proud, ruthless, aggressive spirit."[8]

* * *

THE EYRIE, NEAR BAD NAUHEIM—DECEMBER 12, 1944. *"Eyrie" implied open space, blue sky, fresh air. Freedom. But it was hot in this room, an oppressive, gluey heat. Some of these officers had been working overtime on the plans for the upcoming offensive, bending over their maps for days and nights without end, and they were so exhausted that they nodded off from time to time, caught themselves, nodded off again.[9]*

Then again, HE didn't look so good, either—stooped over, his left hand and arm trembling, sometimes violently, his face pale and puffy. He looked exhausted, mentally and physically. He looked sick. Some of the generals had just seen him nine days previously, at a staff meeting in Berlin, and they thought he had deteriorated noticeably since then.

As always, the Führer relied on a torrent of words—hundreds, thousands of them tumbling out in a rush, some logical, some brilliant, and some puzzling or unintelligible. Prussian military speech used to pride itself on being knapp—*brief and clipped, Spartan—but* knapp *was the last word you would use to describe Hitler once he wound himself up.*

The Führer offered no new information on the offensive, code-named Wacht am Rhein, *nor did they need it. They'd all heard the briefings, had long ago memorized the details, the precise placement of each corps, division, and regiment. As always in the German army, the operational plan had been controversial, with arguments between a "big solution" (Großelösung), a go-for-broke drive across the Meuse River toward Antwerp, and a "small solution" (Kleinlösung), a breakthrough and a quick encirclement of US Army forces east of the Meuse, near Aachen. Hitler and his staff had gone for the former, typically, and the others had gradually fallen into line, not without a certain amount of grumbling.*

But that argument was finished, and the armies were already rolling into their assault sectors for the "big solution." Today was big-picture talk—very big. In the course of ninety minutes, all the old Hitlerian obsessions came tumbling out: the fear of encirclement by Germany's enemies, the need for Lebensraum, the conspiratorial role of "international Jewry," the whole constant paranoid "to be or not to be" of Hitlerian foreign policy.

More than anything, the Führer talked history. He reminded them of the gravity of the struggle. No longer an eighteenth-century conflict over a border province or dynastic succession, the present conflict was a "decisive war for life and death."[10] The roots lay deep: the European powers' attempts to shatter the medieval German empire's dominant position on the continent; the Treaty of Westphalia of 1648; Bismarck's wars of unification. Europe preferred a weak and divided Germany, and it was only Germany's internal fragmentation that "had made possible the rise of the British empire," had ensured that "the American continent was English instead of German," and had allowed France to assume "its dominant position on the continent."[11] He had launched a "preventive war" in 1939 to break out of this stifling international framework once and for all. "All successful wars in history, gentlemen, have been preventive," he told them.[12] The timing had been right. His gigantic rearmament program had given the Reich a potentially decisive advantage, though a temporary one, and so he had no choice but to strike in 1939. They'd heard all this before, and no doubt by the hour mark their eyes were glazing over, and not only from fatigue.

But he also said some things that hit home with them, phrases that corresponded to their bedrock principles of warfighting, words to which history had conditioned them to respond. He spoke of willpower, of tenacity (Zähigkeit), of perserverance (Beharrlichkeit), and of persistence (Dauerhaftigkeit). He went beyond the material realm, spoke of the need to rob the enemy of his "confidence in victory" by launching offensive blows, letting the foe know that "the success of his plans is impossible from the outset":

> *It will never be as possible to do this from a successful defensive as it will be from successful offensive blows. We cannot in the long run, therefore, hold to the principal that the defensive, the defense, is the stronger form of warfare. That can benefit the other side. . . . We must be clear: long periods spent strictly on the defensive can undermine one's endurance, and they must always be relieved by successful [offensive] strikes.[13]*

It had always been his intention, he stated, to "conduct the war offensively, to conduct it operationally," in order to avoid the static warfare of World

War I. Even when events had forced the Wehrmacht onto the defensive, periodic offensives were necessary "to convince the opponent that whatever he does, he can never count on our surrender, never, ever."[14]

He also mentioned Frederick the Great, as he always did. They had all heard variations of Hitler's Frederician rhetoric. Germany would carry on the struggle until, as Frederick once said, "one of our goddamn enemies gets tired."[15] This time out, the Führer made a point that may seem absurd to those reading his words decades later, but it might have made perfect sense to the men in that room at that time. In the seventh year of the Seven Years' War, every one of Frederick's advisers were telling him to give up: generals, provincial governors, his minister in Berlin, even his own brother, Prince Henry. All wanted him to end the unwinnable war. But the king had refused. He had endured. The accusation that Frederick had merely been lucky, that the death of the Tsarina had been the real turning point, the Führer declared, was "irrelevant." Frederick's willpower, "the steadfastness of one man," had been the difference, leading to the miraculous turning point. "If the capitulation had occurred in the fifth year of the war, the change of throne in the seventh year—two years later—would have been irrelevant. It's all about the timing."[16]

* * *

Indeed, the Führer, the generals in that room, and the entire Wehrmacht alike had all been biding their time, standing on the defensive in an increasingly hopeless war, since 1943. Nearly eighteen months had lapsed since the previous German offensive—the failed strike at Kursk. Now the time had come for one last "offensive blow" to show the Allies that their plans were hopeless, that their confidence was misplaced, and that they would never succeed in crushing the German Reich "never, ever."

Planning the Offensive

Operation *Wacht am Rhein* ("Watch on the Rhine," the title of the traditional German patriotic hymn) was months in the planning.[17] A massive, three-army strike at a weak sector of the Allied line in the Ardennes Forest, the plan generated an intense debate within German command circles as to its precise location, scope, and purpose.

Planning for these offensives began back in August, that is, at the very time the German front in the west was entering its phase of collapse. The original conception for a counterblow against the Allies envisioned a strike from the Langres Plateau in the region of Dijon.

The thrust from Langres was aimed at the right flank of Patton's US 3rd Army, then badly overextended in its bold drive across central France.[18] The OKW duly transferred the headquarters of 5th Panzer Army, recently extracted from the Falaise Pocket, to the Langres sector, along with a handful of mechanized remnants that had somehow managed to survive the maelstrom. Patton's spearheads were advancing so rapidly, however, that they overran the German deployment zones for the offensive. The 5th Panzer Army did launch an attack, to be sure, but it was stillborn. Not only did the assault from the Langres Plateau fail to halt the Allied advance, or even to slow it appreciably; the US situation reports from the time barely seemed to notice it. The failure was an indignity indeed for the Wehrmacht, an army that had historically hit hard in the early stages of an assault.

Despite the misfire, long-term planning continued for an offensive against the Allies sometime in the late fall. By then, Hitler and the OKW believed, the Allied armies would have outrun their logistics, the weather would turn sloppy and ground the Allied air forces, and the combination would halt the enemy in a weakened forward position.[19] The endless parade of catastrophic defeats had transformed the Wehrmacht into a new version of the 1941 Red Army, a force that was able to go toe to toe with its adversary only in bad weather. "Muddy ground and foggy weather," Hitler told General Hermann Balck in October, "are the prerequisites to exclude the enemy's air force and tanks, or at least to limit them."[20] The Wehrmacht had no choice, the Führer stated bluntly: "We have to make like the Russians until we are strong once again in the air."[21] If he could bring the Allies to a standstill and assemble ten good Panzer divisions, the time would be ripe for a counterattack. "The Americans have nothing behind them," he said. "No reserves. If we break through anywhere, he has nothing to oppose us."[22]

In mid-September, the OKW formed a new army, the 6th SS Panzer Army under *SS-Oberst-Gruppenführer* Sepp Dietrich, and gave it the mission of overseeing the rebuilding of both SS and army Panzer formations shattered in the recent fighting.[23] Dietrich was aware that his *Panzerarmee* was intended for some special mission but received no specific information as to when or where he might be fighting. Indeed, Hitler was keeping that information close to his vest. Just a month out of the assassination attempt, he felt he couldn't trust his generals to keep military secrets. This was the era when staff officers and field commanders alike had to surrender their sidearms before they were allowed into the Führer's presence. Those present actually had to sign documents swearing not to reveal the details of what they were about to discuss, an offense to the honor of officers in almost any military in the world. Within his small inner circle, however, Hitler was already mentioning a strike against Antwerp, which had fallen to the Allies in early September. Not only would the conquest of the great port wreck the already precarious Allied supply situation; it might very well lead to the destruction of large enemy formations, perhaps even to a "new Dunkirk."[24] Retaking the initiative on the Western Front was crucial if the Wehrmacht was to be ready to meet the anticipated Soviet offensive in the east. But Antwerp was not yet set in stone. Acting on the Führer's orders, Jodl and his deputy operations officer, General Horst von Buttlar-Brandenfels, spent September 1944 working out five operational scenarios for an offensive in the west, essentially covering the entire front. Moving from north to south, they included:

1. Operation Holland: a single thrust offensive from the region of the Maas (Meuse) River bridgehead at Venlo in the Netherlands. The objective would be the reconquest of Antwerp.
2. Operation Liège-Aachen: a dual thrust from the region northwest of Aachen (heading southwest) and from northern Luxembourg (heading northwest). The two pincers would converge on Liège and trap most of the US 1st Army, commanded by General Courtney Hodges.
3. Operation Luxembourg: another dual thrust from central Luxembourg and the Metz region, with the pincers converging on Longwy. The objective was the destruction of portions of both Hodges's 1st Army and Patton's 3rd.
4. Operation Lorraine: dual pincers emerging from Metz and Baccarat, converging on Nancy and trapping Patton's 3rd Army.
5. Operation Alsace: dual thrusts from Épinal and Montbéliard, linking up at Vesoul and destroying elements of the US 6th Army Group.[25]

The first impression the list yields is one of total predictability—and it was no wonder. The war was now in its sixth year, and the joint staff of the OKW was planning a large-scale ground offensive for the first time.[26] All previous offensives had been the work of the Great General Staff of the Army, working through its Operations Section (*Operationsabteilung*). The OKW had done nothing up to now but defend in place, declare various towns and cities to be *feste Plätze* in Hitler's name, and respond to emergencies and collapsed defenses. The OKW had been a sleepy place, in other words, and suddenly having to produce an innovative plan for combined-arms warfare was, apparently, beyond them all. Jodl, in particular, displayed no record whatsoever of insight, flexibility, or operational creativity. He grew increasingly prickly during the planning process and responded to even minor suggestions for revision with the mantra that the Führer's plan was "immutable" (*unabänderlich*).[27] This was clearly not the voice of ownership or of operational confidence.

The list of potential offensives that Jodl and Buttlar drew up, therefore, was a by-the-numbers approach to operational planning. They had so many miles of front and divided it into so many potential offensives. The duo provided virtually no analysis of enemy strength or intentions, relying instead on a great deal of wishful thinking about the state of the Allied armies (described as far weaker than they actually were), along with an optimistic view of the German formations launching the assault. Many of the latter were newly formed *Volksgrenadier* divisions, about whom the jury was still out. As to the Panzers, Jodl expected them to reach the Meuse in a single day, 125 miles or so. Overall, the schema seemed more of a staff college map exercise than a plan to wage a successful offensive campaign, proof that the OKW was an utterly inadequate instrument for operational planning in 1944. The Allies had long ago developed their war planning into an attenuated and systemic process involving hundreds of officers, advisers, and civilian specialists. For its last great test of strength in World War II, the Wehrmacht still relied on a brief sequence of all-nighters by a handful of red-eyed and overtasked staff officers.

Eventually, Jodl and Buttlar settled on a variant of scenario two: a blow against Allied defenses in a sector of the Ardennes Forest between Monschau and Echternach, currently held by US 1st Army. The operation involved three armies. A pair of Panzer formations, the 6th SS Panzer and 5th Panzer Armies, would launch a surprise assault, shatter the US defensive position in the Ardennes, and pass through the dense forest. The Panzers would cross the Meuse River and seize a series of bridgeheads between Liège and Givet—the 6th SS Panzer on both sides of Liège, the 5th Panzer between Huy and Givet. From here 6th SS Panzer would wheel north, cross the Albert Canal between Maastricht and Antwerp, and seize the area north of Antwerp. The 5th Panzer Army, meanwhile, was to reach the Brussels-Dinant line and protect its neighboring army's left flank and rear. A third, smaller formation (7th Army) would deploy on the southern flank of the operation, attack westward toward Luxembourg and Arlon, and provide flank protection for the advance of the two Panzer armies.

When the initial tiny planning circle of the OKW put the relevant field commanders into the picture, however—the men who had actually been conducting operations in the west—they got back an earful. The OB-West, Field Marshal von Rundstedt, first heard an outline of the plan for a strike against US 1st Army on October 12, although once again he received few details. Ten days later the chiefs of staff of *OB-West* and Army Group B (Generals Siegfried Westphal and Hans Krebs, respectively) received their first briefings from Hitler for a strike against Antwerp. Within weeks, Rundstedt (actually, Chief of Staff Westphal) submitted a response. While a drive on Antwerp was theoretically desirable, it was also a "big solution," a maximal and perhaps unrealistic objective attainable only if everything went right and if enemy reactions were sluggish. The Antwerp plan also required a major river-crossing of the Meuse, which multiplied the complexities and uncertainties. In the place of the OKW plan, OB-West suggested a more limited and reasonable conception, one that soon became known as the "small solution." Operation *Martin* had a narrower assault sector (just 25 miles wide) near Simmerath, northeast of Monschau. Once the Panzer forces had broken through the initial American defensive position in the Ardennes, they would wheel north to encircle and destroy all US divisions concentrated in the Aachen sector. All action would take place east of the Meuse—there would be no river-crossing, thus greatly reducing the complexity and length of the operation. Such a blow might disrupt Allied plans for reaching the Rhine and breaking into Germany proper for months, and since the "small solution" did not call for crossing the Meuse, it seemed far more feasible with the forces at hand.[28]

By mid-November, Field Marshal Walter Model, commanding Army Group B, had come up with a smaller solution of his own. This was Operation *Herbstnebel* ("Autumn Mist"), an attack on a 35-mile front southwest of Hürtgenwald. With minor adjustments, Model's plan was identical to Rundstedt's, aiming to clean up all US forces east of the Meuse, but not to go deep. Eventually, he came around to supporting Rundstedt's plan in all its details, perhaps as a way to present a stronger front against Hitler. The agreement represented a victory of sorts for Rundstedt, since he and Model rarely saw eye to eye. Rundstedt was the conservative traditionalist, while Model was the man in a hurry who knew how to exploit his high standing with Hitler in order to bend peers and subordinates alike to his will. Rundstedt distrusted Model as "too temperamental" for comfort. Indeed, he and Westphal had even minted a new slang verb: "to Model" (*modeln*), meaning to go too fast, get muddled, and mess things up. Sorting things out at that point, getting the situation "de-Modeled," wasn't easy.[29] While Model always treated his senior Rundstedt with deference and respect, the two men came from different worlds. Still, Model was a capable operator, and his doubts about the OKW plan were genuine. He and Rundstedt agreed that Hitler's ambitious plan lacked sufficient manpower and that reserves would be lacking to hold the shoulders of the intended penetration. Moreover, the promised reinforcements were unlikely to be present by the time of the offensive, since the Allies themselves were still launching continual and vigorous attacks toward the Roer dams, the Saar, and Lorraine.

Hitler and the OKW staff were adamant, however. The Führer mocked the small solution as a weak "half-solution."[30] A sharp wheel to the north and an operational victory over US forces near Aachen, no matter how successful, amounted to a mere diversion in the grand scheme of things. Antwerp had to be the target, the only spot where the Wehrmacht could possibly deal the Allies a serious wound. Despite our tendency to reject each and every word that came out of his mouth as a commander, Hitler was absolutely correct on this point. Alone in the upper German planning echelon, the Führer seemed to realize the centrality of logistics to Allied momentum in the drive toward Germany. An assault on distant Antwerp was risky, yes, but the current emergency required the Wehrmacht to do nothing less, to risk everything on the "draw of a single card," as Jodl liked to say,[31] and to seek a decisive victory, not a temporary stay of execution.[32] If 6th SS Panzer and 5th Panzer Armies got to Antwerp, they could put all the Allied formations north of the Bastogne–Brussels–Antwerp line out of communications and supply. Success could mean the destruction of twenty to thirty Allied divisions: the entire 21st Army Group, as well as US 9th and 1st Armies. Crushing anywhere from a third to a half of all Western Allied formations on this front would constitute nothing less than a "turning point in the war," Hitler claimed.[33] (See Map 8.1.)

Popular histories of the war usually describe Model and Rundstedt as rejecting Hitler's plan outright. Certainly they raised objections and made counterproposals, as we have seen, but the notion that they "opposed" *Wacht am Rhein* is a very thin one, relying upon a very small number of quotes that historians use as proof texts. "The damn plan doesn't have a leg to stand on," Model complained to Krebs.[34] Rundstedt could always maintain a certain politesse (he agreed that it was time to "stake all on a single card," for example) but was equally unimpressed. He later remembered thinking that the plan was nonsensical,

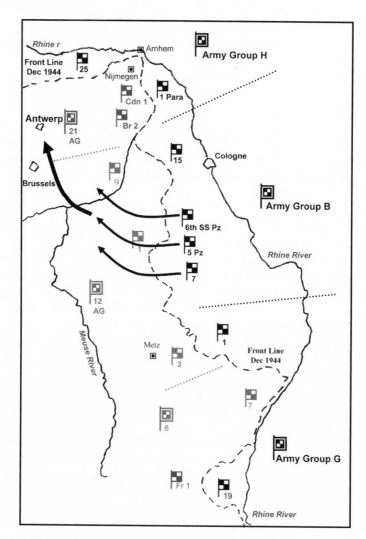

Map 8.1 *Wacht am Rhein*: The "Big Solution" (December 1944)

especially "the setting of Antwerp as the target. If we had reached the Meuse, we should have got down on our knees and thanked God—let alone try to reach Antwerp."[35] While both commanders continued to argue and agitate for their smaller Aachen operation, however, they both gave *Wacht am Rhein* formal support, declaring "full agreement" with the big solution and a drive on Antwerp.[36] There might have been a certain cynicism at work here. Big solution or small solution: either one required a drive to the Meuse as the first stage. If the armies got there, the two field marshals could always restart the argument with Hitler.

Historians tend to give Model and Rundstedt the benefit of the doubt in their conflict with Hitler, and certainly their plans were superficially more reasonable since they set more limited objectives. Nevertheless, we can doubt that a smaller drive toward Aachen would have been any more effective in wounding the Allies in the long term. A partial victory—the only kind that the smaller solution could have yielded—was hardly a victory at all by this point in the war. Moreover, all the variants of the Model-Rundstedt plan rested on the same sorts of assumptions as Hitler's vision for a more grandiose blow: overestimation of German fighting power, underestimation of the Allies, blithe disregard for logistics, the requirement for bad weather to keep the Allied air forces grounded. For all these reasons, Rundstedt and Model weren't being any more realistic in their planning than the Führer was.

But the real reason the Wehrmacht decided to launch the "big solution" was history. Since the days of the Great Elector of Brandenburg in the seventeenth century, the Prussian state had exhibited a tendency to go for broke in military affairs. Bold maneuvers, risky stratagems, surprise attacks: these were the coin of the realm in wartime. Frederick the Great had reified and reinforced the tendency, with his call for "short and lively" wars; his famous standing order to the cavalry promising to fire any officer who failed to charge the enemy when he was within sight; and his bold flanking and encircling maneuvers in the battles of Rossbach, Leuthen, and Zorndorf. Certainly the Prussian-German way of war had its cerebral side, with great philosophers and thoughtful operators like Clausewitz, Helmuth von Moltke the Elder, and Hans von Seeckt. Standing alongside those men of thought were more forceful personalities of action and deed, commanders who were prepared to charge in and get the business done *koste es was er wolle.* Their corporate ethos was "actionist," we might say, urging the commander to do something, even at the risk of it being the wrong thing.[37] They really did believe, as a body, that their bias for action was at the heart of their success, and that they would triumph in the end because they were less squeamish, less "blood-shy" (*blutscheu*) than their adversaries.[38] For all these reasons, anyone expecting the Wehrmacht to adopt the "small solution," as plausible as that idea might sound, simply wasn't paying enough attention to the way that the war had unfolded so far or to the long-term and well-established patterns of German military history. This army, and these commanders, never looked for a small solution to their problems.

Like everything the Wehrmacht tried to do in the 1944, of course, launching *Wacht am Rhein* was more difficult than it seemed to be on paper. The American offensives on both the central front (Bradley's 12th Army Group) and the southern front (Devers's 6th) continued to draw blood and to consume German reserves. The roads leading into the Ardennes were inadequate, and German transport capacity was insufficient. There never seemed to be enough fuel to go around, a constant and pressing problem ever since the loss of the Ploesti oil fields in Romania. Allied airpower forced German assault forces to carry out all of their principal approach marches by night, the same situation that had obtained in the west since D-Day. Finally, the Germans actually had to pray for inclement weather. Clouds and rain or snow were a key component in the operational design, since they would ground the Allied air forces. All these factors added up to delays. The original time frame was mid-November, keyed into the fact that the Allies were about to bring the port facilities of Antwerp online. That target date soon slipped to November 27, then to December 10. Finally, Hitler and the OKW had to settle for December 16—a full month after the original date.

Students of the war will recognize a familiar pattern. In the spring of 1943, the Germans planned to launch a quick counterstrike against the Red Army in the Kursk Salient.[39] Many of the same problems mentioned above played a role in 1943, as well: the need to rest and refresh the assault units with new equipment and personnel, bad roads and communications, lack of transport. All military operations benefit from preparation, of course, and no army should ever launch a great offensive half-cocked. But the paradox—a classic example of Clausewitz's "reciprocal action"—is that preparation takes time, and the enemy, too, can use that time to prepare his defenses.[40] While Kursk might have worked early (let us say, in June 1943), by the time the Wehrmacht actually launched it a month later the Panzer formations ran into a brick wall of deeply echeloned and redundant Soviet defenses. In the fall of 1944, had the Germans been prepared to launch a full-bore counterstroke at the precise moment that the Allied supply network seized up, they might have gained a significant success. But they hadn't been, and they didn't.

Now, in December, they were ready. Despite all their problems planning the resourcing of the operation, the Wehrmacht managed to deploy an impressive operational package for *Wacht am Rhein*. Three complete armies would launch the assault. From north to south they included the 6th SS Panzer Army under *SS-Oberst-Gruppenführer* Sepp Dietrich; the 5th Panzer Army under General Hasso von Manteuffel; and the 7th Army under General Erich Brandenberger—all fighting under the aegis of Model's Army Group B. The first wave alone was to attack the roughly 100-mile front between Monschau and Echternach with 200,000 men: thirteen newly formed *Volksgrenadier* divisions getting their first taste of combat and five Panzer divisions, containing 600 tanks in all and supported by 1,600 guns of all calibers. For the entire operation, Model could call upon nineteen divisions (including seven Panzer divisions), and he could, if necessary, draw on a further ten divisions (including two Panzer Divisions) from other sectors from the front of Army Group B and from the reserve. All told, Model had no fewer than twenty-nine divisions, nine of them Panzer formations. Even airpower was, for once, present in abundance. The Luftwaffe concentrated over 1,700 fighter aircraft—two-thirds of the total number of fighters left in the German arsenal—at airfields in Western Europe.[41] Their purpose was to cover the Panzer spearheads during the race to the Meuse and to attack Allied airfields in the vicinity of the breakthrough sectors. At any rate, bad weather over the front precluded the employment of the Luftwaffe during the opening phase of the offensive, while low stocks of aviation fuel meant that the Germans could only marshal one great blow in the air, rather than perform continuing and sustained operations.

The force assembled for *Wacht* was also notable for a comprehensive scheme of deception, disinformation, and subterfuge. By and large these had not been strengths of the Wehrmacht in this war, and historians usually see Allied activities in this realm (Soviet *maskirovka* and the Allied deception operation known as Operation Fortitude) as the gold standard. But the Germans could play the game, too. False radio traffic informed the Allies that a new 25th Army was being formed and deployed for a major operation farther to the north, along the mouth of the Maas River in Holland. The new formation generated a great deal of paperwork and radio messages, and the Allies seemed to have fallen for at least some of them—not bad for an army that could barely scrape together three divisions in the fall of 1944. German communications and planning documents also used coded references to the *Abwehrschlacht im Westen* ("defensive battle in the west") then in preparation, and even the operational designation "Watch on the Rhine" spoke more of guardianship, protection, and vigilance than aggressive intent.[42] At the front, straw and foliage and other forms of camouflage hid the Panzers from prying Allied reconnaissance flights. German *Landsers* were ordered to fuel their fires with charcoal only, in order to reduce smoke. Horses dragged forward as much of the heavy equipment as they could, and low-flying aircraft muffled the inevitable rumbling and clanking of a modern army being deployed for battle.

The campaign plan, too, incorporated guile and deception in the form of a subsidiary operation code-named *Greif* ("Griffin"). Led by the swashbuckling *SS-Obersturmbannführer* Otto Skorzeny, *Greif* was a false-flag operation that involved perhaps the most unusual unit of the war: the 150th Panzer Brigade. Equipped with captured American jeeps (or "Jiips," as Skorzeny called them) and German Panther tanks souped up to resemble M10 tank destroyers, the 150th was to create just enough confusion among US defenders to allow for a speedy pass through the lines.[43] The brigade would lunge to the Meuse, prevent the Americans from blowing the bridges, and capture and hold them open for Dietrich and Manteuffel. The plan also involved *Einheit Stielau* commandos, ten four-man teams of German soldiers who were fluent in all the exotic idioms of American English. The *Einheit*'s mission was to infiltrate and spread confusion behind American lines. Finally, the offensive featured Operation *Stösser*, the last German *Fallschirmjäger* drop of the war, with an 800-man battalion under Lieutenant Colonel Friedrich August von der Heydte securing the 20-mile stretch of north-south road from Eupen to Malmedy.[44]

Against this imposing combination of force and guile, American defenses were a second-rate array on an economy-of-force sector. Holding the 100-mile stretch of front in the Ardennes Forest against those twenty-nine German divisions were precisely six overstretched US divisions. The defending array included elements of the two corps on the right flank of US 1st Army: General Leonard Gerow's V Corps (to the north, or left) and General Troy Middleton's VIII (on the right, to the south). The latter included, left to right, four divisions: 106th and 28th Infantry, two combat commands of 9th Armored, and 4th Infantry. The first two had the misfortune to be standing in the direct path of the German assault. While they were part of a US Army that historians love to describe as the richest and best equipped in the world, both units had enough problems to fill a book, problems that the Germans would turn into opportunity during the opening days of their new offensive.

Consider the 106th.[45] The Golden Lion Division was an utterly green outfit, the last of the sixty-six US infantry divisions activated in

World War II, a new unit just arrived from the United States and being worked into the field in a quiet sector where nothing much seemed to be happening. Since the division's activation in March 1943, the Golden Lions had been training soldiers and then, as American casualties began to mount in Europe, losing them to the replacement pool. Indeed, in the course of 1944 alone, the division had to give up over 7,000 men, about 60 percent of its allotted strength. In their place had come a diverse parade of human material: 1,100 air cadets, 1,500 from other divisions still stationed in the United States, 2,500 from various disbanded units, and men combed out of the supply and quartermaster services. The rush of events threw them all together hastily, and some of them were still in-processing mere weeks before the division itself departed for Europe—hardly a recipe for unit bonding or cohesion under fire. The 106th, in other words, was very much an assembly-line US Army division: a pack of raw draftees thrown together with a handful of experienced officers and NCOs. It had no real tradition, either old Regular Army or National Guard. It could not forge ahead boldly into battle crying "Rock of the Marne!" or "Texas!" It had to be content with what one analyst called a "prefabricated tradition" that probably didn't go beyond loyalty to a buddy or to the man in the next foxhole.

Or consider General Norman Cota's 28th Division, lying immediately to the right of the 106th. The Bloody Bucket Division had landed in Europe in July and made the exhilarating but exhausting lunge all the way to the German border. It then came to a screeching halt in the Hürtgen Forest and was one of the divisions that received a real mauling. Cota became an instant American hero for his brave leadership on D-Day (as the assistant divisional commander for the 29th, the Blue and Gray Division). Now, however, he stood under a cloud, accused of uncertain leadership with his own division in the Hürtgen. To be fair, however, that tough grind didn't leave anyone covered in glory. At any rate, like the 106th, Cota and his men were in the Ardennes not so much to defend the place as to get a rest and refit that only a quiet sector of the front could provide.

Disaster was looming for the 106th, the 28th, and other American troops in the Ardennes, but they didn't know it. Allied intelligence noted signs of a German buildup but failed completely in interpreting what they saw. After the war, a parade of US intelligence chiefs (General Kenneth W. D. Strong for Eisenhower, Colonel Benjamin A. "Monk" Dickson for the 1st Army, and General Oscar W. Koch for

the 3rd Army) would claim that they had uncovered German preparations, had sent the appropriate warnings upstairs, and had been ig-
nored. Then again, G-2s almost always say that, as anyone conversant
in twentieth-century military operations can attest. US commanders
employed a pair of excuses in their postwar writings. One was the "calculated gamble": they knew they were accepting risk in the Ardennes
but did it anyway, in the confidence that they could beat back any offensive the Germans launched. The other was the "insane opponent":
the decision to launch the offensive ran so contrary to good sense and
military logic that they simply could not believe the Germans would
do so.[46] They often linked this second justification with an admission
that they were misreading the situation within the German high command, believing that Rundstedt (sensible) was in overall charge, while
in fact it was Hitler (irrational). Finally, many blamed the elements.
Bad flying weather grounded the dominant Allied air forces in the
month before *Wacht am Rhein*, and the consequent lack of reconnaissance flights was a key factor allowing the Wehrmacht's buildup to
continue free from prying Allied eyes.

Perhaps the simplest explanation is the best. By late 1944, the two
greatest enemies of sound intelligence work, groupthink and confirma-
tion bias (when everyone thinks alike and discards information that
does not conform to the preconceived notions), had taken hold in the
various Allied headquarters from Eisenhower on down. This problem
was especially true on the critical question of the state of the German army. After the punishing defeats the Wehrmacht had suffered in
the past three months, during which the Allies had inflicted hundreds
of thousands of casualties and whipped it back to the German border, there seemed no way that the Germans had the ability to launch
another large-scale offensive. Indeed, this very consideration under-
pinned Eisenhower's broad-front strategy in the fall. He ordered all
six (and eventually seven) of his Allied armies to continue their attacks
along the entire front—even if they were bloody, low-odds frontal
assaults—in order to prevent the Wehrmacht from accumulating an
operational reserve large enough to mount a new offensive. The Supreme Allied Commander believed he had succeeded, his army group
and army commanders fell into line, and any information to the contrary was unlikely to win a sympathetic hearing from one's superiors.

Superior forces, stealth, intelligence, special operations—it added
up to one word, a sweet one for the Wehrmacht and an ugly one to
the Allies. The word was also shocking, given the relative strengths of
these adversaries just a few months ago: *overmatch*.

Battle of the Bulge: Opening Act

Operation *Wacht am Rhein* was modern German military history in microcosm. Like so many offensive operations in the past, this one came as a surprise and hit the enemy hard. The assault forces tore a great gap in the American defenses in the Ardennes. Soon, massed Panzer formations were exploiting through the gap. The first operational target—the crossings over the Meuse (Maas) River—appeared to be within reach. The US Army was momentarily reeling, with survivors of the initial onslaught swept up in a rout and spreading the wildest rumors to those in the rear. Eisenhower's headquarters was trying desperately to get a fix on things, still unsure whether the blow was some sort of short, sharp spoiling attack or the real thing: a grand offensive seeking a decisive outcome. In the meantime, Eisenhower did some reshuffling of the battle array, detaching US 1st Army (General Courtney Hodges) from General Omar Bradley's 12th Army Group and placing it under the command of General Bernard Montgomery's 21st. Montgomery was now responsible for holding the northern flank of the German assault, Bradley the southern.

And yet, like so many other offensives of both world wars—the opening drive to the Marne in 1914 and the Ludendorff offensives of 1918, Operation Barbarossa in 1941, and Operations Blue and Edelweiss in 1942—*Wacht* petered out short of achieving anything decisive. Once the initial aggressive fury of the attack had spent itself, the systemic weaknesses took hold. In this war, they included an undersupplied army deficient in the logistics to sustain the force of the assault; infantry formations consisting of second-rate, late-war levies; a dried-up manpower pool and consequent lack of replacements; and of course lack of an air force. Just days after the onslaught, US defenses were already beginning to coalesce. German spearheads got close to the Meuse but never did cross it. In that sense, *Wacht am Rhein* joins the list of the other offensives mentioned above: all of them had come teasingly close to success. But "coming close" and "winning" are very different things. Early victories, lack of staying power, ultimate defeat: *Wacht am Rhein* was the latest and final embodiment of the German way of war.

As always, this German offensive opened with a bang. Three armies were lined up abreast. Dietrich's 6th SS Panzer Army stood in the northern sector, opposite Monschau. The most powerful of the armies on paper, it contained three corps (moving from north to south):

LXVII Army Corps (General Otto Hitzfeld)
   272th *Volksgrenadier* Division
   326th *Volksgrenadier* Division
I SS Panzer Corps (*SS-Gruppenführer* Hermann Priess)
   277th *Volksgrenadier* Division
   12th *Volksgrenadier* Division
   3rd *Fallschirmjäger* Division
   12th SS Panzer Division *Hitlerjugend*
   1st SS Panzer Division *Leibstandarte Adolf Hitler*
II SS Panzer Corps (*SS-Obergruppenführer* Wilhelm Bittrich)
   2nd SS Panzer Division *Das Reich*
   9th SS Panzer Division *Hohenstaufen*

At nine divisions, Dietrich's army was not only the strongest but also the best supported, equipped with three newly raised artillery corps (388th, 402nd, and 405th, designated *Volksartillerie* Corps, in keeping with the new, supposedly more ideologically reliable *Volksgrenadier* divisions), as well as three rocket artillery brigades (4th, 9th, and 17th *Volkswerfer* Brigades).[47]

Manteuffel's 5th Panzer Army faced the *Schnee Eifel* Ridge and the Our River between St. Vith and Diekirch. The army was smaller than Dietrich's but still imposing enough. Once again, it contained three corps, moving north to south along the front:

LXVI Corps (General Walther Lucht)
   18th *Volksgrenadier* Division
   62nd *Volksgrenadier* Division
LVIII Panzer Corps (General Walter Krüger)
   116th Panzer Division
   560th *Volksgrenadier* Division
XXXXVII Panzer Corps (General Heinrich Freiherr von Lüttwitz)
   2nd Panzer Division
   26th *Volksgrenadier* Division
   Panzer *Lehr* Division

Manteuffel, too, enjoyed solid support: the 766th and 401st *Volksartillerie* Corps and the 7th, 15th, and 16th *Volkswerfer* Brigades.

The final army was the 7th, under General Brandenberger, facing Echternach on the southern assault sector. Here we may receive a first glimpse of *Wacht am Rhein*'s problems. The two armies lying to

Brandenberger's north were, arguably, well manned and well equipped for their assault mission. While 7th Army was not the *Schwerpunkt* of the offensive, its mission was equally important. As Dietrich and Manteuffel headed toward the Meuse and then wheeled north, their forward motion was going to create a long and vulnerable flank in the south, where the US 3rd Army was, under the most aggressive commander in the American stable, General George Patton.[48] Brandenberger's task was to guard that flank—moving westward, maintaining a firm and cohesive defensive position, and probing aggressively to keep the Americans in this sector off balance. Victory on the Meuse, or even the complete occupation of Antwerp, was going to be useless if the German assault forces were the victim of a vigorous flank attack from the south. Unfortunately, with the German cupboard running dry, the OKW didn't have much to spare for Brandenberger. He commanded three corps, to be sure, but two of them weren't worth much, and the third one existed mainly on paper:

> LXXXV Corps (General Baptist Kniess)
>> 5th *Fallschirmjäger* Division
>> 352nd *Volksgrenadier* Division
> LXXX Corps (General Franz Beyer)
>> 276th *Volksgrenadier* Division
>> 212th *Volksgrenadier* Division
> LIII Corps (General Edwin Graf von Rothkirch und Trach)
>> Security formations only

Brandenberger, too, had a pair of *Volksartillerie* Corps (406th, 408th) in support, along with another two *Volkswerfer* Brigades (8th and 18th). But he possessed neither a single mechanized division nor modern bridging equipment. With such manifestly inferior fighting strength and engineering support, getting forward wasn't going to be easy. Indeed, even if he did get forward and managed to extend all four of his infantry divisions fully and face them south, they would not have sufficed to protect the elongated flank of the attacking wedge. The weakness of the 7th Army is an afterthought in most histories of the Ardennes offensive, since the focus tends to be on the Panzer battles raging to the north within Dietrich and Manteuffel's sectors. While the emphasis is understandable, the inability of the German High Command to form a third robust assault army, or at least to equip 7th Army with a Panzer Division or two, was a critical problem in the plan. The long, open southern flank was eventually going to lead to trouble, no matter how well the operational situation developed elsewhere.

Defending the open southern flank was a worry for another day, however. The Wehrmacht had business at the front. The first target in the path was the unfortunate 106th US Infantry Division. It was 5:35 A.M. on that wintry Saturday, December 16, 1944, and US Army troops atop the *Schnee Eifel* in the Ardennes Forest weren't expecting much in the way of action. The 106th had arrived on the high ground only days before, relieving the 2nd Infantry Division in a sector that had been so quiet up to now that the GIs had taken to calling it the "ghost front."[49] The vast wilderness of the Ardennes reaches into Belgium, Germany, France, and Luxembourg; in late 1944 the region lay roughly at the center of the Allied position in the European Theater. Given the combination of terrain and bad weather, the Allied command considered a German offensive in the region unlikely. Indeed, the Ardennes seemed perfect for acclimating green units like the 106th to the rigors of life in the field and to the routine of frontline duty. The division dutifully occupied the *Schnee Eifel*, the "Snowy Eifel Ridge," centrally located in the wilderness region.

The Ardennes was old-growth forest, in places still primeval. Cities were rare, located mainly along the Meuse River that formed the western boundary of the forest, but small towns dotted a largely unpopulated landscape of woods, rolling hills, and ridges. Winding trails and paths linked hamlet to hamlet, but paved roads were scarce and precious. Narrow, steeply banked rivers sliced the forest into dozens of isolated districts. As the men of the 106th climbed the ridge, their surroundings had to have impressed them. With fresh snow dusting the tall stands of pine, the *Schnee Eifel* was a quiet place, even a beautiful one. The *Schnee* was also light on enemy activity—and that was a good thing. The approach march of the 106th Division had been no thing of beauty. As the division entered the line, its young rookies committed all the snafus borne of inexperience, making a gigantic racket, accidentally setting afire first a regimental command post and then a battalion motor pool, and generally announcing their arrival. Poor hygiene and lax march discipline also laid up seventy soldiers with trench foot soon in the course of the approach.

Thankfully, the Germans seemed to be in a cooperative mood. The German unit directly to the front (18th *Volksgrenadier* Division) seemed to be engaged in the same activity as the US 106th: getting used to the field. A brief artillery barrage, random machine-gun bursts, an occasional German combat patrol—"social calls," the GIs termed them—these were the extent of the action. Occasional German vehicles could be heard, the distant clatter muffled by snow. When the 106th's commander, Major General Alan W. Jones, told his superiors at VIII Corps headquarters that he was hearing the clank of German panzers on his front, he got back a rocket. "Don't be so jumpy, general."[50]

Perhaps Jones had reason to be jumpy. His tactical positions were not of his choosing. Rather, he had inherited them, and they were not necessarily the most favorable in terms of terrain or road coverage or field of fire. They were instead the line that US forward units happened to be occupying when they ran out of gas in the fall. Indeed, the 106th began the battle holding a front that meandered 18 miles as the crow flew, or 21 miles on the ground—twice the recommended length for a divisional frontage. It also had the Our River at its back, rarely a good thing unless one is holding a fortified bridgehead, which the 106th most definitely was not. The positions were random, in other words, one of the many startling factors that distinguishes war in reality from the tidy verities of war in theory. General Jones laid out the division as well as he could, with three regiments (422nd, 423rd, and 424th) arrayed north to south and his divisional reconnaissance troop holding a gap between the first two and the last. The entire American line constituted a tiny salient, or bulge, jutting into the German lines, with the Our at its base. But again, it hardly seemed to matter. The sector was a quiet one.

And then, suddenly, it wasn't quiet all. The German offensive opened with a brief but furious hurricane bombardment, followed by infantry infiltrating through the 106th's indifferently arranged outpost line. Finally came the Panzers, thrusting through the gaps created by the infantry assault. The attack shredded the defenses of the 106th Division within hours. Command and control on the US side broke down almost immediately. The "decision cycle"—to observe, orient, decide, and act—vanished into thin air, and so did the imperatives of risking life and limb for the mission. Hundreds of US servicemen abandoned their positions without firing a shot. US artillery to the rear of the defensive position, normally the American margin of victory, remained silent. Even the best guns and sharpest crews require orders to fire, and none were forthcoming. Some of the 106th's frontline positions were barely touched by either bombardment or assault, but the GIs at the front could make out the sound of firing on both flanks, a roar that soon receded into the distance. These rookie soldiers did not know it—they lacked the battlefield experience to recognize it—but they were hearing the sound of a *Kesselschlacht:* German columns driving deep around both defensive flanks and into the rear. By the end of that first day, the German assault had broken an entire US infantry division, perhaps the one item in the US arsenal that was in short supply in late 1944.

The next morning, the German columns linked up at the village of Schönberg in the American rear, encircling the 422nd and 423rd Infantry Regiments, along with units attached to them: the 589th and 590th Field Artillery Battalions, Companies A and B of the 81st Engineer Battalion, and Company C of the 820th Tank Destroyer Battalion. The linkup at Schönberg surrounded 9,000 US soldiers in a *Kessel* six miles wide and four miles deep. The encircled regiments made two half-hearted attempts to break out of their trap on the *Schnee Eifel*, one each on December 18 and 19, but both failed. A relief attempt by Combat Command B of the US 7th Armored Division (Brigadier General Bruce C. Clarke) likewise came up short. At the start of the German offensive, 7th Armored Division was at Heerlen in the Netherlands, 70 miles from St. Vith. Like all US armor commanders, Clarke moved with impressive dispatch, getting his tankers up to St. Vith, just seven miles away from Schönberg. There he immediately came under German attack by the armored spearheads of Manteuffel's 5th Panzer Army and had to spend the next three days merely holding a "fortified goose-egg" around St. Vith, rather than riding to the rescue of the 106th Division.[51] The debacle ended on December 20 with the surrender of the encircled force. The 106th Division had been in the line nine days; four days of combat had shredded it. The mass surrender—some 7,000 men—marked the worst blow to the US Army in the European campaign. Save for the fall of Bataan, it was the largest surrender by American troops since the Civil War. The victors in this encounter, we should note, were not elite German formations, such as *Fallschirmjäger* or Panzer or SS divisions, but the newly raised 18th *Volksgrenadier* Division, a unit that was in many ways as unready, inexperienced, and half-trained as the US 106th.

The rapid dismantling of 106th Division was just one of many successes enjoyed by the Manteuffel's 5th Panzer Army during the opening days of *Wacht am Rhein*. Facing a US line that was more of a security cordon than a full-fledged defensive position, 5th Panzer broke through almost everywhere, shattering the defenses of General Middleton's US VIII Corps along the Our River, building a bridge at Dasburg, and passing the advance guard of 2nd Panzer Division over the river on day one.[52] US forces performed ably on the tactical level, often fighting to the death to hold the most obscure crossroads or bridges. At the Baraque de Fraiture crossroads, for example, an ad hoc assemblage of US personnel drawn from the 589th Field Artillery Battalion, the 203rd Anti-Aircraft Artillery Battalion, D Troop of the 87th Cavalry Reconnaissance Squadron (7th Armored Division), and the 643rd Tank Destroyer Battalion held the crucial crossing for three days, holding open the supply line to elements of the 7th Armored Division fighting to hold St. Vith.[53] Nevertheless, the view from the operational level—the movement of corps and armies—was that of a German victory. The left and center of Mantueffel's army were driving west at speed, heading toward the Meuse. While his right wing in the north still hung back, the delay was because it was liquidating the main body of the US 106th Division in the cauldron on the *Schnee Eifel.*

All in all, 5th Panzer Army had led things off nicely on day one, fulfilling even Hitler's most optimistic hopes. The situation was otherwise in the north. Here, 6th SS Panzer Army—two complete Panzer corps, with no fewer than four full Panzer divisions—never did get themselves untracked. The first objective was the Elsenborn Ridge on the northern edge of the assault sector. Here lay General Gerow's US V Corps, defending a much narrower sector with much more sensible divisional frontages. Gerow's defensive positions were also deeper and better fortified than Middleton's, and the initial German bombardment inflicted surprisingly few US casualties. As Dietrich's assault formations moved forward toward Elsenborn village, they met a solid wall of steady American infantry from 2nd and 99th Infantry Divisions, backed by the world-class artillery that had been the US Army's calling card ever since the fighting in Tunisia. The German LXVII Corps advanced less than a mile toward Elsenborn before coming to a complete halt. To its left, the I SS Panzer Corps did no better. The 277th *Volksgrenadier* Division, attacking toward Büllingen, met with an immediate US counterattack that threw it back to its original position. The 12st SS Panzer Division *Hitlerjugend* took over the attack sector, going into battle to open a breach rather than to exploit a breach already opened by the infantry.

As hard as the Americans fought, in fact, the attack by the SS had been inept in the extreme. Dietrich, an unpolished, tough-talking brawler whom Rundstedt once described as "decent, but stupid," had no business whatsoever commanding an army, a fact that he himself seemed to realize in his more lucid moments.[54] Inefficient and underroutinized staff work had been the bane of Waffen-SS units throughout the war, and the deficiency was in full flower here. In particular, Dietrich's staff was unprepared to deal with the vast problem of traffic control and the difficulty of passing a gigantic armored formation through the narrow trails of the Ardennes Forest. The scenes in the 6th SS Panzer Army's rear areas simply beggared description, a mind-boggling jam of trucks, tanks, wagons, horses, guns, and supplies: going nowhere and contributing nothing. Likewise, initial attacks by the green *Volksgrenadier* divisions had been amateurish in the extreme—infantry bunching up into a mass, charging forward into the teeth of an unbroken defense, and reeling back with heavy casualties.

The task of the 6th SS Panzer Army's northernmost corps, Hitzfeld's LXVII, was first to penetrate the US line toward Elsenborn and then to immediately wheel north. The corps was to put a roof over the offensive, in a sense, establishing an east-west defensive line from Monschau through Eupen and Verviers to Liège. The point was to protect the northern flank of the offensive against any Allied counterthrust from that direction, an analog to the mission of Brandenberger's 7th Army. But attacks by the LXVII, consisting of a mere two *Volksgrenadier* divisions, failed to achieve any operational momentum, never came close to a breakthrough, and came to a halt by the middle of day one. In a broader sense, Dietrich intended to use his army's four infantry divisions and one *Fallschirmjäger* division to punch a hole through which the mobile formations of I SS Panzer Corps would pass, preferably either on the first day, perhaps on the second. From there the I SS would head west along the Rollbahn though Stavelot and Werbemont, and thence to Huy on the Meuse. But the fighting at Elsenborn frustrated every one of these expectations, limiting the space for the Germans to deploy their heavy armored formations. Dietrich's decision to introduce the 12th SS Panzer Division *Hitlerjugend* prematurely into the fight for the ridge, as an improvised means of effecting the breakthrough, made the congestion worse, not better.

Only on the army's left (southern) wing was there success. Here, elements of the 1st SS Panzer Division *Leibstandarte* Adolf Hitler broke through the seam between US V and VIII Corps in the relatively flat terrain around Losheim. Defending the so-called Losheim Gap was the mission of the 14th Mechanized Cavalry Group under Colonel Mark A. Devine.[55] By contrast with the inexperienced 106th Division or the exhausted 28th, the 14th had characteristics that should have given it an advantage. A cavalry group was a high-mobility, high-firepower formation roughly the size of a regiment, designed to hold the flanks of a division, corps, or army. Throughout the campaign thus far, the groups had played a crucial role, holding vast sections of flank on either side of the main force units and thereby allowing the various corps in the US Army to concentrate on extremely narrow frontages to conduct the assault and continue the advance. They were not so much a part of the US Army's operational art—they allowed the army to practice operational art. They also had high levels of aggression and a tight esprit de corps based on the US Army's long-standing and heroic cavalry tradition.[56]

Assigned the Losheim Gap as his group's sector, Devine was about four miles to the west, at Manderfeld. The colonel had two cavalry reconnaissance squadrons (CRSs—equivalent to battalions in infantry parlance) under his command. He placed one up front (18th CRS) and the other (32nd CRS) in reserve, some 20 miles behind the line at Vielsalm. His frontage was some 9,000 yards, or nearly six miles, his manpower about 1,600 men. The frontage approached that recommended for an entire infantry division in the defense, and covering it in any meaningful sense with a single battalion was probably impossible. Devine gave it a shot, however, dispersing 18th CRS into a number of isolated and immobile "sugar bowl" strongpoints.[57] While the static deployment negated the real strength of a mechanized cavalry group (its mobility) and ran contrary to the doctrine and training of mechanized cavalry, Devine probably made the only decision he could given the disparity between his frontage and his combat power.

Unfortunately, 14th Cavalry Group didn't do much better than 106th Division in the opening phases of the fighting. When the German offensive opened, 14th Cavalry found itself under attack from elements of two German armies: 3rd *Fallschirmjäger* Division (from Dietrich) and the 62nd *Volksgrenadier* Division (from Manteuffel). Devine's sugar bowls functioned as little more than speed bumps for the onrushing Germans, compromising (fatally, as it turned out) the security of the 106th Division to its south. The Germans overran the strongpoints they chose and encircled the others. Devine considered bringing up his second squadron, but events soon overtook that possibility. The Germans penetrated the Losheim Gap within 48 hours, and the stand of 14th Cavalry Group barely deserved the title of "delaying action."

While the reasons for the debacle seem fairly obvious (open terrain, a large assigned frontage, the German numerical advantage in assault), the bigger, usually unexplored issue was the nature of the mechanized cavalry group itself. Built light and designed for extremely rapid movement, it was ideal for offensive warfare against an enemy who was off balance and reeling backward. No one had ever envisioned one of these light units having to defend itself in a toe-to-toe fight with a heavy, mechanized adversary. Viewed in hindsight, the US Army had a great deal of trouble shifting from the exhilarating offensive warfare of the late summer to the nitty-gritty positional fight of the autumn. Now, as winter came down, it found itself transitioning once again, this time pivoting to the defense. The 14th Mechanized Cavalry Group was just one of the casualties of the failure to adapt to a changing battlefield and one more proof of the danger of underestimating one's enemy—a crime to which both adversaries had to plead guilty in the Ardennes. Devine was another casualty. The destruction of his command, and the shelling of his headquarters at Manderfeld, was a trauma. He spent the morning in 106th Division headquarters, eating multiple breakfasts. He was "almost incoherent," an officer observed. "He was nervous, could barely control his actions." Increasingly disheveled, Devine experienced a breakdown. The medics sedated him with sodium amytal and evacuated him to the rear.[58]

With the Losheim Gap compromised, the Germans took advantage. The 3rd *Fallschirmjäger* Division drove through Devine's former command post at Manderfeld, heading toward Lanzerath. With the original schema for the attack (infantry breakthrough followed by armored exploitation) momentarily restored in this sector, several *Kampfgruppen* of the 1st SS Panzer Division could now climb onto the various Rollbahnen and head west. Foremost was *Kampfgruppe* Peiper, a regimental-size formation under one of the Waffen-SS's toughest young commanders. *SS-Standartenführer* Jochen Peiper was a prodigy, young and handsome, ruthless and even cruel: the very model of a Waffen-SS man.[59] At first a trusted adjutant to Himmler, then a company commander on the Don, Peiper was promoted to battalion commander at Kharkov (where his unit earned the sobriquet "Blowtorch Battalion" for its propensity to burn Soviet villages). He later took part in Operation Axis, the strike against the Italians in 1943, where the Boves massacre of September 1943 became part of his résumé, with a number of Italian civilians killed when Peiper called down artillery fire on their town, a punishment for sheltering anti-German partisans. By November he was back in the Soviet Union, taking over command of the 1st SS Panzer Regiment, which he would hold for the rest of the war. Since then he had been stationed in the west, fighting throughout the grinding attritional struggle against the British and Canadians in the Caen sector and seeing his regiment suffer massive casualties. Even the hardest SS man wasn't immune to the stress. He was hospitalized for a month in the fall of 1944, officially for jaundice, but in fact the cause may have been a case of nervous exhaustion.[60]

Now he was back, commanding his old regiment plus Panzer reinforcements and operating under the designation *Kampfgruppe* Peiper. Forming the Panzer spearhead of the 1st SS Panzer Division, Peiper's group spent most of December 16 stuck in the same rear-area traffic jam as the rest of the division. Now, for the first time, he could glimpse operational space. He was as ruthless as ever, elbowing his way forward, running other, slower friendly forces off the road. By the early morning of December 17, he was pushing through the Losheim Gap near Lanzerath, taking the village of Honsfeld, and blasting into the clear. He also had the enormous good fortune to capture some 50,000 gallons of precious fuel for his Panzers at Honsfeld, and they would fuel his *Kampfgruppe* for the next two days.

The second day of the offensive, December 17, found Peiper pushing hard to the west, heading toward Malmedy and Stavelot on the Amblève River, small but steeply banked and typical of the watercourses in the Ardennes. By now he was operating well into the rear of US forces still fighting to the east and was also separated by 30 miles from the rest of his division. The mass of the *Leibstandarte*, including most of the division's infantry formations, was following Peiper's advance guard in four separate columns. Their progress was much slower, however, and it remained to be seen if the division would be able to close up and restore its cohesion on the twisting roads and narrow, hairpin turns of the Ardennes. Peiper himself complained that his sector was more suitable for bicycles than Panzers. Stavelot was an important administrative center, containing the map depot for the US 1st Army (the "1st Army Map Store") and a vehicle repair unit. Just north of the town, along the road to Francorchamps, lay the main dump of Fuel Depot 3, holding nearly a million gallons of gasoline. Indeed, there may have been as many as 4 million gallons within a 25-mile radius of Peiper's position. The American command was already putting into place frantic plans to evacuate the fuel, but moving fuel safely is a time-consuming process, and the dump wouldn't be empty for two more days.[61]

It's a tantalizing possibility: Peiper overrunning a major depot and solving the Wehrmacht's fuel problem in a single stroke. He had no idea that there was fuel on the Francorchamps Road, however, and while he reached Stavelot on the evening of December 17, he encountered just enough resistance from elements of US 117th Regiment (30th Infantry Division), supported by M10s of the 823rd Tank Destroyer Battalion, to convince him to postpone a general assault until the next day.[62] By then, US defenses strengthened enough that Peiper had a tough fight on his hands for the next two days, December 18 and 19. Fighting in tandem with a light *Kampfgruppe* under *SS-Obersturmbannführer* Gustav Knittel (based around the 1st SS Panzer Division's reconnaissance battalion), Peiper eventually got his group across the Amblève by the evening of December 19.[63] But any chance he had of getting much farther to the west had vanished. Indeed, the original plans had called for *Kampfgruppe* Peiper to be on the Meuse by December 18. The main result of Peiper's ride, therefore, was to burn through a great deal of fuel for little result. His Tiger II tanks were monsters—impervious to most Allied fire, the nightmare of Allied tank crews—but slaking their insatiable thirst for fuel would have been difficult enough on a peacetime maneuver. Peiper was running dry, in other words, and if someone didn't untangle the traffic mess in the rear of 6th SS Panzer Army and break through the Elsenborn Ridge, he was finished.

Peiper was responsible for one other dramatic event on December 17. Prowling about the US rear areas, his *Kampfgruppe* inevitably took US prisoners, first dozens and then hundreds at Honsfeld, at Büllingen, at the crossroads village of Baugnez, and at Ligneuville. His soldier-fanatics were under orders to move quickly, and caring for prisoners was not part of the charge. *Kampfgruppe* Peiper shot virtually all the prisoners it took: 19 at Honsfeld, 59 at Büllingen, 86 at Baugnez (the incident, usually named for the larger nearby town, became known as the Malmedy massacre), 44 at Stoumont, 58 more at Ligneuville. They also shot 93 Belgian civilians at Stavelot. Here was the ethos of the Waffen-SS in a nutshell: aggression, drive, and operational acumen combined with brutal behavior and even outright criminality. The number of victims was small, a drop in the bucket compared to what Waffen-SS divisions had been doing in the Soviet Union for the past three years. In the east, a shooting of this size might barely register in the documentation or the historical record. But a mass killing was shocking for this front—so shocking, in fact, that US troops began routinely killing any German prisoner they took in the course of the fighting.[64]

For the big mechanized formations, then, the first days had brought mixed success. The 5th Panzer Army had exceeded expectations and was still rolling to the west, while 6th SS Panzer Army had generally fallen short, save for Peiper's regiment. That left one army—the modest and undermanned 7th—and there, too, the first day had brought mixed fortunes. The army's infantry formations came up in a dense wave, crossing the Our and Sauer Rivers that marked the front line. The LXXXV Corps encountered minimal opposition in the opening attack, crossing the Our with light casualties using light assault boats.

The corps's vanguard, the 5th *Fallschirmjäger*, took Vianden, formed a bridgehead over the river, and was soon on the prowl to the west. The paratroopers even managed to keep pace with 5th Panzer Army to their immediate north and thus fulfilled their mission of protecting the flank of the Panzers' drive. But otherwise, 7th Army had a frustrating day. The 352nd Infantry Division hit tough Allied resistance from the start and never did reach its objective, the village of Ettelbrück. The neighboring LXXX Corps (276th and 212th *Volksgrenadier* Divisions) did no better. The 276th made no headway at all against Combat Command A of the US 9th Armored Division, and while the 212th *Volksgrenadier* Division managed to blast into Echternach and advance as far as Berdorf, four miles away, it could not overcome stubborn resistance from elements of the US 4th Infantry Division in either town. The army's lack of engineering assets was particularly frustrating. Lack of bridging equipment, insufficient transport, inexperienced and half-trained Pioneers, the tortuous path of the swollen Our River in this sector: all added up to a failure to lay down a bridge on the first day. Contributing to Brandenberger's frustration was constant and accurate US artillery fire on all the likely bridging sites. Failure to build the bridge meant that 7th Army's artillery and heavy weapons languished on the eastern side of the Our even as the infantry formations of the army were attempting to drive to the west. Indeed, it is no exaggeration to say that, for 7th Army at least, Operation *Wacht am Rhein* failed during the first two days: for want of a bridge.

Wacht am Rhein: The Brake

While the Wehrmacht had managed to shock the US Army in the opening days of the Ardennes offensive, it came to a screeching halt within days. The adversaries would wrangle for the next two weeks over this or that tiny village, and both sides would manage to inflict monstrous casualties on one another in bitter winter fighting, but in operational terms the offensive was finished. The Germans had come to a full stop.

Four interrelated factors were at work in the forest, all of which worked against the Germans. First, the Allied command recognized the threat posed by *Wacht am Rhein* and soon reacted to thwart it. While the corps commanders weren't quite sure what was happening at the front, and the army and army group commanders were still trying to get a fix on things in the first forty-eight hours, one man seemed to recognize the reality. The Germans had launched neither an attack with limited objectives nor a spoiling operation but rather a full-fledged offensive with far-reaching aims. His snap judgment was a classic example of the coup d'oeil possessed by all great commanders, especially since it emerged more from intuition than from firm data or active reconnaissance. It was the finest hour of the war for a man usually described more as a chairman of the board than a field commander. The Ardennes showed Eisenhower as a first-class operator, among his many administrative and political talents.[65]

Like all great commanders, Eisenhower followed up his quick judgment with a series of decisive orders. Since the Germans had launched a great offensive, other Allied operations along the front had to cease in order to meet it. He ordered Devers's 6th Army Group to extend its front to the Mosel River, relieving the burden on Bradley's 12th. He ordered Patton to suspend his offensive into the Saar. In a decision that rankled many in the US command, he decided to transfer overall command of all forces north of the German penetration to British control, temporarily shearing them off of Bradley's army group and assigning them to Montgomery's 21st. With regard to the Ardennes itself, Eisenhower hewed close to US Army doctrine, giving orders to hold the shoulders of the German penetration at all costs and keep the German penetration narrow. He was willing to allow the Germans to punch a bulge in the Allied line as long as he held them well short of a true breakthrough. Most important, he wanted to set up the Germans for a great pincer maneuver once their momentum had stalled and the battle line had stabilized. Eisenhower recognized that, by coming out of the Siegfried Line, the Wehrmacht had done him a favor. "Yesterday morning," he wrote on December 17, "the enemy launched a rather ambitious counterattack out of the Luxembourg area where we have been holding very thinly. . . . However, we have some armor that is now out of the line and resting. It is closing in on the threat from each flank. If things go well we should not only stop the thrust but should be able to profit from it."[66] Indeed, by the fourth day of the offensive (December 19), Eisenhower, Bradley, and Patton met to discuss the potential for a counterattack from the south against the bulge. Eisenhower was thinking, perhaps, of a week. Patton responded that he'd be ready in three days.[67]

Finally, even before Eisenhower knew the exact shape of the German thrust through the Ardennes, he summoned the divisions from the SHAEF reserve to the front. They included the 82nd and 101st

Airborne Divisions, both stationed around Reims, along with the headquarters of the XVIII Airborne Corps. He dispatched the 82nd to Werbomont, placing it in the path of *Kampfgruppe* Peiper, and the 101st to the key crossroads town of Bastogne, already threatened by the advance of the German 2nd Panzer Division. The orders went out on December 17; the divisions were on the road on December 18 and in place by December 19. The airborne march was an impressive display of US strategic mobility—Bastogne was over 100 miles away from the starting point at Reims. The arrival of the airborne was yet another crucial element in halting German momentum. Bastogne would serve as the great American breakwater. The mechanized elements of Manteuffel's 5th Panzer Army could lap around the town to the north and south, but such a maneuver was operationally sterile. As long as Bastogne remained in US possession, blocking the principal Rollbahn through the central Ardennes, any German advance was unsustainable. German forces located west of Bastogne and heading toward the Meuse would be out of communications, outside of command and control, and very quickly out of supply and fuel. With US forces also hanging tough at St. Vith in the opening week of the offensive, blocking yet another east-west road through the forest, German options were limited. There are only so many roads to the Meuse, and one by one the German staff officers were crossing them off the list.

If any one event served to clarify the operational problem, it was the fall of St. Vith to the Germans. The town finally fell on December 21, as a well-blooded US 7th Armored Division withdrew in good order. But the same attribute that made St. Vith vital to the defense—its position along so many crucial roads—now made it nearly impossible for the Germans to advance through it quickly. German formations that found themselves blocked on other routes of advance now surged toward St. Vith, as if of one mind.[68] The LXVI Corps and the mechanized *Führer Begleit* Brigade (part of the OKW reserve at the start of the offensive but inserted into the St. Vith front early on) had led the assault, but their storm units had become badly intermingled in the fight. Unscrambling them wasn't easy, especially with the arrival of thousands of service and army personnel, some with orders and some without. And now, into this already seething mass came mechanized columns of the 6th SS Panzer Army, balked at Elsenborn and points north and now looking for a good road—any road—to the west. By the next day (December 22), "the flood of vehicles streaming into St. Vith was out of control," completely ignoring the efforts of the military police to direct traffic and restore order.[69] When Field Marshal Model came forward to take a look, the tangle was so bad that he had to dismount well short of St. Vith and make way on foot.

In general, in 1940, German forces had driven through an undefended Ardennes. Now they were trying to fight their way through it against a well-supplied enemy. The results were frustrating at every level. By December 18 Peiper's Kampfgruppe had come to a halt, but on December 19 it ran out of fuel, and by December 20 it was encircled. The sizable US force encircled in Bastogne—elements not only of the 101st Airborne but also of the 9th and 10th Armored Divisions—was tying up two German of XXXXVII Panzer Corps's three divisions: the Panzer *Lehr* Division and the 26th *Volksgrenadier*, along with the corps headquarters. It was the commander of the XXXXVII, General Lüttwitz, who issued the surrender demand to the defenders of Bastogne and received Brigadier General Anthony McAuliffe's tart rejoinder: "Nuts." There was puzzlement all around in German headquarters, up to and including Rundstedt, the OB-West, until a bilingual staff officer translated it as "Quatsch!"—"Rubbish!"[70]

The Americans in Bastogne intended to fight on. With Bastogne standing like a rock, Manteuffel ordered two Panzer divisions—the 2nd and 116th—to bypass the town, but lapping around an obstruction in such dense terrain meant time-consuming detours on a network of secondary roads. To the north, 6th SS Panzer Army launched one attack after another on the Elsenborn Ridge, failing to make any appreciable dent in the defenses. Rundstedt issued repeated orders to Dietrich to get a move on and finally sent a staff officer to Dietrich's command post to act as a kind of monitor over a clearly incompetent commander. Failure to take Elsenborn also made it impossible to relieve Peiper's beleaguered *Kampfgruppe* to the west. The weeklong slugfest for the ridge did achieve one thing, however: massive bloodshed on both sides, as heavy as any in the war. To the south, 7th Army finally bridged the Our, fetched its heavy weapons, and was inching forward. But here, too, it was a low-speed chase through very difficult terrain. The LXXXV Corps on the right, spearheaded by the 5th *Fallschirmjäger* Division, made some progress, but LXXX Corps on the left barely moved at all. A significant gap soon opened between the two corps, and closing it had to be a priority, with the US 3rd Army under Patton already stirring to the south. Overall, after a solid week of heavy fighting, any trained German officer could read the signs. The war of movement (*Bewegungskrieg*) had come to halt, and the equilibrium of the war of position (*Stellungskrieg*) was reestablishing itself.

The shift to static conditions, as always, had a demoralizing effect on German troops and commanders alike. General Siegfried von Waldenburg, commander of 116th Panzer Division, could sense the deflation, especially after the offensive's artificially hyped expectations. "Slowly it began to dawn on the troops," he wrote, "that the great plan had failed, or at least could not lead to a decisive success that would ward off fate. Both their mood and their performance began to suffer under the realization."[71]

Divisions halted; Peiper encircled; gas gauges on empty; a whole Panzer army still on its start line: *Wacht am Rhein* was a mess. And now, as if to set the seal on this disaster of a campaign, even nature changed sides. For a solid week of fighting, the elements had been an ally to the Wehrmacht, with "rain, clouds, and widespread fog" hanging heavy over the forest.[72] Now, all too suddenly, the fog dissipated, the clouds lifted, and the skies turned sunny. Sunny skies are almost always good news. For the Wehrmacht, sunshine meant death.

The Fall and Fall of the German Luftwaffe

Theoretically, clear weather should have been good news for both sides, allowing for more efficient movement, easier supply, and the introduction of airpower. But theory and actual battle are two different worlds. Every single German officer and man at the front knew that the arrival of the air forces would be a highly one-sided affair, with one side dominating and the other barely present. "The weather cleared up—for the first time since the start of the offensive," wrote Colonel Heinz Kokott, commander of the 26th *Volksgrenadier* Division during the Bastogne fight. "This had been dreaded by everybody, for it was well known what a clear day would mean! . . . From now on the enemy was able to bring a dreaded and very effective weapon into action."[73] RAF Bomber Command led things off with a series of heavy raids on the railroad bridges over the Rhine River at Koblenz, Bingerbrück, and Trier—all essential links in the German logistical chain into the Ardennes. American tactical air from the IX, XIX, and XXIX Tactical Air Commands began to range over the battlefield in ground support, shooting up German columns on the road, raiding headquarters, and interdicting supplies to the forward units. On December 24, the Allies flew some 5,000 sorties, compared to fewer than 800 for the Luftwaffe. Even that later number is deceiving. German aircraft might take off and thus count as a sortie. Running a gauntlet of Allied aircraft and antiaircraft guns was a hazardous business, however, especially for poorly trained pilots with a limited fuel supply, and very few of these sorties ever touched their intended targets. "This day was the day of the air forces," wrote General Ludwig Heilmann, commander of 5th *Fallschirmjäger* Division, "but unfortunately it was not ours." The Allied air forces almost always overstated the number of enemy tanks they destroyed, and the Ardennes was no exception. The three US tactical air commands, together with the British 2nd Tactical Air Force, claimed to have killed 413 armored vehicles in the course of the fighting. The real number may have been as little as a tenth of that. Nevertheless, it would be difficult to overstate the disruption that air attacks caused to German ground operations: delays, shattered timetables, the sense of constantly swimming upriver. The real impact of air supremacy was to give the Wehrmacht a case of the slows, robbing it of mobility and thus rendering it incapable of victory. Field Marshal Model recognized as much when, on December 26, he issued an order banning all major movement during the day.

But how had it come to this? How had the Luftwaffe become so enervated that the ground force had to cede daylight hours to the enemy and scurry around like a fugitive at night? Certainly, the war had not begun that way. Luftwaffe aircraft flying ground-support missions had been crucial to all the early victories—in Poland, Scandinavia, France, the Balkans, North Africa, and all the way up to the opening rounds of the 1942 offensive in the Soviet Union. But the Allies had managed to stymie the Luftwaffe over both Tunisia and Kursk in 1943—and then crush it altogether in 1944. The last two years of the war found the Germans outnumbered ten to one in the air, with the Allies routinely flying thousands of sorties while the Germans flew hundreds. German *Landsers* often note that they spied not a single German aircraft overhead during the campaigns they fought, while the Allied air forces loom large and omnipresent in the German memoirs. The devolution of the Luftwaffe was a tale of woe, which helps explain at least partially why so many of its leaders wound up killing themselves. The procurement chief Ernst Udet was the first to go, in November 1941, followed by the Chief of the Luftwaffe General Staff, General Hans Jeschonnek, in August 1943. Of ninety-eight air force generals, fourteen killed themselves in the last days of the war. And finally, the death list included the Luftwaffe's high commander (*Oberbefehlshaber*), the man who, more than any other, embodied the service: the *Reichsmarschall*, Hermann Göring, who killed himself in October 1946 while in Allied custody.

It is common to argue that the Luftwaffe was simply overtaxed, that it was a tactical (or perhaps an operational) air force designed primarily for ground support, that in the course of the war it had to accept a number of missions for which it was simply not equipped. Exhibit A in this argument has long been the hopeless strategic bombing campaign against Great Britain, where the Luftwaffe employed a completely inadequate complement of aircraft for such a vast strategic mission: the single-seat Messerschmitt Bf-109 fighter, the single-engine Junkers Ju-87 Stuka (from *Sturzkampfflugzeug*, or "dive-bomber"), the twin-engine Bf-110 destroyer (*Zerstörer*), and medium bombers like the Heinkel He-111.

While there is some truth to the argument, the Lufwaffe's problems went far deeper.[74] Hitler came to power in 1933 and immediately plunged Germany into a breakneck rearmament program, with the share of national output going to the military rising from 1 percent to 20 percent in just six years. There has never really been anything like it before or since. Even though a lack of raw materials such as coal, iron ore, and bauxite soon started to bite, Hitler's head start gave the Germans a real strategic advantage in the power constellation of the late 1930s. The realization that he had the upper hand for the moment but that the other powers—France, Great Britain, even the United States—were waking up and would soon catch Germany was one of the reasons that Hitler decided to go to war in 1939, an argument he would make dozens of times in various public forums during the war.

As a result of all that spending, the 1939–1940 Luftwaffe had some of the best planes in the world flown by the world's best-trained pilots. Both the Bf-109 and the Stuka had seen action in the Spanish Civil War of 1936–1939, and both were revolutionary designs for their day. The Bf-109 was the first stressed-skin, low-wing, production-model monoplane—it even *looked* modern. The other powers had advantages, too, however, the kind that accrue from doing something second instead of having to pioneer it. The British Hawker Hurricane fighter was a match for the Bf-109, and the Supermarine Spitfire fighter was much more than a match—the latter arriving in the field just in time for the Battle of Britain.

When the Luftwaffe stumbled with its next generation of aircraft designs (the He-177 bomber and Me-210 fighter-bomber), Germany's lead in the air vanished. One of the problems may have been reliance on a relatively small number of gifted designers. In Germany, if Willy Messerschmitt or Ernst Heinkel didn't design it, it probably didn't get produced, and their reputation stood so high that the Luftwaffe often ordered their models into production without sufficient testing. This, perhaps, was a systemic cultural factor, part of the National Socialist ethos that the man of genius was everything, the collective nothing. The He-177, for example, was a high-performance bomber with a very complex powerplant: two twinned engines, with each twin driving an extra-long four-blade propeller. The aircraft was rushed into mass production despite having a tendency to blow up in midair, during level flight, and received the grim nickname of the *Luftwaffenfeuerzeug*— "Luftwaffe's lighter." It killed so many crews that the Germans then rushed it out of production in favor of the previous model, the obsolete He-111. Specifications calling for this huge aircraft to have dive-bombing capability certainly didn't help, and this, too, was systemic. Göring's mind wandered during meetings, and he often said things or commissioned items that he may have forgotten later on. The Luftwaffe also ordered the Me-210 into production, before thorough testing, based on its confidence in Messerschmitt. Unstable in level flight and tending to lurch into a spin at high angles of attack, it, too, was yanked out of production, this time with no real backstop or replacement.

Certainly, German designers yielded to no one in terms of expertise or innovation. In the course of World War II, they revolutionized military aviation. The Germans designed the first operational jet aircraft (the Me-262), the first rocket powered aircraft (Me-163), the ancestor of the cruise missile (the V-1 "buzz bomb"), and the prototype of the intercontinental ballistic missile (the V-2 rocket). They built every manner of innovative aircraft: push-pull layouts like the Dornier Do-335 Arrow or jet aircraft made from nonstrategic materials (wood, mainly) like the He-162 *Volksjäger*. Their drawing boards in 1945 had even wilder designs: the four-engine Me-264 *Amerika* (or "New York bomber"), one of the planes that had so many cancellations, restarts, and design changes that Göring had to be reminded repeatedly in meetings just which aircraft they were talking about; the enormous six-engine Focke-Wulf Ta-400; and the Ho-18, an ahead-of-its-time design by the Horten brothers that would have been the first flying wing. Perhaps most amazing was the Silverbird, a bomber designed by Eugen Sänger. A 100-ton winged rocket launched from a sled on a 2-mile-long track, the Silverbird would shoot up to 130,000 feet, putting it slightly above the 25-mile level of denser atmosphere, then dive down into the thicker air and "bounce" into another long and steep climb. The process would repeat until reaching an altitude of 175 miles, hence the sobriquet "atmosphere skipper." German engineers also envisioned delta-wing aircraft, drone carriers, and ramjets. All in all, it was an astonishing body of theoretical work.[75]

After 1941, none of these innovative designs really mattered. The Reich was now at war with the world's three greatest industrial economies, which in the aggregate could employ the advantages of mass production and economies of scale in a way that Germany could only imagine. The conflict was no longer a short and lively war of maneuver but a war of attrition, and the Luftwaffe's only option was to mass-produce whatever aircraft it had at the moment. That meant sticking with the Bf-109, a plane that was state of the art in 1936 but far from it in 1944. Its G-variant (produced in 1943) was so sluggish and unforgiving that Allied pilots would try to provoke it into a low-altitude dogfight, because there was a good chance they could get it to crash. But Germany really had no choice.

Even mass production was easier said than done. The Wehrmacht could not fight a manpower-intensive war in the Soviet Union *and* man the factories needed to keep up with the Allies in industrial production. Here, the Nazi solution was typically brutal: exploiting slave labor by prisoners of war and concentration camp inmates on an unimaginable scale, working them to death in vast underground factories like the tunnel complex of Mittelbau-Dora at the Nordhausen camp. The production numbers were impressive enough. In 1944, Germany produced 34,000 combat aircraft of all types, nearly tripling the 13,000 figure from 1942. Of course, the Allies built 127,000 aircraft that year, and of that total, the United States built 71,000, more than double the German number, all by itself.[76] This comparison leaves aside altogether the question of quality, an area in which the Allies held a clear lead. The real image that the Luftwaffe of 1944–1945 has left to posterity is not one of visionary jet fighters or rocket planes but of starving human skeletons chained to their drill presses and lathes, banging out parts for one obsolete Me-109 after the other.

Wacht am Rhein: Postmortem

And this is why it really didn't matter if Stavelot or Stoumont or Trois Ponts fell to the Germans. St. Vith could have held out one day longer or a day shorter. German attacks might have finally compromised US defenses on the Elsenborn Ridge. Bastogne could have fallen to the Germans. *Kampgruppe* Peiper could have reached the Meuse on the first day or the second and, frankly, even crossed the river. At some point, the law of averages declares that the weather will clear, and if something as simple as sunshine is a deal-breaker for one of the adversaries, it probably has no business still being in the field. Likewise, if one side cannot fight during the day, it may well be time to face the facts.

Wacht am Rhein was already having its problems when that first clear day dawned (December 23). Not a single German unit had come close to its timetable, not one had reached the Meuse, and those that had made the most forward progress were having grave supply difficulties. But once the bad weather lifted, whatever hope there was of some sort of favorable outcome to the offensive vanished. The front now froze into a bitter *Stellungskrieg*, in which the Germans could measure their forward progress, if any, in yards. Peiper and his *Kampgruppe* had to abandon their vehicles and try as best they could to make it back to the safety of their lines on foot. *Kampfgruppe* Knittel came under a series of heavy Allied air attacks that would eventually claim Knittel himself, who suffered a concussion from a direct hit on his command tank and had to be hospitalized.

Christmas Eve was the high-water mark. Three German mobile formations were approaching the Meuse: the 2nd Panzer, Panzer *Lehr*, and 116th Panzer Divisions. The spearhead of the 2nd Panzer got as far as Foy-Notre-Dame, just three miles from the Meuse crossing at Dinant, a 15-minute drive at most under regular conditions. Panzer *Lehr* stood at Celles, a mile farther back, and 116th Panzer was attacking toward Marche and Hotton, protecting the right flank of the first two.[77] But over the next two days, all three divisions found themselves under constant air attack while a dragnet of US divisions drew tightly around them on both flanks: the 4th Armored, 9th Armored, 2nd Armored, 84th Infantry, and 75th Infantry Divisions. US counterattacks mauled the 116th and Panzer *Lehr* and drove them back while encircling and destroying the advanced guard of 2nd Panzer.[78] And even if somehow those US divisions had vanished, the most meticulous commander in the Allied stable, General Montgomery, had constructed a solid defensive wall on the western bank of the Meuse, consisting of the divisions of the British XXX Corps.

But no one on the German side was going anywhere after December 23. The Battle of the Bulge demonstrated, one more time, just "how the Allies won" the war against the Wehrmacht.[79] Tactical airpower—not numbers of men and tanks, or logistical and economic dominance—was the decisive weapon for the Anglo-Americans. General Manteuffel, the commander of 5th Panzer Army, knew it better than anyone:

The effect of the enemy air forces was decisive for the failure on the German side. With the clearing of the weather after December 21–22, the Anglo-American air forces completely dominated our supply routes. Despite the dedication of the Luftwaffe crews, they were limited to extremely modest actions, which in no way eased the burden on our troops. A further consequence of these air attacks was the extraordinarily crucial delays with which the most urgently needed supplies and materiel got to the troops, since the mass of the supplies were stored east of the Rhine for purposes of deception. Hit especially hard was the transport of sufficient amounts of fuel. From the start of the offensive, therefore, the troops were living hand to mouth.

The battlefield, he concluded, "was in fact isolated."[80]

Consider the fate of the division that had achieved the most in *Wacht am Rhein*: 2nd Panzer. On December 24 the division's 2nd Reconnaissance Battalion (*Aufklärungs-Abteilung*) reached Foy-Notre-Dame, although they were practically out of fuel and far ahead of the rest of the division. For the next two days, P-47 Thunderbolts, the *Jabo* par excellence, flew continuous sorties over the division's main body to the rear, severely reducing its movement and preventing it from closing up to its advanced guard. The isolation of the reconnaissance force allowed US 2nd Armored Division under General Ernest Harmon to launch a series of successful attacks into Foy-Notre-Dame.[81] Thunderbolts played a role in the fight for the town, as well, flushing Panther tanks out into the open where US tanks and tank destroyers could engage them. When German relief columns came up to rescue the beleaguered battalion of 2nd Panzer, they ran into rocket-firing British fighter-bombers: the fearsome Typhoons. Through it all, the German force under attack barely maneuvered; indeed, it hardly moved at all. The battalion formed up into a laager—an immobile and very vulnerable position—encircled and under heavy fire from all sides and from above. Indeed, Foy-Notre Dame wasn't much of a battle at all.

Forced to operate under Allied air supremacy in the Ardennes, German ground forces were no longer *angriffsfähig*, no longer capable of conducting an offensive. The heroic, all-conquering days at the start of the war, when the Panzers swept all before them, might as well have been ancient history. The Wehrmacht had gone from vicious predator to helpless prey, sheltering in fear during the day and paralyzed by the screech of the *Jabo*.

9

Five Minutes Past Midnight

Introduction: The Führer Speaks

Historians live to reassess people and events. It's their calling. Their research often strikes down long-revered idols and raises up the previously obscure or despised—and the process is often an uncomfortable one. It seems unlikely, however, that later generations will ever fundamentally reassess the character of Adolf Hitler. The self-styled "Führer" was a twisted man, a psychotic so consumed with his own racist hatreds that he plunged the world into the greatest war in its history. He was directly responsible for the deaths of at least 50 million people in the course of the fighting, including 6 million Jewish victims of what is now generally recognized as the greatest mass murder of all time: the Shoah, or Holocaust.

In the interests of fairness, however, we should say one more thing about Hitler. He rarely lied about his intentions. Of all the world statesmen of the twentieth century, he may have been the most honest of all. He proclaimed his goals to the German people and to the world, leaving a dense trail of written statements and public proclamations behind him that are still remarkable for their candor.

Adolf Hitler: Führer. *Reichskanzler*. An honest man.

* * *

THE REICHSTAG—SEPTEMBER 1, 1939. *Hitler is speaking to the representatives of the German people assembled in the Reichstag.*[1] *It is the first day of a war that will make or break them all. Those listening in the audience will later say that they notice a certain strain in his voice, a rare tension in his bearing. One of Hitler's many biographers will later describe the speech as "less than top form."*[2] *Is he bewildered at the path of events in the days leading up to this momentous occasion? Or is he already doubtful of the path on which he has embarked? Certainly his words say otherwise:*

"If I call upon the armed forces and the German people to sacrifice, and if

necessary to make the ultimate sacrifice, then I have a right to do so. For I am today just as ready, as I have always been, to make that sacrifice myself."[3]

. . .

As a National Socialist and a German soldier, I enter this war with a strong heart. My entire life has been nothing other than a struggle for my people, for its rebirth, for Germany. This struggle has always been about a profession of faith in this people. One word that I have never learned is capitulation.[4]

If anyone believes that we have a difficult time ahead of us, then I just ask you to contemplate how once a Prussian king with a laughably small state came up against a great coalition and was successful in three conflicts, precisely because he had that same faithful, strong heart we require today.[5]

He pauses for breath, as if to gather strength for the culminating idea:

And I would also assure the whole wide world: a November 1918 will never again be repeated in German history![6]

On January 1, 1945, the Führer issues his last "New Year's Proclamation" (Neujahrsaufruf), one to the German people and one to the Wehrmacht.[7] The tone is sharper than in 1939, more ideological. Under the pressure of battlefield defeat, perhaps, the phobias are tumbling out: the guilt of the "Jewish-international conspiracy" for starting the war,[8] the enemy's intention to "dismember" the German state, "transporting 15–20 million Germans to foreign lands" and "enslaving" the rest, "corrupting our youth," "starving millions."[9] As always, there is the stark either-or of Hitlerian rhetoric, the eternal "to be or not to be," the choice between "living in freedom or dying in slavery" (in der Freiheit leben oder in der Knechtschaft sterben).[10]

Eventually he returns to his bedrock principle, the same idea he stated so vividly at the start of the war. It has been an obsession since his days as a soldier. Indeed, it may have been the very idea that brought him to power in 1933 and the reason he went to war in 1939:

My declaration of September 1, 1939, is still in place. Specifically, neither time nor force of arms can defeat the German people in this war. Above all, a November 1918 will never happen again![11]

The German official history of World War II claims that, during the last days of the war, Hitler was "choreographing his own downfall."[12] He knew that the war was lost. Indeed, "in comparison to the vast majority of his generals he had a much more modern and complex image of and a sharper conception of the requirements of a war in its broader social dimension."[13] And so he played the role of the warrior-hero who refused to say die. He had no strategy, no means to escape his fate. And so he substituted a creed: "an absolute and unlimited belief in German victory."[14] More a pontiff than a politician or strategist, he could not show a smidgen of doubt or hopelessness. Rather, he repeated certain formulas until they became dogma, especially the strange and inherently unstable nature of the Bolshevik-capitalist coalition facing Germany, the "miracle weapons" (*Wunderwaffen*), new jet fighters and submarines that would arrive soon to save them all, and above all the references to Frederick the Great and the miracle of the House of Brandenburg. In so doing, he was consciously creating an imperishable legend of courage, willpower, and endurance, a heroic example that would some day be "the seed of a brilliant rebirth of the National Socialist movement and thereby the realization of a true national community (*Volksgemeinschaft*)."[15]

Such notions of the Führer as a choreographer hearken back to much of the early analysis of his career and persona, particularly that of biographer Alan Bullock, who labeled Hitler the "consummate actor"

> with the actor's and orator's ability for absorbing himself in a role and convincing himself of the truth of what he was saying at the time he said it. In the early years he was often awkward and unconvincing, but with practice the part became second nature to him, and with the immense prestige of success behind him, and the resources of a powerful state at his command, there were few who could resist the impression of the piercing eyes, the Napoleonic pose, and the "historic" personality.[16]

Both lines of argument share a common notion that the surface Hitler is false, that we must dig deeper to unpack his true motives.

Certainly, human beings are complex creatures, driven through life by multiple beliefs and urges. Hitler was no exception. Notions that turn him into an actor or choreographer or poseur, however, seem essentially misguided. They try too hard. There is another, plainer explanation for Hitler's words and deeds up to the end of the war. It has the advantage of simplicity and requires less overt psychoanalysis or subliminal theorizing: perhaps Hitler really believed what he was saying. He was a fanatic, after all, the very essence of a true believer: in himself, in his star, in his belief that the world had "encircled" Germany; in his hatred of the shadowy groups who had stabbed the army in the back in 1918; above all, in his apocalyptic notion of a global Jewish conspiracy that only he could break—and only through war and mass murder. He believed in miracles, but only if you held out long enough to earn one.

After Midnight: Operation *Nordwind*

The end was near, although getting there would require four long months of high-intensity fighting. In the course of those 120 days, Soviet armies brawled their way from Budapest to Vienna and from the Vistula River into Berlin, wading through an ocean of blood to raise the red flag on the Reichstag building. They smashed German defenses in East Prussia, Pomerania, and Silesia—Germany's three advanced eastern ramparts—and stormed the cities of Königsberg, Danzig, and Breslau. The old kingdom of Prussia was one of the many casualties of Hitler's war in the east. Today Königsberg sits in Russia and is known as Kaliningrad, while Danzig and Breslau belong to Poland and are known as Gdańsk and Wrocław.[17] The British and Canadians made themselves masters of the North German Plain, driving clear to the shore of the Baltic Sea and actually placing the Nazi government of Hitler's successor, Grand Admiral Karl Dönitz, under arrest. The US Army encircled and destroyed Army Group B in the Ruhr and thence sped east to the Elbe River and south to Prague. The linkup between Germany's western and eastern enemies took place on April 25, as Soviet and US troops met at Torgau on the left (western) bank of the Elbe, cutting the Reich in half. The Ardennes offensive played no small role in the Wehrmacht's rapid collapse, chewing up all the carefully husbanded reserves "like a broke man spending his last penny," as the former Chief of Staff of the Army, General Franz Halder, later put it.[18] In all that time, the Wehrmacht did not launch any real counterblow to ward off the pummeling; without a sufficient mechanized reserve, it could not have done so even if it wanted.

While Hitler obviously had no strategy to turn the tide, neither did his generals. Their more superficially sensible solutions usually consisted of shortening the line, forming a reserve, fighting in a more mobile fashion, and surrendering ground occasionally in order to launch a counterstroke at a suitable time. *Kleine Lösungen* ("small solutions"), they called them. Such scaled-down plans were no more realistic than Hitler's, however, and no more likely to end well. Decades of problematic developments within German military and strategic doctrine were now coming home to roost. As far back as the 1920s, the notion that Germany had lost World War I in part because of a lack of unified command had become an article of faith with all of them. Rather than separate services—army, navy, air force—they needed a unified armed force. The very term *Wehrmacht* ("defense force") had first appeared during the interwar era. The corollary to creating a unified, joint Wehrmacht was to place it under one supreme leader and strategist—one Führer—a man would reign in the divergent tendencies of the various services.[19] In the 1930s, most of them had hitched their wagon to Hitler, helping him rearm the country and unleash the war that was now ending so disastrously.

The last months of the war saw the Allies chewing up a new cohort of hastily raised infantry formations, for the most part, a one-sided contest indeed. German manpower took one last turn of the downward spiral in these months. If 1944 was the year of the *Volksgrenadier* divisions, 1945 was the year of the *Volkssturm* ("People's Storm") battalions, units manned by civilian conscripts unfit for military duty, old men, and boys.[20] Given a rudimentary training, handed a *Panzerfaust*, and sent out to halt the advance of fully mechanized Allied armies who were now coming on in full stride, they died (or deserted) in droves. The *Volkssturm* was not merely the last nihilistic gesture of a psychotic regime—although it was that. It was also a key component to a uniquely National Socialist strategy to win the war. The idea was to make total victory over Germany so expensive by forcing the Allies to fight for every inch of ground against fanatical popular resistance that eventually their morale would crack. The collapse would probably take place in Britain or America first and thus free up German troops to mass against the enemy in the east. A fanatical people's army thoroughly drenched in Nazi ideology was the key to this strategy—thus the *Volkssturm*.

Although the army was the logical institution to train and equip such a force, the *Volkssturm* was a party creation, administered by Martin Bormann nationally and by the Nazi Gauleiters—portly, comfortably middle-aged, and largely indolent—in the provinces. Bormann, as was his wont, was more concerned with protecting his new piece of turf from encroachment by other groups (the Hitler Youth, the SS, and the army) than he was with preparing the force for combat.[21] His vision of a fanatical people's army, however, foundered on popular fears that the Allies would consider it an illegal partisan organization and execute any of its members taken prisoner. In other words, getting the Germans to join a militia required arming and training it along regular army lines, which ironically gave the Wehrmacht more and more control over it at the expense of the party. The *Volkssturm*, then, was one more example of the administrative chaos inherent in a polycracy like the Third Reich. Competing officials and groups all tried to get their hands on the new force, and in the process they limited whatever utility it might have had. But more than anything, few of the intended soldiers wanted to be there. The regime had dragooned these men, and so they tended to keep their heads down in combat and to steal away when they could. The party's exhortations to fanaticism had little impact on a population that, by this time, recognized that the war was lost and wanted only an end to it. One of the supposedly inspirational slogans of the Volkssturm was *Ein Volk steht auf!* ("The People Rise Up!"). Many did, but most of them sat right back down again.

Despite all the problems, the High Command of the Wehrmacht opened 1945—its final new year—in highly predictable fashion: launching an offensive. Operation *Nordwind* ("Northern Wind") followed hard on the heels of the Ardennes offensive.[22] While it will probably never escape the shadow of *Wacht am Rhein*, *Nordwind* was almost as large. Elements of two German army groups (General Johannes von Blaskowitz's Army Group G and the new Army Group Upper Rhine under the *Reichsführer-SS* himself, Heinrich Himmler) took part, staging a vast concentric operation against US forces in Alsace. As in *Wacht am Rhein*, the *Nordwind* commanders even received their own audience with the Führer at the Eyrie, replete with a long prebattle oration and all the obligatory references to Frederick the Great.[23] And, in fact, *Nordwind* went much more smoothly than the abortive attack in the Ardennes. In the course of a month of bitter winter fighting, *Nordwind* mauled a US field army and came close to breaking it altogether. A German army that seemed all but finished somehow managed to rise up for one last, late encore: the time, we might say, was five minutes after midnight.

For the Americans, this was the sector of General Jacob Devers's 6th Army Group, which had fought its way from the Riviera to the Rhine in the late summer and fall of 1944. Devers was the first to reach the German Rhine but since then had met with nothing but frustration. Eisenhower had refused him permission to cross the Rhine when it appeared that few German formations were on the other side, and German defenders of the 19th Army were still clinging tenaciously to a pocket west of the river—a "trans-Rhine enclave" around the town of Colmar.[24] With the start of the German offensive in the Ardennes,

Eisenhower had ordered him to cease all offensive activities and to surrender division after division to feed the US defensive stand to the north. Naturally, those units came from just one of 6th Army Group's two armies, the US 7th, under the command of General Alexander M. Patch; the other army was the French 1st, under General Jean de Lattre de Tassigny.[25] To make matters worse, Patch received orders to take over sectors of the front previously belonging to Patton's 3rd Army, now in the process of wheeling north. By the end of December, 7th Army was in a bad way: just six weak divisions spread out over a 126-mile front from Sarregemuines (Saargemünd) in the west, then heading east through the Vosges Mountains to Wissembourg and Lauterbourg on the Rhine, and finally bending back sharply to the southwest to Strasbourg. Intelligence of German attack preparations was flowing in to both Devers and Patch. Believing their most vulnerable sector lay in the west, where the Germans could easily punch through to the north-south Sarre River valley, they deployed the three infantry divisions of XV Corps on a very narrow, 35-mile front west of the Vosges Mountains, with the brand-new US 12th Armored Division in reserve.[26] The neighboring corps on its right, the VI, had three divisions as well, but it had to defend the other 90 miles of front, and one of them, the 36th, was spread out along 40 miles on the western bank of the Rhine from Lauterbourg to Strasbourg. Again, a single division stood in reserve (the 14th Armored). Devers could see the weakness and was rushing new divisions into the sector, hustling the first regiment that arrived up to the front as a task force under the divisional commander without their artillery or heavy weapons. Eisenhower had already ordered the evacuation of the sprawling Lauterbourg Salient and perhaps even the surrender of Strasbourg back to the Germans. (See Map 9.1.)

The Wehrmacht struck this weak army just before midnight on December 31, 1944. The German 1st Army, under the command of General Hans von Obstfelder, led things off in the north with a three-corps battle array, right to left:

XIII SS Corps (*SS-Gruppenführer* Max Simon)
    17th SS *Panzergrenadier* Division *Götz von Berlichingen*
    36th *Volksgrenadier* Division
XC Corps (General Erich Petersen)
    257th *Volksgrenadier* Division
    559th *Volksgrenadier* Division
LXXXIX Corps (General Gustav Höhne)
    256th *Volksgrenadier* Division

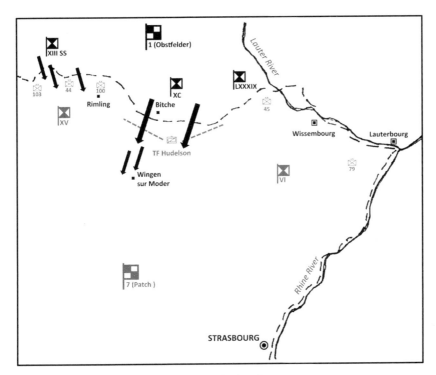

Map 9.1 Last Gasp in the West, Part 1: *Nordwind*

361st *Volksgrenadier* Division
245th *Volksgrenadier* Division

All three corps were heavily reinforced with the new *Volksartillerie* and *Volkswerfer* brigades, self-propelled artillery, assault guns, and even the 653rd Very Heavy Antitank Battalion (*Überschwere Panzerjäger-Abteilung 653*), the first and only antitank unit equipped with the 71-ton *Jagdtiger*, a behemoth mounting a 128mm gun on a King Tiger chassis. Moreover, Obstfelder had another corps still in reserve, XXXIX Panzer, consisting of the 21st and 25th *Panzergrenadier* Divisions, under the command of General Karl Decker.[27]

Just as Devers expected, the XIII SS Corps struck on the extreme German right, heading toward the valley of the Sarre. After a brief bombardment, Simon's two divisions came up in the assault but immediately ran into stiff resistance in front of the prepared defenses of the 103rd, 44th, and 100th Infantry Divisions. The Germans managed to make only a small dent in the American lines in three days of bloody fighting, resulting in a small German salient near the village of Rimling and a corpse-strewn battlefield that the GIs dubbed "Morgue Valley."[28] Waffen-SS divisions have a reputation as elite fighters, but one wouldn't have known it from observing the 17th SS *Panzergrenadier* in action in Alsace. Inadequate staff work, sloppy traffic control, haphazard coordination of fires: *Götz von Berlichingen* suffered from all of them.[29] Perhaps the fact that the division was serving under its fifth commander in four months had something to do with its clumsiness. Its partner, the humble 36th *Volksgrenadier* Division, outfought "Götz" and was responsible for what little progress the corps made.

Nordwind had much better success to the east, however. There, XI and LXXXIX Corps launched their attack south from Bitche through the Low Vosges Mountains. Four *Volksgrenadier* divisions led off the attack, with the 6th SS Mountain Division *Nord* coming down from the Finnish front and joining the attack later. Surprise was total here, US main-force units absent. The attack hit the seam between the two US corps, XV to the left and VI to the right. Patch had a small cavalry screening force here, Task Force Hudelson, consisting largely of jeeps and armored cars, supported by a handful of tank destroyers.[30] The situation was all too reminiscent of the 104th Mechanized Cavalry Group in the Losheim Gap, and the results were about the same. The four divisions penetrated Hudelson's weak front, isolated and reduced his strongpoints one by one, and easily fended off his counterattacks. Having dismantled the US cavalry screen, the attackers pushed south through the Vosges Mountains, penetrating 10 miles and heading for the crucial mountain exits. If they were allowed to debouch from the mountains onto the Alsatian Plain, they could reach the Saverne Gap, from which German mechanized reserves could wheel either right to the Sarre River valley or left along the Marne-Rhine Canal to Strasbourg.

Just three days into the fight, the stakes were already high, a sharp contrast to the Ardennes offensive, which was already terminal by day three. Patch and Devers reacted rapidly, transferring 103rd Division from the extreme left of the line to the eastern shoulder of the German advance. In cooperation with the 100th Division on the western shoulder, Patch and Devers managed to contain the size of the breach, although the Germans were still heading south at speed. Standing in their way and tasked with stopping them was the US 45th Infantry Division under General Robert Frederick. Patch reinforced him, transferring a regiment from 79th Infantry Division, shifting individual battalions from the still-quiet Lauterbourg and Rhine sectors to fill the gap created by the demise of Task Force Hudelson, and even temporarily converting an entire engineer regiment into infantry and throwing them into the battle. At one point, General Frederick had no fewer than eight regiments serving under him, four of which had never before been in combat, and some of which were barely trained.[31] "American Volkssturm Grenadiers," the more experienced GIs called them.[32] The Germans, too, raised the stakes by inserting 6th SS Mountain Division *Nord* into the battle, which by now had devolved into a hamlet-by-hamlet brawl along the mountain trails and tracks of the Low Vosges. US strength was growing by the day, since getting reinforcements to the Alsatian Plain (the American logistical task) was much easier than passing them over the Vosges (the German task). Patch's 7th Army managed to slow down the Germans and then stop them before they reached the mountain exits. By January 5, 1945, a lull had fallen over the front as a fresh blanket of snow covered the exhausted adversaries. The Americans were staggering, but so were the Germans, and apparently *Nordwind* had failed. (See Map 9.2.)

Or perhaps not. No sooner had the guns died down than a new series of German offensives broke over the front, conducted by Himmler's Army Group Upper Rhine. On January 5, the 553rd *Volksgrenadier* Division under General Gerhard Hüther (part of XIV SS Corps) crossed the Rhine River just north of Gambsheim, only 10 miles north of Strasbourg. The landing force contained "an incredibly ragtag assortment" of forces, according to one authority.[33] With only one of its three regiments (1119 Grenadier Regiment) even close to full strength, the 553rd was filled out with youngsters from the NCO Training School at Esslingen, a regiment from a nearby training division, and an SS Police regiment. Himmler was a man without any operational acumen whatsoever, but he did have one positive attribute. The *Reichsführer-SS* was such a terrifying figure that no one in the districts on the Rhine would dare resist his demands for manpower or equipment. At the urging of the XIV SS Corps commander, General Erich von dem Bach-Zelewski, Himmler even found some armor, slapping together the *Jagdpanzer Abteilung von Lüttichau* and attaching it to the assault force. Thus reinforced, the 553rd got over the river on its rubber assault boats, quickly dispersed the weak US covering forces on the western bank, and carved out a sizable bridgehead. Defense along the Rhine had originally been the task of the US 36th Division, but it had long ago departed for the SHAEF reserve on Eisenhower's orders. Now a completely new force, Task Force Linden (comprising elements of the inexperienced 42nd Division) stood the American watch on the

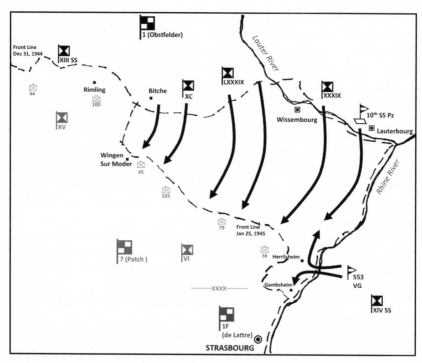

Map 9.2 Last Gasp in the West, Part 2: *Nordwind*

Rhine. As the US official history puts it, Task Force Linden tried to resist the landing:

> But with no organic signal, artillery, or transportation units of its own, and with only a few platoons of 79th Division armor in direct support, the scattered rifle battalions of the task force were overmatched. Ferrying troops and armored vehicles across the Rhine as quickly as possible, the initial assault force was able to brush aside the weak American counterattacks and rapidly extend the width of the bridgehead to about ten miles.[34]

Task Force Linden, in other words, was a "static unit" in everything but name and enjoyed about the same level of success as the typical German *bodenständig* division in Normandy. The landing compromised the right flank of VI Corps and took place at almost the same time as 6th SS Mountain Division *Nord* appeared on the corps's extreme left, driving US troops out of the village of Wingen on the Moder River and threatening to reopen mobile conditions in the Vosges sector. The VI Corps had been weak to begin with, was under attack on both flanks, and almost out of reserves. Patch could see the danger of the "Gambsheim cancer" and immediately ordered Combat Command B of the 12th Armored Division to do something about it.[35] Attacking into the heart of the bridgehead, at the town of Herrlisheim, the 12th ran into a buzz saw of German fire. The division's own inexperience, as well as the general unsuitability of the US armored division for town battle (it possessed one-third the amount of infantry as an US infantry division), led to big problems. Numerous waterways including the Zorn River, which bisected the town, frustrated and channelized US tank movements, while German *Panzerfaust* fire mauled the 714th Tank Battalion in the course of the fighting. The cancer remained.

But the catalog of German attacks was still not done. On January 7, forces of the 19th Army under General Siegfried Rasp launched Operation *Sonnenwende* ("Solstice"), attacking north out of the Colmar Salient and heading toward Strasbourg.[36] Essentially a single thrust by LXIV Corps under the command of General Helmut Thumm, it aimed either to punch through forces of the French 1st Army and head to Strasburg from the south, or perhaps to thrust toward Molsheim, 10 miles away, and close on the city from the west. But LXIV Corps wasn't a particularly powerful force. The 198th Volksgrenadier Division and the 106th Panzer Brigade (some fifty heavy tanks and assault guns) were in the van, thrusting past Rhinau and breaking through the front of the French II Corps on the first day. Thumm's corps headed north, making 10 miles the first day, crossing the Ill River, and reaching Erstein. Here, just 12 miles from Strasbourg, the attack came to a halt. French defenses stiffened over the next few days, aided by the difficult terrain on the southern approaches to Strasbourg, a tangle of rivers, streams, and canals along the western bank of the Rhine. Nevertheless, *Sonnenwende* had opened up one more front and added one more problem to Devers's list.

Make that one more still. Also on January 7, Blaskowitz inserted the 1st Army reserve—the XXXIX Panzer Corps under General Decker. Made up of the 21st Panzer, 25th *Panzergrenadier*, and 245th *Volksgrenadier* Divisions, Decker's corps attacked on a broad front from the Lauter River, between Wissembourg in the west and Lauterbourg in the east. Neither German Panzer division was at full strength. Indeed, it is doubtful that where was a single full-strength Panzer division left in the Wehrmacht by January 1945. Nevertheless, grouped into *Kampfgruppe* Feuchtinger (for the commander of the 21st Panzer Division), the two mobile formations represented a major commitment of force. US strength in the big Lauterbourg Salient, meanwhile, was at a low ebb. The need to plug holes elsewhere on 7th Army's front had sucked troops out of this sector for a week now, making the defense of the salient the very definition of an economy-of-force mission. The VI Corps commander, General Edward Brooks, had replaced the lost units with a miscellaneous jumble of task forces, infantry battalions, elements of the French 23rd Algerian Division, tank destroyers, engineers, and cavalry remnants, all grouped under the commander of the 79th Infantry Division, General Ira Wyche. Like General Frederick to his west, Wyche had no fewer than eight disparate units under his command, and controlling them was easier said than done. At VI Corps headquarters, Brooks had already planned a three-phase retreat, mapping out a series of phase lines for each stage. He had just given orders for stage one, a 10-mile retreat back to some old fortresses of the Maginot Line, when Decker's attack hit. The US front line along the Lauter was nothing more than a handful of rifle battalions of the 45th and 79th Infantry Divisions, and they caved in almost immediately. By January 8, the Germans were moving at speed to the south and west, making 10 miles in two days and slowed down by minefields and bad weather more than by US resistance. Brooks saw no choice but to commit his final reserve. The 14th Armored Division took up position squarely in the path of the German advance between the villages of Hatten and Rittershofen, two villages a mile apart just above the Haguenau Forest, on January 9.[37]

The stage was set for ten days of some of the bitterest fighting of the war. During January 10–20, 14th Armored took on Kampfgruppe *Feuchtinger*. Tanks stalked each other in the narrow streets of Hatten and Rittershofen, and both sides learned not to pop around corners too quickly. There always seemed to be someone waiting—and heavily armed. With both sides focused on such a narrow killing ground, artillery, too, had its day. The Americans had the superior artillery and much more ammunition, as they always did in this war, and their barrages were enormous. The Germans countered with fresh bodies (reinforcements drawn from 20th *Fallschirmjäger* Regiment and 104th Infantry Regiment). With hard fighting still raging in the Ardennes, where the Allies were reducing the bulge, the Americans were momentarily tapped out of new units. The battlespace was flat as a pancake or, better yet, a "pool table" as the GIs dubbed it, save for the ruins of the two villages and a series of big bunkers that had originally been part of the Maginot Line and were now incorporated into the

US defense.[38] German storm troopers had to reduce them the old way, with teams and infantry and pioneers supported by flamethrowers and flamethrower tanks. Temperatures hovered near zero, snow continued to fall, and men fought, froze, and died on both sides. Gradually, however, German momentum began to flag, as losses mounted among their irreplaceable Panzers, assault infantry, and support formations. The ragged band of American units fighting as VI Corps managed to hold the Hatten-Rittershofen Line, but the cost—30 percent casualties—had been heavy.

And yet, the so-called New Year offensives (*Sylwesterschlachten*) were still not complete. The High Command had its own reserve forces in the area and had been husbanding them for a blow against the flank of Patton's US 3rd Army, which was still entangled in flattening the bulge in the Ardennes. But Hitler and Jodl now decided to cancel the strike on 3rd Army, code-named Operation *Zahnarzt* ("Dentist") and utilize the forces in Alsace. New units included the 10th SS Panzer Division *Frundsberg* and the 7th *Fallschirmjäger* Division, fighting under Decker's XXXIX Panzer Corps headquarters, which now moved from Blaskowitz's Army Group G to Himmler's Army Group Upper Rhine. "Frundsberg" would bear the main burden and, with fifty Mark IV and forty Mark V Panther tanks, was as well equipped as any German unit still in the field. The plan was the oldest of all Prussia-German military constructs: a concentric attack—down from the Haguenau Forest and over from the Gambsheim-Herrlisheim bridgehead. The operational target was still VI Corps. If this new assault—the last assault—could break the American front at Haguenau and get into its rear from Gambsheim, VI Corps would be trapped in a *Kessel*.[39]

Opening on January 16, this latest Panzer assault slashed through the US line north of the Haguenau Forest, held by an intermingled assortment of units from Task Force Linden (elements of the 42nd Division) and Wyche's 79th Division—whoever happened to be left in the sector. Commander Brooks had the corps in retrograde motion by this time, but there is no doubt that the new German thrust had caught him, and his superiors, by surprise. More surprising still was an attack out of the Gambsheim-Herrlisheim bridgehead by elements of 10th SS Panzer. While part of the division spearheaded the fight on the Haguenau front, a large part of its Panzer regiment had ferried across the Rhine the night before—and it now erupted into an attack. Here, it hit the unfortunate 12th Armored Division, which had already had its troubles in the January 8–9 attack into Herrlisheim. The 12th had just begun another thrust into the bridgehead with Combat Command A as German Panther tanks were preparing to attack out of it. The American plans were for the 17th Armored Infantry Battalion to push into Herrlisheim from the west while 43rd Tank Battalion came up from the south. The two would rendezvous in the center of the town. Both columns came under heavy fire of all sorts—tank, antitank, small arms, artillery—and the battle almost immediately degenerated into a melee without higher direction. The commander of the US 43rd Tank Battalion, Lieutenant Colonel Nicholas Novosel, sent a cryptic radio message describing the town as "a circus" crawling with German infantry. "Things are hot," he said, before going silent.[40] In the confused fighting that followed over the next two days, Novosel's battalion was destroyed, largely by *Panzerfaust*-wielding German infantry.

The situation facing US VI Corps was now dire. Both flanks were caving, and German attacks were bending the corps back into a crescent. Brooks had seen enough and ordered a general retreat through the forest to a good defensive position along the Zorn, Moder, and Rothbach Rivers. The maneuver took place on the night of January 20–21 and apparently took the German command by surprise. German infantry who woke up expecting one more day of fighting for the ruins of Hatten and Rittershofen were puzzled and relieved in equal measure. Unshaven and unkempt, looking for all the world like U-boat sailors at the end of a long cruise, they pinched themselves. Was it really over?

Getting them back into battle wasn't easy, and their pursuit of the Americans was tentative. Indeed, XXXIX Panzer Corps took four full days to close up to the new line. By then, Brooks had things well in hand: four divisions abreast (45th, 103rd, 79th, and 36th), backed by a robust force of artillery and the remnants of the 12th and 14th Armored Divisions in reserve. With the fighting in the Ardennes finally done, Eisenhower could even deal out one of his high cards: dispatching the 101st Airborne Division to Alsace to backstop Patch's position. The Germans made one last play on January 24, ran into a solid wall of US infantry and artillery, and were done.

The Germans' New Year offensive ended in a mutual mauling, exhausted the adversaries, and inflicted heavy casualties on both sides, perhaps 14,000 American to 23,000 German. American tank losses appear to have been much higher than the Germans (understandable for a battle that featured German Mark V Panthers fighting US M4 Shermans), although no definitive numbers exist. Nevertheless, the extended *Nordwind* sequence was a tactical victory for the Wehrmacht, what the Germans call an "ordinary victory." From a purely technical standpoint, the initiative (*Gesetz des Handelns*) had remained squarely in German hands throughout; US forces had done little but react to what their opponent was doing, and in the end they had abandoned their initial positions and fallen well back. A tactical victory is just that, however: a win that brings with it no real change to the strategic or operational situation. So it was with *Nordwind*. Monstrous Allied armies were on the march in the east and the west, pressing to the very borders of the Reich. Western Allied air forces were in the "smithereens" phase of their bombing campaign, churning up the rubble of German cities they had already destroyed and complaining about a lack of fresh targets. The bomber stream would torch one more city—Dresden—in mid-February, just two weeks after the offensive ended. *Nordwind* changed nothing.

But what a wild ride. Counted out and left for dead a half-dozen times, facing not only battlefield defeat but also the destruction of the state it represented, the German Wehrmacht had risen from the grave one more time. In executing *Nordwind*, it remained true not only to its sense of duty but also to a centuries-old way of war that stressed aggressive attack, boldness, concentric operations, and *Kesselschlacht*. In the process, it threatened US forces in Alsace, especially the overextended VI Corps, with serious defeat, perhaps even destruction. Attacking with widely separated and independent columns, seeking to cave in both enemy flanks, seeking a linkup of the pincers far in the rear: this was war as Frederick the Great or Moltke or Schlieffen understood it. For the last time, the Wehrmacht fought a campaign according to its time-honored precepts. For one final time—months before it was ushered from the historical stage—the Germans showed that they still knew how to fight *Bewegungskrieg*, the war of movement.

Historians celebrate German armies for their planning, administration, and staff work, and, indeed, virtually every army in the world today has a central planning organ based upon the old Prussian-German Great General Staff. But perhaps we err in placing too much stock in the General Staff and the supposed virtues of German planning. The *Wacht am Rhein* offensive in the Ardennes took months of intensive planning and operational debate and wound up becoming a complete misfire: a disaster from start to finish. *Nordwind* was apparently conceived around December 21, 1944, given a little over a week of planning, and then sent into action on December 31. Command and staff relationships—the essence of military planning—were an absolute mess throughout the entire month of the offensive. Army Group G and Army Group Upper Rhine barely seemed to speak with one another, either before or during the fight. Himmler almost certainly felt his inadequacy when conferencing with the military professionals, and Blaskowitz—a card-carrying member of the Prussian officer corps and under a dark cloud indeed since July 20—probably tried to avoid appearing on Himmler's radar screen if at all possible. If they had only launched any of those half-dozen powerful but separate thrusts and landed blows simultaneously, the results might well have been dramatic.

The planning may have been mediocre. As to the fighting, that was a different story. German infantry showed boldness in the attack, steadfastness in the defense, and a willingness to die in both. German tank crews and mechanized formations continued to fight with verve, spirit, boldness, and a frightening level of lethality. Command coordination, logistics, sensibly matching ends and means: those were someone else's tasks. The *Nordwind* offensives of January 1945 saw the Wehrmacht doing the one thing it knew how to do. In its last great offensive, fighting within the narrow confines of Alsace—a cockpit for Prussian and German armies for centuries—the army of the new superpower gave it all that it could handle.

As the fighting ended in Rittershofen, a regimental commander of 21st Panzer Division stood in the ruins of the city. An aide had just informed Lieutenant Colonel Hans von Luck that the "Amis" (the Americans) had gone. Stumbling around the rubble and the reeking streets, he spied a partially demolished church and entered.

> Through a gaping hole in the wall we went in. I stood facing the altar, which lay in ruins, and looked up at the organ. It seemed to be unharmed. A few more of our men came in.
>
> "Come," I called to a lance-corporal, "we'll climb up to the organ."
>
> On arriving above, I asked the man to tread the bellows. I sat down at the organ and—it was hardly believable—it worked.

Luck was a passable musician, and he began to play an air instantly recognizable to his officers and men, a hymn that had resounded at similar times and places in the long history of German arms. Frederick the Great's grenadiers had sung it on the victorious field at Leuthen, and so had Field Marshal Helmuth von Moltke's triumphant infantry on the Chlum Heights at Königgrätz. Now it rang out again—one last encore of *Nun danket alle Gott* ("Now Thank We All Our God")—one more requiem for a dying army.[41]

From Warsaw to the Oder: Planning for the Inevitable

In early 1945, the Eastern Front was what it had been since the Wehrmacht launched Operation Barbarossa: a German graveyard, the theater that claimed the lion's share of the army's divisions and generated the most casualties. The German strategic decision in 1944 to prioritize the Western Front, deal the Anglo-Americans a sharp blow, and then turn back with redoubled fury to the east was also the same thing it had been all along: nonsense. Errors on the strategic level are always the most serious, trumping operational brilliance and tactical acumen. Indeed, strategic errors have a way of being fatal. The Wehrmacht's dramatic path in 1944 from defeat to catastrophe to rebirth on the Western Front was an epic in its way, but an empty one. By late 1944, the Eastern Front had gone into free fall.

The Red Army had spent the autumn mercilessly gouging into the flanks of the German strategic position. A series of offensives smashed Army Group North—always the weakest and most undersupported of the army groups—and herded its two component armies (the 16th and 18th) into one of the most senseless military positions of all time: the Courland Pocket.[42] The small hump of western Latvia from Libau in the west to Tuckum in the east held over thirty German divisions that were cut off from the rest of the Wehrmacht and from the homeland—a force that had to be supplied by sea. The Soviets launched three great offensives into Courland in 1944, two in October and one in December, and then three more in 1945 (January, February, and March). The German force, renamed Army Group Courland in January 1945, warded off all of them, a masterpiece of defensive positional warfare against a powerful enemy, but in the end these thirty divisions stayed right where the Red Army wanted them: in a self-imposed prison camp. Indeed, the defense of the Courland Pocket benefited from the large number of German divisions packed like sardines into a very tiny front. For once on the Eastern Front, German divisions didn't have to defend outrageously extended fronts, and under such conditions they gave a good accounting of themselves. From time to time, General Heinz Guderian, Chief of the General Staff since July 21, 1944, pleaded with Hitler to evacuate Courland and bring the lost armies home to bolster the defenses of the homeland. Over and over again, Hitler refused, and he could always count on a reliable ally in the argument: Admiral Dönitz. He claimed that keeping a toehold in the Baltic Sea was essential to testing Germany's new, fully submersible Type XXI U-boats, one of those miracle weapons that Hitler claimed was eventually going to win the war. At any rate, as 1945 dawned, it was unlikely that Germany could have scrounged up enough ships, transport capacity, and fuel to evacuate Army Group Courland—even if Hitler had agreed.

Likewise, in the south, the Red Army spent the autumn leveraging the advantages gained by Romania's defection. The Soviets overran the Ploesti oil fields, coerced Bulgaria to declare war on Germany, drove into Yugoslavia, and captured Belgrade in October.[43] These successes fatally compromised the position of German forces in Yugoslavia and Greece, and the German occupation force in the southern Balkans, General Alexander Löhr's Army Group E, received orders to evacuate Greece, southern Albania, and southern Macedonia in October.[44] Löhr brought his force north, with Tito's Partisan forces nipping at their heels the whole way.[45] Over and over again, German forces had to fight their way out of encirclements, but they could always amass sufficient force against the lighter-armed Partisans to do so. The Wehrmacht was less well equipped to deal with Allied air attacks, however, especially on the twisting mountain roads of central Bosnia, and the entire march north was an exercise in misery.

The next target in line—and Soviet strategy in this period of the war has all the meticulous sense of purpose of a clerk checking off boxes on an inventory sheet—was Hungary. After the huge losses the Hungarians suffered in the Soviet Union since Stalingrad, the country had clearly been wavering in its allegiance to the Axis. On March 12, 1944, the Germans had carried out Operation Margarethe, occupying the country to prevent an Italian- or Romanian-style defection. By October, Soviet forces had driven deep into Hungary, and fierce armored battles were raging around Debrecen in the Great Hungarian Plain.[46] The Hungarian head of state, Admiral Miklós Horthy, negotiated an armistice with the Soviets.[47] His announcement of the armistice on October 15, 1944, led the Germans to carry out Operation Panzerfaust, a coup by fascist fanatics of the Arrow Cross movement. Horthy was out, and Arrow Cross leader Ferenc Szálasi was in. The Germans purchased Horthy's acquiescence by kidnaping his son, Miklós Jr., beating him senseless, rolling him up in a rug, and transporting him to the Mauthausen concentration camp in Germany (Operation Mickey Mouse): a suitably gangsterish event that tells us all we need to know about the nature of Nazi foreign policy. Keeping Hungary loyal had little impact on the military side, however. After clearing the plain on the eastern bank of the Tisza River, the Soviets stormed toward Budapest. On December 5 they launched an offensive on both sides of the capital and encircled Budapest on Christmas Eve 1944. The siege, with four full German divisions inside the ring, would rage well into 1945.[48]

All of these attacks in the northern and southern sector of the front left the center more or less untouched. Soviet forces still stood where they had since August: along the Vistula River, opposite Warsaw. And for anyone who had been paying attention to Soviet strategy thus far in the war, clearing the flanks could mean only one thing as 1945 began: an offensive along the central Warsaw-Berlin axis and a drive into the heart of Berlin.[49] The end of the fighting back in August had seen Soviet armies seize three great bridgeheads over the Vistula south of Warsaw: at Magnuszew, at Pulawy, and on a long stretch of the Vistula between Baranow and Sandomierz, moving north to south. To the north of Warsaw, the Soviets held three more bridgeheads over the Narew River, two around Pultusk and a third at Lomza. Again, to anyone cognizant in Soviet battle planning, the maintenance of such numerous and expansive bridgeheads was a clear expression of operational intent. Unlike past offensives, the Soviets did not go to great lengths to employ *maskirovka* or deception. There could be no fooling the Germans as to the site of an attack so monstrous in size, and with German reserves chewed up in the Ardennes and in the fighting in Hungary, it hardly mattered how sly the Soviets tried to be. Most of the massive preparations for the great offensive—the Vistula-Oder operation—took place in the open.[50]

And massive they were: two Soviet fronts bursting with men, tanks, and guns. On the Soviet right, directly opposite and to the south of Warsaw, 1st Byelorussian Front (Marshal G. K. Zhukov) assembled ten armies (eight combined-arms armies for the initial penetration, two tank armies, and two cavalry corps for exploitation along the attack axis) plus an air army. Such a robust force offered unlimited operational possibilities, and Zhukov seemed determined to try them all. He envisioned no fewer than three penetrations: the major one from the Magnuszew bridgehead, a 15-mile-wide by 6-mile-deep bulge over the river just south of Warsaw. Zhukov crammed three armies into Magnuszew, the 8th Guards Army under General V. I. Chuikov (formerly the 62nd Army, the heroes of Stalingrad), 5th Shock Army, and 61st Army. They would make the penetration, setting the stage for the 1st Guards Tank Army and the 2nd Guards Tank Army to launch the exploitation to the west. Zhukov designed a second, smaller penetration north of Warsaw, where 47th Army would take advantage of the general rupturing of the German line to cross the Vistula, loop around Warsaw to the north, and link up with the 61st Army coming up out of Magnuszew to encircle the city. Finally, a third drive would emerge out of Pulawy, in the southern reaches of Zhukov's sector: 69th Army and 33rd Army would penetrate the German lines and link up with forces coming down out of Magnuszew, creating a series of tactical encirclements.

To the south (left) of Zhukov lay Marshal I. S. Konev's 1st Ukrainian Front. Here, too, stood ten full armies at the commander's disposal, eight combined-arms armies and two tank armies. Konev's plan was the opposite of Zhukov's, however, and much simpler: while Zhukov was attacking in many places at once, Konev planned on one single great thrust. He jammed no fewer than five of his armies—half the total force—into the Baranow-Sandomierz bridgehead (the 6th, 13th, 52nd, 3rd Guards, and 5th Guards). Moreover, Konev planned to insert 3rd Guards Tank Army and 4th Guards Tank Army into the breakout from the Baranow-Sandomierz bridgehead on day one. The assault of Konev's 1st Ukrainian Front might well have been the single greatest concentration of land power in all of World War II.

Taken together, the two Soviet fronts amassed shocking numbers for the upcoming offensive. Konev and Zhukov had no fewer than 134 rifle divisions, 33,000 guns, 7,000 tanks, and 4,700 aircraft. In all, they commanded 2.25 million men. The two fronts contained about one-third of all infantry formations on the entire front and almost one-half of all the tanks. One authority calls the Soviet advantage "both absolute and awesome, fivefold in manpower, fivefold in armor, over sevenfold in artillery, and seventeen times the German strength in the air."[51] As always, the prelude to deep battle was concentration of massive force on extremely narrow fronts, and the Vistula-Oder operation was no different. The Soviets were able to lay on 220–250 guns per kilometer of front, a (theoretical) artillery piece every 4 meters, along with 21–25 tanks. It was a devastating concentration of offensive power, beyond anything the Soviets had yet achieved, even in their megavictory in Byelorussia the previous summer. A five-to-one advantage in armor across the entire front can easily become a superiority of ten- or even twenty-to-one in certain chosen assault sectors.

Moreover, the Soviet Stavka constructed this behemoth force while simultaneously planning another two-front offensive against East Prussia. The 2nd Byelorussian (Marshal K. K. Rokossovsky) and 3rd Byelorussian (General I. D. Cherniakhovsky) Fronts would launch a vast concentric operation against the exposed province. The operational scheme was essentially that of the Tannenberg campaign in 1914. Cherniakhovsky's force would launch a frontal blast due west, driving on a direct route through Gumbinnen and Insterburg toward Königsberg. Once he had pinned German forces in place, Rokossovsky would come up from the south though Osterode and Allenstein, head toward the Baltic Sea at Elbing, and drive into the deep flank and rear of the German defenders. German forces in the province belonged to Army Group Center, under the command of General Georg-Hans Reinhardt. He had three weak armies (from left to right: 3rd Panzer, 4th, and 2nd) and a badly distended position, with 4th Army occupying a lazy, indefensible bulge looping out toward the east.[52] The initial Soviet attacks intended to *Kessel* 4th Army by smashing the two armies on its flanks. Launching two vast offensives at once, the Soviet Union had become a military superpower by 1945, the purveyor of strategic land power par excellence.

And what of the German force defending the Vistula line? Here stood Army Group A (formerly Army Group North Ukraine, renamed after its brusque eviction from Ukrainian soil in July 1944), under the same officer who had commanded it during that previous catastrophe: General Joseph Harpe. Army Group A contained four relatively threadbare armies stretched over a 420-mile front and deployed along a more or less straight line stretching from north to south:

9th Army (General Smilo Freiherr von Lüttwitz)
—opposite the Magnuszew and Pulawy bridgeheads
4th Panzer Army (General Fritz-Hubert Gräser)
—opposite the Baranow-Sandomierz bridgehead
17th Army (General Friedrich Schulz)
—south of the Vistula to the Beskid Range in the Carpathians
Armeegruppe Heinrici: 1st Panzer Army and 1st Hungarian Army (both under the command of General Gotthard Heinrici)
—holding the army group's right wing in the Carpathians.[53]

Altogether, Harpe's army group could call upon a mere twenty-five divisions on line to hold this long front (standing against 134 Soviet divisions), along with 1,300 tanks (against 6,500). Twelve panzer divisions stood in reserve, but few were at full strength and fuel was in short supply—the Wehrmacht's "new normal" since the loss of the Ploesti fields. Air support for the front, courtesy of VIII *Fliegerkorps* flying out of Kraków, was minimal. The *Fliegerkorps* could barely put 300 aircraft into the air (against 4,700), and those that were theoretically available to fly often didn't, due again to serious fuel constraints. Army Group A also suffered from a serious shortage of munitions of all sorts, and many of Harpe's units in January 1945 had an ammunition load for only two or three days of high-intensity combat.

All these numbers were indicative of the Soviet strategic edge: resources, industrial capacity, and increases in productivity, of course. They were also a product of German decision-making over the last six months. Hitler and the OKW had made a particularly fateful choice the previous fall when they decided to form a new army (the 6th SS Panzer Army under *SS-Oberst-Gruppenführer* Sepp Dietrich) rather than transfer newly raised units to strengthen German armies already holding the line against the Soviets. We might say the same for their decision to deploy that new army in the west for the Ardennes offensive. That choice meant that German defenses in the east would lack a reserve army that Harpe or the General Staff and the OKH could insert to smash a Soviet breakthrough with a bold Panzer counterstroke. Finally, once it was clear that *Wacht am Rhein* was finished, Hitler and the OKW decided to transfer the 6th SS Panzer Army not to the east, as originally promised, but rather to the southeast, to Hungary, where it launched a series of three failed relief offensives to break the Soviet siege of Budapest (Operations Konrad I–III). All of these choices meant starving Army Group A and the other German forces currently defending the long line from the Baltic Sea to the Carpathian Mountains.[54] And yet, we cannot merely label these decisions "wrong." However Hitler or anyone else shuffled them, there simply were not enough German divisions, corps, or armies to do all that needed to be done. Whether 6th SS Panzer Army fought in Budapest or on the Baranow bridgehead line was hardly going to change the ultimate verdict of the war—not at this late date.

We could say the same thing about the operational scheme mooted by Harpe's chief of staff, the young and energetic General Wolfdietrich Ritter von Xylander. In the current conformation of the front, the Baranow and Magnuszew bridgeheads jutted into German-held territory. German forces deployed on that sector of the front, therefore, were in a salient pointing east, nearly encircled even before the start of the fighting. Xylander devised a plan he dubbed *Schlittenfahrt* ("Sleighride," named, incidentally, for the signature maneuver of the Great Elector of Brandenburg in the Winter Campaign of 1678–1679).[55] Just before the offensive, German forces would evacuate the bulge, moving back in three stages to the previously prepared Hubertus Line. The immense Soviet bombardment would therefore strike air—and so would the irresistible momentum of the initial Soviet attack. They would still come forward, but without their usual power. German forces would be standing in good order on a well-prepared, fortified line and be able either to hold the Soviet drive or even to strike a counterblow if conditions were favorable. Moreover, Xylander calculated that *Schlittenfahrt* would free up, at a minimum, four divisions, which he could use to form a strategic reserve for the army group.[56]

Guderian presented *Schlittenfahrt* to Hitler at a conference at the Eyrie on January 9, along with a demand for reinforcements from the west and the by now obligatory demand for the evacuation of the Courland Pocket. While the scheme seems sensible enough, the Führer wasn't having it. The proposed operation was just another retreat, he said, just another refusal to follow his orders to hold the line. Manuever wasn't important to the outcome of the upcoming battle. Determination and strength of will: those were the keys. Hitler responded to Guderian's presentation of the dire situation at the front with all the contempt he had built up for years against the generals, their propensity to "operate," their constant demands for retreat. He didn't believe Guderian's intelligence estimates on Soviet tanks and guns, labeling them "completely idiotic."[57] Guderian responded that they came from the intelligence service, particularly from General Reinhard Gehlen in the *Fremde Heere Ost* (Foreign Armies East) office. "If you think he belongs in a madhouse, then lock me up, too!"[58] Even though the rage on both sides subsided, and the discussion returned to a more civil space, the entire experience "was extremely unpleasant," Guderian wrote.[59] Hitler had reverted to an "ostrich strategy."[60] Meanwhile, the Eastern Front had become "a house of cards. If the front is penetrated at any point, the whole thing would fall apart."[61] Hitler's response had all the charm of a funeral bell tolling: "The East must rely on itself and survive on what it has."[62]

Guderian's account of the January meeting has become the accepted narrative, and no indications that he was lying, or even exaggerating, have ever come to light. Indeed, in a nighttime conference after the Chief of the General Staff departed, Hitler expanded on his skepticism of the reports he had heard earlier that day:

> I looked at the numbers today, and we have 3,000 tanks and assault guns in the east. Since we usually shoot up enemy tanks at a 3–1 ratio, the Soviets need 9,000 tanks to destroy us. They need a 3–1 superiority. But they don't have 9,000 tanks, not at the moment.
>
> . . .
>
> And here: if we look at the whole front, they're supposed to have 150 guns every kilometer. That's 1,500 guns on a ten-kilometer

front. There is no way that can be true! That would mean 15,000 guns on a 100-kilometer front, and 20,000 guns on a 150-kilometer front. The Russians aren't made of artillery![63]

In fact, we can say that they *were* made of artillery. Hitler's departure from reality—born either of ignorance or of willful self-deception—is striking. The time had long passed when the Führer's intuition and amateurish luck could lead to positive battlefield outcomes. His "un-professional and defective" decisions were leading them all to doom, and they were directly responsible for the senseless deaths of hundreds of thousands of German soldiers.[64]

But in the interests of historical accuracy and fairness, let us note that Xylander's plan was no more realistic than Hitler's. The notion that the proposed *Schlittenfahrt* or any similar operational stratagem could ward off the dark fate awaiting Army Group A on the Vistula belongs to the realm of fantasy. Consider the words of the German official history. The controversy over *Schlittenfahrt* was "irrelevant," the author argues:

> Plans of this sort could not replace the German army's losses in materiel and personnel or reduce the opponent's superiority, neither on the Vistula nor weeks later on the Oder.
>
> . . .
>
> On the basis of the numbers alone, the outcome of the upcoming offensive was not in doubt. For the Wehrmacht of the Third Reich, the time for brilliant maneuver was over, since space was lacking. The depth required [for a war of maneuver] lay to the east, not west, of the Vistula. Each retreat brought the eastern opponent to the borders of the Reich. The danger loomed of ground operations on the soil of the homeland.[65]

Indeed, like Model and Rundstedt pressing their point with Hitler and Jodl for the "small solution" during the 1944 Ardennes planning cycle, Xylander, Harpe, and Guderian were declaring allegiance to a way of war they had learned in the War Academy and then tested in the field in the early days of World War II: that war consists above all of a series of cleverly designed and boldly executed military operations, devoid of context, politics, or economics.

Handed impossible orders to hold out to the last man but lacking enough men to do so, Guderian attempted to compensate by digging a series of fortified positions on and behind the Vistula line. Hundreds of thousand of civilians, both German and Polish, as well as prisoners of war, went to work digging trenches and artillery emplacements, felling trees for roadblocks, and protecting the major towns and cities with all-around fortifications. The system was impressive enough on paper, including a *Hauptkampflinie* (main battle line) backstopped by no fewer than four lines (designated "a" through "d") extending to a depth of 150 miles, with intermediate positions between them. A final barrier, the *Nibelungen-Stellung* (Nibelung Position), stretched from Bratislava in the south to the Stettin on the Baltic Sea coast. East Prussia, too, had an impressive system of prepared defenses.[66] Many of them, like the Lötzen Triangle in the lakes district, were of great antiquity but still useful as defensive force multipliers within the dark forests of the province.[67] Nevertheless, the Wehrmacht lacked many of the necessary materiel to build and hold a modern fortified line, including concrete, construction tools, fuel for the tractors, and, above all, artillery to place in the new bunkers; the works remained inadequate and incomplete on the eve of the Soviet offensive.

Mobilizing civilian labor was a double-edged sword for the army, moreover, since it brought the civil administration into play. As they had with the formation of the *Volkssturm*, the Gauleiters sensed that that their moment had come. They could see that fortification-building and civilian mobilization meant access to greater power and funding. Nazi officials in the eastern provinces soon began to intervene in the process of fortification building. The results were catastrophic. Arguments over jurisdiction and precedence arose between the army and the civilian authorities, resulting in confusion, waste, and redundancy of effort. Erich Koch, for example, former Gauleiter of occupied Ukraine and now holding the same office in East Prussia, was an energetic fellow—in all the worst ways. While he knew nothing of fortification or military affairs in general, he was certain that he "was smarter than a trained commander."[68] East Prussia wound up with a haphazard gaggle of poorly placed bunkers, trenches that meandered off into nowhere, and observation posts without a line of sight through the forest. Koch also came up with one of the war's most absurd inventions: a concrete tube two feet in diameter, sunk into the earth so it could allow enemy tanks to pass; a man would then open its lid to spray enemy infantry with machine-gun fire. The test of battle soon showed the problems: the man inside the tube was terrified, he had no real contact with the outside world once he'd gone underground, and any sort of artillery strike on his position led to shattered concrete and the grisliest wounds imaginable. The infantry called it the *Koch-Topf* ("cooking pot").[69]

Lacking manpower, materiel, and suitable fortifications, Army Group A cracked apart on the first day of the Soviet offensive (within hours, actually). As always, the Soviets staggered the start. Coordinated front-level offensives on this continental scale require more than a starter's pistol. Local variations in weather, the ground, and the state of preparations can lead to delays. In previous weeks, the Stavka had been the recipient of urgent requests from the western powers to advance the date of the offensive, scheduled originally for January 16. Stalin had obliged. Indeed, there was nothing he seemed to enjoy more than advancing a starting date on his commanders.[70] The result was a certain amount of last-second scrambling that some commanders handled more smoothly than others:

January 12th	1st Ukrainian Front (Konev)
January 13th	1st Baltic Front (Bagramyan)
	2nd Byelorussian Front (Rokossovsky)
	3rd Byelorussian Front (Cherniakhovsky)
January 14th	1st Byelorussian Front (Zhukov)

At any rate, staggering the attacks brought a benefit—as the Soviets well knew by now. With German field commanders confused as to the location of the Soviet *Schwerpunkt*, they were uncertain or tentative in their reactions and often inserted their meager reserves prematurely or into the wrong place. The impact of receiving one massive blow after another also had a paralyzing effect on the High Command, including both Hitler and the OKH alike.

The Vistula-Oder operation, then, began as Marshal Konev's show, with Zhukov's front following two days later. Konev's assault out of the Baranow-Sandomierz bridgehead married brute force to a sophisticated tactical approach, and it remains a model of modern offensive operations.[71] The offensive opened with a brief but monstrous 15-minute bombardment at 4:45 A.M., with 300 guns per kilometer arranged quite literally hub to hub, targeting 4th Panzer Army opposite the bridgehead. Joining in at 5:00 A.M. were the "forward battalions," probing the German front for weak spots and driving ahead 600 meters into the German defensive zone over the next few hours, occupying the German frontline trenches and even parts of the second. Most of the defending German infantry thought that they were facing the main attack by now, and they came up from their bunkers, where they'd been waiting out the Soviet bombardment, to engage the Soviet assault troops. That decision was fatal, leaving them open and vulnerable to the big one: an all-guns-at-once, 107-minute plastering of every worthwhile target at and behind the German front.[72] Soon the entire battlefield was a seething mass of high explosives, deadly chunks of shrapnel, and clods of frozen dirt, covered in a thick, choking, acrid smoke. A whole series of direct hits destroyed the headquarters of 4th Panzer Army, and the commander, a shaken General Gräser, might as well have been back in Berlin for all the control he was able to exert on the battle. And now, just before noon, it was the turn of the main body of Soviet infantry, moving up in 150-meter-wide sectors deliberately left untouched by the bombardment. Within hours they had penetrated as deep as five miles, and Konev hadn't even played his trump card: the more than 2,000 tanks of the 3rd Guards and 4th Tank Armies. They came up at 2:00 P.M., passing through their own infantry and driving deep, smashing German defenses beyond hope of repair. By nightfall, they had torn a 25-mile-wide gash and in some sectors had penetrated up to 20 miles deep.

Through it all 4th Panzer Army hadn't reacted and, indeed, hadn't been able to react. Like a patient lying on an operating table, the initiative was out of its hands. The formation in the front line, XXXXVIII Panzer Corps, had three divisions stretched very thinly, and the opening Soviet attack had vaporized it. Analysts who have studied German dispositions carefully note that the reserve Panzer formations of 4th Panzer Army (the 16th and 17th Panzer Divisions belonging to General Walther Nehring's XXIV Panzer Corps) were deployed too close to the front line. The decision belonged to Hitler, suspicious as ever of his commanders' operational intentions and willingness to retreat. Located just a few thousand yards behind the *Hauptkampflinie*, however, Nehring's corps suffered mightily in the opening bombardment, especially in terms of command, control, and radio facilities. Within an hour, Nehring was out of communication with his divisions, and as much as General Gräser, he was commanding blindly for the entire opening sequence. He finally received orders in the late afternoon to close up his two divisions to the town of Kielce—dead center in the path of the onrushing Soviet tank armies. His signal troops had restored communications with his divisions by now, but it hardly mattered: the orders were already obsolete. Soviet armor had already overrun the assembly areas for his Panzers, catching one Tiger tank battalion being refueled out in the open and destroying it completely.

The two divisions struggle gamely toward Kielce in disconnected and isolated fragments, and the commander of 17th Panzer Division, Colonel Albert Brux, was wounded in a Soviet bombardment and taken prisoner.

Not that it mattered. Soviet armored spearheads had already taken Kielce. Nehring's corps never did manage to launch a counterattack. Rather, it found itself fighting for its life against superior forces from the start. Soon, 4th Panzer Army had ceased to exist as a military formation. It had degenerated into an onrushing stream of men and vehicles, along with thousands of ethnic German refugees, all heading west and northwest, desperately trying to get to safety. This almost always meant off-road movement, however, since Soviet armor was prowling all the good highways. In the course of the first few days, small groups of survivors from the neighboring XXXXII Corps and XXXXVIII Panzer Corps coalesced around the remnants of Nehring's Panzer corps to form *Gruppe Nehring*—all that was left of the army.

Nehring was a tested commander and managed to form the motley command into a "roving *Kessel*" (*wandernden Kessel*). Surrounded on all sides by Soviet units heading west at top speed and barely thinking it worthwhile to stop and fight a pitched battle with German forces who were already obviously defeated, under constant air attack, and low on supplies and ammunition, Nehring's little band (fewer than 10,000 men all told) managed to thread the needle again and again over the next ten days. Unbeknownst to him, he had hit the seam between the two Soviet fronts, Zhukov to his north and Konev to his south. Moving mainly by night, hiding the tanks and vehicles among the houses and barns of this rural land, Nehring avoided Soviet concentrations, launching the occasional attack only when absolutely necessary and crashing through roadblocks. Kielce to Piotrków, Lask to the crossing over the Warthe River at Sieradz, and finally crossing the Oder River to safety at Glogau: *Gruppe Nehring* had traveled nearly 200 miles to safety. Like the *Rückkämpfer* of 1944, Nehring had beaten the odds—but his saga is impressive only within the context of yet another miserable German operational collapse.[73]

On January 14, Zhukov's 1st Byelorussian Front joined in the offensive. Coming out of the Magnuszew bridgehead, Zhukov meted out the same punishment to German 9th Army as Konev had to 4th Panzer. Here, too, the Soviet commander displayed finesse along with crushing strength. He opened with a furious 25-minute barrage and followed it up with a massive reconnaissance actions. It was of such size, scope, and ferocity (thirty-two reinforced rifle battalions and twenty-five additional rifle companies to reduce German strongpoints) that most of the German defenders believed once again that the main attack had begun. Soon they were falling back, abandoning the front line and then the second. A simultaneous attack out of the Pulawy bridgehead had equal success, and by the end of the day Zhukov's armor was 20 miles inside the German defenses. The commander of 9th Army, General Lüttwitz, inserted his Panzer reserves with impressive dispatch, and 19th and 25th Panzer Divisions duly entered the fray on the first day. Given the collapse of the defenses in front of both bridgeheads, however, Lüttwitz had no choice but to split the divisions, directing 19th Panzer toward the Pulawy bridgehead and the 25th against Magnuszew. Here, too, the impression was not so much of being defeated as simply being swallowed up, and both Panzer divisions were soon reeling back with heavy losses. The next day, Zhukov directed 47th Army to begin its envelopment of Warsaw from the north, while 61st Army and 1st Polish Army drove up from the south. A few days of fighting and it was over: German troops evacuated Warsaw on January 17, and the victorious Polish formations were parading through their liberated capital.

With both 4th Panzer and 9th Armies in tatters, and both Soviet fronts pushing hard, the Vistula-Oder Offensive entered its travelogue phase. Warsaw began the parade, and now the cities and towns fell in a rush: Kraków and Częstochowa to Konev, Łódź to Zhukov. While there was the occasional skirmish, this was top-speed movement, limited only by logistical constraints and supply, ammunition, and fuel. By January 31, the two Soviet fronts had overrun the entire vast Posen Bulge, known as the *Reichsgau Wartheland* or *Warthegau* during Nazi occupation. On January 12—the very night that Soviet forces had smashed the German 4th Panzer Army—the provincial Gauleiter, Arthur Greiser, had promised the local population that victory was certain, that "the Bolshevist flood would bleed itself to death on the borders of the Warthegau," and that "the Bolshevist marauders (*Soldateska*) would not set a single foot on our land."[74] But these had been empty words, and Greiser knew it. Sitting on a flat, featureless plain, he had done nothing to fortify the *Warthegau*, and only very late in the game, on January 20, did he approve an evacuation of the civilian population. While desperate families—women, children, and the elderly— loaded themselves and their possessions onto wagons and sleighs and scurried in the freezing cold, Greiser had a berth on a safe private train to Frankfurt on the Oder, one of many despicable flights carried out by party officials in those last days. Fighting an overmatched military and an utterly negligent civilian authority, the Soviet campaign had been one of the most successful and dramatic in history. Elements of the 1st Tank Army, part of Zhukov's front, were already on the Oder River near Küstrin and Frankfurt, having lunged nearly 250 miles in just over two weeks. Konev's spearheads likewise had driven deep into Silesia, reaching the Oder and seizing sizable bridgeheads on the left bank of the river at Steinau and Ohlau, northwest and southeast of the provincial capital, Breslau. Silesia, Prussia's ur-conquest from two hundred years before, now stood under threat. The Wehrmacht's losses in all this had been colossal: no fewer than 300,000 men. "The catastrophe at the front was coming down on us like an avalanche," as Guderian put it.[75]

Under Guderian's continual urging, Hitler did finally order reinforcements to the front: five divisions and a corps headquarters from the Courland Pocket, the *Grossdeutschland* Panzer Corps from East Prussia. The former involved evacuation by sea and would take time, if it happened at all. The latter had minimal impact. *Grossdeutschland* began to detrain at Łódź on January 16 and immediately sent one of its divisions, the Hermann Göring *Fallschirmjäger* Panzer Division, into action east of the city. But the division had massive Soviet forces hurtling at it from all directions and had no choice but to fall back. Łódź itself fell to elements of Chuikov's 8th Army—largely consisting of infantry but moving just as rapidly as the tank armies—on January 19. Subsequent Soviet attacks caught the German trains carrying much of the *Grossdeutschland* Corps's equipment and destroyed them. Within days of arriving at the front, the corps commander, General Dietrich von Saucken, saw his force reduced to the size of a battlegroup. And like Nehring, he sound found himself surrounded and in command of a wandering cauldron (*Gruppe Saucken*), heading south and west toward the Warthe. Nehring's group was all that was left of 4th Panzer Army, Saucken's the remnant of the 9th.

While the front disintegrated, not just between the Vistula and the Oder but in East Prussia as well, business as usual went on at Führer Headquarters. The same interminable situation conferences took place. Guderian and Hitler continued to argue over the same trivial particulars of operations, administration, and personnel, all of which the general describes in detail in his memoirs. They even redesignated their army groups, hardly the most pressing need at the moment:

Old		*New*
Army Group A (Oder Front)	=======>	Army Group Center

Army Group Center =======>	Army Group North
(East Prussia)	
Army Group North =======>	Army Group Courland
(Courland Pocket)	

And in his by now traditional response to disaster at the front, Hitler fired his generals in droves. General Harpe, the commander of Army Group A, got the axe first, followed by General Lüttwitz, commander of 9th Army. The ostensible reason was the hasty evacuation of Warsaw—yet another fallen city that Hitler had ordered held to the last man. After the fall of the fortress complex of Lötzen in East Prussia on January 23 essentially without a fight, the dismissals gained momentum. General Reinhardt, commanding Army Group Center, went next, followed by General Hossbach of 4th Army. The new army group commanders were Field Marshal Ferdinand Schörner, perhaps Hitler's most fanatic servant, at Army Group A (now redesignated Army Group Center) and General Lothar Rendulic for Army Group Center (now Army Group North).

Their appointments continued a long-standing devolution within Hitler's marshalate. Like Field Marshal Model in the west, neither Schörner nor Rendulic could make a claim to any particular operational brilliance or innovative style of leadership. Both were loyal to the core, however. Schörner, in particular, viewed terrorizing the men underneath him as a legitimate tool of National Socialist command, executed thousands of his own soldiers to keep the others in the line, and would remain with his command until the end of the war. Rendulic managed to touch all the command bases: Army Group Courland, Army Group North, back to Courland, and then Army Group South until the end of the war (with one last redesignation at Army Group *Ostmark*), all in the course of four months. They were men upon whom the Führer could rely: ruthless, grim commanders who were determined to throw their men into the fire by the hundreds of thousands for as long as Hitler felt they should.

Death in the West: The Battle of the Ruhr Pocket

A powerful coalition defeated the Wehrmacht in World War II, particularly on the Western Front. Occasionally, however, the fighting boiled down to a one-on-one affair—and so it was in the Ruhr in 1945. (See Map 9.3.)

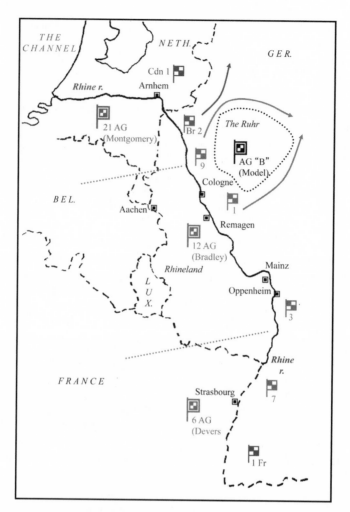

Map 9.3 Annihilation: Encirclement in the Ruhr (March–April 1945)

Let us begin by comparing the character arc of the two adversaries. The German Wehrmacht had dominated the fighting early in the war by rewriting the book on mechanized operations, but it had gone downhill ever since. By 1945, losses were soaring, replacements weren't keeping up, and second-rate *Volksgrenadier* and third-rate *Volkssturm* formations formed an increasing percentage of the order of battle. Indeed, the Wehrmacht wouldn't have been in the field at all were it not for non-German foreigners. They ran the gamut: entire allied field armies (Romanians, Hungarians, Italians, and Finns); smaller volunteer "legions" recruited from the occupied countries (France, Belgium, the Netherlands, the Baltic states) or from enemy POWs (many of the Soviet Union's Baltic and Caucasian peoples, for example, Armenians and Georgians, Azeris and Turkmen); and finally the *Hiltswilligen* or *Hiwis*, hundreds of thousands of Soviet auxiliary volunteers who formed and manned much of the Wehrmacht's logistical network.[76] German weapons—Tiger tanks and Me-262 jet aircraft—might be quite advanced, but the men at the front rarely saw enough of them to make a difference. Field Marshal Albert Kesselring, appointed German supreme commander in the west (OB-West) in March 1945, once complained that leading German armies this late in the war was like "being a pianist asked to play a Beethoven sonata before a large audience on an old, rickety, out of tune piano," and for all the self-serving and self-exculpatory pathos, he was telling the truth.[77]

The US Army, by contrast, joined the war late and stumbled in its debuts in North Africa, Sicily, and Italy. That last campaign, in particular, exposed grave weaknesses in command, maneuver, and combined arms. It had come of age during the great campaign of 1944, which was based around a cadre of hard-hitting and aggressive corps commanders. By 1945, the Americans were as seasoned and professional as anyone in the field. Their material support—weapons, fuel, ammunition, food—was lavish, and US officials liked to brag that the GI was "the best-paid and best-fed soldier" of all time.[78] Bristling with modern equipment and vehicles—tanks, halftracks, self-propelled artillery—the US Army was the most mobile in history—and one of the most lethal. If an American unit found a seam in enemy defenses, it could slash through like lightning, and once in contact it could hurl more brute firepower than any force in history. The amount of artillery the Americans rained down on their enemies never ceased to shock the Germans, who had to be more selective about what they obliterated. Finally, US commanders had a truly Olympian weapon upon which they could call: wave after wave of fighters and fighter-bombers like the P-47 Thunderbolt and P-51 Mustang. US airpower made it nearly impossible for the Germans to move by day.[79] In March, all these advantages came together in the greatest American victory of World War II. The battle of the Ruhr Pocket has never won the attention it deserves, but it was something rare in military history. World War II was messy and unpredictable, and plans rarely worked out in the way the generals had conceived them. In the Ruhr, however, the US Army lived the dream: establishing full-spectrum dominance to win a decisive victory at minimal cost.[80]

The Western Allies were a bit slow off the mark in 1945. The supreme commander, General Dwight D. Eisenhower, had a huge force under his command, some 5 million men in three army groups: 21st in the north, consisting of British, Canadian, and US forces under Field Marshal Bernard Law Montgomery; the all-American 12th in the center under General Omar Bradley; and 6th in the south, with US and French forces under General Jacob L. Devers. But January saw the Allies still trying to shake off the after-effects of the great German offensive in the Ardennes Forest—the Battle of the Bulge. Even after they righted themselves and resumed the advance, the going was slow, with a month of gritty fighting needed to clear the densely populated Rhineland and close up to the great river itself. Allied armies were still 300 miles from Berlin, however, and final victory seemed a long way off.

The Rhine was a serious obstacle. River-crossing operations are highly complex by nature, requiring careful planning, tight cooperation between infantry, engineers, and artillery, and time to prepare. But in one of the war's most dramatic moments, the looming barrier suddenly vanished. As General John W. Leonard's 9th Armored Division (a component of US III Corps under General John Milliken, part of General Courtney Hodges's 1st Army) approached the Rhine at Remagen on March 7, the Americans were astonished to see that the Ludendorff Bridge over the river was still standing. American tanks rushed it just as the Germans set off explosives. The bridge lifted off its foundations, then settled back down again—intact. Suddenly and incredibly, the Allies were over the Rhine. "Hot dog, Courtney!" Bradley responded when Hodges told him the news. "This will bust him wide open." Within the hour, Hodges was pushing every man and vehicle he could across the bridge, forming a powerful bridgehead on the eastern bank of the Rhine.

The Germans' loss of the bridge at Remagen is one of the most famous episodes of the war, a seemingly miraculous piece of good luck for the enemy.[81] But a closer inspection tells a different story. Like all the Rhine bridges, Remagen had its own dedicated defensive force, a special staff under General Joachim von Kortzfleisch and a small mixed forced of infantry and engineers. Their primary task was to defend the bridge or, failing that, to destroy it. But the Rhine was still a rear area at this point in the war. Instead of sheltering behind the mighty river, German armies in the west were fighting well in front of it, defending themselves along smaller watercourses like the Roer and the Ahr. Even the smallest tactical retreat required permission from the top, and no one was allowed to prepare rear-area defensive works on the fighting bank of the Rhine. A general retreat across the Rhine—an operation involving millions of soldiers and tens of thousands of vehicles—required just as much planning as an assault across it. It was a strategic redeployment of the first order, not a minor tactical maneuver to be improvised in a day or two.

And therein lay the problem. Ordered to defend every last village west of the Rhine, the German army was dug in, flatfooted, and no longer capable of maneuver. All it would take was for one those highly mobile, fully motorized Allied armies to crack open a seam and it would be full speed ahead to the Rhine. That had been the US 9th Armored Division. And once the 9th arrived in front of Remagen, it found not a prepared defensive position but merely a river—plus a great deal of confusion on the far side as the Germans frantically tried to improvise their defenses or blow the bridge. But given the speed of the US advance, it is not surprising that they found a big bridge rigged with an insufficient explosive charge, with wiring that probably could have used a few more days to install and test. So the Allies had gotten lucky, certainly. But if it hadn't happened at Remagen, it might well have happened somewhere else.

Nevertheless, the loss of the bridge at Remagen led to a furious reaction from Hitler—and not just from Hitler. The final year of the war was a time in which a soldier of the Wehrmacht might be executed for any number of activities under the general heading of "cowardice" (*Feigheit*) or "criminal neglect of duty" (*Dienstpflichtverletzung*). After receiving a preliminary report, the Führer ordered the arrest of four officers involved in the action: Majors Hans Scheller, Herbert Strobel, and August Kraft, as well as Lieutenant Karl-Heinz Peters. Certainly none of the four had acted particularly heroically. Scheller, for example, was the officer in charge at the bridge on March 7. He reacted slowly to the onrush of the Americans, failed to hold them up on the western bank as originally planned, and was sheltering in a nearby tunnel rather than supervising on site while engineers under his command tried to blow the bridge. That was enough for Hitler to dispatch a "flying tribunal" (*fliegendes Standgericht*), essentially a drumhead court-martial, to Remagen. Field Marshal Walter Model of Army Group B, the field commander most directly concerned with the affair, now intervened, however. He did so not to save the lives of his men, as one might expect, but rather to try the accused himself—and to order their execution. The trials took place on March 13–14 in Model's presence, without benefit of attorney or ever a stenographer, and Model had all four men shot on March 14.[82]

Getting over the Rhine allowed the US Army to reopen mobile operations. Blocking the American path was Model's Army Group B, with 5th Panzer Army on his right and 15th Army on the left. The 5th Panzer was defending the Ruhr, one of the Reich's last remaining heavy industrial centers, home to the massive Krupp Steel Works at Essen, while 15th Army was hastily redeploying against the expanding US bridgehead at Remagen. For all the troubles the Germans were having by this point in the war, those two armies were still strong enough to cause trouble—and mass casualties—to any attacker foolish enough to launch a frontal assault. Seizing the Ruhr and striking a blow at German heavy industry had been part of the Allied operational plan even before D-Day. But fighting *through* the Ruhr—with all its cities, factories, and millions of civilians—had real bloodbath potential and could easily turn into a super-Stalingrad, an urban battle on an unimaginable scale. For that very reason, Eisenhower's plan had always been to encircle German forces in the Ruhr, not blast through them frontally. Often maligned as a somewhat dull, broad-front strategist—keeping all his armies moving forward in lockstep—Ike could spot a battlefield opportunity—and he got one at Remagen.

His operational plan called for a classic pincer maneuver by two armies. Hodges's 1st Army would break out of the Remagen bridgehead and drive east. Meanwhile, 90 miles north, US 9th Army under General Walter H. Simpson would cross the Rhine at Wesel, part of Montgomery's multiarmy crossing operation code-named Operation Plunder. Once over the river, the 9th, too, would motor east. Essentially, the Americans would have one army on the Ruhr's northern flank and another on its southern. At this point, both armies would wheel inward, turn toward one another, and link up behind German Army Group B to encircle and destroy it. The plan was risky, since the two US armies would be out of contact with one another as they came forward. It relied on surprise, speed, and the immobility of German forces due to fuel shortages and Allied air attacks. Speed was essential. No one in the world was better than Model at stamping a reserve force out of nothing and whipping together a fighting force out of infantry replacements, march battalions, and rear-area clerks. If he managed to do so now, he could make a great deal of trouble for Hodges and Simpson.

Every plan has its risks, however, and the Allies had calculated this one expertly. Allied intelligence had drawn a remarkably detailed and accurate portrait of the German defenders by now. In the south, Hodges would target German LXVII Corps under General Otto-Maximilian Hitzfeld, holding the left (southern) flank of the 15th Army. Hitzfeld had been through hard fighting in the Rhineland, then had been the corps commander responsible for losing Remagen. His corps was understrength, undersupplied, and especially underfueled and had largely ceased daily reconnaissance patrols—a sure sign that élan was ebbing. In the north, however, 9th Army was certain to move more slowly. Hodges was coming out of a bridgehead over the Rhine, but Simpson's forces were not yet over the river, and he was serving under Montgomery, a congenitally cautious commander who liked to line things up and take his time. Moreover, the terrain east of Wesel was marshy and wooded, and reconnaissance flights had just identified a German Panzer division (the 116th under General Siegfried von Waldenburg) in reserve in this sector. Indeed, Montgomery had already decided to expand his crossing operation to include a two-division airborne drop, Operation Varsity, to disrupt the defenses and keep German mobile reserves from getting to the front.

Montgomery launched Operation Plunder (now Plunder-Varsity) on March 23, kicking things off with a massive, 4-hour, 4,000-gun artillery barrage, followed by airborne drops by British 6th and US 17th Airborne Divisions. Although the parachute troops took heavy casualties, the crossing forces got over the Rhine against weak resistance and formed a bridgehead on the far bank. Simpson's US 9th Army now prepared for a breakout offensive to the east, with 8th Armored and 2nd Armored Divisions probing for weak spots in the German line. As predicted, the going was slow, and 9th Army took a full week to chew through the Germans and the terrain, aided every step of the way by heavy US artillery fire and nonstop attacks by tactical airpower. Not until March 29 did Simpson break through into the clear, heading east.

While 9th Army was fighting forward, 1st Army at Remagen put on one of the greatest American shows of the war.[83] Hodges had three heavy corps arrayed abreast north to south: VII under General J. Lawton "Lightning Joe" Collins; III (General James Van Fleet); and V (General Clarence R. Huebner)—all crowded into a 35-mile strip on the eastern bank of the Rhine. All three corps were bulging with manpower and equipment, and, as always, firepower support was extravagant. The attack opened before dawn on March 25 and simply vaporized the German defenders. Even the weather cooperated, offering a crystal-clear day that allowed XIX Tactical Air Command to roam the skies and swoop down at will on the hapless Germans below. By noon, all three US corps had made a clean breakthrough out of the Remagen bridgehead, advancing 12 miles the first day and 20 miles on the second. The pace was frenetic, and US infantry often hitched a ride on the nearest Sherman tank to keep up rather than wait for their trucks. Already, US columns were taking the surrender of thousands of Germans, including 17,000 by III Corps on March 26 alone. A few German units attempted to launch counterattacks, but US momentum smothered them before they got started, and most GIs probably never even noticed them.

Onward came the Americans, reaching Giessen and Marburg on day four (March 28). With 1st Army already 80 miles from the starting line, the time had come to make its great wheel to the north, cutting across the rear of Army Group B, linking up with 9th Army, and encircling the entire German force in the Ruhr. The commander of 3rd Armored Division, General Maurice Rose, assembled a task force under Lieutenant Colonel Walter B. Richardson and gave a simple order. "Just go like hell," he ordered.[84] The objective was Paderborn, 60 miles due north.

The ride of Task Force Richardson was an epic in miniature. Slashing north, firing on the run, and cutting across columns of German stragglers, Richardson rode his column hard. He eluded roadblocks where he could and blasted through the others, making 45 miles in one day. But when the task force reached Brilon, 15 miles south of Paderborn, the column halted while Richardson's exhausted force did a thorough reconnaissance of a champagne warehouse. Next morning, his groggy crews finally met actual German resistance, an ad hoc battalion thrown together by cadets from an SS training center, supported by sixty Tiger and Panther tanks. A tough scrap ensued over the next two days, and when General Rose came up to supervise the fight on March 30 he was killed when his personal reconnaissance column—two jeeps, a motorcycle, and an armored car—had the bad luck to bump into German Tiger tanks from the 507th Battalion. Nevertheless, US forces kept coming up, sidestepping SS defenses at Paderborn and heading west toward Lippstadt. As always by this point of the war, the Germans could not keep up with American speed.

At Lippstadt, the lead elements of the two US armies—the 9th coming over from Wesel and the 1st coming up from Remagen—made contact. It was April 1, Easter Sunday, just after noon. The pincers snapped shut—and the US Army had its greatest encirclement of the war. Model's Army Group B—5th Panzer and 15th Armies, including seven corps and nineteen divisions, with all their support troops and headquarters—was surrounded, trapped in an egg-shaped pocket 30 miles by 75 miles in diameter. Enclosed in the ring were no fewer than twenty-six generals and even a naval officer, Admiral Werner Scheer, commander of Defense District I in Essen.

While the Americans maneuvered, Model and his army group sat still. Since 1945, historians have drawn up a litany of reasons why. Half-strength divisions, low fuel, Allied command of the air, morale collapse among the rank and file, and of course, the refusal of the Führer, Adolf Hitler, to countenance even the smallest tactical retreat: Model was caught in a perfect storm of military disaster. But one other fact deserves mention: the blistering tempo of the American rush had forced German headquarters on all levels to flee their posts or dive for cover. By the second day, Model had lost contact with the commander of his 15th Army, General Gustav-Adolf von Zangen, whom he presumed captured or killed. Zangen was neither, but he was equally unable to raise Model by radio. Model appointed another commander and ordered him to launch a counterattack with units from 15th Army—at the precise moment that Zangen was trying to form his stragglers into a new defensive position to the east. No wonder so many German soldiers were confused. Inside the pocket, Model himself first wanted to fight on, then gradually came to see the hopelessness. From outside, the High Command in Berlin demanded that Model stay put and defend Fortress Ruhr. Hitler promised to send a newly formed army, the 12th under General Walther Wenck, to relieve the Ruhr and hinted that new wonder weapons were on the way that would turn the tide of battle. But it soon became clear to Model that neither 12th Army nor miracle weapons were going to show up anytime soon.

During the week following Easter, the Americans solidified the ring around Army Group B, placing four corps along the perimeter. All four immediately launched concentric drives against the outmanned and unsupplied enemy, herding the Germans into a smaller and smaller space, packing them together, and making them an even more lucrative target for US firepower. By April 11, the pocket was half as large as it had been on April 1; by April 14, US attacks toward the town of Hagen had sliced the pocket in half again. Here and there, German troops were already surrendering, often under the urging of the local civilian population. The locals soon learned that any sign of resistance—a German sniper shot, an infantry skirmish, or a random mortar round— seemed to madden the "Amis." The result was almost always the same: a hailstorm of US fire flattened the town and killed German soldiers and civilians alike. Artillery units attached to US XVI Corps on the northwestern edge of the pocket, for example, fired no fewer than 259,000 rounds in fourteen days. Assuming that the other three corps kept pace, American guns may well have fired a million shells during the two-week battle.

To the people of the Ruhr, the Americans seemed to arrive out of the blue. The good burghers of Gesseln, near Paderborn, were attending a delayed Easter Mass on Tuesday, April 3, when they heard the clanking and roaring of engines in the streets of their little village. "Herr Vicar, they are here," a woman whispered to the priest, "they are already here." At that very moment a 76mm cannon from an American Sherman tank poked through the church door, trained directly at the altar. US soldiers defused the situation by entering the church, kneeling, and praying the Mass with the parishioners.[85]

Things didn't always end so happily. The battle wrought enormous physical destruction. Factories closed and production ceased, as did the distribution of food and goods to the region's cities and suburbs. Electricity, water, and sewage all broke down in this densely populated area—a recipe for disease if the battle dragged on. The Ruhr's prosperous middle classes rushed to their local banks to pull out their *Reichmarks*, currency that would soon be worthless. Meanwhile, bands of Russian and Polish laborers from the Nazi empire roamed the countryside, pillaging what they could. When to run up the white flag and surrender to the Americans became a crucial question for German civilians. Doing so too early meant falling afoul of the Nazi authorities who were demanding a fight to the finish; doing so too late could mean a violent introduction to the American way of war. All too often, the local Nazi bigwig called upon his townsmen to fight to the death and then fled just before the enemy attacked.

On April 14, with the pocket torn in two and German units running out of ammunition and food, mass surrenders began. The 116th Panzer Division, for example, had neither a single serviceable tank nor an artillery round left to its name. Thousands and then tens of thousands of German soldiers responded to US loudspeaker calls to surrender or simply made for the nearest US unit, white flag or handkerchief in hand. The number of prisoners exceeded all expectations, amounting to 317,000 men, twice the US intelligence estimate. The human herd rolled in, held in POW cages that were little more than open fields with inadequate food and facilities. *Rheinwiesenlager*, the Germans called them—"Rhine meadow camps"—stretched as far as the eye could see.[86]

One man didn't surrender, however. Field Marshal Model, crushed by the totality of the defeat, as well as the news that the Soviet government had listed him as a war criminal, was growing more despondent by the hour. "What is left for a defeated general?" he asked his chief of staff, General Carl Wagener, on April 17. "In ancient times they took poison." Like Hitler, Model had often complained about the "cowardice" of Field Marshal Friedrich Paulus in letting himself be taken prisoner by the Soviets at Stalingrad. "A field marshal does not become a prisoner," Model had muttered. "Such a thing is just not possible." By April 19, Model was on the run from the Americans, a fugitive commander without an army. He was sitting in a forest clearing, "repeatedly stung by mosquitos," when a radio broadcast came on the air. Josef Goebbels always spoke to the German people on the eve of Hitler's birthday. Model listened on a portable radio as Goebbels condemned those who waved "the white flag of surrender." Only "unshakeable faith" in Hitler would do now. "We stand by him as he has stood by us in Germanic loyalty," the doctor proclaimed. "He shall remain for us what he is and always was: Our Hitler!"[87]

Something snapped in Model as he heard that last line.[88] Was it the scales falling from the field marshal's eyes? A guilty conscience for giving up the fight? Or just the depression of defeat? He began to rage:

And those are the men one has trusted, blindly trusted, closing one's eyes to retain their trust. I had blindly taken the responsibility for compliance with soldierly duty in a just war. A just war led by those frauds? And how many sacrifices have I demanded from my soldiers only to serve these swine?[89]

Certainly, no one in the officer corps had served Hitler more faithfully. Two days later, the field marshal took leave of his aides in a beautiful copse of tall oaks outside of Duisburg and shot himself with his Walther 6.35mm service pistol.

10

The Last Stand

Introduction: And the Two Become One

The two-front war (*Zweifrontenkrieg*) had long been the German strategic nightmare. Planning to avoid one—and to fight one successfully if necessary—lay at the foundation of the German way of war. Fighting on interior lines, taking advantage of the central position, fighting *Bewegungskrieg*, achieving a *Kesselschlacht:* as we have seen, these were the keys to German success. German planners had not simply chosen these methods from a menu of options. As the power in the middle of Europe (*Macht in die Mitte*), surrounded on all sides by powerful neighbors and occupying a relatively flat plain, Prussia-Germany had to make a virtue out of necessity.[1] German commanders had to identify the most dangerous enemy pressing in on them, concentrate against him while leaving other, less threatened portions of the front weak, and destroy the enemy in a climactic battle as rapidly as possible. A two-front war could, under the right circumstances, become a manageable series of one-front wars.[2]

But what happened if this approach failed? What if—despite superior aggression and high mobility and the successful application of mission command—*Bewegungskrieg* failed to produce victory? It was, after all, an operational technique, not a politically grounded strategy—and only strategy can win a war. What if, for example, the enemy state whose army you had just smashed refused to come to terms? What if your adversaries were so well coordinated that they were able to offer material support to one another? What if one of them took advantage of your deployment against another to launch a great offensive precisely where *you* were weak? What if your multiple adversaries began to press you so closely that you could not move, or if (as in 1945) they had a technological advantage—airpower—that rendered you immobile?

In 1945, the Wehrmacht had to contemplate all these thorny questions. Driven back from all sides, compressed into a smaller and smaller fighting area, bereft of fuel and air cover, drafting men who clearly had no business being in uniform, the German army could no longer maneuver effectively. Once in contact with the foe, it didn't fight all that well, either. The nature of modern industrialized warfare and the sheer size of the forces involved meant heavy casualties for everyone concerned, of course, but certainly not enough to reverse the ultimate verdict of the war. The Prussian army had invented the *Kesselschlacht*, and the German army had later patented it in a series of highly successful campaigns. Now the war had turned the entire country into one vast *Kessel*. The two fronts had become one.

In the first four months of 1945, the Wehrmacht made its last stand. However, unlike many backs-to-the-wall episodes—which we often steep in tales of personal heroism and the imperishable glory of defending hearth and home—the last stand of 1945 was hardly what we would describe as epic. The Allies came on inexorably, and nowhere could the tattered German army stop them. Civilians and soldiers alike died in the hundreds of thousands, and millions more found themselves on the road as homeless refugees, or "displaced persons."[3] Given the criminal nature of the Hitler regime and the taint it left on Germany's armed forces, it is unlikely that any future poet will choose to immortalize this fight to the finish in verse, or to provide this downfall with its "Dulce et Decorum Est."[4]

It was nearly over. "You know what would be practical?" Berliners joked sardonically in February 1945 as the ring around Germany was growing tighter. "If you could just take the S-Bahn from the Eastern to the Western Front."[5]

It was a bitter joke, yes, but two months later, with the city itself under siege, a variant was already in circulation—this one with an even sharper edge: "You know what would be practical? If you could *run* from the Eastern to the Western Front."[6] Not a few soldiers of the Wehrmacht were about to test that hypothesis.

The Holdup

The Vistula-Oder campaign had ended almost as suddenly as it had begun. As Zhukov's 1st Byelorussian Front and Konev's 1st Ukrainian Front hurtled toward the Oder, they encountered stiffening resistance on their flanks. For Konev, the threat came from his left (southern) flank, from German forces in Silesia; for Zhukov, it came from Pomerania on his right (northern) flank. In the first weeks of February,

German garrisons were resisting Zhukov's advance stubbornly inside a number of older fortresses like Thorn (Toruń), Schneidemühl (Pila), Deutsch Krone (Wałcz), and Arnswalde (Choszczno). As always, Soviet fronts attempting to fight deep battle weakened a bit more each day, as each forward bound took them farther from their base of supply. Konev, too, found the going much slower the more deeply he advanced into the urban and industrial districts of Silesia.[7]

Moreover, a new German army group appeared on Zhukov's maps: Army Group Vistula, assembled in Pomerania on January 24. The new formation was a typical late-war creation, made up of broken units from the Vistula Front (remnants of General Busse's 9th Army), as well as from East Prussia (the 2nd Army of General Walther Weiss), along with a newly formed 11th SS Panzer Army under *SS-Obergruppenführer* Felix Steiner. All these formations were thrown together hastily and were vastly understrength, and the entire army group barely possessed the fighting strength of a corps. Guderian and Hitler wrangled over the commander, with Guderian recommending Field Marshal Maximilian Weichs. The Wehrmacht currently had two army group staffs in the Balkans (Weichs's Army Group F and General Alexander Löhr's Army Group E), and Weichs seemed the logical choice—a man with "soldierly" qualities who was "clever, upright, and brave," as Guderian put it. "If anyone could master the situation, Weichs could."[8] Being soldierly was the last thing Hitler cared about by this point in the war, and he instead proposed Himmler, then commanding Army Group Upper Rhine in the wind-down phase of Operation *Nordwind*.[9] Weichs, the Führer said, "made a tired impression" and "didn't appear up to the mission," which was how he felt about the entire officer corps by now.[10] Himmler was hopeless as a commander, but just as in Alsace, he was able to terrorize enough officials and civilians to fill the ranks and to scrounge up scarce supplies, even if he hadn't the faintest idea of what to do with either one. (See Map 10.1.)

At any rate, Soviet reconnaissance patrols detected increasing activity out of Pomerania, and Zhukov had to detach troops from his forward drive to protect his northern flank. That task had originally been the mission of his neighbor to the right, Rokossovsky's 2nd Byelorussian Front. Tough fighting in East Prussia had diverted Rokossovsky to the north, however, leaving Zhukov's long flank open and vulnerable. On February 15, 1st SS Panzer Army actually launched a counteroffensive south from the Stargard region. Operation *Sonnenwende* ("Solstice") looked impressive enough on the map—a three-pronged advance with every division and mechanized formation that the Germans could

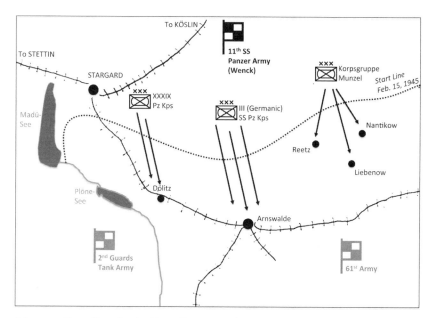

Map 10.1 Last Gasp in the East: Operation *Sonnenwende* (February 1945)

scrounge.[11] The quality was mixed, including the 281st Infantry Division, a converted security formation just evacuated from Courland, and the 4th SS *Polizei Panzergrenadier* Division, which despite its name had almost no heavy weapons. Much of the army's fighting strength lay with the III (Germanic) SS Panzer Corps under General Martin Unrein. The corps consisted of three non-German volunteer divisions of the Waffen-SS, recruited from nationalities that were acceptably "Aryan," according to National Socialism's bogus racial theories:

11th SS Volunteer Panzergrenadier Division *Nordland*— Norwegian and Danish
23rd SS Volunteer Panzergrenadier Division *Nederland*—Dutch
27th SS Volunteer Division *Langemarck*—Flemish

Another of the participating formations, XXXIX Panzer Corps, contained a foreign volunteer division, the 28th SS Volunteer Grenadier Division *Wallonien*, consisting of French-speaking Belgians, or Walloons. Commanded by the Belgian Rexiste leader Léon Degrelle, this "division" was never larger than a brigade and perhaps less than that in *Sonnenwende*.[12]

Despite the disparate nature of the manpower, the planning was solid enough. Guderian had won a point with Hitler in the prebattle planning stage, urging the Führer to appoint Himmler's chief of staff, General Walther Wenck, as the actual field commander (*Feldkommando*) for the offensive. Where Himmler was uncertain and indolent, Wenck was energetic and capable and, at forty-four years old, the youngest general in the German army. He launched the attack on a 30-mile front, with XXXIX Panzer on the right, III (Germanic) SS Panzer Corps in the center, and the ad hoc *Korpsgruppe* named for General Oskar Munzel providing flank protection on the left. The timing and precise location of the attack caught forward units of the Soviet 61st Army by surprise. With its assortment of Danes, Norwegians, and Flemings in the lead, *Sonnenwende* drove south seven miles and actually managed to relieve the besieged German garrison of Arnswalde. But this relatively impressive opening soon petered out into tough positional fighting over the next two days—the last thing the Wehrmacht could afford. The infantry component—German and non-German alike—was half-trained, and the precious Panzers suffered heavy and irreplaceable losses to Soviet antitank guns, mines, and artillery. Bad luck also played a role. After briefing Hitler personally on February 17, Wenck was driving back to headquarters. His exhausted driver had been on duty for two days straight, so Wenck took over, promptly fell asleep at the wheel, and slammed into a bridge. He spent the next few weeks convalescing in a hospital, and *Sonnenwende* never did get restarted. Whether Wenck's presence would have made difference is an open question, but losing a good commander days into an operation is rarely a positive.

Failure or not, the counterstroke had an impact. *Sonnenwende* gave both Zhukov and the Stavka a case of the nerves. Final victory was in sight, so this was no time to be courting senseless risk. With a major river (the Oder) in front of Zhukov and unknown troubles brewing on his flanks, the time had come to halt. Konev's front, as well, was going to be needed for the drive on Berlin, and he could hardly fight in Berlin and Silesia at the same time. Put simply, before the two Soviet fronts could strike at Berlin they had housecleaning duties to tend to on their flanks. Zhukov, along with Rokossovsky's 2nd Byelorussian Front, spent the next two months squashing the remains of German resistance in eastern Pomerania (*Hinterpommern*—"Pomerania east of the Oder"). The campaign featured a tricky degree of interfront cooperation, with Zhukov's right wing and Rokossovsky's left wing doing most of the fighting. At first, the two fronts drove straight north, heading toward Kolberg and Köslin. After reaching the Baltic coast and splitting the province in two, Zhukov wheeled left toward Stettin and the mouth of the Oder, while Rokossovsky wheeled right toward Danzig and the Gotenhafen fortifications. By now, the German civilian population in this region was on the move, with hundreds of thousands fleeing their homes, desperate to evade rampaging Soviet tank columns. All the German military formations in Pomerania took in immense masses of civilians. Indeed, helping civilians flee to the west became the army's unofficial raison d'être for continuing the war to the bitter end.

While Zhukov reduced Pomerania, Konev fought a bitter campaign to reduce German resistance in Silesia.[13] On February 8, 1st Ukrainian Front launched a vast, two-pronged operation out of the Steinau and Ohlau bridgeheads (the Lower Silesian Operation). Field Marshal Ferdinand Schörner of Army Group Center had two understrength "armies" under his command in Silesia: 17th Army standing opposite the Ohlau bridgehead and 4th Panzer Army guarding Steinau. Both were the remnants of German forces smashed on the Vistula, however, and Schörner had "only about as many field divisions as Konev had armies," in the words of one analyst.[14] Both German forces gave way within hours, and Konev's tank armies were motoring 40 miles past their starting line by the end of the first day. Rather than push west toward Germany, however, Konev decided first to encircle Breslau, diverting 1st Guards Tank Army from its original westward axis, wheeling it 180 degrees to the east, and looping it around Breslau from the south. Breslau was encircled (and would withstand a siege and assault for three full months, until May 6—outliving even Hitler himself).[15] But Konev's decision gave the Germans just enough time for elements of 4th Panzer Army to firm up their defenses along the Neisse River (*Lausitzer Neisse*, or "Lusatian Neisse"). Konev's attempts to establish bridgeheads over the Neisse led to fierce fighting against the six German divisions on the western bank and resulted in a bare sliver of a lodgment between Forst in the south and Guben in the north.

Konev now faced a German army immediately to his west (4th Panzer) and a second immediately to his south (17th) and was, for the moment, "contained inside a right angle of German forces."[16] He had pushed up to the Neisse on a 60-mile front and encircled Breslau, but German forces were still in the field and still active, launching a pair of small but vigorous counterattacks at Lauban (March 2) and at Striegau (March 9) that, although failing to achieve lasting success, served notice to Konev that the front was still active. Moreover, activity on his deep-left flank seemed threatening. Here lay *Armeegruppe* Heinrici (later, 1st Panzer Army), and once again Konev couldn't concentrate on the Berlin axis far to the west when a threat lay this deep on his opposite flank. He now decided to redeploy 4th Tank Army from the Neisse front and insert it into battle 100 miles to the southeast in Upper Silesia. On March 15, he launched another massive offensive (the Upper Silesian Operation), both sides battling away in the mountains and industrial districts north of Mährisch-Ostrau (Moravska Ostrava). The initial breakthroughs managed to encircle the German LVI Panzer Corps southwest of Oppeln. The corps managed to break out of the ring—just in time for 4th Ukrainian Front to join the offensive on March 22—launching an attack on 1st Panzer Army from the east. Heinrici parried both thrusts, and the Soviets called off their offensive on March 31. They had pushed back, but not destroyed, 1st Panzer Army, and that may be all they wanted to do in the first place. Konev had neutralized the threat from Silesia, but it had taken him nearly two months, almost exactly the time Zhukov needed to overrun Pomerania.

Berlin

Over the centuries, humanity has amassed a great deal of folk wisdom about vengeance. "What goes around comes around," we warn. "Revenge is sweet," we might claim, sometimes "best served cold"—but not here, not in this case. (See Map 10.2.)

The masters of the Third Reich—Adolf Hitler and his paladins—might have been pondering such notions early on the morning of April 16, 1945, as the sprawling city of Berlin awakened to an ominous heavy rumble from the east. To the practiced ear it was the sound of artillery fire. The Red Army had shaken off its two-month slumber along the Oder River and was once again on the march. Nearly four years had passed since the Wehrmacht invaded the Soviet Union in Operation Barbarossa, waging the most brutal war in history by murdering, starving, and enslaving millions of Soviet civilians. It was, perhaps, the only true *Vernichtungskrieg* (war of annihilation) in human history. To the people of Berlin, that distant din of battle no doubt appeared as an omen. A grim reckoning was at hand.[17]

On April 1—the day after the close of the Upper Silesian Operation—Stalin convened a planning session in the Kremlin to discuss the final drive on Berlin. The meeting took place in Stalin's study, with portraits of the great Russian generals of the past—Alexander

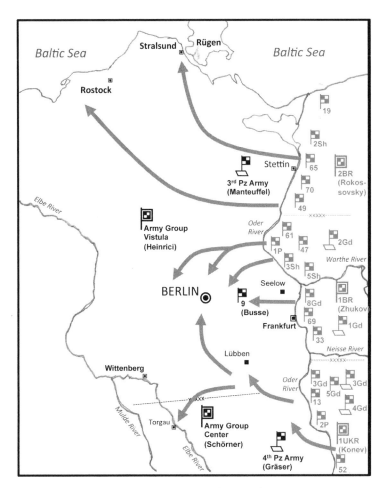

Map 10.2 Endgame: The Soviet Drive on Berlin (April–May 1945)

Suvorov and Mikhail Kutuzov—staring down on them all. Whereas in late January 1945 the German capital seemed within the Soviets' grasp, the situation had changed utterly by March. On the Western Front, Anglo-American armies were now over the Rhine, finishing up the Ruhr encirclement, and driving east deep into central Germany. The day before, Stalin had received a note from Eisenhower indicating that Berlin was not a priority western target. Instead, Eisenhower intended to thrust along the Erfurt–Leipzig–Dresden axis and effect an early junction with Soviet armies on the Elbe River, along with a secondary thrust near Regensburg and Linz for a linkup on the Danube (Donau, to the Germans). Ike's note seemed to hand over Berlin to the Soviet operational sphere. But Stalin had also apparently received a contradictory intelligence report warning that the Western Allies were about to launch an operation to seize Berlin, with forces under General Montgomery attacking north of the Ruhr along the shortest route to Berlin. Stalin split the difference between these two irreconcilable reports, sending Eisenhower a reply agreeing to the general strategy of a linkup on the Elbe and the Danube—but also lying to the supreme commander, stating that Berlin wasn't a Soviet priority either and that, at any rate, Soviet armies wouldn't be ready to march until mid-May.

In attendance at the April 1 conference were Zhukov, Konev, General A. I. Antonov (newly appointed Chief of the Soviet General Staff), and General S. M. Shtemenko, Antonov's operations chief. Stalin opened the conference by having Shtemenko read the confidential telegram aloud, intimating that the Western Allies intended to capture Berlin.

> Stalin turned to Zhukov and Konev: "Well then, who is going to take Berlin, we or the Allies?"[18]
>
> Konev claims to have responded first: "It is we who will be taking Berlin, and we shall take it before the Allies."[19] Zhukov agreed.
>
> "All right. The two of you must work out your plans right here in Moscow, at the General Staff, and as soon as they are ready, say, in a day or two, report them back to General Headquarters, so that you may go back to your front with approved plans."[20]

In a few days Stalin and his generals worked out plans for a hasty redeployment of three Soviet fronts to the Oder-Neisse front: Rokossovsky's 2nd Byelorussian Front in the north, from the Baltic Sea coast to Schwedt on the Oder River; 1st Byelorussian Front around Küstrin in the center, directly opposite Berlin; and Konev's 1st Ukrainian Front, facing the Neisse between Guben and Muskau. Together they would launch the last great Soviet offensive of the war. Zhukov would drive out of his bridgeheads across the Oder and head due west toward Berlin while Konev crossed the Lausitzer Neisse River on Zhukov's left and came up from the south, and Rokossovsky crossed the Oder near Stettin, overran the Mecklenburg Plain, and protected Zhukov's northern flank from any German counterthrust. Flank protection for the main thrust was crucial. Indeed, it was the very operational problem that had eventually short-circuited the Vistula-Oder offensive. In addition, Rokossovsky and Konev were crucial not only operationally but also strategically. Passing north and south of Berlin, their mission was to drive west at speed, link up with the Western Allies as far west as possible, and overrun the Soviet occupation zone in Germany before the end of hostilities.

Stalin convened another meeting on April 3 to discuss these various plans. The dictator always had a sharp eye for operational possibilities, and it had become sharper in the course of the war. After hashing out the various front directives, however, Stalin did something unusual. He leaned over the map and erased the sector line between the 1st Byelorussian and 1st Ukrainian Fronts, just west of the town of Lübben in the Spreewald District, 35 miles southeast of Berlin. In other words, Berlin no longer "belonged" to Zhukov's sector—or to anyone's. In case the Germans managed to parry Zhukov's blow, Stalin wanted Konev to be ready to attack Berlin from the south. Stalin's erasure was a not-very-subtle attempt to stoke a rivalry between his two commanders and get both of them moving with maximum dispatch. "He did not say anything," Konev later reported, "but I think Marshal Zhukov also saw a certain implication in this." Konev certainly did: "The line of demarcation was cut short at about the point we were supposed to reach on the third day of the operation. Subsequently (apparently depending on the situation), it was tacitly assumed, the commanders of the fronts could display their own initiative."[21] The operation still centered on Zhukov, in other words, and Konev's and Rokossovsky's fronts were essentially flanking guards, but Stalin wanted to provide the operation with maximum flexibility. "Let the one who is first to break in take Berlin," he told his staff later.[22]

Finally, with the international situation changing by the day and not necessarily to Soviet advantage, Stalin wanted speed. He set April 16 as the start date for the Berlin operation, along with a maximum duration of just 12–15 days. Calling the time frame compressed was an understatement, especially given the geography involved. While Zhukov's redeployment essentially consisted of compressing his front along the Oder, Rokossovsky was still embroiled in the fighting for eastern Pomerania, Danzig, and Gotenhafen and had a long way to go just to get to the Oder. Likewise, Konev's front was still tied down in heavy fighting in Silesia, and he would need time to regroup for the new operation, especially the difficult problem of shifting his tank armies from his extreme left to his extreme right. Nevertheless, over the course of the next two weeks the Soviets managed to assemble no fewer than eighteen field armies in their three fronts, a total of 2.5

million men, 41,600 guns, 6,250 tanks, and 7,500 aircraft. While such massive concentrations of force were a well-practiced drill for the Red Army, never had the Soviet command had to perform the complex act so rapidly. The Berlin concentration stands as the most prodigious feat of Soviet planning, administration, and logistics in the entire war.

The German position facing Zhukov on the *Oderbruch* (the flood plain of the Oder) was no better or worse than any other by this point in the war. Army Group Vistula held a line from the Baltic Sea to the confluence of the Oder and the Neisse. Its commander, General Gotthard Heinrici, had replaced the utterly incompetent Himmler as army group commander in March. He had a well-earned reputation as a defensive specialist, and he had recently held his ground against an offensive by multiple Soviet fronts in Upper Silesia. "Our tough little bastard" (*unser Giftzwerg*), his men called him. He had 3rd Panzer Army under General Hasso von Manteuffel deployed on his left (to the north) and 9th Army (General Theodor Busse) on his right, each with three corps. The 9th Army, standing directly in Zhukov's path, had CI Corps on the left, XI SS Corps on the right, and LVI Panzer Corps (General Helmuth Weidling) in reserve. To the right of Heinrici's army group right stood Field Marshal Schörner's Army Group Center. Schörner's operational responsibility extended well to the south, curving in a protective semicircle around Bohemia, but his left-wing army, the 4th Panzer under General Fritz-Hubert Gräser, stood on the Neisse just across from Konev and would bear the brunt of 1st Ukrainian Front's initial assault. All in all, the German line was at least cohesive, with a wide river in front, and a Panzer corps standing behind in reserve. The matchups were symmetrical:

3rd Panzer Army	v.	2nd Byelorussian Front
9th Army	v.	1st Byelorussian Front
4th Panzer Army	v.	1st Ukrainian Front

By the Wehrmacht's standards of 1945, it seemed like a textbook defensive position. It was, at any rate, as much as this threadbare military establishment could afford.

Closer inspection showed the flaws, of course. Three weak German armies faced fully fleshed and well-supplied Soviet fronts. In general, these German armies contained the same number of *divisions* as their counterpart Soviet fronts had *armies*. Busse's 9th Army, for example, contained 14 divisions. Its adversary, Zhukov's 1st Byelorussian Front, had no fewer than 18 armies (breaking down into 77 rifle divisions, 7 tank/mechanized corps, and 8 artillery divisions). On the German left, 3rd Panzer Army possessed 11 weak divisions; 2nd Byelorussian Front facing it had 8 armies (33 rifle divisions, 4 tank/mechanized corps, and 3 artillery divisions). The numbers told the same sad story they had been telling since late 1943. The 1st Byelorussian Front had over 3,000 tanks and nearly 17,000 artillery pieces; German 9th Army had 500 tanks and 344 guns. Not one of Heinrici's units was at approved strength, and most of his divisions were little more than battalion-size battlegroups. His guns had only a few dozen rounds apiece. His force was a motley crew: foreign volunteer divisions of the Waffen-SS (*Nordland* and *Nederland*), plus a Panzer division (*Müncheberg*) that could barely scrounge up 50 tanks. No one on his staff expected the line to hold against a major Soviet assault, and a certain fatalism was taking root. Morale can hardly be described as adequate when a regimental commander in the 303rd Infantry Division (a unit only just formed out of raw infantry replacements at the Döberitz Training Ground) feels compelled to instruct his battalion commanders: "You have to hold the front at any cost. You're responsible. If a few soldiers start to run away, then you must shoot them. If you see many soldiers taking off, and you can't stop them and the situation is hopeless, then you'd better shoot yourself."[23]

The battle to take Berlin unfolded in three distinct phases. The first was the Soviet offensive along the Oder and Neisse, starting on April 16. Zhukov led things off at 3:00 A.M. with a furious bombardment by 9,000 guns that left his own crews bleeding from the ears. Channeling Stalin's desires, the marshal based his plan on speed and shock—stunning the defenders with a quick, 30-minute hurricane of fire, bursting out of the Küstrin bridgehead with his infantry while hundreds of searchlights blinded the defenders, then inserting his mobile reserves (1st and 2nd Guards Tank Armies) for the pursuit to Berlin.

Despite Zhukov's overwhelming strength, the plan fell apart early. The bombardment was too short, and Heinrici had pulled back his frontline troops so they could avoid the initial storm. He had worked out the tactic in previous battles, even though he often had to explain himself to Hitler, who saw it as a form of retreat. Once the bombardment lifted, Zhukov's infantry had an uphill fight versus German forces on the Seelow Heights (the high ground on the Oder's western bank), plus a secondary river crossing over the old course of the Oder (*Alte Oder*). The heights gave the Germans an advantage in observation, and they used it to call down a killing fire on the advancing Soviets below. The searchlights also misfired, as smoke from Soviet artillery reflected the light back into the eyes of the attackers.[24] Losses were heavy, and Zhukov later admitted that he had underestimated the strength of the German position. Knowing that no plan survives contact with the enemy, the marshal now changed the operation on the fly. He inserted his two tank armies into the fray as breakthrough elements, rather than holding them back for the pursuit. In the short term, the tanks only increased the congestion on a very crowded battlefield, however, and Zhukov's day ended on a frustrating note. His failure to secure the Seelow Heights on the first day led to a testy midnight phone call from Stalin—rarely good news for a Soviet field commander.

Konev, by contrast, slashed through German defenses with ease. Lacking a bridgehead, he planned crossings at multiple sites across the Neisse (over 130 in all). While military dispersion is rarely a good idea, it was just the ticket against a German force spread so thinly. Just to make sure, Konev also bombarded the defenders for a full two and a half hours. With 250 guns per kilometer, the fire smashed the defensive position, killing thousands of defenders and leaving others stupefied. Once the bombardment lifted, the lead units spilled into their assault boats and paddled across the river behind a thick smokescreen laid down by the Red Air Force. The Soviets soon had bridgeheads on the far bank and were marking landing zones for the follow-on waves. Within hours, sappers had lashed cables over the river, the first ferries were in operation, and T-34 tanks were crossing the Neisse. By noon, Konev's two tank armies (3rd and 4th Guards) were across the Neisse and by nightfall heading at speed for the next river line, the Spree. It was a textbook river crossing, as smooth and seamless as any in the entire war, and Konev's phone chat with Stalin that night could not have been warmer. "With Zhukov things are not going so well yet," the boss stated gravely, before ordering Konev to wheel his tank armies to the right and race directly for Berlin.[25]

The next few days saw Zhukov continue to struggle on the direct line to Berlin. The next two days (April 17–18) were much like the first. The Germans held the Seelow Heights as Heinrici slowly fed in his reserve, mainly elements of SS Division *Nordland*. Hopes began to rise in the Führerbunker. General Keitel had always preached that an offensive failed if it did not achieve a breakthrough on the third day, and this was day three.[26] Zhukov's monstrous superiority in artillery, aircraft, and tanks gradually began to tell, however, and he started to slowly chew through 9th Army's left flank on April 19. He moved cautiously, however, since 2nd Byelorussian Front had not yet launched its attack to his north, and every mile he advanced to the west lengthened his unprotected flank.

The great breakthrough came on April 20. Zhukov's 2nd Guards Tank Army smashed through the German lines to Bernau, looping down on Berlin from the northeast. At virtually the same time, his 1st Guards Tank Army broke through at Diedersdorf, heading west on Highway 1. Moreover, Rokossovsky's 2nd Byelorussian Front had launched its attack, crossing the Oder near Stettin, pressing the German defenders hard, and relieving Zhukov from having to worry about his right flank. Zhukov's own front had suffered heavy losses on the Seelow Heights, with perhaps 30,000 men killed in action, but he was not a commander who cared all that much about his own casualties. At any rate, he had broken into the clear, and no German force in the field was capable of stopping him. On April 21, Zhukov had the honor of being the first to bombard Berlin, with his 203mm howitzers firing at extreme range and striking the city's eastern outskirts 10 miles away.[27]

Konev, meanwhile, was on a wild ride of his own. His two tank armies (3rd Guards and 4th Guards) were motoring in the clear and wheeling to the right, coming up on Berlin from the south. The advance guard of 3rd Guards Tank Army crossed the Spree River without even slowing down and penetrated another 20 miles beyond it, still without meeting any serious resistance. On April 21, Konev's tanks actually overran the immense underground bunker complex at Zossen, the headquarters and communications center of the German General Staff. So rapid had been their advance that the German staff barely got out of the building. The machinery was still humming, as it were, with telephones ringing off the hook and teleprinters clattering out urgent messages to recipients who would never read them. By now, Konev was just 12 miles from Berlin.

These twin Soviet breakthroughs were decisive to the Battle of Berlin. Not only had they opened a path to the German capital; the converging Soviet drives had broken through both flanks of German 9th Army, trapping the army's mass in a pocket near Halbe in the Spreewald, the deep forest southeast of Berlin.[28] The battle of encirclement meant that 9th Army's divisions would be unavailable for the defense of the capital itself. Most of them were now hors de combat, herded into the ever-shrinking Halbe *Kessel*, under constant Soviet bombardment, and enduring an enormous slaughter. As Konev's tank armies ran around his right flank and then came up behind him, the 9th Army commander, General Busse, was receiving the most senseless orders from Führer Headquarters. First he was to hold his ground along the Oder, then launch an attack to the south, and finally reverse his front altogether, face west, and attack to the north. The orders struck him as "unworkable," indeed, as "completely insane."[29] Only LVI Panzer Corps under General Weidling managed to escape the trap, carrying out a skillful but costly fighting retreat to Berlin against direct orders from Hitler.

From April 22 to April 24, the armies from both sides converged on Berlin, marking the second phase of the battle. Konev brought up his 4th Guards Tank Army, 3rd Guards Tank Army, and 28th Army from the south, while a finally unchained Zhukov drove on the eastern approaches to the city (5th Shock Army, 8th Guards Army, and 1st Guards Tank Army), lapped around it to the north (2nd Guards Tank Army and 3rd Shock Army), and even came down its western side toward Spandau and Potsdam (47th Army). On April 23, Konev and Zhukov's spearheads linked up near Potsdam, closing the trap around Berlin. On the German side, Weidling and LVI Panzer Corps also managed to reach the city, slipping in just ahead of the Soviets on the night of April 23. Weidling's reception was one of the classic examples of the toxic nature of Nazi command. Hitler summoned the general to the Führerbunker, apparently to have him arrested and executed for carrying out an unauthorized retreat. Ignoring his staff's advice to flee, Weidling responded to the summons in person. He appeared before the Führer, presented a forceful briefing of the dire situation, and acquitted himself well during the cross-examination. Hitler was so impressed that he canceled the execution and appointed Weidling commander of the Berlin Defense Area (*Verteidigungsberich*).[30]

Weidling later said he wished he'd been shot rather than "have this chalice passed to him."[31] The city's defenses were a mess. On paper, Berlin had eight defensive sectors, labeled "A" through "H," starting in the east and moving clockwise. The perimeter and suburbs formed the first defensive position. The line of the S-Bahn formed the second defensive ring farther inside the city proper, while the inner citadel known as Sector Z (for *Zentrum*, "center") formed the third and final defensive position. Sector Z was the heart of the city, bounded by the Spree River in the north and the Landwehr Canal in the south, containing the government sector, the Reichstag, and the Chancellery. Finally, dominating the landscape were three gargantuan *Flak* towers—one in the Berlin Zoo, and one each in the parks of Humboldthain and Friedrichshain—made of reinforced concrete and nearly indestructible.

Weidling knew that he had nowhere near enough troops to man these positions. He calculated that a city the size of Berlin required at least eight full-strength divisions, grouped into multiple corps. It needed a field army, in other words. But with 9th Army dying in the *Halbe Kessel*, Weidling had to rely on a quilt of second-rate manpower: "emergency units" (*Alarmeinheiten*) made up of unassigned replacements, cadets from the various military schools, armed postmen and utility workers, and the usual coterie of Hitler Youth and *Volkssturm*. Weidling did bring with him the battered remnants of five divisions, however, and he deployed them as logically as he could: 20th *Panzergrenadier* in the southwest, near the Wannsee; 9th *Fallschirmjäger* in the north; Panzer Division *Müncheberg* in the south; SS *Nordland* in the east; and 18th *Panzergrenadier* in Sector Z. But the array was shaky— and Weidling knew it. He had no faith at all in his Hitler Youth battalions, sixteen-year-old boys on bicycles, armed only with a single-shot antitank weapon, the *Panzerfaust*. The *Faust* was a fearsome weapon, firing a shaped charge that could kill any tank in the field. The combination of its one-shot limitation and its short range, however, meant almost certain death for the soldier wielding it. Nor could Weidling's mood have brightened at the news that one of his divisional commanders, General Georg Scholze of 20th *Panzergrenadier*, had killed himself upon entering the city.[32] Scholze had recently heard the news that his wife and four of their five children had died in an Allied bombing raid on Potsdam. His suicide was no doubt a reminder to Weidling that, even if the battle went well, they were all doomed.

For all these reasons, Weidling never was able to form a firm defensive perimeter. The Soviets arrived hard on his heels, and often his weary soldiers were taking up positions in a building or block only moments before it came under Soviet bombardment or attack. Konev blasted his way into southern Berlin on April 24, with 3rd Guards Tank Army crossing the Teltow Canal after a 3,000-gun bombardment on a 5-kilometer sector pulverized the hapless *Volkssturm* defenders opposite. Zhukov's forces reached the southeastern perimeter on that same day, with 5th Shock Army fighting its way into Treptow Park and driving up to the S-Bahn. From April 24 to April 28, the Red Army overran 90 percent of Berlin, and while the battles were extremely bloody for both sides, Soviet momentum was unrelenting.

Riding point for the Soviets by this time was the 8th Guards Army. The commander, General V. I. Chuikov, had defended Stalingrad in 1942 and knew urban combat as well as any man alive. Careful reconnaissance, combined arms, avoiding the middle of the streets, and spraying every window and doorway in his path with fire from automatic weapons: this was Chuikovian warfare. His battle cycle ran twenty-four hours, launching night attacks to rob the defenders of rest. In daylight, he made prodigious use of smoke, covering his assault groups until they were within 30 meters of the objective. Chuikov's men also knew how to improvise. Tank losses to the German *Panzerfaust* were heavy in the early going, and Soviet crews worked out a number of expedients by festooning their vehicles with mattresses or bedsprings to disrupt the geometry of the warhead and thus disperse the blast. Soviet infantry also found that a captured *Panzerfaust* made an ideal blockbuster—a quick way to blast a hole in a brick wall and kill the defenders inside. Above all, Chuikov knew that defenders held all the trump cards in a city fight—terrain, protection, invisibility—and that the only way to overcome them was to accept massive casualties on his side. Finally, if the Germans did try to make a serious stand, Chuikov simply wheeled up his big guns and blasted away over open sights.[33]

By April 28, all that was left of Berlin—and by extension of the Third Reich—was Sector Z: the citadel. The Battle of Berlin now shifted into its third and final phase. Historians often describe the German defenders in Berlin as "fanatics," but up until this point they had been anything but. They had fought hard, certainly, but they never held a position for long and retreated as soon as Soviet infantry began to work around their flanks. Inside the citadel, things changed. Retreat was no longer an option, and it was time to do or die. It would be interesting to interview Weidling's men today: a seemingly arbitrary collection of old men who had last seen action in World War I, boys who were barely shaving, grizzled NCOs fighting their fiftieth battle, and a large contingent of non-German fighters—idealists enlisted in the anti-Bolshevik crusade, Scandinavians in *Nordland*, a battalion of right-wing Frenchmen from the SS Charlemagne Division, and Latvian infantrymen.[34] The defenders of the island were a polyglot cross-section of the 1945 Wehrmacht, drawn to this final battle by little else, seemingly, than the bad luck of the historical draw.

Still, enough soldiers had crowded into Sector Z that the Germans for once had sufficient manpower, with some 10,000 men packed into an area three miles from north to south and nine miles from east to west. In such close quarters the Germans were able to fortify the most important buildings and to block the most obvious avenues of approach. The *Panzerfaust* came into its own, since the urban terrain offered better opportunities than the open field for ambush-style shoot-and-scoot tactics, and the Germans managed to take a heavy toll of attacking armor. Meanwhile, the Soviets were no longer able to employ their entire strength. Stalin had already pulled Konev's front out of the battle on April 27–28, sending it west to meet the US Army on the Elbe River and southward toward Prague. Meanwhile, only two of Zhukov's ten armies were still active in the struggle: 3rd Shock Army (General V. I. Kuznetsov) coming down from the northern front on the Spree and Chuikov's 8th Guards coming up from the south across the Landwehr Canal.

The final five days from April 28 through May 2 have fixed the Battle of Berlin in our historical consciousness. Some of the starkest images of the war come to mind: the murderous building-by-building fight, with no quarter granted by either side; the bodies of hundreds, perhaps thousands, of German soldiers hanging from lampposts, executed for "desertion" or "cowardice" or simply for being in the wrong place at the wrong time; SS squads prowling the streets, shooting anyone unlucky enough to be caught flying a white surrender flag in the window; the desperate slogans chalked on the walls of the dying city—*Berlin bleibt deutsch!* ("Berlin Stays German!"). General Weidling had to cross town to confer with General Erich Bärenfänger, one of his tactical zone commanders. "Heavy artillery fire struck the Potsdamer Platz and the Leipziger Strasse. The grit from stone and brick hung like a thick fog in the air." His car made its way slowly forward, now rushing for a quick bound during a lull in the shelling, now screeching to a halt as the shelling resumed. "Shells were bursting on all sides of us, and we were covered with shards of stone." Finally, he decided to abandon the vehicle and make his way to Alexanderplatz on foot: "In the spacious, two-level underground U-Bahn station the population was seeking refuge and protection. Masses of terrified civilians stood or lay closely packed together on the ground. It was a shocking sight."[35] Like the inhabitants of Warsaw, Stalingrad, Budapest, and so many other cities, Berliners now sat in the line of fire, millions of them huddling in air-raid shelters, train stations, or in the mammoth *Flak* towers, helplessly awaiting their fate. In the course of the fight, one of the underground tunnels of the S-Bahn under the Landwehr Canal was blown up—at whose order is still unclear—and the tunnel soon filled with water. Other demolitions led to flooding in significant portions of the underground rail, both S-Bahn and U-Bahn. While grisly tales of thousands of unfortunates drowned in a rushing wall of water are certainly apocryphal, the fact is that the tunnels were holding wounded soldiers, the old, and the young; the flooding only added to the misery.[36]

On April 28, Chuikov's 8th Guards Army crossed the Landwehr Canal near a park (the Tiergarten), while 3rd Shock lunged across the Spree directly into the government district. The by now standard blizzard of fire preceded each attack—howitzers and siege guns and Katyusha rocket-launchers—and the defenders had to give way. By the end of the day, the two Soviet spearheads were less than a mile apart. Incredibly, it would take the Soviets four full days of fierce fighting to cross that final mile. The assault on the Reichstag was the signature moment of the battle. Crossing the Spree over Moltke Bridge (which the Germans tried but failed to blow up), elements of 3rd Shock Army came under heavy fire from the Ministry of the Interior building. Soviet assault teams stormed the ministry, with heavy losses, as well as the nearby Swiss Embassy building just across the street. From here, they could see the Reichstag just a few hundred yards across the open Königsplatz. Flanking fire from the Kroll Opera House to the south held up the advance, however, as did a collapsed tunnel traversing the Königsplatz. Flooded with water seeping in from the Spree, it formed a protective moat.

The 150th Rifle Division spent April 30 fighting across the Königsplatz, which by now was a killing ground. The first assault teams crossing the open space ran into a vicious crossfire that shot them to pieces. As always, Soviet tactical solutions were brutal and effective. The commander of the 150th Rifle, General V. M. Shatilov, wheeled up ninety guns on a 400-meter front and started blasting away—at the Kroll, at the Reichstag, and at anything that moved. Slowly, with progress measured by yards and casualties, Shatilov's men fought their way into the Reichstag building, defended by a menagerie of sailors, SS, and Hitler Youth. The Soviets would need yet another day, May 1, to smash resistance in the basement, secure the prize, and plant the red flag on the Reichstag dome. Weidling surrendered the Berlin garrison on May 2, although it took another day or two for resistance in the city to cease altogether.

For the soldiers of the Red Army, it was a sweet moment of revenge. They had, in the words of Soviet propaganda, "slain the Fascist beast in its own lair"—at a cost of 350,000 casualties.[37] They promptly sullied themselves by a rampage of looting and killing inside the city, not to mention the rape of every German woman or girl they could get their hands on. No explanation will ever suffice for this horror: that it was not frontline troops but the follow-on echelons, for example, or that the perpetrators were recruited from the Asian ethnic groups of the Soviet Union. The former doesn't appear to be true, and the latter is simple racism. Equally unacceptable are stammering, tu quoque rationalizations that "the Germans did it too" in the Soviet Union.[38] Rape is rape, a vicious crime and equally contemptible under any circumstances. A man who rapes cannot possibly be avenging the original victim, however he may rationalize. He rapes because he wants to, and because he can. Historians have fixated on these mass assaults—and for good reason. In terms of their impact on world opinion, the Soviets may well have lost the Cold War in the first week after they seized Berlin.[39]

One other fixation is more misguided, however, and that is our lurid obsession with Hitler's last days in his bunker: the ranting and raving, the nonsensical orders, the death sentences against those deemed disloyal. The Führerbunker is a distorting lens, given how little control Hitler actually exerted over the battle. He spent most of his last days ordering three chimerical relief operations from outside the city. The first consisted of General Walther Wenck's newly formed 12th Army from the west.[40] The second was *SS-Obergruppenführer* Felix Steiner's weak *Armeegruppe* ("army detachment") from the north.[41] The third was Busse's 9th Army trapped in the Halbe Pocket to the southeast.[42] Not one had a chance of reaching Berlin (Steiner, for example, had just three understrength divisions and mocked the attack order as "senseless")—and none obeyed the call.[43] Indeed, Hitler's communications with the outside world were so sporadic that his staff had to resort to bizarre improvisations to gain even basic intelligence on the fighting: dialing random phone numbers near the front to see whether a German or Russian voice picked up.[44] Hitler was a passive observer in Berlin, and it was no wonder. He had long ago decided to kill himself when the end was near, and he did just that on April 30, along with Eva Braun, his new wife; General Hans Krebs, his last Chief of the General Staff; and General Wilhelm Burgdorf, the chief of the *Heerespersonalamt* (Army Personnel Office) and Hitler's personal adjutant. Soviet assault units on the surface were probably no more than 500 yards away.

The German Way of War: A Retrospective

And so ended World War II in Europe. What Rommel had called the "unequal struggle" had mercifully come to an end.[45] The war that Hitler started and the Wehrmacht conducted so tenaciously killed at least 50 million people and destroyed a continent, all for naught. Hitler was dead. Germany was occupied and divided, a pariah among nations for its crimes, especially the attempted genocide against the Jews. The war shattered Germany's reputation, transforming the land of *Dichter und Denker* (the poet and the thinker) to the land of *Richter und Henker* (the judge and the hangman). The country has yet to live down that reputation, and it probably never will. Anytime the reunited Germany—today a robust and powerful player in Europe—performs some controversial act on the international scene, someone will throw down the word "Nazi."[46] The German experience in World War II should be an object lesson against the notion of "rolling the iron dice" and resorting to a war of aggression.

And yet, for all the pain and suffering it caused, the Wehrmacht emerged from the war with its reputation intact. Its victories early in the war—Case White in Poland, Exercise Weser in Scandinavia, Case Yellow in the west, Operation Mercury, the airborne conquest of Crete—will always stand as innovative examples of modern mechanized operations.[47] German generals rushed into print with their memoirs, and those written by Guderian, Field Marshal Erich von Manstein, and staff officer Friedrich Wilhelm von Mellenthin won a vast and fascinated reading audience in the West among those eager to learn the secrets of blitzkrieg. Likewise, a large body of popular West German authors like Franz Kurowski, Erich Kern, Jürgen Thorwald, and above all Paul Carell extolled the fighting qualities of the army, the level of comradeship within the ranks, and its heroic struggle against the odds. Their publishers were affiliated with the political far right, and they often wrote under pseudonyms to hide their past—either as soldiers of the Wehrmacht or as officials of the Nazi regime—but these details mattered little in the English-speaking West.[48] All these authors painted a picture of commanders of genius and a heroic army with "clean hands," that is to say, men who would never have dreamed of carrying out atrocities against civilians and who condemned in no uncertain terms the Nazi Party and SS monsters who did so. With the West locked in a frightening new struggle against global communism, the Wehrmacht looked not so much like a former enemy but rather a forerunner: the first to take on the Red Army and the only force in the world with deep experience fighting the Russians. Wehrmacht worship in the West reached a peak in the 1980s, as the US Army began rereading Clausewitz, studying the campaigns of Moltke the Elder, and rediscovering Königgrätz and Case Yellow.

That pleasant consensus on the Wehrmacht has now unraveled, and the notion of the army's "clean hands" is gone forever. Scholars have meticulously catalogued the crimes of the Wehrmacht, the military's participation in the Shoah, and the merciless slaughter of civilians on the Eastern Front and in the Balkans. A traveling exhibition with that very title—"War of Annihilation: Crimes of the Wehrmacht"—moved across Germany beginning in 1995 and was seen by almost a million Germans.[49] The damning photographs and textual evidence generated rage in some of the visitors, including those who thought that the exhibition slandered the memory of their fathers and grandfathers, but it caused shock and horror in many more. Scholarly interest in the Wehrmacht today is more likely to center around its participation in mass murder than its military operations. Our reassessment has likewise extended to the memoirs that formed so much of the historical memory of the Wehrmacht, and historians working in the primary documents have had a field day deconstructing some of Manstein's or Guderian's more fanciful claims and blatant omissions—especially their tendency to heap all blame on Hitler for decisions and failed operations in which they were deeply complicit.

Claims of the Wehrmacht's war-fighting qualities have been more resistant. Indeed, they should be. As an instrument of war, the German army displayed considerable strengths during World War II. The generalship was consistently solid and often brilliant. The command system was flexible enough to permit wide latitude to the field- and company-grade officers at the sharper end, even in the war's later years. All ranks fought with an aggressive spirit and generated a great deal of combat power (*Kampfkraft*) as a result. Coordination of movement and fires remained impressive until the end. Above all, this army managed to maintain its cohesion, remaining in the field and combat-effective during three years of the most grievous defeats in military history. Model's counterattack in front of Warsaw in August 1944, as well as his resurrection of the defeated army of the west the very next month, were proof that, even at bay, the Wehrmacht was still a lethal force. Anyone who fought against it in World War II would agree.[50]

Analyzing the campaigns of 1944–1945 on the European continent helps us reach a more balanced view of the Wehrmacht's fighting qualities. During roughly eighteen months, the Wehrmacht suffered from a multitude of weaknesses that more than outweighed its virtues, militarily speaking. The German army during this epic battle was outnumbered, undersupplied, and out of fuel. And frankly, there were times when it didn't look all that different from the French in the 1940 campaign or the Italians in the Western Desert of North Africa. Defenders of the army's honor can deflect such criticisms onto Hitler, of course, but Hitler's deficiencies as a strategist tell only part of the story. German field marshals and general officers focused relentlessly on operations—by which they meant usually one thing: the maneuver scheme. That one-sided fixation often meant problems in nonkinetic aspects of the fight: supply, logistics, and intelligence. For example, one amazing aspect of Operation *Wacht am Rhein*, the German offensive in the Ardennes (the Battle of the Bulge), was the principle that since there was not enough fuel to go around for all the Panzer formations the advance would have to rely upon captured enemy stocks. *Wacht am Rhein* was not a sound operational plan at all, then, but a prayer. German officers were also unconcerned with broader questions of war, such as international politics, overall strategy, and economics. They took refuge in the excuse that Hitler held all those threads in his hand so they could concentrate on their narrower métier. And so, for example, Wehrmacht commanders paid no real attention to the Axis-allied armies fighting at their side—the Italians, Romanians, Finns, and Hungarians without whom continuation of the war was impossible.

A second problem in the last years of the war in Europe was the politicization of the German officer corps. Present in embryo ever since Hitler came to power, and reified in 1934 (when the Wehrmacht took an oath to Hitler directly rather than to the German constitution) and 1938 (during the so-called Blomberg-Fritsch Crisis, when Hitler abolished the defense ministry and created the OKW), the nazification of the German generals triumphed completely in 1944–1945. Despite posing as anti-Hitlerites in their postwar memoirs, the generals remained loyal to the core. Guderian and Field Marshal Gerd von Rundstedt sat on misnamed "Courts of Honor" and judged fellow officers implicated in the July 20 plot to assassinate Hitler. Virtually all of them took huge bribes (so-called dotations) from the Nazi regime. These dotations were allegedly gifts from a grateful nation—a ridiculous and offensive notion during this period of bloody defeats. Manstein used his money to purchase an estate in Pomerania in October 1944, at the very moment the Soviets were massing troops to scour the entire region, and all the senior officers received a double bonus share on May 1, 1945—the day after Hitler's suicide.[51]

Conclusion: Schörner's War

Those who see the Wehrmacht as an army of brilliant operators like Guderian, Rommel, and Manstein need to clear a space in the memory palace for one field marshal whom we have all but forgotten. Ferdinand Schörner was the *typos* of the late-war Nazi general. He came to the fore late in the conflict, holding a series of increasingly hopeless commands as Germany's strategic situation deteriorated: Army Group A and Army Group South Ukraine in the spring of 1944; Army Group North (later renamed Army Group Courland) in the summer; Army Group Center in January 1945, which he led until the end. He never won a battle, but failure wasn't fully his fault. While Schörner was competent enough in a technical sense, nothing short of nuclear weapons could have evened up the fight on the Eastern Front against a Soviet army vastly superior in numbers and equipment.

If we take as the first rule of generalship "do no harm," however, then Schörner was a disaster.[52] His art of war consisted of loyalty to Hitler. He was a true believer, a fanatic about holding out to the end, even as things fell apart. Of all the Führer's minions, Schörner was the most enthusiastic, a National Socialist if ever there was one. Schörner's bedrock conception of command was to shoot or hang large numbers of his own men for "cowardice" in order to terrorize the others into obeying him. He led through fear—flying his little Fieseler Storch aircraft around the rear areas of his army groups, landing suddenly in a divisional or corps area of responsibility, and handing down death sentences on the flimsiest of evidence—all the while staring down at his immaculately manicured fingernails. The phrase "*der Ferdl kommt!*" ("Here comes Ferd!") always meant trouble for the rank and file. He once scolded his chief of staff that "you handle the operations, I'll keep order," and in the weeks after the attempt on Hitler's life he opened staff meetings by asking, "How many men did you hang today?"[53] It is no surprise that Goebbels admired Schörner for his "political insight" and for his "entirely new, modern methods." To be specific:

> He takes special aim at the so-called regular stragglers. By "regular stragglers," he means those soldiers, who always seem to understand how to remove themselves from their unit in critical situations and vanish back into the rear under some kind of pretext. He deals with such figures quite brutally, has them hanged from the nearest tree wearing a placard that says, "I am a deserter and was too cowardly to protect German women and children."

"Naturally," Goebbels concluded, "this has a terrifying impact on other deserters or those who are thinking about it."[54] Hitler, too, appreciated these methods and named Schörner his successor as Commander in Chief of the Army—Nazi Germany's last.

Like all tyrants, Schörner assembled a posse of thugs around him who did the dirty work. His security troops once came upon a tank workshop where a crew was waiting to get its reconnaissance vehicle fixed. The crew's actions seem logical enough, but Schörner had the vehicle commander shot for "malingering." On other occasions, as at Lednice on May 7, 1945, Schörner was reportedly present when his military police shot twenty-two German soldiers for "standing around without orders."[55] Hitler had been dead for a week by then and the war was all but over, but Schörner was still executing his own men to encourage the others.

Schörner's excuse for his crimes was that he had to maintain discipline in the ranks so that his army group could escape to the west (toward the Americans) rather than be overrun by the Soviets. His strategy was an organized flight to the west, a maneuver that had to proceed systematically. Just two days before the murders at Lednice, Schörner had issued his last order of the day to Army Group Center. Excoriating the "traitors and cowards" in their midst, he urged his men to be steadfast. "In these hard days, we must not lose our nerves or become cowardly," he declared. "Any attempt to find your own way back to the homeland is a dishonorable betrayal of your comrades and of our people . . . and will be punished."[56]

Powerful words—and stirring words! A few days later, on May 9, Schörner bundled himself into his little Storch and flew away, abandoning his post and leaving the men of Army Group Center to their fate as Soviet prisoners. The commander who hanged "traitors" and "cowards" from lampposts and fences and who let his men know that "they might die at the front, but they definitely would die in the rear"[57] had apparently reached his limit, making us wonder whether all the threats, all the abuse he heaped on others, all the summary executions were not merely a compensatory mechanism for some inner weakness.[58] Schörner managed to fly to the safety of American lines, but US troops handed him over to the Soviets, who put him on trial and put him in prison for the next ten years. Schörner did his time next to some of the very men he had left in the lurch—and they didn't hesitate to let him know what they thought of him. Released in late 1954, he returned to West Germany, provoking angry outbursts from many former soldiers and their families. He went on trial there, too, and spent four more years in prison.

In the end, Schörner had proven his loyalty, but only in the narrowest sense. He had stayed loyal to Hitler to the very end and beyond. To his troops, however, he had shown only callousness, if not outright cruelty. Consider this admonition toward Germany's former generals from a German author in 1949:

> How astonishing that the generals always speak only of their soldierly duty to those above them, never of their duty to those soldiers whose lives are in their hands, the blood of their own nation. No one can demand that you kill a tyrant if your conscience forbids it. But mustn't we demand the same care and seriousness toward the lives of each of your subordinates?[59]

A particularly good question—and not only for Schörner! Let us recall that he wasn't the only one "guilty of the senseless death of German soldiers" in the last year of the war.[60] World War II will always be "Hitler's war," but Hitler had an officer corps filled with hundreds and thousands of Schörners: the key enablers who helped their Führer launch the war, fight it, and keep fighting it long after any hope of victory had vanished.

Until five minutes past midnight.

Notes

Introduction

1. The classic evocation of this scene is H. R. Trevor-Roper, *The Last Days of Hitler* (New York: Macmillan, 1947), 96–100.

2. The quote is from the diary of Johann Ludwig "Lutz" Graf Schwerin von Krosigk, in ibid., 98.

3. The best analysis of Frederick the Great in the Seven Years' War, combining deep insight and sharp writing, is Dennis E. Showalter, *The Wars of Frederick the Great* (New York: Longman, 1996). For the improbable end game ("Prussia's situation was restored by an event no reviewer of historical fiction would credit as a novel's plot"), see 311–316.

4. For the dramatic change in Russian policy, see Robert Asprey, *Frederick the Great: The Magnificent Enigma* (New York: History Book Club, 1986), 551–553.

5. Albert Speer, *Erinnerungen* (Frankfurt am Main: Ullstein, 1969), 44: "Für einen grossen Bau hätte ich wie Faust meine Seele verkauft. Nun hatte ich meinen Mephisto gefunden." The memoirs appear in English as *Inside the Third Reich: Memoirs by Albert Speer* (New York: Macmillan, 1970). The quote is on page 31.

6. See Helmut Lindemann, "Die Schuld der Generale," *Deutsche Rundschau* (January 1949): 20–26: "Der Vorwurf, die Abschlachtung von vielen Hunderttausenden deutscher Soldaten nicht verhindert zu haben, muss schwer auf dem Gewissen jedes einzelnen deutschen Generals lasten" (24).

7. Jörg Muth, *Command Culture: Officer Education in the U.S. Army and the German Armed Forces, 1901–1940, and the Consequences for World War II* (Denton: University of North Texas Press, 2011), 100.

8. The works of Omer Bartov were seminal in the rise of the ideological school: *The Eastern Front, 1941–45: German Troops and the Barbarisation of Warfare* (New York: St. Martin's Press, 1986), and *Hitler's Army: Soldiers, Nazis, and War in the Third Reich* (New York: Oxford University Press, 1991). See also Stephen G. Fritz, *Frontsoldaten: The German Soldier in World War II* (Lexington: University Press of Kentucky, 1995), and Wolfram Wette, *Die Wehrmacht: Feindbilder, Vernichtungskrieg, Legenden* (Frankfurt: S. Fischer, 2002).

9. See Robert M. Citino, *The German Way of War: From the Thirty Years' War to the Third Reich* (Lawrence: University Press of Kansas, 2005).

10. Michael Stürmer, *The German Empire: A Short History* (New York: Modern Library, 2000), 12–13.

11. Waldemar Erfurth, "Die Zusammenwirken getrennter Heeresteile," 4 parts, *Militärwissenschaftliche Rundschau* 4, nos. 1–4 (1939): 14–41, 156–78, 290–314, and 472–499.

12. See, for example, W. Bigge, "Ueber Selbstthätigkeit der Unterführer im Kriege," *Beihefte zum Militär-Wochenblatt* 1894 (Berlin: E. S. Mittler, 1894), 17–55, from the text of a lecture given to the Military Society in Berlin on November 29, 1893. See also Wilhelm Hermann von Blume, "Selbstthätigkeit der Führer im Kriege," *Beihefte zum Militär-Wochenblatt* 1896 (Berlin: E. S. Mittler, 1896), 479–534.

13. Still the best book on the topic is Dirk W. Oetting, *Auftragstaktik: Geschichte und Gegenwart einer Führungskonzeption* (Frankfurt: Report Verlag, 1993). A representative example from literally hundreds in the professional military literature is Wilhelm Meyer-Detring, "Vorzüge und Grenzen der Auftragstaktik," *Allgemeine Schweizerische Militärzeitschrift* 136, no. 11 (1970): 824–831.

14. For the dramatic operational sequence from Prague to Zorndorf—the crucible of Frederick's career and historical reputation—see Showalter, *Wars of Frederick the Great*, 135–221, and Citino, *German Way of War*, 67–100.

15. For a fine period account of Frederick's disaster at Hochkirk, see Ernst Friedrich Rudolf von Barsewisch, "The Battle of Hochkirch," in Peter Paret, ed., *Frederick the Great: A Profile* (New York: Hill and Wang), 121–128.

16. The phrase "Krieg des armen Mannes" is ubiquitous in the professional German discourse on World War II. For one example, see Walter Görlitz, *Model: Strategie der Defensive* (Wiesbaden: Limes, 1977), 177.

17. Any inquiry into Barbarossa and the drive on Moscow must begin with the works of David Stahel: *Operation Barbarossa and Germany's Defeat in the East* (Cambridge: Cambridge University Press, 2009), *Kiev 1941: Hitler's Battle for Supremacy in the East* (Cambridge: Cambridge University Press, 2009), and *Operation Typhoon: Hitler's March on Moscow, October 1941* (Cambridge: Cambridge University Press, 2013). Combining exhaustive research and a sharply etched thesis (i.e., that Barbarossa was unwinnable and that the wheels had come off the German effort almost immediately after crossing the border), they represent the state of the question today. For a more popular but still very erudite approach, see Andrew Nagorski, *The Greatest Battle: Stalin, Hitler, and the Desperate Struggle for Moscow That Changed the Course of World War II* (New York: Simon & Schuster, 2007). For the disastrous Stalingrad-Alamein nexus, see Robert M. Citino, *Death of the Wehrmacht: The German Campaigns of 1942* (Lawrence: University Press of Kansas, 2007).

18. The preeminent German-language work on the Mediterranean campaign is Ralf Georg Reuth, *Entscheidung im Mittelmeer: Die südliche Peripherie Europas in der deutschen Strategie des Zweiten Weltkrieges, 1940–1942* (Koblenz: Bernard & Graefe, 1985), including the introduction by Andreas Hillgruber (7–8). See also Douglas Porch, *The Path to Victory: The Mediterranean Theater in World War II* (New York: Farrar, Straus and Giroux, 2004). (For the Tunisian campaign, see 370–414.)

For detailed operational analysis of the fighting, see Robert M. Citino, *The Wehrmacht Retreats: Fighting a Lost War, 1943* (Lawrence: University Press of Kansas, 2012), 75–109.

19. The indispensable work on the deterioration and collapse of the Axis is Josef Schröder, *Italiens Kriegsaustritt 1943: Die deutschen Gegenmassnahmen im italienischen Raum: Fall "Alarich" und "Achse"* (Göttingen: Musterschmidt-Verlag, 1969).

20. The crucial German-language work on Kursk is Ernst Klink, *Das Gesetz des Handelns: Die Operation Zitadelle 1943* (Stuttgart: Deutsche Verlags-Anstalt, 1966), especially the appendices (*Anlagen*). Read Klink in conjunction with the pertinent portions of the German official history, *Das Deutsche Reich und der Zweite Weltkrieg*, volume 8, *Die Ostfront 1943/44* (München: Deutsche Verlags-Anstalt, 2007), part 1, Bernd Wegner, "Von Stalingrad nach Kursk," 1–79; part 2, Karl-Heinz Frieser, "Die Schlacht im Kursker Bogen," 81–208; and part 3, Bernd Wegner, "Die Aporie des Krieges," 209–274. Together, these three sections add up to a major scholarly monograph on Kursk, its origins, course, and aftermath, written by two of the deans of operational military history in Germany. "Official history," with all its negative connotations of reputation-protecting and special pleading, this is not. The third indispensable volume is Roland G. Foerster, ed., *Gezeitenwechsel im Zweiten Weltkrieg? Die Schlachten von Ch'arkow und Kursk im Frühjahr und Sommer 1943 in operativer Anlage, Verlauf und politischer Bedeutung* (Berlin: E. S. Mittler, 1996), the edited papers of the 35th International Military History Day, a 1993 scholarly conference in Ingolstadt sponsored by the Federal German Militärgeschichtliches Forschungsamt (Military History Research Office).

21. For Balck's swirling fight between Zhitomir and Brussilov, see F. W. von Mellenthin, *Panzer Battles: A Study of the Employment of Armor in the Second World War* (New York: Ballantine, 1971), 301–20.

22. Earl D. Ziemke, *Stalingrad to Berlin: The German Defeat in the East* (Washington, DC: Center of Military History, 1987), 197–205, covers the fighting at Nevel in typically concise fashion. For "Schweinerei," see page 203.

23. "Herr Feldmarschall," declared Conrath to his superior, Field Marshal Albert Kesselring, "das sofortige Drauflosmarschieren ist meine Stärke." Albert Kesselring, *Soldat bis zum letzten Tag* (Bonn: Athenäum, 1953), 221. The English translation of Kesselring's memoirs is, "If you mean to go for them, Field-Marshal, then I'm your man." Kesselring, *A Soldier's Record* (New York: William Morrow, 1954), 194.

24. For the battle of Mars-la-Tour, see Geoffrey Wawro, *The Franco-Prussian War: Germany Conquers France, 1970–71* (Cambridge: Cambridge University Press, 2005), 151–163, by one of the best writers in the field. Dennis Showalter, *The Wars of German Unification* (London: Arnold, 2004), 258–263, offers insightful commentary as always. The narrative in Michael Howard, *The Franco-Prussian War* (New York, Macmillan, 1962), 144–166, still shapes the discussion of the battle.

25. Hans von Kretschman, "The Battle of Vionville—Mars-la-Tour," in Major General Sir F. Maurice, ed., *The Franco-German War, by Generals and Other Officers Who Took Part in the Campaign* (London: Allen & Unwin, 1899), 146.

26. Howard, *Franco-Prussian War*, 157.

27. For the French origins, see Lieutenant Colonel Walter Obkircher, "General Constantin von Alvbensleben: Zu Seinem 50. Todestag, 28 März," *Militär-Wochenblatt* 126, no. 39 (March 7, 1942): 1113.

28. "Es ist keine Schlacht verloren, solange man nicht das Gefühl hat, geschlagen zu sein. Und ich wollte dies Gefühl nicht haben." Quoted in Lieutenant Colonel Wolfgang Foerster, "Prinz Friedrich Karl," *Militärwissenschaftliche Rundschau* 8, no. 2 (1943): 90. For the best biography of Blücher, one that challenges much of the traditional narrative of the career of "Marschall Vorwärts," see Michael V. Leggiere, *Blücher: Scourge of Napoleon* (Norman: University of Oklahoma Press, 2014).

29. For examples of the "Kesselring as genius" trope, see Carlo D'Este, *Fatal Decision: Anzio and the Battle for Rome* (New York: Harper Perennial, 1992), 87–88, Porch, *Path to Victory*, 423, and Dominick Graham and Shelford Bidwell, *Tug of War: The Battle for Italy* (London: Hodder & Stoughton, 1986), 38.

30. See Alan F. Wilt, *The Atlantic Wall: Hitler's Defenses in the West, 1941–1944* (New York: Enigma Books, 2004), as well as Walter Warlimont, *Im Hauptquartier der deutschen Wehrmacht 1939 bis 1945: Grundlagen, Formen, Gestalten*, vol. 2 (Augsburg: Weltbild Verlag, 1990): 434–438.

31. Preeminently in the works of the late Stephen E. Ambrose: *Band of Brothers: E Company, 506th Regiment, 101st Airborne; From Normandy to Hitler's Eagle's Nest* (New York: Simon & Schuster, 1992); *D-Day, June 6, 1944: The Climactic Battle of World War II* (New York: Simon & Schuster, 1994); and *Citizen Soldiers: The U.S. Army from the Normandy Beaches to the Bulge to the Surrender of Germany, June 7, 1944–May 7, 1945* (New York: Simon & Schuster, 1997), all works that paved the way for Tom Brokaw, *The Greatest Generation* (New York: Random House, 1998).

32. Compared to the mountain of books on Operation Overlord, Bagration has generated essentially two. Paul Adair, *Hitler's Greatest Defeat: The Collapse of Army Group Center* (London: Brockhampton, 1994), offers a worthy narrative without a grounding in the foreign-language documents or scholarship. For a far superior work, see Walter S. Dunn Jr., *Soviet Blitzkrieg: The Battle for White Russia, 1944* (Boulder, CO: Lynne Rienner, 2000), a meticulous analysis based firmly on Russian-language works.

33. "Es war eine weit grössere Katastrophe als diejenige von Stalingrad." Walter Görlitz, *Der zweite Weltkrieg 1939–1945*, vol. 2 (Stuttgart: Steingrüben, 1952), 252.

34. There is a copious literature on the suffering of German civilians in the last year of the war, often linked to the politics of expellee groups in the postwar Federal Republic. See, for representative examples, Kurt Dieckert and Horst Grossmann, *Der Kampf um Ostpreussen: der umfassende Dokumentarbericht über das Kriegsgeschehen in Ostpreussen* (Stuttgart: Motorbuch, 1960), Hans von Ahlfen, *Der Kampf um Schlesien 1944–1945* (Stuttgart: Motorbuch, 1963), and Egbet Kieser, *Danziger Bucht 1945: Dokumentation einer Katastrophe* (Esslingen am Neckar: Bechtle, 1978).

35. See Krisztián Ungváry, *The Siege of Budapest: 100 Days in World War II* (New Haven: Yale, 2005).

36. See, for example, Dr. Erich Weniger, "Die Selbständigkeit der Unterführer und ihre Grenzen," an older article reprinted in the *Militärwissenschaftliche Rundschau* 9, no. 2, (1944): 101–115, stressing the "limits" of independent command.

37. For the discourse of the late war period, see Richard Lakowski, "Das Zusammenbruch der deutschen Verteidigung zwischen Ostsee und Karpaten," in *Das Deutsche Reich und der Zweite Weltkrieg*, volume 10/1, *Der Zusammenbruch des deutschen Reiches 1945: die Militärische Niederwerfung der Wehrmacht* (München: Deutsche Verlags-Anstalt, 2008), 493–494. For period examples of the same language, see "Clausewitz über Beharrlichkeit im Kriege," *Militärwissenschaftliche Rundschau* 9, no. 1 (1944): 56, and Helmut Beck-Broichsitter, "Über Beharrlichkeit im Angriff," *Militärwissenschaftliche Rundschau* 9, no. 1 (1944): 57–64.

38. "Oft genug nicht nur unkonventioneller, sondern auch unprofessioneller und fehlerhafter operativer Entschlüsse Hitlers." See Bernd Wegner, "Der Krieg gegen Die Sowjetunion, 1942–43," in *Das Deutsche Reich und der Zweite Weltkrieg*, volume 6, *Die Ausweitung zum Weltkrieg und der Wechsel der Initiative, 1941–1943* (Stuttgart: Deutsche Verlags-Anstalt, 1990), 954.

39. "Um jeden Meter Boden zu ringen." Adolf Heusinger, *Befehl im Widerstreit: Schicksalsstunden der deutschen Armee 1923–1945* (Tübingen: Rainer Wunderlich Verlag, 1950), 283.

40. "Halten um jeden Preis." See General Peter von der Groeben, "Der Zusammenbruch der Heeresgruppe Mitte und ihr Kampf bis zur Festigung der Front (22.VI. bis 1.IX.1944)," Foreign Military Studies (FMS) series, published by the US Department of the Army and based upon interviews with captured German generals. The German originals remain unpublished but are available for consultation at the US Army Heritage and Education Center (USAHEC) in Carlisle, PA, manuscript T-31, 39.

41. Trevor-Roper, *Last Days of Hitler*, 97, has Schwerin-Krosigk's touching narrative: Goebbels is reading Hitler passages from the Führer's favorite book, Thomas Carlyle's *History of Frederick the Great*, with the king suffering and contemplating suicide, and then hearing of the death of the Tsarina and the "miracle of the house of Brandenburg." As Goebbels would later report, "tears stood in the Führer's eyes." See also John Clive, "Editor's Introduction," in Thomas Carlyle, *History of Frederick the Great* (Chicago: University of Chicago Press, 1969), xiii.

42. For the role that the "Dotationen" ("bribes" in plain English) played in keeping the war going, see Olaf Groehler, "Die Güter der Generale: Dotationen im zweiten Weltkrieg," *Zeitschrift für Geschichtswissenschaft* 19, no. 5 (1971): 655–663, a blast by an East German scholar not only against the Wehrmacht generals but also at their "fascist" successors in the Bundeswehr. Groehler gives a detailed account of the truly massive sums the regime gave to all the field marshals, boosting their salaries to 48,000 Reichsmarks, at a time when the average German worker or professional made 2,100–2,900 per annum, as well as gifts for birthdays and other special events (250,000 Reichsmarks to Field Marshal Keitel for his fiftieth birthday, for example, or the same amount to von Kluge for his sixtieth). See also Gerhard Weinberg, "Some Thoughts on World War II," in Gerhard Weinberg, *Germany, Hitler & World War II* (Cambridge: Cambridge University Press,

1995), 307–309. As Weinberg puts it, the end of the war saw "huge bribes for many at the top and bullets for thousands at the bottom" (309). For one scholar who answered Weinberg's call for research into this point, see Norman J. W. Goda, "Black Marks: Hitler's Bribery of his Senior Officers during World War II," *Journal of Modern History*, 72, No. 2 (June 2000): 413–452, later reprinted in Emmanuel Kreike and William Chester Jordan, eds., *Corrupt Histories* (Rochester, NY: University of Rochester Press, 2004), 96–137. For the role that bribery played in General Heinz Guderian's career, and his acquisition of the estate at Gut Diepenhof in West Prussia, see Russell A. Hart, *Guderian: Panzer Pioneer or Myth Maker* (Washington, DC: Potomac, 2006), 82–84.

43. For the relationship between the German army and the surrender of 1918, as well as the most nuanced discussion of the *Dolchstoss*, see Scott Stephenson, *The Final Battle: Soldiers of the Western Front and the German Revolution of 1918* (Cambridge: Cambridge University Press, 2009).

44. "Krieg bis fünf Minuten nach zwölf," Lakowski, "Das Zusammenbruch der deutschen Verteidigung zwischen Ostsee und Karpaten," 491.

Chapter 1. In the Cauldron: The Battle of the Korsun Pocket

1. The vignette is taken from diary entries in Anonymous, "Im Kessel," *Allgemeine schweizerische Militärzeitschrift* 115, nos. 4–6 (April–June 1949): 259–69, 328–337, 410–421. The specific quote is found in no. 4 (April 1949): 261. The author was a German intelligence officer inside the Korsun Pocket.

2. For an overview of the concept and its execution, see Edgar Röhricht, *Probleme der Kesselschlacht: dargestellt an Einkreisungs-Operationen im Zweiten Weltkrieg* (Karlsruhe: Condor-Verlag, 1958). Röhricht also published his memoirs, *Pflicht und Gewissen: Erinnerungen eines deutschen Generals 1932 bis 1944* (Stuttgart: W. Kohlhammer Verlag, 1965).

3. For the campaigns of Frederick William, the Great Elector of Brandenburg, it is necessary to rely upon the older secondary literature and biographies, especially Martin Philippson, *Der Grosse Kurfürst Friedrich Wilhelm von Brandenburg*, 3 volumes (Berlin: Verlag Siegfried Cronbach, 1897–1903); Gerhard von Pelet-Narbonne, *Der Grosse Kurfürst* (Berlin: B. Behr, 1905); and Hans Kania, *Der Grosse Kurfürst* (Leipzig: Teubner, 1930). Curt Jany, *Geschichte der königlich preussischen Armee*, 4 volumes (Berlin: Karl Siegismund, 1928–1933), is still useful. For Frederick the Great, begin with Dennis E. Showalter, *The Wars of Frederick the Great* (London: Longman, 1996). Older biographies of Frederick include the comprehensive work by Reinhold Koser, *Geschichte Friedrichs des Grossen* (Berlin: J. G. Cotta, 1912–13); Lieutenant Colonel W. von Bremen, *Friedrich der Grosse* (Berlin: B. Behr, 1905); and the classic English-language account by Thomas Carlyle, *History of Friedrich the Second, Called Frederick the Great* (Albany, NY: J. B. Lyon, 1900). Useful modern works include Gerhard Ritter, *Frederick the Great: A Historical Profile* (Berkeley: University of California Press, 1968); Walther Hubatsch, *Frederick the Great of Prussia: Absolutism and Administration* (London: Thames and Hudson,

1973); and Theodor Schieder, *Frederick the Great* (London: Longman, 2000). For a synthesis of the scholarly literature, see Robert M. Citino, *The German Way of War: From the Thirty Years' War to the Third Reich* (Lawrence: University Press of Kansas, 2005), especially 1–103.

4. There is a large and vibrant literature on Moltke's wars. Begin with Dennis E. Showalter, *The Wars of German Unification* (London: Arnold, 2004), a marriage of fine scholarship and elegant writing, and Arden Bucholz, *Moltke and the German Wars, 1864–1871* (New York: Palgrave, 2001). For the primary source, head to Helmuth von Moltke, *Strategy, Its Theory and Application: The Wars for German Unification, 1866–1871* (Westport, CT: Greenwood, 1971), a reprint of his selected correspondence, as well as Daniel Hughes, ed., *Moltke on the Art of War: Selected Writings*, (Novato, CA: Presidio, 1993). For 1866, begin with Gordon Craig, *The Battle of Königgrätz: Prussia's Victory over Austria, 1866* (Philadelphia: Lippincott, 1964), although it has been superseded by Geoffrey Wawro, *The Austro-Prussian War: Austria's War with Prussia and Italy in 1866* (Cambridge: Cambridge University Press, 1996), a work of meticulous research and sharp analysis. The professional German view is found in Major General Oscar von Lettow-Vorbeck, *Geschichte des Krieges von 1866 in Deutschland*, 3 volumes (Berlin: E. S. Mittler, 1896–1902). For a general account by one of Germany's most brilliant and renowned literary figures, see Theodor Fontane, *Der deutsche Krieg von 1866*, 2 volumes (Berlin: R. v. Decker, 1870–71). For the war with France, start with the leading authority, Geoffrey Wawro, *The Franco-Prussian War* (Cambridge: Cambridge University Press, 2003), which has now largely superseded the previous standard work by Michael Howard, *The Franco-Prussian War* (New York: Macmillan, 1962). The primary source is Helmuth von Moltke, *The Franco-German War of 1870–71* (New York: Howard Fertig, 1988). Theodor Fontane, *Der Krieg gegen Frankreich, 1870–1871*, 4 volumes (Zürich: Manesse, 1985), is beautifully written and typically perceptive.

5. The Schlieffen Plan is more than a century old but continues to generate fierce controversy. For the book that started it all, see Gerhard Ritter, *Der Schlieffenplan: Kritik eines Mythos* (Munich: R. Oldenbourg, 1956), especially 13–81, which included Schlieffen's *Denkschrift* of early 1906, the first time it had appeared in published form. Ritter's verdict ("the Schlieffen Plan was never a sound recipe for victory" but "a bold, even over-bold gamble, whose success depended on many lucky breaks," 68) endured in the literature until the appearance of Terence Zuber, *Inventing the Schlieffen Plan: German War Planning, 1871–1914* (Oxford: Oxford University Press, 2002). Presented first in his article, "The Schlieffen Plan Reconsidered," *War in History* 6, no. 3 (July 1999): 262–305, Zuber's argument is that the Schlieffen Plan was a postwar construction and that Schlieffen never had a firm plan to march an army corps around the west of Paris to encircle the entire French army. Noting that there is no reference at all to the plan until 1920, and that the first operational history of the war, the Swiss historian Hermann Stegemann's *Geschichte des Krieges* (Stuttgart: Deutsche Verlags-Anstalt, 1918), doesn't even mention it, Zuber posits that German officers, anxious to preserve their reputations, attempted to heap the blame onto General Helmuth von Moltke (the Younger) by claiming that he had failed to carry out the plan bequeathed to him by

his genius-predecessor, Schlieffen. The book generated an enormous controversy that played out in the scholarly journals. For an overview of the *Schlieffenstreit*, see Hans Ehlert, Michael Epkenhans, and Gerhard P. Gross, eds., *The Schlieffen Plan: International Perspectives on the German Strategy for World War I* (Lexington: University Press of Kentucky, 2014), a collection of papers from a conference at the federal German *Militärgeschichtliches Forschungsamt* in 2004. The volume also includes a useful appendix including German mobilization plans from 1893 to 1914. Unfortunately, the paper that Zuber delivered at the conference is not included, although it was in the original German version of the book, *Der Schlieffenplan: Analysen und Dokumente* (München: Odenberg, 2006).

6. On Tannenberg, Dennis E. Showalter's *Tannenberg: Clash of Empires* (Washington, DC: Brassey's, 2004), currently reigns supreme, along with Holger H. Herwig's *The First World War: Germany and Austria-Hungary, 1914–1918* (London: Arnold, 1997), and Norman Stone's older but still very useful work, *The Eastern Front, 1914–1917* (London: Hodder and Stoughton, 1975).

7. Any study of the Eastern Front from the Soviet side must begin with the body of work by David M. Glantz, some of it written alone, some with Jonathan House. A partial list includes *When Titans Clashed: How the Red Army Stopped Hitler* (Lawrence: University Press of Kansas, 1995), *The Battle of Kursk* (Lawrence: University Press of Kansas, 1999), *To the Gates of Stalingrad: Soviet-German Combat Operations, April–August 1942* (Lawrence: University Press of Kansas, 2009), and *Armageddon in Stalingrad: September–November 1942* (Lawrence: University Press of Kansas, 2009), all with Jonathan House; and, as a solitary author, *Zhukov's Greatest Defeat: The Red Army's Epic Disaster in Operation Mars* (Lawrence: University Press of Kansas, 1999), *The Battle for Leningrad, 1941–1944* (Lawrence: University Press of Kansas, 2002), *Colossus Reborn: The Red Army at War, 1941–1943* (Lawrence: University Press of Kansas, 2005), and *Red Storm over the Balkans: The Failed Soviet Invasion of Romania, Spring 1944* (Lawrence: University Press of Kansas, 2007). Glantz's entire oeuvre is data-intensive, hyperdetailed, and authoritative. His only current rival from the German side is the equally authoritative David Stahel, author of *Operation Barbarossa and Germany's Defeat in the East* (Cambridge: Cambridge University Press, 2009), *Kiev 1941: Hitler's Battle for Supremacy in the East* (Cambridge: Cambridge University Press, 2012), and *Operation Typhoon: Hitler's March on Moscow* (Cambridge: Cambridge University Press, 2013).

8. For the German view of Kasserine Pass, see Robert M. Citino, *The Wehrmacht Retreats: Fighting a Lost War, 1943* (Lawrence: University Press of Kansas, 2012), 75–109.

9. As opposed to *exzentrisch*, with friendly formations moving away from one another, representing a loss of combat power and thus undesirable. See, for example, Robert M. Citino, *Death of the Wehrmacht: The German Campaigns of 1942* (Lawrence: University Press of Kansas, 2007), 155–158.

10. For the use of "ordinary victory" in German military literature, see, for example, Hermann Jung, *Die Ardennen-Offensive 1944/45: Ein Beispiel für die Kriegführung Hitlers* (Göttingen: Muster-Schmidt Verlag, 1971): "[Die] deutschen An-

griffsdivisionen der Einkesselung entgingen und die Alliierten nur einen 'ordinären Sieg' errangen" (199).

11. Stahel is the authority on the battle of Moscow, with *Operation Typhoon* analyzing the opening stages of the German drive on the capital and *The Battle for Moscow* (Cambridge: Cambridge University Press, 2014) examining the final grind to a halt. The Soviet counteroffensive has not received the attention it deserves in the English-language scholarship. For the Soviet staff study, see Richard W. Harrison, ed., *The Battle of Moscow 1941–1942: The Red Army's Defensive Operations and Counteroffensive along the Moscow Strategic Direction* (Solihull, UK: Helion, 2015). Andrew Nagorski, *The Great Battle: Stalin, Hitler, and the Desperate Struggle for Moscow That Changed the Course of World War II* (New York: Simon & Schuster, 2007), is a nicely written popular account.

12. For Stalingrad, the campaign that led up to it, the fighting within the city itself, and the Soviet counteroffensive that ended it, see Citino, *Death of the Wehrmacht*, 152–182, 223–258, and 289–302.

13. For Paulus's "Armee eingeschlossen" dispatch, see Manfred Kehrig, *Stalingrad: Analyse und Dokumentation einer Schlacht* (Stuttgart: Deutsche Verlags-Anstalt, 1974), 559–560.

14. The issues involved in the breakout versus air supply argument are handled very ably in Joel S. A. Hayward, *Stopped at Stalingrad: The Luftwaffe and Hitler's Defeat in the East, 1942–1943* (Lawrence: University Press of Kansas, 1998).

15. The primary source on the winter counteroffensive of 1943 is Erich von Manstein, *Verlorene Siege* (Bonn: Athenäum-Verlag, 1955), 397–472, "Der Winterfeldzug 1942/42 in Sudrüssland," although the entire book needs to be read with a healthy skepticism. See also Friedrich Schulz, "Der Rückschlag im Süden der Ostfront 1942/43," Manuscript T-15 in the Foreign Military Studies series. The original is available in the US Army Heritage and Education Center (AHEC) in Carlisle, PA. The report is also available in English translation as "Reverses on the Southern Wing." Two indispensable English-language works are David M. Glantz, *From the Don to the Dnepr: Soviet Offensive Operations, December 1942–August 1943* (London: Frank Cass, 1991), and Dana V. Sadarananda, *Beyond Stalingrad: Manstein and the Operations of Army Group Don* (Mechanicsburg, PA: Stackpole, 2009). From the German side, see Eberhard Schwarz, *Die Stabilisierung der Ostfront nach Stalingrad: Mansteins Gegenschlag zwischen Donez und Dnjepr im Frühjahr 1943* (Göttingen: Muster-Schmidt Verlag, 1985). See also two works by the dean of German military historians, Karl-Heinz Frieser: "Schlagen aus der Nachhand—Schlagen aus der Vorhand: Die Schlachten von Char'kow und Kursk 1943," in Roland G. Foerster, ed., *Gezeitenwechsel im Zweiten Weltkrieg? Die Schlachten von Char'kov und Kursk im Frühjahr und Sommer 1943 in operativer Anlage, Verlauf und politischer Bedeutung* (Berlin: E. S. Mittler, 1996), and "Mansteins Gegenschlag am Donez: Operative Analyse des Gegenangriffs der Heeresgruppe Süd im Februar/März 1943," *Militärgeschichte* 9 (1999): 12–18 (written with Friedhelm Klein).

16. For a critical discussion of this sobriquet, see Robert M. Citino, *The Wehrmacht Retreats*, 113–116.

17. For an account of Kutuzov by one of the German commanders, see Lothar Rendulic, "Die Schlacht von Orel, Juli 1943: Wahl und Bildung des Schwerpunktes," *Österreichische Militärische Zeitschrift* 1, no. 3 (1963): 130–138.

18. For the Belgorod operation, see the chapter, virtually a monograph in itself, in Glantz, *From the Don to the Dnepr*, 215–365.

19. "Die Enttäuschung der Truppe war riesengross, war erschütternd mitzuerleben." Nikolaus von Vormann, *Tscherkassy* (Heidelberg: Kurt Vowinckel Verlag, 1954), 12.

20. "Auch ich als Kommandeur der 23. Pz.D. glaubte daran. Auch ich wollte nachts mal wieder schlafen, ohne befürchteten zu müssen, dass russische Panzer das Wecken übernahmen." Ibid.

21. "Dann sehen meine Generale nur nach hinten." Ibid.

22. "Erschwerend kam hinzu, dass die Nogaische Steppe ohne Baum und Strauch keine Deckung bot und kaum natürliche Hindernisse besass. So fühlten sich die Soldaten wie auf einem Präsientierteller dem feindlichen Feuer ausgesetzt." Karl-Heinz Frieser, "Der Rückzugsoperationen der Heeresgruppe Süd in der Ukraine," in *Das Deutsche Reich und der Zweite Weltkrieg*, volume 8, *Die Ostfront 1943/44: Der Krieg im Osten und an den Nebenfronten* (München: Deutsche Verlags-Anstalt, 2011), 382.

23. See the discussion in Ferdinand Heim, "Stalingrad und der Verlauf des Feldzuges der Jahre 1943–1945," in Alfred Philippi and Ferdinand Heim, *Der Feldzug gegen Sowjetrussland 1941 bis 1945: ein operativer Überblick* (Stuttgart: W. Kohlhammer, 1962), especially 225–229.

24. Manstein, *Verlorene Siege*, 535.

25. For an eyewitness account of the debate between Hitler and Zeitzler over a retreat to the *Pantherstellung*, see Adolf Heusinger, *Befehl im Widerstreit: Schicksalsstunden der deutschen Armee 1923–1945* (Tübingen: Rainer Wunderlich Verlag, 1950), 250–254.

26. "Eine blosse Fortsetzung der Politik mit anderen Mitteln." Carl von Clausewitz, *Vom Kriege: Ungekürzter Text* (München: Cormoran, 2000), Book I, Chapter I, no. 24 (p. 44).

27. "Wir sehen also erstens: dass wir uns den Krieg unter allen Umständen als kein selbständiges Ding, sondern als ein politisches Instrument zu denken haben." Clausewitz, *Vom Kriege*, Book I, Chapter I, no. 27 (p. 45).

28. For the primary source on "consecutive operations," "deep battle," and "operational art," see the seminal work by Georgii Samoilovich Isserson, *The Evolution of Operational Art* (Fort Leavenworth, KS: Combat Studies Institute Press, 2013). Richard W. Harrison, *The Russian Way of War: Operational Art, 1904–1940* (Lawrence: University Press of Kansas, 2001), is a penetrating synthesis. See also Harrison's biography of Isserson: *Architect of Soviet Victory in World War II: The Life and Theories of G. S. Isserson* (Jefferson, NC: McFarland, 2010).

29. The figures are from Frieser, "Der Rückzugsoperationen der Heeresgruppe Süd," 385–387.

30. Natzmer was the operations officer (Ia) of the *Panzergrenadier* Division

Grossdeutschland. Frieser, "Der Rückzugsoperationen der Heeresgruppe Süd," 385–386.

31. "Kommentar überflüssig." Frieser, "Der Rückzugsoperationen der Heeresgruppe Süd," 386.

32. "Immerhin blieb gewiss, dass sich auf diesem Flügel der Heeresgruppe ein neues schweres Gewitter zusammenbraue." Manstein, *Verlorene Siege,* 565.

33. See the section titled "Blunting the Christmas Offensive" in Steven H. Newton, ed., *Panzer Operations: The Eastern Front Memoir of General Raus, 1941–1945* (New York: Da Capo, 2003), 262–268. For the course of operations, see also Gotthard Heinrici, "Der Feldzug in Russland: ein operativer Überblick," part 2, chapter 14, "Deutsch Rückschläge, Oktober 1943-Mai 1944," Manuscript T-9 in the Foreign Military Studies series. The original is available in the AHEC in Carlisle, PA.

34. For the vigorous Soviet employment of "forward detachments," see Glantz and House, *When Titans Clashed,* 183–184.

35. Insertion of the tank armies was always a dramatic moment in Soviet offensives, representing the commitment of the most powerful formation in the order of battle and clearly revealing Soviet operational intentions. See Richard N. Armstrong, *Red Army Tank Commanders: The Armored Guards* (Atglen, PA: Schiffer, 1994).

36. For the most comprehensive biographies of Manstein, see the highly critical accounts by Marcel Stein, *Generalfeldmarschall Erich von Manstein: Kritische Betrachtung des Soldaten und Menschen* (Mainz: v. Hase & Koehler, 2000), and *Der Januskopf—Feldmarschall von Manstein: Eine Neubewertung* (Bissendorf: Biblio Verlag, 2006), as well as the English translation of the latter, *Field Marshal von Manstein: The Janus Head / A Portrait* (Solihull, UK: Helion, 2007). See also the favorable but balanced biography by Mungo Melvin, *Manstein: Hitler's Greatest General* (London: Phoenix, 2010). To Melvin, Manstein "was ambitious, bordering on the arrogant, impatient with the slow and intolerant of the less gifted" (508)—and this in a generally positive character analysis.

37. For the *Rochade,* see Manstein, *Verlorene Siege,* 405–406, as well as Frieser, "Der Rückzugsoperationen der Heeresgruppe Süd," 390.

38. Dennis E. Showalter, *Hitler's Panzers: The Lightning Attacks That Revolutionized Warfare* (New York: Berkley Caliber, 2009), 195. Hitler sometimes mocked Hube's nickname. "Und darunter: 'Hube—der Mann!'" in Helmut Heiber, ed., *Hitlers Lagebesprechungen: Die Protokollfragmente seiner militärischen Konferenzen 1942–1945* (Stuttgart: Deutsche Verlags-Anstalt, 1962), "Mittagslage vom 1. Februar 1943 in der Wolfsschanze," 125.

39. Frieser, "Der Rückzugsoperationen der Heeresgruppe Süd," 391.

40. "'Operation,'—ich hasse die geschwollenen Ausdrücke. Das its gar keine Operation, das ist nur ein geschwollener Ausdruck." Heiber, *Hitlers Lagebesprechungen,* "Besprechung des Führers mit General Jodl und—Später Anwesend—General Zeitzler am 28. Dezember 1943," 489.

41. "Operieren gleichbedeutend mit Ausreissen." Heim, "Stalingrad und der Verlauf des Feldzuges der Jahre 1943–1945," 231.

42. "Wenn er (Manstein) selber die Verantwortung für die Krim hätte, würde er diese Entscheidung schwerer treffen." Heiber, *Hitlers Lagebesprechungen*, "Besprechung des Führers mit General Zeitzler am 27. Dezember 1943," 485.

43. "In der Tat waren sie in seinem sonst grobzügigen Gesicht wohl das einzig anziehende." Manstein, *Verlorene Siege*, 573.

44. "Blitzartig durchzuckte mich der Gedanke an einen indischen Schlangenbeschwörer." Ibid.

45. "Es war so zusagen ein wortloser Kampf." Ibid.

46. "Nachdem alle Anwesenden ausser dem General Zeitzler den Raum verlassen hatten, bat ich Hitler, ganz offen sprechen zu dürfen. Mit ziemlich eisiger, jedenfalls verschlossener Miene antwortete Hitler 'Bitte sehr.'" Ibid., 572.

47. "Sie ist auch die Folge der Art, in der bei uns geführt wird." Ibid.

48. "Glauben Sie, dass sie zum Beispiel etwa Ihnen besser gehorchen würden?" Ibid., 573.

49. "Ich kann sie notfalls absetzen, kein anderer würde diese Autorität haben." Ibid.

50. "Meine Antwort, dass die Befehle, die ich gäbe, befolgt würden, nahm er ohne weitere Gegenäusserung hin und brach dann das Gespräch ab." Ibid.

51. "Bewegungsfreiheit unseres rechten Heeresgruppen-Flügels." Ibid., 574.

52. "Wer Wen einkesselt." Frieser, "Der Rückzugsoperationen der Heeresgruppe Süd," 392.

53. The exploits of Bäke's heavy regiment are a staple of popular work on the Wehrmacht. Walter Görlitz, *Der Zweite Weltkrieg* (Stuttgart: Steingrüben-Verlag, 1952), vol. 2, 241, lists 34 Tigers and 47 Panthers, as does Franz Kurowski, *Panzer Aces: German Tank Commanders of World War II* (Mechanicsburg, PA: Stackpole, 2004), 61. The concept of "tank ace" seems to have been invented by popular authors like Kurowski. It has no provenance in the wartime documents. Frieser, "Der Rückzugsoperationen der Heeresgruppe Süd" 400, gives Bäke 34 Tigers and 46 Panthers.

54. There is precisely one English-language scholarly study of the Soviet VVS (*Voyenno-vozdushnyye sily*, or "Soviet Air Force"): Von Hardesty and Ilya Grinberg, *Red Phoenix Rising: The Soviet Air Force in World War II* (Lawrence: University Press of Kansas, 2012). An updated and expanded version of Hardesty's original *Red Phoenix: The Rise of Soviet Air Power, 1941–1945* (Hopkins, MN: Olympic, 1982), the new edition benefits from a large body of newly available Soviet documentation.

55. "Wir standen in der Tat einer Hydra gegenüber, der für jeden abgeschlagenen Kopf zwei neue zu wachsen schienen." Manstein, *Verlorene Siege*, 509, 514.

56. Frieser, "Der Rückzugsoperationen der Heeresgruppe Süd," 392–393.

57. Literature on the Korsun (or Korsun-Shevchenkovsky, or Tscherkassy) Pocket is a mixed bag. One dedicated monograph exists: Niklas Zetterling and Anders Frankson, *The Korsun Pocket: The Encirclement and Breakout of a German Army in the East, 1944* (Philadelphia: Casemate, 2008), a detailed tactical account, typical of Zetterling's oeuvre; along with an unpublished master's thesis, Douglas E. Nash, "No Stalingrad on the Dnieper: The Korsun-Shevchenkovsky Operation, January to February 1944" (Fort Leavenworth, KS: US Army Command

and General Staff College, 1995). See also Frieser, "Der Rückzugsoperationen der Heeresgruppe Süd," 394–419, and Alex Buchner, *Ostfront 1944* (Friedberg: Podzun-Pallas-Verlag, 1988), 15–72. After these four essential works, see the primary source by the commander of the 23rd Panzer Division, Vormann, *Tscherkassy*. Then turn to the journal and chapter literature: the three-part "Im Kessel" (see note 1, above); O. Jaggi, "Der Ausbruch aus Kesseln," *Allgemeine schweizerische Militärzeitschrift* 130, nos. 4–5, 12 (April–May and December 1964): 224–231, 295–302, and 811–812; Hans Speidel, "Der Ausbruch aus dem Kessel von Tscherkassy," *Allgemeine schweizerische Militärzeitschrift* 115, no. 6 (June 1949): 391–410; Oberst Randewig, Willi Rothhaar, "Im Kessel von Tscherkassy," in Hanns Möller-Witten, *Männer und Taten: Ritterkreuzträger erzählen* (München: J. F. Lehmanns Verlag, 1959), 117–126, and the commemorative booklet from the 5th SS Panzer Division, *Wiking*, "Die Flut verschlang sich selbst, nicht uns!" (Hannover: Truppenkameradschaft "Wiking," n.d.). Still extremely useful is Oldwig von Natzmer et al., "Das Zurückkämpfen eingekesselter Verbände zur eigenen Front," Manuscript T-12 in the Foreign Military Studies series. The original is available in the AHEC in Carlisle, PA. See, in particular, "Kämpfe des XI. und XXXXII. A.K. Entsatzoperation und Ausbruch," Einzelbearbeitung Nr. 2, and "Die Kesselschlacht von Tscherkassy, Dez. 43—Jan. 44," Einzelbearbeitung Nr. 3. For the oft-neglected topic of signals and intelligence, see Kunibert Randewig, "Die Sowjet Funktäuschung in der Schlacht von Tscherkassy," *Allgemeine schweizerische Militärzeitschrift* 119, no. 6 (June 1953): 429–437. And finally, two worthy articles from the Soviet camp are G. Vorontsov, "The Art of Troop Control," *Soviet Military Review*, no. 7 (1972): 36–39, and I. S. Konev, "The Korsun-Shevchenkovsky Pocket," *Soviet Military Review*, no. 2 (1974): 46–49.

58. "Diesen 'Sack' im Süden abzuschnüren." Manstein, *Verlorene Siege*, 576.

59. Frieser, "Der Rückzugsoperationen der Heeresgruppe Süd," 393–394.

60. Vormann, *Tscherkassy*, 37.

61. The numbers are from Frieser, "Der Rückzugsoperationen der Heeresgruppe Süd," 395. Total numbers on the Eastern Front, according to Glantz and House, *When Titans Clashed*, 184, were 2,468,500 for the Germans (plus 706,000 satellite troops) for a total of 3,174,500, versus 6,394,500 Soviets, a little over a 2:1 ratio overall. Zetterling and Frankson, *Korsun Pocket*, 51–54, give 2,528,000 Germans, 6,100,000 Soviets, a Soviet advantage of 2.4:1. Overall, they note, 40 Soviet divisions were attacking 15 German.

62. "Keine Mittel, um dieses Manöver zu verhindern." Frieser, "Der Rückzugsoperationen der Heeresgruppe Süd," 395–396.

63. "Ein verblüffendes, in seiner Dramatik erschütterndes Bild!" Vormann, *Tscherkassy*, 60.

64. Konev, "Korsun-Shevchenkovsky Pocket," 47, claimed to have encircled "ten divisions and one brigade—some 80,000 officers and men, up to 1,600 guns and mortars, over 230 tanks and assault guns," but his figures are wildly exaggerated. Zetterling and Frakson, *Korsun Pocket*, 111, give a figure of 59,000 men. The equipment numbers are from Frieser, "Der Rückzugsoperationen der Heeresgruppe Süd," 397. For the *Wallonie* Brigade, see the memoirs of the Belgian Rexiste

leader, Léon Degrelle, *La Campagne de Russie, 1941–1945* (Paris: La Diffusion du Livre, 1949).

65. Frieser, "Der Rückzugsoperationen der Heeresgruppe Süd," 400–401.

66. See Zetterling and Frankson, *Korsun Pocket*, 153–168, "Breith's III Panzer Corps Attacks."

67. "Die Versorgung machte grösste Schwierigkeiten. Die Truppe war seit einigen Tagen ohne Verpflegung, den Panzern fehlte Betriebsstoff und Munition." In Frieser, "Der Rückzugsoperationen der Heeresgruppe Süd," 404.

68. Speidel, "Ausbruch aus dem Kessel von Tscherkassy," 399. For the text of one of the *Freies Deutschland*'s pamphlets, see Felix Steiner, *Die Freiwilligen: Idee und Opfergang* (Göttingen: Pless Verlag, 1958), 247, and Peter Strassner, *Europäische Freiwillige: Die Geschichte der 5. SS-Panzerdivision Wiking* (Osnabrück: Munin Verlag, 1968), 236–237.

69. Ibid., 399–400. For Seydlitz's own account of his dramatic transformation, see Walther von Seydlitz, *Stalingrad: Konflikt und Konsequenz: Erinnerungen* (Oldenburg: Stalling, 1977). See also Hans Marten, *General von Seydlitz 1942–1945: Analyse eines Konfliktes* (Berlin: von Kloeden Verlag, 1971).

70. For details of the Soviet visitation, see "Im Kessel," 333–334.

71. "Weshalb is der Kessel im Wehrmachtbericht unerwähnt geblieben?" See "Im Kessel," part 1 (April 1949), 266.

72. "Es wird kritisiert, getadelt, und in Landknechtsart geschimpft." Ibid., 265.

73. For the breakout, see Zetterling and Frankson, *Korsun Pocket*, 255–281, as well as "Im Kessel," part 3 (June 1949), and Speidel, "Ausbruch aus dem Kessel von Tscherkassy," 405–410.

74. "Soldaten haben die Schlacht zu gewinnen und nicht Träger von Uniformen." "Im Kessel," part 3 (June 1949), 411.

75. Speidel, "Ausbruch aus dem Kessel von Tscherkassy," 407.

76. For the formal protest of Colonel Schulze, the chief medical officer of the XI Corps, see *Frieser*, "Der Rückzugsoperationen der Heeresgruppe Süd," 408–409. Speidel, "Ausbruch aus dem Kessel von Tscherkassy," 407, doesn't mention the protest.

77. "Damit endet die planmässige Führung der Gruppe Stemmermann und ihre Existenz überhaupt." Vormann, *Tscherkassy*, 120. For Stemmermann's death, see Speidel, "Ausbruch aus dem Kessel von Tscherkassy," 408, and "Im Kessel," 420.

78. "Das elementare Nachströmen der Massen." Vormann, Tscherkassy, 120.

79. "Blankes Entsetzen." Frieser, "Der Rückzugsoperationen der Heeresgruppe Süd," 411.

80. Konev, "Korsun-Shevchenkovsky Pocket," 48–49.

81. Nash, "No Stalingrad on the Dnieper," 132.

82. For Hube's *wandernden Kessel*, see Carl Wagener, "Der Ausbruch der 1. Panzerarmee aus dem Kessel von Kamenez-Podolsk, März/April 1944, *Wehrwissenschaftliche Rundschau* 9, no. 1 (1959): 16–48; Oldwig von Natzmer, "Ausbruch der 1. Panzer-Armee aus der Kessel im Raum Kamenez-Podolsk im Frühjahr 1944," Einzelbearbeitung Nr. 1 in Oldwig von Natzmer, et al., "Das Zurückkämpfen

eingekesselter Verbände zur eigenen Front," as well as the pertinent passages in Frieser, "Der Rückzugsoperationen der Heeresgruppe Süd," 432–447. Finally, see Peter Erlau, *Flucht aus der weissen Hölle: Erinnerungen an die grosse Kesselschlacht der 1. Panzerarmee Hube im Raum um Kamenez-Podolsk vom 8. März bis 9. April 1944* (Stuttgart: Kulturhistorischer Verlag Dr. Riegler, 1960), the memoir of the radio company commander in the 169th Infantry Division.

83. For the castrophe at Ternopol, see Alex Buchner, *Ostfront 1944* (Friedberg: Podzun-Pallas-Verlag, 1988), an operational analysis of all the great encirclement battles in the last two years of the war: Tscherkassy, Ternopol, Krim, Vitebsk, Bobruisk, Brody, Jassy, and Kishinev. Frieser, "Der Rückzugsoperationen der Heeresgruppe Süd," 424–431, is typically incisive in his analysis.

84. For *Führerbefehl* No. 11, see Walther Hubatsch, ed., *Hitlers Weisungen für die Kriegführung 1939–1945* (Frankfurt: Bernard & Graefe Verlag, 1962), 243–250.

85. The chapter on Ternopol in Buchner, *Ostfront*, is titled "Von 4 600 Soldaten kamen 55 zurück."

Chapter 2. In the Mountains: The Battle for Italy

1. This vignette draws upon the memoirs of the German *Oberbefehlshaber-Südwest* (OB-Südwest), Field Marshal Albert Kesselring, *Soldat bis zum letzten Tag* (Bonn: Athenäum-Verlag, 1953), 265–267. The English translation is *The Memoirs of Field-Marshal Albert Kesselring* (Novato, CA: Presidio, 1989), 191–192.

2. "Seinen ausgrebrannten Kompanien stünden zwei häufig abgelöste alliierte Divisionen gegenüber." Kesselring, *Soldat bis zum letzten Tag*, 265.

3. "Ich wäre Bayer, müsste ihn aber als Preussen darauf hinweisen, dass die Preussen nie fragten, wie stark der Feind sei, sondern wo er sei." Kesselring, *Soldat bis zum letzten Tag*, 265. The same exact claim was once made for the Prussian Field Marshal Gebhard Leberecht von Blücher. See Eberhard Kessel, "Blücher: Zum 200. Gebürtstag am 16. Dezember," *Militärwissenschaftliche Rundschau* 7, no. 4 (1942): 312.

4. For the Allied campaign in the Mediterranean, begin with Michael Howard, *The Mediterranean Strategy in the Second World War* (New York: Praeger, 1968), Douglas Porch, *The Path to Victory: The Mediterranean Front in World War II* (New York: Farrar, Straus and Giroux, 2004), and Carlo D'Este, *World War II in the Mediterranean, 1942–1945* (Chapel Hill, NC: Algonquin Books, 1990). For American participation, see the US Army official histories, the "Green Book Series," especially George F. Howe, *Northwest Africa: Seizing the Initiative in the West* (Washington, DC: Center of Military History, 2002); Albert N. Garland and Howard McGaw Smyth, *Sicily and the Surrender of Italy* (Washington, DC: Center of Military History, 1991); Martin Blumenson, *Salerno to Cassino* (Washington, DC: Center of Military History, 1969); and Ernest R. Fisher, *Cassino to the Alps* (Washington, DC: Center of Military History, 1993). Other official US sources include the series *American Forces in Action*, a series of fourteen studies first published by the War Department's Historical Division (1944–1948, republished in 1990). The four

dealing with Italy are *Salerno: American Operations From the Beaches to the Volturno, 9 September–6 October 1943* (Washington, DC: Center of Military History, 1990); *From the Volturno to the Winter Line, 6 October–15 November 1943* (Washington, DC: Center of Military History, 1990); *Fifth Army at the Winter Line, 15 November 1943– 15 January 1944* (Washington, DC: Center of Military History, 1990), and *Anzio Beachhead, 22 January–25 May 1944* (Washington, DC: Center of Military History, 1990). While these predecessors of the Green Books did not yet have the full body of archival documentation available, they make up that deficiency with immediacy and originality. The authors are not restating an already well-established narrative but rather are forming it. Authorship of individual volumes remains anonymous. See also the British official history, C. J. C. Molony, *The Mediterranean and Middle East*, volume 5, *The Campaign in Sicily, 1943, and the Campaign in Italy, 3rd September 1943 to 31st March 1944* (London: Her Majesty's Stationery Office, 1973). For German strategy in the Mediterranean, see Ralf Georg Reuth, *Entscheidung im Mittelmeer: die südliche Peripherie Europas in der deutschen Strategie des Zweiten Weltkrieges, 1940–1942* (Koblenz: Bernard & Graefe, 1985), and, for more general questions of German strategy, Andreas Hillgruber, *Der 2. Weltkrieg: Kriegsziele und Strategie der grossen Mächte* (Stuttgart: W. Kohlhammer, 1985). Dominick Graham and Shelford Bidwell, *Tug of War: the Battle for Italy* (London: Hodder & Stoughton, 1986), is an excellent operational and strategic history, as is W. G. F. Jackson, *The Battle for Italy* (New York: Harper & Row, 1967); and Eric Linklater, *The Campaign in Italy* (London: His Majesty's Stationery Office, 1951). John Strawson, *The Italian Campaign* (New York: Carroll & Graf, 1988), remains a good, brief introduction. Two journalistic accounts remain invaluable for the Italian campaign: Christopher Buckley, *The Road to Rome* (London: Hodder and Stoughton, 1945), by a correspondent for the *Daily Telegraph*, and Richard Tregaskis, *Invasion Diary* (Lincoln, NE: Bison Books, 2004). Tregaskis has already made his reputation with the wildly popular *Guadalcanal Diary* (New York: Random House, 1943). *Invasion Diary*, published in 1944, was a harrowing work in which Tregaskis suffers a serious head wound in combat—a grown man learning to read, write, and speak again. It never won the audience of his earlier work. Buckley's jeep drove over a mine in Korea in 1950, killing him instantly.

5. For the debate over Sledgehammer and Roundup, see Richard W. Steele, *The First Offensive, 1942: Roosevelt, Marshall, and the Making of American Strategy* (Bloomington: Indiana University Press, 1973).

6. See Elena Agarossi, *A Nation Collapses: The Italian Surrender of September 1943* (Cambridge: Cambridge University Press, 2006).

7. For Operation Axis, see Robert M. Citino, *The Wehrmacht Retreats: Fighting a Lost War, 1943* (Lawrence: University Press of Kansas, 2012), 244–249. The most comprehensive scholarly account is Josef Schröder, *Italiens Kriegsaustritt, 1943: Die deutschen Gegenmassnahmen im italienischen Raum: Fall "Alarich" und "Achse"* (Göttingen: Musterschmidt-Verlag, 1969). Gerhard Schreiber, *Die italienischen Militärinternierten im deutschen Machtbereich, 1943–1945: Verraten—Verachtet—Vergessen* (München: Oldenbourg-Verlag, 1990), describes the sad aftermath, with hundreds of thousands of former Italian soldiers "interned" as industrial workers in the

Reich. Schreiber also penned the portions of the German official history dealing with the Italian campaign, "Das Ende des nordafrikanischen Feldzugs und der Krieg in Italien 1943 bis 1945," in *Das Deutsche Reich und der Zweite Weltkrieg*, volume 8, *Die Ostfront, 1943/44: Der Krieg im Osten un an den Nebenfronten*, 1100–1162.

8. During the Allied advance into the so-called Winter Line, US 5th Army advanced eight miles in six weeks. Mark W. Clark, *Calculated Risk* (New York: Enigma, 2007), 210.

9. Siegfried Westphal, *Heer in Fesseln: Aus den Papieren des Stabchefs von Rommel, Kesselring und Rundstedt* (Bonn: Athenäum-Verlag, 1950), 238, translated into English as *The German Army in the West* (London: Cassell, 1951).

10. For the German debate over where to hold the line in the Italian peninsula, see Ralph S. Mavrogordato, *Command Decisions: Hitler's Decision on the Defense of Italy* (Washington, DC: Center of Military History, 1990), the only dedicated historical work dealing with this crucial topic.

11. For recent works on Allied dominance in the ground and air domains during the Mediterranean fighting, see Steven Thomas Barry, *Battalion Commanders at War: U.S. Army Tactical Leadership in the Mediterranean Theater, 1942–1943* (Lawrence: University Press of Kansas, 2013), and Robert S. Ehlers, *The Mediterranean Air War: Airpower and Allied Victory in World War II* (Lawrence: University Press of Kansas, 2015).

12. The classic analysis of the concept of *Kampfkraft* within the German army is Martin van Creveld, *Fighting Power: German and U.S. Army Performance, 1939–1945* (Westport, CT: Praeger, 2007).

13. See Eberhard von Mackensen, *Vom Bug zum Kaukasus: Das III Panzerkorps im Feldzug gegen Sowjetrussland 1941–42* (Neckargemünd: Kurt Vowinckel, 1967). Mackensen had led III Panzer Corps and 1st Panzer Army on the Eastern Front. See Robert M. Citino, *Death of the Wehrmacht: The German Campaigns of 1942* (Lawrence: University Press of Kansas, 2007), 103–104, 110–111, 176–180, and 229–232.

14. See Frido von Senger und Etterlin, *Krieg in Europa* (Köln: Kiepenheuer & Witsch, 1960). The English translation is *Neither Fear nor Hope: The Wartime Career of General Frido von Senger und Etterlin, Defender of Cassino* (Novato, CA: Presidio, 1989). For a précis of his experience in Italy, see "Die Cassino-Schlachten," *Allgemeine schweizerische Militärzeitschrift* 117, nos. 6 and 7 (1951): 397–413 and 469–486. Senger wrote widely on doctrine, as well. See *Der Gegenschlag: Kampfbeispiele und Führungsgrundsätze der beweglichen Abwehr* (Neckargemünd: Kurt Vowinckel Verlag, 1959).

15. Herr has neither memoir nor biographer. He commanded 13th Panzer Division in the Caucasus campaign (as part of Mackensen's III Panzer Corps), suffering a severe head wound in the fight for Ordzhonikidze. See Citino, *Death of the Wehrmacht*, 241–243.

16. See, for example, Helmut Beck-Broichsitter, "Über die Beharrlichkeit im Angriff," *Militärwissenschaftliche Rundschau* 9, no. 1 (1944): 57–64.

17. Schreiber, "Das Ende des nordafrikanischen Feldzugs und der Krieg in Italien 1943 bis 1945," 1131.

18. For German operations in Italy, see Senger, *Krieg in Europa*, 225–327, and

Rudolf Böhmler, *Monte Cassino* (Damrstadt: E. S. Mittler & Sohn, 1956). The English translation of Böhmler's work has the same title, *Monte Cassino* (London: Cassell, 1956); it omits paragraphs included in the original version on an apparently random basis. Compare, for example, 163 in the German version to 70 in the English—one more example of why the researcher should always consult the original whenever possible. All references hereafter are to the original German edition. Turn then to the massive report written after the war by the German commanders themselves, with Siegfried Westphal in the lead, under the title, "Der Feldzug in Italien," Foreign Military Studies, Manuscript T-1a, Foreign Military Studies series. See especially Chapter 6, Heinrich von Vietinghoff, "Die Kämpfe der 10. Armee in Süd- und Mittelitalien unter besonderer Berücksichtigung der Schlachten bei Salerno, am Volturno, Garigliano, am Sangro und um Cassino"; Chapter 12, Wolf Hauser, "Der Kampf der 14. Armee bei Anzio-Nettuno bis Anfang Mai 1944"; Eberhard Mackensen, "Stellungnahme zu 'Der Feldzug in Italien' von Gen. Major Wolf Hauser: Anlage zu Kapitel 12"; Chapter 13, Siegfried Westphal, "Die Auffassung der Heeresgruppe"; and Chapter 14, Torsten Christ, "Die Luftlage im Frühjahr 1944." For the crucial question of supply in the peninsula, see "Sonderthemen: Die Versorgunglage," especially Chapter 3, Ernst Fähndrich, "Die Entwicklung der Versorgungslage im Frühjahr 1944 (von Mitte März) bis zum Beginn der Alliierten Offensive"; Chapter 4, Ernst Eggert, "Die Entwicklung der Versorgungslage im Sommer 1944 während der Mai-Offensive und der Rückzugskämpfe (bis Juli 1944 einschl.)"; and Chapter 6, Ernst Eggert, "Die Versorgungslage vom Beginn des Jahres 1945 bis zur Kapitulation." For the views of *OB-Südwest*, see Manuscript T-1a K1, Albert Kesselring, "Kesselring's Comments on MS #T-1a." All of the originals are available in the AHEC in Carlisle, PA.

19. For the tough street battle in Ortona, see Mark Zuehlke, *Ortona: Canada's Epic World War II Battle* (Vancouver: Douglas & McIntyre, 2004.

20. For the various lines, see Böhmler, *Monte Cassino*, 161–164, and Vietinghoff, "Die Kämpfe der 10. Armee in Süd- und Mittelitalien," 75–76.

21. "Ein typischer preussischer Offizier." Senger, *Krieg in Europa*, 229. See also Böhmler, *Monte Cassino*, 182, who calls Gräser "ein tadelsfreier Soldat" ("a soldier *sans reproche*").

22. "Vermisstenzahlen, die mit der Schwere der Kämpfe nicht im Einklang standen." Senger, *Krieg in Europa*, 230.

23. "Volksliste 3," to be precise. See Böhmler, *Monte Cassino*, 183.

24. "Diese Sonderbehandlung nach 'rassischen Prinzipien' war nicht dazu angetan, die Moral der Truppe zu heben." Senger, *Krieg in Europa*, 230.

25. "Gutgläubige und hitlertreue Soldat." Senger, *Krieg in Europa*, 230. Böhmler states that "their hearts hardly beat for Germany" ("Dieser Soldaten schlug das Herz kaum für Deutschland"), *Monte Cassino*, 183.

26. For the three "Stalingrad divisions," see Böhmler, *Monte Cassino*, 181–182 (for the 94th Division), 182 (for the 305th), and 263–264 (for the 44th).

27. "Die sogenannten Stellungen." Senger, *Krieg in Europa*, 230–231.

28. "Frontalen Abwehrkampf." Ibid., 231.

29. "Hinten werde es besser." Ibid.

30. Vietinghoff, "Die Kämpfe der 10. Armee in Süd- und Mittelitalien," 83–84.

31. "Es gibt kein Rezept; zum Teil ist es Gefühlssache!" Kesselring, *Soldat bis zum letzten Tag*, 263 (note).

32. For the importance of the coup d'oeil, see Carl von Clausewitz, *Vom Kriege: Ungekürzter Text* (München: Cormoran, 2000), Book I, Chapter 3, 64–65.

33. For the ups and downs of the Anglo-American coalition in World War II, see the splendid trilogy by Rick Atkinson, *An Army at Dawn: The War in North Africa, 1942–1943* (New York: Henry Holt, 2002); *The Day of Battle: The War in Sicily and Italy, 1943–1944* (New York: Henry Holt, 2007); and *The Guns at Last Light: The War in Western Europe, 1944–1945* (New York: Henry Holt, 2013). To label them "popular history" is absolutely correct. They are hugely popular, but they are also excellent history—well grounded in the primary and secondary sources, judiciously argued, and beautifully written. Ostensibly a history of the US Army, the books are, in fact, broadly conceived histories of the war in the European theater, embracing strategy, operations, and tactics, with coalition politics standing at the heart of the narrative, as it must. See also the pertinent volume of the US Army's official history: Maurice Matloff and Edwin M. Snell, *Strategic Planning for Coalition Warfare, 1941–1942* (Washington, DC: Center of Military History, 1953), one of the still-authoritative Green Books.

34. The Rapido/Gari disaster has made a far greater impression on the US historiography than the German. For the primary source, see Clark, *Calculated Risk*, 218–221, as well Clark's sympathetic biographer, Martin Blumenson, *Mark Clark* (London: Jonathan Cape, 1985), 166–170. Both imply that the need to plan the Anzio landing pushed sensible and timely planning for the Rapido crossing into the background. See also *Fifth Army History*, part 4: *Cassino and Anzio* (Italy: Headquarters Fifth Army, 1944), 39–58. The most detailed account of the actual crossing is still Blumenson, *Salerno to Cassino*, 322–351. Carlo D'Este, *Fatal Decision: Anzio and the Battle for Rome* (New York: Harper Perennial, 1992), 79–84, blames Clark's "paranoid mistrust" of the British as the reason for his ill-fated decision to attack (79). Readers would do well to read *Fatal Decision* in tandem with D'Este's *Bitter Victory: The Battle for Sicily, 1943* (New York: Harper Perennial, 1991), to form as complete a picture of operations in Italy as possible. From the German side, see Senger, *Krieg in Europa*, 193, as well as Vietinghoff, "Die Kämpfe der 10. Armee in Süd- und Mittelitalien," 106–107.

35. For the British crossing of the Garigliano, and the real danger it posed to the German defensive position, see Blumenson, *Salerno to Cassino*, 315–321.

36. Quoted in Atkinson, *Day of Battle*, 333.

37. Quoted in Blumenson, *Salerno to Cassino*, 327.

38. Westphal, "Auffassung der Heeresgruppe," 4–6.

39. Kesselring, *Soldat bis zum letzten Tag*, 269.

40. "Im Zick-zack dahinter angelegt." Senger, *Krieg in Europa*, 243.

41. Ibid.

42. D'Este, *Fatal Decision*, 83, provides a total of 1,681: 143 killed, 663 wounded, and 875 missing (about 500 of whom were captured).

43. "Ein erbittertes Ringen." Westphal, "Auffassung der Heeresgruppe," 5.

44. "Weil sie ihr keine Sorge machte." Senger, *Krieg in Europa*, 243.

45. Operation Shingle has generated a large historiography for what was, after all, a mere corps-size operation. See the authoritative works by Martin Blumenson, both the official entry in the Green Book series: *Salerno to Cassino*, and the monograph *Anzio: The Gamble That Failed* (Philadelphia: Lippincott, 1963). Carlo D'Este's *Fatal Decision* is a typically excellent entry from this master historian. See also John S. D. Eisenhower, *They Fought at Anzio* (Columbia: University of Missouri Press, 2007), for a synthesis of recent research. Finally, Steven J. Zaloga, *Anzio 1944: The Beleaguered Beachhead* (NY: Osprey, 2005), is yet another excellent entry in Osprey's Campaign Series, with solid research, erudite text, and superb maps.

46. Atkinson, *Day of Battle*, 353.

47. Ibid., 353–354. For a defense of Lucas, see also the article by Steven L. Ossad, "Major General John P. Lucas at Anzio: Prudence or Boldness?" in *Global War Studies* 8, no. 1 (2011): 35–56, who makes a strong case for Lucas and a strong case against higher command echelons (especially Clark and Churchill), who concocted a muddled, undersupported mission. "In the final analysis, the operation was doomed from the start and should never have been mounted. All the justifications since are based on arguments about attrition, or diversion of forces, and other strategically bankrupt excuses" (54).

48. Quoted in Atkinson, *Day of Battle*, 355, and many other sources. The precise nature of Clark's orders to Lucas continue to excite controversy, but the fact that they are still controversial reveals their lack of precision.

49. D'Este, *Fatal Decision*, 111.

50. Ibid., 112.

51. So Lucas claimed in a postwar interview, but verifying the quote has proven impossible. Quoted in Atkinson, *Day of Battle*, 355.

52. "No son of a bitch, no commander" is well attested. See, for example, Carlo D'Este, "Soldier's Soldier," *World War II* 30, no. 5 (January–February 2016): 30–39. Regarding Anzio, Truscott wondered if Anzio was going to be a "suicide sashay." D'Este, *Fatal Decision*, 109.

53. "Sozusagen friedens- und übungsmässig." Walter Fries, "Einsatz der 29. Panzer Grenadier Division während des deutschen Gegenangriffes zur Beseitigung des Landekopfes Anzio-Nettuno im Februar 1944," Foreign Military Studies, Manuscript D-141, 3. The original is available in AHEC in Carlisle, PA.

54. "Deswegen können Sie ruhig schlafen." Siegfried Westphal, *Erinnerungen* (Mainz: v. Hase & Koehler Verlag, 1975), 248. Kesselring is ambivalent on Canaris's role, implying that he gave an all-clear, while at the same time providing evidence of increased transport tonnage in Naples Harbor. *Soldat bis zum letzten Tag*, 269.

55. Quoted in Blumenson, *Salerno to Cassino*, 358.

56. "Dieses sehr stark auf Sicherheit bedachte Vorgehen." Fries, "Einsatz der 29. Panzer Grenadier Division während des deutschen Gegenangriffes," 3.

57. For Case "Richard" and the scramble to build a new defensive front, see Kesselring, *Soldat bis zum letzten Tag*, 270–272, and Westphal, *Erinnerungen*, 249–250.

58. "Mir kam es dabei auf jeden Meter an." Kesselring, *Soldat bis zum letzten Tag*, 270.

59. "Ein buntes Gemisch verschiedenster Truppenteile." Hauser, "Der Kampf der 14. Armee bei Anzio-Nettuno," 9.

60. "Der Kampfgeist und Wert der Truppenteile darunter leidet." Ibid.

61. See Walter Kühn, "Die Artillerie bei Anzio-Nettuno," Foreign Military Studies, Manuscript D-158. The original is available in the AHEC in Carlisle, PA. The report contains the entire order of battle for the German artillery at Anzio and a schematic rendering of the battery positions.

62. Atkinson, *Day of Battle*, 368–369. For airpower at Anzio, including the use of radio-guided bombs, see James S. Corum, *Wolfram von Richtofen: Master of the German Air War* (Lawrence: University Press of Kansas, 2008), 348–353.

63. Atkinson, *Day of Battle*, 370.

64. Quoted in Eisenhower, *They Fought at Anzio*, 140.

65. For the Ranger disaster at Cisterna, see D'Este, *Fatal Decision*, 160–169, and Blumenson, *Salerno to Cassino*, 390–391.

66. Hauser, "Der Kampf der 14. Armee bei Anzio-Nettuno," 13–14. In the report, "Conrath" is misspelled "Konrad."

67. "Die feindlichen Angriff v. 30.1. lag folgende Absicht zugrunde." Ibid., 14.

68. "Die Kämpfe haben wiederum gezeigt, dass ein Angriff gegen das weitüberlegen feindliche Artl. Feuer und bei der feindlichen Luftherrschaft mit ihrem starken Bomber- und Jaboeinsatz nur unter Inkaufnahme hoher Verluste geführt werden konnte." Ibid., 23. For the course of the first German attack from the perspective of the Americans, see Blumenson, *Salerno to Cassino*, 294–396.

69. Hauser, "Der Kampf der 14. Armee bei Anzio-Nettuno," 24.

70. Ibid., 27.

71. See, for example, Mackensen, "Stellungnahme zu 'Der Feldzug in Italien' von Gen. Major Wolf Hauser," which describes in some detail the "conditions" (*Auflagen*) Hitler imposed on the general's operational scheme.

72. "Dem kürzesten Weg an den entscheidenden Punkt der Küste." Hauser, "Der Kampf der 14. Armee bei Anzio-Nettuno," 26.

73. Blumenson, *Salerno to Cassino*, 431–432.

74. "5 Minuten vor 12." Hauser, "Der Kampf der 14. Armee bei Anzio-Nettuno," 36.

75. For the "Flyover" and "the Caves," see Eisenhower, *They Fought at Anzio*, 173–190. For the difficulty experienced by the German panzers in this harsh terrain, see Martin Schmidt, "Gegenangriff gegen den Landekopf Anzio-Nettuno," Manuscript D-204 in the Foreign Military Studies series. The original is available in the AHEC in Carlisle, PA. Schmidt was the *Höherer Panzerabwehr-Offizier* (antitank supervisor) on Kesselring's staff at OB-Südwest.

76. "Einen erheblichen Nachlassen der körperlichen und seelischen Widerstandskraft." Hauser, "Der Kampf der 14. Armee bei Anzio-Nettuno," 38.

77. For the struggle for Cassino town and monastery from the German side, especially from that of the *Fallschirmjäger*, see Böhmler, *Monte Cassino*, 252–426,

and Senger, *Krieg in Europa*, 254–299. In general, Fred Majdalany, *The Battle of Cassino* (Boston: Houghton Mifflin, 1957), has stood the test of time, supplemented by Matthew Parker, *Monte Cassino: The Hardest-Fought Battle of World War II* (New York: Anchor Books, 2005).

78. "Zahlmeister, Schreiber, und Kraftfahrer." Böhmler, *Monte Cassino*, 418.

79. A good place to start for the Diadem operational sequence is *Fifth Army History*, part 5, *The Drive to Rome* (Italy: Fifth Army Headquarters, 1944). For Böhmler, *Cassino*, 245–286, Diadem is "the Third Battle of Cassino." For Diadem, see Fisher, *Cassino to the Alps*, 19–38; D'Este, *Fatal Decision*, 347–382; and Parker, *Monte Cassino*, 292–340. For the role of I Corps, squeezed by XIII Corps on the right and the French on the left, see Mark Zuehlke, *The Liri Valley: Canada's World War II Breakthrough to Rome* (Vancouver: Douglas & McIntyre, 2001).

80. For the primary source memoir, see Reinhard Gehlen, *Der Dienst: Erinnerungen 1942–1971* (München: Knaur, 1971). The English translation is *The Service: The Memoirs of General Reinhard Gehlen* (New York: World Publishing, 1972).

81. D'Este, *Fatal Decision*, 333–334.

82. "As if someone had switched on the lights." Quoted in Parker, *Monte Cassino*, 293. For the fighting on Monte-Majo, see Captain Meister, "Die Kämpfe am Monte Maio: vom 10.-13. Mai 1944," *Allgemeine schweizerische Militärzeitschrift* 117, no. 8 (1951): 545–558.

83. See A. Zajac, "Der Angriff des 2. karpatischen Schützenbataillons vom 12. Mai 1944 auf die Höhe 593 (NE Montecassino)," *Allgemeine schweizerische Militärzeitschrift* 127, no. 1 (1961): 24–27.

84. For the Borga Grappa linkup, see Clark, *Calculated Risk*, 283.

85. For an able presentation of the anti-Clark indictment, see D'Este, *Fatal Decision*, 366–382: "Clark's decision on May 25 was a calculated act that was to prove as militarily stupid as it was insubordinate" (366), he writes, asserting that Clark's order to Truscott "destroyed any hope of trapping von Vietinghoff's retreating army" (370). Williamson Murray and Allan R. Millett, *A War to Be Won: Fighting the Second World War* (Cambridge, MA: Harvard University Press, 2000), are blunt in condemning "Clark's insubordination" and "vainglorious pursuit of publicity and prestige" (385), while Thomas W. Zeiler, *Annihilation: A Global Military History of World War II* (Oxford: Oxford University Press, 2011), references "Clark's showboating" (280).

86. See Parker, *Monte Cassino*, 377–338; Zaloga, *Anzio: the Beleaguered Beachhead*, 85; and d'Este, *Fatal Decision*, 365.

87. For Clark's own reasonable defense of his decision to go for Rome, see *Calculated Risk*, 282–291.

88. "Trotzdem kann daraus nicht gefolgert werden, Feldmarschall Alexanders Plan, mit stärkeren Kräften aus dem Brückenkopf Richtung Valmontone anzugreifen, wäre erfolgreicher gewesen." Senger, *Krieg in Europa*, 320.

89. For the rest of the war in Italy, a truly forgotten campaign within the literature of World War II, see the belated volume in the Green Book Series, *The U.S. Army in World War II*, and Ernest F. Fisher Jr., *Cassino to the Alps* (Washington, DC: Center of Military History, 1977), with its appropriately dreary conclusion

on this campaign of 602 days, the longest of World War II: "Each day had seemed an eternity, as many a veteran of the campaign on both sides has testified. Almost always at a foot slogger's pace—a pace rendered all the more interminable by the infrequent exhilaration of pursuit—and seemingly always approaching precipitous heights controlled by a well-concealed enemy, Allied troops, under a broiling sun or in numbing cold, had slowly pushed ahead." It was, Fisher writes, "a cruel, bitter campaign that all too often seemed to be going nowhere" (545). For a popular history that manages to distill a very complex narrative, see Thomas R. Brooks, *The War North of Rome, June 1944–May 1945* (Edison, NJ: Castle Books, 2001). For a divisional account from the German side, see Heinrich Greiner, "Schlacht um Rom und Rückzugskämpfe nördlich Rom (362. I.D.)," Manuscript D-169 in the Foreign Military Studies series. The original is available in the AHEC in Carlisle, PA.

90. Westphal, "Auffassung der Heeresgruppe," 15–16.

91. Westphal, *Erinnerungen*, 251.

92. Westphal, "Auffassung der Heeresgruppe," 15.

93. Fries, "Einsatz der 29. Panzer Grenadier Division während des deutschen Gegenangriffes," 12–15.

Chapter 3. On the Beach: Normandy and Beyond

1. The vignette is based on Bodo Scheurig, *Alfred Jodl, Gehorsam und Verhängnis: Biographie* (Berlin: Propyläen, 1991), 265–266.

2. T. N. Dupuy, *A Genius for War: The German Army and General Staff, 1807–1945* (Englewood Cliffs, NJ: Prentice-Hall, 1977).

3. Samuel Mitcham Jr., *Hitler's Legions: The German Army Order Battle, World War II* (New York: Stein and Day, 1990).

4. David Downing, *Devil's Virtuosos: German Generals at War, 1940–5* (New York: Dorset Press, 1977).

5. The most biting commentary on the arcane nature of the German command system remains Geoffrey Megargee, *Inside Hitler's High Command* (Lawrence: University Press of Kansas, 2000). A book that swam against the tide of Wehrmacht-worship when it appeared, it was one of the few scholarly works that we can legitimately say redefined the terms of the debate over the character of the German army in World War II.

6. For the role of the German navy in the establishment of the OKW, see the fine scholarly biography by Keith Bird, *Erich Raeder: Admiral of the Third Reich* (Annapolis, MD: Naval Institute Press, 2006), which notes the inconsistencies in the memoirs of Erich Raeder, *Grand Admiral* (Annapolis, MD: Naval Institute Press, 1960).

7. For *Weserübung* ("Exercise Weser"), the German invasion of Norway and Denmark, see Adam R. A. Claasen, *Hitler's Northern War: The Luftwaffe's Ill-Fated Campaign, 1940–1945* (Lawrence: University Press of Kansas, 2001), as well as Jack Greene and Alessandro Massignani, *Hitler Strikes North: The Invasion of Norway and Denmark, 9 April 1940* (London: Frontline Books, 2013).

8. Still preeminent in the literature is Richard Muller, *The German Air War in Russia* (Baltimore, MD: Nautical & Aviation, 1992). See also Williamson Murray, *Luftwaffe* (Baltimore, MD: Nautical & Aviation, 1983), 72–111, "The Turn to Russia."

9. Neither Halder nor Zeitzler published memoirs, but see Franz Halder, *Hitler als Feldherr* (München: Munchener Dom-Verlag, 1949), as well as Peter Bor, *Gespräche mit Halder* (Wiesbaden: Limes-Verlag, 1950). As is the case with so many German writers on the Wehrmacht, "Peter Bor" is a pseudonym for Paul Egon Lüth, founder of the extreme right-wing *Bundes deutscher Jugend* in 1950. Lüth was later implicated in the scandal surrounding Operation Gladio, a CIA plan to form a "stay behind organization" in the event of a Soviet invasion and conquest of West Germany. The purpose would be to launch a partisan war against the occupation regime and to kill pro-Soviet officials. For Zeitzler, see "Die Ringen um die grossen Entscheidungen im zweiten Weltkriege," part 1, "Stalingrad: der Wendepunkt des Krieges," and part 2, "Abwehrschlachten im Russland nach dem Wendepunkt im Kriege," Manuscripts D-405 and D-406, respectively, in the Foreign Military Studies series. Together, they amount to a monograph-length work. See also Zeitzler, "Die oberste Führung des Heeres im Rahmen der Wehrmachtführung (Zukunftsgedanken)," Manuscript C-026 in the Foreign Military Studies series. Zeitzler discusses the functioning of the German High Command during the war, "wie es tatsächlich war" (how it was) and also "wie es hatte sein sollen" (how it should have been). For an overview, see Kurt Dittmar, "Das Verhältnis OKW-OKH," Manuscript B-512 in the Foreign Military Studies series. Dittmar is particularly revelatory on the anger of OKH officers against the "Adoranten" in the OKW, which they mocked as the "militärischen Büro des Gefreiten Hitler" (7). Both originals are available in the AHEC in Carlisle, PA.

10. For German defensive preparations in the west, see Alan F. Wilt, *The Atlantic Wall: Rommel's Plan to Stop the Allied Invasion* (New York: Enigma Books, 2004).

11. For Führer Directive No. 40, "Befehlsbefügnisse an den Küsten," see Walther Hubatsch, ed., *Hitlers Weisungen für die Kriegführung 1939–1945* (Frankfurt: Bernard & Graefe, 1962), 176–182.

12. For Rundstedt's life, career, and new command, see Charles Messenger, *The Last Prussian: A Biography of Field Marshal Gerd Rundstedt, 1875–1953* (London: Brassey's, 1991), 158–159.

13. The joke within the German military was that the country had lost World War I because of its "fleet in being" and was now losing World War II because of an "army in being." See Bernd Wegner, "Deutschland am Abgrund," in *Das Deutsche Reich und der Zweite Weltkrieg*, volume 8, *Die Ostfront 1943/44: Der Krieg im Osten und an den Nebenfronten* (München: Deutsche Verlags-Anstalt, 2011), 1165.

14. See Freiherr Treusch von Buttlar Brandenfels, "Stellungnahme zu dem Bericht des Generalleutnant z.V. Bodo Zimmermann (MS #B-308) über die Operationen des OB. West von den Vorbereitungen gegen die Invasion bus zum Rückzug auf den Westwall," 11, Manuscript B-672 in the Foreign Military Studies

series. The original is available in the AHEC in Carlisle, PA. Buttlar was the army operations chief (Ia) in the *Wehrmachtführungsstab*.

15. For Dieppe, see Ronald Atkin, *Dieppe 1942: The Jubilee Disaster* (London: Book Club Associates, 1980); J. P. Campbell, *Dieppe Revisited: A Documentary Investigation* (London: Cass, 1993), as well as the entry in Osprey's always reliable Campaign Series by Ken Ford, *Dieppe 1942* (London: Osprey, 2010).

16. For the raid on St. Nazaire, a fiasco for the commandos involved but a success in closing the dry dock, see James Dorrian, *Storming St. Nazaire: The Gripping Story of the Dock-Busting Raid, March 1942* (Annapolis, MD: Naval Institute Press, 1998), and another Osprey entry by Ken Ford, *St. Nazaire 1942: The Great Commando Raid* (London: Osprey, 2001).

17. See Gerd von Rundstedt, "Beurteilung der Lage Ob. West am 25.10.1943," available on microfilm from the National Archives and Records Administration, Serial T-311, Reel 27, Frames 7032424–7032474. See also the comprehensive report by Bodo Zimmermann, "Bericht über die Operationen des OB. West von den Vorbereitungen gegen die Invasion bis zum Rückzug auf den Westwall," Manuscript B-308 in the Foreign Military Studies series, as well as the series of commentaries on it: Gerd von Rundstedt, "Bemerkungen zur Ausarbeitung des General Zimmermann," B-633; Hans Speidel, "Stellungnahme zu dem Bericht des Generalleutnant z.V. Bodo Zimmermann (MS #B-308) über die Operationen des OB. West von den Vorbereitungen gegen die Invasion bus zum Rückzug auf den Westwall," B-718; Günther Blumentritt, "Drei Marschälle, Volkscharakter, und der 20. Juli," B-344; and Buttlar, "Stellungnahme zu dem Bericht des Generalleutnant z.V. Bodo Zimmermann," B-672.

18. "Trotzdem wird es dem Feind an vielen Stellen eben doch gelingen, mit starken Kräften zu landen, besonders an Fronten, wo nur eine 'Sicherung' möglich war." Rundstedt, "Beurteilung der Lage Ob. West," 14. See also Zimmermann, "Bericht über die Operationen des OB. West," 42 ("dem Gegner die Anlandung immer gelingen wird").

19. "Etwa vorhandene örtliche Reserven sind zum Gegenstoss anzusetzen, der sofort erfolgen muss." Rundstedt, "Beurteilung der Lage Ob. West," 14. See also Zimmermann, "Bericht über die Operationen des OB. West," 43.

20. "Wenn der Feind erst Zeit hat, sich festzustezen, ist das Hinauswerfen meist schwierig." Rundstedt, "Beurteilung der Lage Ob. West," 14.

21. A picket for the 1st Army and a mere watch for the 19th Army. Ibid., 12.

22. "Mit stärksten Mitteln amerikanischen Ausmasses." Ibid., 16.

23. "Mit den dann vorhandenen Mitteln." Ibid., 49.

24. For Führer Directive No. 51, see Hubatsch, *Hitlers Weisungen für die Kriegführung*, 233–238. "Anders der Westen!" 233.

25. "Alle im Westen und in Dänemark liegenden Truppenteile und Verbände sowie alle im Westen neuafzustellenden Panzer-, Sturmgeschütz- und Panzerjägereinheiten dürfen ohne meine Genehmigung nicht für andere Fronten abgezogen werden." Ibid., 235.

26. "Hochwertigen, angriffsfähigen, und voll beweglichen." Ibid., 234.

27. Annexes 51a, 51b, and 51c are included in ibid., 238–241.

28. For Führer Directive No. 52, see ibid., 241–242. Walter Warlimont, the deputy chief of the operations staff at OKW, described Directive No. 52 as a "fanatical revolutionary appeal," calling for "a hard and merciless struggle, not only against the enemy but also against each unit and commander who fails in this decisive hour." See Walter Warlimont, *Im Hauptquartier der deutschen Wehrmacht 1939 bis 1945: Grundlagen, Formen, Gestalten*, 2 vols. (Koblenz: Bernard & Graefe Verlag, 1990). The quote is from volume 2, 441. The English translation of Warlimont's memoirs is *Inside Hitler's Headquarters, 1939–45* (Novato, CA: Presidio, 1964).

29. For the "fester Platz," see Führer Directive No. 53, in Hubatsch, *Hitlers Weisungen für die Kriegführung*, 243–250.

30. "Innerhalb seines Heeresgruppen-Bereichs Freiheit des Handelns." Zimmermann, "Bericht über die Operationen des OB. West," 40.

31. Ibid.

32. "Kompetenzengerangel." Detlef Vogel, "Deutsche und Alliierte Kriegführung im Westen," in *Das Deutsche Reich und der Zweite Weltkrieg*, volume 7, *Das Deutsche Reich in der Defensive: Strategischer Luftkrieg in Europa, Krieg im Westen und in Ostasien 1943–1944/45* (München: Deutsche Verlags-Anstalt, 2001), 473.

33. For a balanced and well-modulated discussion of the Rommel-Rundstedt rivalry, see Wilt, *Atlantic Wall*, 103–106.

34. Charles P. Stacey, *The Victory Campaign: The Operations in Northwest Europe, 1944–1945*, 58–59. The volume is volume 1 in the *Official History of the Canadian Army in the Second World War* (Ottawa: Queen's Printer, 1957).

35. Vogel, "Deutsche und Alliierte Kriegführung im Westen," 473.

36. Blaskowitz had raised low-key objections to the massacre of Jewish and Polish civilians during the 1939 campaign. See Samuel W. Mitcham Jr., *Defenders of Fortress Europe: The Untold Story of the German Officers during the Allied Invasion* (Washington, DC: Potomac, 2009), 91, as well as Alexander B. Rossino, *Hitler Strikes Poland: Blitzkrieg, Ideology, and Atrocity* (Lawrence: University Press of Kansas, 2003), 175.

37. "Nirgends für eine Verteidigung im Grosskampf ausreichend schmal und tief genug gegliedert." Zimmermann, "Bericht über die Operationen des OB. West," 25. See also Rundstedt, "Beurteilung der Lage Ob. West," 11, 21–34. Rundstedt notes the differences between 1914–1918 and 1944. "Die Divisionsabschnitte an den Schwerpunkten waren schmal im Vergleich zu heute" (11).

38. Zimmermann, "Bericht über die Operationen des OB. West," 25.

39. For the static divisions, see Hans Speidel, *Invasion 1944: Ein Beitrag zu Rommels und des Reiches Schicksal* (Tübingen: Rainer Wunderlich, 1949), 51–52. Speidel was Army Group B's chief of staff under Rommel and, more than any single individual, was responsible for the creation of the postwar Rommel myth. The English translation is *Invasion 1944: Rommel and the Normandy Campaign* (Chicago: Henry Regnery, 1950). Prior to publication as a book, Speidel serialized the work as "Die alliierte Invasion in Europa 1944: eine deutsche Darstellung," *Allgemeine schweizerische Militärzeitschrift* 115, nos. 9–12 (1949): 646–652, 712–723, 778–791, 864–875, and 116; and nos. 1–2 (1950): 27–39, 93–111. For Rommel generally, see

Ralf Georg Reuth, *Rommel: Das Ende einer Legende* (München: Piper, 2004), translated into English as *Rommel: The End of a Legend* (London: Haus, 2005). Equally good, as sophisticated in its interpretation as it is marvelous in its writing, is the comparative biography by Dennis Showalter, *Patton and Rommel: Men of the War in the Twentieth Century* (New York: Berkley Caliber, 2005). For a short biographical profile of Rommel, see Robert M. Citino, *Armored Forces: History and Sourcebook* (Westport, CT: Greenwood Press, 1994), 266–269.

40. For the 709th Division, see the absolutely essential work by Niklas Zetterling, *Normandy 1944: German Military Organization, Combat Power and Organizational Effectivenesss* (Winnipeg: J. J. Federowicz, 2000), 292–294. Discussing German performance in Normandy is impossible without the statistics and attention to detail that Zetterling brings. See also Gordon A. Harrison, *Cross-Channel Attack* (Washington, DC: Center of Military History, 2007), an entry in the venerable Green Book series, 146–147.

41. Among the niche works on D-Day, none is more useful than James Foster Tent, *E-Boat Alert: Defending the Normandy Invasion Fleet* (Annapolis, MD: Naval Institute Press, 1996), especially 108–128, the chapter on Operation Neptune.

42. "Angriff—ran—versenken!" Dönitz quoted in Vogel, "Deutsche und Alliierte Kriegführung im Westen," 486. "Es erinnert ein wenig an die Einsatzgrundsätze japanischer Kamikazeflieger."

43. The precise numbers vary by individual source, but the order of magnitude does not: a few hundred Luftwaffe aircraft meeting thousands of Allie counterparts. Hans Speidel, *Aus unserer Zeit: Erinnerungen* (Berlin: Propyläen, 1977), makes a good point in correlating Luftwaffe personnel with the number of operational aircraft: 450,000 men in the west (17,000 stationed in Paris), supporting a grand total of 520 operational aircraft (167–168). For the overall problem of airpower in the western campaign, see Walter Gaul, "Die deutsche Luftwaffe während der Invasion 1944," *Wehrwissenschaftliche Rundschau* 3 (1953): 134–144.

44. "Der OB. West auf diese Weise niemals zu einer einheitlichen und straffen Führung im Westen kommen konnte." Zimmerman, "Bericht über die Operationen des OB. West," 9.

45. See Friedrich Ruge, *Rommel und die Invasion: Erinnerungen* (Stuttgart: K. F. Koehler Verlag, 1959), a remarkably detailed and candid memoir by the naval adviser (*Marinesachverständiger*) to Field Marshal Rommel. For the origins of the "Czech hedgehog" (*Tschechenigel*) as a means of coastal defense, see 12–13.

46. For coastal artillery, see Speidel, *Invasion 1944*, 60–65. See also Ernst Goettke, "Die Vorbereitung der Küstenverteidigung," Manuscript B-663, in the Foreign Military Studies series, available in the AHEC in Carlisle, PA. Goettke specifically mentions the difficulty of navy and army officers speaking a different "language of command" (*Kommandosprache*), 12.

47. "Mit rücksichtsloser Energie und Härte die tausenden Nichtstuer zu Befestigungsarbeiten zu zwingen." Jodl quoted in Vogel, "Deutsche und Alliierte Kriegführung im Westen," 466.

48. "Schärfere Massnahmen." Ibid., 491.

49. "*Unser* Vorfeldhindernis ist das Meer, der *beste* Panzergraben!" Ibid., 463.

50. "Im Bereich West gibt es kein Ausweichen." Ibid., 463.

51. For the fortifications on Guernsey, see the three-part article by Pierre Renier, "*Festung Guernsey 1944*: An Analysis of the Official German Handbook on Their Island Fortress," *Channel Islands Occupation Review*, nos. 20, 22, and 24 (February 1995, March 1997, and March 1998): 5–29, 5–50, and 5–36. The article reprints much of the official German report *Festung Guernsey*, compiled in 1944 on the orders of General Rudolf Graf von Schmettow, commander of 319th Infantry Division, the Wehrmacht division occupying the island. Only two copies of the report are extant, both held on Guernsey.

52. Erwin Rommel, *Krieg ohne Hass* (Heidenheim: Heidenheimer Zeitung, 1950), 219–220, 233.

53. "Es mag sein, dass seine oft berufene 'Intuition' dabei im Spiele gewesen ist." Warlimont, *Im Hauptquartier der deutschen Wehrmacht* 2, 439.

54. Zimmermann, "Bericht über die Operationen des OB. West," 11.

55. For Fortitude, see Mary Kathryn Barbier, *D-Day Deception: Operation Fortitude and the Normandy Invasion* (Westport, CT: Praeger Security, 2007), a fine and balanced evaluation without any of the breathless enthusiasm that historians tend to bring to questions of intelligence and deception operations. In the final analysis, Barbier argues, the impact of Operatio Fortitude "was minimal" (195). Indeed, Allied bombing of Normandy was so comprehensive and effective that any attempt to redeploy 15th Army and shift it laterally to the left was probably doomed to failure. "By attacking rail and road bridges across the Seine and Loire rivers, locomotives, and marshaling yards before and after the invasion, Allied air forces effectively isolated the Normandy area long enough for the Allied invasion forces to establish and reinforce bridgeheads" (194).

56. For General Marcks's LXXXIV Corps in Normandy, see the monograph by his intelligence officer (Ic), Friedrich Hayn, *Die Invasion: Von Cotentin bis Falaise* (Heidelberg: Kurt Vowinckel Verlag, 1954).

57. The literature on D-Day and the Normandy Campaign is massive and shows no signs of slowing down. Too much of the literature wallows in the tiresome "greatest generation" trope and offers little that is new in the way of information or insight. A partial list of essential books should start with Harrison, *Cross-Channel Attack*, and Martin Blumenson, *Breakout and Pursuit* (Washington, DC: Center of Military History, 1961). The magisterial scholarly account is, and will likely remain, Russell F. Weigley, *Eisenhower's Lieutenants: The Campaign of France and Germany, 1944–1945* (Bloomington: Indiana University Press, 1981), supplemented by Carlo D'Este, *Decision in Normandy* (New York: Harper, 1994). See also the standard popular account—still extremely useful—by Max Hastings, *Overlord: D-Day and the Battle for Normandy* (New York: Simon & Schuster, 1984), supplemented by Antony Beevor, *D-Day: the Battle for Normandy* (NY: Penguin Books, 2010), a carefully crafted narrative, and John Prados, *Normandy Crucible: The Decisive Battle That Shaped World War II in Europe* (New York: NAL Caliber, 2011), which combines archival research and sophisticated discussion of intelligence issues with the use of old commercial wargames, especially the old gem by Simulations Publications, Inc. (SPI), *Cobra* (designed by Brad J. Hessel, 1977),

in order to test various hypotheses about the course of the campaign. For the role of wargaming in operational analysis in general, see Robert M. Citino, "Lessons from the Hexagon: Wargames and the Military Historian," in Pat Harrigan and Matthew G. Kirschenbaum, eds., *Zones of Control: Perspectives on Wargaming* (Cambridge, MA: MIT Press, 2016), 439–446. Specialized studies can also be rewarding. Steve R. Waddell, *United States Army Logistics: The Normandy Campaign* (Westport, CT: Greenwood Press, 1994), is still the only volume on this crucial area—the single most important factor in the conduct of the landing and the subsequent operations—and is therefore indispensable. Roman Johann Jarymowycz, *Tank Tactics: From Normandy to Lorraine* (Boulder, CO: Lynne Rienner, 2001), is an interesting addition to the literature: a Canadian author highly critical of Allied armored doctrine in general, the US tank-destroyer concept in particular, and the British and Canadian preference for the set-piece battle. For the best of the "greatest generation" literature, see Stephen E. Ambrose, *Citizen Soldiers: The U.S. Army from the Normandy Beaches to the Bulge to the Surrender of Germany, June 7, 1944– May 7, 1945* (New York: Touchstone, 1997), supplemented by Kenneth D. Rose, *Myth and the Greatest Generation: A Social History of Americans in World War II* (New York: Routledge, 2008). For the D-Day landing itself, see Adrian Lewis, *Omaha Beach: A Flawed Victory* (Chapel Hill: University of North Carolina Press, 2001), supplemented by Stephen E. Ambrose, *D-Day: June 6, 1944: The Climactic Battle of World War II* (New York: Simon & Schuster, 1994); Joseph Balkoski, *Omaha Beach: D-Day, June 6, 1944* (Mechanicsburg, PA: Stackpole, 2004), and Antony Beevor, *D-Day: The Battle for Normandy* (New York: Viking, 2009).

58. Hans Speck, "Die Machtmittel Zweier Weltreiche," *Die Wehrmacht* 13 (1944), 132–133, reprinted in *Die Wehrmacht: Herausgegeben vom Oberkommando der Wehrmacht*, 5 vols. (Hamburg: Verlag für Geschichtliche Dokumentation, 1978). See also Friedrich Zschäckel, "Es begann am 6.6.," *Die Wehrmacht* 13 (1944): 130– 131, and Hans Feitl, "Invasionsfront Normandie," Die Wehrmacht 14 (1944): 138– 139. Speck, Zschäckel, and Feitl all had the title *Kriegsberichter* ("war reporter"), an early form of officially sanctioned, embedded journalism. All page references are to the five-volume reprint from 1978.

59. For the 716th Infantry Division, see Zetterling, *Normandy 1944*, 297–300, in particular the amount of captured Czech and French artillery, as well as Wilhelm Richter, "716. Infanterie-Division in Normandy (6. Juni-23. Juni-1944)," Manuscript B-621 in the Foreign Military Studies series. The original is available in the AHEC in Carlisle, PA. Particularly helpful for non-German readers is David C. Isby, ed., *Fighting the Invasion: The German Army at D-Day* (London: Greenhill, 2000), an edited compendium of translated Foreign Military Studies reports.

60. Stephen E. Ambrose, *Pegasus Bridge: D-Day; The Daring British Airborne Raid* (London: Pocket Books, 2003), offers a typically brilliant narrative.

61. For the 352nd Infantry Division, see Fritz Ziegelmann, "Die Geschichte der 352. Infanterie-Division," Manuscript B-432 in the Foreign Military Studies series, available in the AHEC in Carlisle, PA, as well as Zetterling, *Normandy 1944*, 277–280.

62. Of the hundreds of books on the US landing at Omaha, two are essential:

Lewis, *Omaha Beach*, which criticized Allied planning with authority and a surprising amount of passion, and Balkoski, *Omaha Beach: D-Day*, for the immediacy, the "you-are-there" feel, and the incisive operational and tactical analysis.

63. Hein Severloh, *WN 62: Erinnerungen an Omaha Beach: Normandie, 6. Juni 1944* (Garbsen: HEK Creativ Verlag, 2000), translated into English as *WN 62: A German Soldier's Memories of the Defense of Omaha Beach: Normandy, June 6, 1944* (Garbsen: HEK Creativ Verlag, 2011).

64. "Wer alles verteidigen will, verteidigt nichts." Speidel, *Invasion 1944*, 66, or perhaps "Wer alles decken will, deckt nichts," Rudolf-Christoph Freiherr von Gersdorff, "Allgemeine Bemerkungen zur deutschen Invasionsabwehr," Manuscript B-122 in the Foreign Military Studies series, 6. The original is available in the AHEC, Carlisle, PA. Or perhaps more likely, given the king's eighteenth-century Latinized German, "Wer alles defendieren will, defendieret gar nichts!"

65. The man of the hour was Group Captain James Martin Stagg, Eisenhower's chief meteorologist. See John Ross, *The Forecast for D-Day: And the Weatherman Behind Ike's Greatest Gamble* (Guilford, CT: Lyons Press, 2014), as well as Doyle Rice, "D-day: The Most Important Weather Forecast in History," *USA Today* (June 6, 2014).

66. "Es gibt keine menschliche Tätigkeit, welche mit dem Zufall so beständig und so allgemein in Berührung stände als der Krieg." Carl von Clausewitz, *Vom Kriege: Ungekürzter Text* (München: Cormoran, 2000), Book I, Chapter I, no. 20, 41.

67. Hayn, *Die Invasion*, 16–17.

68. Ibid., 17.

69. For Falley, see Mitcham, *Defenders of Fortress Europe*, 34–35, as well as Hayn, *Die Invasion*, 17. Paul Carell, *Sie Kommen! Der Deutsche Bericht über die Invasion und die 80tägige Schlacht um Frankreich* (Oldenburg: Gerhard Stalling Verlag, 1960), 51–52, offers a typically novelistic account—correct in its essentials, with invented conversations and dubious internal monologues. Carell (actually Paul Karl Schmidt, an *Obersturmbannführer* in the *Allgemeine-SS* and a press spokesman for the German Foreign Ministry, the *Auswärtiges Amt*, during World War II) clearly had his own sources of information, but readers should tread with care. This is history of a sort, with strong fictive overtones. The very popular English translation is *Invasion—They're Coming! The German Account of the Allied Landings and the 80 Days' Battle for France* (New York: E. P. Dutton, 1963). For the authoritative exposé of Schmidt/Carell's career, see Wigbert Benz, *Paul Carell: Ribbentrops Pressechef Paul Karl Schmidt vor und nach 1945* (Berlin: WVB, 2005).

70. For Rommel's trip home, see Rick Atkinson, *The Guns at Last Light: The War in Western Europe, 1944–45* (New York: Henry Holt, 2013), 78–80, the third installment in his magisterial *Liberation* trilogy.

71. For Feuchtinger, see Mitcham, *Defenders of Fortress Europe*, 37–39.

72. "Küsten-Verteidigungs-Abschnitt 'Bayeux.'" Ziegelmann, "Die Geschichte der 352. Infanterie-Division," 7.

73. "Stärkere Luftlandungen in der Vire-Niederung südlich Carentan." Ibid.,

21. The precise wording of the messages varies by source, depending on the level of command. See Hayn, *Die Invasion*, 13–15.

74. "Eine planmässige Landung stärkerer Kräft . . . Die 'Invasion' hatte wirklich begonnen!" Ziegelmann, "Die Geschichte der 352 Infanterre-Division," 23.

75. "Auf dem Strande legen sehr viele Verwundete und Tote." The verbatim report from WN 76—the Wehrmacht's declaration that it had defeated the landing—is included in ibid., 25. See also Harrison, *Cross-Channel Attack*, 319–320, although Harrison, too, is basing his account on Ziegelmann.

76. "Das verst. G.R. 915 (ohne 1 Btl.) zum Gegenangriff auf Crépon." Ziegelmann, "Die Geschichte der 352. Infanterie-Division," 27.

77. "Nach kurzer Zeit erschienen die ersten Jabos." Ibid., 28–29.

78. The notion of "polycracy" or "polycratic rule" was a useful corrective to the notion that the entire Third Reich was dependent on Hitler's personal will and orders from above. It was a structuralist interpretation that restored a sense of agency to the numerous offices and administrators of the Reich. The ur-texts are Hans Mommsen, *Beamtentum im Dritten Reich: Mit ausgewählten Quellen zur nationalsozialistischen Beamtenpolitik* (Stuttgart: Deutsche Verlagsanstalt, 1966), and Martin Broszat, *Der Staat Hitlers: Grundlegung und Entwicklung seiner inneren Verfassung* (München: Deutscher Taschenbuch-Verlag, 1969). A more recent expression is found in Ian Kershaw's notion of "working towards the Führer," in *Hitler*, 2 vols. (New York: Norton, 1998–2000), especially volume 1, *1889–1936: Hubris*, 527–589. "In the Darwinist jungle of the Third Reich, the way to power and advancement was through anticipating the 'Führer will,' and, without waiting for directives, taking initiatives to promote what were presumed to be Hitler's aims and wishes" (530). For a discussion of the impact on German military history, see Robert M. Citino, *The German Way of War: From the Thirty Years' War to the Third Reich* (Lawrence: University Press of Kansas, 2005), 277–278.

79. See Leo Freiherr Geyr von Schweppenburg, "Reflections on the Invasion," 2 parts, *Military Review* (February and March 1961): 2–11 and 12–21, as well as "Zu Problemen der Invasion von 1944 (mit einleitenden Bemerkungen von Fritz Ernst)," in *Die Welt als Geschichte* 22 (1962): 79–87.

80. "Es ist alles im Kriege sehr einfach, aber das Einfachste ist schwierig." Clausewitz, *Vom Kriege*, Book I, Chapter 7, 86.

81. See Stephen A. Bourque, "Operational Fires Lisieux and Saint-Lô: The Destruction of Two Norman Towns on D-Day," *Canadian Military History* 19, no. 2 (2010): 25–40.

82. Hans von Luck, *Panzer Commander* (Westport, CT: Praeger, 1989), 149.

83. Oppeln was known to come to his office drunk at 8:00 A.M., but he was also an Olympic gold medalist in dressage at the 1936 Summer Olympics in Berlin. Mitcham, *Defenders of Fortress Europe*, 38.

84. Carell, *Sie Kommen!*, 102, has Marcks declaring, "Oppeln, if you don't succeed in throwing the English into the sea, we've lost the war" ("Oppeln, wenn es Ihnen nicht gelingt, die Engländer ins Meer zu werfen, haben wir den Krieg verloren"), but there is no attribution, and the quote has shown up in none of the

other literature. Carell also has Oppeln respond, in classic Prussian style, "Ich greife an!" ("I attack!"), but again, the author gives no citation. Mitcham, *Defenders of Fortress Europe*, 39, includes the same quote from Marcks, but his source is Carell.

85. "Es bleibt dahingestellt, ob dieser Entschluss richtig war." Zimmermann, "Bericht über die Operationen des OB. West," 67.

Chapter 4. In the Middle: The Smashing of the Central Front

1. This famous bon mot leads off Karl Marx, *The Eighteenth Brumaire of Louis Bonaparte* (New York: Mondial, 2005), 1. The original German renders it as "eine Mal als Tragödie, das andere Mal als Farce."

2. For Mars-la-Tour (sometimes "Mars-la-Tour-Vionville"), see Geoffrey Wawro, *The Franco-Prussian War* (Cambridge: Cambridge University Press, 2003), 138–163; David Ascoli, *A Day of Battle: Mars-la-Tour, 16 August 1870* (London: Harrap, 1987); and Hans von Kretschman, "The Battle of Vionville—Mars-la-Tour," in Major General Sir F. Maurice, ed., *The Franco-German War, by Generals and Other Officers Who Took Part in the Campaign* (London: Allen & Unwin, 1899), 131–153. For a view from within the World War II officer corps, see Lieutenant Colonel Obkircher, "General Constantin von Alvensleben: Zu Seinem 50. Todestag, 28 März," *Militär-Wochenblatt* 126, no. 39 (March 7, 1942): 1111–1115.

3. Quoted in Wawro, *Franco-Prussian War*, 156. Michael Howard, *The Franco-Prussian War* (New York: Doerset, 1990), 157, calls Bredow's ride "perhaps the last successful cavalry charge in Western European warfare" (157).

4. The account is based on a series of vignettes in Adolf Heusinger, *Befehl im Widerstreit: Schicksalsstunden der deutschen Armee 1923–1945* (Tübingen: Rainer Wunderlich Verlag, 1950), 326–329 ("6. Juni 1944: Tag der Invasion. Der Chef des Generalstabes des Heeres mit dem Chef der Operationsabteilung auf der Rückfahrt vom Lagevortrag bei Hitler"), 330–341 ("Anfang Juli 1944: Der Chef der Operationsabteilung als Vertreter des erkrankten Chefs des Generalstabes des Heeres beim Lagevortrag im Führerhauptquartier auf dem Obersalzberg"), 342–345 ("Anfang Juli 1944: Im Berchtesgaden. Im Zimmer des Chefs des Generalstabes des Heeres"), and 346–349 ("Mitte Juli 1944: Hauptquartier des Oberkommando des Heeres im Mauerwald bei Angerburg in Ostpreussen. Im Zimmer des Chefs des Generalstabes des Heeres").

5. "Anstelle des Zweifrontenkrieges, des ständigen Alptraums deutscher Strategen, drohet ein Allfrontenkrieg." Karl-Heinz Frieser, "Irrtümer und Illusionen: Die Fehleinschätzung der deutschen Führung im Frühsommer 1944," in *Das Deutsche Reich und der Zweite Weltkrieg*, volume 8, *Die Ostfront 1943/44: Der Krieg im Osten und an den Nebenfronten* (München: Deutsche Verlags-Anstalt, 2011), 496.

6. "Ich kriege immer einen Horror, wenn ich so etwas höre, dass man sich irgendwo absetzen muss, um dann 'operieren' zu können." Quoted in Ferdinand Heim, "Stalingrad und der Verlauf des Feldzuges der Jahre 1943–1945," in Alfred Philippi and Ferdinand Heim, *Der Feldzug gegen Sowjetrussland 1941 bis 1945* (Stuttgart: W. Kohlhammer, 1962), 228.

7. For one example among many dozens of using "ruthless" as a positive attribute, see Hitler's electoral speech at Eberswalde (July 27, 1932), in which he contrasts the Nazi Party's determination with the waffling of his enemies: "Sie verwechseln mich immer mit einem bürgerlichen oder einem marxistischen Politiker, der heute SPD und morgen USPD und übermorgen KPD und dann Syndikalisten oder heute Demokraten und morgen deutsche Volkspartei und dann [. . .] Wirtschaftspartei . . . Sie verwechseln uns mit Ihresgleichen selbst! Wir haben ein Ziel uns gewählt und verfechten es fanatisch, rücksichtslos bis ins Grab hinein!" For the complete text of the speech, see de.metapedia.org/wiki/Quelle_/ _Rede _vom_27._Juli_1932_(Adolf_Hitler)#Quellennachweis.

8. Heusinger never admitted to error; in his defense, the Soviets did eventually launch a highly destructive offensive to the south of Army Group Center, against Army Group North Ukraine. See *Befehl im Widerstreit*, 328–329.

9. "Dazwischen, also von der Gegend westlich Bobruisk bis nördlich Minsk, klafft ein Loch, in dem an einzelnen Stellen unzusammenhängend örtlich gekämpft wird." Heusinger, *Befehl im Widerstreit*, 331

10. "Dann können Sie ihr 4 Divisionen wegnehmen." Ibid., 335.

11. "Wichtig erscheint mir, dass die Generale ihre Pflicht tun oder dazu gezwungen werden." Ibid., 332.

12. Ibid., 339.

13. "Da gehört ein besonders harter Mann hin." Ibid.

14. "Koste es, was es wolle!" Ibid.

15. "So geriet der Aufmarsch an der Ostfront allmählich zu einem grotesken Täuschungsmanöver." Frieser, "Irrtümer und Illusionen," 493.

16. For the long, slow Soviet dismemberment of Army Group North—always the most undermanned and underfunded of the German army groups in the east—see Hans Meier-Welcker (Militärgeschichtliches Forschungsamt), ed., *Abwehrkämpfe am Nordflügel der Ostfront 1944–1945* (Stuttgart: Deutsche Verlags-Anstalt, 1963), especially Helmuth Forwick, "Der Rückzug der Heeresgruppe Nord nach Kurland," 99–214. The volume also includes useful extended essays by Karl Köhler, "Der Einsatz der Luftwaffe im Bereich der Heeresgruppe Nord von Ende Juni bis Mitte Oktober 1944," 15–98, and Rudolf Kabath, "Die Rolle der Seebrückenköpfe beim Kampf um Ostpreussen 1944–1945," 215–451. See also David M. Glantz, *The Battle for Leningrad, 1941–1944* (Lawrence: University Press of Kansas, 2002), 328, 330–334, as well as David M. Glantz and Jonathan House, *When Titans Clashed: How the Red Army Stopped Hitler* (Lawrence: University Press of Kansas, 1995), 192–193. For the tough battles on Army Group North's front, see Burkhart Müller-Hillebrand, "Die Rückzugskämpfe der Heeresgruppe Nord im Jahre 1944," Manuscript P-035 in the Foreign Military Studies series, as well as the larger study, Burkhart Müller-Hillebrand et al., "Der Feldzug gegen die Sowjetunion in Nordabschnitt der Ostfront, 1941–1945," Manuscript P-114a, especially part 3, Friedrich Sixt, "Die Übergang der Initiative an den Russen (Kriegsjahr 1943)," part 4, Friedrich Sixt, "Der Rückzug der Heeresgruppe Nord in die Baltischen Länder und das Ringen um den Zusammenhang mit der Gesamtfront (Januar bis Mitte September 1944)," and part 5, Friedrich Sixt, "Einschliessung

in Kurland und Endkampf der Heeresgruppe Nord (Mitte September 1944 bis Mai 1945)." All of the German-language originals are available in the US Army Heritage and Education Center (AHEC) in Carlisle, PA. Steven H. Newton, ed., *Retreat from Leningrad: Army Group North 1944/1945* (Atglen, PA: Schiffer, 1995), is a useful edited collection of the various Foreign Military Studies reports.

17. Glantz and House, *When Titans Clashed*, 193.

18. For the relief of Kovel, see Hermann Gackenholz, "Der Zusammenbruch der Heeresgruppe Mitte 1944," in Hans-Adolf Jacobsen and Jürgen Rohwer, eds., *Entscheidungsschlachten des zweiten Weltkrieges* (Frankfurt: Verlag für Wehrwesen Bernard & Graefe, 1960), 450. Gackenholz was one of the editors of the *Kriegstagebuch* (war diary) for Army Group Center.

19. For the "weissrussiche Balkon" and the "ukrainische Balkon," see Heim, "Stalingrad und der Verlauf des Feldzuges der Jahre 1943–1945," 246. Frieser, "Irrtümer und Illusionen," 501–505, hews closely to Heim's original analysis.

20. "Galizische Lücke." Frieser, "Irrtümer und Illusionen," 502.

21. "Vielleicht kriegsentscheidende." Quoted in ibid., 504.

22. Frieser, the leading scholarly expert on the 1940 campaign, places great weight on this point. "Irrtümer und Illusionen," 504. See Karl-Heinz Frieser, *Blitzkrieg-Legende: Der Westfeldzug 1940* (München: R. Oldenbourg, 1995).

23. For the historiography on Field Marshal Model, see three works. Begin with the breezy account by Walter Görlitz, *Model: Strategie der Defensive: von Russland bis zum Ruhrkessel* (Bergisch Gladbach: Gustav Lübbe Verlag, 1977), reprinted as *Model: Der Feldmarschall und sein Endkampf an der Ruhr* (Frankfurt: Ullstein, 1992). Görlitz was a journalist and popularizer who has somehow won a reputation among many Western scholars as a scholarly and official authority. The biography by the always reliable Steven H. Newton, *Hitler's Commander: Field Marshal Walther Model—Hitler's Favorite General* (New York: Da Capo, 2006), is a favorable account, taking note of Model's operational acumen and his willingness to disagree with the Führer. Marcel Stein, *A Flawed Genius: Field Marshal Walter Model: A Critical Biography* (Solihull, UK: Helion, 2010), gives Model his due on the battlefield, but scores him for his blind spots regarding Hitler and the Nazi regime, and also provides chapter and verse on the field marshal's war crimes. Stein is the author of the equally scathing biography *Field Marshal von Manstein: The Janus Head/A Portrait* (Solihull, UK: Helion, 2007). For a solid (if relatively unproblematized) introduction to Model, see Carlo d'Este, "Model," in Correlli Barnett, ed., *Hitler's Generals* (New York: Quill, 1989), 318–333.

24. "Beide Heeresgruppen haben sich dort zu schlagen, wo sie stehen und nunmehr endgültig den russisichen Vormarsch aufzuhalten." Peter von der Groeben, "Der Zusammenbruch der Heeresgruppe Mitte und ihr Kampf bis zur Festigung der Front (22.VI. bis 1.IX.1944)," Manuscript T-31 in the Foreign Military Studies series. As with the entire series, the original is available at the US Army Heritage and Education Center in Carlisle, PA. The quote in taken from page 40.

25. "Wo nunmehr 'zum ersten Mal Schwerpunkt gegen Schwerpunkt' stände," Hermann Gackenholz, "Zum Zusammenbruch der Heeresgruppe Mitte im Sommer 1944," *Vierteljahrshefte für Zeitgeschichte* 3, no. 3 (Juli 1955): 321.

26. For Manstein's tendency to deal from the backhand, see Karl-Heinz Frieser, "Schlagen aus der Nachhand—Schlagen aus der Vorhand: Die Schlachten von Char'kow und Kursk 1943," in Roland G. Foerster, ed., *Gezeitenwechsel im Zweiten Weltkrieg? Die Schlachten von Char'kov und Kursk im Frühjahr und Sommer 1943 in operativer Anlage, Verlauf und politischer Bedeutung* (Berlin: E. S. Mittler, 1996), and "Mansteins Gegenschlag am Donez: Operative Analyse des Gegenangriffs der Heeresgruppe Süd im February/März 1943," *Militärgeschichte* 9 (1999): 12–18, the latter coauthored with Friedhelm Klein.

27. "Anstelle des in der Tradition des deutschen Generalstabes favorisierten Operierens a posteriori blieb nun nur die Möglichkeit, in einem Operieren a priori die eigenen Kräfte von vorherein festzulegen." Frieser, "Irrtümer und Illusionen," 506.

28. For a comprehensive view of Soviet planning in the spring of 1944, see Soviet General Staff, *Operation Bagration: The Rout of the German Forces in Belorussia, 23 June–29 August 1944*, edited and translated by Richard W. Harrison (Solihull: Helion, 2016), as well as Glantz and House, *When Titans Clashed*, 195–196. "The Defeat of the Germans in Belorussia (Summer 1944)," *Journal of Slavic Military Studies* 7, no. 4 (December 1994): 809–810, describes Operation Bagration as "the fifth blow executed by the Red Army."

29. For the reports flowing from the various German armies, see Gackenholz, "Zum Zusammenbruch der Heeresgruppe Mitte im Sommer 1944," 520–521.

30. "Befand sich die deutsche Abwehr in der Rolle jenes vielbeschriebenen Jagdhundes, dessen Instinkt dadurch blockiert wird, dass er sich drei gleich weit entfernten Hasen gegenübersieht." See Frieser, "Irrtümer und Illusionen," 506.

31. "Wie so oft hatte sich Hitler in eine autosuggestive Euphorie hineingeredet." Albert Speer, *Spandauer Tagebücher* (Frankfurt: Ullstein, 1978), 34. The English translation of the diaries is *Spandau: The Secret Diaries* (New York: Macmillan, 1976). The mood could easily snap, however. In the same passage, Speer has Hitler suddenly break off and say, "Wenn wir aber, meine Herren, diesen Krieg verlieren sollten, tun Sie gut daran, sich alle einen Strick zu besorgen" ("Gentlemen, if we lose this war, you'll all do well to get yourself a rope.")

32. "Also,—anganga is." Walter Warlimont, *Im Hauptquartier er deutschen Wehrmacht 1939 bis 1945: Grundlagen, Formen, Gestalten* (Augsburg: Weltbild Verlag, 1990), volume 2, 457.

33. Hugo von Freytag-Loringhoven, *Feldherrngrösse: Von Denken und Handeln hervorragender Heerführer* (Berlin: E. S. Mittler, 1922), 56.

34. "Als Erlösung aus einer unerträglichen Spannung und drückenden Ungewissheit empfunden." Frieser, "Irrtümer und Illusionen," 497.

35. Ibid., 499.

36. Gackenholz, "Zum Zusammenbruch der Heeresgruppe Mitte im Sommer 1944," 321–322.

37. "Fenster der Verwundbarkeit." Frieser, "Irrtümer und Illusionen," 496.

38. For a solid analysis of Soviet *maskirovka*, see William M. Connor, "Analysis of Deep Attack Operations: Operation Bagration; Belorussia 22 June–29 August 1944," a student paper from the US Army Command and General Staff College,

Fort Leavenworth, KS (March 1987), 22–30. See also Graham Jenkins, "The Mask of the Bear: Soviet Deception in Operation Bagration," on Jenkins's website *Automatic Ballpoint*, automaticballpoint.com/2010/05/04/the-mask-of-the-bear-soviet -deception-in-operation-bagration (accessed August 2016).

39. See Hermann Teske, *Die silbernen Spiegel: Generalstabsdienst unter der Lupe* (Heidelberg: Kurt Vowinckel, 1952), for a description of false Soviet rail traffic toward Brest: "ein vorbildliches Beispiel der Ausnutzung der Eisenbahn als operativem Führungsmittel" (211). Teske was *General des Transportwesens* for Army Group Center in 1944.

40. For the order of battle for 3rd Panzer Army, see Rolf Hinze, *Der Zusammenbruch der Heeresgruppe Mitte im Osten 1944* (Stuttgart: Motorbuch Verlag, 1980), 34–35, 278–280.

41. "Er (Hitler) habe bisher nicht gewusst, dass Busch auch zu den Generalen gehöre, die stets nach hinten blickten." Gerd Niepold, *Mittlere Ostfront Juni '44: Darstellung, Beurteilung, Lehren* (Herford und Bonn: Verlag E. S. Mittler & Sohn, 1985), 20. Niepold was the operations officer (Ia) of the XXXXVII Panzer Corps.

42. Gackenholz, "Der Zusammenbruch der Heeresgruppe Mitte 1944," 452. Frieser, "Irrtümer und Illusionen," 518, describes Busch as a "gläubiger Nationalsozialist und absolut Gefolgsmann des 'Führers.'"

43. "Unmissverständlichen Willen des Führers." Gackenholz, "Der Zusammenbruch der Heeresgruppe Mitte 1944," 452.

44. Frieser, "Irrtümer und Illusionen," 518.

45. Quoted in Paul Adair, *Hitler's Greatest Defeat: The Collapse of Army Group Center, June 1944* (London: Arms and Armour Press, 1994), 62; this is still the best short narrative introduction to the sprawling Soviet offensive.

46. The numbers for men and weapons employed in Operation Bagration vary wildly by source and are often based on different fundamental calculations and whether or not to include various reserves and second- or third-echelon forces in the initial total. For the discrepancies, often quite dramatic, see John Erickson, *The Road to Berlin: Stalin's War with Germany* (New Haven, CT: Yale University Press, 1983), 214–215; Lee Baker, "Explaining Defeat: a Reappraisal of 'Operation Bagration,' 1944," *Journal of Slavic Military Studies* 21 (2008): 129–130, Karl-Heinz Frieser, "Der Zusammenbruch der Heeresgruppe Mitte im Sommer 1944," in *Das Deutsche Reich und der Zweite Weltkrieg*, volume 8, *Die Ostfront 1943/44: Der Krieg im Osten und an den Nebenfronten* (München: Deutsche Verlags-Anstalt, 2011), 526–527, and Glantz and House, *When Titans Clashed*, 201–202.

47. The phrase belongs to David Stahel, *Operation Barbarossa and Germany's Defeat in the East* (Cambridge: Cambridge University Press, 2009, a superbly researched work and currently the authoritative work on the German invasion of the Soviet Union. Stahel places the date of the Soviet transformation into a "militarised juggernaut" much earlier than most scholars—to late summer of 1941, in fact.

48. "Die Gesamtfront war zu weit gespannt." Gackenholz, "Der Zusammenbruch der Heeresgruppe Mitte 1944," 449.

49. For the relevant details, see Baker, "Explaining Defeat," 134–136.

50. The current expert on the various German "Stärke" (strengths) is Gregory Liedtke. See his first book, *Enduring the Whirlwind: The German Army and the Russo-German War 1941–1943* (Solihull, UK: Helion, 2016). Liedtke's strengths are extremely deep research and an obsessive devotion to precision and detail, and no research into the Eastern Front can proceed without considering his findings on actual battlefield strengths.

51. Baker, "Explaining Defeat," 138.

52. Frieser, "Zusammenbruch der Heeresgruppe Mitte," 531. Fifty-two of those 118 belonged to 20th Panzer Division, newly transferred from Army Group North Ukraine.

53. The problem of "Entmotorisierung" had arisen long before 1944. See the discussion in Robert M. Citino, *Death of the Wehrmacht: The German Campaigns of 1942* (Lawrence: University Press of Kansas, 2007), 152–153. In June 1942, OKW issued a report titled *Wehrkraft* (Military Strength), which included the ominous words "Entmotorisierungsmassnahmen nicht zu umgehen" (demotorization measures unavoidable). See Warlimont, *Im Hauptquartier er deutschen Wehrmacht*, volume 2, 251, n. 29.

54. Frieser, "Zusammenbruch der Heeresgruppe Mitte," 535.

55. "Die russische Offensive begann am 22. Juni 1944—dem 3. Jahrestag von 'Barbarossa.'" Gackenholz, "Der Zusammenbruch der Heeresgruppe Mitte 1944," 457. See also Earl F. Ziemke, *Stalingrad to Berlin: The German Defeat in the East* (Washington, DC: Center of Military History, 1987), 319 ("On the morning of 22 June, the third anniversary of the invasion, the offensive against Army Group Center began"), and Frieser, "Zusammenbruch der Heeresgruppe Mitte," 538 ("Wie allgemein erwartet, begann die Rote Armee ihre Offensive gegen die Heeresgruppe Mitte am 22. Juni, dem dritten Jahrestag des deutschen Überfalls auf die Sowjetunion"). Soviet General Staff, *Operation Bagration*, gives June 23 as the starting date of the offensive.

56. Glantz and House, *When Titans Clashed*, 294.

57. Quoted in Erickson, *Road to Berlin*, 216.

58. Frieser, "Zusammenbruch der Heeresgruppe Mitte," 536.

59. Rokossovsky's operational design for 1st Byelorussian Front was the most controversial aspect of the planning for Bagration. See Erickson, *Road to Berlin*, 202–203.

60. Gackenholz, "Zum Zusammenbruch der Heeresgruppe Mitte," 321, refers to "in der Auffrischung befindlichen nicht einsatzbereiten Pz. Gren. Div. 'Feldherrnhalle.'"

61. For Soviet airpower in Bagration, see Von Hardesty and Ilya Grinberg, *Red Phoenix Rising: The Soviet Air Force in World War II* (Lawrence: University Press of Kansas, 2012), 300–310.

62. For the fighting in and around Vitebsk, see Otto Heidkämper, *Witebsk: Kampf und Untergang der 3. Panzerarmee* (Heidelberg: Kurt Vowinckel Verlag, 1954), 144–171, as well as Alex Buchner, *Ostfront 1944: Tscherkassy, Tarnopol, Krim, Witebsk, Bobruisk, Brody, Jassy, Kischinew* (Eggolsheim: Podzun-Pallas Verlag, 1988),

150–159. The English translation of the book is similarly titled *Ostfront 1944: The German Defensive Battles on the Russian Front 1944* (Atglen, PA: Schiffer, 1995). All references in these notes are to the original German-language version.

63. "Sieger von Vitebsk." Frieser, "Zusammenbruch der Heeresgruppe Mitte," 540.

64. Buchner, *Ostfront*, 151.

65. "Melden Sie dem Führer, dass ich mich weigere, einen Generalstabsoffizier oder irgendeinen anderen Soldaten über Witebsk abspringen zu lassen." Quoted in Heidkämper, *Witebsk*, 160.

66. "Bis zur Entsetzung." Gackenholz, "Der Zusammenbruch der Heeresgruppe Mitte," 463.

67. Adair, *Hitler's Greatest Defeat*, 96. The Luftwaffe field divisions (*Luftwaffenfelddivisionen*) remain a cipher in the history of the war—every scholar knows of them, but no one has written on them. There is no central repository of documents, and the researcher will be reduced to reading documentation on every level of command (army group, army, corps) in order to glean what information s/he can. This was a problem recognized years ago by the dean of World War II historians, Gerhard L. Weinberg, "Unexplored Questions about the German Military During World War II," *Journal of Military History* 62 (April 1998): 371–380. As of now, René Gurtner, "Deutsche Luftwaffen-Felddivisionen im Weltkrieg 1939–1945," *Allgemeine schweizerische Militärzeitschrift* 122, no. 8 (1956): 592–608, remains the starting point. Weinberg wrote a similar piece a year earlier, "World War II Scholarship, Now and in the Future," *Journal of Military History* 61 (April 1997): 335–346, and it is amazing how much of the agenda he outlined in those two seminal pieces remains undone.

68. "Wie Hasen bei einer Treibjagd liefen wir im Zirpen der Geschosse über das freie Gelände." Buchner, *Ostfront*, 155.

69. "Nächtlicher Durchbruch unter pers. Einsatz des K[ommandierenden] G[enerals] günstig angelaufen." Quoted in Frieser, "Zusammenbruch der Heeresgruppe Mitte," 542.

70. "Entartete der Rückzug zur wilden Flucht." Ibid.

71. For the ordeal of 4th Army at Orsha and Mogilev, broken down to the encirclement of individual divisions, see Buchner, *Ostfront*, 159–190.

72. "Auf kleinen Fahrzeugen und zu Fuss erreichten die Reste der Division am 5. Juli den Raum südostwärts von Minsk. Völlig vom Gegner umstellt und ständig von Partisanen bedrängt, lösten sich die Regimenter in kleine Gruppen auf, die sich unter ständigen Kämpfen durch Wälder und Getreidefelder nach Westen durchzuschlagen versuchten, was den meisten aber nicht glückte." Buchner, *Ostfront*, 182.

73. "Ihr Befehl ist ein Handeln gegen die Befehle Hitlers." Quoted in Frieser, "Zusammenbruch der Heeresgruppe Mitte," 544.

74. "Volzug ist zu melden." Quoted in Niepold, *Mittlere Ostfront Juni '44*, 102.

75. "Ein unbeschreibliches Durcheinander." Frieser, "Zusammenbruch der Heeresgruppe Mitte," 544.

76. "Truppen haben an allen nicht angriffnen Frontteilen stehen zu bleiben,

bis sie vom Feinde überlegen angegriffen und zurückgedrückt werden." Quoted in Niepold, *Mittlere Ostfront Juni '44*, 102.

77. "Hintertür." Frieser, "Zusammenbruch der Heeresgruppe Mitte," 544.

78. "Hitler genehmigt ein schrittweises Absetzen der 4. Armee auf die Beresina." Niepold, *Mittlere Ostfront Juni '44*, 118.

79. "Es wurde kein Rückmarsch mehr, nicht einmal ein geordneter Rückzug, sondern nur noch aufgelöstes Züruckkämpfen durch ein ausgedehntes Wald- und Sumpfgebiet." Buchner, *Ostfront*, 163.

80. For the epic rear guard of the "gallant Gascon" Ney, see David G. Chandler, *The Campaigns of Napoleon* (New York: Macmillan, 1966), 830.

81. "Unaufhörlich lud die Rote Luftwaffe über uns ab." Quoted in Hinze, *Der Zusammenbruch der Heeresgruppe Mitte*, 225. Reprinted in Buchner, *Ostfront*, 165–166.

82. "Deutschsprechende Russen in den Uniformen gefangengenommener deutscvher Offiziere, die man diesen abgenommen hatte, tauchteauf." Buchner, *Ostfront*, 162–163.

83. For the "Kesselbildung bei Pekalin," see Hinze, *Der Zusammenbruch der Heeresgruppe Mitte*, 233–236. See also Frieser, "Zusammenbruch der Heeresgruppe Mitte," 553–554.

84. For the dolorous *Kommandeurbesprechung* at Pekalin, see Hinze, *Der Zusammenbruch der Heeresgruppe Mitte*, 236–238.

85. Buchner, *Ostfront*, note on 168.

86. For the success of the first *Welle*, see Hinze, *Der Zusammenbruch der Heeresgruppe Mitte*, 238–241.

87. The classic analysis of the phenomenon is Rolf Hinze, *Rückkämpfer 1944: Eine Studie* (Self-published, 1988). Hinze was a staff officer, a *Rückkämpfer* himself, one of the men hardy (or lucky) enough to survive. See his own judgment: "Einer Gruppe 'Erfolgreichen'—besser gesagt 'Glückspilzen'" (53).

88. Still the most useful study on the concept of "annihilation" is Jehuda L. Wallach, *The Dogma of the Battle of Annihilation: The Theories of Clausewitz and Schlieffen and Their Impact on the German Conduct of Two World Wars* (New York: Praeger, 1986), along with the informed discussion in Robert T. Foley, *German Strategy and the Path to Verdun: Erich von Falkenhayn and the Development of Attrition, 1870–1916* (Cambridge: Cambridge University Press, 2005).

89. For the travails of the 9th Army in the Bobruisk Kessel, see Buchner, *Ostfront*, 190–225, as well as Hinze, *Der Zusammenbruch der Heeresgruppe Mitte*, 188–223.

90. For Rokossovsky, see the profile by Stuart D. Goldman, "Russia's Rock," *World War II* (September–October 2015): 40–49.

91. For this highly fraught commanders' conference, see Erickson, *Road to Berlin*, 202–203.

92. For Rokossovsky's expert preparations, see ibid., 221–222.

93. "Eine Dreiviertelstunde lang prasselten und hämmerten Granaten aller Kaliber jaulend, heulend und zischend." Buchner, *Ostfront*, 190.

94. Frieser, "Zusammenbruch der Heeresgruppe Mitte," 546–547.

95. "Kommandeur der 134. Division hat sich erschossen." Buchner, *Ostfront*, 210–211.

96. "Völlig durchgedreht!" and "Irrenhaus!" Both quoted in Frieser, "Zusammenbruch der Heeresgruppe Mitte," 547.

97. "Die 9. Armee hat als Kampfverband praktisch zu bestehen aufgehört." Quoted in Niepold, *Mittlere Ostfront Juni '44*, 138.

98. Written by Ludwig Bauer in 1859. The first verse runs:

O Deutschland hoch in Ehren,	Oh Germany high in honor
Du heil'ges Land der Treu,	Thou holy loyal land,
Stets leuchte deines Ruhmes Glanz	May the glory of thy fame
In Ost und West aufs neu!	shine always in East and West.
Du stehst wie deine Berge fest	You stand as firm as your a mountains
Gen Feindes Macht und Trug,	Against the foe's power and deception,
Und wie des Adlers Flug vom Nest	And like an eagle flying from the nest
Geht deines Geistes Flug.	may your spirit take wing.

99. Quoted in Frieser, "Zusammenbruch der Heeresgruppe Mitte," 551.

100. "Dieser Anachronismus sollte den folgenden Ereignissen das Gepräge geben." Edgar Röhricht, *Probleme der Kesselschlacht: dargestellt an Einkreisungs-Operationen im zweiten Weltkrieg* (Karlsruhe: Condor-Verlag, 1958).

101. "Die Ostfront stand noch immer, aus tausend Wunden blutend, doch sie war an vielen Stellen aufgerissen, sie drohte gänzlich einzustürzen, und niemand vermochte mehr zu sagen, was der´nächste Tag bringen würde." Walter Görlitz, *Der zweite Weltkrieg 1939–1945* (Stuttgart: Steingrüben-Verlag, 1952), volume 2, 252. Görlitz's two-volume work is often accepted as authoritative by Western readers, but he was a publicist rather than a scholar, and quotes and statistics are unsourced. The writing is superb throughout.

102. "Was den wirklichen Krieg von dem auf dem Papier unterscheidet" and "das scheinbar Leichte schwer macht." Carl von Clausewitz, *Vom Kriege: Ungekürzter Text* (München: Cormoran, 2000), Book 1, Chapter 7, 86 and 88. For operational considerations of friction, see Johann Tretter, "Friktionen: ein lehrreiches Beispiel aus dem zweiten Weltkrieg über Friktionen, oder was hier so genannt ist, die das scheinbar Leichte schwer machen," *Allgemeine schweizerische Militärzeitschrift* 131, no. 6 (1965): 336–344.

103. The narrative is based on the account by Adolf Heusinger, "20. Juli 1944: Lagevortrag im Führerhauptquartier bei Rastenburg in Ostpreussen," *Befehl im Widerstreit: Schicksalsstunden der deutschen Armee 1923–1945* (Tübingen: Rainer Wunderlich Verlag, 1950), 352–355.

104. "Mit seinen schweren Kriegsverstümmelungen eine Inkarnation des Kriegers, schreckerregend und achtunggebietend zugleich." Walter Warlimont, *Im Hauptquartier er deutschen Wehrmacht 1939 bis 1945: Grundlagen, Formen, Gestalten* (Augsburg: Weltbild Verlag, 1990), volume 2, 472.

105. "Wenn jetzt nicht endlich die Heeresgruppe vom Peipussee zurückgenommen wird, dann werden wir eine Katastrophe." Heusinger, *Befehl im Widerstreit*, 355.

106. "Wo ist der Führer?" Ibid.

107. For an introduction to the resistance, the key players, and the figure of Stauffenberg, see *Vierteljahrshefte für Zeitgeschichte* 12, no. 3 (July 1964), the journal issue marking the twentieth anniversary of the attempt on Hitler's life. Articles include Peter Hoffmann, "Zu dem Attentat im Führerhauptquartier 'Wolfsschanze' am 20. Juli 1944" (254–284), Eberhard Zeller, "Claus und Berthold Stauffenberg" (223–249), Wolfgang von Groote, "Bundeswehr und 20. Juli" (285–299), Paul Graf Yorck von Wartenburg, "Gedenkrede zur Einweihung der Stauffenbergkapelle" (250–253), and a reprint of documents on the foreign policy plans of Adam von Trott, a diplomat involved in the plot, "Trott und die Aussenpolitik des Widerstands" (300–323). See also, among many other sources, Helmut Krausnick, "Erwin Rommel und der deutsche Widerstand gegen Hitler," *Vierteljahrshefte für Zeitgeschichte* 1, no. 1 (January 1953): 65–70.

108. "Die Front kämpfte weiter, als ob nichts geschehen sei." Bodo Zimmermann, "Bericht über die Operationen des OB. West von den Vorbereitungen gegen die Invasion bis zum Rückzug auf den Westwall," Manuscript B-308 in the Foreign Military Studies series, available in the AHEC in Carlisle, PA, 105.

109. "Gott sei dank, dass es kein Landser war!" Hermann Teske, *Die silbernen Spiegel: Generalstabdiesnt under der Lupe* (Heidelberg: Kurt Vowinckel, 1952), 226

110. "Dann erschien Hitler. Nach kurzem Gruss setze er sich nachlässig auf seinen Stuhl, zog in sichtlicher Verlegenheit an seinen Fingern und war zunächst unfähig, ein Gespräch zu eröffnen.... Als er geendet hatte, wischte er sich den Schweiss von der Stirn und löffelte dann mit aufgelegten Armen hörbar eine Gemüsesuppe." Rudolf-Christoph Freiherr von Gersdorff, *Soldat im Untergang* (Frankfurt: Ullstein, 1977), 66.

111. "Der Narr macht krieg." Quoted in Zeller, "Claus und Berthold Stauffenberg," 237.

112. "Allzu oft schon war aus der Empörung, tagtäglich am Ursprungsort dem Unheil zusehen zu müssen, das die militärische 'Führung' Hitlers über Wehrmacht, Volk und Land brachte, die Versuchung in einem selber aufgestanden, wenn auch ohne je über die 'Blässe des Gedankens' hinauszugelangen." Warlimont, *Im Hauptquartier er deutschen Wehrmacht*, volume 2, 472.

113. Siegfried Westphal, "Die Auffassung der Heeresgruppe," Chapter 13 in "Der Feldzug in Italien," Manuscript T-1a in the Foreign Military Studies series, 89 and 90. The German originalis available in the AHEC in Carlisle, PA.

114. "Die Truppe kämpft allerorts heldenmütig, jedoch der ungleiche Kampf neigt dem Ende entgegen." Rommel's' letter to Hitler is reproduced in Hans Speidel, *Invasion 1944: Ein Beitrag zu Rommels and des Reiches Schicksal* (Tübingen: Rainer Wunderlich Verlag, 1949), 137–138, as well as Friedrich Ruge, *Rommel und die Invasion: Erinnerungen von Friedrich Ruge* (Stuttgart: K. F. Koehler, 1959), 280–281. See also Alfred Schickel, "Generalfeldmarschall Erwin Rommel: Eine Würdigung zu seinem Geburts- und Todestag," *Wehrkunde* 18, no. 11 (1969): 552–555, and Helmut Krausnick, "Erwin Rommel und der deutsche Widerstand gegen Hitler," *Vierteljahrshefte für Zeitgeschichte* 1, no. 1 (1955): 65–70, for examples of Rommel speaking plainly in opposition to Hitler. More recent research has exploded the notion of Rommel as a proto–resistance fighter. See Ralf Georg Reuth, *Rommel:*

Das Ende einer Legende (München: Piper, 2004), translated into English as *Rommel: The End of a Legend* (London: Haus, 2005).

115. See Nicolaus von Below, *At Hitler's Side: The Memoirs of Hitler's Luftwaffe Adjutant 1937–1945* (London: Greenhill, 2001), 212.

116. "Nachdem die Generäle bisher nichts erreicht haben, müssen sich nun die Obersten einschalten." Quoted in Bodo Scheurig, *Henning von Tresckow: eine Biographie* (Frankfurt: Ullstein, 1980), 175. On the number of generals in the resistance, see Romedio Galeazzo graf Thun-Hohenstein, "Wehrmacht und Widerstand," in Hans Poeppel, Wilhelm-Karl Prinz von Preussen, and Karl-Günther von Hase, eds., *Die Soldaten der Wehrmacht* (München: Herbig, 1998), 113. The volume assembles articles and authors of diverse backgrounds from outside the academy, almost always a good thing, and while the entries are generally conservative in tone, they rarely fall into 1950s-style apologetics. See especially Gustav-Adolf Caspar, "Ethische, politische und militärische Grundlagen der Wehrmacht"; Horst Rohde, "Politische Indoktrination in höheren Stäben und in der Truppe—untersucht am Beispiel des Kommissarbefehls"; Franz W. Seidler, "Das Justizwesen der Wehrmacht"; Andreas Broicher, "Die Wehrmacht in ausländischen Urteilen"; and Walter Post, "Die Proportion der sogennanten 'Täter' in der Millionenarmee—Versuch einer Quantifizierung am Beispiel der 6. Armee im Russlandfeldzug 1941."

117. "Wenn Sie mich fragen, meine Herren—die grösste Blamage für den preussisch-deutschen Generalstab." Quoted in Walter Görlitz, *Model: Strategie der Defensive: von Russland bis zum Ruhrkessel* (Wiesbaden: Limes Verlag, 1975), 201.

118. "Noch schlechter vorbereitet als der Kapp-Putsch." Teske, *Die Silbernen Spiegel*, 226, as well as Görlitz, *Model: Strategie der Defensive*, 201.

119. "Bald konnte ich auch feststellen, dass die Truppen der Kampffront ihn dahin auffassten, das ihr gewisse Kreise in den Rücken fallen wollten." Lothar Rendulic, *Gekämpft, Gesiegt, Geschlagen* (Wels: Verlag Welsermühl, 1952), 266.

120. F. W. von Mellenthin, *Panzer Battles: A Study of the Employment of Armor in the Second World War* (Norman: University of Oklahoma Press, 1956), 363.

121. "Von der Heimat wusste er wenig." Teske, *Die silbernen Spiegel*, 225. Teske writes of himself in the third person (as "der damalige Generalstabsoffizier.")

122. "Es wäre viel eher verstanden worden, wenn die Attentäter mir offenenem Visier, mit der Pistole in her Hand, zur Tat geschritten wäre." Zimmermann, "Bericht über die Operationen des OB. West," 109.

123. "Das ist der Anfang vom Ende, ein führchterliches Fanal!" Ibid., 106.

124. For the elusive origins, development, and modern conception of *Auftragstaktik*, the starting point is still Dirk W. Oetting, *Auftragstaktik: Geschichte und Gegenwart einer Führungskonzeption* (Frankfurt: Report Verlag, 1993). For the derivation of the term, see Antulio J. Echevarria II, *After Clausewitz: German Military Thinkers before the Great War* (Lawrence: University Press of Kansas, 2000), 32–42, and 94–103, who warns that "the term *Auftragstaktik* has been greatly abused in military publications in recent years." See also Roger A. Beaumont, "On the Wehrmacht Mystique," *Military Review* 66, no. 7 (July 1986): 44–56; Antulio J. Echevarria II, "*Auftragstaktik*: In Its Proper Perspective," *Military Review* 66, no. 10 (October 1986): 50–56; Daniel J. Hughes, "Abuses of German Military History,"

Military Review 66, no. 12 (December 1986): 66–76; and Martin van Creveld, "On Learning from the Wehrmacht and Other Things," *Military Review* 68, no. 1 (January 1988): 62–71. The Hughes article, especially, is essential, a warning against borrowing foreign terms when the US officer corps has so little knowledge of foreign languages.

125. Or sometimes "Selbsttätigkteit" (or "Selbstthätigkeit" in older texts). See, for example, Major Bigge, "Ueber Selbstthätigkeit der Unterführer im Kriege," *Beihefte zum Militär-Wochenblatt* 1894 (Berlin: E. S. Mittler, 1894), 17–55, from the text of a lecture given to the Military Society in Berlin on November 29, 1893, or General von Blume, "Selbstthätigkeit der Führer im Kriege," *Beihefte zum Militär-Wochenblatt* 1896 (Berlin: E. S. Mittler, 1896), 479–534.

126. See Robert M. Citino, *The German Way of War: From the Thirty Years' War to the Third Reich* (Lawrence: University Press of Kansas, 2005).

127. The dramatic events of November 1918 have been grist for the historian's mill for almost a century now. For decades, pride of place went to J. W. Wheeler Bennett, *The Nemesis of Power: The German Army in Politics, 1918–1945* (New York: Viking Press, 1964), especially part I, chapter 1 ("From Spa to Kapp, November 1918–March 1920"), 3–82, but he has now been superseded by Scott Stephenson, *The Final Battle: Soldiers of the Western Front and the German Revolution of 1918* (Cambridge: Cambridge University Press, 2009).

128. Quoted in Stephenson, *Final Battle*, 94–95. See also Maurice Baumont, *The Fall of the Kaiser* (London: George Allen & Unwin, 1931), 111–112.

129. "Der Faheneid ist jetzt nur eine Idee." Quoted in numerous sources, especially Wheeler-Bennett, *Nemesis of Power*, 22, n. 1. See Baumont, *Fall of the Kaiser*, 112, and Stephenson, *Final Battle*, 95.

130. For a devastating indictment about the ways in which the supposedly apolitical army suborned the Weimar Republic, see F. L. Carsten, *The Reichswehr and Politics, 1918 to 1933* (Berkeley: University of California Press, 1966). Compare Casten's approach to Harold J. Gordon Jr., *The Reichswehr and the German Republic 1919–1926* (Princeton, NJ: Princeton University Press, 1957), which defends the Reichswehr and scores Republican leaders for having little sympathy and even less knowledge of security concerns.

131. Peter Gay, *Weimar Culture: The Outsider as Insider* (New York: Harper Torchbooks, 1970), especially Chapter 2, "The Community of Reason," 23–45.

132. Quoted in Robert G. L. Waite, *Vanguard of Nazism: The Free Corps Movement in Postwar Germany 1918–1933* (New York: Norton, 1952), 155.

133. Any investigation of the Prussian army in the Napoleonic Wars must now begin with the works of Michael V. Leggiere. See especially *Napoleon and the Struggle for Germany: The Franco-Prussian War of 1813* (Cambridge: Cambridge University Press, 2015), 2 volumes, which weds monumental, even obsessive, research to sound judgment and brilliant operational insight. The new volumes build upon his earlier, still very sound work, *Napoleon and Berlin: The Franco-Prussian War in North Germany* (Norman: University of Oklahoma Press, 2002). Leggiere does warn that "the story of General Yorck's defection and the Convention of Tauroggen (Tauragė) is shrouded in conjectures and assumptions to such an ex-

tent that the truth may never be known." *Napoleon and the Struggle for Germany*, volume 1, 75.

134. Quoted in Leggiere, *Napoleon and the Struggle for Germany*, volume 1, 76, from Johann Droysen's monumental biography of Yorck, *Das Leben des Feld-marschalls Grafen Yorck von Wartenburg*, 2 volumes (Leipzig: Insel-Verlag, 1913).

135. Leggiere, *Napoleon and the Struggle for Germany*, volume 1, 77.

136. For personality sketches of the various personalities involved, see Fabian von Schlabrendorff, *Offiziere gegen Hitler* (Zurich: Europa Verlag, 1946). Published in English as *The Secret War against Hitler* (Boulder, CO: Westview Press, 1994).

137. From a radio broadcast of July 22, 1944. See, for example, Gerhard Rings-hausen, *Hans-Alexander von Voss: Generalstabsoffizier im Widerstand 1907–1944* (Berlin: Lukas Verlag, 2008), 132, n. 15, as well as Irene Zarina White, *Fire Burn: World War II Diaries* (Bloomington, IN: Xlibris, 2006), entry for July 22, 1944.

138. For the "dotations," see documents in Olaf Groehler, "Die Güter der Generale: Dotationen im zweiten Weltkrieg," *Zeitschrift für Geschichtswissenschaft* 19, no. 5 (1971): 655–663, as well as Norman J. W. Goda, "Hitler's Bribery of his Senior Officers During World War II," *Journal of Modern History* 72 (June 2000): 413–452.

139. Quoted in Agostino von Hassell and Sigrid MacRae with Simon Ames-kamp, *Alliance of Enemies: The Untold Story of the Secret American and German Collaboration to End World War II* (New York: Thomas Dunne, 2006), 233.

140. See Kenneth A. E. Sears, *Opposing Hitler: Adam von Trott zu Solz, 1909–1944* (Brighton, UK: Sussex, 2009), 80.

141. "Gersdorff, der Feldmarschall v. Kluge ist kein grosser Mann." Gersdorff, *Soldat im Untergang*, 151–152.

Chapter 5. In the West: The Campaign in France

1. The chapter "Der kriegerische Genius" is one of Clausewitz's most fully realized essays. Carl von Clausewitz, *Vom Kriege: Ungekürzter Text* (München: Cormoran, 2000), Book 1, Chapter 3, 61–81.

2. "Gemüts- oder Seelenstärke." Ibid., 70.

3. "Drittens sehr Reizbare, deren Gefühle sich schnell und heftig wie Pulver entzünden, aber nicht danernd sind." Ibid., 71.

4. "Die aufbrausenden, aufflammenden Gefühle sind an sich für das praktische Leben und also auch für den Krieg nicht sehr geeignet." Ibid.

5. For this vignette, see Albert Speer, *Spandauer Tagebücher* (Frankfurt: Ullstein, 1978), 34–35.

6. "Den nächsten Schlag können sis nicht überleben! Werden sie nicht überleben!" Ibid.

7. "Unsere Lage ist nicht mit der von 1918 zu vergleichen. Auch wenn die Gegner das Glauben." Ibid.

8. "Auch Friedrich der Grosse hat mit unbezähmbarer Energie in hoffnungs-loser Lage weitergekämpft." Ibid., 35.

9. "Der Wille, meine Herren, siegt immer!" Ibid.

10. "Wenn wir aber, meine Herren, diesen Krieg verlieren sollten, tun Sie gut daran, sich alle einen Strick zu besorgen." Ibid., 34.

11. "Ablenkungsoperation." Detlef Vogel, "Deutsche und Alliierte Kriegführung im Westen," in *Das Deutsche Reich und der Zweite Weltkrieg*, volume 7, *Das Deutsche Reich in der Defensive: Strategischer Luftkrieg in Europa, Krieg im Westen und in Ostasien 1943–1944/45* (München: Deutsche Verlags-Anstalt, 2001), 543.

12. For the ordeal of *Kampfgruppe* Heintz, see the entry in the Green Book series, Gordon Harrison, *Cross-Channel Attack* (Washington, DC: Center of Military History, 2002), 378–379.

13. All figures for 12th SS Panzer and Panzer Lehr taken from the indispensable work by Niklas Zetterling, *Normandy 1944: German Military Organization, Combat Power and Organizational Effectiveness* (Winnipeg: J. J. Fedorowicz, 2000), 350–359, and 384–392, respectively.

14. For Panzer Lehr's ride to the front, see Fritz Bayerlein, "An Interview with Genlt Fritz Bayerlein: Pz Lehr Division (Jan-28 July 1944)," Manuscript ETHINT 66 (7–9 August 1945). The original is available in the US Army Heritage and Education Center (AHEC) in Carlisle, PA, and many other repositories (including online). Part two of the Bayerlein interview also exists ("An Interview with Genlt Fritz Bayerlein: Critique of Normandy Breakthrough Pz Lehr Div from St Lo to the Ruhr," Manuscript ETHINT 67. See also the separate interview with Bayerlein, "A Crack German Panzer Division and What Allied Air Power Did to It between D-Day and V-Day," Military Intelligence Service, 9th Air Force (May 29, 1945). The original is in the Library of Congress in Washington, DC, and many other repositories. See also Paul Carell, *Sie Kommen! Der Deutsche Bericht über die Invasion und die 80tägige Schlacht um Frankreich* (Oldenburg: Gerhard Stalling Verlag, 1960), 51–52, a novelistic account with thick overtones of heroicism, but it's based on Carell's own sources (diaries and interviews) and correct in the operational essentials. Carell was actually Paul Karl Schmidt, an *Obersturmbannführer* in the *Allgemeine-SS* and a press spokesman for the German foreign ministry. The quotation from Bayerlein ("Aber die Kolonnen werden immer weiter auseinandergerissen") is included in Carell, *Sie Kommen!*, 108, the events corroborated in "An Interview with Genlt Fritz Bayerlein," part 1, and "Crack German Panzer Division."

15. "Es ist taghell—von Bränden und Explosionen." Quotation from Bayerlein in Carell, *Sie Kommen!*, 109.

16. "Das Städtchen Condé war nur noch ein rauchender Trümmerhaufen." Quotation from Hartdegen in ibid., 109.

17. "Den Gefechtsstand von Sepp Dietrich, dem Korpskommandeur, hatten wir die ganze Nacht gesucht, um uns über seine Absichten zu erkundigen und Befehle zu holen." Quotation from Hartdegen in ibid., 110.

18. The numbers are from Bayerlein, "Pz Lehr Division," 8.

19. For the reaction of 12th SS Panzer Division *Hitlerjugend* to the invasion, see Michael Reynolds, *Steel Inferno: I SS Panzer Corps in Normandy* (Staplehurst, UK: Spellmount, 1997), 52–91. Reynolds is an expert on the operations of the Waffen-SS

and author of a second volume on the I SS Panzer Corps, *Men of Steel: I SS Panzer Corps; The Ardennes and Eastern Front, 1944–45* (Staplehurst, UK: Spellmount, 1999), as well as *Sons of the Reich: II SS Panzer Corps; Normandy, Arnhem, Ardennes, Eastern Front* (Staplehurst, UK: Spellmount, 2002), and a biographer of one of the most infamous SS commanders, *The Devil's Adjutant: Jochen Peiper, Panzer Leader* (New York: Sarpedon, 1995). See also the memoir of one of the division's most aggressive regimental commanders: Kurt Meyer, *Grenadiere* (München: Schild-Verlag, 1957), 208–230; the English translation is *Grenadiers: The Story of Waffen SS General Kurt "Panzer" Meyer* (Mechanicsburg, PA: Stackpole, 2005). Kurt Meyer is not to be confused with Hubert Meyer, the division's operations officer (Ia) and historian, author of *Kriegsgeschichte der 12. SS-Panzerdivision "Hitlerjugend,"* 2 vols. (Osnabrück: Munin-Verlag, 1982), translated into English as *The History of the 12th SS Panzer Division "Hitlerjugend"* (Winnipeg: J. Fedorowicz, 1994). For a propagandistic account of the *Hitlerjugend* Division, its character, and its mission, see Bruno Wundshammer, "Sie nennen sie 'Crack Babies,'" in *Signale* (Berlin: Oberkommando der Wehrmacht, n.d. [1944?], 270–272. *Signale* was a bound volume of selected articles published previously in the glossy magazine *Signal*. And for the militarized Prussian culture of the *Hitlerjugend* organization in general, see Fritz Gerlach, "Schöpfer und Lenker deutscher Wehrkraft: Acht grosse Soldaten in vier Jahrhunderten deutcher Geschichte," in Wilhelm Utermann, ed., *Junger—eure Welt! Das Jahrbuch der Hitler-Jugend* (München: Zentralverlag der NSDAP, 1941), 155–169, featuring character profiles of Georg von Frundsberg, Prince Eugene, the Old Dessauer, Friedrich Wilhelm I, Frederick the Great, Scharnhorst, Gneisenau, and Clausewitz.

20. For years, scholars accepted Meyer, *Grenadiere*, 216–230, as the primary source on the engagement between the North Novas and the *Hitlerjugend*. But see Marc Milner, *Stopping the Panzers: The Untold Story of D-Day* (Lawrence: University Press of Kansas, 2014), which combines fine-grain research and sharp writing to debunk much of Meyer's account and (per the book's stated purpose) to rehabilitate the fighting reputation of the Canadian army. For a précis, see Milner's original article, "Stopping the Panzers: Reassessing the Role of 3rd Canadian Infantry Division in Normandy, 7–10 June 1944," *Journal of Military History* 74, no. 2 (April 2010): 291–522.

21. Quoted in Milton Shulman, *Defeat in the West* (Waldenbury, East Sussex, UK: Masquerade, 1986), 14, Reynolds, *Steel Inferno*, 60, and Milner, *Stopping the Panzers*, 132.

22. "Doch was ist das? Sehe ich recht?" Meyer, *Grenadiere*, 216.

23. "Die Einheit bietet ungeschützt ihre Flanke dar . . . Nicht schiessen! Feueröffnung nur auf meinen Befehl!" Ibid., 217.

24. "Ein ungeheurer Druck lastet auf uns. Jetzt muss es gleich geschehen." Ibid., 218.

25. A crime for which Meyer would be tried and convicted, although he always maintained his innocence. See Peter Kikkert, "Kurt Meyer and Canadian Memory: Villain and Monster, Hero and Victim or Worse—a German?" *Canadian Military History* 21, no. 2 (Spring 2012): 33–44.

26. "Angriffsziel: Küste." Meyer, *Grenadiere*, 217.

27. Milner, *Stopping the Panzers*, p 138.

28. Quoted in ibid., 285.

29. Ibid.

30. The primary source account of this highly successful decapitation assault is Leo Geyr von Schweppenburg, "Panzer-Gruppe West," Manuscript B-466 in the Foreign Military Studies series (available at the AHEC in Carlisle, PA). See also Harrison, *Cross-Channel Attack*, 373–374, and Carell, *Sie Kommen!*, 151.

31. For Witt's death, see Meyer, *Grenadiere*, 236: "Ein letzter Blick in sein Gesicht ist mir verwehrt—es existiert nicht mehr."

32. For the toll the fighting took on the German officer corps, see Josef Folttmann and Hanns Möller-Witten, *Opfergang der Generale: Die Verluste der Generale and Admirale und der im gleichem Dientsrang stehenden sonstigen Offiziere und Beamten im Zweiten Weltkrieg* (Berlin: Bernard & Graefe, 1959). Folttmann and Möller-Witten give a total of 963 dead generals: 676 from the army, 113 from the Luftwaffe, 73 from the Kriegsmarine, 63 from the Waffen-SS, and 39 from the police (26). See also the paper by US Army Major French L. MacLean, "German General Officer Casualties in World War II—Harbinger for U.S Army General Officer Casualties in Airland Battle?" (Fort Leavenworth, KS: School of Advanced Military Studies, 1988).

33. "Arme Leute sollen eben keinen krieg führen." Quoted in Friedrich Ruge, *Rommel und die Invasion: Erinnerungen von Friedrich Ruge* (Stuttgart: K. F. Koehler Verlag, 1959), 189.

34. For the battle of Cherbourg, see the chapter in Ruge, *Rommel und die Invasion* titled "Der Verlust von Cherbourg" (176–192), the chapter in Harrison, *Cross-Channel Attack* entitled "The Capture of Cherbourg (8 June–1 July)," 386–449, with its excellent maps; and the chapter in Carell, *Sie Kommen!* ("Der Kampf um Cherbourg"), 169–206. Finally, see the very readable popular history by William B. Breuer, *Hitler's Fortress Cherbourg: The Conquest of a Bastion* (New York: Stein and Day, 1984). No current scholarly monograph or article analyzes the battle from the German side.

35. "Beharrten das OKW und auch Hitler darauf, keinen Meter Boden kampflos preiszugeben." Vogel, "Deutsche und Alliierte Kriegführung im Westen," 546.

36. Harrison, *Cross-Channel Attack*, 428.

37. Ibid.

38. They were, in Schlieben's formulation, "Verbunkert." Ibid., 430. Ruge, in *Rommel und die Invasion*, calls the defenders "zusammengewürfelt, überaltert, und schlecht ausgerüstet" (187).

39. Quoted in Harrison, *Cross-Channel Attack*, 430.

40. Quoted in ibid., 432.

41. Quoted in Breuer, *Hitler's Fortress Cherbourg*, 219.

42. Quoted in Harrison, *Cross-Channel Attack*, 430.

43. Quoted in Breuer, *Hitler's Fortress Cherbourg*, 252.

44. William M. Hammond, *Normandy* (Washington, DC: Center of Military History, n.d.), pamphlet in *The Campaigns of World War II* series, 34.

45. A problem emphasized strongly in Carlo D'Este, *Decision in Normandy* (New York: Harper Perennial, 1994), 271–273.

46. Analysis taken from *St-Lo (7 July–19 July 1944)* (Washington, DC: Center of Military History, 1994), a reprint of the original entry in the venerable *American Forces in Action* series issued by the Historical Division of the War Department, 126.

47. Quoted in Martin Blumenson, *Breakout and Pursuit* (Washington DC: Center of Military History, 2005), 177, part of the Green Books series.

48. For Wittmann and Villers-Bocage, see Este, *Decision in Normandy*, 178–183, as well as the fine work by David Porter, *7th Armoured Division at Villers-Bocage, 13 June 1944* (London: Amber Books, 2012). Wittmann has become a legend, with all the pitfalls to understanding the actual historical figure. The notion of the "tank ace," for example, seems to be a postwar construction in military literature of the West German political right. Buff literature like Will Fey, *Armor Battles of the Waffen-SS 1943–45* (Mechanicsburg, PA: Stackpole, 2003), and Patrick Agte, *Michael Wittmann and the Waffen SS Tiger Commanders of the Leibstandarte in World War II*, 2 vols. (Mechanicsburg, PA: Stackpole, 2006), are hagiographical in tone and often maddeningly imprecise in detail and must be used with caution.

49. Porter, *7th Armoured Division at Villers-Bocage*, 136.

50. The primary source on the Margival conference remains Hans Speidel, *Invasion 1944: Ein Beitrag zu Rommels und des Reiches Schicksal* (Tübingen: Rainer Wunderlich Verlag, 1949), 112–124. See also the briefer account in Speidel's memoirs, *Aus unserer Zeit: Erinnerungen* (Berlin: Propyläen Verlag, 1977), 178–183, but note the accusations of misremebering or outright falsehood in "So war das Schicksal dazwischengetreten: die Legenden und Verdrängungen des Generals Hans Speidel," *Der Spiegel*, no. 5 (1978): 70–81. See also Peter Margaritis, *Crossroads at Margival: Hitler's Last Conference in France, June 17, 1944* (Self-published, n.d.).

51. "Mit erhobener und bitterer Stimme." Speidel, *Invasion 1944*, 114.

52. "Er sah fahl und übernächtig aus." Ibid., 113.

53. "Seine frühere Suggestivkraft schien geschwunden." Ibid., 114.

54. "Bis zum letzten Atemzug gekämpft." Ibid.

55. "Uneingeschränkte Operationsfreiheit." Ibid., 116.

56. "Sie verlangen, wir sollen Vertrauen haben, und man traut uns selber nicht!" Ibid., 117.

57. "Kümmern Sie sich nicht um den Weitergang des Krieges, sondern um Ihre Invasionsfront." Ibid., 118.

58. Reynolds, *Sons of the Reich*, 16–18.

59. Vogel, "Deutsche und Alliierte Kriegführung im Westen," 548, text and note 42.

60. For Dollmann's departure, Hausser's arrival, and the rest of the German command shuffle in the west, see Samuel W. Mitcham Jr., *Defenders of Fortress Europe: The Untold Story of the German Officers During the Allied Invasion* (Washington, DC: Potomac Books, 2009), 81–84, as well as Vogel, "Deutsche und Alliierte Kriegführung im Westen," 546. See also Hausser's memoirs, *Soldaten wie andere auch: Der Weg der Waffen-SS* (Osnabrück: Munin Verlag, 1966). For a personality

profile of the SS-commander, see Enrico Syring, "Paul Hausser: 'Türöffner' und Kommandeur 'seiner' Waffen-SS," in Ronald Smelser and Enrico Syring, eds., *Die SS: Elite under dem Totenkopf: 30 Lebensläufe* (Paderborn: Ferdinand Schöningh, 2000), 191–207.

61. "Solange der FM. schimpft, ist alles in Ordnung." Horst Freiherr Treusch von Buttlar Brandenfels, "Stellungnahme zu dem Bericht des Generalleutnant z.V. Bodo Zimmermann über die Operationen des O.B. West von den Vorbereitungen gegen die Invasion bis zum Rückzug auf den Westwall," Manuscript B-672 in the Foreign Military Studies series, available in the AHEC in Carlisle, PA, 7.

62. For a comparison between Kluge, Rundstedt, and Rommel, see Günther Blumentritt, "Three Marshals, National Character, and the 20 July Complex," Manuscript B-344 in the Foreign Military Studies series. The German manuscript is apparently untitled, but the English translation bears the title listed above.

63. "Es wird gehalten, und wenn kein Aushilfsmittel unsere Lage grundsätzlich verbessert, muss anständig gestorben werden." Quoted in Vogel, "Deutsche und Alliierte Kriegführung im Westen," 552. Hitler later responded typically: "Sagen Sie dem Feldmarschall von Kluge, er habe seine Augen ausschliesslich nach vorn und auf den Feind zu richten und nicht nach rückwärts zu blicken." Walter Warlimont, *Im Hauptquartier er deutschen Wehrmacht 1939 bis 1945: Grundlagen, Formen, Gestalten* (Augsburg: Weltbild Verlag, 1990), volume 2, 477.

64. For the Allied backlog (*Rückstand*), see Vogel, "Deutsche und Alliierte Kriegführung im Westen," 547.

65. The primary source for Operation Cobra planning is Omar N. Bradley, *A Soldier's Story* (New York: Holt, 1951), 326–346. Turn then to the two pertinent chapters in Blumenson, *Breakout and Pursuit*, still models of informed and incisive operational military history: "Cobra Preparations" (197–223) and "Cobra" (224–246). See also James Jay Carafano, *After D-Day: Operation Cobra and the Normandy Breakout* (Boulder, CO: Lynne Rienner, 2000), which looks at the campaign through the lens of the "combat command, regimental and battalion commanders, the 'field-grade' leaders" (4) and argues that "the ability to understand and exploit the full capabilities of the U.S. Army" was the key to the eventual breakout, rather than a magic technological bullet like the Culin hedgerow cutter or the brute firepower of carpet-bombing (260); Russell A. Hart's exhaustive and meticulously researched *Clash of Arms: How the Allies Won in Normandy* (Boulder, CO: Lynne Rienner, 2001), especially 247–264; Roman Johann Jarymowycz, *Tank Tactics: From Normandy to Lorraine* (Boulder, CO: Lynne Rienner, 2001), 107–202; and two books by United States Military Academy historian Steve R. Waddell: *United States Army Logistics: The Normandy Campaign* (Westport, CT: Greenwood Press, 1994), and *United States Army Logistics: From the American Revolution to 9/11* (Westport, CT: Greenwood Press, 2009).

66. Figures taken from Bradley, *A Soldier's Story*, 341. For a useful study of carpet-bombing effectiveness in Operations Charnwood, Goodwood, Cobra, Totalize, and Tractable, see E. Wehrli, "Taktische Bombenteppiche," *Allgemeine schweizerische Militärzeitscrift* 130, no. 7 (1964): 445–455.

67. Bradley, *A Soldier's Story*, 341.

68. *"The bombers, I reasoned, could fly parallel to it without danger of mistaking our front line."* Ibid., 330. Bradley thought the sentence important enough to place it in italics.

69. "Die eigene Kampfkraft an Menschen und Material (Waffen, Funkgerät) ist durch die ungeheure Überlegenheit des Gegners stark geschwächt." Paul Hausser, "Normandie. 7. Armee vom 29./6.—24./7.1945," Manuscript A-974 in the Foreign Military Studies series, 33–34.

70. "Junge Truppen ohne Kampferfahrung sind den Einwirkungen des Materialkrieges nicht gewachsen." Ibid., 34.

71. Bradley, *A Soldier's Story*, 341.

72. Bayerlein's testimony in "A Crack German Panzer Division and What Allied Air Power Did to It between D-Day and V-Day," 7.

73. Ibid.

74. The quotation is omnipresent in the literature. See, for example, John Prados, *Normandy Crucible: The Decisive Battle the Shaped World War II in Europe* (New York: NAL Caliber, 2012), 133; Harry Yeide, *Fighting Patton: George S. Patton Jr. through the Eyes of His Enemies* (New York: Zenith, 2011), 235; Samuel W. Mitcham Jr., *The Desert Fox in Normandy: Rommel's Defense of Fortress Europe* (Westport, CT: Praeger, 1997), 188; Samuel W. Mitcham Jr., *Retreat to the Reich: The German Defeat in France, 1944* (Mechanicsburg, PA: Stackpole, 2007), 91; and Mark Perry, *Partners in Command: George Marshall and Dwight Eisenhower in War and Peace* (New York: Penguin, 2007), 317. It is worth noting, therefore, that the original source of the quote seems to be the oft-maligned Carell, *Invasion—Sie Kommen!*, 238. In this case, we do have corroborating sources regarding Bayerlein's sour, defeated mood at the time of Cobra.

75. Bayerlein, "A Crack German Panzer Division and What Allied Air Power Did to It between D-Day and V-Day," 50–51.

76. Prados, *Normandy Crucible*, 133.

77. Quoted in Bodo Zimmermann, "Bericht über die Operationen des OB. West von den Vorbereitungen gegen die Invasion bis zum Rückzug auf den Westwall," Manuscript B-308 in the Foreign Military Studies series, 115–116. For the Avranches counteroffensive in general, see the monograph by Mark J. Reardon, *Victory at Mortain: Stopping Hitler's Panzer Counteroffensive* (Lawrence: University Press of Kansas, 2002), plus the numerous entries in the Foreign Military Studies series: Rudolf-Christoph Freiherr von Gersdorff, "Der Feldzug in Nordfrankreich," B and II, 2. Kapitel, "Der Amerikanische Durchbruch auf Avranches" (Manuscript B-723); Rudolf-Christoph Freiherr von Gersdorff, "Der Feldzug in Nordfrankreich," Band IV, 4. Kapitel, "Der deutsche Gegenangriff auf Avranches" (B-725); Rudolf-Christoph Freiherr von Gersdorff, "Kommentar zum Kriegstagebuch der 7. Armee" (Manuscript A-918); Rudolf-Christoph Freiherr von Gersdorff, "Der Kessel von Falaise" (A-919); Rudolf-Christoph Freiherr von Gersdorff, "Vom Gegenangriff auf Avranches zum Kessel von Falaise" (A-920); Rudolf-Christoph Freiherr von Gersdorff, "Der Gegenangriff auf Avranches" (A-921); and Heinrich Eberbach, "Panzergruppe Eberbach bei Alencon und beim Durchbruch aus dem Kessel von Falaise" (A-922), besides many others. Gersdorff was chief of staff of

the 7th Army in Normandy, was deeply involved in the anti-Hitler resistance, and, indeed, had tried to kill Hitler on an earlier occasion.

78. Quoted in Blumenson, *Breakout and Pursuit*, 464. See also Rudolf-Christoph Freiherr von Gersdorff, "Kommentar zum Kriegstagebuch der 7. Armee," Manuscript A-918 in the Foreign Military Studies series.

79. For the Schwerin-Funck imbroglio, see Blumenson, *Breakout and Pursuit*, 462–464. For Schwerin, see Marcel Stein, *A Flawed Genius: Field Marshal Walter Model; A Critical Biography* (Solihull, UK: Helion, 2010), 250–253.

80. See Reardon, *Victory at Mortain*, 160–161, and Prados, *Normandy Crucible*, 183.

81. Stein, *A Flawed Genius*, 250, describes Schwerin as "one of the few German commanders endowed with genuine guts."

82. Blumenson, *Breakout and Pursuit*, 537. For Falaise in general, William B. Breuer, *Death of a Nazi Army: The Falaise Pocket* (New York: Scarborough House, 1985), remains an adequate narrative account. For the force that finally closed the Falaise Pocket, see the memoir by General Stanislaw Maczek, *Avec mes Blindés: Pologne, France, Belgique, Hollande, Allemagne* (Paris: Press de la Cité, 1967).

83. For Kluge's end, see Mitcham, *Defenders of Fortress Europe*, 145–147.

84. "Feldmarschall von Kluge hat zu melden, nach welcher Gegend Deutschlands er zu gehen gedenkt." Quoted in Gert Buchheit, *Hitler der Feldherr: die Zerstorung einer Legende* (Rastatt: Grote, 1958), 439.

85. "Ich scheide von Ihnen, mein Führer, als einer, der Ihnen in dem Bewusstsein, seine Pflicht bis zum äussersten getan zu haben, näher stand, als Sie das vielleicht erkannt haben." For Kluge's letter to Hitler in its entirety, see Percy Ernst Schramm, ed., *Kriegstagebuch des Oberkommandos der Wehrmacht (Wehrmachtführungsstab)*, volume 4, *1. Januar 1944–22. Mai 1945, Zweiter Halbband* (Frankfurt: Bernard & Graege Verlag, 1961), 1573–1576.

86. A point made forcefully in Helmut Lindemann, "Die Schuld der Generale," *Deutsche Rundschau* (January 1949): 20–26: "Der Vorwurf, die Abschlachtung von vielen Hundertausenden deutscher Soldaten nicht verhindert zu haben, muss schwer auf dem Gewissen jedes einzelnen deutschen Generals lasten" (24). The article is a review of B. H. Liddell Hart, *The Other Side of the Hill: Germany's Generals, Their Rise and Fall, with Their Account of Military Events, 1939–1945* (London: Cassell, 1948). The American edition of Liddell Hart's book is *The German Generals Talk* (New York: Quill, 1979).

Chapter 6. On the Run: The East

1. See the transcript of the *Lagebesprechung* with General Jodl, dated July 31, 1944, in Helmut Heiber, ed., *Lagebesprechungen im Führerhauptquartier: Protokollfragmente aus Hitlers militärischen Konferenzen 1942–1945* (München: DTV, 1962), 242–271. For the English translation, see Robert L. Miller, ed., *Hitler at War: Meetings and Conversations, 1939–1945* (New York: Enigma, 2015), 247–267.

2. "Das Problem der Stabilisierung der Ostfront—zu mehr kann man im Moment ja nicht kommen." Heiber, *Lagebesprechungen*, 243.

3. "Dann wird das eine Kraft werden." Ibid. Translated in Miller, *Hitler at War*, 243, as: "Then it will be a real force."

4. "Aber nur durch eine Voraussetzung: dass wir das, was wir in diesem Riesenraum angebaut haben oder verbraucht haben an Menschen, wirklich dem Kampf zuführen." Heiber, *Lagebesprechungen*, 243.

5. "Die Verbände sind weder in ihrer Bewaffnung noch ihrer sonstigen Ausrüstung nach überhaupt zu einer beweglichen Kriegführung geeignet." Ibid., 244. Miller, *Hitler at War*, 249, translates the sentence as: "The units are not suited to mobile battle."

6. "Ich habe hier eine gewisse Anzahl von Kräften. Diese Kräfte genügen kaum, um diese schmale Front hier zu verteidigen." Heiber, *Lagebesprechungen*, 245.

7. "Wir führen einen Revolutionskrieg!" Ibid., 265.

8. "Das ist auf einmal durch diesen Schlag fast völlig verschwunden; wobei ich nicht sagen möchte, dass ich das für die richtige Kur halte." Ibid., 271.

9. For the near encirclement of 9th Army, as well as Model's Büffel-Bewegung, see Earl F. Ziemke, *Stalingrad to Berlin: The German Defeat in the East* (Washington, DC: Center of Military History, 1987).

10. For Model's role in blunting Operation Kutuzov and the evacuation of the Orel Salient, see Walter Bussmann, "Kursk—Orel—Dnjepr: Erlebnisse und Erfahrungen im Stab des XXXXVI Panzerkorps während des 'Unternehmens Zitadelle.'" *Vierteljahrshefte für Zeitgeschichte* 41, no. 4 (October 1993): 503–518; Peter von der Groeben, "Die Schlacht der 2. Panzer-Armee und 9. Armee im Orel-Bogen vom 5. Juli bis 18. August 1943," Manuscript T-26 in the Foreign Military Studies series; and Lothar Rendulic, "Die Schlacht von Orel, Juli 1943: Wahl und Bildung des Schwerpunktes." *Österreichische Militärische Zeitschrift* 1, no. 3 (1963): 130–138, although recent research indicates that Rendulic polishes his operational record beyond recognition in the course of the article. For a précis, see Robert M. Citino, *The Wehrmacht Retreats: Fighting a Lost War, 1943* (Lawrence: University Press of Kansas, 2012), 217–221.

11. "Haben Sie das Auge gesehen? Dem Mann traue ich es zu, dass er es schafft. Aber ich selber möchte nicht unter ihm dienen." Quoted in Walter Görlitz, *Model: Strategie der Defensive: Von Russland bis zum Ruhrkessel* (Wiesbaden: Limes, 1975), 124.

12. "Mein Führer, führen Sie die 9. Armee oder ich?" Quoted in ibid., 125–126. Görlitz gives no citation, but the account has worked its way into virtually all of the secondary literature. See, for example, Steven H. Newton, *Hitler's Commander: Field Marshal Walther Model—Hitler's Favorite General* (New York: Da Capo, 2006), 181–182. Marcel Stein, *A Flawed Genius: Field Marshal Walter Model; A Critical Biography* (Solihull, UK: Helion, 2010), 90, tracks down the provenance to Model's orderly, Lieutenant Fabian von Bonin und Ostau.

13. "Noch nie hatte Hitler so viel militärische Verantwortung in die Hand eines einzelnen Generals gegeben." Karl-Heinz Frieser, "Der Zusammenbruch der Heeresgruppe Mitte im Sommer 1944," in *Das Deutsche Reich und der Zweite Weltkrieg*, volume 8, *Die Ostfront 1943/44: Der Krieg im Osten und an den Nebenfronten* (München: Deutsche Verlags-Anstalt, 2011), 558.

14. A fact that still goes generally unrecognized: Model helped cause the disaster he was later called upon to rescue. See Adolf Heusinger, *Befehl im Widerstreit: Schicksalsstunden der deutschen Armee 1923–1945* (Tübingen: Rainer Wunderlich, 1950). When Model was commanding Army Group North Ukraine, Heusinger tells Hitler, "konnte er dorthin nicht genug Kräfte holen und zeterte Stein and Bein"—that is, he fought tooth and nail for every division he could get (330–331).

15. Stein, *A Flawed Genius*, 141.

16. Peter von der Groeben, "Der Zusammenbruch der Heeresgruppe Mitte und ihr Kampf bis zur Festigung der Front (22.VI. bis 1.IX.1944)," Manuscript T-31 in the Foreign Military Studies series. See page 37, which speaks of a change in the enemy's operational approach: "drängte er von jetzt ab auf breiter Front planmässig von Abschnitt zu Abschnitt nach."

17. For the Soviet thrusts toward Molodeczno and Baranowitschi, see Hermann Gackenholz, "Zum Zusammenbruch der Heeresgruppe Mitte im Sommer 1944," *Vierteljahrshefte für Zeitgeschichte* 3, no. 3 (Juli 1955): 339–332, especially the map on page 331, as well as Gackenholz's chapter, "Der Zusammenbruch der Heeresgruppe Mitte 1944," in Hans-Adolf Jacobsen and Jürgen Rohwer, eds., *Entscheidungsschlachten des zweiten Weltkrieges* (Frankfurt: Verlag für Wehrwesen Bernard & Graefe, 1960), 466–471.

18. "Nur noch mit Regimentern und Bataillonen gegen Armeen kämpfen." Quoted in Frieser, "Der Zusammenbruch der Heeresgruppe Mitte im Sommer 1944," 559.

19. For the Vilna controversy, see Heusinger, *Befehl im Widerstreit*, 330–341 and 348–351.

20. A case of a *Himmelfahrtskommando*—allowing for a certain theological confusion; we might call it a "Hail Mary" in English. See Frieser, "Der Zusammenbruch der Heeresgruppe Mitte im Sommer 1944," 563.

21. "Das verlangt man auch von jedem Kriegsschiffkommandanten. Eine Feigheit, das! Lächerlich! Der Herr hat seine Pflicht zu tun. Funken Sie ihm das!" Heusinger, *Befehl im Widerstreit*, 348.

22. "Machen Sie, was Sie wollen! Das Leben retten Sie niemand. . . ." Ibid., 349.

23. The smashing of Army Group North Ukraine—a devastating and decisive battlefield defeat for the Wehrmacht but an episode that is every much a subsidiary chapter to Operation Bagration—has barely registered on the historical consciousness. Even the usually reliable German official history, *Das Deutsche Reich und der Zweite Weltkrieg*, volume 8, *Die Ostfront 1943/44: Der Krieg im Osten und an den Nebenfronten*, fumbles the ball here, discussing the offensive in two separate sections, apparently without realizing it. See Frieser, "Der Zusammenbruch der Heeresgruppe Mitte im Sommer 1944," 566–569, and Klaus Schönherr, "Die Kämpfe um Galizien und die Beskiden," 679–730, both in the official history. Otherwise, see Rolf Hinze, *To the Bitter End: The Final Battles of Army Groups North Ukraine, A, and Center—Eastern Front, 1944–45* (Philadelphia: Casemate, 2010), although its treatment of the Soviet offensive in July 1944 is cursory (15–23). See also the Soviet army study, "1st Ukrainian Front's Lvov-Peremyshl' Operation (July–August 1944)," *Journal of Slavic Military Studies* 9, no. 1 (March 1996): 198–252, and 9, no.

3 (September 1996): 617–664. Otherwise, individual chapters and portions of the secondary literature have to suffice. See, for example, John Erickson, *The Road to Berlin: Stalin's War with Germany* (New Haven, CT: Yale University Press, 1983), 230–247, and David M. Glantz and Jonathan House, *When Titans Clashed: How the Red Army Stopped Hitler* (Lawrence: University Press of Kansas, 1995), 210–214.

24. Schönherr, "Die Kämpfe um Galizien und die Beskiden," 685.

25. Ibid., 683.

26. "Vorprogrammierte Einschliessung." Frieser, "Der Zusammenbruch der Heeresgruppe Mitte im Sommer 1944," 567.

27. Ziemke, *Stalingrad to Berlin*, 332.

28. Quoted in Erickson, *Road to Berlin*, 207; Glantz and House, *When Titans Clashed*, 201.

29. For the attack on the Rava Russkaya axis, see Erickson, *Road to Berlin*, 232–234.

30. Schönherr, "Die Kämpfe um Galizien und die Beskiden," 688; Glantz and House, *When Titans Clashed*, 211.

31. For the attack on the Lvov axis, see Erickson, *Road to Berlin*, 234–235.

32. For the encirclement of XIII Corps at Brody, see Alex Buchner, *Ostfront 1944: Tscherkassy, Tarnopol, Krim, Witebsk, Bobruisk, Brody, Jassy, Kischinew* (Eggolsheim: Podzun-Pallas Verlag, 1988), 2344–264. The English translation of the book is similarly titled *Ostfront 1944: The German Defensive Battles on the Russian Front 1944* (Atglen, PA: Schiffer, 1995). References are to the original German-language version.

33. For one of the units inside the Brody Pocket, see Wolfgang Lange, *Korpsabteilung C vom Dnjeper bis nach Polen (November 1943 bis Juli 1944): Kampf einer Infanterie-Division auf breiter Front gegen grosse Übermacht—Kampf im Kessel und Ausbruch* (Neckargemünd: Kurt Vowinckel Verlag, 1961), 97–125.

34. "Vielleicht nochmals die Nacht abwarten. Die Lage ist hoffnungslos!" Quoted in Buchner, *Ostfront*, 259.

35. Ibid., 259–260.

36. "So ein Ende ist bitter wie der Tod und schrecklich wie das Weltende." Quoted in Lange, *Korpsabteilung C*, 116.

37. For Konev's offensive and the German countermeasures, see the account from the commander of 1st Panzer Army: Erhard Raus, "Die Schlacht bei Lemberg," *Allgemeine schweizerische Militärzeitschrift* 121, no. 11 (1955): 833–844; F. W. von Mellenthin, *Panzer Battles: A Study of the Employment of Armor in the Second World War* (Norman: University of Oklahoma Press, 1956), 282–287. See also Steven H. Newton, ed., *Panzer Operations: The Eastern Front Memoir of General Raus, 1941–1945* (New York: Da Capo, 2003), 283–291.

38. "So betrug die Angriffsbreite einer Schützendivision etwa einen Kilometer." Frieser, "Der Zusammenbruch der Heeresgruppe Mitte im Sommer 1944," 567.

39. "Geradezu überrollt." Ibid.

40. Erickson, *Road to Berlin*, 237–238.

41. See Frieser, "Der Zusammenbruch der Heeresgruppe Mitte im Sommer

1944," 571–572, as well as the map, "Die Offensive des linken Flügels der 1. Weiss-russischen Front von Kovel' bis Warschau (18. bis 31 Juli 1944)," 645.

42. "Bis zur Vernichtung der Besatzung." Ibid., 569.

43. "Die Ereignisse des 20. Juli dürften dabei indirekt eine gewisse Rolle gespielt haben." Ibid., 568.

44. "Aus der Bewegung." Ibid., 571.

45. The standard works on the Warsaw Uprising, both exhaustively researched and unlikely to be superseded anytime soon, are Alexandra Richie, *Warsaw 1944: Hitler, Himmler, and the Warsaw Uprising* (New York: Farrar, Straus and Giroux, 2013), and Norman Davies: *Rising '44: The Battle for Warsaw* (New York: Viking, 2003).

46. "Wie aus dem Nichts" and "Er nahm sie sich einfach." Frieser, "Der Zusammenbruch der Heeresgruppe Mitte im Sommer 1944," 581.

47. "Nun griffen vier deutsche Panzerdivisionen konzentrisch aus vier Richtungen an." Ibid., 582.

48. "Bin für rücksichtsloses Abbrennen, 1000 Meter rechts und links der Strasse. Sonst kommen wir nicht durch." Quoted in Görlitz, *Model: Strategie der Defensive*, 204.

49. Quoted in Frieser, "Der Zusammenbruch der Heeresgruppe Mitte im Sommer 1944," 585.

50. The aphorism "der Hieb die beste Parade sei" appears in German planning documents from the time: "The thrust attack is the best parry." We might render it in English as "the best defense is a good offense." See ibid., 568, as well as Ferdinand Heim, "Stalingrad und der Verlauf des Feldzuges der Jahre 1943–1945," in Alfred Philippi and Ferdinand Heim, *Der Feldzug gegen Sowjetrussland 1941 bis 1945* (Stuttgart: W. Kohlhammer, 1962), 253, which renders the original German as "der Angriff ist die beste Parade."

51. For Strachwitz, see Günter Fraschka, *Der Panzer-Graf: General Graf Strachwitz—ein Leben für Deutschland* (Rastatt: Erich Pabel Verlag, 1962), as well as Raymond Bagdonas, *The Devil's General: The Life of Hyazinth von Strachwitz, "The Panzer Graf"* (Havertown, PA: Casemate, 2013).

52. "Der letzte Kavallerist in dieser Welt . . . Gänzlich unorthodox in seiner Angriffsweise, immer mit neuen Ideen—eine verrückter als die andere." Quoted in Fraschka, *Der Panzer-Graf*, 210.

53. "Merken Sie sich, Carius, wenn dieser Graben als Panzerhindernis für mich nicht existiert, dann existiert er auch für Sie nicht." Quoted in ibid., 202.

54. Frieser, "Der Zusammenbruch der Heeresgruppe Mitte im Sommer 1944," 591. For details of the attack, see also Bagdonas, *The Devil's General*, 293–300.

55. "Obwohl er nur über 60 Kampfwagen verfügte, griff er in einer wilden Attacke an." Frieser, "Der Zusammenbruch der Heeresgruppe Mitte im Sommer 1944," 590.

56. "Sie sprechen heir nicht mit einem Leutnant, sondern mit einem leibhaftigen General!" Quoted in Fraschka, 223.

57. For Operation Axis, see Citino, *The Wehrmacht Retreats*, 244–249.

58. Gerhard von Pelet-Narbonne, *Der Grosse Kurfürst* (Berlin: B. Behr, 1905), 86.

59. For German attitudes toward coalition warfare, see the series of articles by General Georg Wetzell, "Bismarck-Moltke und der Bündniskrieg." *Militär-Wochenblatt* 122, no. 45 (May 6, 1938); "Der Bündniskrieg: Eine militärpolitisch operative Studie des Weltkrieges," 5 parts, *Militär-Wochenblatt* 122, nos. 14–18 (October 1, 1937, October 8, 1937, October 15, 1937, October 22, 1937, and October 29, 1937); and "'Der Bündniskrieg' und die Kritik," 2 parts, *Militär-Wochenblatt* 122, nos. 28–29 (January 7, 1938 and January 14, 1938). Wetzell was at the time the editor of the semiofficial journal.

60. The current standard on the Habsburg army in World War I is Geoffrey Wawro, *A Mad Catastrophe: The Outbreak of World War I and the Collapse of the Habsburg Empire* (New York: Basic Books, 2015). As in all his books, Wawro weaves exhaustive research, take-no-prisoners argumentation, and extremely sharp writing into a formidable package. Holger H. Herwig, *The First World War: Germany and Austria-Hungary, 1914–1918* (London: Arnold, 1997), is still extremely useful for strategic and operational planning.

61. For the planning, course, and significance of the Brusilov offensive, see Timothy C. Dowling, *The Brusilov Offensive* (Bloomington: Indiana University Press, 2008).

62. Erich von Manstein, *Verlorene Siege* (Bonn: Athenäum-Verlag, 1955). Translated into English as *Lost Victories* (Novato, CA: Presidio, 1982).

63. Albert Kesselring, *Soldat bis zum letzten Tag* (Bonn: Athenäum-Verlag, 1953). Translated into English as *The Memoirs of Field-Marshal Kesselring* (Novato, CA: Presidio, 1989).

64. Hans Friessner, *Verratene Schlachten: Die Tragödie der deutschen Wehrmacht in Rumänien und Ungarn* (Hamburg: Holsten-Verlag, 1956). As yet untranslated into English, the title is "Battles Betrayed."

65. Maximilian Fretter-Pico, *Missbrauchte Infanterie: Deutsche Infanteriedivisionen im osteuropäischen Grossraum 1941 bis 1944: Erlebnisskizzen, Erfahrungen und Erkenntnisse* (Frankfurt: Bernard & Graefe, 1957). Not yet translated into English, the title is "Misused Infantry."

66. Lothar Rendulic, *Gekämpft, Gesiegt, Geschlagen* (Wels: Verlag 'Welsermühl,' 1952). Not yet translated into English, the title might be rendered as "Fought, Won, Beaten."

67. The dominant work on the Romanian experience in World War II remains Mark Axworthy, *Third Axis, Fourth Ally: Romanian Armed Forces in the European War, 1941–1945* (London: Arms and Armour, 1995).

68. Ibid., 9.

69. Ibid., 119.

70. For the course of this disastrous campaign, see the scholarly account by Andreas Hillgruber, *Die Räumung der Krim 1944: eine Studie zur Entstehung der deutschen Führungsentschlüsse* (Berlin: E.S. Mittler & Sohn, 1959), the article by Freiherr von Weitershausen, "Die Verteidigung und Räumung von Sevastopol im Mai 1944," *Wehrwissenschaftliche Rundschau* 4, 2 parts (1954): 209–216 and 326–336, and the entry in the German official history, Klaus Schönherr, "Der Rückzug der

Heeresgruppe A über die Krim bis Rumänien," *Das Deutsche Reich und der Zweite Weltkrieg*, volume 8, *Die Ostfront 1943/44: Der Krieg im Osten und an den Neben-fronten* (München: Deutsche Verlags-Anstalt, 2011), 450–490.

71. "Nach seiner Überzeugung sei die Verteidigung auf der Krim auch auf län-gere Zeit gewährleistet." Quoted in Hillgruber, *Die Räumung der Krim 1944*, 32.

72. "Das er die Nerven verloren habe." Quoted in ibid., 36.

73. He also sent out a stirring order of the day to his new army hectoring them to stand fast and fight to the last: "Der Stolz der Armee hängt an jedem Meter Bodens des ihr anvertrauten Raumes." Quoted in ibid., 58.

74. "Macht euch bloss keine Illusionen. Ich warte hier schon zwei Tage, und kein Schiff lässt sich blicken." Heusinger, *Befehl im Widerstreit*, "Auf der Krim," 311–312.

75. Quoted in Hillgruber, *Die Räumung der Krim 1944*, 84.

76. For the *Totila* and *Teja* disasters, see ibid., 71–72.

77. Ibid., 85.

78. For the extremely brief Romanian campaign of August 1944, begin with the memoir by the commander of Army Group South Ukraine, Hans Friessner, *Verratene Schlachten*—filled with distortions and special pleading of all sorts, but nonetheless essential. The entry in the German official history, Klaus Schönherr, "Der Rückzugskämpfe in Rumänien und Siebenbürgen," *Das Deutsche Reich und der Zweite Weltkrieg*, volume 8, *Die Ostfront 1943/44: Der Krieg im Osten und an den Nebenfronten* (München: Deutsche Verlags-Anstalt, 2011), 731–848, is the size of a small monograph and contains much new information as well as a critical analysis of Friessner's account. See also Hans Kissel, *Die Katastrophe in Rumänien* (Darm-stadt: Wehr und Wissen, 1964), as much for the documents in the appendices as for the lucid text. For a Soviet account, steeped in Cold War rhetoric but nonethe-less accurate, see W. A. Mazulenko, *Die Zerschlagung der Heeresgruppe Südukraine* (Berlin [Ost]: Verlag des Ministeriums für Nationale Verteidigung, 1959). For a detailed analysis of tactical and operational level combat on a critical portion of the front, Walter Rehm, *Jassy: Schicksal einer Division oder einer Armee?* (Neck-argemünd: Kurt Vowinckel Verlag, 1959), is indispensable. David M. Glantz, *Red Storm over the Balkans: The Failed Soviet Invasion of Romania, Spring 1944* (Lawrence: University Press of Kansas, 2006), does the favor of reminding us that the Soviets made their share of errors and ran their share of slipshod campaigns. And for the unlucky 6th Army—destroyed twice in under two years—see E. Léderrey, "Le 6e armée allemande sur le front de l'Est, de 1941 à 1944: son engagement; sa capitula-tion; sa resurrection; sa fin," *Revue Militaire Suisse* 104, no. 11 (1959): 525–539.

79. For a transcript of the Hitler-Antonescu meeting on August 5, see Kissel, *Die Katastrophe in Rumänien*, Anlage 2, 182–187.

80. "Wenn nicht, müsste der Verbündete dies sagen, damit Deutschland die nötigen Konsequenzen ziehen könne." Quoted in ibid., 182–183.

81. "Es würde an Deutschlands Seite bleiben und das letzte Land sein, was das Reich verliesse, denn es wisse, dass Deutschlands Ende auch das Ende Rumäniens bedeute." Quoted in ibid., 187.

82. Schönherr, "Der Rückzugskämpfe in Rumänien und Siebenbürgen," 781–782.

Chapter 7. On the Run: The West

1. The vignette is taken from "Ende Januar 1945: An der Westfront," in Adolf Heusinger, *Befehl im Widerstreit: Schicksalsstunden der deutschen Armee 1923–1945* (Tübingen: Rainer Wunderlich, 1950), 376–379.

2. "Das Vertrauen meiner Männer will ich nicht verlieren." Ibid., 376.

3. "Je ernster die Lage ist, um so härter muss durchgegriffen werden." Ibid.

4. "Wir müssen durchhalten, koste es, was es wolle." Ibid., 377.

5. "Sie sagen, man dürfe nicht 5 Minuten vor 12 die Nerven verlieren." Ibid., 378.

6. "Als alter Soldat wirft man nicht die Flinte ins Korn." Ibid.

7. "Sie machen sich nicht viel Gedanken." Ibid.

8. "Man fiel ihm und der Front in den Rücken." Ibid., 379.

9. Operation Dragoon (originally Anvil) was once a subject of great scholarly interest. Over time the notion that it had been a nonevent took in both the academic and the public sphere—perhaps a casualty of our increasing obsession with D-Day and the Normandy landing, and, indeed, with only two events that day: Omaha Beach and Point-du-Hoc. As a result nothing new on Dragoon has appeared in years, and our overall view of the European theater has become distorted. Nevertheless, the researcher has her/his work cut out simply reading the considerable body of secondary literature. Begin with Jeffrey J. Clarke and Robert Ross Smith, *Riviera to the Rhine* (Washington, DC: Center of Military History, 1993), one of the best and most concise of the Green Book series, and supplement the reading with the fine monograph by Alan F. Wilt, *The French Riviera Campaign of August 1944* (Carbondale: Southern Illinois University Press, 1981), along with the shorter pamphlet, Jeffrey Clarke, *Southern France* (Washington, DC: Center of Military History, n.d.), part of the *Campaigns of World War II* series. See also "Operation Anvil/Dragoon" (Fort Leavenworth, KS: Combat Studies Institute, 1984), part of the CSI Battlebook Series (no. 3-D). From the German side, begin with the pertinent section in one of the most venerable one-volume histories of the war, Kurt von Tippelskirch, *Geschichte des zweiten Weltkrieges* (Bonn: Athenäum-Verlag, 1956), 442–446, then turn to the modern official history, Detlef Vogel, "Deutsche und Alliierte Kriegführung im Westen," in *Das Deutsche Reich und der Zweite Weltkrieg*, volume 7, *Das Deutsche Reich in der Defensive: Strategischer Luftkrieg in Europa, Krieg im Westen und in Ostasien 1943–1944/45* (München: Deutsche Verlags-Anstalt, 2001), 581–605, titled "Die Landung in Südfrankreich," as well as Joachim Ludewig, *Der deutsche Rückzug aus Frankreich 1944* (Freiburg: Verlag Rombach, 1995), 61–98. Ludewig's book is available in English as *Rückzug: The German Retreat from France* (Lexington: University Press of Kentucky, 2012). The victorious Americans were quite interested in this campaign and conducted numerous interviews with the German commanders involved in it, with reports issued under the Foreign Military Studies series and available in the original German in the US

Army Heritage and Education Center in Carlisle, PA. See, for example, Johannes Blaskowitz, "German Reaction to the Invasion of Southern France: Questions for Generaloberst Johannes Blaskowitz" (Manuscript A-868); Herbert Büchs, "Stärke und Dislozierung der deutschen Luftwaffe in Südfrankreich" (A-869); Horst Wilutzky, "Der Kampf der Heeresgruppe G im Westen" (A-882); Horst Wilutzky, "Beilage zu 'Der Kampf der Heeresgruppe G im Westen'" (A-883); Johannes Blaskowitz, "Fragebogen an Generaloberst Blaskowitz" (A-916); Hans Röttiger, "Geschichte Südfrankreich/OB West" (B-330); Fritz Schulz, "Bericht über die Kämpfe der 19. Armee in Südfrankreich vom 15. August bis 15. September 1944" (B-514); Walter Botsch, "Südfrankreich: 19. Armee" (B-515); Georg von Sodernstern, "Stellungnahme zum Bericht Botsch v. 10.7.46 (MS #B-515)" (B-516); Walter Botsch, "Stellungnahme zur Geschichte der 7. amerikanischen Armee (von der deutschen 19. Armee aus gesehen") (B-518); Hans Schmidt, "Zum Fragebogen vom 3.3.47" (B-519); Friedrich Wiese, "Die 19. Armee in Süd-Frankreich vom 1.7. bis 15.9.44: Betrachtungen und Beurteilungen des O.B. der 19. Armee" (B-787); and Johannes Blaskowitz, "Kampf der Armeegruppe 'G' in Südfrankreich bis Mitte September 1944" (B-800). Finally, for the best of the journal literature, see Richard von Donat, "Logistische Probleme beim Rückzug aus Südfrankreich: August/ September 1944," 2 parts, *Truppenpraxis* 7 (1963): 946–951, and 8 (1964): 27–31; David Wingeate Pike, "Les forces Allemandes dans le Sud-Ouest de la France mai-juillet 1944," in *Guerres Mondiales et Conflits Contemporains* no. 152 (1988): 3–24, and, by the same author, "La retraite des forces allemandes du sud-ouest de la France août 1944," in *Guerres Mondiales et Conflits Contemporains* no. 164 (1991): 49–73, and Rainer Mennel, "Landung der Alliierten an der Küste der Provence und Durchbruch durch das Rhônetal bis zur Burgundischen Pforte 1944: Ein Beitrag zur Militär- und Wehrgrographie," in *Wehrforschung* 23 (1974): 110–117.

10. Vogel, "Die Landung in Südfrankreich," 597, or "between Cavalaire-sur-Mer and Agay." Wilt, *The French Riviera Campaign*, 81.

11. For the horrifying details of the massacre at Oradour, see Max Hastings, *Das Reich: The March of the 2nd SS Panzer Division through France* (New York: Holt, Rinehart and Winston, 1981), 162–181.

12. Vogel, "Die Landung in Südfrankreich," 588.

13. Ludewig, *Der deutsche Rückzug*, 62.

14. "Noch nicht einsatzfähig." Botsch, "Südfrankreich: 19. Armee," 30–31.

15. Vogel, "Die Landung in Südfrankreich," 591. Critical support assets such as antitank companies (*Panzerjägerkompanien*), moreover, were still being transferred to the battle in northern France at the time of the Allied landing (Ludewig, *Der deutsche Rückzug*, 63).

16. "Die H[aupt]-K[ampf]-L[inie] ist und bleibt der Strand. Jeder Kommandant [u.a.] haben den Befehl, ihren Platz bis zum letzten Mann und zur letzten Patrone zu halten." Quoted in Vogel, "Die Landung in Südfrankreich," 592.

17. Wilt, *The French Riviera Campaign*, 106.

18. "Den im Abschnitt Cap Nègre, St. Tropez und St. Maxime gelandeten Gegner ins Meer zurück." Quoted in Vogel, "Die Landung in Südfrankreich," 597–598.

19. "Zur eigenen späteren Absicherung und Rechtfertigung." Ibid.

20. Ludewig, *Der deutsche Rückzug*, 127–128.

21. For a study of the isolated ports, many of which held out until the end of the war, see Jacques Mordal, *Les poches de l'Atlantique* (Paris: Presses de la Cité, 1965), translated into German as *Die letzten Bastionen: das Schicksal der deutschen Atlantikfestungen 1944/45* (Oldenburg: Gerhard Stalling Verlag, 1966). For a study of one fortress in depth, see Hartwig Pohlman, "Die Festung Gironde Nord (Royan) 1944/45," 5 parts, *Feldgrau* 7 (1959): 1–4, 44–47, 68–70, 100–103, and 129–132.

22. Ludewig, *Der deutsche Rückzug*, 135.

23. "Geradezu erschütternde Bilder." Quoted in ibid.

24. For the formation and ride of Task Force Butler, see the master's thesis by Michael J. Volpe, "Task Force Butler: A Case Study in the Employment of an Ad Hoc Unit in Combat Operations, during Operation Dragoon, 1–30 August 1944" (Fort Leavenworth, KS: US Army Command and General Staff College, 1996), along with Clarke and Smith, *Riviera to the Rhine*, 80, 84, 132–133, 144–157, and Wilt, *The French Riviera Campaign*, 134–138.

25. Rick Atkinson, *The Guns at Last Light: The War in Western Europe, 1944–1945* (New York: Henry Holt, 2013), 207.

26. Ibid., 208.

27. "Es musste einseitig blind geführt werden, wie im vortechnischen Zeitalter." Blaskowitz, "Kampf der Armeegruppe 'G' in Südfrankreich," 16–17.

28. For the 11th Panzer Division's logistics in this difficult campaign, see Donat, "Logistische Probleme beim Rückzug aus Südfrankreich," part 2, 27–28, "Die Führung der Instandsetzungsdienste der 11. Panzerdivision."

29. "Bis zum 28. August, verblieb der Division gerade noch ein Drittel ihrer ursprünglich über 100 Panzer." Vogel, "Die Landung in Südfrankreich," 600.

30. Quoted in Clarke and Smith, *Riviera to the Rhine*, 169.

31. Atkinson, *The Guns at Last Light*, 212.

32. Vogel, "Die Landung in Südfrankreich," 604.

33. The units involved were French, the true forgotten army of the European Theater of Operations, at least in English-language accounts. "At 7:00 AM on the twelfth, reconnaissance troops of the 1st French Division met Le Clerc's division near Châtillon on the Seine River, halfway between Dijon and Troyes, and the permanent link between north and south was now forged." Wilt, *French Riviera Campaign*, 154.

34. "Jedes deutsche Dorf [in Elsass-Lothringen] muss zu einer Festung werden." Quoted in Vogel, "Die Landung in Südfrankreich," 603.

35. See the orders to the garrison in the Bresk-Litovsk *fester Platz* in August 1944: they were to fight "bis zur Vernichtung der Besatzung." Karl-Heinz Frieser, "Der Zusammenbruch der Heeresgruppe Mitte im Sommer 1944," in *Das Deutsche Reich und der Zweite Weltkrieg*, volume 8, *Die Ostfront 1943/44: Der Krieg im Osten und an den Nebenfronten* (München: Deutsche Verlags-Anstalt, 2011), 569.

36. Quoted in Erich Kern, *Generalfeldmarschall Schörner* (Rosenheim: Deutscvhe Verlagsgesellschaft, n.d.), 78, 99. See also "Schörner: der laute Kamerad," in *Der Spiegel* (9 February 1955), 14.

37. For the retreat from Finland in general, see H. R., "Rückzugskämpfe in

Finnland (vom 28. September bis 14. Oktober 1944): eine deutsche Darstellung," in *Allgemeine schweizerische Militärzeitschrift* 125, no. 4 (1959): 281–295. Rendulic's wartime memoirs are *Gekämpft, Gesiegt, Geschlagen* (Wels, "Welsermühl," 1952). For the general's postwar career, see his second memoir, *Glasenbach–Nürnberg–Landsberg. Ein Soldatenschicksal nach dem Krieg* (Graz: Leopold Stocker Verlag, 1953).

38. "Tagesbefehl von Model: Der Feind steht an Ostpreussens grenzen!" Facsimile in Hansgeorg Model and Dermot Bradley, *General Feldmarschall Walter Model (1891–1945): Dokumentation eines Soldatenlebens* (Osnabrück: Biblio Verlag, 1991), 237. The book is a collection of documents, many presented in facsimile. For Model's increasingly strident orders of the day in general, see Marcel Stein, *Flawed Genius: Field Marshal Walter Model; A Critical Biography* (Solihull, UK: Helion, 2010), 233–242.

39. "Die Truppe ist ausgebrannt. Ohne Erfüllung nachstehender Mindestforferungen sind von ihr keine Kampfleistungen zu erwarten." In "Lagebeurteilung Models an GO Jodl zur unverzüglichen Vorlage beim Führer (18. 8. 1944)," Model and Bradley, *Generalfeldmarschall Walter Model*, 251. See also Ludewig, *Der deutsche Rückzug*, 121–122.

40. The primary source for Hitler's intention to destroy Paris is still Dietrich Choltitz, *Brennt Paris? Adolf Hitler: Taschenberich des letzten deutschen Befehlshabers in Paris* (Frankfurt: R. G. Fischer Verlag, 2014). A facsimile of the original order is reprinted on page 7 and also appears in "Brennt Paris?—ja oder nein?" a seventieth-anniversary article in *Die Welt* (August 24, 2014).

41. The world authority on the liberation of Paris calls Choltitz "one of the most difficult personalities in the liberation of Paris to understand." Michael Neiberg, *The Blood of Free Men: The Liberation of Paris, 1944* (New York: Basic Books, 2012), 86.

42. "Den schwersten Auftrag, den ich je durchgeführt habe—allerdings dann mit grösster Konsequenz durchgeführt habe—ist die Liquidation der Juden. Ich habe diesen Auftrag allerdings auch bis zur letzten Konsequenz durchgeführt." Quoted in Sönke Neitzel, *Abgehört: Deutsche Generäle in britischer Kriegsgefangenschaft 1942–1945* (Berlin: List Taschenbuch, 2007), 258. The book's English translation is *Tapping Hitler's Generals: Transcripts of Secret Conversations, 1942–45* (St. Paul, MN: Frontline Books, 2007). A useful companion volume is Wassili S. Christoforow, Wladimir G. Makarow, and Matthias Uhl, eds., *Verhört: Die Befragungen deutscher Generale und Offiziere durch die sowjetischen Geheimdienste 1945–1952* (Oldenbourg: De Gruyter, 2015).

43. "Anscheinend lag Montgomery mehr an einem sauberen Innehalten der Vormarschstreifen als an dem weiteren Vorstoss der Amerikaner, der sich für den deutschen Rückzug vernichtend ausgewirkt hätte. Man war für diese Form eines Bewegungskrieges noch nicht wendig genug." Tippelskirch, *Geschichte des zweiten Weltkrieges*, 441.

44. "Schwimm-Volkswagen." Ludewig, *Der deutsche Rückzug*, 185. Tippelskirch, *Geschichte des zweiten Weltkrieges*, 441, speaks of "Fähren, Dampfer, und Kähne" ("ferries, steamers, and barges").

45. "Er sei kein Schulbub, mit dem man [so] umspringen könne." Quoted in Ludewig, *Der deutsche Rückzug*, 143. Accounts from the era of Model's peremptory

behavior, unreasonable demands, and threats to court-martial his subordinates—all accompanied by sarcastic laughter—are legion. Perhaps General Bodo Zimmermann, the operations chief for OB-West, put it best: "Er verlangte oft zu viel u. dies zu schnell." Bodo Zimmermann, "Bericht über die Operationen des OB. West von den Vorbereitungen gegen die Invasion bis zum Rückzug auf den Westwall," manuscript B-308 in the Foreign Military Studies series (German original available in the US Army Heritage and Education Center in Carlisle, PA), 135.

46. "Die Panzer-Div nur noch Torsos [sic] seien." Quoted in Ludewig, *Die deutsche Rückzug*, 143.

47. Ludewig, *Der deutsche Rückzug*, 184, speaks of the "sogennanten Seinefront" (the "so-called front along the Seine").

48. The most vivid account of this great offensive, which blew apart the entire German position in France within a matter of days, remains Martin Blumenson, *Breakout and Pursuit* (Washington, DC: Center of Military History, 1961), 657–675, a classic entry in the Green Book series.

49. "Die Amerikaner trafen am Südflügel der 1. Armee lediglich auf eine weitgespannte, von zwei Divisionen (48. Inf., 17. SS-Pz.Gren.Div.) verteidigte 'Sicherungslinie.'" Ludewig, *Der deutsche Rückzug*, 188.

50. For a lucid outline of this complex and highly mobile operational sequence, see Vogel, "Die Landung in Südfrankreich," 572–573.

51. Ludewig, *Der deutsche Rückzug*, 228.

52. For the Schelde Estuary campaign, see the article by French naval historian Jacques Mordal, "Das deutsche 'Dünkirchen' an der Schelde," *Marine-Rundschau* 61, no. 3 (1964): 121–130, a German translation of the French original "Le 'Dunkerque' allemand de l'Escaut," in *Revue Militaire d'Information* (May 1963): 24–31.

53. The advance of Hodges's 1st Army has barely registered on the modern historical consciousness, which is odd, since 1st Army actually did most of the fighting against the Germans on the Western Front. Hodges's colorless personality—compared to, let us say, Patton—has no doubt contributed to the problem, but that is hardly an excuse for scholarly historians. To date, the most detailed work on 1st Army operations is the unpublished doctoral dissertation by Adam J. Rinkleff, "American 'Blitzkrieg': Courtney Hodges and the Advance from Villedieu to Aachen" (University of North Texas, 2012). See also William C. Sylvan and Francis G. Smith Jr. (John T. Greenwood, ed.), *Normandy to Victory: The War Diary of General Courtney H. Hodges and the First U.S. Army* (Lexington: University Press of Kentucky, 2008), as well as the lone biography of the general, Stephan T. Wishnevsky, *Courtney Hicks Hodges: From Private to Four-star General in the United States Army* (Jefferson, NC: McFarland, 2006).

54. For the Mons Pocket, see Blumenson, *Breakout and Pursuit*, 676–684, as well as Rinkleff, "American 'Blitzkrieg,'" 270–272.

55. Blumenson, *Breakout and Pursuit*, 668.

56. *Through Combat: 314th Infantry Regiment* (314th Infantry Association, n.p., n.d.), 32. Quoted in Blumenson, *Breakout and Pursuit*, 673.

57. For the German view of Allied logistical problems, see Vogel, "Die Landung in Südfrankreich," 567–572. The primary source from the Allied side is still the

pertinent chapter in Dwight D. Eisenhower, *Crusade in Europe* (Garden City, NY: Doubleday, 1948), 288–320, titled "Pursuit and the Battle of Supply."

58. Vogel, "Die Landung in Südfrankreich," 571.

59. Harry L. Coles and Albert K. Weinberg, *Civil Affairs: Soldiers Become Governors* (Washington, DC: Center of Military History, 2014), 745. Overall, the Allies had to divert 37 percent of their airlift tonnage—their principal improvisatory means of keeping forward units supplied—to feed the French capital. Ludewig, *Der deutsche Rückzug*, 172–173.

60. Mordal, "Das deutsche 'Dünkirchen' an der Schelde," 127.

61. Ibid., 128.

62. "Ein für das deutsche Heer unwürdiges und beschämendes Bild." Quoted in Ludewig, *Der deutsche Rückzug*, 224–225.

63. "An die Soldaten des Westheeres! Aufruf Generalfeldmarschalls Model," in Model and Bradley, *General Feldmarschall Walter Model*, 282–283.

64. "Wir haben eine Schlacht verloren, aber ich sage Euch: Wir werden diesen Krieg doch gewinnen!" Ibid., 282.

65. The word is *Waschlappen*. Ibid., 283.

66. "Was in dieser Lage das Beste und Richtigste ist." Ibid., 282.

67. "Ein ruhiges Wort, ein vernünftiger Gedanke, ein handfester Rat im rechten Augenblick wird unzähligen anderen die notwendige Unterstützung, Zuversicht, Selbsstützung, Selbstvertrauen und Haltung geben." Ibid., 283.

68. "Der Feind had vier Jahre lang Schlachten verloren. Er hat zum erstenmal eine Schlacht gegen uns gewonnen. Er hat sie nicht gewonnen, weil er klüger, tapferer und besser ist. Er kann auch nicht zaubern. Er ist nicht überall da." Ibid.

69. "Soldaten, wir müssen dem Führer diese Zeit schaffen." Ibid.

70. Steven H. Newton, *Hitler's Commander: Field Marshal Walther Model—Hitler's Favorite General* (New York: Da Capo, 2006), 307.

71. For a lucid operational of the situation in the west in September 1944, see the pertinent chapter in Siegfried Westphal, *Heer in Fesseln: Aus den Papieren des Stabchefs von Rommel, Kesselring und Rundstedt* (Bonn: Athenäum-Verlag, 1950), 260–269.

72. These were divisions of the 29th–32nd *Welle* ("waves"), originally *Sperr-Divisionen* (blocking divisions), then grenadier divisions, and finally (in line with a supposedly more ideological prosecution of the war) *Volksgrenadier*. See Wolf Keilig, *Das deutsche Heer 1939–1945: Gliederung, Einsatz, Stellenbesetzung* (Bad Nauheim: Verlag Hans-Henning Podzun, 1956), Section 101, 1–9. For the experience of one unit, a regular division and then a rebuilt *Volksgrenadier*, see *Die 62. Infanterie-Division 1938–1944, Die 62. Volks-Grenadier-Division 1944–1945* (Fulda: Kamaradenhilfswerk der ehemaligen 62. Division, 1968).

73. Ludewig, *Der deutsche Rückzug*, 250.

74. Omar N. Bradley, *A Soldier's Story* (New York: Modern Library, 1999), 415–416.

75. Operation Market Garden is one of the best-known episodes of the war, thanks largely to the film *A Bridge Too Far* (dir. Richard Attenborough, 1977). For the literature, see the classic narrative by Cornelius Ryan, also entitled *A Bridge*

Too Far (New York: Simon & Schuster, 1974), the capper on his great World War II trilogy, along with *The Longest Day*, on D-Day (Greenwich, CT: Fawcett, 1959), and *The Last Battle*, on Berlin (New York: Simon & Schuster, 1966). For a more scholarly evocation and a more balanced focus on the British, see William F. Buckingham, *Arnhem 1944* (Stroud, UK: Tempus, 2004). For a detailed analysis of Waffen-SS operations during the battle, see Michael Reynolds, *Sons of the Reich: II SS Panzer Corps: Normandy, Arnhem, Ardennes, Eastern Front* (Staplehurst, UK: Spellmount, 2002), 99–177. Finally, the commander of the British 1st Airborne Division wrote his memoirs: R. E. Urquhart, *Arnhem: Britain's Infamous Airborne Assault of WW II* (London: Cassell, 1958), as did the commander of the US 82nd Airborne, James Gavin, *On to Berlin: Battles of an Airborne Commander 1943–1946* (New York: Viking, 1978), the commander of the US 101st Airborne, Maxwell D. Taylor, *Swords and Plowshares* (New York: Norton, 1972), and the commander of the Polish parachute brigade, Stanislaw Sosabowski, *Freely I Served: The Memoir of the Commander, 1st Polish Independent Parachute Brigade 1941–1944* (Barnsley, UK: Pen and Sword, 2014). For analysis from the professional journal literature, see A. D. Besterbreurtje, "Die Luftlandeoperationen in den Niederlanden im Herbst 1944," 2 parts, *Allgemeine schweizerische Militärzeitung* 92, no. 6 (1946): 363–374, and no. 7 (1946): 416–426.

76. Reynolds, *Sons of the Reich*, 99. See also Bernard Law Montgomery, *The Memoirs of Field-Marshal the Viscount Montgomery* (London: Collins, 1958), 297.

77. "Abhauen! Treffpunkt Terborg." Quoted in Ludewig, *Der deutsche Rückzug*, 328. Walter Görlitz, *Model: Strategie der Defensive: Von Russland bis zum Ruhrkessel* (Wiesbaden: Limes, 1975), 222, has a minor variation: "Alles raus—Treffpunkt Terborg!"

78. Reynolds, *Sons of the Reich*, 117–119.

79. Ludewig, *Der deutsche Rückzug*, 328–329.

80. Reynolds, *Sons of the Reich*, 170.

81. R. E. Urquhart, *Arnhem*, 204.

82. Quoted in John Terraine, "Haig," in Michael Carver, ed., *The Warlords* (Barnsley: Pen & Sword, 2005), 41.

83. "Keine Drahtsperren, keine Verminung, die Bauwerke ohne Armierung mit Festungswaffen, überdies zum Teil völlig verkommen u. verwahrlost, das Nachrichtennetz was grössenteils abgebaut, die technischen Einrichtungen fehlten oder waren unbrauchbar geworden, eine Sicherheitsbesatzung was nicht vorhanden, ausgebildetes technisches Personal u. Festungstruppen fehlten." Zimmermann, "Bericht über die Operationen des OB. West," 164. For one example of West Wall propaganda, see Frid Muth, *Gepanzerter Westen* (Berlin: Verlag für Sozialpolitik, Wirtschaft und Statistik, 1939), and Deutsche Arbeitsfront, *Unbezwinglicher Westwall: Ein Volksbuch vom Ringen um Deutschlands Westmark* (Wiesbaden: Deutsche Volksbücher, 1940).

84. For an operational analysis of the fight for the ports, with the German troops isolated and sitting in a "huge, carefully monitored prisoner of war camp," see Sönke Neitzel, "Der Kampf um die deutschen Atlantik- und Kanalfestungen

und sein Einfluss auf den alliierten Nachschub während der Befreiung Frankreichs 1944/45," *Militärgeschichtliche Mitteilungen* 55 (1996): 381–430. See also Reinhold Mueller, *Unter weisser Flagge von Saint-Nazaire 1944–1945* (Bad Neuheim: Podzun-Verlag, 1966).

85. For the battle of Aachen from the German perspective, see Bernhard Poll, ed., *Das Schicksal Aachens im Herbst 1944: authentische Berichte* (Aachen: Verlag des Aachener Geschichtsvereins, 1955). Poll labels the battle "the big catastrophe" in Aachen's long history, comparable only to the burning of the city in 1656 (193).

86. The two indispensable monographs on the Hürtgen are Edward G. Miller, *A Dark and Bloody Ground: The Hürtgen Forest and the Roer River Dams, 1944–1945* (College Station: Texas A&M University Press, 1995), and Robert Sterling Rush, *Hell in Hürtgen Forest* (Lawrence: University Press of Kansas, 2001). Both are meticulous accounts that go down to the platoon level, with Miller examining what he sees as a US command failure and Rush emphasizing sources of unit cohesion. From the German perspective, see Rudolf-Christoph Freiherr von Gersdorff, "Der Kampf um den Hürtgenwald (November-Anfang Dezember 44)," Manuscript A-891 in the Foreign Military Studies series.

87. For Patton's travails in Lorraine, see John Nelson Rickard, *Patton at Bay: The Lorraine Campaign, 1944* (Washington, DC: Brassey's, 2004).

88. For the most vigorous presentation of this thesis, see David P. Colley, *Decision at Strasbourg: Ike's Strategic Mistake to Halt the Sixth Army Group at the Rhine in 1944* (Annapolis, MD: Naval Institute Press, 2008).

89. For details of the Schwerin case, see Stein, *A Flawed Genius*, 250–253.

90. "Der Art. Reg. Kdr. sei völlig betrunken, die Bewegungen könnten nicht durchgeführt werden . . . Als sein Div. Kdr. ihn holen liess, war er so betrunken, dass er nicht mehr alleine stehen konnte." Hermann Balck, *Ordnung im Chaos: Erinnerungen 1893–1948* (Osnabrück: Biblio Verlag, 1981), 587–588, translated into English as *Order in Chaos: The Memoirs of General of Panzer Troops Hermann Balck* (Lexington: University Press of Kentucky, 2015). The artillery officer in question was Lieutenant Colonel Johann Schottke. Balck was tried and convicted for his murder in 1948, since the execution was conducted without any regular procedure or military tribunal.

91. "Als ich den Namen las, stutzte ich und sah die Akte kurz durch und sagte: ich bin ja nicht Jurist, aber meines Erachtens nach ist es Versicherungsbetrug, Missbrauch der Dienstgewalt und Bestechung." The general in question was the problematic Edgar Feuchtinger, 21st Panzer Division. Ibid., 391–392.

Chapter 8. The Last Battle

1. The speech has come down to us in varying versions—some shorter, some longer, with alternate wording and organization. This account bases itself on the "Rede des Königs vor der Schlacht bei Leuthen (3. Dezember 1757)," found online in the Œuvres de Frédéric le Grand—Werke Friedrichs des Großen (Trier: Digi-

tale Ausgabe der Universitätsbibliothek Trier, 2016). See friedrich.uni-trier.de/de /volz/3/id/003016000/text.

2. "Wir müssen den Feind schlagen oder uns vor ihren Batterien alle begraben lassen."

3. "Es ist beinahe keiner unter Ihnen, der sich nicht durch eine große und ehrebringende Handlung ausgezeichnet hätte."

4. "Ist einer oder der andere unter Ihnen, der nicht so denkt, der fordere hier auf der Stelle seinen Abschied. Ich werde ihm selbigen ohne den geringsten Vorwurf geben."

5. "Ja, das müßte ein infamer Hundsfott sein; nun wäre es Zeit!" The witness for Billerbeck's intervention is the king's page, Georg Karl zu Putlitz.

6. "Ich habe vermuthet, daß mich keiner von Ihnen verlassen würde."

7. "Nun leben Sie wohl, meine Herren, morgen um diese Zeit haben wir den Feind geschlagen, oder wir sehen uns nie wieder."

8. "Ansprache Hitlers vor Divisionskommandeuren am 12. Dezember 1944," in Helmut Heiber, ed., *Lagebesprechungen im Führerhauptquartier: Protokollfragmente aus Hitlers militärischen Konferenzen 1942–1945* (München: DTV, 1962), 281–294. For the English translation, see Robert L. Miller, ed., *Hitler at War: Meetings and Conversations, 1939–1945* (New York: Enigma, 2015), 272–281.

9. "In dem Raum herrschte eine stickige Hitze. Wir beide waren so übermudet, dass wir trotz grösster Anstrengungen die Augen nicht offen halten konnten und von Zeit zu Zeit einnickten." Siegfried Westphal, *Erinnerungen* (Mainz: von Hase & Koehler Verlag, 1975), 307. Westphal is speaking of himself and Field Marshal Walter Model.

10. "Entscheidungskrieg auf Leben und Tod." "Ansprache Hitlers vor Divisionskommandeuren am 12. Dezember 1944," 281.

11. "Dass das britische Weltreich entstehen konnte, dass der amerikanische Kontinent englisch statt deutsch wurde, und dass aber auch Frankreich auf dem Kontinent selbst seine überragende Stellung erhielt." Ibid., 282.

12. "Alle erfolgreichen Kriege der Menschheit, meine Heeren, sind Präventivkriege gewesen." Ibid., 284.

13. "Trotzdem muss man sich darüber klar sein, dass zu lange Perioden einer nur defensiven Standhaftigkeit auf die Dauer zehren, dass sie auf all Fälle wieder durch erfolgreiche Schläge abgelöst werden müssen." Ibid., 290.

14. "Ebenso ist es wichtig, diese psychologischen Momente dadurch noch zu verstärken, dass man keinen Augenblick vorübergehen lässt, um [ohne?] dem Gegner klarzumachen, dass, ganz gleich, was er auch tut, er nie auf eine Kapitulation rechnen kann, niemals, niemals." Ibid., 291.

15. "Wir werden unter allen Umständen diesen Kampf so lange führen, bis, wie Friedrich der Grosse gesagt hat, einer unserer verfluchten Gegner es müde wird." In "Besprechung Hitlers mit Generalleutnant Westphal und Generalleutnant Krebs am 31. August 1944," Heiber, *Lagebesprechungen im Führerhauptquartier*, 280. Frederick's words were actually, "Wir werden uns solange herumschlagen bis unsere verfluchten Feinde sich zum Frieden bequemen." Letter from the king to his friend Jean-Baptiste de Boyer, the Marquis d'Argens, Littau (May 7, 1758), found

online in the Œuvres de Frédéric le Grand—Werke Friedrichs des Großen (see note 1, above). See friedrich.uni-trier.de/de/hein/2/33-02/?h=d%27Argens|1758. For another variant on Frederick's original words, see Josef Goebbels, writing in *Das Reich*, the weekly newspaper (October 19, 1944): "Wie jener grosse Friedrich werden wir um uns schlagen, bis unsere verfluchten Feinde sich zum Frieden bequemen." Quoted in Hermann Jung, *Die Ardennen-Offensive 1944/45: ein Beispiel für die Kriegführung Hitlers* (Göttingen: Muster-Schmidt Verlag, 1971), 82.

16. "Denn wenn im fünften Jahr des Krieges kapituliert worden wäre, wäre auch der Wechsel des Throns im siebenten Jahr, also zwei Jahre später, völlig belanglos gewesen. Man muss die Zeit abwarten." In "Ansprache Hitlers vor Divisionskommandeuren am 12. Dezember 1944," 292.

17. The literature on Operation *Wacht am Rhein* (the Ardennes offensive, or the "Battle of the Bulge" in American vernacular) is prodigious, especially in English. Sprawling one-volume histories abound: Charles B. MacDonald, *Time for Trumpets: The Untold Story of the Battle of the Bulge* (New York: HarperCollins, 1997); John Toland, *Battle: The Story of the Bulge* (Lincoln, NE: Bison Books, 1999); Antony Beevor, *Ardennes 1944: Hitler's Last Gamble* (New York: Viking, 2015); and most recently Peter Caddick-Adams, *Snow and Steel: The Battle of the Bulge, 1944–45* (Oxford: Oxford University Press, 2015). All are wonderful and nearly interchangeable. The starting point for research into the US Army in the battle is Hugh M. Cole, *The Ardennes: Battle of the Bulge* (Washington, DC: Center of Military History, 1965), part of the Green Book series. Robert E. Merriam, *Dark December: The Full Account of the Battle of the Bulge* (Yardley, PA: Westholme, 2011), is still recommended for its proximity to the event (it appeared originally in 1947). Alex Kershaw, *The Longest Winter: The Battle of the Bulge and the Epic Story of WWII's Most Decorated Platoon* (New York: Da Capo, 2005), is a worthy entry for its tight focus on the sharp end of combat. Danny Parker is the authoritative source on all things Bulge in the United States, both as a wargame designer (his earlier incarnation) and as a very astute researcher and writer. See his *Battle of the Bulge: Hitler's Ardennes Offensive, 1944–1945* (New York: Da Capo, 1991). Harold R. Winton, *Corps Commanders of the Bulge: Six American Generals and Victory in the Ardennes* (Lawrence: University Press of Kansas, 2007), fills an important niche, focusing on the US Army's actual war fighters (as opposed to the more administratively focused field army commanders). For sources in German, begin with Jung, *Die Ardennen-Offensive*, for its meticulous research and hefty documentary appendices, along with a sizable body of journal literature, including Carl Wagener, "Strittige Fragen zur Ardennenoffensive," *Wehrwissenschaftliche Rundschau* 11, no. 1 (January 1961): 26–54; Martin Voggenreiter, "Frühjahrsoffensive 1918 und Ardennenoffensive 1944," *Wehrwissenschaftliche Rundschau* 14, no. 12 (December 1964): 731–745; and Hasso von Manteuffel, "Die Schlacht in den Ardennen 1944–1945," in Hans-Adolf Jacobsen and Jürgen Rohwer, eds., *Entscheidungsschlachten des zweiten Weltkrieges* (Frankfurt: Verlag für Wehrwesen Bernard & Graefe, 1960), 527–560. See also Eugen Bircher, "Die militärgeographischen Grundlagen der deutschen Gegenoffensive in der Eifel und in den belgisch-französischen Ardennen: Dezember 1944/Januar 1945," *Allgemeine schweizerische Militärzeitung* 91–111, no. 2 (1945): 65–96, as well as Rainer

Mennel, *Der Schlussphase des zweiten Weltkrieges im Westen: eine Studie zur politischen Geographie* (Osnabrück: Biblio Verlag, 1981). Useful unpublished documentation includes an immense number of entries into the Foreign Military Studies series, available at the US Army Heritage and Education Center in Carlisle, PA. Often criticized for a Cold War focus with how to beat the Russians in a future conflict, the vast majority of the FMS series in fact deals with the Western Front, not the Eastern Front, with the US Army naturally eager to get feedback from German officers on its performance against the Wehrmacht. There is nothing particularly sinister about it, and in fact the FMS series is the US military establishment at its best—willing and even eager to learn from any source that might be helpful. See, for a very partial listing, Siegfried von Waldenburg, "Einsatz der 116. Pz. Div. in den Ardennen vom 16.12. bis 26.12.44 (Teil I und II)," Manuscript A-873; Siegfried von Waldenburg, "Einsatz der 116. Pz. Div. in den Ardennen 1944/1945, III. Teil vom 27.XII.44 bis 16.I.45" (A-874); Erich Brandenberger and Rudolf-Christoph Freiherr von Gersdorff, "Die Ardennen-Offensive im Abschnitt der deutschen 7. Armee (16. Dezember 1944—25. Januar 1945)" (A-876); Hermann Priess, "Ardennen. Einsatz des I. SS-Panzer-Corps während der Ardennen-Offensive, Dezember–January, 1944–1945" (A-877); Fritz Kraemer, "Einsatz der 6. Panzer-Armee in den Ardennen 1944/45" (A-924); Hasso von Manteuffel, "Die 5. Panzer-Armee in der Ardennen-Offensive (16. Dezember 1944 bis 25. Januar 1945), I-III" (B-151); Hasso von Manteuffel, "Die 5. Panzer-Armee in her Ardennen-Offensive (16. Dezember 1944 bis 25. Januar 1945), IV-VII" (B-151a); Carl Wagener, "Einsatz der 5. Panzer-Armee in der Ardennen-Offensive Winter 1944/45" (B-235); Karl Tholholte, "Ardennen" (Army Group B artillery) (B-311); Hugo Kraas, "Die 12. SS-Panzer-Division 'Hitler-Jugend' in der Ardennen-Offensive" (B-522); and Günter Reichhelm, "Thema: Stellungnahme zum Bericht Kraemer vom Oktober 1945, 'Einsatz der 6. Panzer-Armee in den Ardennen 1944/1945'" (B-676).

18. Walter Warlimont, *Im Hauptquartier der deutschen Wehrmacht 1939 bis 1945: Grundlagen, Formen, Gestalten* (Augsburg: Weltbild Verlag, 1990), volume 2, 505.

19. On August 19, Hitler told Jodl that he should "darauf einstellen, dass man im November offensiv wird—wenn der Feind nicht fliegen kann." Quoted in Jung, *Ardennen-Offensive*, 101.

20. "Voraussetzung ist schlammiger Boden und nebeliges Wetter." Hermann Balck, *Ordnung im Chaos: Erinnerungen 1893–1948* (Osnabrück: Biblio Verlag, 1981), 557.

21. "Wir müssen es machen wie die Russen, bis wir wieder in der Luft stark sind." Ibid.

22. "Die Amerikaner hat nichts hinter sich. Keine Reserven." Ibid.

23. Indeed, the original manpower of Dietrich's army was two-thirds army and one-third Waffen-SS. See Kraemer, "Einsatz der 6. Panzer-Armee," 1-2.

24. "Neues Dünkirchen." Detlef Vogel, "Deutsche und Alliierte Kriegführung im Westen," in *Das Deutsche Reich und der Zweite Weltkrieg*, volume 7, *Das Deutsche Reich in der Defensive: Strategischer Luftkrieg in Europa, Krieg im Westen und in Ostasien 1943–1944/45* (München: Deutsche Verlags-Anstalt, 2001), 619–634, titled

"Die Ardennenoffensive (Operation 'Wacht am Rhein')." The quote is taken from page 619.

25. See Cole, *Battle of the Bulge*, 20; Parker, *Battle of the Bulge*, 10; and Jung, *Die Ardennen-Offensive*, 106–107.

26. "War der WFStab zu Beginn der 6. Kriegsjahres zum ersten Male berufen, eine grosse Angriffsoperation anzulegen und dazu alle Vorbereitungen zu treffen, wie sie bis dahin allein dem Generalstab des Heeres und seiner Operationsabteilung zugefallen waren." Warlimont, *Im Hauptquartier der deutschen Wehrmacht*, 512.

27. Manteuffel, "Die Schlacht in den Ardennen," 535.

28. "Big solution" versus "small solution" forms the heart of the debate over the Bulge. Siegfried Westphal, *Heer in Fesseln* (Bonn: Athenäum-Verlag, 1950), 269–285, is an appropriate starting point, augmented by his memoirs, *Erinnerungen*, 298–307. See also Percy Ernst Schramm, "Der Führungsgegensatz zwischen der Obersten Führung und den Kommandostellen des Westens," in Percy Ernst Schramm, ed., *Kriegstagebuch des Oberkommandos der Wehrmacht (Wehrmachtführungsstab)*, volume 4, *1. Januar 1944—22. Mai 1945*, zweiter Halbband (Frankfurt: Bernard & Graege Verlag, 1961), 1705–1712.

29. Charles Messenger, *The Last Prussian: A Biography of Field Marshal Gerd von Rundstedt 1875–1953* (London: Brassey's, 1991), 210.

30. "Halbe Lösung." Manteuffel, "Die Schlacht in den Ardennen," 536.

31. "Alles auf eine Karte setzen." Quoted in Jung, *Ardennen-Offensive*, 111.

32. To Hitler, the small solution "würde nur den Tag der Abrechnung hinausschieben und die Westmächte nicht verhandlungsbereit machen." Manteuffel, "Die Schlacht in den Ardennen," 534.

33. "Eine Wende des Krieges." Vogel, "Die Ardennenoffensive," 620.

34. "Mir scheint die ganze Sache auf verdammt hölzernen Füssen zu stehen." Walter Görlitz, *Model: Strategie der Defensive: von Russland bis zum Ruhrkessel* (Bergisch Gladbach: Basatei Lübbe), 235.

35. Widely quoted, originally in Milton Shulman, *Defeat in the West* (Waldenbury, East Sussex, UK: Masquerade, 1986), 290.

36. "Voll einverstanden." Quoted in Vogel, "Die Ardennenoffensive," 620.

37. For an argument regarding the "actionist" ethos of the German officer corps of an earlier era, see Isabel V. Hull, *Absolute Destruction: Military Culture and the Practices of War in Imperial Germany* (Ithaca, NY: Cornell University Press, 2005).

38. "Sollten sie sich etwa einem Feind ergeben, den man als 'blutscheu,' militärisch inkompetent, ja oft als dekadent hingestellt hatte?" Vogel, "Die Ardennenoffensive," 637.

39. For the attenuated and halting run-up to the Kursk offensive, see Robert M. Citino, *The Wehrmacht Retreats: Fighting a Lost War, 1943* (Lawrence: University Press of Kansas, 2012), 116–129.

40. "Wechselwirkung." See Carl von Clausewitz, *Vom Kriege: Ungekürzter Text* (München: Cormoran, 2000), Book 1, Chapter 1, 29. The standard English translation, Carl von Clausewitz, *On War*, edited and translated by Michael Howard and

Peter Paret (Princeton, NJ: Princeton University Press, 1976), renders the term as "interaction." For the use of the term during World War II, see Heinz Guderian, "Die Wechselwirkungen zwischen Ost- und West-Front," Manuscript T-42 in the Foreign Military Studies series, as well as Albert Kesselring, "Antworten zu den Fragen über Wechselbeziehungen zwischen der operativen und propagandistischen Kriegführung" (B-280).

41. Vogel, "Die Ardennenoffensive," 622.

42. The term was already in use in German radio traffic, reducing Allied worries that anything new was taking place. See Cole, *Battle of the Bulge*, 21.

43. See Klaus-Dietmar Henke, *Die amerikanische Besetzung Deutschlands* (München: R. Oldenbourg, 2009), 319.

44. An operation whose existence, extent, and purpose remained unknown to the commander of the 5th Panzer Army. Manteuffel, "Die Schlacht in den Ardennen," 537 ("Stärke, Einsatzort und -zeitpunkt der Fallschirmjäger blieben ihm bis zu Beginn des Angriffs unbekannt"). Manteuffel writes of himself in the third person.

45. For the unhappy fate of the 106th Infantry Division, see Robert M. Citino, "First Blood on the Ghost Front: How the Bulge Began," *World War II 29*, no. 4 (November/December 2014): 38–45. Alan W. Jones, "The Operations of the 423D Infantry (106th Infantry Division) in the Vicinity of Schonberg During the Battle of the Ardennes, 16–19 December 1944 (Ardennes-Alsace Campaign) (Personal Experience of a Battalion Operations Officer" (Fort Benning, GA: Infantry School, 1949), is a very useful supplement.

46. For both the "calculated gamble" and "insane opponent" constructs in the Allied intelligence failure, see the thought-provoking article by Paul H. Van Doren, "Decision Making and Cognitive Analysis Track: A Historic Failure in the Social Domain," available online at the Department of Defense Command and Control Research Program website: dodccrp.org/events/10th_ICCRTS/CD/papers/035.pdf.

47. For the German order of battle on the army, corps, and division level, along with a complete command roster, see Jung, *Die Ardennen-Offensive*, 334–339. See also Parker, *Battle of the Bulge*, 343–365.

48. A problem recognized by Rundstedt early on: "Die Kräfte der 7. Armee reichten für die vorgesehene, weit südlich auf der Höhe von Luxemburg liegende Abwehrfront nicht aus" (Jung, *Die Ardennen-Offensive*, 112).

49. See Charles Whiting, *The Ghost Front: The Ardennes before the Battle of the Bulge* (New York: Da Capo, 2002).

50. Quoted in Citino, "First Blood on the Ghost Front," 40.

51. For the "fortified goose egg" and the battle of St. Vith, see the typically excellent work by Steven Zaloga, *Battle of the Bulge 1944 (1): St Vith and the Northern Shoulder* (London: Osprey, 2013).

52. Wagener, "Strittige Fragen zur Ardennenoffensive," 31.

53. For the fight at Baraque de Fraiture (or "Parker's Crossroads"), see Cole, *Battle of the Bulge*, 388–392, as well as the informative website maintained

by the US 7th Armored Division Association, located online at 7tharmddiv.org /baraque-87-589.htm.

54. Quoted in Messenger, *The Last Prussian*, 162–163.

55. An action ably analyzed in Matthew Darlington Morton, *Men on Iron Ponies: the Death and Rebirth of the Modern U.S. Cavalry* (DeKalb: Northern Illinois University Press, 2009), 171–176.

56. See William Stuart Nance, *Forgotten Glory: U.S. Corps Cavalry in the ETO* (Lexington: University Press of Kentucky, 2016).

57. Rick Atkinson, *Guns at Last Light: The War in Western Europe, 1944–1945* (New York, Henry Holt, 2013), 433.

58. Ibid., 433–434.

59. For Peiper, see the magisterial work by Jens Westemeier, *Himmlers Krieger: Joachim Peiper und die Waffen-SS in Krieg und Nachkriegszeit* (Paderborn: Ferdinand Schöningh, 2014). In English, see Michael Reynolds, *The Devil's Adjutant: Jochen Peiper, Panzer Leader* (New York: Sarpedon, 1995).

60. Peiper's medical record indicates splinter wounds to the left thigh, a bullet graze on the left hand, jaundice, and damage to the gallbladder. Reynolds, *The Devil's Adjutant*, 34.

61. For Peiper's ride, see Parker, *Battle of the Bulge*, 77–78, 100–101, 105–106, as well as Cole, *Battle of the Bulge*, 260–269.

62. For Peiper at Stavelot, see Reynolds, *The Devil's Adjutant*, 160–166, as well as Parker, *Battle of the Bulge*, 121–122.

63. For Knittel's battle, see Reynolds, *The Devil's Adjutant*, 164–166.

64. For Malmedy, see James J. Weingartner, *Crossroads of Death: The Story of the Malmédy Massacre and Trial* (Berkeley: University of California Press, 2004).

65. "Im Gegensatz zu manchen anderen hohen Offizieren glaubte Eisenhower nicht an ein kleineres Unternehmen, sondern ging von einer grossangelegten deutschen Offensive aus." Vogel, "Die Ardennenoffensive," 627.

66. Quoted in the magisterial work on the European theater, Russell F. Weigley, *Eisenhower's Lieutenants: The Campaign of France and Germany, 1944–1945* (Bloomington: Indiana University Press, 1981), 496.

67. The iconic moment in General Patton's career. See George S. Patton Jr., *War as I Knew It* (New York: Bantam, 1980), 181, along with Carlo D'Este, *Patton: A Genius for War* (New York: HarperPerennial, 1995), 679–680, and Ladislas Farago, *Patton: Ordeal and Triumph* (Yardley, PA: Westholme, 1964), 707–711. See also the discussion in John Nelson Rickard, *Advance and Destroy: Patton as Commander in the Bulge* (Lexington: University Press of Kentucky, 2011), 106–107. Rickard, a Canadian scholar, is the finest historian of Patton's operations in World War II.

68. For the fall of St. Vith and the ensuing German traffic jam, see Cole, *Battle of the Bulge*, 405–413.

69. Ibid., 411.

70. Jung, *Die Ardennen-Offensive*, 162. In today's cruder vernacular, it might be "Bullshit!" The battle for Bastogne, usually reduced to one pithy word, was actually a very complicated operational sequence in which the attacking German

formations suddenly had to transition to the defensive. See Manteuffel, "Die 5. Panzer-Armee in der Ardennen-Offensive," 90–112.

71. "Langsam fing die Truppe an zu empfinden, dass der grosse Plan wohl gescheitert war oder nicht mehr zu einem das Schicksal wendenden Erfolg führen würde; Stimmung und Leistung begannen unter dieser Erkenntnis zu leiden." Quoted in Jung, *Die Ardennen-Offensive*, 159.

72. "Bedeckt, trübe, verbreitet Nebel." Ibid., 161.

73. Quoted in Christer Bergström, *The Ardennes, 1944–1945: Hitler's Winter Offensive* (Havertown, PA: Casemate, 2014), 223.

74. For a brilliant dissection of the Luftwaffe's design, procurement, and production problems, see Adam Tooze, *The Wages of Destruction: The Making and Breaking of the Nazi Economy* (New York: Penguin, 2006), 440–452, 576–584, and 627–634.

75. See James P. Duffy, *Target: America—Hitler's Plan to Attack the United States* (Westport, CT: Praeger, 2004), and Manfred Griehl, *Luftwaffe over America: The Secret Plans to Bomb the United States in World War II* (Mechanicsburg, PA: Stackpole, 2004).

76. Tooze, *Wages of Destruction*, 639.

77. Wagener, "Strittige Fragen zur Ardennenoffensive," 43–44.

78. For the triumph of Allied airpower in the Ardennes, see Harold R. Winton, "Airpower in the Battle of the Bulge: A Case for Effects-Based Operations?" *Journal of Military and Strategic Studies* 14, no. 1 (Fall 2011): 1–22.

79. Richard Overy, *Why the Allies Won* (New York: Norton, 1997).

80. "Die Einwirkung der gegnerischen Luftstreitkräfte war entscheidend für den Ablauf auf deutscher Seite . . . Die Truppe lebte daher von Beginn der Offensive an praktisch von der Hand in den Mund. Das Schlachtfeld war in der Tat 'isoliert.'" Manteuffel, "Die Schlacht in den Ardennen," 552.

81. Winton, "Airpower in the Battle of the Bulge," 15.

Chapter 9. Five Minutes Past Midnight

1. "'Und von jetzt ab wird Bombe mit Bombe vergolten!' Reichstagsrede vom 1. September 1939," in Erhard Klöss, ed., *Reden des Führers: Politik und Propaganda Adolf Hitlers, 1922–1945* (München: Deutscher Taschenbuch Verlag, 1967), 208–216.

2. Ian Kershaw, *Hitler*, volume 2, *1936–1945 Nemesis* (New York: Norton, 2000), 222.

3. "Wenn ich diese Wehrmacht aufrief, und wenn ich nun vom deutschen Volk Opfer und, wenn notwendig, all Opfer fordere, denn habe ich ein Recht dazu." Klöss, *Reden des Führers*, 215.

4. "Ein Wort habe ich nie kennengelernt, es heisst: Kapitulation." Ibid.

5. "Ein preussischer König mit einem lächerlich kleinen Staat." Ibid.

6. "Und ich möchte deher jetzt der ganzen Umwelt gleich versichern: Ein November 1918 wird sich niemals mehr in der deutschen Geschichte wiederholen!" Ibid.

7. "Rede vom 1. Januar 1945 (Adolf Hitler)," in *Sonderdruck zu Mitteilungen der Deutschen Gesandtschaft in Bern*, Rundschreiben No. 2 (13. Januar 1945). Available online at de.metapedia.org/wiki/Quelle_/_Rede_vom_1._Januar_1945_(Ad olf_Hitler)#Quellennachweis.

8. "Die hinter allem stehenden internationalen Juden." Ibid.

9. "Ihre erfolgreiche Durchführung würde nicht nur die völlige Zerreißung des Deutschen Reiches, den Transport von 15 oder 20 Millionen Deutscher in das Ausland, die Versklavung des Restteiles unseres Volkes, die Verderbung unserer deutschen Jugend, sondern vor allem das Verhungern unserer Millionen-Massen mit sich bringen." Ibid.

10. "Davon abgesehen kann man aber entweder nur in der Freiheit leben oder in der Knechtschaft sterben." Ibid.

11. "Ich habe damit nur in dem Sinne gehandelt, dem ich in der denkwürdigen Reichstagssitzung am 1. September 1939 mit der Erklärung Ausdruck verlieh, daß in diesem Kampfe Deutschland weder durch Waffengewalt noch durch die Zeit jemals würde niedergezwungen werden, daß sich aber ein 9. November im Deutschen Reich niemals mehr wiederholen wird." Ibid.

12. Bernd Wegner, "Die Choreographie des Untergangs," in *Das Deutsche Reich und der Zweite Weltkrieg*, volume 8, *Die Ostfront 1943/44: Der Krieg im Osten und an den Nebenfronten* (München: Deutsche Verlags-Anstalt, 2011), 1192–1209.

13. "Hitler verfügte schon seit Kriegsbeginn über ein im Vergleich zur grossen Mehrheit seiner Generale sehr viel moderneres und komplexeres Kriegsbild sowie über ein relativ schärferes Bewustsein von den Anforderungen eines gesamtgesellschaftlichen Krieges." Ibid., 1193.

14. "Uneingeschränktes Glaubensbekenntnis zum deutschen Sieg." Ibid., 1198.

15. "Aus dem Opfer unserer Soldaten und aus meiner eigenen Verbundenheit mit ihnen bis zum Tod, wird in der deutschen Geschichte so oder so einmal der Same aufgehen zur strahlenden Wiedergeburt der nationalsozialistischen Bewegung und damit zur Verwirklichung einer wahren Volksgemeinschaft." Quoted in ibid., 1208.

16. Alan Bullock, *Hitler: A Study in Tyranny* (New York: Konecky & Konecky, 1962), 377.

17. Prit Buttar, *Battleground Prussia: The Assault on Germany's Eastern Front, 1944–45* (Oxford: Osprey, 2010), offers an adequate survey of these operations. For the war arriving with a vengeance on Germany's eastern doorstep, see Alastair Noble, "The Phantom Barrier: *Ostwallbau* 1944–1945," *War in History* 8, no. 4 (2001): 442–467, and Alastair Noble, "The First Frontgau: East Prussia, July 1944," *War in History* 13, no. 2 (2006): 200–216.

18. "Aber die für die Ardennenoffensive verwendeten Kräfte waren die letzten Groschen eines bettelarm gewordenen Mannes." Franz Halder, *Hitler als Feldherr* (München: Münchener Dom-Verlag, 1949), 59.

19. A major theme of Erich Ludendorff, *Der totale Krieg* (München: Ludendorffs Verlag, 1936). Ludendorff believed that the *Feldherr* should also be the political master. War was no longer the continuation of politics, he wrote. "Alle Theorien von Clausewitz sind über den Haufen zu werfen . . . Darum hat die Poli-

tik der Kriegsführung zu dienen" (10). For a comparison between Ludendorff and Hitler's success in the "spiritual mobilization of Germany," see Jürgen Förster, "Ludendorff and Hitler in Perspective: The Battle for the German Soldier's Mind, 1917–1944," *War in History* 10, no. 3 (2003): 321–334.

20. The *Volkssturm* phenomenon has generated one very fine scholarly book. See David K. Yelton, *Hitler's* Volkssturm: *The Nazi Military and the Fall of Germany, 1944–1945* (Lawrence: University Press of Kansas, 2002). Otherwise, see the journal literature, including Hans Kissel, "Der deutsche Volkssturm 1944–1945," *Wehrwissenschaftliche Rundschau* 10, no. 4 (1960): 209–226, and Klaus Schönherr, "Der deutsche Volkssturm im Reichsgau Wartheland 1944/45," *Militärgeschichtliches Beiheft zur Europäischen Wehrkunde* 2 (1967): 1–16. Perry Biddiscombe, "Into the Maelstrom: German Women in Combat, 1944–45," *War & Society* 30, no. 1 (March 2011): 61–89, analyzes the regime's incomplete and last-ditch recruitment of female troops, regarded by many German soldiers as a form of "moral castration" (88).

21. On one occasion, Bormann warned one of his rivals in the *Volkssturm* to "take his fingers out of my organizational sphere." Yelton, *Hitler's Volkssturm*, 42.

22. *Nordwind* is seriously underserved in the scholarly literature on World War II. Begin with the pertinent chapter in the Green Book series: Jeffrey J. Clarke and Robert Ross Smith, *Riviera to the Rhine* (Washington, DC: Center of Military History, 1993), 492–512. Keith Bonn, *When the Odds Were Even: The Vosges Mountains Campaign, October 1944–January 1945* (New York: Ballantine, 1994), offers a workable narrative, even if the "even odds" metaphor is a dubious analytical framework; Wolf T. Zoepf, *Seven Days in January: With the 6th SS-Mountain Division in Operation Nordwind* (Bedford, PA: Aberjona, 2001), offers a detailed memoir from the German side; Steven J. Zaloga, *Operation Nordwind 1945: Hitler's Last Offensive in the West* (Oxford: Osprey, 2010), is another of the author's typically excellent battle books. Perhaps the most useful item is the pamphlet by Roger Cirillo, *Ardennes-Alsace, 16 December 1944–25 January 1945* (Washington, DC: Center of Military History, n.d.), part of the *Campaigns of World War II* series. Finally, see the pertinent portions in the memoir by Jean de Lattre de Tassigny, *The History of the French First Army* (London: George Allen and Unwin, 1949), 181–401.

23. "Ansprach des Führers vor Divisionskommandeuren am 28. Dezember 1944 im Adlerhorst," in Helmut Heiber, ed., *Hitlers Lagebesprechungen: Die Protokollfragmente seiner militärischen Konferenzen 1942–1945* (Stuttgart: Deutshe Verlags-Anstalt, 1962), 738–758.

24. Clarke and Smith, *Riviera to the Rhine*, 485.

25. See De Lattre, *French First Army*, 295–296.

26. Cirillo, *Ardennes-Alsace*, 40.

27. Order of battle taken from Zaloga, *Operation Nordwind*, 36.

28. Rick Atkinson, *The Guns at Last Light: The War in Western Europe, 1944–1945* (New York: Henry Holt, 2013), 477. See also John A. Adams, *General Jacob Devers: World War II's Forgotten Four Star* (Bloomington: Indiana University Press, 2015), 302.

29. Entry in the diary of the 7th Army chief of staff, General Arthur White: "German offensive began on Seventh Army Front about 0030 am. Krauts were howling drunk. Murdered them." Quoted in Zaloga, *Operation Nordwind*, 44.

30. For the demise of Task Force Hudelson, see Clarke and Smith, *Riviera to the Rhine*, 505–508.

31. Ibid., 508–509.

32. Bonn, *When the Odds Were Even*, 191–193.

33. Zaloga, *Operation Nordwind*, 57.

34. Clarke and Smith, *Riviera to the Rhine*, 515.

35. Zaloga, *Operation Nordwind*, 65–76.

36. Clarke and Smith, *Riviera to the Rhine*, 516–518.

37. For Hatten-Rittershofen, see Zaloga, *Operation Nordwind*, 59–65.

38. Ibid., 64.

39. Clarke and Smith, *Riviera to the Rhine*, 523–527.

40. Zaloga, *Operation Nordwind*, 70–73.

41. Hans von Luck, *Panzer Commander* (New York: Dell, 1989), 235–236.

42. For the long but hopeless defensive stand in the Courland Pocket (*Kurland Kessel*), see Werner Haupt, *Kurland: die letzte Front—Schicksal für zwei Armeen* (Bad Nauheim: Podzun-Verlag, 1964), as well as Heinz-Günther Koch, "Kamperfahrung in der Verteidigung: Deutsche Erfahrungen in den Kurlandschlachten 1945," *Allgemeine schweizerische Militärzeitschrift* 123, no. 1 (1957): 31–41. For Dönitz's naval strategy, see Jak P. Mallmann Showell, ed., *Führer Conferences on Naval Affairs 1939–1945* (Mechanicsburg, PA: Stackpole, 2005), along with the books by Henrik O. Lunde, *Hitler's Wave-Breaker Concept: An Analysis of the German End Game in the Baltic* (Havertown, PA: Casemate, 2013), and Howard D. Grier, *Hitler, Donitz, and the Baltic Sea: The Third Reich's Last Hope, 1944–1945* (Annapolis, MD: Naval Institute Press, 2013).

43. See, for example, Peter Gosztony, "Der Krieg zwischen Bulgarien und Deutschland 1944/45," 3 parts, *Wehrwissenschaftliche Rundschau* 17 (1967): nos. 1–3, 22–38, 89–99, and 163–176.

44. See Gerhard Hümmelchen, "Balkanräumung 1944," *Wehrwissenschaftliche Rundschau* 9 (1959): 565–583.

45. See H. K. Frank, "Rückzugskämpfe in Serbien," *Allgemeine schweizerische Militärzeitschrift* 125, nos. 2–3 (1959): 118–130 and 201–212.

46. For the tactical and operational details of this great armored conflagration in the heart of the Danubian breadbasket, see Hans Kissel, *Die Panzerschlachten in der Pußta im Oktober 1944* (Neckargemünd: Kurt Vowinckel Verlag, 1960).

47. For the political details, see Andreas Hillgruber, "Das deutsch-ungarisch Verhältnis im letzten Kriegsjahr: vom Unternehmen 'Margarethe I' (19. März 1944) bis zur Räumung Ungarns durch die deutschen Truppen (4. April 1945)," *Wehrwissenschaftliche Rundschau* 10 (1960): 78–104, a companion to his earlier "Die letzten Monate der deutsch-rumänischen Waffenbruderschaft," *Wehrwissenschaftliche Rundschau* 7 (1957): 377–397. For more recent analysis that blends political and military developments, see Krisztián Ungváry, "Kriegsschauplatz Ungarn,"

in *Das Deutsche Reich und der Zweite Weltkrieg,* volume 8, *Die Ostfront 1943/44: Der Krieg im Osten und an den Nebenfronten* (München: Deutsche Verlags-Anstalt, 2011), 849–958.

48. Peter Gosztony, "Der Kampf um Budapest 1944/45," 5 parts, *Wehrwissenschaftliche Rundschau* 13 and 14 (1963 and 1964): 575–585, 654–672, 729–839, 46–61, and 92–105. Published as *Der Kampf um Budapest 1944/45* (München: Schnell und Steiner, München, 1964). Now superseded by Krisztián Ungváry, *The Siege of Budapest: 100 Days in World War II* (New Haven, CT: Yale University Press, 2005).

49. The great Soviet offensive out of the Vistula bridgeheads usually warrants a mention in western histories with little in the way of specificity or detail. As a point of departure, see Christopher Duffy, *Red Storm on the Reich: The Soviet March on Germany, 1945* (New York: Atheneum, 1991), 67–86. From the German side, see Eike Middeldorf, "Die Abwehrschlacht am Weichselbrückenkopf Baranow: eine Studie über neuzeitliche Verteidigung," *Wehrwissenschaftliche Rundschau* 3, no. 4 (1953): 187–203; Kurt von Tippelskirch, *Geschichte des zweiten Weltkriegs* (Bonn: Athenäum-Verlag, 1956), 534–551; and Ferdinand Heim, "Stalingrad und der Verlauf des Feldzuges der Jahre 1943–1945," in Alfred Philippi and Ferdinand Heim, eds., *Der Feldzug gegen Sowjetrussland 1941 bis 1945* (Stuttgart: W. Kohlhammer, 1962), 271–281. For the primary source that still tends to define the historical narrative in the English-speaking world, see the memoir of the Chief of the General Staff at the time, Heinz Guderian, *Erinnerungen eines Soldaten* (Heidelberg: Kurt Vowinckel, 1951), 353–385 (the section titled "Der russische Stoss"), translated into English as *Panzer Leader* (New York: Ballantine, 1957). Just as influential in Germany is the popular history by Jürgen Thorwald, *Es begann an der Weichsel* (München: Knaur, 1965). Originally appearing in 1948, it painted an image of a helpless German population in the eastern provinces, first betrayed by the Nazi regime and then crucified (sometimes literally) by the Soviets. It continues to inform German historical memory to this day. See Thorwald's later volume as well, *Das Ende an der Elbe* (Stuttgart: Steingrüben Verlag, 1953). "Jürgen Thorwald" is a pseudonym for Heinz Bongartz, a journalist and writer of military propaganda during the Third Reich. For critiques of Thorwald's work, including its accuracy and historicity, see David Oels, "'Dieses Buch ist kein Roman': Jürgen Thorwalds 'Die grosse Flucht' zwischen Zeitgeschichte und Erinnerungspolitik," *Zeithistorische Forschungen* 6 (2009), 367–390; David Oels, "Schicksal, Schuld und Gräueltaten: populäre Kriegspropaganda: Jürgen Thorwalds ewiger bestseller 'Die grosse Flucht,'" *Die Zeit* (July 22, 2010); and Anna M. Parkison, "Afterlives of a Nazi Sabotage Blunder: Jürgen Thorwald's Der Fall Pastorius," in *Non Fiktion* 6, nos. 1/2 (2011): 49–70.

Turn then to the German official history, Richard Lakowski, "Der Zusammenbruch der deutschen Verteidigung zwischen Ostsee und Karpaten," in *Das Deutsche Reich und der Zweite Weltkrieg,* volume 10/1, *Der Zusammenbruch des Deutschen Reiches 1945: Die Militärisen Niederwerfung der Wehrmacht* (München: Deutsche Verlags-Anstalt, 2008), 491–679. Hans Mangenheimer, "Die Abwehrschlacht an der Weichsel 1945: Planung und Ablauf aus der Sicht der deutschen operative Führung," *Vorträge zur Militärgeschichte* 9: *Operatives Denken und Handeln in deutschen Streitkräften im 19. und 20. Jahrhundert,* issued by the *Militargeschichtliches Forschungsamt* (Herford: Verlag E. S. Mittler & Sohn, 1988), 161–182, is valuable for its technical analysis of the German defensive posture on the Vistula. Other worthy entries in this very useful volume include Karl-Heinz Frieser, "Der Vorstoss der Panzergruppe Kleist zur Kanalküste (10. bis 21. Mai 1940): Führungsprobleme beim erstmaligen operativen Einsatz der Panzerwaffe" (123–148), a response to Frieser by Johann Adolf Graf von Kielmansegg, "Bemerkungen zum Referat von Hauptmann Dr. Frieser aus der Sicht eines Zeitzeugen" (149–160), and Christian Greiner, "General Adolf Heusinger (1887–1982): Operatives Denken und Planen 1948 bis 1956" (225–261). Finally, see Hans von Ahlfen, "Rückzug von der Weichsel zur Oder in Januar 1945 infolge des russischen Durchbruchs aus der Baranov und Pulawy-Brückenkopf," Manuscript D-368, part of the Foreign Military Studies series and available at the AHEC in Carlisle, PA.

50. For the Vistula-Oder operation, see David M. Glantz and Jonathan House, *When Titans Clashed: How the Red Army Stopped Hitler* (Lawrence: University Press of Kansas, 1995), 238–247, as well as John Erickson, *The Road to Berlin: Stalin's War with Germany* (New Haven, CT: Yale University Press, 1983), 447–469.

51. Erickson, *Road to Berlin,* 447.

52. For the East Prussian campaign, begin with the commander of the German 4th Army, Friedrich Hossbach, "Aus den Kämpfen der 4. deutschen Armee um Ostpreussen: in der Zeit vom 15.8.1944 bis 28.1.1945," 3 parts, *Allgemeine schweizerische Militärzeitschrift* 116, nos. 2, 4, 5 (1950): 138–148, 278–286, and 351–363. Published the next year as *Schlacht um Ostpreussen: Aus den Kämpfen der 4. deutschen Armee um Ostpreussen in der Zeit vom 19.7.1944 bis 30.1.1945* (Überlingen: Otto Dikreiter Verlag, 1951). Prit Buttar, *Battleground Prussia: The Assault on Germany's Eastern Front, 1944–45* (London: Osprey, 2010), offers a cogent summary of the complex battles for the Baltic littoral.

53. Lakowski, "Der Zusammenbruch der deutschen Verteidigung zwischen Ostsee und Karpaten," 498.

54. Guderian, *Erinnerungen eines Soldaten,* 345–349 ("Um das zu können, bedurfte es der sofortigen Überführung der Truppen vom Westen nach dem Osten," 347).

55. For the original *Schlittenfahrt,* see Robert M. Citino, *The German Way of War: From the Thirty Years' War to the Third Reich* (Lawrence: University Press of Kansas, 2005), 22–33.

56. See Duffy, *Red Storm on the Reich,* 60–61. Xylander would be killed on February 14, 1945, when the aircraft in which he was riding was shot down over Dresden (50).

57. "Völlig idiotisch." Guderian, *Erinnerungen eines Soldaten,* 351.

58. "Wenn Sie verlangen, dass der General Gehlen in ein Irrenhaus kommt, dann sperren Sie auch mich gleich dazu." Ibid.

59. "Das ganze war höchst unerfreulich." Ibid.

60. "Vogel-Strauss-Politik und -Strategie!" Ibid., 352.

61. "Die Ostfront ist wie ein Kartenhaus. Wird dir Front an einer einzigen Stelle durchstossen, so fällt sie zusammen." Ibid.

62. "Der Osten muss sich allein helfen und mit dem auskommen, was er hat." Ibid.

63. The published English translation renders the last line, "And the Russian forces don't consist only of artillery, either." See "Evening Situation Report, January 9, 1945, in Adlerhorst," in Helmut Heiber and David M. Glantz, eds., *Hitler and His Generals: Military Conferences, 1942–1945* (New York: Enigma, 2003), 595.

64. The phrase is from the German official history ("oft genug nicht nur unkonventioneller, sondern auch unprofessioneller und fehlerhafter operativer Entschlüsse Hitlers"). Bernd Wegner, "Der Krieg gegen Die Sowjetunion, 1942–43," in *Das Deutsche Reich und der Zweite Weltkrieg,* volume 6, *Die Ausweitung zum Weltkrieg und der Wechsel der Initiative, 1941–1943* (Stuttgart: Deutsche Verlags-Anstalt, 1990), 954.

65. "Die Gefahr des Bodenkrieges auf dem Reichsgebiet war unübersehbar geworden." Lakowski, "Der Zusammenbruch der deutschen Verteidigung zwischen Ostsee und Karpaten," 510.

66. Mangenheimer, "Die Abwehrschlacht an der Weichsel," 171–175. Lakowski, "Der Zusammenbruch der deutschen Verteidigung zwischen Ostsee und Karpaten," 499.

67. For a discussion of the old East Prussian fortifications, see Robert M. Citino, *The Evolution of Blitzkrieg Tactics: German Defends Itself against Poland, 1919–1933* (Westport, CT: Greenwood Press, 1987), 61–63.

68. "Herr Koch, Gauleiter von Ostpreussen und Reichskommissar für die Verteidigung, wusste natürlich über alles besser Bescheid als ausgebildete soldatische Führer." Otto Lasch, *So fiel Königsberg: Kampf und Untergang von Ostpresussens Hauptstadt* (München: Gräfe und Unzer Verlag, n.d.), 28. Lasch was the last commandant of Königsberg fortress and led the defense of the city against the Soviets.

69. Or sometimes the "Mausefalle" (mousetrap). Ibid., 29.

70. Erickson, *Road to Berlin,* 455.

71. Duffy, *Red Storm on the Reich,* 67–72.

72. Glantz, *When Titans Clashed,* 242.

73. Duffy, *Red Storm on the Reich,* 81–86.

74. "Wir haben niemals daran gezweifelt, dass die bolshewistische Flut vor den Grenzen des Warthegaues verbluten und ihre entscheidende Niederlage erfahren wird" and "nach dem festen Willen des Führers kein Fuss der bolshewistischen Soldateska dieses Land betreten wird." Quoted in in Thorwald, *Es begann on der Weichsel,* 37.

75. "Die Katastrophe an der Front entwickelte sich bis dahin lawineartig." Guderian, *Erinnerungen eines Soldaten,* 365.

76. See Rolf-Dieter Müller, *An der Seite der Wehrmacht: Hitlers ausländische Helfer beim 'Kreuzzug gegen den Bolschewismus' 1941–1945* (Frankfurt: Fischer Taschenbuch Verlag, 2010). Translated into English as *The Unknown Eastern Front: The Wehrmacht and Hitler's Foreign Soldiers* (London: I. B. Tauris, 2012).

77. "Nachdem ich Einblick in die Gesamtlage gewonnen hatte, kam ich mir wie ein Klavierspieler vor, der auf einem alten, verbrauchten und verstimmten Klavier

eine Beethoven-Sonate vor einem grossen Publikum spielen sollte." Albert Kesselring, *Soldat bis zum letzten Tag* (Bonn: Athenäum-Verlag, 1953), 375–376.

78. Charles B. MacDonald, *The Last Offensive* (Washington, DC: Center of Military History, 1993), 10, part of the Green Book series.

79. For US intellectual and doctrinal developments before the war and their relation to the wartime evolution of the army, see Peter J. Schifferle, *America's School for War: Fort Leavenworth, Officer Education, and Victory in World War II* (Lawrence: University Press of Kansas, 2010), as well as Jörg Muth, *Command Culture: Officer Education in the US Army and the German Armed Forces, 1901–1940, and the Consequences for World War II* (Denton: University of North Texas Press, 2011), for a comparative analysis. See also Walter E. Kretchik, *U.S. Army Doctrine: From the American Revolution to the War on Terror* (Lawrence: University Press of Kansas, 2011), linking the army's battlefield evolution to its doctrinal documents. For James Jay Carafano, the key to wartime success was ingenuity; see *GI Ingenuity: Improvisation, Technology, and Winning World War II* (Westport, CT: Praeger Security International, 2006).

80. The US triumph and German collapse in the Ruhr has one dedicated scholarly monograph—and a fine one: Derek S. Zumbro, *Battle for the Ruhr: The German Army's Final Defeat in the West* (Lawrence: University Press of Kansas, 2006). Zumbro is a former US Navy SEAL officer and a deep thinker with formidable foreign-language (German) skills. From the German side, see Carl Wagener, "Kampf und Ende der Heeresgruppe B im Ruhrkessel 22. März bis 17. April 1945," *Wehrwissenschaftliche Rundschau* 7, no. 10 (1957): 535–564.

81. For Remagen, see Ken Hechler, *The Bridge at Remagen* (New York: Ballantine, 1957). Hechler was a combat historian in the European theater and was attached to the 9th Armored Division for the dramatic events at Remagen. He was later elected to the US Congress as a representative from West Virginia. See also Larry Izzo, "An Analysis of German Mistakes Leading to the Capture of the Ludendorff Bridge at Remagen," in *Military History Anthology* (Fort Leavenworth, KS: Combat Studies Institute, 1984), as well as Robert J. C. Osborne et al., "The 9th Armd Div in Exploitation of Remagen Bridgehead" (Fort Knox, KY: The Armored School, 1949–1950). E. Bircher, "Die militärische Bedeutung des Rheins in seiner militär/geographischen Beziehungen im Laufe der Geschichte," in *Allgemeine schweizerische Militärzeitung* 91, 4 parts, nos. 5, 9, 10, 11 (1945): 217–233, 459–478, 505–519, and 548–555, offers the full historical panorama of the conquerors, hosts, and raiders who have had to take the Rhine into their operational calculations.

82. See Marcel Stein, *A Flawed Genius: Field Marshal Walter Model; A Critical Biography* (Solihull, UK: Helion, 2010), 179–184.

83. For the US "breakout offensive," see MacDonald, *The Last Offensive*, 346–350.

84. Ibid., 350.

85. Zumbro, *Battle for the Ruhr*, 311–312.

86. Ibid., 395–396.

87. For the full text of Goebbels's 1945 speech, the last of his twelve "Unser Hitler" speeches (one for every year of the Third Reich except 1934), see Thorwald, *Das Ende an der Elbe*, 74–75.

88. For a discussion of what Model heard and didn't hear, see Stein, *A Flawed Genius*, 187. Walter Görlitz, *Model: Strategie der Defensive: von Russland bis zum Ruhrkessel* (Wiesbaden: Limes, 1975), 285, is mistaken in claiming that Goebbels uttered the phrase "verräterischen Ruhrarmee" (traitorous Ruhr army) and seeing those words as the proximate cause of Model's suicide: they appear nowhere in this very famous and oft-quoted speech.

89. Staff officer Winrich Behr, quoted in Stein, *A Flawed Genius*, 285.

Chapter 10. The Last Stand

1. See, among other sources, Michael Stürmer, *The German Empire: A Short History* (New York: Modern Library, 2000), 12–13.

2. For a particularly brilliant exposition of German military culture and the classic traditions of German operational thought, see Gerhard P. Gross, *Mythos und Wirklichkeit: Geschichte des operativen Denkens im deutschen Heer von Moltke d. Ä. bis Heusinger* (Paderborn: Schöningh Ferdinand, 2012), recently translated into English as *The Myth and Reality of German Warfare: Operational Thinking from Moltke the Elder to Heusinger* (Lexington: University Press of Kentucky, 2016).

3. For the saga of the "displaced persons," or "DPs," which flooded Europe with "a tidal wave of nomad peoples," see the pertinent chapter in William I. Hitchcock, *The Bitter Road to Freedom: The Human Cost of Allied Victory in World War II Europe* (New York: Free Press, 2008), 249–280, as well as Gregory Dallas, *1945: The War That Never Ended* (New Haven, CT: Yale University Press, 2005), 428–431.

4. "Dulce et decorum est, pro patria mori." (It is a sweet and fitting thing to die for your country.) Horace, *Odes* (III.2.13). Mocked, famously, by British war poet Wilfred Owen in his posthumously published poem "Dulce et Decorum Est," wherein the poet depicts Horace's phrase as "the old Lie."

5. "Was ist praktisch? Wenn man mit der S-Bahn von der Ost- zur Westfront fahren kann." Sven Felix Kellerhoff, "Im Kessel von Halbe starb Hitlers letzte Hoffnung," *Die Welt* (April 24, 2016).

6. "Was ist praktisch? Wen mann zu Fuss von der Ost- zur Westfront laufen kann." Ibid.

7. For classic expositions of these flank battles in Pomerania and Silesia, see Christopher Duffy, *Red Storm on the Reich: The Soviet March on Germany, 1945* (New York: Atheneum, 1991), 114–198, and John Erickson, *The Road to Berlin: Stalin's War with Germany* (New Haven, CT: Yale University Press, 1983), 431–469. For the German perspective, see Richard Lakowski, "Der Zusammenbruch der deutschen Verteidigung zwischen Ostsee und Karpaten," in *Das Deutsche Reich und der Zweite Weltkrieg*, volume 10/1, *Der Zusammenbruch des Deutschen Reiches 1945: Die Militärisen Niederwerfung der Wehrmacht* (München: Deutsche Verlags-Anstalt, 2008), 531–568.

8. "Ich schätzte ihn charakterlich wie soldatisch besonders hoch. Er war ein ebenso kluger wie aufrechter und tapferer Mann und sicher besonders geeignet,

eine so schwere Situation zu meistern, wenn sie überhaupt zu meistern war." Heinz Guderian, *Erinnerungen eines Soldaten* (Heidelberg: Kurt Vowinckel, 1951), 366.

9. See the tart comment in Earl F. Ziemke, *Stalingrad to Berlin: The German Defeat in the East* (Washington, DC: Center of Military History, 1987), 425: "Hitler professed to see signs of authentic if late-blooming military talent in Himmler's recent handling of Army Group Oberrhein."

10. "Der Feldmarschall von Weichs macht auf mich einen müden Eindruck. Ich glaube nicht, dass er dieser Aufgabe noch gewachsen ist." Quoted in Guderian, *Erinnerungen eines Soldaten*, 366.

11. For *Sonnenwende* (not to be confused with the operation of the same name that occurred as part of Operation *Nordwind*), see Duffy, *Red Storm on the Reich*, 181–185. And for tactical details of the fighting in Pomerania, see Joachim Schulz-Naumann, "Ein Pommersche Infanterie-Division im Kampf um die Heimat: Anfang 1945," *Allgemeine schweizerische Militärzeitschrift* 123, no. 10 (1957): 737–752.

12. See Léon Degrelle, *La Campagne de Russie, 1941–1945* (Paris: La Diffusion du Livre, 1949), 401–448, 277–209, translated into English by the Holocaust-denying Institute for Historical Review as *Campaign in Russia: The Waffen SS on the Eastern Front* (Newport Beach, CA: Institute for Historical Review, 1985), 277–309. For the Wallonien Division's role in the Pomeranian fighting, see the unpublished manuscript "Bataille de la Baltique/Pommernfront 1945: 28. Pa. Gren. Div. SS 'Wallonien.'" A copy is on file in the US Army Heritage and Education Center in Carlisle, PA.

13. The loss of Silesia, the eastern province whose original seizure by Frederick the Great had made Prussia a great power in the first place, loomed large in the historiography of Germany's postwar trauma. See, for example, Johannes Kaps, ed., *Die Tragödie Schlesiens 1945/46 in Dokumenten: unter besonderer Berücksichtigung des Erzbistums Breslau* (München: Verlag "Christ Unterwegs," 1952/3). For the fight itself, see Hans von Ahlfen, *Der Kampf um Schlesien, 1944/1945* (Stuttgart: Motorbuch Verlag, 1963). Ahlfen was the commandant of Fortress Breslau at the beginning of the Soviet siege.

14. Duffy, *Red Storm on the Reich*, 128.

15. Much of the literature on the fighting in Silesia actually deals only with the long siege of the provincial capital, Breslau. See Hans von Ahlfen, "Der Kampf der Festung Breslau," *Wehrwissenschaftliche Rundschau* 1, *Sonderdruck* (1956): 20–39; Joachim Konrad, "Das Ende von Breslau," *Vierteljahrshefte für Zeitgeschichte* 4, no. 4 (October 1956): 387–390; and Ernst Hornig, "Festung Breslau 1945," *Schweizer Monatshefte* 48, no. 4 (1968–1969): 356–365. Konrad was a leading evangelical clergyman (the *Stadtdekan*); Hornig became evangelical bishop of Breslau in 1946, although he had to carry out his duties from Görlitz.

16. Duffy, *Red Storm on the Reich*, 134.

17. The Battle of Berlin occupies a special place in the history of World War II, for all the obvious reasons: the end of the war, the collapse of the Third Reich, Hitler's suicide. As a part of the mythos of the war, it will never cease to compel. As an actual operation and battle, it is much less interesting: a sad-sack collection of second- and third-rate German (and non-German allied) formations with no hope

of stopping the Soviet offensive. The literature is copious. In English, Cornelius Ryan, *The Last Battle* (New York: Fawcett, 1966), is a typically brilliant page-turner and dominated the field, but it now faces stiff competition from the equally brilliant work by Antony Beevor, *The Fall of Berlin 1945* (New York: Penguin, 2002), who is meticulously working his way through the entire war with one fine book after another. German-language materials include a vast literature in the professional military journals, as well as anniversary articles in popular journals. Begin with the testimony of the last German commandant in Berlin, Helmuth Weidling, "Der Endkampf in Berlin (23.4—2.5 1945)," 3 parts, in *Wehrwissenschaftliche Rundschau* 12, no. 1 (1962), no. 2. (1962) and no. 3 (1962): 40–52, 111–118, and 169–174; as well that of staff officer Gerhard Boldt, *Die letzten Tage der Reichskanzlei* (Hamburg: Rowohlt Verlag, 1947), including the later expanded edition, *Hitler: die letzten zehn Tage in der Reichskanzlei: der authentische Bericht* (München: Wilhelm Heyne Verlag, 1976); and the last keeper of the OKW war diary, Joachim Schultz, "Die Schlacht um Berlin," 2 parts, in *Allgemeine schweizerische Militärzeitschrift* 121 (1955), no. 4 and no. 5 (1955): 277–291 and 349–363. See also Joachim Schultz, *Die letzten 30 Tage: Aus dem Kriegstagebuch des OKW: Dokumente zur Zeitgeschichte* (Stuttgart: Steingrüben-Verlag, 1951), available in various editions, some under the name Joachim Schulz-Naumann, *Die letzten dreissig Tage: Das Kriegstagebuch des OKW, April bis Mai 1945* (Frankfurt: Ullstein, 1995). Twentieth-anniversary literature includes Erich Kuby, "Die Russen in Berlin 1945," *Der Spiegel*, no. 21 (1965): 57–74; Peter Gosztony, "Die Eroberung Berlins durch die Rote Armee im Frühjahr 1945," 2 parts, *Allgemeine schweizerische Militärzeitschrift* 131, no. 4 and no. 5 (1965): 196–205 and 273–283; as well as Walther Wenck, "Berlin war nicht zu mehr zu retten," in *Stern*, April 1965, 62–69. Wenck was the commander of 12th Army, given the impossible mission of relieving Berlin. For the fortieth anniversary, see Peter Gosztony, "Stalin, die Rote Armee und das Kriegsende 1945," *Allgemeine schweizerische Militärzeitschrift* 151, no. 5 (1985): 261–266. For details of the actual military operation, see Karl-Heinz Frieser, "Die Schlacht um die Seelower Höhen," in Roland G. Foerster, ed., *Seelower Höhen 1945* (Hamburg: E. S. Mittler & Sohn, 1998), 129–143. A collection of symposium papers, this is an omnibus volume that goes well beyond the limited scope suggested by its title, with contributions on American strategy (Alfred C. Mierzejewski, "Die Strategie der Vereinigten Staaten und das Ende des Zwetien Weltkrieges in Europa," 15–26), British strategy (John A. S. Grenville, "Wettlauf nach Berlin? Britische Ziele und Strategie im letzten Kriegsjahr," 27–38), and Soviet strategy (John Erickson, "Soviet Strategy 1941–1945: Surprise, Survival, Attrition, Annihilation," 39–62), plus a concluding summation on the continued meaning of the war (Gerhard Weinberg, "Der historische Ort des Zweiten Weltkrieges," 175–190). Finally, see Wilhelm Willemer, "The German Defense Plan for Berlin," Manuscript P-136 in the Foreign Military Studies series at the US Army Heritage and Education Center, Carlisle, PA. Despite its English title, the document is in the original German.

18. "Tak kto zhe budet brat Berlin, my ili soyuzniki?" Transliterated in Erickson, *Road to Berlin*, 531.

19. I. S. Konev, *Year of Victory* (Moscow: Progress Publishers, 1984), 79.

20. Ibid., 80.

21. Ibid., 83.

22. Quoted in Tony Le Tissier, *Zhukov at the Oder: The Decisive Battle for Berlin* (Mechanicsburg, PA: Stackpole, 1996), 109.

23. Quoted in Beevor, *Fall of Berlin*, 209.

24. Orders first went out to douse the searchlights, followed quickly by a countermand, and the chaos was total. Erickson, *Road to Berlin*, 563–564.

25. Quoted in Konev, *Year of Victory*, 105.

26. A rule that Ziemke, in *Stalingrad to Berlin* (475), labels "dubious."

27. Erickson, *Road to Berlin*, 577.

28. See the article by the 9th Army commander, Theodor Busse, "Die letzte Schlacht der 9. Armee," *Wehrwissenschaftliche Rundschau* 5, no. 4 (1955): 145–168. See also the ancillary materials relating to the rapid fall of the fortress of Landsberg to the Soviets during the Vistula-Oder campaign. Busse's article accused the commander there, General Gerhard Kegler, of dereliction of duty. For the accused's response, see Gerhard Kegler, "Die letzte Schlacht der 9. Armee: eine Entgegnung," *Wehrwissenschaftliche Rundschau* 5, no. 7 (1955): 294–296, which includes the testimony of the army judge who presided over Kegerl's court-martial, Ernst Freiherr von Dörnberg. For 9th Army's attenuated collapse even before the Berlin battle, see Richard Lakowski, "Die Lage der 9, deutschen Armee von Beginn der offensive der Roten Armee (16. April 1945)," in Foerster, ed., *Seelower Höhen 1945*, 111–128.

29. "Undurchführbaren" and "völlig abwegige." Busse, "Die letzte Schlacht der 9. Armee," 165–166.

30. Weidling tells the tale in "Der Endkampf in Berlin," 41–46. Hitler offered both Heinrich and Busse the command, and they turned it down. See Lakowski, "Der Zusammenbruch der deutschen Verteidigung zwischen Ostsee und Karpaten," 658.

31. "Es wäre besser, wenn Sie befohlen hätten, mich zu erschiessen, dann ginge dieser Kelch an mir vorüber." Weidling, "Der Endkampf in Berlin," 46.

32. "An den Fernsprecher kam aber der Ia und meldete, dass sich der Divisionskommandeur bei der Truppe befände. Nach einer halbe Stunde meldete er mir dann, dass sich der Divisionskommandeur, Generalmajor Scholz erschossen hätte." Ibid., 112. Weidling has misspelled the name of the deceased officer.

33. For the Soviet approach to urban warfare, see V. I. Chuikov, *The End of the Third Reich* (Moscow: Progress Publishers, 1978), 198–210. Like all the Soviet military memoirs, this one almost certainly had a ghostwriter, but it contains enough of Chuikov's personal papers and reminiscences to make it worthwhile to the modern researcher. See also Beevor, *Fall of Berlin*, 316–319.

34. For the strange story of the French fighting to defend the German capital against the Russians, see the French right-wing author Marc Augier, writing as "Saint-Loup," *Les Hérétiques* (Paris: Presses de la Cité, 1965), 416–445. See also "Saint-Loup," *Les Volontaires* (Paris: Presses de la Cité, 1963), for the anti-Bolshevik movement in France more generally.

35. "Massen von aufgeschreckten Menschen standen und lagen eng aneinan-

dergedrückt. Es war ein erschütterndes Bild." Weidling, "Der Endkampf in Berlin," 111.

36. Willemer, "The German Defense Plan for Berlin," 56–58. See Boldt, *Die letzten Tage der Reichskanzlei*, 76–77, who calls the demolition order "the most inhuman of all his [Hitler's] orders" ("der unmenschlichste aller seiner Befehle"). See also the excerpted text in Hans Dollinger, ed., *Die letzten hundert Tage: Das Ende des Zweiten Weltkrieges in Europea und Asien* (München: Verlag Kurt Desch, 1965), 233, a marvelous collection of photographs and period documents. For the English translation, see Hans Dollinger, ed., *The Decline and Fall of Nazi Germany and Imperial Japan: A Pictorial History of the Final Days of World War II* (New York: Bonanza Books, 1965).

37. This phrase is usually attributed to Soviet journalist Ilya Ehrenburg, but sourcing it has not been easy. The oft-quoted passage is "Tötet, tötet! Es gibt nichts, was an den Deutschen unschuldig ist, an den Lebenden nicht und nicht an den Ungeborenen! Folgt der Weisung des Genossen Stalin und zerstampft für immer das Faschistische Tier in seiner Höhle. Brecht mit Gewalt den Rassenhochmut der germanischen Frauen. Nehmt sie als rechtmässige Beute. Tötet, ihr tapferen, vorwärtsstürmenden Rotarmisten!" (Kill! Kill! In the German race there is nothing but evil; not one among the living, not one among the yet unborn but is evil! Follow the precepts of Comrade Stalin. Stamp out the fascist beast once and for all in its lair! Use force and break the racial pride of these German women. Take them as your lawful booty. Kill! As you storm onward, kill, you gallant soldiers of the Red Army.) But the primary source for almost all non–Russian language scholarship is the memoir of Nazi naval chief (and Hitler's successor) Karl Dönitz, *Zehn Jahre und zwanzig Tage: Erinnerungen 1935–1945* (Bonn: Bernard & Graefe Verlag, 1997), 424, translated into English as *Memoirs: Ten Years and Twenty Days* (Annapolis, MD: Naval Institute Press, 2012), 431. Ryan, *The Last Battle*, 27–28, and Buttar, *Battleground Prussia*, 21–22, both discuss Ehrenburg, in books written over forty years apart, but both are actually discussing Dönitz's version of Ehrenburg. Catherine Merridale, *Ivan's War: Life and Death in the Red Army, 1939–1945* (New York: Picador, 2006), 301–302, usually taken as authoritative, provides a few hair-raising quotes from Ehrenburg (though without the encouragement to rape German women and without the specific quote of the "fascist beast"). Even here, however, Merridale's source is Duffy, *Red Storm on the Reich*, 274 (which gives only the quote "Soldiers of the Red Army! Kill the Germans! Kill all Germans! Kill! Kill! Kill!"), and which, in turn, is unsourced but almost certainly based on Dönitz.

38. The mass rape of German women in the wake of the Soviet victory receives a generally nuanced discussion in Beevor, *Fall of Berlin*, 326–237 and 409–471, along with startling admonitions not to privilege the "victim's perspective" (326). See also Antony Beevor, "They Raped Every German Female from Eight to 80," *The Guardian* (May 2002), theguardian.com/books/2002/may/01/news.features11.

39. For the way in which rape became "a fitting symbol for Russia's foreign policy" in the postwar era, see Michael C. C. Adams, *The Best War Ever: America and World War II* (Baltimore: Johns Hopkins University Press, 2015), 111.

40. The single extant monograph on 12th Army is Franz Kurowski, *Armee*

Wenck: die 12. Armee zwischen Elbe und Oder 1945 (Neckargemünd: Kurt Vowinckel Verlag, 1967), but like all of Kurowski's popular histories, this one should generate caution in the scholarly historian. The essential narrative and the direct quotes are safe enough. Modern scholarship has eviscerated the bipolar metanarrative of a noble Wehrmacht and an insane Nazi political leadership, however, and, indeed, Kurowski is probably most problematic in what the author has decided to omit.

41. For Armeegruppe Steiner and its role in the Battle of Berlin, see Felix Steiner, *Die Armee der Geächteten* (New York: Ishi Press, 2011), 214–229, with Steiner's reasonable verdict on his hastily assembled command: "Zu einem Angriff auf Berlin waren sie völlig unzulänglich" (228).

42. "Die 9. Armee hatte damit aufgehört zu bestehen." Busse, "Die letzte Schlacht der 9. Armee," 168.

43. "Undurchführbar und sinnlos." Steiner, *Die Armee der Geächteten*, 228.

44. "Sagen Sie, gnädige Frau, waren die Russen schon bei Ihnen?" Boldt, *Die letzten Tage der Reichskanzlei*, 71.

45. "Die Truppe kämpft allerorts heldenmütig, jedoch der ungleiche Kampf neigt sich dem Ende entgegen." For Rommel's letter to Hitler in its entirety, see Percy Ernst Schramm, ed., *Kriegstagebuch des Oberkommandos der Wehrmacht (Wehrmachtführungsstab)*, volume 4, *1. Januar 1944—22. Mai 1945*, zweiter Halbband (Frankfurt: Bernard & Graege Verlag, 1961), 1572–1573.

46. Indeed, the Germans do it often. See, for example, the cover of *Der Spiegel*, no. 13 (2015): an image of Angela Merkel superimposed onto a group of Nazi officers, with the title, "The German Übermacht: Wie Europäer auf die Deutschen blicken."

47. *Military Review*, published by the US Army Command and General Staff College at Fort Leavenworth, Kansas, was the epicenter of this phenomenon. For a mere sampling, see the articles by Roger A. Beaumont, "On the Wehrmacht Mystique," *Military Review* 66, no. 7 (July 1986): 44–56; Antulio Echevarria II, "*Auftragstaktik:* In Its Proper Perspective," *Military Review* 66, no. 10 (October 1986): 50–56; Daniel J. Hughes, "Abuses of German Military History," *Military Review* 66, no. 12 (December 1986): 66–76; and Martin van Creveld, "On Learning from the Wehrmacht and Other Things," *Military Review* 68, no. 1 (January 1988): 62–71.

48. "Franz Kurowski" has employed a number of pseudonyms over the years, including Karl Alman, *Panzer vor: Die dramatische Geschichte der deutschen Panzerwaffe und ihre tapferen Soldaten* (Bochum: Heinrich Pöppinghaus Verlag, 1974), as well as Heinrich H. Bernig, Karl Kollatz, Rüdiger Greif, Franz K. Kaufmann, and others. "Erich Kern" is actually *SS-Sturmbannführer* Erich Johann Kernmayr, "Jürgen Thorwald" is Heinz Bongartz, former journalist and Luftwaffe publicist, and "Paul Carell" is, of course, the former *SS-Obersturmbannführer* Paul Karl Schmidt. To sample the oeuvre of the unrepentant Nazi Erich Kern, see *Der Grosse Rausch: Russlandfeldzug 1941–1945* (Göttingen: Plesse-Verlag, 1961), a title that we may translate reasonably into modern English as "The Big Rush."

49. The original name of the exhibition, which ran from 1995 to 2000, was *Vernichtungskrieg: Verbrechen der Wehrmacht 1941 bis 1944*. Complaints from scholars

(especially Bogdan Musial and Krisztián Ungváry) about inaccuracies in photos' captioning and attribution led the Hamburg Institute for Social Research, the exhibition's sponsor, to suspend the display. Indeed, some of the dead in the photos appear to have been victims not of the Wehrmacht but of the Soviet security force, the NKVD. After an internal review, which admitted to a small number of errors and agreed to minor changes but defended the basic point of view (i.e., that the Wehrmacht had carried out a criminal war against civilians, partisans, and Jews in the east), the exhibition reopened under the title *Verbrechen der Wehrmacht: Dimensionen des Vernichtungskrieges 1941–1944* in 2001. For accompanying texts, see Hannes Heer, ed., *Vernichtungskrieg: Verbrechen der Wehrmacht 1941 bis 1944* (Hamburg: Hamburger Edition, 1995), and the exhibition catalog, Hamburger Institut für Sozialforschung, ed., *Verbrechen der Wehrmacht: Dimensionen des Vernichtungskrieges 1941–1944* (Hamburg: Hamburger Institut für Sozialforschung, 2002). The controversy became a part of the never-ending German culture wars and generated a blizzard of articles in the German press. See, for example, Klaus Wiegrefe, "Wir nehmen Vorwürfe ernst," *Der Spiegel* 43 (1999), 112–113; Klaus Wiegrefe, "Alles, alles, alles überprüfen," *Der Spiegel* 45 (1999), 107–109; and Klaus Wiegrefe, "Lansder vor Leichenbergen," *Der Spiegel* 46 (2000), 102–105. Günter Grass's 2006 admission that he had joined the Waffen-SS late in the war shared many of the same touch points of past crimes and modern memory. See "Ich war Mitglied der Waffen-SS," *Frankfurter Allgemeine Zeitung* (August 11, 2006). It was, truly, an amazing moment: Grass was a prickly, irascible personality, and he had spent a career accusing others of hiding their Nazi pasts and, indeed, accusing the entire German nation of doing so. See also Henryk M. Broder, "Günter Grass: der Herr der Binse," *Der Spiegel Online* (August 14, 2006), spiegel.de/ kultur/gesellschaft/guenter-grassist -der-herr-der-binse-a-431695.html. See also the interview by Daniel Haas with leftist historian Hannes Heer (the scholar who assembled the original version of the *Wehrmachtausstellung*), in which Heer asks an equally amazing question: "Wie hat Grass damals zum Holocaust gestanden?" Grass would have been seventeen at the end of the war. *Spiegel Online* (August 15, 2006), spiegel.de/kultur/literatur/ss -bekenntnis-wie-hat-grass-damals-zum-holocaust-gestanden-a-431646.html. One certain prediction: the German culture wars will continue.

50. Certainly, recent scholarship has cast a more critical eye on the Wehrmacht's fighting qualities. Geoffrey P. Megargee, *Inside Hitler's High Command* (Lawrence: University Press of Kansas, 2000), offers chapter and verse on the command and planning muddle within the German High Command, the strategic idiocy of the OKH/OKW split, the inattention to supply and logistics, and the relative paucity of assets devoted to intelligence and counterintelligence. David Stahel has mined the primary sources to demonstrate the slipshod nature of planning for Barbarossa, the casual, almost haphazard approach that officers of the Wehrmacht took to executing the greatest military campaign of all time, and the serious problems in the field that resulted within weeks of the opening of the campaign. See David Stahel: *Operation Barbarossa and Germany's Defeat in the East* (Cambridge: Cambridge University Press, 2009), *Kiev 1941: Hitler's Battle for Supremacy in the East* (Cambridge: Cambridge University Press, 2009), and *Opera-*

tion Typhoon: Hitler's March on Moscow, October 1941 (Cambridge: Cambridge University Press, 2013). Jörg Muth, *Command Culture: Officer Education in the US Army and the German Armed Forces, 1901–1940, and the Consequences for World War II* (Denton: University of North Texas Press, 2011), is not only a feisty comparison of US and German officer training programs but also takes serious issue with Western worship of the German General Staff. German operational plans in World War II were clumsy, predictable, and inflexible, he argues, and only the army's war-fighting virtues—flexible command and the aggression of the men in the field—rescued them. Finally, young scholar Gregory Liedtke is the first to challenge the Wehrmacht's claim of being swamped by superior numbers. Meticulously researching the primary documents, Liedtke paints an often surprising portrait of an army far better able to replace its combat losses than it admitted. See Gregory Liedtke, *Enduring the Whirlwind: The German Army and the Russo-German War, 1941–1943* (Solihull, UK: Helion, 2016), as well as his earlier, seminal article, "Furor Teutonicus: German Offensives and Counter-Attacks on the Eastern Front, August 1943 to March 1945," *Journal of Slavic Military Studies* 21 (2008): 563–587.

51. For a spirited demolition of the Guderian mythos, see Russell A. Hart, *Guderian, Panzer Pioneer or Myth Maker* (Washington, DC: Potomac, 2006). Hart mentions the final big payoff on page 113. See also Gerd R. Ueberschaer and Winfried Vogel, *Dienen und Verdienen: Hitler's Geschenke und Seine Eliten* (Frankfurt am Main: Fischer Verlag, 1999).

52. On Schörner generally, see the two apologetic biographies: Roland Kaltenegger, *Schörner: Feldmarschall der letzten Stunde* (München: Herbig, 1994), and Erich Kern, *Generalfeldmarschall Schörner: ein deutsches Soldatenschicksal* (Rosenheim: Deutsche Verlagsgesellschaft, 1993). A large body of articles appeared in the German press at the time of Schörner's return from Soviet captivity. See "Schörner: der laute Kamerad," in *Der Spiegel* (9 February 1955), which formed the contemporary consensus. See also "Ein General spielt falsch: zum 'Fall Schörner' zu Protokoll gegeben," *Die Gegenwart* 10, no. 6 (1955): 175–178; "Wer half Schörner?" *Der Spiegel* (October 16, 1957), 22–24; and the counterargument found in "Gerechtigkeit für Schörner!" *Nation Europa* no. 4 (1955): 48–51.

53. "Wieviel Leute haben Sie schon aufgehängt?" Quoted in "Schörner: der laute Kamerad," 15–16.

54. "Das wirkt natürlich auf die anderen Deserteure oder solche, die es werden wollen, sehr abschreckend." Josef Goebbels, *Tagebücher 1945: die letzten Aufzeichnungen* (Bergisch Gladbach: Bastei Lubbe, 1977), 169–170.

55. "Ohne Befehl herumziehende Soldaten werden erschossen." Quoted in "Schörner: der laute Kamerad," 17.

56. For Schörner's last order of the day, see Goebbels, *Tagebücher 1945*, 542–543.

57. "Jedenfalls weisst der Soldat im Kampfraum Schörners, dass er vorne sterben kann und hinten sterben muss." Goebbels's formulation, in ibid., 201.

58. Jürgen Thorwald, *Das Ende an der Elbe* (Stuttgart: Steingrüben Verlag, 1953), 252–258, is still the dominant narrative for Schörner's attempted flight to freedom.

59. Helmut Lindemann, "Die Schulde der Generale," *Deutsche Rundschau* (January 1949), 24.

60. "Vergessen scheint auf einmal zu sein, dass dieser Schörner nicht die einzige war, der am sinnlosen Tod deutscher Soldaten schuld ist." The words of theologian Helmut Gollwitzer, quoted in Bert-Oliver Manig, "Der Bluthund ist zurück," *Die Zeit* (September 8, 2005), 4. Gollwitzer was affiliated with the Confessing Church (*Bekennende Kirche*), which opposed the Nazi regime's attempts to coordinate the Protestant churches. He would eventually succeed Martin Niemöller as pastor of the congregation at Berlin-Dahlem. For Gollwitzer's wartime experience, including his long years in Soviet captivity, see Helmut Gollwitzer, *Und führen wohin du nicht willst: Bericht einer Gefangenschaft* (München: Chr. Kaiser Verlag, 1953). The book title is a scriptural reference: "Amen, amen, I say to you, when you were younger, you used to dress yourself and go where you wanted; but when you grow old, you will stretch out your hands, and someone else will dress you and lead you where you do not want to go" (*The New American Bible*, John 21:18).

Bibliography

"Ausbruch der 1. Panzer-Armee aus der Kessel im Raum Kamenez-Podolsk im Frühjahr 1944." Einzelbearbeitung Nr. 1. In Oldwig von Natzmer et al. "Das Zurückkämpfen eingekesselter Verbände zur eigenen Front." Manuscript T-12. US Army Heritage and Education Center (USAHEC) Foreign Military Studies series. Carlisle, PA.

"Bataille de la Baltique/Pommernfront 1945: 28. Pa. Gren. Div. SS 'Wallonien.'" No manuscript number. US Army Heritage and Education Center (USAHEC) Foreign Military Studies series. Carlisle, PA.

"Die Kesselschlacht von Tscherkassy, Dez. 43–Jan. 44." Einzelbearbeitung Nr. 3. In Oldwig von Natzmer et al. "Das Zurückkämpfen eingekesselter Verbände zur eigenen Front." Manuscript T-12. US Army Heritage and Education Center (USAHEC) Foreign Military Studies series. Carlisle, PA.

"Ein General spielt falsch: zum 'Fall Schörner' zu Protokoll gegeben." *Die Gegenwart* 10, no. 6 (1955).

"Gerechtigkeit für Schörner!" *Nation Europa* no. 4 (1955).

"Ich war Mitglied der Waffen-SS." *Frankfurter Allgemeine Zeitung* (August 11, 2006).

"Im Kessel." *Allgemeine Schweizerische Militärzeitschrift* 115, nos. 4–6 (1949).

"Kämpfe des XI. und XXXXII. A.K. Entsatzoperation und Ausbruch." Einzelbearbeitung Nr. 2. In Oldwig von Natzmer et al. "Das Zurückkämpfen eingekesselter Verbände zur eigenen Front." Manuscript T-12. US Army Heritage and Education Center (USAHEC) Foreign Military Studies series. Carlisle, PA.

Œuvres de Frédéric le Grand—Werke Friedrichs des Großen. Online. Trier: Digitale Ausgabe der Universitätsbibliothek Trier, 2016. Address friedrich.uni-trier.de.

"Operation Anvil/Dragoon." *CSI Battlebook.* Fort Leavenworth, KS: Combat Studies Institute, 1984.

"Schörner: der laute Kamerad." *Der Spiegel* (9 February 1955).

"So war das Schicksal dazwischengetreten: die Legenden und Verdrängungen des Generals Hans Speidel." *Der Spiegel*, no. 5 (1978).

"The German Übermacht: Wie Europäer auf die Deutschen blicken." *Der Spiegel*, no. 13 (2015).

"Wer half Schörner?" *Der Spiegel* (October 1957).

5th SS Panzer Division *Wiking.* "Die Flut verschlang sich selbst, nichts un!" Hannover: Truppenkameradschaft "Wiking," n.d.

Adair, Paul. *Hitler's Greatest Defeat: The Collapse of Army Group Center*. London: Brockhampton, 1994.

Adams, John A. *General Jacob Devers: World War II's Forgotten Four Star*. Bloomington: Indiana University Press, 2015.

Adams, Michael C. C. *The Best War Ever: America and World War II*. Baltimore: Johns Hopkins University Press, 2015.

Agarossi, Elena. *A Nation Collapses: The Italian Surrender of September 1943*. Cambridge: Cambridge University Press, 2006.

Agte, Patrick. *Michael Wittmann and the Waffen SS Tiger Commanders of the Leibstandarte in World War II*. 2 Volumes. Mechanicsburg, PA: Stackpole, 2006.

Ahlfen, Hans von. "Der Kampf der Festung Breslau." *Wehrwissenschaftliche Rundschau 1, Sonderdruck* (1956).

———. *Der Kampf um Schlesien, 1944/1945*. Stuttgart: Motorbuch Verlag, 1963.

———. "Rückzug von der Weichsel zur Oder in Januar 1945 infolge des russischen Durchbruchs aus der Baranov und Pulawy-Brückenkopf." Manuscript D-368. US Army Heritage and Education Center (USAHEC) Foreign Military Studies series. Carlisle, PA.

Alman, Karl. *Panzer vor: Die dramatische Geschichte der deutschen Panzerwaffe und ihre tapferen Soldaten*. Bochum: Heinrich Pöppinghaus Verlag, 1974.

Ambrose, Stephen E. *Band of Brothers: E Company, 506th Regiment, 101st Airborne; From Normandy to Hitler's Eagle's Nest*. New York: Simon & Schuster, 1992.

———. *Citizen Soldiers: The U.S. Army from the Normandy Beaches to the Bulge to the Surrender of Germany, June 7, 1944–May 7, 1945*. New York: Simon & Schuster, 1997.

———. *D-Day: June 6, 1944: The Climactic Battle of World War II*. New York: Simon & Schuster, 1994.

———. *Pegasus Bridge: D-Day: The Daring British Airborne Raid*. London: Pocket Books, 2003.

Anzio Beachhead, 22 January–25 May 1944. Washington, DC: Center of Military History, 1990.

Armstrong, Richard N. *Red Army Tank Commanders: The Armored Guards*. Atglen, PA: Schiffer, 1994.

Ascoli, David. *A Day of Battle: Mars-la-Tour, 16 August 1870*. London: Harrap, 1987.

Asprey, Robert. *Frederick the Great: The Magnificent Enigma*. New York: History Book Club, 1986.

Atkin, Ronald. *Dieppe 1942: The Jubilee Disaster*. London: Book Club Associates, 1980.

Atkinson, Rick. *An Army at Dawn: The War in North Africa, 1942–1943*. New York: Henry Holt, 2002.

———. *The Day of Battle: The War in Sicily and Italy, 1943–1944*. New York: Henry Holt, 2007.

———. *The Guns at Last Light: The War in Western Europe, 1944–1945*. New York: Henry Holt, 2013.

Axworthy, Mark. *Third Axis, Fourth Ally: Romanian Armed Forces in the European War, 1941–1945*. London: Arms and Armour, 1995.

Bagdonas, Raymond. *The Devil's General: The Life of Hyazinth von Strachwitz, "The Panzer Graf."* Havertown, PA: Casemate, 2013.

Baker, Lee. "Explaining Defeat: A Reappraisal of 'Operation Bagration,' 1944." *Journal of Slavic Military Studies* 21 (2008).

Balck, Hermann. *Order in Chaos: The Memoirs of General of Panzer Troops Hermann Balck.* Lexington: University Press of Kentucky Press, 2015.

———. *Ordnung im Chaos: Erinnerungen 1893–1948.* Osnabrück: Biblio Verlag, 1981.

Balkoski, Joseph. *Omaha Beach: D-Day, June 6, 1944.* Mechanicsburg, PA: Stackpole, 2004.

Barbier, Mary Kathryn. *D-Day Deception: Operation Fortitude and the Normandy Invasion.* Westport, CT: Praeger Security, 2007.

Barnett, Correlli, ed. *Hitler's Generals.* New York: Quill, 1989.

Barry, Steven Thomas. *Battalion Commanders at War: US Army Tactical Leadership in the Mediterranean Theater, 1942–1943.* Lawrence: University Press of Kansas, 2013.

Barsewisch, Ernst Friedrich Rudolf von. "The Battle of Hochkirch." In Peter Paret, ed. *Frederick the Great: A Profile.* New York: Hill and Wang, 1972.

Bartov, Omer. *The Eastern Front, 1941–45: German Troops and the Barbarisation of Warfare.* New York: St. Martin's Press, 1986.

———. *Hitler's Army: Soldiers, Nazis, and War in the Third Reich.* New York: Oxford University Press, 1991.

Bayerlein, Fritz. "A Crack German Panzer Division and What Allied Air Power Did to It between D-Day and V-Day." Military Intelligence Service, 9th Air Force (May 29, 1945). Library of Congress. Washington, DC.

———. "An Interview with Genlt Fritz Bayerlein: Critique of Normandy Breakthrough Pz Lehr Div from St Lo to the Ruhr." Manuscript ETHINT 67. US Army Heritage and Education Center (USAHEC) Foreign Military Studies series. Carlisle, PA.

———. "An Interview with Genlt Fritz Bayerlein: Pz Lehr Division (Jan–28 July 1944)." Manuscript ETHINT 66 (7–9 August 1945). US Army Heritage and Education Center (USAHEC) Foreign Military Studies series. Carlisle, PA.

Beaumont, Roger A. "On the Wehrmacht Mystique." *Military Review* 66, no. 7 (1986).

Beck-Broichsitter, Helmut. "Über die Beharrlichkeit im Angriff." *Militärwissenschaftliche Rundschau* 9, no. 1 (1944).

Beevor, Antony. *Ardennes 1944: Hitler's Last Gamble.* New York: Viking, 2015.

———. *D-Day: The Battle for Normandy.* NY: Penguin Books, 2010.

———. *The Fall of Berlin 1945.* New York: Penguin, 2002.

———. "They Raped Every German Female from Eight to 80." *The Guardian.* theguardian.com/books/2002/may/01/news.features11.

Below, Nicolaus von. *At Hitler's Side: The Memoirs of Hitler's Luftwaffe Adjutant, 1937–1945.* London: Greenhill, 2001.

Benz, Wigbert. *Paul Carell: Ribbentrops Pressechef Paul Karl Schmidt vor und nach 1945.* Berlin: WVB, 2005.

Bergström, Christer. *The Ardennes, 1944–1945: Hitler's Winter Offensive.* Havertown, PA: Casemate, 2014.

Besterbreurtje, A. D. "Die Luftlandeoperationen in den Niederlanden im Herbst 1944." 2 Parts. *Allgemeine schweizerische Militärzeitung* 92, no. 6 and no. 7 (1946).

Biddiscombe, Perry. "Into the Maelstrom: German Women in Combat, 1944–45." *War & Society* 30, no. 1 (2011).

Bigge, W. "Ueber Selbstthätigkeit der Unterführer im Kriege." *Beihefte zum Militär-Wochenblatt.* Berlin: E. S. Mittler, 1894.

Bircher, Eugen. "Die militärgeographischen Grundlagen der deutschen Gegenoffensive in der Eifel und in den belgisch-französischen Ardennen: Dezember 1944/Januar 1945." *Allgemeine schweizerische Militärzeitung* 91–111, no. 2 (1945).

———. "Die militärische Bedeutung des Rheins in seiner militär/geographischen Beziehungen im Laufe der Geschichte." *Allgemeine schweizerische Militärzeitung* 91, 4 parts, nos. 5, 9, 10, 11 (1945).

Bird, Keith. *Erich Raeder: Admiral of the Third Reich.* Annapolis, MD: Naval Institute Press, 2006.

Blaskowitz, Johannes. "Fragebogen an Generaloberst Blaskowitz." Manuscript A-916. US Army Heritage and Education Center (USAHEC) Foreign Military Studies series. Carlisle, PA.

———. "German Reaction to the Invasion of Southern France: Questions for Generaloberst Johannes Blaskowitz." Manuscript A-868. US Army Heritage and Education Center (USAHEC) Foreign Military Studies series. Carlisle, PA.

———. "Kampf der Armeegruppe 'G' in Südfrankreich bis Mitte September 1944." Manuscript B-800.

Blume, Wilhelm Hermann von. "Selbstthätigkeit der Führer im Kriege." *Beihefte zum Miltär-Wochenblatt.* Berlin: E. S. Mittler, 1896.

Blumenson, Martin. *Anzio: The Gamble That Failed.* Philadelphia: Lippincott, 1963.

———. *Breakout and Pursuit.* Washington, DC: Center of Military History, 1961.

———. *Mark Clark.* London: Jonathan Cape, 1985.

———. *Salerno to Cassino.* Washington, DC: Center of Military History, 1969.

Blumentritt, Günther. "Drei Marschälle, Volkscharakter, und der 20. Juli." Manuscript B-344. US Army Heritage and Education Center (USAHEC) Foreign Military Studies series. Carlisle, PA.

———. "Three Marshals, National Character, and the 20 July Complex." Manuscript B-344. US Army Heritage and Education Center (USAHEC) Foreign Military Studies series. Carlisle, PA.

Böhmler, Rudolf. *Monte Cassino.* Darmstadt: E. S. Mittler & Sohn, 1956.

———. *Monte Cassino.* London: Cassell, 1956.

Boldt, Gerhard. *Die letzten Tage der Reichskanzlei.* Hamburg: Rowohlt Verlag, 1947.

———. *Hitler: die letzten zehn Tage in der Reichskanzlei: der authentische Bericht.* München: Wilhelm Heyne Verlag, 1976.

Bonn, Keith. *When the Odds Were Even: The Vosges Mountains Campaign, October 1944–January 1945.* New York: Ballantine, 1994.

Bor, Peter. *Gespräche mit Halder.* Wiesbaden: Limes-Verlag, 1950.

Botsch, Walter. "Stellungnahme zur Geschichte der 7. amerikanischen Armee (von derdeutschen 19. Armee aus gesehen)." Manuscript B-518. US Army

Heritage and Education Center (USAHEC) Foreign Military Studies series. Carlisle, PA.

———. "Südfrankreich: 19. Armee." Manuscript B-515. US Army Heritage and Education Center (USAHEC) Foreign Military Studies series. Carlisle, PA.

Bourque, Stephen A. "Operational Fires Lisieux and Saint-Lô: The Destruction of Two Norman Towns on D-Day." *Canadian Military History* 19, no. 2 (2010).

Bradley, Omar N. *A Soldier's Story*. New York: Holt, 1951.

Brandenberger, Erich, and Rudolf-Christoph Freiherr von Gersdorff. "Die Ardennen-Offensive im Abschnitt der deutschen 7. Armee (16. Dezember 1944–25. Januar 1945)." Manuscript A-876. US Army Heritage and Education Center (USAHEC) Foreign Military Studies series. Carlisle, PA.

Bremen, W. von. *Friedrich der Grosse*. Berlin: B. Behr, 1905.

Breuer, William B. *Death of a Nazi Army: The Falaise Pocket*. New York: Scarborough House, 1985.

———. *Hitler's Fortress Cherbourg: The Conquest of a Bastion*. New York: Stein and Day, 1984.

Broder, Henryk M. "Günter Grass: der Herr der Binse." *Der Spiegel Online* (August 14, 2006). spiegel.de/kultur/gesellschaft/guenter-grass-der-herr-der-binse-a-431 695.html.

Broicher, Andreas. "Die Wehrmacht in ausländischen Urteilen." In Hans Poeppel, Wilhelm-Karl Prinz von Preussen, and Karl-Günther von Hase, eds. *Die Soldaten der Wehrmacht*. München: Herbig, 1998.

Brokaw, Tom. *The Greatest Generation*. New York: Random House, 1998.

Brooks, Thomas R. *The War North of Rome, June 1944–May 1945*. Edison, NJ: Castle Books, 2001.

Broszat, Martin. *Der Staat Hitlers: Grundlegung und Entwicklung seiner inneren Verfassung*. München: Deutscher Taschenbuch-Verlag, 1969.

Buchheit, Gert. *Hitler der Feldherr: die Zerstorung einer Legende*. Rastatt: Grote, 1958.

Buchner, Alex. *Ostfront 1944: The German Defensive Battles on the Russian Front 1944*. Atglen, PA: Schiffer, 1995.

———. *Ostfront 1944: Tscherkassy, Tarnopol, Krim, Witebsk, Bobruisk, Brody, Jassy, Kischinew*. Eggolsheim: Podzun-Pallas Verlag, 1988.

Bucholz, Arden. *Moltke and the German Wars, 1864–1871*. New York: Palgrave, 2001.

Büchs, Herbert. "Stärke und Dislozierung der deutschen Luftwaffe in Südfrankreich." Manuscript A-869. US Army Heritage and Education Center (USAHEC) Foreign Military Studies series. Carlisle, PA.

Buckingham, William F. *Arnhem 1944*. Stroud: Tempus, 2004.

Buckley, Christopher. *The Road to Rome*. London: Hodder and Stoughton, 1945.

Bullock, Alan. *Hitler: A Study in Tyranny*. New York: Konecky & Konecky, 1962.

Busse, Theodor. "Die letzte Schlacht der 9. Armee." *Wehrwissenschaftliche Rundschau* 5, no. 4 (1955).

Bussmann, Walter. "Kursk—Orel—Dnjepr: Erlebnisse und Erfahrungen im Stab des XXXXVI Panzerkorps während des 'Unternehmens Zitadelle.'" *Vierteljahrshefte für Zeitgeschichte* 41, no. 4 (1993).

Buttar, Prit. *Battleground Prussia: The Assault on Germany's Eastern Front, 1944–45.* Oxford: Osprey, 2010.

Buttlar Brandenfels, Freiherr Treusch von. "Stellungnahme zu dem Bericht des Generalleutnant z. V. Bodo Zimmermann (MS #B-308) über die Operationen des OB. West von den Vorbereitungen gegen die Invasion bus zum Rückzug auf den Westwall." Manuscript B-672. US Army Heritage and Education Center (USAHEC) Foreign Military Studies series. Carlisle, PA.

Caddick-Adams, Peter. *Snow and Steel: The Battle of the Bulge, 1944–45.* Oxford: Oxford University Press, 2015.

Campbell, J. P. *Dieppe Revisited: A Documentary Investigation.* London: Cass, 1993.

Carafano, James Jay. *After D-Day: Operation Cobra and the Normandy Breakout.* Boulder, CO: Lynne Rienner, 2000.

———. *GI Ingenuity: Improvisation, Technology, and Winning World War II.* Westport, CT: Praeger Security International, 2006.

Carell, Paul. *Invasion—They're Coming! The German Account of the Allied Landings and the 80 Days' Battle for France.* New York: E. P. Dutton, 1963.

———. *Sie Kommen! Der Deutsche Bericht über die Invasion und die 80tägige Schlacht um Frankreich.* Oldenburg: Gerhard Stalling Verlag, 1960.

Carlyle, Thomas. *History of Frederick the Great.* Chicago: University of Chicago Press, 1969.

———. *History of Friedrich the Second, Called Frederick the Great.* Albany, NY: J. B. Lyon, 1900.

Carsten, F. L. *The Reichswehr and Politics, 1918 to 1933.* Berkeley: University of California Press, 1966.

Carver, Michael, ed. *The Warlords.* Barnsley: Pen & Sword, 2005.

Caspar, Gustav-Adolf. "Ethische, politische und militärische Grundlagen der Wehrmacht." In Hans Poeppel, Wilhelm-Karl Prinz von Preussen, and Karl-Günther von Hase, eds. *Die Soldaten der Wehrmacht.* München: Herbig, 1998.

Chandler, David G. *The Campaigns of Napoleon.* New York: Macmillan, 1966.

Choltitz, Dietrich. *Brennt Paris? Adolf Hitler: Taschenbericht des letzten deutschen Befehlshabers in Paris.* Frankfurt: R. G. Fischer Verlag, 2014.

Christ, Torsten. "Die Luftlage im Frühjahr 1944." In "Der Feldzug in Italien." Manuscript T-1a. US Army Heritage and Education Center (USAHEC) Foreign Military Studies series. Carlisle, PA.

Christoforow, Wassili S., Wladimir G. Makarow, and Matthias Uhl, eds. *Verhört: Die Befragungen deutscher Generale und Offiziere durch die sowjetischen Geheimdienste 1945–1952.* Oldenbourg: De Gruyter, 2015.

Chuikov, V. I. *The End of the Third Reich.* Moscow: Progress Publishers, 1978.

Cirillo, Roger. *Ardennes-Alsace, 16 December 1944–25 January 1945.* Washington, DC: Center of Military History, n.d.

Citino, Robert M. *Armored Forces: History and Sourcebook.* Westport, CT: Greenwood Press, 1994.

———. *Death of the Wehrmacht: The German Campaigns of 1942.* Lawrence: University Press of Kansas, 2007.

————. *The Evolution of Blitzkrieg Tactics: German Defends Itself Against Poland, 1919–1933*. Westport, CT: Greenwood Press, 1987.

————. "First Blood on the Ghost Front: How the Bulge Began." *World War II* 29, no. 4 (2014).

————. *The German Way of War: From the Thirty Years' War to the Third Reich.* Lawrence: University Press of Kansas, 2005.

————. "Lessons from the Hexagon: Wargames and the Military Historian." In Pat Harrigan and Matthew G. Kirschenbaum, eds. *Zones of Control: Perspectives on Wargaming.* Cambridge, MA: MIT Press, 2016.

————. *The Wehrmacht Retreats: Fighting a Lost War, 1943.* Lawrence: University Press of Kansas, 2012.

Claasen, Adam R. A. *Hitler's Northern War: The Luftwaffe's Ill-Fated Campaign, 1940–1945.* Lawrence: University Press of Kansas, 2001.

Clark, Mark W. *Calculated Risk.* New York: Enigma, 2007.

Clarke, Jeffrey J. *Southern France.* Washington, DC: Center of Military History, n.d.

Clarke, Jeffrey J., and Robert Ross Smith. *Riviera to the Rhine.* Washington, DC: Center of Military History, 1993.

Clausewitz, Carl von. "Clausewitz über Beharrlichkeit im Kriege." *Militärwissenschaftliche Rundschau* 9, no. 1 (1944).

————. *On War.* Edited and translated by Michael Howard and Peter Paret. Princeton, NJ: Princeton University Press, 1976.

————. *Vom Kriege: Ungekürzter Text.* München: Cormoran, 2000.

Cole, Hugh M. *The Ardennes: Battle of the Bulge.* Washington, DC: Center of Military History, 1965.

Coles, Harry L., and Albert K. Weinberg. *Civil Affairs: Soldiers Become Governors.* Washington, DC: Center of Military History, 1992.

Colley, David P. *Decision at Strasbourg: Ike's Strategic Mistake to Halt the Sixth Army Group at the Rhine in 1944.* Annapolis, MD: Naval Institute Press, 2008.

Connor, William M. "Analysis of Deep Attack Operations: Operation Bagration: Belorrussia 22 June–29 August 1944." Fort Leavenworth, KS: US Army Command and General Staff College, 1987.

Corum, James S. *Wolfram von Richtofen: Master of the German Air War.* Lawrence: University Press of Kansas, 2008.

Craig, Gordon. *The Battle of Königgrätz: Prussia's Victory over Austria, 1866.* Philadelphia: Lippincott, 1964.

Creveld, Martin van. *Fighting Power: German and U.S. Army Performance, 1939–1945.* Westport, CT: Praeger, 2007.

————. "On Learning from the Wehrmacht and Other Things." *Military Review* 68, no. 1 (1988).

Dallas, Gregory. *1945: The War That Never Ended.* New Haven, CT: Yale University Press, 2005.

Das Deutsche Reich und der Zweite Weltkrieg. Volume 6. *Die Ausweitung zum Weltkrieg und der Wechsel der Initiative, 1941–1943.* Stuttgart: Deutsche Verlags-Anstalt, 1990.

Das Deutsche Reich und der Zweite Weltkrieg. Volume 7. *Das Deutsche Reich in der Defensive: Strategischer Luftkrieg in Europa, Krieg im Westen und in Ostasien 1943–1944/45.* München: Deutsche Verlags-Anstalt, 2001.

Das Deutsche Reich und der Zweite Weltkrieg. Volume 8. *Die Ostfront 1943/44: Der Krieg im Osten und an den Nebenfronten.* München: Deutsche Verlags-Anstalt, 2011.

Das Deutsche Reich und der Zweite Weltkrieg. Volume 10/1. *Der Zusammenbruch des deutschen Reiches 1945: die Militärische Niederwerfung der Wehrmacht.* München: Deutsche Verlags-Anstalt, 2008.

Das Deutsche Reich und der Zweite Weltkrieg. Volume 8. *Die Ostfront 1943/44.* München: Deutsche Verlags-Anstalt, 2007.

Davies, Norman. *Rising '44: The Battle for Warsaw.* New York: Viking, 2003.

Degrelle, Léon. *Campaign in Russia: The Waffen SS on the Eastern Front.* Newport Beach, CA: Institute for Historical Review, 1985.

———. *La Campagne de Russie, 1941–1945.* Paris: La Diffusion du Livre, 1949.

D'Este, Carlo. *Bitter Victory: The Battle for Sicily, 1943.* New York: Harper Perennial, 1991.

———. *Decision in Normandy.* New York: HarperPerennial, 1994.

———. *Fatal Decision: Anzio and the Battle for Rome.* New York: HarperPerennial, 1992.

———. "Model." In Correlli Barnett, ed. *Hitler's Generals.* New York: Quill, 1989.

———. *Patton: A Genius for War.* New York: HarperPerennial, 1995.

———. "Soldier's Soldier." *World War II* 30, no. 5 (2016).

———. *World War II in the Mediterranean, 1942–1945.* Chapel Hill, NC: Algonquin Books, 1990.

Deutsche Arbeitsfront. *Unbezwinglicher Westwall: Ein Volksbuch vom Ringen um Deutschlands Westmark.* Wiesbaden: Deutsche Volksbücher, 1940.

Dieckert, Kurt, and Horst Grossmann. *Der Kampf um Ostpreussen: der umfassende Dokumentarbericht über das Kriegsgeschehen in Ostpreussen.* Stuttgart: Motorbuch, 1960.

Die 62. Infanterie-Division 1938–1944, Die 62. Volks-Grenadier-Division 1944–1945. Fulda: Kamaradenhilfswerk der ehemaligen 62. Division, 1968.

Die Wehrmacht: Herausgegeben vom Oberkommando der Wehrmacht. 5 Volumes. Hamburg: Verlag für Geschichtliche Dokumentation, 1978.

Dittmar, Kurt. "Das Verhältnis OKW-OKH." Manuscript B-512. US Army Heritage and Education Center (USAHEC) Foreign Military Studies series. Carlisle, PA.

Dollinger Hans, ed. *The Decline and Fall of Nazi Germany and Imperial Japan: A Pictorial History of the Final Days of World War II.* New York: Bonanza Books, 1965.

———. *Die letzten hundert Tage: Das Ende des Zweiten Weltkrieges in Europa und Asien.* München: Verlag Kurt Desch, 1965.

Donat, Richard von. "Logistische Probleme beim Rückzug aus Südfrankreich: August/September 1944." 2 Parts. *Truppenpraxis* 7 and 8 (1963–1964).

Dönitz, Karl. *Memoirs: Ten Years and Twenty Days.* Annapolis, MD: Naval Institute Press, 2012.

———. *Zehn Jahre und zwanzig Tage: Erinnerungen 1935–1945*. Bonn: Bernard & Graefe Verlag, 1997.

Dorrian, James. *Storming St. Nazaire: The Gripping Story of the Dock-Busting Raid, March 1942*. Annapolis, MD: Naval Institute Press, 1998.

Dowling, Timothy C. *The Brusilov Offensive*. Bloomington: Indiana University Press, 2008.

Downing, Downing. *Devil's Virtuosos: German Generals at War, 1940–1945*. New York: Dorset Press, 1977.

Droysen, Johann. *Das Leben des Feldmarschalls Grafen Yorck von Wartenburg*. 2 Volumes. Leipzig: Insel-Verlag, 1913.

Duffy, Christopher. *Red Storm on the Reich: The Soviet March on Germany, 1945*. New York: Atheneum, 1991.

Duffy, James P. *Target: America—Hitler's Plan to Attack the United States*. Westport, CT: Praeger, 2004.

Dunn, Walter S. Jr. *Soviet Blitzkrieg: The Battle for White Russia, 1944*. Boulder, CO: Lynne Rienner, 2000.

Dupuy, T. N. *A Genius for War: The German Army and General Staff, 1807–1945*. Englewood Cliffs, NJ: Prentice-Hall, 1977.

Eberbach, Heinrich. "Panzergruppe Eberbach bei Alencon und beim Durchbruch aus dem Kessel von Falaise." Manuscript A-922. Foreith Military Studies. Carlisle, PA.

Echevarria, Antulio J., II. *After Clausewitz: German Military Thinkers before the Great War*. Lawrence: University Press of Kansas, 2000.

———. "*Auftragstaktik:* In Its Proper Perspective." *Military Review* 66, no. 10 (1986).

Eggert, Ernst. "Die Entwicklung der Versorgungslage im Sommer 1944 während der Mai-Offensive und der Rückzugskämpfe (bis Juli 1944 einschl.)." Chapter 4. "Sonderthemen: Die Versorgunglage." In "Der Feldzug in Italien." Manuscript T-1a. US Army Heritage and Education Center (USAHEC) Foreign Military Studies series. Carlisle, PA.

———. "Die Versorgungslage vom Beginn des Jahres 1945 bis zur Kapitulation." Chapter 6. "Sonderthemen: Die Versorgunglage." In "Der Feldzug in Italien." Manuscript T-1a. US Army Heritage and Education Center (USAHEC) Foreign Military Studies series. Carlisle, PA.

Ehlers, Robert S. *The Mediterranean Air War: Airpower and Allied Victory in World War II*. Lawrence: University Press of Kansas, 2015.

Ehlert, Hans, Michael Epkenhans, and Gerhard P. Gross, eds. *Der Schlieffenplan: Analysen und Dokumente*. München: Odenberg, 2006.

———. *The Schlieffen Plan: International Perspectives on the German Strategy for World War I*. Lexington: University Press of Kentucky, 2014.

Eisenhower, Dwight D. *Crusade in Europe*. Garden City, NY: Doubleday, 1948.

Eisenhower, John S. D. *They Fought at Anzio*. Columbia: University of Missouri Press, 2007.

Erfurth, Waldemar. "Die Zusammenwirken getrennter Heeresteile." 4 Parts. *Militärwissenschaftliche Rundschau* 4 (1939).

Erickson, John. *The Road to Berlin: Stalin's War with Germany*. New Haven, CT: Yale University Press, 1983.

———. "Soviet Strategy, 1941–1945: Surprise, Survival, Attrition, Annihilation." In Roland G. Foerster, ed. *Seelower Höhen 1945*. Hamburg: E. S. Mittler & Sohn, 1998.

Erlau, Peter. *Flucht aus der weissen Hölle: Erinnerungen an die grosse Kesselschlacht der 1. Panzerarmee Hube im Raum um Kamenez-Podolsk vom 8. März bis 9. April 1944*. Stuttgart: Kulturhistorischer Verlag Dr. Riegler, 1960.

Fähndrich, Ernst. "Die Entwicklung der Versorgungslage im Frühjahr 1944 (von Mitte März) bis zum Beginn der Allierten Offensive." Chapter 3. "Sonderthemen: Die Versorgunglage." In "Der Feldzug in Italien." Manuscript T-1a. US Army Heritage and Education Center (USAHEC) Foreign Military Studies series. Carlisle, PA.

Farago, Ladislas. *Patton: Ordeal and Triumph*. Yardley, PA: Westholme, 1964.

Feitl, Hans. "Invasionsfront Normandie." *Die Wehrmacht* 14 (1944). In *Die Wehrmacht: Herausgegeben vom Oberkommando der Wehrmacht*. 5 Volumes. Hamburg: Verlag für Geschichtliche Dokumentation, 1978.

Fey, Will. *Armor Battles of the Waffen-SS, 1943–45*. Mechanicsburg, PA: Stackpole, 2003.

Fifth Army at the Winter Line, 15 November 1943–15 January 1944. Washington, DC: Center of Military History, 1990.

Fifth Army History. Part 4. *Cassino and Anzio*. Italy: Headquarters Fifth Army, 1944.

———. Part 5. *The Drive to Rome*. Italy: Fifth Army Headquarters, 1944.

Fisher, Ernest R. *Cassino to the Alps*. Washington, DC: Center of Military History, 1993.

Foerster, Roland G., ed. *Gezeitenwechsel im Zweiten Weltkrieg? Die Schlachten von Ch'arkow und Kursk im Frühjahr und Sommer 1943 in operativer Anlage, Verlauf und politischer Bedeutung*. Berlin: E. S. Mittler, 1996.

———, ed. *Seelower Höhen 1945*. Hamburg: E. S. Mittler & Sohn, 1998.

Foerster, Wolfgang. "Prinz Friedrich Karl." *Militärwissenschaftliche Rundschau* 8, no. 2 (1943).

Foley, Robert T. *German Strategy and the Path to Verdun: Erich von Falkenhayn and the Development of Attrition, 1870–1916*. Cambridge: Cambridge University Press, 2005.

Folttmann, Josef and Hanns Möller-Witten. *Opfergang der Generale: Die Verluste der Generale and Admirale und der im gleichem Dientsrang stehenden sonstigen Offiziere und Beamten im Zweiten Weltkrieg*. Berlin: Bernard & Graefe, 1959.

Fontane, Theodor. *Der deutsche Krieg von 1866*. 2 Volumes. Berlin: R. v. Decker, 1870–71.

———. *Der Krieg gegen Frankreich, 1870–1871*. 4 Volumes. Zürich: Manesse, 1985.

Ford, Ken. *Dieppe 1942*. London: Osprey Publishing, 2010.

———. *St. Nazaire 1942: The Great Commando Raid*. London: Osprey, 2001.

Förster, Jürgen. "Ludendorff and Hitler in Perspective: The Battle for the German Soldier's Mind, 1917–1944." *War in History* 10, no. 3 (2003).

Forwick, Helmuth. "Der Rückzug der Heeresgruppe Nord nach Kurland." In Hans Meier-Welcker, ed. *Abwehrkämpfe am Nordflügel der Ostfront 1944–1945.* Stuttgart: Deutsche Verlags-Anstalt, 1963.

Frank, H. K. "Rückzugskämpfe in Serbien." *Allgemeine schweizerische Militärzeitschrift* 125, nos. 2–3 (1959).

Fraschka, Günter. *Der Panzer-Graf: General Graf Strachwitz—ein Leben für Deutschland.* Rastatt: Erich Pabel Verlag, 1962.

Fretter-Pico, Maximilian. *Missbrauchte Infanterie: Deutsche Infanteriedivisionen im osteuropäischen Grossraum 1941 bis 1944: Erlebnisskizzen, Erfahrungen und Erkenntnisse.* Frankfurt: Bernard & Graefe, 1957.

Freytag-Loringhoven, Hugo von. *Feldherrngrösse: Von Denken und Handeln hervorragender Heerführer.* Berlin: E. S. Mittler, 1922.

Fries, Walter. "Einsatz der 29. Panzer Grenadier Division während des deutschen Gegen-angriffes zur Beseitigung des Landekopfes Anzio-Nettuno im Februar 1944." Manuscript D-141. US Army Heritage and Education Center (USAHEC) Foreign Military Studies series. Carlisle, PA.

Frieser, Karl-Heinz. *Blitzkrieg-Legende: Der Westfeldzug 1940.* München: R. Oldenbourg, 1995.

———. "Der Rückzugsoperationen der Heeresgruppe Süd in der Ukraine." In *Das Deutsche Reich und der Zweite Weltkrieg.* Volume 8. *Die Ostfront 1943/44: Der Krieg im Osten und an den Nebenfronten.* München: Deutsche Verlags-Anstalt, 2011.

———. "Der Vorstoss der Panzergruppe Kleist zur Kanalküste (10. bis 21. Mai 1940): Führungsprobleme beim erstmaligen operativen Einsatz der Panzerwaffe." *Vorträge zur Militärgeschichte 9: Operatives Denken und Handeln in deutschen Streitkräften im 19. und 20. Jahrhundert.* Herford: Verlag E. S. Mittler & Sohn, 1988.

———. "Der Zusammenbruch der Heeresgruppe Mitte im Sommer 1944." In *Das Deutsche Reich und der Zweite Weltkrieg.* Volume 8. *Die Ostfront 1943/44: Der Krieg im Osten und an den Nebenfronten.* München: Deutsche Verlags-Anstalt, 2011.

———. "Die Schlacht im Kursker Bogen." In *Das Deutsche Reich und der Zweite Weltkrieg.* Volume 8. *Die Ostfront 1943/44.* München: Deutsche Verlags-Anstalt, 2007.

———. "Die Schlacht um die Seelower Höhen." In Roland G. Foerster, ed. *Seelower Höhen 1945.* Hamburg: E. S. Mittler & Sohn, 1998.

———. "Irrtümer und Illusionen: Die Fehleinschätzung der deutschen Führungim Frühsommer 1944." In *Das Deutsche Reich und der Zweite Weltkrieg.* Volume 8. *Die Ostfront 1943/44: Der Krieg im Osten und an den Nebenfronten.* München: Deutsche Verlags-Anstalt, 2011.

———. "Schlagen aus der Nachhand—Schlagen aus der Vorhand: Die Schlachten von Char'kow und Kursk 1943." In Roland G. Foerster, ed. *Gezeitenwechsel im Zweiten Weltkrieg? Die Schlachten von Char'kov und Kursk im Frühjahr und Sommer 1943 in operativer Anlage, Verlauf und politischer Bedeutung.* Berlin: E. S. Mittler, 1996.

Frieser, Karl-Heinz, and Friedhelm Klein. "Mansteins Gegenschlag am Donez:

Operative Analyse des Gegenangriffs der Heeresgruppe Süd im February/ März 1943." *Militärgeschichte* 9 (1999).

Friessner, Hans. *Verratene Schlachten: Die Tragödie der deutschen Wehrmacht in Rumänien und Ungarn.* Hamburg: Holsten-Verlag, 1956.

Fritz, Stephen G. *Frontsoldaten: The German Soldier in World War II.* Lexington: University Press of Kentucky, 1995.

From the Volturno to the Winter Line, 6 October–15 November 1943. Washington, DC: Center of Military History, 1990.

Gackenholz, Hermann. "Der Zusammenbruch der Heeresgruppe Mitte 1944." In Hans-Adolf Jacobsen and Jürgen Rohwer, eds. *Entscheidungsschlachten des zweiten Weltkrieges.* Frankfurt: Verlag für Wehrwesen Bernard & Graefe, 1960.

———. "Zum Zusammenbruch der Heeresgruppe Mitte im Sommer 1944." *Vierteljahrshefte für Zeitgeschichte* 3, no. 3 (1955).

Garland, Albert N., and Howard McGaw Smyth. *Sicily and the Surrender of Italy.* Washington, DC: Center of Military History, 1991.

Gaul, Walter. "Die deutsche Luftwaffe während der Invasion 1944." *Wehrwissenschaftliche Rundschau* 3 (1953).

Gavin, James. *On to Berlin: Battles of an Airborne Commander, 1943–1946.* New York: Viking, 1978.

Gay, Peter. *Weimar Culture: The Outsider as Insider.* New York: Harper Torchbooks, 1970.

Gehlen, Reinhard. *Der Dienst: Erinnerungen 1942–1971.* München: Knaur, 1971.

———. *The Service: The Memoirs of General Reinhard Gehlen.* New York: World Publishing, 1972.

Gerlach, Fritz. "Schöpfer und Lenker deutscher Wehrkraft: Acht grosse Soldaten in vierjahrhunderten deutcher Geschichte." In Wilhelm Utermann, ed. *Jungen—eure Welt! Das Jahrbuch der Hitler-Jugend.* München: Zentralverlag der NSDAP, 1941.

Gersdorff, Rudolf-Christoph Freiherr von. "Allgemeine Bemerkungen zur deutschen Invasionsabwehr." Manuscript B-122. US Army Heritage and Education Center (USAHEC) Foreign Military Studies series. Carlisle, PA.

———. "Der Feldzug in Nordfrankreich." Band II. 2. Kapitel, "Der Amerikanische Durchbruch auf Avranches." Manuscript B-723. US Army Heritage and Education Center (USAHEC) Foreign Military Studies series. Carlisle, PA.

———. "Der Feldzug in Nordfrankreich." Band IV. 4. Kapitel, "Der deutsche Gegenangriff auf Avranches." Manuscript B-725. US Army Heritage and Education Center (USAHEC) Foreign Military Studies series. Carlisle, PA.

———. "Der Gegenangriff auf Avranches." Manuscript A-921. US Army Heritage and Education Center (USAHEC) Foreign Military Studies series. Carlisle, PA.

———. "Der Kampf um den Hürtgenwald (November-Anfang Dezember 44)." Manuscript A-891. US Army Heritage and Education Center (USAHEC) Foreign Military Studies series. Carlisle, PA.

———. "Der Kessel von Falaise." Manuscript A-919. US Army Heritage and Education Center (USAHEC) Foreign Military Studies series. Carlisle, PA.

————. "Kommentar zum Kriegstagebuch der 7. Armee." Manuscript A-918. US Army Heritage and Education Center (USAHEC) Foreign Military Studies series. Carlisle, PA.

————. *Soldat im Untergang*. Frankfurt: Ullstein, 1977.

————. "Vom Gegenangriff auf Avranches zum Kessel von Falaise." Manuscript A-920. US Army Heritage and Education Center (USAHEC) Foreign Military Studies series. Carlisle, PA.

Glantz, David M. *The Battle for Leningrad, 1941–1944*. Lawrence: University Press of Kansas, 2002.

————. *Colossus Reborn: The Red Army at War, 1941–1943*. Lawrence: University Press of Kansas, 2005.

————. *From the Don to the Dnepr: Soviet Offensive Operations, December 1942–August 1943*. London: Frank Cass, 1991.

————. *Red Storm Over the Balkans: The Failed Soviet Invasion of Romania, Spring 1944*. Lawrence: University Press of Kansas, 2007.

————. *Zhukov's Greatest Defeat: The Red Army's Epic Disaster in Operation Mars*. Lawrence: University Press of Kansas, 1999.

Glantz, David M., and Jonathan House. *Armageddon in Stalingrad: September–November 1942*. Lawrence: University Press of Kansas, 2009.

————. *The Battle of Kursk*. Lawrence: University Press of Kansas, 1999.

————. *To the Gates of Stalingrad: Soviet-German Combat Operations, April–August 1942*. Lawrence: University Press of Kansas, 2009.

————. *When Titans Clashed: How the Red Army Stopped Hitler*. Lawrence: University Press of Kansas, 1995.

Goda, Norman J. W. "Black Marks: Hitler's Bribery of His Senior Officers during World War II." *Journal of Modern History* 72, No. 2 (2000).

Goebbels, Josef. *Tagebücher 1945: die letzten Aufzeichnungen*. Bergisch Gladbach: Bastei Lubbe, 1977.

Goettke, Ernst. "Die Vorbereitung der Küstenverteidigung." Manuscript B-663. US Army Heritage and Education Center (USAHEC) Foreign Military Studies series. Carlisle, PA.

Goldman, Stuart D. "Russia's Rock." *World War II* (2015).

Gollwitzer, Helmut. *Und führen wohin du nicht willst: Bericht einer Gefangenschaft*. München: Chr. Kaiser Verlag, 1953.

Gordon, Harold J. Jr. *The Reichswehr and the German Republic, 1919–1926*. Princeton, NJ: Princeton University Press, 1957.

Görlitz, Walter. *Der zweite Weltkrieg 1939–1945*. 2 Volumes. Stuttgart: Steingrüben, 1952.

————. *Model: Der Feldmarschall und sein Endkampf an der Ruhr*. Frankfurt: Ullstein, 1992.

————. *Model: Strategie der Defensive*. Wiesbaden: Limes, 1977.

————. *Model: Strategie der Defensive: von Russland bis zum Ruhrkessel*. Bergisch Gladbach: Gustav Lübbe Verlag, 1977.

Gosztony, Peter. "Der Kampf um Budapest 1944/45." 5 Parts. *Wehrwissenschaftliche Rundschau* 13 and 14 (1963 and 1964).

————. *Der Kampf um Budapest 1944/45*. München: Schnell und Steiner, 1964.

————. "Der Krieg zwischen Bulgarien und Deutschland 1944/45." 3 Parts. *Wehrwissenschaftliche Rundschau* 17. Nos. 1, 2, 3. (1967).

————. "Die Eroberung Berlins durch die Rote Armee im Frühjahr 1945." 2 Parts. *Allgemeine schweizerische Militärzeitschrift* 131, nos. 4–5 (1965).

————. "Stalin, die Rote Armee und das Kriegsende 1945." *Allgemeine schweizerische Militärzeitschrift* 151, no. 5 (1985).

Graham, Dominick, and Shelford Bidwell. *Tug of War: The Battle for Italy*. London: Hodder & Stoughton, 1986.

Greene, Jack, and Alessandro Massignani. *Hitler Strikes North: The Invasion of Norway and Denmark, 9 April 1940*. London: Frontline Books, 2013.

Greiner, Christian. "General Adolf Heusinger (1887–1982): Operatives Denken und Planen 1948 bis 1956." *Vorträge zur Militärgeschichte 9: Operatives Denken und Handeln in deutschen Streitkräften im 19. und 20. Jahrhundert*. Herford: Verlag E. S. Mittler & Sohn, 1988.

Greiner, Heinrich. "Schlacht um Rom und Rückzugskämpfe nördlich Rom (362. I.D.)." Manuscript D-169. US Army Heritage and Education Center (USAHEC) Foreign Military Studies series. Carlisle, PA.

Grenville, John A. S. "Wettlauf nach Berlin? Britische Ziele und Strategie im letzten Kriegsjahr." In Roland G. Foerster, ed. *Seelower Höhen 1945*. Hamburg: E. S. Mittler & Sohn, 1998.

Griehl, Manfred. *Luftwaffe over America: The Secret Plans to Bomb the United States in World War II*. Mechanicsburg, PA: Stackpole, 2004.

Grier, Howard D. *Hitler, Donitz, and the Baltic Sea: The Third Reich's Last Hope, 1944–1945*. Annapolis, MD: Naval Institute Press, 2013.

Groeben, Peter von der. "Der Zusammenbruch der Heeresgruppe Mitte und ihr Kampf bis zur Festigung der Front (22.VI. bis 1.IX.1944)." Manuscript T-31. US Army Heritage and Education Center (USAHEC) Foreign Military Studies series. Carlisle, PA.

————. "Die Schlacht der 2. Panzer-Armee und 9. Armee im Orel-Bogen vom 5. Juli bis 18. August 1943." Manuscript T-26. US Army Heritage and Education Center (USAHEC) Foreign Military Studies series. Carlisle, PA.

Groehler, Olaf. "Die Güter der Generale: Dotationen im zweiten Weltkrieg." *Zeitschrift für Geschichtswissenschaft* 19, no. 5 (1971).

Groote, Wolfgang von. "Bundeswehr und 20. Juli." *Vierteljahrshefte für Zeitgeschichte* 12, no. 3 (1964).

Gross, Gerhard P. *The Myth and Reality of German Warfare: Operational Thinking from Moltke the Elder to Heusinger*. Lexington: University Press of Kentucky, 2016.

————. *Mythos und Wirklichkeit: Geschichte des operativen Denkens im deutschen Heer von Moltke d. Ä. bis Heusinger*. Paderborn: Schöningh Ferdinand, 2012.

Guderian, Heinz. "Die Wechselwirkungen zwischen Ost- und West-Front." Manuscript T-42. US Army Heritage and Education Center (USAHEC) Foreign Military Studies series. Carlisle, PA.

————. *Erinnerungen eines Soldaten*. Heidelberg: Kurt Vowinckel, 1951.

————. *Panzer Leader*. New York: Ballantine, 1957.

Gurtner, René. "Deutsche Luftwaffen-Felddivisionen im Weltkrieg 1939–1945." *Allgemeine schweizerische Militärzeitschrift* 122, no. 8 (1956).

Haas, Daniel. "Wie hat Grass damals zum Holocaust gestanden?" *Der Spiegel Online* (August 15, 2006). spiegel.de/kultur/literatur/ss-bekenntnis-wie-hat-grass-damals-zum-holocaust-gestanden-a-431646.html.

Halder, Franz. *Hitler als Feldherr.* München: Munchener Dom-Verlag, 1949.

Hamburger Institut für Sozialforschung, ed. *Verbrechen der Wehrmacht: Dimensionen des Vernichtungskrieges 1941–1944.* Hamburg: Hamburger Institut für Sozialforschung, 2002.

Hammond, William M. *Normandy.* Washington, DC: Center of Military History, n.d.

Hardesty, Von. *Red Phoenix: The Rise of Soviet Air Power, 1941–1945.* Hopkins, MN: Olympic, 1982.

Hardesty, Von, and Ilya Grinberg. *Red Phoenix Rising: The Soviet Air Force in World War II.* Lawrence: University Press of Kansas, 2012.

Harrigan, Pat, and Matthew G. Kirschenbaum, eds. *Zones of Control: Perspectives on Wargaming.* Cambridge, MA: MIT Press, 2016.

Harrison, Gordon A. *Cross-Channel Attack.* Washington, DC: Center of Military History, 2007.

Harrison, Richard W. *Architect of Soviet Victory in World War II: The Life and Theories of G. S. Isserson.* Jefferson, NC: McFarland, 2010.

———. *The Russian Way of War: Operational Art, 1904–1940.* Lawrence: University Press of Kansas, 2001.

———, ed. *The Battle of Moscow, 1941–1942: The Red Army's Defensive Operations and Counteroffensive along the Moscow Strategic Direction.* Solihull, UK: Helion, 2015.

Hart, Russell A. *Clash of Arms: How the Allies Won in Normandy.* Boulder, CO: Lynne Rienner, 2001.

———. *Guderian: Panzer Pioneer or Myth Maker.* Washington, DC: Potomac, 2006.

Hassell, Agostino von, and Sigrid MacRae with Simon Ameskamp. *Alliance of Enemies: The Untold Story of the Secret American and German Collaboration to End World War II.* New York: Thomas Dunne, 2006.

Hastings, Max. *Das Reich: The March of the 2nd SS Panzer Division through France.* New York: Holt, Rinehart and Winston, 1981.

———. *Overlord: D-Day and the Battle for Normandy.* NY: Simon & Schuster, 1984.

Haupt, Werner. *Kurland: die letzte Front—Schicksal für zwei Armeen.* Bad Nauheim: Podzun-Verlag, 1964.

Hauser, Wolf. "Der Kampf der 14. Armee bei Anzio-Nettuno bis Anfang Mai 1944." Chapter 12. "Der Feldzug in Italien." Manuscript T-1a. US Army Heritage and Education Center (USAHEC) Foreign Military Studies series. Carlisle, PA.

Hausser, Paul. "Normandie. 7. Armee vom 29./6.–24./7.1945." Manuscript A-974. US Army Heritage and Education Center (USAHEC) Foreign Military Studies series. Carlisle, PA.

———. *Soldaten wie andere auch: Der Weg der Waffen-SS.* Osnabrück: Munin, 1966.

Hayn, Friedrich. *Die Invasion: Von Cotentin bis Falaise.* Heidelberg: Kurt Vowinckel, 1954.

Hayward, Joel S. A. *Stopped at Stalingrad: The Luftwaffe and Hitler's Defeat in the East, 1942–1943.* Lawrence: University Press of Kansas, 1998.

Heer, Hannes, ed. *Vernichtungskrieg: Verbrechen der Wehrmacht 1941 bis 1944.* Hamburg: Hamburger Edition, 1995.

Heiber, Helmut, ed. *Hitlers Lagebesprechungen: Die Protokollfragmente seiner militärischen Konferenzen 1942–1945.* Stuttgart: Deutsche Verlags-Anstalt, 1962.

———, ed. *Lagebesprechungen im Führerhauptquartier: Protokollfragmente aus Hitlers militärischen Konferenzen 1942–1945.* München: DTV, 1962.

Heiber, Helmut, and David M. Glantz, eds. *Hitler and His Generals: Military Conferences, 1942–1945.* New York: Enigma, 2003.

Heidkämper, Otto. *Witebsk: Kampf und Untergang der 3. Panzerarmee.* Heidelberg: Kurt Vowinckel, 1954.

Heim, Ferdinand. "Stalingrad und der Verlauf des Feldzuges der Jahre 1943–1945." In Alfred Philippi and Ferdinand Heim, eds. *Der Feldzug gegen Sowjetrussland 1941 bis 1945: ein operativer Überblick.* Stuttgart: W. Kohlhammer, 1962.

Heinrici, Gotthard. "Der Feldzug in Russland: Ein operativer Überblick." Chapter 14. "Deutsch Rückschläge, Oktober 1943-Mai 1944." Manuscript T-9. US Army Heritage and Education Center (USAHEC) Foreign Military Studies series. Carlisle, PA.

Henke, Klaus-Dietmar. *Die amerikanische Besetzung Deutschlands.* München: R. Oldenbourg, 2009.

Herwig, Holger H. *The First World War: Germany and Austria-Hungary, 1914–1918.* London: Arnold, 1997.

Heusinger, Adolf. *Befehl im Widerstreit: Schicksalsstunden der deutschen Armee 1923–1945.* Tübingen: Rainer Wunderlich Verlag, 1950.

Hillgruber, Andreas. "Das deutsch-ungarisch Verhältnis im letzten Kriegsjahr: vom Unternehmen 'Margarethe I' (19. März 1944) bis zur Räumung Ungarns durch die deutschen Truppen (4. April 1945)." *Wehrwissenschaftliche Rundschau* 10 (1960).

———. *Der 2. Weltkrieg: Kriegsziele und Strategie der grossen Mächte.* Stuttgart: W. Kohlhammer, 1985.

———. "Die letzten Monate der deutsch-rumänischen Waffenbruderschaft." *Wehrwissenschaftliche Rundschau* 7 (1957).

———. *Die Räumung der Krim 1944: eine Studie zur Entstehung der deutschen Führungsentschlüsse.* Berlin: E. S. Mittler & Sohn, 1959.

Hinze, Rolf. *Der Zusammenbruch der Heeresgruppe Mitte im Osten 1944.* Stuttgart: Motorbuch Verlag, 1980.

———. *Rückkämpfer 1944: Eine Studie.* Self-published, 1988.

———. *To the Bitter End: The Final Battles of Army Groups North Ukraine, A, and Center—Eastern Front, 1944–45.* Philadelphia: Casemate, 2010.

Hitchcock, William I. *The Bitter Road to Freedom: The Human Cost of Allied Victory in World War II Europe.* New York: Free Press, 2008.

Hoffmann, Peter. "Zu dem Attentat im Führerhauptquartier 'Wolfsschanze' am 20. Juli 1944." *Vierteljahrshefte für Zeitgeschichte* 12, no. 3 (July 1964).

Hornig, Ernst. "Festung Breslau 1945." *Schweizer Monatshefte* 48, no. 4 (1968–1969).

Hossbach, Friedrich. "Aus den Kämpfen der 4. deutschen Armee um Ostpreussen: in der Zeit vom 15.8.1944 bis 28.1.1945." 3 Parts. *Allgemeine schweizerische Militärzeitschrift* 116, nos. 2, 4, 5. (1950).

———. *Schlacht um Ostpreussen: Aus den Kämpfen der 4. deutschen Armee um Ostpreussen in der Zeit vom 19.7.1944 bis 30.1.1945.* Überlingen: Otto Dikreiter Verlag, 1951.

Howard, Michael. *The Franco-Prussian War.* New York: Macmillan, 1962.

———. *The Mediterranean Strategy in the Second World War.* New York: Praeger, 1968.

Howe, George F. *Northwest Africa: Seizing the Initiative in the West.* Washington, DC: Center of Military History, 2002.

H. R. "Rückzugskämpfe in Finnland (vom 28. September bis 14. Oktober 1944): eine deutsche Darstellung." *Allgemeine schweizerische Militärzeitschrift* 125, no. 4 (1959).

Hubatsch, Walther. *Frederick the Great of Prussia: Absolutism and Administration.* London: Thames and Hudson, 1973.

———, ed. *Hitlers Weisungen für die Kriegführung 1939–1945.* Frankfurt: Bernard & Graefe Verlag, 1962.

Hughes, Daniel J. "Abuses of German Military History." *Military Review* 66, no. 12 (1986).

———, ed. *Moltke on the Art of War: Selected Writings.* Novato, CA: Presidio, 1993.

Hull, Isabel V. *Absolute Destruction: Military Culture and the Practices of War in Imperial Germany.* Ithaca, NY: Cornell University Press, 2005.

Hümmelchen, Gerhard. "Balkanräumung 1944." *Wehrwissenschaftliche Rundschau* 9 (1959).

Isby, David C., ed. *Fighting the Invasion: The German Army at D-Day.* London: Greenhill, 2000.

Isserson, Georgii Samoilovich. *The Evolution of Operational Art.* Fort Leavenworth, KS: Combat Studies Institute Press, 2013.

Izzo, Larry. "An Analysis of German Mistakes Leading to the Capture of the Ludendorff Bridge at Remagen." In *Military History Anthology.* Fort Leavenworth, KS: Combat Studies Institute, 1984.

Jackson, W.G.F. *The Battle for Italy.* New York: Harper & Row, 1967.

Jacobsen, Hans-Adolf, and Jürgen Rohwer, eds. *Entscheidungsschlachten des zweiten Weltkrieges.* Frankfurt: Verlag für Wehrwesen Bernard & Graefe, 1960.

Jaggi, O. "Der Ausbruch aus Kesseln." *Allgemeine schweizerische Militärzeitschrift* 130, nos. 4–5, 12 (1964).

Jany, Curt. *Geschichte der königlich preussischen Armee.* 4 Volumes. Berlin: Karl Siegismund, 1928–1933.

Jarymowycz, Roman Johann. *Tank Tactics: From Normandy to Lorraine.* Boulder, CO: Lynne Rienner, 2001.

Jenkins, Graham. "The Mask of the Bear: Soviet Deception in Operation Bagration." Found on *Automatic Ballpoint.* automaticballpoint.com/2010/05/04/the -mask-of-the-bear-soviet-deception-in-operation-bagration.

Jones, Alan W. "The Operations of the 423d Infantry (106th Infantry Division) in the Vicinity of Schonberg during the Battle of the Ardennes, 16–19 December

1944 (Ardennes-Alsace Campaign) (Personal Experience of a Battalion Operations Officer." Fort Benning, GA: Infantry School, 1949.

Jung, Hermann. *Die Ardennen-Offensive 1944/45: Ein Beispiel für die Kriegführung Hitlers*. Göttingen: Musterschmidt Verlag, 1971.

Kabath, Rudolf. "Die Rolle der Seebrückenköpfe beim Kampf um Ostpreussen 1944–1945." In Hans Meier-Welcker, ed. *Abwehrkämpfe am Nordflügel der Ostfront 1944–1945*. Stuttgart: Deutsche Verlags-Anstalt, 1963.

Kaltenegger, Roland. *Schörner: Feldmarschall der letzten Stunde*. München: Herbig, 1994.

Kania, Hans. *Der Grosse Kurfürst*. Leipzig: Teubner, 1930.

Kaps, Johannes, ed. *Die Tragödie Schlesiens 1945/46 in Dokumenten: unter besonderer Berücksichtigung des Erzbistums Breslau*. München: Verlag "Christ Unterwegs." 1952/3.

Kegler, Gerhard. "Die letzte Schlacht der 9. Armee: eine Entgegnung." *Wehrwissenschaftliche Rundschau* 5, no. 7 (1955).

Kehrig, Manfred. *Stalingrad: Analyse und Dokumentation einer Schlacht*. Stuttgart: Deutsche Verlags-Anstalt, 1974.

Keilig, Wolf. *Das deutsche Heer 1939–1945: Gliederung, Einsatz, Stellenbesetzung*. Bad Nauheim: Verlag Hans-Henning Podzun, 1956.

Kellerhoff, Sven Felix. "Im Kessel von Halbe starb Hitlers letzte Hoffnung." *Die Welt* (April 24, 2016).

Kern, Erich. *Der Grosse Rausch: Russlandfeldzug 1941–1945*. Göttingen: Plesse-Verlag, 1961.

———. *Generalfeldmarschall Schörner*. Rosenheim: Deutscvhe Verlagsgesellschaft, n.d.

Kershaw, Alex. *Hitler*. 2 Volumes. New York: Norton, 1998–2000.

———. *The Longest Winter: The Battle of the Bulge and the Epic Story of WWII's Most Decorated Platoon*. New York: Da Capo, 2005.

Kessel, Eberhard. "Blücher: Zum 200. Gebürtstag am 16. Dezember." *Militärwissenschaftliche Rundschau* 7, no. 4 (1942).

Kesselring, Albert. "Antworten zu den Fragen über Wechselbeziehungen zwischen der operativen und propagandistischen Kriegführung." Manuscript B-280. US Army Heritage and Education Center (USAHEC) Foreign Military Studies series. Carlisle, PA.

———. "Kesselring's Comments on MS #T-1a." Manuscript T-1a K1. US Army Heritage and Education Center (USAHEC) Foreign Military Studies series. Carlisle, PA.

———. *The Memoirs of Field-Marshal Albert Kesselring*. Novato, CA: Presidio, 1989.

———. *Soldat bis zum letzten Tag*. Bonn: Athenäum, 1953.

Kielmansegg, Johann Adolf Graf von. "Bemerkungen zum Referat von Hauptmann Dr. Frieser aus der Sicht eines Zeitzeugen." *Vorträge zur Militärgeschichte 9: Operatives Denken und Handeln in deutschen Streitkräften im 19. und 20. Jahrhundert*. Herford: Verlag E. S. Mittler & Sohn, 1988.

Kieser, Egbert. *Danziger Bucht 1945: Dokumentation einer Katastrophe*. Esslingen amNeckar: Bechtle, 1978.

Kikkert, Peter. "Kurt Meyer and Canadian Memory: Villain and Monster, Hero and Victim or Worse—a German?" *Canadian Military History* 21, no. 2 (2012).

Kissel, Hans. "Der deutsche Volkssturm 1944–1945." *Wehrwissenschaftliche Rundschau* 10, no. 4 (1960).

———. *Die Katastrophe in Rumänien.* Darmstadt: Wehr und Wissen, 1964.

———. *Die Panzerschlachten in der Pußta im Oktober 1944.* Neckargemünd: Kurt Vowinckel Verlag, 1960.

Klink, Ernst. *Das Gesetz des Handelns: Die Operation Zitadelle 1943.* Stuttgart: Deutsche Verlags-Anstalt, 1966.

Klöss, Erhard, ed. *Reden des Führers: Politik und Propaganda Adolf Hitlers, 1922–1945.* München: Deutscher Taschenbuch Verlag, 1967.

Koch, Heinz-Günther. "Kampferfahrung in der Verteidigung: Deutsche Erfahrungen in den Kurlandschlachten 1945." *Allgemeine schweizerische Militärzeitschrift* 123, no. 1 (1957).

Köhler, Karl. "Der Einsatz der Luftwaffe im Bereich der Heeresgruppe Nord von Ende Juni bis Mitte Oktober 1944." In Hans Meier-Welcker, ed. *Abwehrkämpfe am Nordflügel der Ostfront 1944–1945.* Stuttgart: Deutsche Verlags-Anstalt, 1963.

Konev, I. S. "The Korsun-Shevchenkovsky Pocket." *Soviet Military Review*, no. 2 (1974).

———. *Year of Victory.* Moscow: Progress Publishers, 1984.

Konrad, Joachim. "Das Ende von Breslau." *Vierteljahrshefte für Zeitgeschichte* 4, no. 4 (1956).

Koser, Reinhold. *Geschichte Friedrichs des Grossen.* Berlin: J. G. Cotta, 1912–13.

Kraas, Hugo. "Die 12. SS-Panzer-Division 'Hitler-Jugend' in der Ardennen-Offensive." Manuscript B-522. US Army Heritage and Education Center (USAHEC) Foreign Military Studies series. Carlisle, PA.

Kraemer, Fritz. "Einsatz der 6. Panzer-Armee in den Ardennen 1944/45." Manuscript A-924. US Army Heritage and Education Center (USAHEC) Foreign Military Studies series. Carlisle, PA.

Krausnick, Helmut. "Erwin Rommel und der deutsche Widerstand gegen Hitler." *Vierteljahrshefte für Zeitgeschichte* 1, no. 1 (January 1953).

Kreike, Emmanuel, and William Chester Jordan, eds. *Corrupt Histories.* Rochester, NY: University of Rochester Press, 2004.

Kretchik, Walter E. *U.S. Army Doctrine: From the American Revolution to the War on Terror.* Lawrence: University Press of Kansas, 2011.

Kretschman, Hans von. "The Battle of Vionville—Mars-la-Tour." In F. Maurice, ed. *The Franco-German War, by Generals and Other Officers Who Took Part in the Campaign.* London: Allen & Unwin, 1899.

Kuby, Erich. "Die Russen in Berlin 1945." *Der Spiegel*, no. 21 (1965).

Kühn, Wlater. "Die Artillerie bei Anzio-Nettuno." Manuscript D-158. US Army Heritage and Education Center (USAHEC) Foreign Military Studies series. Carlisle, PA.

Kurowski, Franz. *Armee Wenck: die 12. Armee zwischen Elbe und Oder 1945.* Neckargemünd: Kurt Vowinckel Verlag, 1967.

———. *Panzer Aces: German Tank Commanders of World War II.* Mechanicsburg, PA: Stackpole, 2004.

Lakowski, Richard. "Der Zusammenbruch der deutschen Verteidigung zwischen Ostsee und Karpaten." In *Das Deutsche Reich und der Zweite Weltkrieg*. Volume 10/1. *Der Zusammenbruch des Deutschen Reiches 1945: Die Militärisen Niederwerfung der Wehrmacht*. München: Deutsche Verlags-Anstalt, 2008.

———. "Die Lage der 9, deutschen Armee von Beginn der offensive der Roten Armee (16. April 1945)." In Roland G. Foerster, ed. *Seelower Höhen 1945*. Hamburg: E. S. Mittler & Sohn, 1998.

Lange, Wolfgang. *Korpsabteilung C vom Dnjeper bis nach Polen (November 1943 bis Juli 1944): Kampf einer Infanterie-Division auf breiter Front gegen grosse Übermacht-Kampf im Kessel und Ausbruch*. Neckargemünd: Kurt Vowinckel Verlag, 1961.

Lasch, Otto. *So fiel Königsberg: Kampf und Untergang von Ostpresussens Hauptstadt*. München: Gräfe und Unzer Verlag, n.d.

Lattre de Tassigny, Jean de. *The History of the French First Army*. London: Allen and Unwin, 1949.

Léderrey, E. "Le 6e armée allemande sur le front de l'Est, de 1941 à 1944: son engagement; sa capitulation; sa resurrection; sa fin." *Revue Militaire Suisse* 104, no. 11 (1959).

Leggiere, Michael V. *Blücher: Scourge of Napoleon*. Norman: University of Oklahoma Press, 2014.

———. *Napoleon and Berlin: The Franco-Prussian War in North Germany*. Norman: University of Oklahoma Press, 2002.

———. *Napoleon and the Struggle for Germany: The Franco-Prussian War of 1813*. 2 Volumes. Cambridge: Cambridge University Press, 2015.

Le Tissier, Tony. *Zhukov at the Oder: The Decisive Battle for Berlin*. Mechanicsburg, PA: Stackpole, 1996.

Lettow-Vorbeck, Oscar von. *Geschichte des Krieges von 1866 in Deutschland*. 3 Volumes. Berlin: E. S. Mittler, 1896–1902.

Lewis, Adrian. *Omaha Beach: A Flawed Victory* (Chapel Hill: University of North Carolina Press, 2001).

Liddell Hart, B. H. *The German Generals Talk*. New York: Quill, 1979.

———. *The Other Side of the Hill: Germany's Generals, Their Rise and Fall, with Their Account of Military Events, 1939–1945*. London: Cassell, 1948.

Liedtke, Gregory. *Enduring the Whirlwind: The German Army and the Russo-German War, 1941–1943*. Solihull, UK: Helion, 2016.

———. "Furor Teutonicus: German Offensives and Counter-Attacks on the Eastern Front, August 1943 to March 1945." *Journal of Slavic Military Studies* 21 (2008).

Lindemann, Helmut. "Die Schuld der Generale." *Deutsche Rundschau* (January 1949).

Linklater, Eric. *The Campaign in Italy*. London: Her Majesty's Stationery Office, 1951. London: Collins, 1958.

Luck, Hans von. *Panzer Commander*. New York: Dell, 1989.

Ludendorff, Erich. *Der totale Krieg*. München: Ludendorffs Verlag, 1936.

Ludewig, Joachim. *Der deutsche Rückzug aus Frankreich 1944*. Freiburg: Verlag Rombach, 1995.

———. *Rückzug: The German Retreat from France.* Lexington: University Press of Kentucky, 2012.

Lunde, Henrik O. *Hitler's Wave-Breaker Concept: An Analysis of the German End Game in the Baltic.* Havertown, PA: Casemate, 2013.

MacDonald, Charles B. *The Last Offensive.* Washington, DC: Center of Military History, 1993.

———. *Time for Trumpets: The Untold Story of the Battle of the Bulge.* New York: HarperCollins, 1997.

Mackensen, Eberhard von. "Stellungnahme zu 'Der Feldzug in Italien' von Gen. Major Wolf Hauser: Anlage zu Kapitel 12." Chapter 13. "Der Feldzug in Italien." Manuscript T-1a. US Army Heritage and Education Center (USAHEC) Foreign Military Studies series. Carlisle, PA.

———. *Vom Bug zum Kaukasus: Das III Panzerkorps im Feldzug gegen Sowjetrussland 1941–42.* Neckargemünd: Kurt Vowinckel, 1967.

MacLean, French L. "German General Officer Casualties in World War II— Harbinger for U.S Army General Officer Casualties in Airland Battle?" Fort Leavenworth, KS: School of Advanced Military Studies, 1988.

Maczek, Stanislaw. *Avec mes Blindés: Pologne, France, Belgique, Hollande, Allemagne.* Paris: Press de la Cité, 1967.

Majdalany, Fred. *The Battle of Cassino.* Boston: Houghton Mifflin, 1957.

Mallmann Showell, Jak P., ed. *Führer Conferences on Naval Affairs, 1939–1945.*

Mangenheimer, Hans. "Die Abwehrschlacht an der Weichsel 1945: Planung und Ablauf aus der Sicht der deutschen operative Führung." *Vorträge zur Militärgeschichte 9: Operatives Denken und Handeln in deutschen Streitkräften im 19. und 20. Jahrhundert.* Herford: Verlag E. S. Mittler & Sohn, 1988.

Manig, Bert-Oliver. "Der Bluthund ist zurück." *Die Zeit* (September 8, 2005).

Manstein, Erich von. *Lost Victories.* Novato, CA: Presidio, 1982.

———. *Verlorene Siege.* Bonn: Athenäum-Verlag, 1955.

Manteuffel, Hasso von. "Die 5. Panzer-Armee in der Ardennen-Offensive (16. Dezember 1944 bis 25. Januar 1945), I-III." Manuscript B-151. US Army Heritage and Education Center (USAHEC) Foreign Military Studies series. Carlisle, PA.

———. "Die 5. Panzer-Armee in der Ardennen-Offensive (16. Dezember 1944 bis 25. Januar 1945), IV–VII." Manuscript B-151a. US Army Heritage and Education Center (USAHEC) Foreign Military Studies series. Carlisle, PA.

———. "Die Schlacht in den Ardennen 1944–1945." In Hans-Adolf Jacobsen and Jürgen Rohwer, eds. *Entscheidungsschlachten des zweiten Weltkrieges.* Frankfurt: Verlag für Wehrwesen Bernard & Graefe, 1960.

Margaritis, Peter. *Crossroads at Margival: Hitler's Last Conference in France: June 17, 1944.* Self-published/n.d.

Marten, Hans. *General von Seydlitz 1942–1945: Analyse eines Konfliktes.* Berlin: von Kloeden Verlag, 1971.

Marx, Karl. *The Eighteenth Brumaire of Louis Bonaparte.* New York: Mondial, 2005.

Matloff, Maurice, and Edwin M. Snell. *Strategic Planning for Coalition Warfare, 1941–1942.* Washington, DC: Center of Military History, 1953.

Maurice, F., ed. *The Franco-German War, by Generals and Other Officers Who Took Part in the Campaign*. London: Allen & Unwin, 1899.

Mavrogordato, Ralph S. *Command Decisions: Hitler's Decision on the Defense of Italy*. Washington, DC: Center of Military History, 1990.

Mazulenko, W. A. *Die Zerschlagung der Heeresgruppe Südukraine*. Berlin [Ost]: Verlag des Ministeriums für Nationale Verteidigung, 1959. US ed. Mechanicsburg, PA: Stackpole, 2005.

Megargee, Geoffrey. *Inside Hitler's High Command*. Lawrence: University Press of Kansas, 2000.

Meier-Welcker, Hans, ed. *Abwehrkämpfe am Nordflügel der Ostfront 1944–1945*. Stuttgart: Deutsche Verlags-Anstalt, 1963.

Meister, Captain. "Die Kämpfe am Monte Maio: vom 10.-13. Mai 1944." *Allgemeine schweizerische Militärzeitschrift* 117, no. 8 (1951).

Mellenthin, F. W. von. *Panzer Battles: A Study of the Employment of Armor in the Second World War*. New York: Ballantine, 1971.

Melvin, Mungo. *Manstein: Hitler's Greatest General*. London: Phoenix, 2010.

Mennel, Rainer. *Der Schlussphase des zweiten Weltkrieges im Westen: eine Studie zur politischen Geographie*. Osnabrück: Biblio Verlag, 1981.

———. "Landung der Alliierten an der Küste der Provence und Durchbruch durchdas Rhônetal bis zur Burgundischen Pforte 1944: Ein Beitrag zur Militär- und Wehrgeographie." *Wehrforschung* 23 (1974).

Merriam, Robert E. *Dark December: The Full Account of the Battle of the Bulge*. Yardley, PA: Westholme, 2011.

Merridale, Catherine. *Ivan's War: Life and Death in the Red Army, 1939–1945*. New York: Picador, 2006.

Messenger, Charles. *The Last Prussian: A Biography of Field Marshal Gerd Rundstedt, 1875–1953*. London: Brassey's, 1991.

Meyer, Hubert. *The History of the 12th SS Panzer Division "Hitlerjugend."* Winnipeg: J. Fedorowicz, 1994.

———. *Kriegsgeschichte der 12. SS-Panzerdivision "Hitlerjugend."* 2 Volumes. Osnabrück: Munin-Verlag, 1982.

Meyer, Kurt. *Grenadiere*. München: Schild-Verlag, 1957.

———. *Grenadiers: The Story of Waffen SS General Kurt "Panzer" Meyer*. Mechanicsburg, PA: Stackpole, 2005.

Meyer-Detring, Wilhelm. "Vorzüge und Grenzen der Auftragstaktik." *Allgemeine schweizerische Militärzeitschrift* 136 (1970).

Middeldorf, Eike. "Die Abwehrschlacht am Weichselbrückenkopf Baranow: eine Studie über neuzeitliche Verteidigung." *Wehrwissenschaftliche Rundschau* 3, no. 4 (1953).

Mierzejewski, Alfred C. "Die Strategie der Vereinigten Staaten und das Ende des Zweiten Weltkrieges in Europa." In Roland G. Foerster, ed. *Seelower Höhen 1945*. Hamburg: E. S. Mittler & Sohn, 1998.

Miller, Edward G. *A Dark and Bloody Ground: The Hürtgen Forest and the Roer River Dams, 1944–1945*. College Station: Texas A&M University Press, 1995.

Miller, Robert L., ed. *Hitler at War: Meetings and Conversations, 1939–1945.* New York: Enigma, 2015.

Milner, Marc. "Stopping the Panzers: Reassessing the Role of 3rd Canadian Infantry Division in Normandy, 7–10 June 1944." *Journal of Military History* 74, no. 2 (2010).

———. *Stopping the Panzers: The Untold Story of D-Day.* Lawrence: University Press of Kansas, 2014.

Mitcham, Samuel Jr. *Defenders of Fortress Europe: The Untold Story of the German Officers during the Allied Invasion.* Washington, DC: Potomac, 2009.

———. *The Desert Fox in Normandy: Rommel's Defense of Fortress Europe.* Westport, CT: Praeger, 1997.

———. *Hitler's Legions: The German Army Order of Battle, World War II.* New York: Stein and Day, 1990.

———. *Retreat to the Reich: The German Defeat in France, 1944.* Mechanicsburg, PA: Stackpole, 2007.

Model, Hansgeorg, and Dermot Bradley. *General Feldmarschall Walter Model (1891–1945): Dokumentation eines Soldatenlebens.* Osnabrück: Biblio Verlag, 1991.

Molony, C. J. C. *The Mediterranean and Middle East.* Volume 5. *The Campaign in Sicily, 1943, and the Campaign in Italy, 3rd September 1943 to 31st March 1944.* London: Her Majesty's Stationery Office, 1973.

Moltke, Helmuth von. *The Franco-German War of 1870–71.* New York: Howard Fertig, 1988.

———. *Strategy, Its Theory and Application: The Wars for German Unification, 1866–1871.* Westport, CT: Greenwood, 1971.

Mommsen, Hans. *Beamtentum im Dritten Reich: Mit ausgewählten Quellen zur nationalsozialistischen Beamtenpolitik.* Stuttgart: Deutsche Verlagsanstalt, 1966.

Montgomery, Bernard Law. *The Memoirs of Field-Marshal the Viscount Montgomery.* London: Collins, 1958.

Mordal, Jacques. "Das deutsche 'Dünkirchen' an der Schelde." *Marine-Rundschau* 61, no. 3 (1964).

———. *Die letzten Bastionen: das Schicksal der deutschen Atlantikfestungen 1944/45.* Oldenburg: Gerhard Stalling Verlag, 1966.

———. "Le 'Dunkerque' allemand de l'Escaut." *Revue Militaire d'Information* (May 1963).

———. *Les poches de l'Atlantique.* Paris: Presses de la Cité, 1965.

Morton, Matthew Darlington. *Men on Iron Ponies: The Death and Rebirth of the Modern U.S. Cavalry.* DeKalb: Northern Illinois University Press, 2009.

Mueller, Reinhold. *Unter weisser Flagge von Saint-Nazaire 1944–1945.* Bad Neuheim: Podzun-Verlag, 1966.

Muller, Richard. *The German Air War in Russia.* Baltimore: Nautical & Aviation, 1992.

Müller, Rolf-Dieter. *An der Seite der Wehrmacht: Hitlers ausländische Helfer beim 'Kreuzzug gegen den Bolschewismus' 1941–1945.* Frankfurt: Fischer Taschenbuch Verlag, 2010.

————. *The Unknown Eastern Front: The Wehrmacht and Hitler's Foreign Soldiers.* London: I. B. Tauris, 2012.

Müller-Hillebrand, Burkhart, et al. "Der Feldzug gegen die Sowjetunion in Nordabschnitt der Ostfront, 1941–1945." Manuscript P-114a. US Army Heritage and Education Center (USAHEC) Foreign Military Studies series. Carlisle, PA.

————. "Die Rückzugskämpfe der Heeresgruppe Nord im Jahre 1944." Manuscript P-035. US Army Heritage and Education Center (USAHEC) Foreign Military Studies series. Carlisle, PA.

Murray, Williamson. *Luftwaffe.* Baltimore: Nautical & Aviation, 1983.

Murray, Williamson, and Allan R. Millett. *A War to Be Won: Fighting the Second World War.* Cambridge, MA: Harvard University Press, 2000.

Muth, Frid. *Gepanzerter Westen.* Berlin: Verlag für Sozialpolitik, Wirtschaft und Statistik, 1939.

Muth, Jörg. *Command Culture: Officer Education in the U.S. Army and the German Armed Forces, 1901–1940, and the Consequences for World War II.* Denton: University of North Texas Press, 2011

Nagorski, Andrew. *The Greatest Battle: Stalin, Hitler, and the Desperate Struggle for Moscow that Changed the Course of World War II.* New York: Simon & Schuster, 2007.

Nance, William Stuart. *Forgotten Glory: U.S. Corps Cavalry in the ETO.* Lexington: University Press of Kentucky, 2016.

Nash, Douglas E. "No Stalingrad on the Dnieper: The Korsun-Shevchenkovsky Operation, January to February 1944." Fort Leavenworth, KS: US Army Command and General Staff College, 1995.

Natzmer, Oldwig von, et al. "Das Zurückkämpfen eingekesselter Verbände zur eigene Front." Manuscript T-12. US Army Heritage and Education Center (USAHEC) Foreign Military Studies series. Carlisle, PA.

Neiberg, Michael. *The Blood of Free Men: The Liberation of Paris, 1944.* New York: Basic Books, 2012.

Neitzel, Sönke. *Abgehört: Deutsch Generäle in britischer Kriegsgefangenschaft 1942–1945.* Berlin: List Taschenbuch, 2007.

————. "Der Kampf um die deutschen Atlantik- und Kanalfestungen und sein Einfluss auf den alliierten Nachschub während der Befreiung Frankreichs 1944/45." *Militärgeschichtliche Mitteilungen 55* (1996).

————. *Tapping Hitler's Generals: Transcripts of Secret Conversations, 1942–45.* St. Paul, MN: Frontline Books, 2007.

Newton, Steven H., ed. *Hitler's Commander: Field Marshal Walther Model—Hitler's Favorite General.* New York: Da Capo, 2006.

————. *Panzer Operations: The Eastern Front Memoir of General Raus, 1941–1945.* New York: Da Capo, 2003.

————, ed. *Retreat from Leningrad: Army Group North, 1944/1945.* Atglen, PA: Schiffer, 1995.

Niepold, Gerd. *Mittlere Ostfront Juni '44: Darstellung, Beurteilung, Lehren.* Herford und Bonn: Verlag E. S. Mittler & Sohn, 1985.

Noble, Alastair. "The First Frontgau: East Prussia, July 1944." *War in History* 13, no. 2 (2006).

———. "The Phantom Barrier: *Ostwallbau, 1944–1945.*" *War in History* 8, no. 4 (2001).

Obkircher, Walter. "General Constantin von Alvbensleben: Zu Seinem 50. Todestag, 28 März." *Militär-Wochenblatt* 126, no. 39 (1942).

Oels, David. "'Dieses Buch ist kein Roman': Jürgen Thorwalds 'Die grosse Flucht' zwischen Zeitgeschichte und Erinnerungspolitik." *Zeithistorische Forschungen* 6 (2009).

———. "Schicksal, Schuld und Gräueltaten: populäre Kriegspropaganda: Jürgen Thorwalds ewiger bestseller 'Die grosse Flucht.'" *Die Zeit* (July 22, 2010).

Oetting, Dirk W. *Auftragstaktik: Geschichte und Gegenwart einer Führungskonzeption.* Frankfurt: Report Verlag, 1993.

Osborne, Robert J. C., et al. "The 9th Armd Div in Exploitation of Remagen Bridgehead." Fort Knox, KY: The Armored School, 1949–1950.

Ossad, Steven L. "Major General John P. Lucas at Anzio: Prudence or Boldness?" *Global War Studies* 8, no. 1 (2011).

Overy, Richard. *Why the Allies Won.* New York: Norton, 1997.

Paret, Peter, ed. *Frederick the Great: A Profile.* New York: Hill and Wang, 1972.

Parker, Danny. *Battle of the Bulge: Hitler's Ardennes Offensive, 1944–1945.* New York: Da Capo, 1991.

Parker, Matthew. *Monte Cassino: The Hardest-Fought Battle of World War II.* New York: Anchor Books, 2005.

Parkison, Anna M. "Afterlives of a Nazi Sabotage Blunder: Jürgen Thorwald's Der Fall Pastorius." *Non Fiktion* 6, nos. 1 and 2 (2011).

Patton, George S. Jr. *War as I Knew It.* New York: Bantam, 1980.

Pelet-Narbonne, Gerhard von. *Der Grosse Kurfürst.* Berlin: B. Behr, 1905.

Perry, Mark. *Partners in Command: George Marshall and Dwight Eisenhower in War and Peace.* New York: Penguin, 2007.

Philippi, Alfred, and Ferdinand Heim. *Der Feldzug gegen Sowjetrussland 1941 bis 1945: ein operativer Überblick.* Stuttgart: W. Kohlhammer, 1962.

Philippson, Martin. *Der Grosse Kurfürst Friedrich Wilhelm von Brandenburg.* 3 Volumes. Berlin: Verlag Siegfried Cronbach, 1897–1903.

Pike, David Wingeate. "La retraite des forces allemandes du sud-ouest de la France août 1944." *Guerres Mondiales et Conflits Contemporains* no. 164 (1991).

———. "Les forces Allemandes dans le Sud-Ouest de la France mai-juillet 1944." *Guerres Mondiales et Conflits Contemporains,* no. 152 (1988).

Poeppel, Hans, Wilhelm-Karl Prinz von Preussen, and Karl-Günther von Hase, eds. *Die Soldaten der Wehrmacht.* München: Herbig, 1998.

Pohlman, Hartwig. "Die Festung Gironde Nord (Royan) 1944/45." 5 parts. *Feldgrau* 7 (1959).

Poll, Bernhard, ed. *Das Schicksal Aachens im Herbst 1944: authentische Berichte.* Aachen: Verlag des Aachener Geschichtsvereins, 1955.

Porch, Douglas. *The Path to Victory: The Mediterranean Theater in World War II.* New York: Farrar, Straus and Giroux, 2004.

Porter, David. *7th Armoured Division at Villers-Bocage, 13 June 1944.* London: Amber Books, 2012.

Post, Walter. "Die Proportion der sogennanten 'Täter' in der Millionenarmee— Versuch einer Quantifizierung am Beispiel der 6. Armee im Russlandfeldzug 1941." In Hans Poeppel, Wilhelm-Karl Prinz von Preussen, and Karl-Günther von Hase, eds. *Die Soldaten der Wehrmacht.* München: Herbig, 1998.

Prados, John. *Normandy Crucible: The Decisive Battle That Shaped World War II in Europe.* New York: NAL Caliber, 2011.

Priess, Hermann. "Ardennen. Einsatz des I. SS-Panzer-Corps während der Ardennen-Offensive, Dezember-Januar, 1944–1945." Manuscript A-877. US Army Heritage and Education Center (USAHEC) Foreign Military Studies series. Carlisle, PA.

Raeder, Erich. *Grand Admiral.* Annapolis, MD: Naval Institute Press, 1960.

Randewig, Kunibert. "Die Sowjet Funktäuschung in der Schlacht von Tscherkassy." *Allgemeine schweizerische Militärzeitschrift* 119, no. 6 (1953).

Randewig, Kunibert, and Willi Rothhaar. "Im Kessel von Tscherkassy." In Hanns Möller-Witten, ed. *Männer und Taten: Ritterkreuzträger erzählen.* München: J. F. LehmannVerlag, 1959.

Raus, Erhard. "Die Schlacht bei Lemberg." *Allgemeine schweizerische Militärzeitschrift* 121, no. 11 (1955).

Reardon, Mark J. *Victory at Mortain: Stopping Hitler's Panzer Counteroffensive.* Lawrence: University Press of Kansas, 2002.

Rehm, Walter. *Jassy: Schicksal einer Division oder einer Armee?* Neckargemünd: Kurt Vowinckel Verlag, 1959.

Reichhelm, Günter. "Thema: Stellungnahme zum Bericht Kraemer vom Oktober 1945, 'Einsatz der 6. Panzer-Armee in den Ardennen 1944/1945.'" Manuscript B-676. US Army Heritage and Education Center (USAHEC) Foreign Military Studies series. Carlisle, PA.

Rendulic, Lothar. "Die Schlacht von Orel, Juli 1943: Wahl und Bildung des Schwerpunktes." *Österreichische Militärische Zeitschrift* 1, no. 3 (1963).

———. "Die Schlacht von Orel, Juli 1943: Wahl und Bildung es Schwerpunktes." *Österreichische Militärische Zeitschrift* 1, no. 3 (1963).

———. *Gekämpft, Gesiegt, Geschlagen.* Wels: Verlag Welsermühl, 1952.

———. *Glasenbach–Nürnberg–Landsberg. Ein Soldatenschicksal nach dem Krieg.* Graz: Leopold Stocker Verlag, 1953.

Renier, Pierre. "*Festung Guernsey 1944:* An Analysis of the Official German Handbook on their Island Fortress." *Channel Islands Occupation Review,* nos. 20, 22, and 24 (1995–1998).

Reuth, Ralf Georg. *Entscheidung im Mittelmeer: Die südliche Peripherie Europas in der deutschen Strategie des Zweiten Weltkrieges, 1940–1942.* Koblenz: Bernard & Graefe, 1985.

———. *Rommel: Das Ende einer Legende.* München: Piper, 2004.

———. *Rommel: The End of a Legend.* London: Haus, 2005.

Reynolds, Michael. *The Devil's Adjutant: Jochen Peiper, Panzer Leader.* New York: Sarpedon, 1995.

———. *Men of Steel: I SS Panzer Corps; The Ardennes and Eastern Front, 1944–45.* Staplehurst, UK: Spellmount, 1999.

———. *Sons of the Reich: II SS Panzer Corps; Normandy, Arnhem, Ardennes, Eastern Front.* Staplehurst, UK: Spellmount, 2002.

———. *Steel Inferno: I SS Panzer Corps in Normandy.* Staplehurst, UK: Spellmount, 1997.

Rice, Doyle. "D-Day: The Most Important Weather Forecast in History." *USA Today* (June 6, 2014).

Richie, Alexandra. *Warsaw 1944: Hitler, Himmler, and the Warsaw Uprising.* New York: Farrar, Straus and Giroux, 2013.

Richter, Wilhelm. "716. Infanterie-Division in Normandy (6. Juni-23. Juni-1944)." Manuscript B-621. US Army Heritage and Education Center (USAHEC) Foreign Military Studies series. Carlisle, PA.

Rickard, John Nelson. *Advance and Destroy: Patton as Commander in the Bulge.* Lexington: University Press of Kentucky, 2011.

———. *Patton at Bay: The Lorraine Campaign, 1944.* Washington, DC: Potomac Books, 2004.

Ringshausen, Gerhard. *Hans-Alexander von Voss: Generalstabsoffizier im Widerstand 1907–1944.* Berlin: Lukas Verlag, 2008.

Rinkleff, Adam J. "American 'Blitzkrieg': Courtney Hodges and the Advance from Villedieu to Aachen." Ph.D. diss. Denton: University of North Texas, 2012.

Ritter, Gerhard. *Der Schlieffenplan: Kritik eines Mythos.* Munich: R. Oldenbourg, 1956.

———. *Frederick the Great: A Historical Profile.* Berkeley: University of California Press, 1968.

Rohde, Horst. "Politische Indoktrination in höheren Stäben und in der Truppe— untersucht am Beispiel des Kommissarbefehls." In Hans Poeppel, Wilhelm-Karl Prinz von Preussen, and Karl-Günther von Hase, eds. *Die Soldaten der Wehrmacht.* München: Herbig, 1998.

Röhricht, Edgar. *Pflicht und Gewissen: Erinnerungen eines deutschen Generals 1932 bis 1944.* Stuttgart: W. Kohlhammer Verlag, 1965.

———. *Probleme der Kesselschlacht: dargestellt an Einkreisungs-Operationen im Zweiten Weltkrieg.* Karlsruhe: Condor-Verlag, 1958.

Rommel, Erwin. *Krieg ohne Hass.* Heidenheim: Heidenheimer Zeitung, 1950.

Rose, Kenneth D. *Myth and the Greatest Generation: A Social History of Americans in World War II.* New York: Routledge, 2008.

Ross, John. *The Forecast for D-Day: And the Weatherman Behind Ike's Greatest Gamble.* Guilford, CT: Lyons Press, 2014.

Rossino, Alexander B. *Hitler Strikes Poland: Blitzkrieg, Ideology, and Atrocity.* Lawrence: University Press of Kansas, 2003.

Röttiger, Hans. "Geschichte Südfrankreich/OB West." Manuscript B-330. US Army Heritage and Education Center (USAHEC) Foreign Military Studies series. Carlisle, PA.

Ruge, Friedrich. *Rommel und die Invasion: Erinnerungen.* Stuttgart: K. F. Koehler Verlag, 1959.

Rundstedt, Gerd von. "Bemerkungen zur Ausarbeitung des General Zimmermann." Manuscript B-633. US Army Heritage and Education Center (USAHEC) Foreign Military Studies series. Carlisle, PA.

———. "Beurteilung der Lage Ob. West am 25.10.1943." National Archives and Records Administration. Serial T-311. Reel 27. Frames 7032424–7032474.

Rush, Robert Sterling. *Hell in Hürtgen Forest.* Lawrence: University Press of Kansas, 2001.

Ryan, Cornelius. *A Bridge Too Far.* New York: Simon & Schuster, 1974.

———. *The Last Battle.* New York: Simon & Schuster, 1966.

———. *The Longest Day.* Greenwich, CT: Fawcett, 1959.

Sadarananda, Dana V. *Beyond Stalingrad: Manstein and the Operations of Army Group Don.* Mechanicsburg, PA: Stackpole, 2009.

Saint-Loup, *Les Hérétiques.* Paris: Presses de la Cité, 1965.

———. *Les Volontaires.* Paris: Presses de la Cité, 1963.

Salerno: American Operations from the Beaches to the Volturno, 9 September–6 October 1943. Washington, DC: Center of Military History, 1990.

Scheurig, Bodo. *Alfred Jodl, Gehorsam und Verhängnis: Biographie.* Berlin: Propyläen, 1991.

———. *Henning von Tresckow: eine Biographie.* Frankfurt: Ullstein, 1980.

Schickel, Alfred. "Generalfeldmarschall Erwin Rommel: Eine Würdigung zu seine Geburts- und Todestag." *Wehrkunde* 18, no. 11 (1969).

Schieder, Theodor. *Frederick the Great.* London: Longman, 2000.

Schifferle, Peter J. *America's School for War: Fort Leavenworth, Officer Education, and Victory in World War II.* Lawrence: University Press of Kansas, 2010.

Schlabrendorff, Fabian von. *Offiziere gegen Hitler.* Zurich: Europa Verlag, 1946.

———. *The Secret War against Hitler.* Boulder, CO: Westview Press, 1994.

Schmidt, Hans. "Zum Fragebogen vom 3.3.47." Manuscript B-519. US Army Heritage and Education Center (USAHEC) Foreign Military Studies series. Carlisle, PA.

Schmidt, Martin. "Gegenangriff gegen den Landekopf Anzio-Nettuno." Manuscript D-204. US Army Heritage and Education Center (USAHEC) Foreign Military Studies series. Carlisle, PA.

Schönherr, Klaus. "Der deutsche Volkssturm im Reichsgau Wartheland 1944/45." *Militärgeschichtliches Beiheft zur Europäischen Wehrkunde* 2 (1967).

———. "Der Rückzug der Heeresgruppe A über die Krim bis Rumänien." In *Das Deutsche Reich und der Zweite Weltkrieg.* Volume 8. *Die Ostfront 1943/44: Der Krieg im Osten und an den Nebenfronten.* München: Deutsche Verlags-Anstalt, 2011.

———. "Der Rückzugskämpfe in Rumänien und Siebenbürgen." *Das Deutsche Reich und der Zweite Weltkrieg.* Volume 8. *Die Ostfront 1943/44: Der Krieg im Osten un an den Nebenfronten.* München: Deutsche Verlags-Anstalt, 2011.

———. "Die Kämpfe um Galizien und die Beskiden." *Das Deutsche Reich und der Zweite Weltkrieg.* Volume 8. *Die Ostfront 1943/44: Der Krieg im Osten und an den Nebenfronten.* München: Deutsche Verlags-Anstalt, 2011.

Schramm, Percy Ernst, ed. "Der Führungsgegensatz zwischen der Obersten Führung und den Kommandostellen des Westens." In Percy Ernst Schramm, ed. *Kriegstagebuch des Oberkommandos der Wehrmacht (Wehrmachtführungsstab)*. Volume 4. *1. Januar 1944–22. Mai 1945*. Zweiter Halbband. Frankfurt: Bernard & Graege Verlag, 1961.

———. *Kriegstagebuch des Oberkommandos der Wehrmacht (Wehrmachtführungsstab)*. Volume 4. *1. Januar 1944–22. Mai 1945*. Zweiter Halbband. Frankfurt: Bernard & Graege Verlag, 1961.

Schreiber, Gerhard. "Das Ende des nordafrikanischen Feldzugs und der Krieg in Italien 1943 bis 1945." In *Das Deutsche Reich und der Zweite Weltkrieg*. Volume 8. *Die Ostfront, 1943/44: Der Krieg im Osten un an den Nebenfronten*. München: Deutsche Verlags-Anstalt, 2011.

———. *Die italienischen Militärinternierten im deutschen Machtbereich, 1943–1945: Verraten—Verachtet—Vergessen*. München: Oldenbourg-Verlag, 1990.

Schröder, Josef. *Italiens Kriegsaustritt 1943: Die deutschen Gegenmassnahmen im italienischen Raum: Fall "Alarich" und "Achse."* Göttingen: Musterschmidt-Verlag, 1969.

Schultz, Joachim. *Die letzten 30 Tage: Aus dem Kriegstagebuch des OKW: Dokumente zur Zeitgeschichte*. Stuttgart: Steingrüben-Verlag, 1951.

———. "Die Schlacht um Berlin." 2 Parts. *Allgemeine schweizerische Militärzeitschrift* 121, nos. 4–5 (1955).

Schultz-Naumann, Joachim. *Die letzten dreissig Tage: Das Kriegstagebuch des OKW, April bis Mai 1945*. Frankfurt: Ullstein, 1995.

———. "Ein Pommersche Infanterie-Division im Kampf um die Heimat: Anfang 1945." *Allgemeine schweizerische Militärzeitschrift* 123, no. 10 (1957).

Schulz, Friedrich. "Der Rückschlag im Süden der Ostfront 1942/43." Manuscript T-15. US Army Heritage and Education Center (USAHEC) Foreign Military Studies series. Carlisle, PA.

———. "Reverses on the Southern Wing." Manuscript T-15. US Army Heritage and Education Center (USAHEC) Foreign Military Studies series. Carlisle, PA.

Schulz, Fritz. "Bericht über die Kämpfe der 19. Armee in Südfrankreich vom 15. August bis 15. September 1944." Manuscript B-514. US Army Heritage and Education Center (USAHEC) Foreign Military Studies series. Carlisle, PA.

Schwarz, Eberhard. *Die Stabilisierung der Ostfront nach Stalingrad: Mansteins Gegenschlag zwischen Donez und Dnjepr im Frühjahr 1943*. Göttingen: Muster-Schmidt Verlag, 1985.

Schweppenburg, Leo Freiherr Geyr von. "Panzer-Gruppe West." Manuscript B-466. US Army Heritage and Education Center (USAHEC) Foreign Military Studies series. Carlisle, PA.

———. "Reflections on the Invasion." 2 parts. *Military Review* (1961).

———. "Zu Problemen der Invasion von 1944 (mit einleitenden Bemerkungen von Fritz Ernst)." *Die Welt als Geschichte* 22 (1962).

Sears, Kenneth A. E. *Opposing Hitler: Adam von Trott zu Solz, 1909–1944*. Brighton, UK: Sussex, 2009.

Seidler, Franz W. "Das Justizwesen der Wehrmacht." In Hans Poeppel, Wilhelm-

Karl Prinvon Preussen, and Karl-Günther von Hase, eds. *Die Soldaten der Wehrmacht*. München: Herbig, 1998.

Senger und Etterlin, Frido von. "Die Cassino-Schlachten." *Allgemeine schweizerische Militärzeitschrift* 117, nos. 6 and 7 (1951).

———. *Der Gegenschlag: Kampfbeispiele und Führungsgrundsätze der beweglichen Abwehr*. Neckargemünd: Kurt Vowinckel Verlag, 1959.

———. *Krieg in Europa*. Köln: Kiepenheuer & Witsch, 1960.

———. *Neither Fear nor Hope: The Wartime Career of General Frido von Senger und Etterlin, Defender of Cassino*. Novato, CA: Presidio, 1989.

Severloh, Hein. *WN 62: A German Soldier's Memories of the Defense of Omaha Beach; Normandy, June 6, 1944*. Garbsen: HEK Creativ Verlag, 2011.

———. *WN 62: Erinnerungen an Omaha Beach: Normandie, 6. Juni 1944*. Garbsen: HEK Creativ Verlag, 2000.

Seydlitz, Watlher von. *Stalingrad: Konflikt und Konsequenz: Erinnerungen*. Oldenburg: Stalling, 1977.

Showalter, Dennis E. *Hitler's Panzers: The Lightning Attacks That Revolutionized Warfare*. New York: Berkley Caliber, 2009.

———. *Patton and Rommel: Men of War in the Twentieth Century*. New York: Berkley Caliber, 2005.

———. *Tannenberg: Clash of Empires*. Washington, DC: Brassey's, 2004.

———. *The Wars of Frederick the Great*. New York: Longman, 1996.

———. *The Wars of German Unification*. London: Arnold, 2004.

Shulman, Milton. *Defeat in the West*. Waldenbury, East Sussex, UK: Masquerade, 1986.

Sixt, Friedrich. "Der Rückzug der Heeresgruppe Nord in die Baltischen Länder und das Ringen um den Zusammenhang mit der Gesamtfront (Januar bis Mitte September 1944)." Part 4. Burkhart Müller-Hillebrand, Friedrich Sixt et al. "Der Feldzug gegen die Sowjetunion in Nordabschnitt der Ostfront, 1941–1945." Manuscript P-114a. US Army Heritage and Education Center (USAHEC) Foreign Military Studies series. Carlisle, PA.

———. "Die Übergang der Initiative an den Russen (Kriegsjahr 1943)." Part 3. Burkhart Müller-Hillebrand, Friedrich Sixt et al. "Der Feldzug gegen die Sowjetunion in Nordabschnitt der Ostfront, 1941–1945." Manuscript P-114a. US Army Heritage and Education Center (USAHEC) Foreign Military Studies series. Carlisle, PA.

———. "Einschliessung in Kurland und Endkampf der Heeresgruppe Nord (Mitte September 1944 bis Mai 1945)." Part 5. Burkhart Müller-Hillebrand, Friedrich Sixt et al. "Der Feldzug gegen die Sowjetunion in Nordabschnitt der Ostfront, 1941–1945." Manuscript P-114a. US Army Heritage and Education Center (USAHEC) Foreign Military Studies series. Carlisle, PA.

Smelser, Ronald, and Enrico Syring, eds. *Die SS: Elite unter dem Totenkopf: 30 Lebensläufe*. Paderborn: Ferdinand Schöningh, 2000.

Sodernstern, Georg von. "Stellungnahme zum Bericht Botsch v. 10.7.46 (MS #B-515)." Manuscript B-516. US Army Heritage and Education Center (USAHEC) Foreign Military Studies series. Carlisle, PA.

Sosabowski, Stanislaw. *Freely I Served: The Memoir of the Commander, 1st Polish Independent Parachute Brigade, 1941–1944.* Barnsley, UK: Pen and Sword, 2014.

Soviet General Staff. "1st Ukrainian Front's Lvov-Peremyshl' Operation (July–August 1944)." *Journal of Slavic Military Studies* 9, no. 1 (1996).

———. "The Defeat of the Germans in Belorussia (Summer 1944)." *Journal of Slavic Military Studies* 7, no. 4 (1994).

———. *Operation Bagration: The Rout of the German Forces in Belorussia, 23 June–29 August 1944.* Edited and translated by Richard W. Harrison. Solihull, UK: Helion, 2016.

Speck, Hans. "Die Machtmittel Zweier Weltreiche." *Die Wehrmacht* 13 (1944). In *Die Wehrmacht: Herausgegeben vom Oberkommando der Wehrmacht.* 5 Volumes. Hamburg: Verlag für Geschichtliche Dokumentation, 1978.

Speer, Albert. *Erinnerungen.* Frankfurt am Main: Ullstein, 1969.

———. *Inside the Third Reich: Memoirs by Albert Speer.* New York: Macmillan, 1970.

———. *Spandau: The Secret Diaries.* New York: Macmillan, 1976.

———. *Spandauer Tagebücher.* Frankfurt: Ullstein, 1978.

Speidel, Hans. *Aus unserer Zeit: Erinnerungen.* Berlin: Propyläen, 1977.

———. "Der Ausbruch aus dem Kessel von Tscherkassy." *Allgemeine schweizerische Militärzeitschrift* 115, no. 6 (1949).

———. "Die alliierte Invasion in Europa 1944: eine deutsche Darstellung." 4 Parts. *Allgemeine schweizerische Militärzeitschrift* 115, nos. 9–12 (1949).

———. *Invasion 1944: Ein Beitrag zu Rommels und des Reiches Schicksal.* Tübingen: Rainer Wunderlich, 1949.

———. *Invasion 1944: Rommel and the Normandy Campaign.* Chicago: Henry Regnery, 1950.

———. "Stellungnahme zu dem Bericht des Generalleutnant z.V. Bodo Zimmermann (MS #B-308) über die Operationen des OB. West von den Vorbereitungen gegen die Invasion bus zum Rückzug auf den Westwall." Manuscript B-718. US Army Heritage and Education Center (USAHEC) Foreign Military Studies series. Carlisle, PA.

Stacey, Charles P. *The Victory Campaign: The Operations in Northwest Europe, 1944–1945.* Volume 1. *Official History of the Canadian Army in the Second World War.* Ottawa: Queen's Printer, 1957.

Stahel, David. *Kiev 1941: Hitler's Battle for Supremacy in the East.* Cambridge: Cambridge University Press, 2009.

———. *Operation Barbarossa and Germany's Defeat in the East.* Cambridge: Cambridge University Press, 2009.

———. *Operation Typhoon: Hitler's March on Moscow, October 1941.* Cambridge: Cambridge University Press, 2013.

Steele, Richard W. *The First Offensive, 1942: Roosevelt, Marshall, and the Making of American Strategy.* Bloomington: Indiana University Press, 1973.

Stegemann, Hermann. *Geschichte des Krieges.* Stuttgart: Deutsche Verlags-Anstalt, 1918.

Stein, Marcel. *Der Januskopf—Feldmarschall von Manstein: Eine Neubewertung.* Bissendorf: Biblio Verlag, 2006.

———. *Field Marshal von Manstein: The Janus Head/A Portrait.* Solihull, UK: Helion, 2007.

———. *A Flawed Genius: Field Marshal Walter Model: A Critical Biography.* Solihull, UK: Helion, 2010.

———. *Generalfeldmarschall Erich von Manstein: Kritische Betrachtung des Soldaten und Menschen.* Mainz: v. Hase & Koehler, 2000.

Steiner, Felix. *Die Armee der Geächteten.* New York: Ishi Press, 2011.

———. *Die Freiwilligen: Idee und Opfergang.* Göttingen: Pless Verlag, 1958.

Stephenson, Scott. *The Final Battle: Soldiers of the Western Front and the German Revolution of 1918.* Cambridge: Cambridge University Press, 2009.

St-Lo (7 July–19 July 1944). Washington, DC: Center of Military History, 1994.

Stone, Norman. *The Eastern Front, 1914–1917.* London: Hodder and Stoughton, 1975.

Strassner, Peter. *Europäische Freiwillige: Die Geschichte der 5. SS-Panzerdivision Wiking.* Osnabrück: Munin Verlag, 1968.

Strawson, John. *The Italian Campaign.* New York: Carroll & Graf, 1988.

Stürmer, Michael. *The German Empire: A Short History.* New York: Modern Library, 2000.

Sylvan, William C., and Francis G. Smith Jr. *Normandy to Victory: The War Diary of General Courtney H. Hodges and the First U.S. Army.* Edited by John T. Greenwood. Lexington: University Press of Kentucky, 2008.

Syring, Enrico. "Paul Hausser: 'Türöffner' und Kommandeur 'seiner' Waffen-SS." In Ronald Smelser and Enrico Syring, eds. *Die SS: Elite unter dem Totenkopf: 30 Lebensläufe.* Paderborn: Ferdinand Schöningh, 2000.

Taylor, Maxwell D. *Swords and Plowshares.* New York: Norton, 1972.

Tent, James Foster. *E-Boat Alert: Defending the Normandy Invasion Fleet.* Annapolis, MD: Naval Institute Press, 1996.

Teske, Hermann. *Die silbernen Spiegel: Generalstabsdienst unter der Lupe.* Heidelberg: Kurt Vowinckel, 1952.

Thoholte, Karl. "Ardennen (Army Group B artillery)." Manuscript B-311. US Army Heritage and Education Center (USAHEC) Foreign Military Studies series. Carlisle, PA.

Thorwald, Jürgen. *Das Ende an der Elbe.* Stuttgart: Steingrüben Verlag, 1953.

———. *Es begann an der Weichsel.* München: Knaur, 1965.

Through Combat: 314th Infantry Regiment. 314th Infantry Association, n.p., n.d.

Thun-Hohenstein, Romedio Galeazzo Graf. "Wehrmacht und Widerstand." In Hans Poeppel, Wilhelm-Karl Prinz von Preussen, and Karl-Günther von Hase, eds. *Die Soldaten der Wehrmacht.* München: Herbig, 1998.

Tippelskirch, Kurt von. *Geschichte des zweiten Weltkrieges.* Bonn: Athenäum-Verlag, 1956.

Toland, John. *Battle: The Story of the Bulge.* Lincoln, NE: Bison Books, 1999.

Tooze, Adam. *The Wages of Destruction: The Making and Breaking of the Nazi Economy.* New York: Penguin, 2006.

Tregaskis, Richard. *Guadalcanal Diary.* New York: Random House, 1943.

———. *Invasion Diary.* Lincoln, NE: Bison Books, 2004.

Tretter, Johann. "'Friktionen:' ein lehrreiches Beispiel aus dem zweiten Weltkrieg über Friktionen, oder was hier so genannt ist, die das scheinbar Leichte schwer machen." *Allgemeine schweizerische Militärzeitschrift* 131, no. 6 (1965).

Trevor-Roper, H. R. *The Last Days of Hitler.* New York: Macmillan, 1947.

Trott, Adam von. "Trott und die Aussenpolitik des Widerstands." *Vierteljahrshefte für Zeitgeschichte* 12, no. 3 (July 1964).

Ueberschaer, Gerd R., and Winfried Vogel. *Dienen und Verdienen: Hitler's Geschenke und Seine Eliten.* Frankfurt am Main: Fischer Verlag, 1999.

Ungváry, Krisztián. "Kriegsschauplatz Ungarn." In *Das Deutsche Reich und der Zweite Weltkrieg.* Volume 8. *Die Ostfront 1943/44: Der Krieg im Osten und an den Nebenfronten.* München: Deutsche Verlags-Anstalt, 2011.

———. *The Siege of Budapest: 100 Days in World War II.* New Haven, CT: Yale University Press, 2005.

Urquhart, R. E. *Arnhem: Britain's Infamous Airborne Assault of WW II.* London: Cassell, 1958.

US 7th Armored Division Association. "Troop 'D,' 87th Cavalry Reconnaissance Squadron, Incidents in Memoirs of Men of the 589th Field Artillery Battalion (106th Infantry Division), Battle at Baraque de Fraiture, Belgium ('Parker's Crossroads')," December 20–23, 1944. www.7tharmddiv.org/baraque-87-589.htm.

Utermann, Wilhelm, ed. *Jungen—eure Welt! Das Jahrbuch der Hitler-Jugend.* München: Zentralverlag der NSDAP, 1941.

Van Doren, Paul H. "Decision Making and Cognitive Analysis Track: A Historic Failure in the Social Domain." Department of Defense Command and Control Research Program. dodccrp.org/events/10th_ICCRTS/CD/papers/035.pdf.

Vietinghoff, Heinrich von. "Die Kämpfe der 10. Armee in Süd- und Mittelitalien unter besonderer Berücksichtigung der Schlachten bei Salerno, am Volturno, Garigliano, am Sangro und um Cassino." Chapter 6. "Der Feldzug in Italien." Manuscript T-1a. US Army Heritage and Education Center (USAHEC) Foreign Military Studies series. Carlisle, PA.

Vogel, Detlef. "Deutsche und Alliierte Kriegführung im Westen." In *Das Deutsche Reich und der Zweite Weltkrieg.* Volume 7. *Das Deutsche Reich in der Defensive: Strategischer Luftkrieg in Europa, Krieg im Westen und in Ostasien 1943–1944/45.* München: Deutsche Verlags-Anstalt, 2001.

———. "Die Ardennenoffensive (Operation 'Wacht am Rhein')." In *Das Deutsche Reich und der Zweite Weltkrieg.* Volume 7. *Das Deutsche Reich in der Defensive: Strategischer Luftkrieg in Europa, Krieg im Westen und in Ostasien 1943–1944/45.* München: Deutsche Verlags-Anstalt, 2001.

———. "Die Landung in Südfrankreich." In *Das Deutsche Reich und der Zweite Weltkrieg.* Volume 7. *Das Deutsche Reich in der Defensive: Strategischer Luftkrieg in Europa, Krieg im Westen und in Ostasien 1943–1944/45.* München: Deutsche Verlags-Anstalt, 2001.

Voggenreiter, Martin. "Frühjahrsoffensive 1918 und Ardennenoffensive 1944." *Wehrwissenschaftliche Rundschau* 14, no. 12 (1964).

Volpe, Michael J. "Task Force Butler: A Case Study in the Employment of an

Ad Hoc Unit in Combat Operations, during Operation Dragoon, 1–30 August 1944." Fort Leavenworth, KS: US Army Command and General Staff College, 1996.

Vormann, Nikolaus von. *Tscherkassy*. Heidelberg: Kurt Vowinckel Verlag, 1954.

Vorontsov, G. "The Art of Troop Control." *Soviet Military Review*, no. 7 (1972).

Waddell, Steve R. *United States Army Logistics: From the American Revolution to 9/11*. Westport, CT: Greenwood, 2009.

———. *United States Army Logistics: The Normandy Campaign*. Westport, CT: Greenwood Press, 1994.

Wagener, Carl. "Der Ausbruch der 1. Panzerarmee aus dem Kessel von Kamenez-Podolsk, März/April 1944." *Wehrwissenschaftliche Rundschau* 9, no. 1 (1959).

———. "Einsatz der 5. Panzer-Armee in der Ardennen-Offensive Winter 1944/45." Manuscript B-235. US Army Heritage and Education Center (USAHEC) Foreign Military Studies series. Carlisle, PA.

———. "Kampf und Ende der Heeresgruppe B im Ruhrkessel 22. März bis 17. April 1945." *Wehrwissenschaftliche Rundschau* 7, no. 10 (1957).

———. "Strittige Fragen zur Ardennenoffensive." *Wehrwissenschaftliche Rundschau* 11, no. 1 (1961).

Waite, Robert G. L. *Vanguard of Nazism: The Free Corps Movement in Postwar Germany, 1918–1933*. New York: Norton, 1952.

Waldenburg, Siegfried von. "Einsatz der 116. Pz. Div. in den Ardennen vom 16.12. bis 26.12.44 (Teil I und II)." Manuscript A-873. US Army Heritage and Education Center (USAHEC) Foreign Military Studies series. Carlisle, PA.

———. "Einsatz der 116. Pz. Div. in den Ardennen 1944/1945, III. Teil vom 27.XII.44 bis 16.I.45." Manuscript A-874. US Army Heritage and Education Center (USAHEC) Foreign Military Studies series. Carlisle, PA.

Wallach, Jehuda L. *The Dogma of the Battle of Annihilation: The Theories of Clausewitz and Schlieffen and Their Impact on the German Conduct of Two World Wars*. New York: Praeger, 1986.

Warlimont, Walter. *Im Hauptquartier der deutschen Wehrmacht 1939 bis 1945: Grundlagen, Formen, Gestalten*. 2 volumes. Augsburg: Weltbild Verlag, 1990.

———. *Inside Hitler's Headquarters 1939–45*. Novato, CA: Presidio, 1964.

Wartenburg, Paul Graf Yorck von. "Gedenkrede zur Einweihung der Stauffenbergkapelle." *Vierteljahrshefte für Zeitgeschichte* 12, no. 3 (July 1964).

Wawro, Geoffrey. *The Austro-Prussian War: Austria's War with Prussia and Italy in 1866*. Cambridge: Cambridge University Press, 1996.

———. *The Franco-Prussian War: Germany Conquers France, 1970–71*. Cambridge: Cambridge University Press, 2005.

———. *A Mad Catastrophe: The Outbreak of World War I and the Collapse of the Habsburg Empire*. New York: Basic Books, 2015.

Wegner, Bernd. "Der Krieg gegen Die Sowjetunion, 1942–43." In *Das Deutsche Reich und der Zweite Weltkrieg*. Volume 6. *Die Ausweitung zum Weltkrieg und der Wechsel der Initiative, 1941–1943*. Stuttgart: Deutsche Verlags-Anstalt, 1990.

———. "Deutschland am Abgrund." In *Das Deutsche Reich und der Zweite Weltkrieg*.

Volume 8. *Die Ostfront 1943/44: Der Krieg im Osten und an den Nebenfronten.* München: Deutsche Verlags-Anstalt, 2011.

———. "Die Choreographie des Untergangs." In *Das Deutsche Reich und der Zweite Weltkrieg.* Volume 8. *Die Ostfront 1943/44: Der Krieg im Osten und an den Nebenfronten.* München: Deutsche Verlags-Anstalt, 2011.

———. "Von Stalingrad nach Kursk." In *Das Deutsche Reich und der Zweite Weltkrieg.* Volume 8. *Die Ostfront 1943/44.* München: Deutsche Verlags-Anstalt, 2007.

Wehrli, E. "Taktische Bombenteppiche." *Allgemeine schweizerische Militärzeitscrift* 130, no. 7 (1964).

Weidling, Helmuth. "Der Endkampf in Berlin (23.4–2.5 1945)." 3 Parts. *Wehrwissenschaftliche Rundschau* 12, nos. 1–3 (1962).

Weigley, Russell F. *Eisenhower's Lieutenants: The Campaign of France and Germany, 1944–1945.* Bloomington: Indiana University Press, 1981.

Weinberg, Gerhard L. "Der historische Ort des Zweiten Weltkrieges." In Roland G. Foerster, ed. *Seelower Höhen 1945.* Hamburg: E. S. Mittler & Sohn, 1998.

———. *Germany, Hitler & World War II.* Cambridge: Cambridge University Press, 1995.

———. "Some Thoughts on World War II." In Gerhard L. Weinberg, ed. *Germany, Hitler & World War II.* Cambridge: Cambridge University Press, 1995.

———. "Unexplored Questions about the German Military during World War II." *Journal of Military History* 62 (April 1998).

Weingartner, James J. *Crossroads of Death: The Story of the Malmédy Massacre and Trial.* Berkeley: University of California Press, 2004.

Weitershausen, Georg Freiherr von. "Die Verteidigung und Räumung von Sevastopol im Mai 1944." *Wehrwissenschaftliche Rundschau* 4 (1954).

Wenck, Walther. "Berlin war nicht zu mehr zu retten." *Stern* (April 1965).

Weniger, Erich. "Die Selbständigkeit der Unterführer und ihre Grenzen." *Militärwisseschaftliche Rundschau* 9, no. 2 (1944).

Westemeier, Jens. *Himmlers Krieger: Joachim Peiper und die Waffen-SS in Krieg und Nachkriegszeit.* Paderborn: Ferdinand Schöningh, 2014.

Westphal, Siegfried, "Die Auffassung der Heeresgruppe." Chapter 14. "Der Feldzug in Italien." Manuscript T-1a. US Army Heritage and Education Center (USAHEC) Foreign Military Studies series. Carlisle, PA.

———. *Erinnerungen.* Mainz: v. Hase & Koehler Verlag, 1975.

———. *The German Army in the West.* London: Cassell, 1951.

———. *Heer in Fesseln: Aus den Papieren des Stabchefs von Rommel, Kesselring und Rundstedt.* Bonn: Athenäum-Verlag, 1950.

———, ed. "Der Feldzug in Italien." Manuscript T-1a. US Army Heritage and Education Center (USAHEC) Foreign Military Studies series. Carlisle, PA.

Wette, Wolfram. *Die Wehrmacht: Feindbilder, Vernichtungskrieg, Legenden.* Frankfurt: S. Fischer, 2002.

Wetzell, Georg. "Bismarck-Moltke und der Bündniskrieg." *Militär-Wochenblatt* 122, no. 45, (1938).

———. "Der Bündniskrieg: Eine militärpolitisch operative Studie des Welt-krieges." 5 Parts. *Militär-Wochenblatt* 122 (1937).

———. "'Der Bündniskrieg' und die Kritik." 2 Parts. *Militär-Wochenblatt* 122 (1938).

Wheeler Bennett, J. W. *The Nemesis of Power: The German Army in Politics, 1918–1945.* New York: Viking Press, 1964.

White, Irene Zarina. *Fire Burn: World War II Diaries.* Bloomington, IN: Xlibris, 2006.

Whiting, Charles. *The Ghost Front: The Ardennes before the Battle of the Bulge.* New York: Da Capo, 2002.

Wiegrefe, Klaus. "Alles, alles, alles überprüfen." *Der Spiegel* 45 (1999).

———. "Landser vor Leichenbergen." *Der Spiegel* 46 (2000).

———. "Wir nehmen Vorwürfe ernst." *Der Spiegel* 43 (1999).

Wiese, Friedrich. "Die 19. Armee in Süd-Frankreich vom 1.7. bis 15.9.44: Betrach-tungen und Beurteilungen des O.B. der 19. Armee." Manuscript B-787. US Army Heritage and Education Center (USAHEC) Foreign Military Studies series. Carlisle, PA.

Willemer, Wilhelm. "The German Defense Plan for Berlin." Manuscript P-136. US Army Heritage and Education Center (USAHEC) Foreign Military Stud-ies series. Carlisle, PA.

Wilt, Alan F. *The Atlantic War: Rommel's Plan to Stop the Allied Invasion.* New York: Enigma Books, 2004.

———. *The French Riviera Campaign of August 1944.* Carbondale: Southern Illinois University Press, 1981.

Wilutzky, Horst. "Beilage zu 'Der Kampf der Heeresgruppe G im Westen.'" Man-uscript A-883. US Army Heritage and Education Center (USAHEC) Foreign Military Studies series. Carlisle, PA.

———. "Der Kampf der Heeresgruppe G im Westen." Manuscript A-882. US Army Heritage and Education Center (USAHEC) Foreign Military Studies series. Carlisle, PA.

Winton, Harold R. "Airpower in the Battle of the Bulge: A Case for Effects-Based Operations?" *Journal of Military and Strategic Studies* 14, no. 1 (2011).

———. *Corps Commanders of the Bulge: Six American Generals and Victory in the Ardennes.* Lawrence: University Press of Kansas, 2007.

Wishnevsky, Stephan T. *Courtney Hicks Hodges: From Private to Four-star General in the United States Army.* Jefferson, NC: McFarland, 2006.

Wundshammer, Bruno. "Sie nennen sie 'Crack Babies.'" *Signale.* Berlin: Oberkom-mando der Wehrmacht, n.d. [1944?].

Yeide, Harry. *Fighting Patton: George S. Patton Jr. through the Eyes of His Enemies.* New York: Zenith, 2011.

Yelton, David K. *Hitler's Volkssturm: The Nazi Military and the Fall of Germany, 1944–1945.* Lawrence: University Press of Kansas, 2002.

Zajac, A. "Der Angriff des 2. karpatischen Schützenbataillons vom 12. Mai 1944 auf die Höhe 593 (NE Montecassino)." *Allgemeine schweizerische Militärzeitschrift* 127, no. 1 (1961).

Zaloga, Steven J. *Anzio 1944: The Beleaguered Beachhead.* New York: Osprey, 2005.

———. *Battle of the Bulge 1944 (1): St Vith and the Northern Shoulder.* London: Osprey, 2013.

———. *Operation Nordwind 1945: Hitler's Last Offensive in the West.* Oxford: Osprey, 2010.

Zeiler, Thomas W. *Annihilation: A Global Military History of World War II.* Oxford: Oxford University Press, 2011.

Zeitzler, Kurt. "Die oberste Führung des Heeres im Rahmen der Wehrmachtführung (Zukunftsgedanken)." Manuscript C-026. US Army Heritage and Education Center (USAHEC) Foreign Military Studies series. Carlisle, PA.

———. "Die Ringen um die grossen Entscheidungen im zweiten Weltkriege." Part 1. "Stalingrad: der Wendepunkt des Krieges." Manuscript D-405. Foreign Military Studies. Carlisle. PA.

———. "Die Ringen um die grossen Entscheidungen im zweiten Weltkriege." Part 2. "Abwehrschlachten im Russland nach dem Wendepunkt im Kriege." Manuscript D-406. US Army Heritage and Education Center (USAHEC) Foreign Military Studies series. Carlisle, PA.

Zeller, Eberhard. "Claus und Berthold Stauffenberg." *Vierteljahrshefte für Zeitgeschichte* 12, no. 3 (July 1964).

Zetterling, Niklas. *Normandy 1944: German Military Organization, Combat Power and Organizational Effectiveness.* Winnipeg: J. J. Federowicz, 2000.

Zetterling, Niklas, and Anders Frankson. *The Korsun Pocket: The Encirclement and Breakout of a German Army in the East, 1944.* Philadelphia: Casemate, 2008.

Ziegelmann, Fritz. "Die Geschichte der 352. Infanterie-Division." Manuscript B-432. US Army Heritage and Education Center (USAHEC) Foreign Military Studies series. Carlisle, PA.

Ziemke, Earl D. *Stalingrad to Berlin: The German Defeat in the East.* Washington, DC: Center of Military History, 1987.

Zimmermann, Bodo. "Bericht über die Operationen des OB. West von den Vorbereitungen gegen die Invasion bis zum Rückzug auf den Westwall." Manuscript B-308. US Army Heritage and Education Center (USAHEC) Foreign Military Studies series. Carlisle, PA.

Zoepf, Wolf T. *Seven Days in January: With the 6th SS-Mountain Division in Operation Nordwind.* Bedford, PA: Aberjona, 2001.

Zschäckel, Friedrich. "Es begann am 6.6." *Die Wehrmacht* 13 (1944). In *Die Wehrmacht: Herausgegeben vom Oberkommando der Wehrmacht.* 5 Volumes. Hamburg: Verlag für Geschichtliche Dokumentation, 1978.

Zuber, Terence. *Inventing the Schlieffen Plan: German War Planning, 1871–1914.* Oxford: Oxford University Press, 2002.

———. "The Schlieffen Plan Reconsidered." *War in History* 6, no. 3 (1999).

Zuehlke, Mark. *The Liri Valley: Canada's World War II Breakthrough to Rome.* Vancouver: Douglas & McIntyre, 2001.

———. *Ortona: Canada's Epic World War II Battle.* Vancouver: Douglas & McIntyre, 2004.

Zumbro, Derek S. *Battle for the Ruhr: The German Army's Final Defeat in the West.* Lawrence: University Press of Kansas, 2006.

Index